Please return / renew by date shown.
You can renew at: **norlink.norfolk.gov.uk**
or by telephone: **0344 800 8006**
Please have your library card & PIN ready.

23 Feb 3/3		

SHREDDED

Inside RBS, the Bank That Broke Britain

Ian Fraser

BIRLINN

This edition first published in 2015 by
Birlinn Limited
West Newington House
10 Newington Road
Edinburgh
EH9 1QS

www.birlinn.co.uk

ISBN: 978 1 78027 277 1

British Library Cataloguing-in-Publication Data
A catalogue record for this book is available from the British Library

Typeset by Iolaire Typesetting, Newtonmore
Printed and bound by Grafica Veneta
www.graficaveneta.com

To Gail, Eleanor, John and Flora

Contents

List of Illustrations

RBS's head office at St Andrew Square, 1828 to 1969.

RBS's 'world headquarters' at Gogarburn, near Edinburgh, 2005 to date.

Fred Goodwin speaking at an anti-fraud conference in Beijing.

Santander and RBS directors unveil RBS's £26.4 billion takeover offer for NatWest.

Fred Watt, Sir George Mathewson, George Younger and Fred Goodwin in RBS's Waterhouse Square London HQ.

Sir George Mathewson, Fred Watt and Fred Goodwin unveil record pre-tax profits.

Barclays chief executive John Varley.

The 'three amigos' – Fortis's Jean-Paul Votron, RBS's Goodwin and Santander's Emilio Botín – unveil plans for a bid for ABN AMRO.

Rijkman Groenink of ABN AMRO on his way to an Amsterdam courtroom.

Sir Tom McKillop gives evidence to the Treasury committee in Portcullis House.

Sir Tom McKillop and Fred Goodwin leave a session of the Treasury committee.

Sir Philip Hampton is driven away from RBS's annual general meeting in Edinburgh.

Gordon Brown, Alistair Darling and Mervyn King at a meeting of G20 finance ministers in London.

RBS chief executive Stephen Hester speaking at a session of the Treasury committee.

Bob Diamond emerges from Portcullis House after being grilled by the Treasury committee.

New Zealander Ross McEwan, who became RBS's CEO.

Acknowledgements

Shredded is the product of one-to-one interviews with about 120 current and former employees of the Royal Bank of Scotland and related companies. Most, but not all, had left the bank by the time I interviewed them. In the face of a system of corporate secrecy, underpinned by non-disclosure agreements and a fear of retribution, all but a handful preferred to remain anonymous. Many of the people I interviewed have been severely impoverished as a result of the bank's collapse, given the number of shares they had accumulated over the years. Some have been psychologically scarred.

I am also grateful to numerous former senior advisors to the bank – including investment bankers, accountants and consultants – institutional investors in the bank, former chief executives of rival banks, senior politicians, regulators, financial journalists and corporate 'victims' of the bank. In most cases, they too preferred to remain anonymous. I would like to offer special thanks to RBS's former chief executive and former chairman, Sir George Mathewson, who agreed to be interviewed on several occasions and provided me with all his speeches and a selection of related correspondence ranging from 1987 to 2006. Others who were willing to speak on the record for the purposes of this book included: Mathewson's former colleague Iain Robertson, who was with the bank from 1992 until March 2005 and was latterly non-executive chairman of its corporate banking and financial markets division; the former chairman of the management board of ABN AMRO, Rijkman Groenink; Killian Wawoe, a former human resources head at ABN; the former UK regulator and author of the March 2000 report 'A Review of Banking Services in the UK', Don Cruickshank; Simon Samuels, head of European banks research at Barclays; and the Edinburgh-based financier Peter de Vink.

In terms of direct assistance with the research and writing of this book, I am indebted to Jamie Mann and Frances Coppola who helped me to write specific chapters, as well as to Professor Stewart Hamilton, Richard Smith, Mike Parker, Colin Donald, Michael Campbell, Michael Moss and Nick Kochan who reviewed various chapters, provided moral support and made some valuable suggestions for improvement. Other writers and journalists who have provided insights and assistance include Shanny Basar, Chris Baur, Iain Dey, Simon English, Sean Farrell, Daniel Gross, Marc Hochstein, Patrick Hosking, Bill Jamieson, Kenny Kemp, Peter Thal Larsen, Joris Luyendijk, Richard C. Morais, Ray Perman, Nils Pratley, David Rothnie, Jeroen Smit, Yves Smith, David Torrance, Steven Vass, Siddharth Verma, Harry Wilson, William Wright and Alf Young. The team at Birlinn – Hugh Andrew, Andrew Simmons and Tom Johnstone – have been incredibly supportive throughout and Patricia Marshall has been meticulous in her copy-editing. Finally, I'd like to thank my daughter Eleanor for her sterling work transcribing some of the interviews.

All unattributed quotes come from people, including ex-Royal Bank of Scotland insiders, who wished to remain anonymous.

Any errors are, of course, my own.

Introduction

When I was reporting on the Royal Bank of Scotland for newspapers including the *Sunday Herald* and the *Sunday Times* from 1999 to 2008, I always felt there was something not quite right about the place. It was a company that didn't actually make anything but which had a 'manufacturing' division. It trumpeted its environmental credentials, yet funded some environmentally disastrous activities. It presented its Private Finance Initiative projects as socially responsible, even though most were a rip-off for taxpayers. It employed at least 70 in-house media relations staff, yet rarely told journalists anything. It had a 'dignity at work' policy, yet treated many of its staff abysmally. It claimed that its marketing was responsible, but sent a pre-approved £10,000 credit card to a dog named Monty. It claimed to treat customers who were having trouble repaying their debts fairly and responsibly, but it hounded some of them to within an inch of their lives. Its CEO Fred Goodwin was lionised in the media and by analysts and showered with awards, although he was a sociopathic bully whose achievements had been over-hyped.

Most striking of all was RBS's market value. At times, this seemed to be detached from reality. On the way up, the bank used to boast that, by market capitalisation, it was worth more than Coca-Cola and more than Sony and Apple combined. In April 2007, its market value reached £64 billion – more than all the other listed companies in Scotland put together and about 4.6 per cent of the FTSE-100. Its persistent triumphalism and the greed of its top brass grated with me. And yet, as a Scot living mainly in Edinburgh, part of me was proud to have a seemingly successful global giant on my doorstep. So many other Scottish firms had succumbed to takeover. At least here was one that was bucking the trend, acquiring overseas firms, building a global brand and creating jobs locally.

But RBS is a case study in how not to manage and regulate a bank. Soon after Fred Goodwin became the chief executive on 6 March 2000, things started to go awry. And the most serious problem was foolhardy and excessive lending. For several years, the problems were masked by the gains that came with the acquisition of National Westminster Bank. Sir Philip Hampton, who took over as chairman in February 2009, explained the nature of the problem when speaking to the CBI conference on 4 November 2013. Hampton said, 'We were lending to anyone with a pulse . . . We were taking on clients that other banks were rejecting.'[1] Speaking to the Scottish Parliament in November 2009, Stephen Hester, Goodwin's successor, said, 'RBS was the poster child of excess in the banking industry. That is why we are all having to pick up the pieces.'[2]

There were some shocking governance failures, including that the board was so in awe of Goodwin they let him run the bank as a personal fiefdom, but with some dangerous cult-like characteristics (at least until their somewhat half-hearted attempt to rein him in in June 2005). Institutional shareholders also have a lot to answer for. Having backed Fred Goodwin in the NatWest takeover battle, they egged him on over the next two or three years and 94.5 per cent of them voted in favour of the disastrous ABN AMRO takeover. And, where regulation and banking supervision are concerned, the RBS saga is extraordinary. Why, for example, did the Labour governments of Tony Blair and Gordon Brown allow the bank to grow to a scale that far exceeded anyone's ability to manage it? Why was the bank allowed to leverage itself 70 times, putting itself and the wider UK economy at risk? Why did the Blair and Brown governments invariably side with the bank in its disputes with the regulator, hobbling the FSA's ability to regulate it? Why has nobody been properly held to account for its collapse? I try to answer these questions in the book.

A lot of people are astonished that no one has been prosecuted for destroying RBS. And there is the view that, if the UK state had been so minded, it could readily have prosecuted a number of RBS executives for alleged crimes including fraud, conspiracy to defraud, fraudulent trading, false accounting and regulatory offences under the Companies Act 2006.

Unfortunately, however, prosecuting high-level financial crimes is notoriously difficult, especially if hard evidence like emails and secret recordings are not available. Another reason is that, unlike countries like Iceland and Nigeria, the UK doesn't have much appetite for the prosecution of mainstream bankers. So what we have had instead are diversionary tactics, faux outrage and political bluster.

The damage caused by RBS's collapse and the wider banking crisis have, in terms of human suffering, been immense. As a direct result, unemployment in the UK is still at nearly 7 per cent of the workforce, or 2.24 million. Real wages in the UK have fallen more sharply than any other member of the OECD group of 34 countries, and they still face a long climb back if they are to return to the levels seen before the bank's collapse.

As Cambridge economist Ha-Joon Chang says: 'Steep cuts in welfare spending have hit many of the poorest hard. Increasing job insecurity, symbolised by the rise of zero-hours contracts, has been making workers' lives more stressful. The spread of food banks, the popularity of "poverty recipes" in cookery, and the advance of German discount supermarket chains, such as Aldi and Lidl, are the more visible manifestations of this pressure on the living standards of citizens.'[3]

Interest rates have been stuck at 0.5 per cent since March 2009. Coupled with 'quantitative easing', this has created a nightmare scenario for many pensioners and savers, while also weakening sterling, with the pound plunging to a low of $1.38 against the United States dollar that year. Despite the pain and suffering they have caused at home, the United Kingdom's austerity policies were not enough to dissuade credit rating agencies Moody's and Fitch from stripping the country's AAA status in 2013, which has pushed up the cost of borrowing.

Despite a superficial restructure, RBS's bad debts and massive future litigation liabilities continue to hang over the recovery. The shrinkage that occurred under Stephen Hester was impressive but it came at a huge cost in terms of the destruction of whole swathes of the UK's small and medium-sized enterprise base and it failed to resolve the crisis at the bank because it was not accompanied by cultural change.

If there's one lesson to be learned from the financial crisis, it is that gigantic, world-straddling, 'universal' banks like the one RBS became under Fred Goodwin make little or no economic sense. Rather than helping the broader economy, they tend to exploit implicit government subsidies in order to 'rent seek', with their main raison d'être being to enrich their own management. Not only are they too big to fail, they are also too big to manage, too big to regulate and too big to prosecute.

The only viable long-term solution for such financial behemoths is to break them up into more manageable chunks. That way, they are more likely to focus on serving the needs of the real economy in the geographies on which they focus and less likely to prioritise negative behaviour like rent seeking and empire building. (Rent seeking is what happens when a company uses its resources to obtain an economic gain or 'rent' from others but fails to give any reciprocal benefits back to society through wealth creation.) Smaller banks find it difficult to hold a gun to the government's head over the re-regulation of the banking sector or to hold the government to ransom should they get into difficulties.

RBS has shrunk considerably since the crisis, offloading Direct Line, Williams & Glyn's, RBS Aviation, Sempra Commodities, big chunks of the investment bank and the bulk of its international operations. But, with total assests of £1.027 trillion, equivalent to 64 per cent of the UK's gross domestic product, the bank still has not shrunk enough.

Ian Fraser
April 2014

Preface to the paperback edition

The Royal Bank of Scotland is, like most other banks, in a stronger position than it was five years ago. Not least this is because of a stronger UK economy. Powered by a buoyant services sector, and despite Tory austerity policies, United Kingdom GDP grew by 1.7 per cent 2013, 2.8 per cent in 2014, and is poised grow by some 2.4 per cent in 2015. The recovery may be patchy, with every sector other than services smaller than it was in 2008, and many of the new jobs being in low-paid or part-time roles, but it has boosted asset prices and strengthened demand for credit. RBS like other banks is better capitalised, better managed, more aware of what it is doing, and has more assiduous risk managers and slightly less insane remuneration policies than it had pre-crisis. The bank is better regulated, with both the Financial Conduct Authority and the Prudential Regulation Authority more alert to the risks that are posed by giant, world-straddling institutions than their predecessor, the Financial Services Authority.

However, as I make clear in my new epilogue – 'Osborne's Cunning Plan' – RBS is by no means out of the woods. Ross McEwan, chief executive since October 2013, has made some impressive strides, especially where innovation and technology are concerned, as well as in the bank's headlong retreat from 'casino' banking in international markets. But the tough-talking New Zealander still has a massive task ahead of him. Consistently low interest rates of 0.5 per cent are playing havoc with traditional banks' business models and are going to necessitate further savage job cuts as the bank shrinks back to its UK and Irish core.

McEwan has admitted that RBS's IT systems remain somewhat

flaky, telling the *Financial Times* that they could still 'fall over' at any time – though he says 'if [they do], it will be for much shorter periods of time'. His goal of transforming RBS into the 'UK's most trusted bank by 2020' seems hugely ambitious, not least because it was named the UK's least trusted bank by *Moneywise* in June 2015, largely due to what was described as appalling standards of customer service and shoddy complaints handling. The array of regulatory penalties that hang over the bank for past criminal wrongdoing would demoralize any chief executive. Together with the hundreds, if not thousands, of civil lawsuits and class actions that the bank still faces from aggrieved customers and investors who allege the bank swindled, cheated or abused them, these can be expected to further dent both RBS's reputation and its ability to generate profits in the long term.

The new epilogue also examines the wisdom of Osborne's plan to sell three-quarters of the taxpayer's stake in RBS to private-sector investors by 2020. Emboldened by the general election victory of 7 May 2015, and free from Liberal Democrat interference, the government started offloading its shares during the summer. A stake for which taxpayers had paid £3.2 billion in 2008–9 was on 3 August 2015 sold for just £2.1 billion – in other words, at a thumping £1.1 billion loss. And most of the shares went to hedge funds seeking to speculate on short-term movements in the share price, not committed long-term owners. However, Osborne and his newly appointed City minister, Harriett Baldwin, who spent 22 years as a JPMorgan investment banker before becoming a Tory MP, turned a deaf ear to the chorus of disapproval that greeted the start of a five-to-ten year process of divestment, and to alternative proposals, including the one from the New Economics Foundation which recommended that RBS should be broken up into 130 local banks modelled on Germany's Sparkassen. For Osborne and Baldwin, RBS will be better off in the hands of private investors – even though these are the very people who cheered from the side-lines as Fred Goodwin drove it off a cliff in October 2008.

In this paperback edition, I have left the bulk of original text largely as it was. I have, however, made updates where needed and introduced one or two factual corrections, notably to the date that RBS appointed its first Roman Catholic member of staff in Glasgow (chapter 1); to the nature of the post-NatWest takeover IT integration (chapter 10); and to definitions of capital (chapter 19). I would like to thank all readers who helped with this process. Typographical errors have, hopefully, also been ironed out.

Ian Fraser
September 2015

The battle Royal

The Royal Bank of Scotland owes its origins to the collapse of another failed international business venture that was built on hubris, self-delusion and inadequate planning. Between 1695 and 1700, amid unprecedented Anglophobia and patriotic fervour, the Scots piled one quarter of their national wealth into the shares of the Company of Scotland. The corporation was founded in 1695 by William Paterson, a Dumfries-born visionary financier who also founded the Bank of England, in order to promote Scottish international trade and challenge the might of the London-based East India Company. The Company of Scotland secured the rights to establish a colony, Scotland's first, in Panama and its promoters insisted that business would be brisk and offer investors spectacular financial returns on the back of burgeoning international trade. Scottish investors became intoxicated. The company became one of the biggest speculative and delusional bubbles in financial history. The project was under-researched and poorly planned. The Company of Scotland failed to appreciate that the Panamanian coast was an inhospitable, malaria-ridden swamp. It failed to foresee strong Spanish and English hostility towards the project, which would lead these powers to seek to scupper it using dirty tricks, diplomacy and force. After just two years, the so-called Darien Scheme lay in tatters. Of the 3,700 settlers and crew who sailed to 'New Caledonia', 3,000 lay dead and 11 of the 14 ships that had been commissioned by the Company had been sunk or lost.

Some £153,000 sterling, nearly a quarter of Scotland's liquid capital, had gone up in smoke. The warm embrace of political union with England, sweetened by financial compensation for the company's backers, began to have some appeal. In 1707, after many centuries of discord and mutual distrust, Scotland and England signed the Treaty of Union. And Article XV – known as 'the Equivalent' – of the treaty was the kernel that, eventually, gave rise to the Royal Bank of Scotland. In Article XV, England agreed to pay Scotland a very large sum of money, which was ostensibly to compensate Scotland for taking on a share of England's national debt. In the end, however, the sum of £398,085 and 10 shillings sterling (worth some £44 million today) was extended to the Scots (mainly members of Scotland's upper middle classes and aristocracy) who had lost their shirts in Darien. Whether it was overt bribery is open to debate but Scotland's national poet, Robert Burns, certainly thought it was. In 1791, he wrote that the Scottish people had been:

> bought and sold for English gold –
> Such a parcel of rogues in a nation.

Many of those who received compensation under the Equivalent, known as debenture holders, formed the Equivalent Society to pool their compensation payments and distribute dividends. In 1724, this became the Equivalent Company, founded by royal charter. Soon afterwards, a group of its shareholders, led by the Duke of Argyll, a staunch anti-Jacobite who was one of Scotland's most powerful men at the time, decided the Equivalent Company should branch out into banking. The Bank of Scotland had been established in 1695 and still had a monopoly of banking services in Scotland at the time. But it was seen as suspect by Scotland's Whig establishment as not only had it rebuffed a merger proposal from the Equivalent Company, it was also widely seen as having Jacobite leanings, which, to many Whigs, was little short of treasonous. The Jacobites favoured the restoration of a Stuart king – James Francis Edward Stuart ('The Old Pretender') – to the thrones of England, Scotland and Ireland. James, the only son of the deposed James II and Mary of Modena, was brought up as a Catholic in exile, at the chateau of Saint-Germain-en-Laye near Paris. However, the Jacobite Rising that the Earl of Mar started in his name in 1715 ended in ignominious failure.

In May 1727, the Equivalent Company was instrumental in the foundation of the Royal Bank of Scotland – and the main reason it was launched was as a bulwark against Jacobitism. The new bank, well capitalised from day one, was established by a royal charter approved by the Whig prime minister, Robert Walpole, and the Hanoverian monarch, King George I. In its early years, the 'New Bank' operated from a house in Ship Close on Edinburgh's High Street with a staff of just eight and a total authorised share capital of £111,348 sterling. With many of its directors and officers also sitting on the board of the Equivalent Company (which continued to exist), it was right at the heart of Scotland's burgeoning Whig establishment and aimed to back the country's pro-trade and industry entrepreneurial classes. Its first governor was Archibald Campbell, the Earl of Ilay, who later became Duke of Argyll and was, at the time, Lord Register of Scotland and Keeper of the Privy Seal. The bank's first deputy governor, Sir Hew Dalrymple, was Scotland's most senior judge and many of its inaugural board of directors were either Edinburgh lawyers or members of the judiciary (so if there was to be any litigation against it, the bank was likely to have the upper hand).

For most of the bank's life, its board of directors resembled a roll call of Scotland's 'great and good'. For a 130-year stretch between 1838 and 1968, the Royal Bank of Scotland had a duke of Buccleuch and Queensberry as governor – later chairman, really a titular head. Successive dukes of Buccleuch and Queensberry – whose family name is Montagu-Douglas-Scott and whose estates at Bowhill, Dalkeith, Drumlanrig and Broughton put them among the biggest landowners in Europe – were effectively given the governorship on a hereditary basis, with each succeeding as governor at the time of their father's death.

One of the Royal Bank of Scotland's earliest goals was to put the Bank of Scotland ('The Old Bank') out of business. A number of skulduggerous means were used, including hoarding its rival's banknotes. However, six years after the defeat of Charles Edward Stuart ('The Young Pretender') at the Battle of Culloden in 1746, which ended the Jacobite dream of a Stuart restoration, the feuding banks buried the hatchet. At a clandestine meeting in 1752, they entered a 'non-compete agreement' – really, a cartel – which saw them accept each other's banknotes for the first time, agree to defend each other from outside aggressors and effectively carve up the Scottish market between them. The Bank of Scotland agreed to steer clear of Glasgow, a city that was on the cusp of a boom for which the Royal Bank of Scotland had high hopes, while RBS agreed to steer clear of the rest of Scotland, giving free rein to the 'Old Bank' in the provinces. Under a system called 'free banking', which meant there was no central bank or 'lender of last resort' in Scotland, the two leading Scottish banks were to play a critical part in the development of the Scottish economy during the 18th and 19th centuries. The Royal was the more innovative from an early stage, inventing the overdraft – or 'cash credit' – which enabled trusted Scottish merchants to punch above their financial weight. Writing in *An Inquiry into the Nature and Causes of the Wealth of Nations*, published in 1776, Adam Smith praised Scotland's banking system, which he said had expanded considerably since 1750 with 'new banking companies in almost every considerable town'.[1] Smith wrote:

> The business of the country is almost entirely carried on by means of the paper of those different banking companies . . . Silver very seldom appears except in the change of a twenty shillings banknote, and gold still seldomer. But though the conduct of all those different companies has not been unexceptionable, and has accordingly required an Act of Parliament to regulate it, the country, notwithstanding, has evidently derived great benefit from their trade. I have heard it asserted, that the trade of the city of Glasgow doubled in about fifteen years after the first erection of the banks there; and that the trade of Scotland has more than quadrupled since the first erection of the two public banks [RBS and Bank of Scotland] at Edinburgh.[2]

In February 1793, seventeen years after Smith published *Wealth of Nations* and three and a half years after the storming of the Bastille in Paris, the Royal Bank came close to collapse. News of the outbreak of war with Revolutionary France sent jitters around the Scottish economy, fuelling demand for cash and triggering a slowdown in trade. However, RBS, was unabashed, extending a very large line of credit to one of its Glasgow borrowers. The loan came on the back of lavish, even reckless, lending to Glasgow merchants and manufacturers that had followed the opening of its Glasgow branch in 1783. 'General commercial collapse was a very real and terrifying possibility, and the Royal Bank stood right at the sharp end', say the bank's archives. One of the bank's senior directors travelled to Westminster to plead with the government of Prime Minister William Pitt the Younger for a bailout.

Eventually, the government came up with a neat way of salvaging the failing institution. The RBS archives say, 'The proposal to issue Exchequer bills was passed on 29 April and given Royal Assent on 9 May 1793. On 15 May the Royal Bank resolved to apply for £200,000 of Exchequer bills . . . The British economy in general, and the Royal Bank of Scotland in particular, had been saved by government intervention.'[3] It was not to be the first time.

There was a murkier side to the bailout though. According to American economist Murray Rothbard, in its aftermath Scottish banks, including Royal Bank, treated their customers high-handedly as they struggled to rebuild their tattered balance sheets. Rothbard says that, in 1797, Scotland's banks followed the Bank of England in suspending 'specie' payments – they stopped honouring requests to exchange banknotes for gold and silver coins on demand, even though the refusal meant they were breaking the law. Rothbard added, 'Before the Scottish banks suspended payment, all Scottish bank offices were crowded with depositors demanding gold and small-note holders demanding silver in payment. They were treated with contempt and loathing by the bankers, who denounced them as the "lowest and most ignorant classes" of society, presumably for the high crime of wanting their money out of the shaky and inherently bankrupt banking system.'[4]

Rothbard believes the turning of a blind eye to such wrongdoing led bankers to assume they were above the law. But curiously, the banks' ability to unilaterally suspend specie payments – which Professor Sydney G. Checkland says was never mentioned in public inquiries – also played a major part in Scottish banking's success.[5] It also meant there were fewer bank failures in Scotland than in other countries. Rothbard concluded, 'The less-than-noble tradition of non-redeemability in Scottish banks continued, unsurprisingly, after Britain resumed specie payments in 1821.'[6]

In the 1810s, the Royal Bank was losing credibility with its customers. Its directors were accused of cliquishness and prioritising their own interests and those of a select band of cronies. The manager of the Glasgow branch was found guilty of large-scale fraud, costing the bank £55,000 in bad debts.

In a bid to improve corporate governance and clean up its image, the bank introduced *Rules, Orders and Bye-Laws for the Good Government of the Corporation of the Royal Bank of Scotland* on 2 March 1819. The sixteen-page document was reprinted and circulated, with little revision, for over a century. It was read out to the board every year, immediately after directors had been elected or re-elected. According to the bank's website, the 'important thing about these rules was not so much that they were laid down, but that they were printed and circulated, accessible to anyone with an interest in the bank and its operation . . . [The document] sets out in clear English how the bank will make sure that its assets are kept safe; that its officers are honest; that its board supervises properly; and that branches are appropriately managed. It dictates rules for granting loans, to make sure that directors cannot bypass proper process in their own interests, and to guarantee that all loans are "transacted in the best and safest manner for the bank, avoiding all manner of partiality with the borrowers".[7]

One reason the Commercial Bank of Scotland was founded in 1810 was that Scots were so disenchanted with the nation's three existing players – Royal Bank of Scotland, Bank of Scotland and British Linen Bank. James Anderson, historian of the Commercial Bank of Scotland, says, 'It was felt by many of the Scottish people that the three old Banks had become too . . . devoted to their own interests . . . to be the real promoters of the general good.'[8] (Commercial Bank of Scotland merged with National Bank of Scotland in 1958 and with RBS in 1969–70). The onset of greater competition during the Victorian era was a force for good in Scottish banking, which became more accessible and democratic than in any other country of the world at the time. It was also a time when the bank's shareholders had a strong vested interest in ensuring that its management behaved responsibly. As the Bank of England's Andy Haldane put it, 'Banking was a low-concentration, low-leverage, high-liquidity business . . . Due to unlimited liability, control rights were exercised by investors whose personal wealth was literally on the line. That generated potent incentives to be prudent with depositors' money.'[9]

After the First World War, the Royal Bank of Scotland's board decided Scotland was over-banked and embarked on southward expansion. It didn't help that the Scottish economy was on its knees after Chancellor of the Exchequer Winston Churchill 'imprisoned industry in a golden cage' by returning Britain to the gold standard in 1925. RBS's chief cashier and general manager, Alexander Kemp Wright, acquired four English banks over the next 15 years: Drummond's, which had its origins in Aberdeenshire (1924); Williams Deacon's (1930); and two doyens of private banking – Child & Co (1939) and Glyn, Mills & Co (1939).[10] RBS was on a roll. At a banquet to celebrate its bicentenary in Edinburgh's North British Hotel on 3 June 1927, self-congratulation was the dish of the day. RBS chairman the Duke of Buccleuch said:

> The banking system of Scotland [is] probably the greatest and most original work which the practical genius of the Scottish people [has] produced . . . There is no question that Scotland's system of banking is one of the country's greatest assets . . . In the peaceful development of the country after the risings of the '15 and '45, the banks, although then in the earliest stage of development, played an important part in developing trade and commerce, and thus acted as a civilising and moderating influence . . . The cash credit system, which as all students of the subject know, was introduced by the Royal Bank so far back as 1728, in itself was an evidence of Scotland's more settled outlook, because the principle behind it was faith and trust between man and man.[11]

Important guests, including the Bank of England governor Montagu Norman, controller of finance in the Treasury Sir Otto Niemeyer, Field Marshal Earl Haig and Brendan Bracken, editor of *The Banker*, also spoke of the bank's many achievements.

However, over the next half decade, the Royal Bank of Scotland and, indeed, the whole British banking sector lost their way. Thanks to the Bretton Woods agreement of 1944 – which tied the value of the US dollar to gold, fixed exchange rates and controlled global capital flows – there was a stable economic backdrop as economies sought to rebuild themselves after the Second World War. But a lack of competition in the banking sector caused banks to become complacent. They increasingly became instruments of government policy, helping to impose 'demand management' macroeconomic policies intended to keep inflation in check and alleviate the balance of payments crisis, as opposed to vehicles for serving their customers' financial needs. The resultant credit squeeze seriously weakened the banks, undermining their ability to compete with overseas players. With the decline of traditional heavy industries in the 1960s and 1970s, the Scottish economy and banking sector were in the doldrums. Royal Bank responded by

merging with the larger National Commercial Bank of Scotland in
1969–70. The combined entity became Scotland's biggest bank, with
a 40 per cent market share and nearly 700 branches. In England, it
merged its operations, which had a total of 326 branches, under the
new Williams & Glyn's brand. Williams & Glyn's was more adven-
turous than its Edinburgh-based parent, becoming the first bank in
the UK to offer free-if-in-credit current account banking to its retail
customers in 1974. While the Royal Bank became the dominant brand
on branches, banknotes and chequebooks, the National Commercial
Bank of Scotland name lived on at the holding company level and the
merged entity was run from the National Commercial's head office at
42 St Andrew Square. Conveniently, this was just around the corner
from the Royal Bank's existing head office at number 36. The enlarged
group suffered from a lack of dynamism, arcane internal processes
and hierarchical career paths. It was also starving critical parts of
the economy of funding. In the mid 1970s, the bank's chairman, Sir
James Ogilvy Blair-Cunynghame, told a convention in Aviemore that
the enlarged group saw little merit in supporting the manufacturing
sector. The bank's employees were almost exclusively male, white,
Anglo-Saxon Protestants and it did not employ its first Roman Catholic
in Glasgow until the 1970s. But there was less inequality where pay
was concerned than today. In the 1970s and 1980s, RBS's chief executive earned between six and ten times the pay of the bank's average
employee. By 2007, Fred Goodwin was earning 180 times the pay of
the average employee.

When the board of Royal Bank of Scotland, led by chairman Sir
Michael Herries, agreed to a £334-million takeover offer by Standard
Chartered Bank in March 1981, it had not banked on two things that
would ultimately kill their planned 'white knight' deal. The first was
the vociferous opposition of many Scots who were not prepared to sit
idly by and see their biggest financial institution become a branch of
a larger, London-based aggressor. The second was that, within three
weeks, the Hong Kong and Shanghai Banking Corporation (HSBC)
would jump in with a much higher offer for Royal Bank. Chaired
by Michael Sandberg, HSBC leapt into the fray on 6 April with a
£500-million offer for Royal Bank of Scotland – 49.7 per cent higher
than Standard Chartered's bid. At this point, the willingness of Herries
and his co-directors to sell the pride of Scottish finance on the cheap

made them seem inept. A large number of companies headquartered in Scotland had been taken over by English and overseas firms in the preceding years and there was deep scepticism that the pledges made by Standard Chartered and HSBC that Royal Bank would have autonomy under their ownership would be kept.

Critics of the proposed Standard Chartered deal were largely unaware that, since the late 1970s, Lloyds Bank had been actively pursuing a takeover of Royal Bank, that other banks including Germany's Deutsche Bank were circling and that the main reason Herries had been willing to accept such a low offer from Standard Chartered was to thwart their advances. Lloyds was already part of the way there, with a 16 per cent equity stake in the Edinburgh-based institution. When Standard Chartered's chairman Lord Anthony Barber, whose personal assistant was the future prime minister John Major, first approached Herries at an IMF conference in Manila in October 1979, he was pushing at an open door. Not only would a deal with Standard Chartered enable Royal Bank of Scotland to escape the clutches of the rapacious Lloyds, it would also mean the bank was doing a deal with a near equal, on its own terms.

Eight directors from the Royal Bank would have made it on to the board of the merged entity. The Edinburgh-based bank would also suddenly have gained access to Standard Chartered's international network, with strong connections in the 'Third World', and some rapidly emerging markets too.

Soon after the initial bids, Standard Chartered raised its offer to £500 million to match that of HSBC, and a campaign was launched under the banner 'The Battle Royal' by *The Scotsman* newspaper. The core message was that Scotland was at risk of becoming a 'branch economy' and even an economic wasteland, bereft of high-paying and professional services jobs, if Royal Bank were to be sold. Politicians north of the Border, including Secretary of State for Scotland George Younger and Parliamentary Under-Secretary of State for Scotland Alex Fletcher, lobbied Mrs Thatcher and Trade and Industry Secretary John Biffen with a view to getting the takeover bids referred to the Monopolies and Mergers Commission.

It did not take long for them to get their way. On 1 May 1981, the Thatcher government referred both the bids to the Monopolies and Mergers Commission. This triggered six months of intense lobbying, during which the Commission took evidence from a wide range of organisations and individuals and interested parties, including rival banks, business organisations, lobby groups, trade unions etc. Some of the warnings made to the Commission were stark. The Fraser of Allander Institute said that if the Royal Bank lost its independence Scotland would become 'a society of hewers of wood and drawers of water'.[12] The Campaign for a Scottish Assembly said that economic and financial centralisation of the UK 'has been the curse of Scotland that so many of its best brains have left rather than stay in their own country and make it the land of opportunity. We are not interested in a worldwide freemasonry of rich men who wear a tartan tie once a year and go to pathetic reunions for Burnschmaltz'.[13] The Scottish Development Agency, whose chief executive was George Mathewson, came out vociferously against both bids, saying they were against the public interest and would have 'severe and far-reaching adverse consequences for the Scottish economy'.

But the support for RBS was far from universal. Some in Scottish business and finance believed the bank deserved to be taken over, owing to its lack of dynamism and inadequate products and services. One senior Scottish financier told *The Scotsman*, 'The expanding and outward looking part of the financial sector in Edinburgh is in no way dependent on the Royal and never has been . . . The innovative developments that have taken place in Scottish finance have not derived from the presence of the Royal, but in spite of its presence.'[14]

The day before the Monopolies and Mergers Commission published its report, the Royal Bank held a tetchy annual general meeting at the North British Hotel. Herries and the board came under sustained fire from shareholders, with non-executive director Peter Balfour narrowly avoiding being voted off the board. There was an even bigger humiliation for Herries the next day, 15 January 1982, when the MMC report – which had been widely trailed as likely to block both bids – was published. The 104-page report was unequivocal. Neither Standard Chartered nor HSBC should be allowed to acquire or merge with the Royal Bank. The report argued that any transfer of control outside Scotland would 'be a serious detriment to Scottish morale and the Scottish economy . . . [A] distant management, however intelligent and unprejudiced, may not give the same weight to local concerns as would a manager who is part of the local community and has full responsibility on the spot'.[15] The report concluded that loss of control would 'diminish confidence and morale in Scottish business. It would also, by reducing the number of key independent positions in Edinburgh, weaken the public life and leadership of the city and the country'.[16]

To the surprise of many, given its belief in open borders and free market capitalism, the government of Margaret Thatcher accepted the Monopolies and Mergers Commission's advice and blocked both bids. Some believe this was because Thatcher – distracted and distraught after her son, Mark, went missing in the Sahara desert during the Paris–Dakar rally – delegated the decision to her more malleable Trade and Industry Secretary, John Biffen.

In many companies, the chairman would resign in circumstances like this but Herries and many of his co-directors limped on. Having had 'independence forced upon them', the directors desperately needed a viable alternative strategy for the bank – 'plan B', as they called it.[17] The Bank of England had also suffered a huge loss of prestige as its plan to broker a marriage between Standard Chartered and Royal lay in tatters and now it had scrapped the old demarcations between UK clearing banks and international banks for no reason.

There were mixed views about the 'tartan ring fence' that had effectively sprung up around Scottish banks. To many, it seemed a dangerous anachronism that would lead to banks becoming complacent, lazy and potentially exploitative of their customers.

When US president Richard Nixon unilaterally tore up the Bretton Woods agreement in August 1971, it set the financial markets free, enabling billions of dollars, pounds, Deutschmarks and yen to flow unimpeded around the world. While this would instil greater fiscal discipline among deficit nations, it also created much greater economic volatility – and irrevocably changed global banking. UK inflation peaked at 28 per cent in 1975 and a sterling crisis forced the government of Harold Wilson to go cap in hand to the Washington-based International Monetary Fund for a bailout. Industry and the public sector were plagued by strikes, and inefficiency, culminating in the 'winter of discontent' of 1978–79. The trade unions were blamed for the economic mayhem of the 1970s but the post-bailout austerity and the powerful forces that were unleashed by the end of Bretton Woods also played a considerable part.

Soon after entering Downing Street with a pledge to 'bring har-

mony' in May 1979, Prime Minister Margaret Thatcher set about
trying to rebuild Britain's battered economy. She believed monetarism,
lower taxes, less government spending, the privatisation of state-owned
assets, the sale of council houses and 'rolling back the frontiers of the
state' would restore the country's economic fortunes. She was pin-
ning her hopes on the ability of individualism and unfettered market
forces to cure the UK's economic ills. In October 1979, her inaugural
Chancellor of the Exchequer, Geoffrey Howe, quietly abolished
exchange controls. A belated response to Bretton Woods, this enabled
sterling to float freely, which meant individuals and companies could
take as much money as they liked into and out of the country. Soon
afterwards, the Treasury scrapped the 'Corset' (also known as the
Supplementary Special Deposit Scheme) which restricted the amount
of credit that was allowed in the economy. The move enabled Royal
Bank of Scotland and other clearing banks to enter the UK mortgage
market for the first time, ending mortgage rationing and blowing a first
few puffs of hot air into the UK's housing price bubble.[18] Thatcher's
economic policies included very high interest rates (they ranged
between 10 and 17 per cent between 1979 and 1987), and spending cuts
including the scrapping of the industrial subsidies that her predecessors, Edward Heath and Harold Wilson, had used to prop up 'lame
duck' industries. This helped decimate the industrial base of Scotland
and the north of England. Unemployment soared, peaking at three
million in 1982, leading to pitched battles in the streets. There were
calls for Thatcher to resign. However, Thatcher regained popular support after the British armed forces defeated Argentina in the Falklands
War and went on to triumph in her battles with both inflation and
the coal-miners. Emboldened, the Iron Lady introduced a raft of free
market reforms with a view to promoting 'responsible capitalism' and
a more meritocratic society.

Sensing opportunities on the back of Thatcher's reforms, the Royal
Bank of Scotland acquired Lockerbie Savings Bank in 1982 and Annan
Savings Bank in 1985. The latter included the Dumfriesshire-based
Ruthwell Savings Bank, which was established by parish minister
Reverend Henry Duncan in 1810, to give his humble parishioners access
to deposit accounts. In 1985, the Royal Bank invested £20 million in the
direct-to-consumer insurance start-up Direct Line (for more on this, see
Chapter 4). The bank also sought to cash in on the opportunities thrown

up by 'Big Bang' – a radical series of reforms introduced on 27 October 1986 which aimed to free up finance and enable London to regain its position as the world's pre-eminent international financial centre. The old-fashioned boundaries that once separated different types of activity in the City of London were swept away, jobbers joined forces with stockbrokers to former 'dual capacity firms' and the cosy cartel of fixed commissions was swept away, as financial markets were liberalised. Royal Bank responded by buying merchant bank Charterhouse in 1985 and Liverpool-based stockbrokers Tilney in May 1986. Speaking about these deals the following year, Royal Bank of Scotland chief executive Charlie Winter said, 'In some respects I regret what is happening but you cannot bury your head in the sand.'[19] The bank was well on the road to becoming a financial services supermarket, offering a broad range of services under one roof. In the mid 1980s, Winter also saw virtue in building an international network and laid the groundwork for the purchase of Citizens Bank in Providence, Rhode Island. Other groundbreaking initiatives in the mid 1980s included setting up Royal Bank Development Capital, whose goal was to fund indigenous growth businesses.

However, Royal Bank of Scotland was handicapped by ponderous management, inefficiency and under-investment in its main retail and commercial banking businesses. In this area, it was consistently outflanked by Bank of Scotland. Under Bruce Pattullo's leadership, the 'old' bank had been restructured with a management board and devolved decision-making. It had exceeded its target of doubling its share of the UK market, was being seen as a 'growth' stock by institutional investors and was getting glowing reviews in the *Financial Times*' 'Lex' column.[20]

Mathewson to the rescue

When Margaret Thatcher swept back into 10 Downing Street for a third term as prime minister in June 1987, the City of London breathed a sigh of relief. A victory for Labour leader Neil Kinnock would have seen many of the market-oriented reforms introduced over the previous eight years overturned. Interviewed by the BBC's Nick Clarke, the S.G. Warburg chief economist Ian Harwood welcomed the result. Harwood said, 'The election means there is absolutely no political risk to investing in the UK on a four to five year view, which was not the case twenty-four hours ago. Foreigners will take cognisance of that and [decide] the UK equity market and, quite possibly, the UK gilt market look good value by international standards.' Asked about whether he was relieved self-regulation would continue, Harwood said, 'I don't think we're going to see any more scandals on a very large scale; I think people have learnt their lesson.'

The Thatcher government's economic shock therapy seemed to have offered up an economic miracle, especially if you lived in the south-east of England. The United Kingdom's gross domestic product grew by 4.01 per cent in 1986, 4.56 per cent in 1987 and 5.03 per cent in 1988. Equity investors were in a state of irrational exuberance. The FTSE-100 index of leading shares, launched in January 1984, more than doubled from its starting level of 1000 to reach 2,455 in mid July 1987. Few realised it at the time but it was in classic bubble territory.

In Scotland, Wales, Northern Ireland and northern England, the effects were more patchy. In Scotland, Thatcher's policies cut a swathe through heavy industries and precipitated the closures of vehicle manufacturing plants at Bathgate and Linwood. Hatred of Thatcher, arguably, played a part in robbing the Royal Bank of Scotland of one of its more able economists – Alex Salmond. An economist with the bank since 1980, he quit his job on defeating the Tory MP Sir Albert McQuarrie in 1987 to become MP for Banff and Buchan.

As he strode through the doors of Royal Bank's head office at 42 St Andrew Square on 1 October 1987, three and a half months after the general election, George Mathewson was firmly on the side of progress. The appointment of the 47-year-old Dunfermline-born scientist-turned-technocrat as the bank's director of strategy and development had been announced on 18 March. Although some saw him as the heir apparent, he was one of several potential successors to Charlie Winter, the bank's chain-smoking chief executive who was due to retire in 1993. The board's view was that Mathewson had the calibre to be chief executive but would need to prove himself. He started his career at Royal Bank of Scotland as a 16-year-old apprentice in the bank's Dundee Lochee branch in 1949, still played the organ in his local church in Longniddry. He had been group chief executive since 1985, and was supportive of Mathewson's appointment but many of his colleagues were puzzled, suspicious and fearful. They wondered what someone who had never worked in a bank could teach them about banking and were concerned that the arrival of technocratic non-bankers like Mathewson would block their traditional career paths. There was also some resentment that the Royal Bank had agreed to purchase Mathewson's family home in Banchory for £125,000 in order to facilitate his move to Edinburgh.

Some saw it as a bad omen when, less than three weeks after Mathewson's arrival, the stock market crashed and a huge storm devastated much of southern England. Between 'Black Monday', 19 October 1987, and the end of the month, the FTSE-100 index had tumbled by 26.45 per cent and the Dow Jones Industrial Average fell by a record 23 per cent in a single session. This drove the Bank of England to cut rates from 9.875 per cent before Black Monday to 7.375 per cent in May 1988. Alan Greenspan, appointed chairman of the US Federal Reserve in 1987, vowed to do whatever it took to restore calm, giving rise to talk of the 'Greenspan put' – the notion that he would always open the financial spigots to rescue markets from downturns or crashes. Mathewson, however, was so focused on familiarising himself with the task in hand that, he says, he barely noticed the crash.

Mathewson's background put him at odds with most of the people in the Royal Bank of Scotland. He had degrees in maths, physics and applied physics from University College, St Andrews University. Hardly anyone else at the bank had a degree at all. He had remained at the college, which later became known as Dundee University, for six years after graduation, doing a PhD and lecturing in electrical engineering. In 1967, he moved with his wife Sheila to the United States, where he worked as a professional engineer on weapons systems analysis at Bell Aerospace in Buffalo, New York. In his spare time, he passed a Master of Business Administration degree at the State University of New York. On his return to the UK, Mathewson joined the venture capital firm Industrial and Commercial Finance Corporation (ICFC, later known as 3i), becoming manager of its Aberdeen office, where he channelled investment into smaller companies in the north-east of Scotland. He made his name as a dynamic and forceful chief executive of the Scottish Development Agency (SDA) in 1981–87. At the Glasgow-based development quango, Mathewson succeeded in persuading private sector investors to come in alongside the public sector and boosted the SDA's credibility among leading businessmen and financiers.[1] Under the 'Locate in Scotland' banner, he ran marketing campaigns to attract 'sunrise industries' to Silicon Glen, Scotland's technology corridor in the Central Lowlands. Mathewson also launched urban renewal projects designed to reinvigorate town centres in Glasgow, Leith, Motherwell and Dundee and ran a state-funded venture capital business, Scottish Development Finance, which was modelled on ICFC. He was instrumental in getting new conference and exhibition centres built in Edinburgh and Glasgow. Mathewson won widespread, but not universal, plaudits for his five-year stewardship of the SDA.

During his time there, Mathewson had a close ally in George Younger, the Secretary of State for Scotland from 1979 to 1986, who effectively held the purse strings and had some input into the overall strategy. Younger – who had seen active service in the Korean War with the Argyll and Sutherland Highlanders and was educated at Winchester and Oxford – persuaded Thatcher that uncaring Conservatism would destroy what was left of the Scottish party and successfully wheedled money out of successive chancellors.[2] Mathewson says, 'I struck up a good rapport with George Younger, as I think he appreciated what I did, because this [the SDA] had been a huge problem and, when I came in, it ceased to be a problem.'

After announcing his resignation from the SDA on 2 March 1987,[3] Mathewson was inundated with job offers. Before accepting the director of strategy and development role at the Royal Bank of Scotland, Mathewson sought advice from Ian MacGregor, the Scottish-American tough guy whom Thatcher's government had appointed to run the National Coal Board in 1983. MacGregor said he should accept the RBS offer, telling him it would be 'an historic opportunity'.

When the appointment was unveiled on 18 March 1987, the top brass at the Royal Bank could 'hardly contain their enthusiasm', according to *The Glasgow Herald*.[4] Chief executive Charles Winter said, 'Our dream is to create an international bank run from Edinburgh, and we are well on the way to doing that.'[5]

When Mathewson arrived for work on 1 October 1987, the 'feel-good' factor was at its peak across much of Britain. Social and economic transformation was in the air. But the Royal Bank remained a deeply conservative institution. Nearly all the bank's managers had joined as school leavers and worked their way up. Few had university degrees, though the vast majority sat banking exams administered by the Edinburgh-based Chartered Institute of Bankers in Scotland, the oldest banking institute in the world. The bank's 23,000 staff were predominantly white Anglo-Saxon Protestants (WASPs) and predominantly male, with the bank's management 100 per cent male. As long as staff toed the party line and kept themselves out of mischief, they could expect a job for life. 'The careers of people who did well and those who made lots of mistakes progressed at the same rate,' said one former executive.

An employee had to work his way up a rigid hierarchy of fourteen levels – four of clerk (1 to 4), five of assistant manager (5 to 9), three of manager (M1 to M3) and two of senior manager (M4 to M5) – before they could reach the giddy heights of executive. Different ranks had different privileges, with lending limits increased as staff gained seniority. The top-ranked executives – styled 'E's – had special privileges including the use of chauffeur-driven cars and the 'mess', a suite of dining and reception rooms on the third floor of the bank's 42 St Andrew Square headquarters, where they were waited on by uniformed staff. In the 1970s and 1980s, branch managers enjoyed both social status and a rare amount of autonomy. Many still played by the three-six-three rule – borrowing at 3 per cent, lending at 6 per cent and being on the golf course by three o'clock. One ex-insider, who was there from the 1970s to mid 2000s, said, 'The branch manager was God and was really running his own business. They could set their own opening times and their own holidays. When they provided insurance, managers would help themselves to the commission. It was seen as a fringe benefit. Some managers were making more out of that than they were from their salary.' The measure of a banker's prowess was not how much money they lent but their ability to avoid bad debts.

By the late 1980s, the Duke of Buccleuch was no longer on the board. However, David Ogilvy, the 13th Earl of Airlie, a former chairman of the City merchant bank Schroders, was a non-executive director. Sir Donald Cameron of Lochiel, 26th Chief of Clan Cameron and father of the bank's later head of investment banking, was a non-executive director from 1954–80, spending his last 11 years as vice-chairman. Some of these upper-crust types were talented people but their continuing presence on the board suggested that the bank was choosing its directors for prestige rather than intrinsic ability. 'In the 1980s, the annual general meetings were more like gatherings of the Scottish aristocracy than the decision-making forum of a FTSE-100 company,' said one former *Financial Times* correspondent. 'They had a huge and cumbersome board and a most unusual way of doing things. They were certainly ripe for reform.'

Mathewson had little truck with tradition. He wanted to ensure the bank worked for customers, shareholders and staff, and if having a clutch of aristos on the board was going to hinder this they would have to go. Victor Blank was on the Royal Bank board with Mathewson from 1987 to 1993. A former mergers and acquisitions partner at corporate law firm Clifford Turner (now Clifford Chance) who had come into the Royal Bank's fold after it acquired Charterhouse, he says, 'He [Mathewson] took no prisoners – was not hidebound by the history and the traditions and the practices but wanted to build RBS into a modern bank.' Mathewson says he came with an open mind and without preconceived ideas. A profile in *Business* magazine made clear Mathewson's desire to be seen as a tough guy who had come in to shake things up. The article, headlined 'The Royal's New Strongman', was accompanied by a full-page colour photo of Mathewson in a tank top, pumping iron in an Edinburgh gym (he was hoisting a 7 kilogram dumbbell in each hand) with beads of sweat running down his temple.

One ex-insider said, 'It was distasteful – like Putin showing off his six-pack.' No other director of the bank would have even considered letting themselves be photographed in this way.

The accompanying article described Mathewson as 'crown prince to Royal Bank chief executive Charles Winter' and was disparaging about the bank's approach to corporate governance. Writer Mark Meredith intoned, '[M]anagement sessions have been likened to a séance, decisions produced occasionally by default. Board meetings have been characterised by fussing and fretting over extraneous issues or by frequent and sometimes unwelcome interventions by the group's chairman, Sir Michael Herries.' The article concluded by saying, 'Portraits of past great managers look down from the walls with ready reproach. But George Mathewson will not wait forever. He is an impatient man.'[6] The article, with the implied criticism of existing management and hints of power struggles, caused consternation inside the bank.

In an address to the bank's Fife, Falkirk and Stirling Managers' Association in February 1988, Mathewson said that the bank's diversification into areas like merchant banking, motor insurance and factoring since 1985 was only the beginning – there were lots more changes in the pipeline. He added, in Ronald Reagan-esque style, 'Change brings opportunity. We must not only learn to adjust to change, we must embrace change, and indeed we must manufacture change. We must go with the winds of change because upon them you can fly to the lands of opportunity.' Mathewson later put it more bluntly. The Royal Bank of Scotland was 'overweight' and 'flabby' which would put it at a disadvantage in the more dog-eat-dog banking environment ushered in by Thatcher's liberalisation of the financial sector. It was going to have to go on a workout. 'Forms of behaviour and competition hitherto precluded by statute or custom now constitute normal behaviour. It is legitimate to poach your competitor's staff as well as his customers and to denigrate his products or services in your advertising. In such an environment the overweight organisation is at risk . . .'[7]

At times, as he sought to push changes through, Mathewson felt isolated and frustrated, not least because of a feud with Victor Blank. With the backing of some of the bank's non-executive directors, Blank wanted Charterhouse, where he was chairman and chief executive, to control all of the bank's corporate banking activities. Mathewson thought this a ludicrous idea. He thought it was imperative that the

merchant bank (which he anyway wanted to sell off) should be ring-
fenced from Royal Bank of Scotland's corporate lending arm because
of conflicts of interest between the two and the different mindsets of
their people. For example, having them under the same management
might lead to money being lent just so Charterhouse could get its hands
on an advisory contract.

The Earl of Airlie, a non-executive director of the Royal Bank
of Scotland since 1983, was part of a group of London-based RBS
directors which sided with Blank, going as far as arguing that he and
not Mathewson should become RBS's next chief executive. Other
members of the Blank camp included Sir Carron Greig and Peter
Balfour. Airlie, Balfour and Greig had all been educated at Eton and
served in the Scots Guards, and Balfour was Airlie's brother-in-law.
They all felt Mathewson was too uncouth and aggressive to be officer
material. Blank was unlikely to have been interested if the HQ was in
Edinburgh, so some were even proposing the headquarters should be
moved to London if this was the price that had to be paid for securing
their man.

Robin Duthie, a non-executive director of Royal Bank of Scotland,
who had been instrumental in Mathewson's appointment, led another
group of non-executive directors who championed Mathewson. Aside
from Duthie – a chartered accountant and former managing director of Greenock-based tent makers Black and Edgington – members
of the group included Sir Angus Grossart, Alistair Hamilton, Emilio
Botín and, latterly, George Younger.

The wily Herries – who had been taipan (literally 'chief executive')
of the Hong Kong-based trading group Jardine Matheson from 1963 to
1970 and a non-executive director of Royal Bank of Scotland since 1972
and its chairman since October 1978 – played divide and rule for over
a year before eventually lending his support to Mathewson. In the end,
the Blank camp acquiesced after George Younger persuaded them that
Mathewson would be all right. Airlie says, 'George Younger reassured
me by saying, "I knew him when I was a minister. I can handle him." '

Having won the power struggle, Mathewson went to Michael
Herries and George Younger in early 1990 and told them the bank was
in such a deep hole – because of reckless lending during the 'Lawson
boom' and its archaic structures and processes – that they had to let
him modernise it or else it risked extinction. They had sufficient faith

in Mathewson to let him launch a secret project to examine radical proposals for reshaping the bank. Under the code name Nova Reda (a misspelling of 'new network' in Portuguese), Mathewson and two executives he had brought across from the SDA – Frank Kirwan and Cameron McPhail – together with four rising stars from inside RBS – Michael Mosson (human resources), Norman McLuskie (procurement and systems), Miller McLean (legal) and Grahame Whitehead (finance) – met every Friday for six months to plot a complete overhaul. He and his six co-conspirators met in conditions of the utmost secrecy and the room in which they met, Cameron McPhail's office at 42 St Andrew Square, had to be regularly swept for bugs. It was not quite a coup d'état they were planning – the board and Winter knew something was up – but it was pretty close.

The Scottish economy had fundamentally changed over the course of the 1980s. On 8 March 1990, *The Herald* published series of articles by the Royal Bank's economists, Grant Baird and Jim Walker. In one, they wrote, '[R]ccent indications are of a slowing economy in Glasgow . . . The manufacturing base of Glasgow has collapsed since 1976, falling from 32 per cent of employees working in that sector to just 18 per cent now (below the Scottish average). The jobs which have replaced those in engineering and shipbuilding have largely been in the services sector – in retailing, financial and business services, public administration, and leisure and recreation. With the current economic slowdown in the UK concentrated on consumers' expenditure, some of these areas – as well as the construction industry – are likely to be hit hard.'

In August 1990, five months after the poll tax riots signalled the beginning of the end of Thatcher's premiership, the UK and Scottish economies started to head into recession and Iraq invaded Kuwait. Mathewson decided the time had come to give senior staff a foretaste of his plans for the bank. Addressing the bank's senior executives at an 'offsite' at the bank's Esdaile training centre, a former boarding school for the daughters of Church of Scotland ministers in a south Edinburgh suburb, he said Royal Bank of Scotland was going to have to adapt or die. He said, 'Truly, it is no longer enough for us simply to be as profitable as the "big four" banks [Barclays, Lloyds, Midland and NatWest]. We should be forging ahead of them. We are not. We are not because our marketing is simply not targeted enough. And I have come to the conclusion that our structure needs refining. Frankly – and not least in the clearing bank – we have become too bureaucratic, spending too much time contemplating our own navels.' Mathewson was unable to go into detail but he did hint of a major overhaul and redundancies. 'There are radical changes coming in the way we do business – in the way we sell our products in reporting lines . . . the shape of the jobs many of us do will become quite different. In some cases we shall be asked to do quite different jobs. Nobody likes change but, in the present climate, we change or die, corporately and individually.' With his trademark bluntness, Mathewson then said that a recent rise in bad and doubtful debts in the core banking business was causing him to doubt the competence of its branch banking staff. 'When I see cases where we take our accounts from other banks, only to have the companies concerned go "belly up" within months rather than years . . . I have to question whether we have lost the ability to tell a good risk from a bad one.'8

Mathewson, by now, had the full support of Younger, who became Royal Bank's deputy chairman in January 1990 and chairman of the group's main operating subsidiary in July 1990. By this time, Younger had decided that Mathewson should definitely succeed Winter. Younger suspected that aspects of Blank's personality and lifestyle, which included his comparative ostentation, his passion for cricket, his Englishness and even his Jewishness, might alienate many of the Royal Bank's rank-and-file workers whereas, to him, Mathewson seemed to be blessed with the common touch and was much more likely to be able to understand, relate to and motivate the bank's 25,000-strong team.

In November 1990, the Nova Reda proposals were unveiled to the RBS board. At a historic board meeting in 42 St Andrew Square on Tuesday, 20 November 1990 – the day that Thatcher surprised BBC political correspondent John Sergeant on the steps of the British embassy in Paris during her battle to cling on to power after the Tory Party turned against her, by saying, 'I confirm it is my intention to let my name go forward for the second ballot' – Mathewson told the board that the bank's structure and management team were no longer fit for purpose. He asked them to approve a radical restructuring and a brutal cull of 'dead wood'. 'This bank is in deep trouble. We could cease to exist as independent entity and I would like to propose to you what [is] a rescue plan.'9 The tactics worked. RBS's board rubber-stamped the Nova Reda proposals and Mathewson was appointed deputy chief executive. One non-executive director who was in the room said, '[B]y that time, we had all recognised the existing management was not up to scratch and we unanimously agreed with George's proposals.'

In the months after the meeting, most of the directors who had doubted whether Mathewson should become chief executive had gone. And within a couple of years, Charterhouse had been sold to Paris-based Credit Commercial de France (CCF) and Frankfurt-based BHF-Bank for around £235 million. Blank had gone too.

The bank's chairman, Sir Michael Herries (who died in 1995), stepped down a couple of months later but remained as a non-executive director. Asked how he thought Herries felt about it, Mathewson said, 'When push came to shove, Michael was basically prepared to accept my recommendations. He moved ahead with it.'[10] The situation was harder for the bank's affable chief executive, Charles Winter. According to one senior insider, during this period, 'Charles would get quite down or even overwhelmed. He recognised that the bank needed to be revolutionised and may have thought that he should have grasped the nettle himself, ten years earlier. He probably also wished that the people who were doing it had come from within the bank, rather than having to be brought in from the outside.' However, despite his private doubts and even though he confided in friends that he no longer believed Mathewson should succeed him, Nova Reda was presented with Winter's imprimatur.

The programme was brutal. A key part was that one-third of the Royal Bank's top 300 executives were given their marching orders. The incoming team saw many of the existing staff as time-servers who had been promoted beyond their abilities or else were too dyed in the wool to push through reforms. One ex-manager recalls the fear and trepidation that stalked the bank's corridors and branch networks at the time. 'There were early morning phone calls around the country asking, "Has so-and-so been fired?" It was all fairly brutal. This sort of thing had never happened at Royal Bank of Scotland before.'

A key structural change introduced with Nova Reda was that all lending to larger companies and other large entities was removed from the branches and put into a dedicated new division, called the Corporate and Institutional Banking Division (CIBD). Mathewson believed that would help him undermine the bank's regional fiefdoms and enable Royal Bank to develop a corporate business that would be capable of giving the Bank of Scotland a run for its money and help it to compete with the big boys in London. Another change was that a new Operations Division took control of all back-office functions including IT, human resources, property and procurement. This restructuring meant that the bank was able to provide a cheaper homogenised service to barely profitable mass-market clients while offering a bespoke service to larger and more profitable clients.

Four months after the seminal board meeting, Mathewson conceded that internal blockages had meant his attempts to sell the restructuring had misfired. Addressing the branch banking managers' conference in March 1991, Mathewson said, 'The significance and depth of what we have set out to achieve has still not been brought home to a lot of our staff . . . our internal communications have not been as we would have hoped, largely because those who were briefed did not pass the message on.' Mathewson then said he was determined to drive up sales, adding, 'We must increase our average number of products per customer. To do that, managers will be provided with the necessary management information on average products per customer in their branches and will be incentivised accordingly.' He also said that underperformance would no longer be tolerated at Royal Bank, adding that 'counterproductive misfits must be decisively dealt with. Among the most damaging, in my opinion, are bullies – bullies to their subordinates but sycophants to their superiors . . . those lacking integrity who do not give subordinates credit and who do not promote an open organisation.'[11]

Mathewson believes that, before Nova Reda, 'a great many people in Royal Bank were just in a different world. It is hard for me to explain what RBS was like in those days – except that NatWest was a bit like it when we took it over!'[12] Nova Reda entailed significant job losses. By September 1991, Royal Bank of Scotland's branch banking staff had fallen to 20,660, down from 21,870 the previous year (a 5 per cent fall). In a valedictory interview with the *Financial Times* in April 2006, Mathewson also said, 'All the power was changed – all the executives were changed. The golf courses in Edinburgh started to fill up again in the week.'[13] However, lots of people inside the bank were uncomfortable with the pace of change – which is one reason that positive spin about Nova Reda didn't always filter down the ranks – and, to this day, many of the bankers who were put out to grass resent what he did. Winter was beginning to distance himself from Mathewson's Maoist revolution. In July 1991, he wrote to Younger, who had been chairman for six months, complaining that the new team seemed unable to accept the previous regime had done anything right, and offering to resign two years ahead of his official retirement. In his resignation letter, Winter wrote, 'I have seen over the past few months the culture of the Royal Bank quite destroyed by a series of radical and rapid changes, all apparently generated by a feeling that the management of the bank up to this point had been typified by total incompetence and that revolutionary rather than evolutionary change was necessary.'[14] Winter left six months later, seemingly a broken man.

Britain's 'Big Bang' ended in a spectacular bust. The fun lending party of the Thatcher decade, at which the bank's own managers were among the most generous bartenders, had culminated in the most almighty hangover – and it was jeopardising the very future of several UK banks, including that of the Royal. A great many borrowers were stuck with negative equity, especially after property valuations plunged by 27–30 per cent in 1990–93. There were 75,500 home repossessions in 1991 alone – a UK record.[15] Loans were turning sour at an alarming rate and Mathewson feared the Royal Bank might have to declare a loss for the year to September 1991.

As writer and journalist Anthony Sampson put it: 'The over-lending by the high-street banks had done more than put their own safety at risk. Their wild marketing of loans to students, home-owners and debtaholics had led to countless personal tragedies as interest rates went up and the economy turned down . . . the optimism of the eighties gave way to a pessimism which could be more dangerous, as people lost confidence in credit and preferred to avoid the banks altogether.'[16]

3

Rebuilding the Royal

George Mathewson, then Royal Bank of Scotland's director of group strategic planning, received a surprise phone call from the Bank of England's deputy governor Eddie George in early 1991. The Bank of England, then led by Old Etonian governor Robin Leigh-Pemberton, wanted to know if the Royal Bank would be interested in buying Midland Bank. It was essentially offering the 155-year-old bank, founded in Birmingham in 1836, on a plate. Mathewson was flattered and was even tempted for a few seconds.

Midland, one of the UK's 'big four' banks, was in serious difficulties as a result of its $822-million acquisition the San Francisco-based Crocker National Bank. The 1981 deal had gone horribly wrong for Midland largely because the English bank had failed to conduct any due diligence on Crocker's loan book and had been far too trusting of Crocker's management in the early years of its ownership of Crocker. Abusing Midland's balance sheet, Crocker's bosses had gone on a crazed lending spree to Latin American borrowers and the California real-estate market in the early 1980s.[1] The less-developed-countries' debt crisis of 1982–89 caused it a severe hangover as many of Crocker's borrowers defaulted or went bust.

Midland, whose logo was a griffin surrounded by gold coins, very nearly drowned in a sea of red ink, even after offloading Crocker to Wells Fargo, another San Francisco-based bank. Attempts by new chief executive Sir Kit McMahon to restore Midland to health proved faltering and, in March 1990, it declared a full-year loss. Other banks, including Lloyds Bank, were circling the wounded griffin, while HSBC was blowing hot and cold after acquiring a 14.9 per cent stake in December 1987.[2] The debacle prompted Midland to sell off the Clydesdale Bank, the Glasgow-based bank it had owned since 1919, together with Northern Bank (Northern Ireland) and National Irish Bank (Republic of Ireland). These three banks were bought by Melbourne-based National Australia Bank in a £408-million deal. The Bank of England approached Mathewson as part of a contingency plan in case either of Midland's other suitors got cold feet.

Mathewson put down the phone and wandered round to the office of the Royal Bank of Scotland's Irish-born senior manager of group strategic planning Frank Kirwan, one of a cohort of high flyers he had brought across from the SDA. Mathewson said to Kirwan, 'Hey, the Bank of England just phoned up and asked us if we want to buy Midland – what do you think?' Kirwan told Mathewson, 'It sounds like a fascinating opportunity.' However, Mathewson replied, 'Yeah but we haven't got the management capacity to do it.' Kirwan thought for a moment before agreeing this was a good call.

Kirwan characterises this as something of 'a eureka moment' for the bank – it was the point when the management and particularly Tony Schofield, who was running the retail bank, acknowledged that Nova Reda had been insufficient to turn the Royal Bank of Scotland around. If the bank wanted to be genuinely competitive and able to absorb opportunistic takeovers like Midland (which was eventually bought by HSBC for £3.9 billion in March 1992), more radical change was required.

When he joined the Royal Bank in October 1987, Mathewson saw his first goal as being to 'bring it into the nineteenth century'. Nova Reda – the internal coup d'état he led in November 1990 – was largely designed to achieve that. Having recognised it had not gone far enough, Mathewson and his team then set about reforming Royal Bank's core retail and commercial banking business. The division had really let itself down during 1985–89, when it had lent far too generously to commercial and residential property in England, Scotland and Wales. This pushed provisions for bad debt so high in both 1990 and 1991 that the bank was barely profitable.

Until the late 1980s, the British market for retail banking services was a protected and highly profitable oligopoly and there was a gentlemen's agreement that Scottish and English banks would not encroach on each other's turf. The lack of competition had enabled British banks to continue to overcharge for what at times was a lousy service – something which institutional investors who owned equity stakes in the banks welcomed since it ensured the profits kept rolling in.[3]

But a chill wind of competition started to blow through this cosy club. The Building Societies Act 1986 freed up UK building societies to compete on a level playing field with the banks. Players such as Abbey National and Halifax parked their tanks on the banks' front lawns and started touting the full panoply of consumer finance services. New services included interest-bearing current accounts, unsecured loans, currency exchange, insurance, stockbroking and even personal equity plans (tax-exempt investment accounts). The banks recognised that, if they were to survive the onslaught, they would have to become more efficient and more customer driven.

And, thanks to the efforts of its deputy governor and group chief executive Bruce Pattullo, Bank of Scotland had a massive head start over its younger rival where modernisation of systems, processes, structures and customer service were concerned. One former Royal Bank of Scotland director confided, 'We had a weak executive under Charlie Winter and Bruce Pattullo was able to knock hell out of us. By the time George took over, the Bank of Scotland had increased its share of the Scottish banking market to 40 per cent and we'd fallen back from 48 per cent to 40 per cent. They were on the verge of overtaking us.'

Frank Kirwan and others pulled together some of the existing analysis that had been done about the current state of Royal Bank. The main conclusions were stark – its systems were terrible, nobody knew what was making a profit and what wasn't, Charterhouse had very little to do with the rest of the bank and was actually sucking capital out of the bank and failing to make a return. Project Columbus – an overhaul of the bank's core banking operations – was Mathewson's response to these and other pressures. The bank chose the name Columbus because it was embarking on a voyage of discovery and because 1992, the year the project was launched, was the 500th anniversary of the explorer's first voyage and landfall in the Bahamas. However, the choice of name turned out to be troublesome. Within days of Project Columbus being announced, the Banking, Insurance and Finance Union (BIFU) distributed a leaflet to all 22,000 Royal Bank employees warning them about the project's likely outcome. The leaflet said Columbus didn't know where he was going, lost half his crew and was clapped in irons on his return. They might also have mentioned that, on Columbus's first voyage, his flagship, the *Santa Maria*, was wrecked.

Mathewson quickly diagnosed that the fundamental problem was that RBS's retail and commercial bank was 'operationally and structurally inefficient'. Areas that Mathewson felt needed urgent attention included the surfeit of unprofitable customers in the retail bank, the bank's old-fashioned and creaky operational structure and its expensive and inconsistent lending processes. Mathewson was also eager to overhaul human resources policies, information technology and branches. The latter were uninviting when compared to those accessible and unpretentious high-street outlets of building societies such as Abbey National and Halifax. In a slightly exasperated strategy note to the board dated 26 June 1991, Kirwan wrote, 'The majority of the branches do not have a word processor, far less a personal computer.'[4] Mathewson says, 'The main thing was we wanted to get rid of the local and regional power fiefdoms. In those days, you had an assistant general manager running, say, Manchester – the whole of Manchester. It just didn't work and that's recognised now by all banks . . . it was a total revolution, to the extent that I do not believe you could do it nowadays. We changed the reporting lines, the structures, the offices on the ground. They had never integrated the systems for Williams & Glyn's and so that was a part of Columbus.'[5]

The project was led by Tony Schofield, one of several Mancunians who took senior roles in the Royal Bank of Scotland's Edinburgh head office in the 1980s and 1990s. Schofield had joined Williams Deacon's Bank in Manchester in 1957, which merged with Glyn Mills in 1969 to form Williams & Glyn's. The group of bright young things who had followed Mathewson across from the Scottish Development Agency, including Cameron McPhail, was also instrumental in steering the Columbus project. They were joined by several members of the deputy chief executive's committee established by Mathewson in November 1990.

Mathewson also brought in management consultants McKinsey & Company to assist with the reinvention of the Royal. The lead McKinsey consultant on the project was Australian-born George Feiger. One former Royal Bank of Scotland executive remembers Feiger as 'slightly off the wall', adding, 'Feiger was extremely articulate and extremely charismatic but he sometimes suspended his critical faculties in championing an idea.' Another ex-senior insider said, 'McKinsey drilled right down into what the needs were and then set about restructuring the bank in a way that ensured these could be delivered. The underlying principle was that they should segment the customer base, giving greater focus and specialism to staff.' One of McKinsey's tasks was to redesign the bank's core processes, including its credit processes – the methods by which it decided whether to issue loans.

Banking was changing. In the late 1960s and early 1970s, the University of Chicago economics professor and monetarist champion Milton Friedman argued that the sole social responsibility of any business was to grow its profits. In his narrow, neoliberal vision, the interests of stakeholders – including customers, staff and the wider community – played second or third fiddle to those of shareholders. The so-called 'Friedman Doctrine', essentially a misreading of Adam Smith, entered the mainstream under Margaret Thatcher in the 1980s and became even more entrenched after the fall of the USSR in August 1991. By the mid 1990s, British bankers were among the Friedman doctrine's most ardent disciples and tended to scorn anyone who even suggested different models. In their push to boost short-term shareholder value, new-fangled concepts were introduced to UK high-street banking. Some came from the world of investment banking (including the notion that it didn't matter if customers were ripped off or poorly treated, just as long as profits were made) and some from retailers and fast-moving consumer goods companies such as Unilever and Procter & Gamble (segment the market and then 'sell, sell, sell'). Cross-selling – trying to sell additional financial services and products, notably high-commission insurance products, to existing customers – became banking's holy grail.

Banking ceased to be about service and started to be all about sales and profit. It was part of a wider shift that has been dubbed the 'financialisation' of the UK economy, in which the City of London and financial services sector took an ever larger slice of gross domestic product, as consumers became much more relaxed about getting into debt. David Lascelles, a former *Financial Times* banking correspondent, says, 'Traditional bank managers had been driven out by credit scoring, centralisation and marketing; branch networks had been pared back and reshaped into novel patterns with hubs and spokes and tiers, and few contained anyone who could answer to the title of "banker" any more. Bad debts had become a cost of doing business rather than a measure of banking ability. The marketing drive had reshaped traditional concepts of service, and profit was king.' Lascelles added, 'The clean-out of the old guard meant the custom and wisdom of the ages had been swept away.'⁶

Mathewson outlined his grand vision for the future at the bank's Esdaile training centre on 5 December 1992. He said, 'It is our goal to be the best bank in the UK – to provide the best and most consistent returns to our shareholders, to provide the best possible value to our customers and to provide the best jobs to our employees . . . Customers, like our capital, are the heritage of generations of successful trading. They must be cherished and cared for and, above all, they must be treated with integrity.'⁷ Mathewson is a staunch Scottish Nationalist who believed that a reinvigorated Royal Bank of Scotland would help reinvigorate the ailing Scottish economy. One of his mantras around this time was 'Where is it written that Scotland can't have the world's best bank?' He said that, by the time Project Columbus was completed in 1997, he wanted to increase the retail bank's profit by £200 million, achieve a return on equity of 32 per cent and reduce headcount by 3,500. The intention was for one third of these job losses to be via redundancy. A key element was that Mathewson wanted to build an open and collegiate internal culture at the bank, in which people thought for themselves and were not afraid to speak their minds.

Mathewson struggled to disguise his contempt for many members of the bank's management team. Sleepwalkers who had led a once-great institution to near collapse was how he saw them. They had required the bank to make massive provisions for bad debt – £323 million in 1991 and £401 million in 1992. This had all but wiped out its profits for two years in a row and Mathewson used it as his excuse to hollow out the branches. One former senior manager says, 'The picture that was coming out of Columbus was that everything has to be entirely rejigged because the bank was bust. When the bank was reorganised under Columbus, it became very much sales focused – sales orientation became the name of the game. That was when I realised that this was not a tweak – this was a revolution. I realised that the bank needed to change so I didn't actually mind too much.'

In an article published in *People Management* in 1995, Royal Bank of Scotland's project director Steve Rick and external consultant Dr

Richard Wellins said Project Columbus was a major achievement that had totally transformed the retail bank. They wrote, 'Retail banking, led by Tony Schofield, employed 16,000 people across a network of 750 branches [in 1992]. Infrastructure was poor and bad debts were reaching crisis levels. Re-engineering meant rethinking the fundamentals of the business . . . The challenge facing both the designers and the executive in this case was akin to changing the engines on an aeroplane midway across the Atlantic.'[8]

But Columbus didn't just involve replacing the engines. It also involved jettisoning many of the passengers and crew, especially those aged 50 or over. Before Columbus, many Royal Bank of Scotland branch managers had an aura about them. They put the fear of God into customers who missed a repayment or whose accounts inadvertently went into the red. But Mathewson saw these people as a barrier to progress and wanted them to be emasculated or shown the door. Even though they were given generous redundancy packages and early retirement pensions, many deeply resented the fact that Mathewson was promoting his pals from the SDA into positions of power and disliked what he was doing to the bank. One former Edinburgh-based branch manager recalls, 'It was a bloodbath. Initially that made George Mathewson very unpopular, hated even.' Others were just glad to take the redundancy and spend more time on the golf course. They recognised the bank was changing, did not like the direction it was moving in. Some left confident in the belief that – given the new team's ignorance of banking and impatience for reform – they were bound to come a cropper sooner or later.

Mathewson said the bank's personnel department 'operated like the command economy which has collapsed in Soviet Russia'.[9]

He wanted a free market in talent, where people were promoted on the basis of their merit, not the number of years they had been with the bank, and was determined to end the policy which put retail bankers with no relevant expertise in charge of head office departments like legal, marketing, personnel and communications. Job vacancies began to be advertised internally. Staff started having their performance appraised and assessed according to 'key results' under a new performance management system called 'maximising performance', known internally as 'Max'.[10]

After hundreds of managers had been shown the door, remaining managers were forced to reapply for their jobs in a process known as 'targeted selection' – something which also came from McKinsey. This was traumatic, for many employees had joined the bank aged 16 and had never been interviewed before. Some suspected the interviews were a stitch-up. One RBS senior manager who went through the process three times said, 'I hated it. It always seemed like there was a hidden agenda and it had a very negative impact on internal morale.' The hidden agenda was almost certainly to cut out 'dead wood' and ensure the bank retained only younger, less well-paid and more malleable managers who would not be averse to the notion of becoming glorified salesmen.

From 1993 onwards, there was a daily 'morning huddle' among staff at the landmark domed branch behind the Royal's registered office at 36 St Andrew Square. Each staff member was given a target of how many savings accounts they must sell that day and, if they failed to meet these targets, they risked being named 'dunce of the week'. In some Manchester branches, staff who missed sales targets were given furry toy monkeys which they had to put on their desks as a badge of shame. After segmenting its customer base, the bank prioritised middle- and upper-middle-class customers and didn't mind if it lost the business of less well-heeled customers. Unsurprisingly, the trade union was not happy about Columbus, not least because of the 3,500 job losses but also because of the way the bank was deriding employees who missed their sales targets.

A core part of Columbus was the decision to centralise and computerise credit decisions. Traditionally, these had been taken in the branches, but under Columbus they were centralised in a new credit department based in Drummond House in South Gyle, on the western fringes of Edinburgh. The 500,000-square-foot, £60-million building was opened by the Queen in July 1993 and sported a monumental bronze statue near its entrance. *The Wealth of Nations*, by Leith-born artist Eduardo Paolozzi, commissioned by non-executive director Angus Grossart, reputedly cost Royal Bank half a million pounds. Depicting a gigantic, reclining dismembered 'man machine', it is intended to show how technology was increasingly dominating human life. The inscription on it is a quote from Albert Einstein – 'Knowledge is wonderful, but imagination is even better.' The bank's 40–50 credit experts passed Paolozzi's sculpture every day on their way into work but are unlikely to have followed its message as they used new-fangled, computer-based credit scoring techniques to decide who should get credit. Banking was already becoming more automated and more outwith human control.

For the first time, new technology was making it possible for the Royal Bank of Scotland's management to gauge their exposure to specific categories of borrower such as farmers or speculative property developers at the press of a button. Other processing functions were also gradually stripped out of the branches and centralised in Drummond House. The centralisation process enabled Royal Bank of Scotland to cut costs as it meant repetition was minimised and branch staff's pay could, over time, be cut, as less skill was required. The idea was that, now that they had been freed up from administration or decision making, branch staff could focus exclusively on selling extra financial products to existing customers.

As part of Project Columbus in the mid 1990s, RBS managers had to start typing their own letters. Some 600 secretaries were made redundant and every manager was given a personal computer with some template letters on it and told just to get on with it. Many had never used a computer before and few could even type. A pilot was run in the north of England and, when RBS management saw the savings on stationery and postage, they were overjoyed. However, they hadn't realised that, instead of putting things down on paper, managers were just picking up the phone. One former RBS manager said, 'As I kept pointing out at the time, this meant there was no longer any record of what we were doing!'

Around this time, the bank also adopted a more proactive approach towards its 'distressed assets' – corporate, small and medium-sized enterprises (SME) and commercial property borrowers which were in financial difficulties, in breach of covenant or in default on loans. Mathewson hired former 3i managing director Derek Sach, who had coincided with him at 3i in the late 1970s, to review the approach. Sach established and still oversees the bank's new 'hospital' for such customers – initially it was dubbed 'Specialised Lending Services' (SLS) but now it is known as 'Global Restructuring Group'. The goal was to reduce the £400 million Royal Bank had set aside as provision for bad debts in the year to September 1992 by restructuring debt and nursing corporate assets back to health rather than just putting them into receivership.

To tackle the legacy of troubled loans on the commercial property side, Mathewson also drafted in the property expert Bill Samuel as a consultant. A former chairman of Motherwell Football Club who had run his own steel stockholding firm and a commercial property business, Samuel arrived in 1992 to help 'work out' the bank's portfolio of distressed property assets. These included industrial sheds, office blocks, retail premises, hotels and a ragbag of other properties which had come into the bank's ownership after overextended customers defaulted on loans or went bust during the 1990–92 property crash. Rather than continue selling them at fire-sale prices – the strategy the bank was deploying when he arrived and which was costing the bank £2 million a day – Samuel preferred to hold on to troublesome properties until the market picked up. Samuel assured Mathewson that inflation would come to their rescue sooner or later. Samuel was also behind the creation of a special subsidiary known as 'West Register', which was named after the lane beside the bank's 42 St Andrew Square headquarters. This became a portmanteau for the Royal Bank's property assets, including distressed assets it acquired at knockdown prices from the receivers of bust customers and third-party vendors during the downturn. The structure was innovative but it set a dangerous precedent in that it gave rise to dangerous conflicts of interest within the bank.

Insiders suggest the property situation was looking distinctly 'hairy' by the third quarter of 1992 and putting the whole bank at risk. However, Samuel's punt on a UK commercial property market recovery came good after sterling was ejected from the Exchange Rate Mechanism (ERM) (a precursor of the euro that tied exchange rates to the value of the Deutschmark and a basket of other European currencies) on 'Black Wednesday', 16 September 1992. After that date, the Bank of England, led by its governor, Eddie George, managed to stabilise the value of sterling, bring inflation under control and create a platform for the long boom of 1994–2007. Not long after that, Samuel's portfolio of distressed property assets started to come into its own and, through carefully timed disposals, it became a significant contributor to RBS's group profits from the mid 1990s.

Even younger employees found the quasi-permanent revolution of Columbus and subsequent 'change' programmes disorientating and hard to cope with. The changes continued in October 1995 when Royal

Bank embarked on yet another major restructuring by splitting its business customer base into three categories, based on the sophistication of their needs and their size. In a speech in December 1995, Mathewson said the revised structure was intended to ensure customers got better services, since more specialised managers would be more *au fait* with their individual needs.

One ex-RBS executive said that, however painful, the reorganisation was essential. 'Before Columbus, there was a huge amount of waste. There were too many people doing very, very inefficient processes. There was a lot of rekeying of data. It wasn't that people were being lazy or inefficient before – it was just that people were working with processes that were anachronistic and hadn't been updated for a very long time. RBS was the first bank to do this systematically.' Another manager, who left the bank in 2011, said, 'Nervousness about Mathewson started to dispel once Columbus was in place. To be blunt, the older managers were not switched on – many of them were just coasting along – and a clear-out was probably overdue. Mathewson and the people who came in with him were forward thinking – they recognised that the bank had to change or die a slow death. They could see the potential for increased profits and reduced staff costs. George was quite a visionary – but he was quite ruthless with it.'

Mathewson believes the bank would have faced a very uncertain future and probably have been taken over without Columbus. He sees the effects mainly in financial terms, saying, 'The outcome was far better performance, with the bank's cost-to-income ratio [going] from 65–70 down [to] below 50. The dividends and share price kept growing. Royal Bank became the first Scottish business to be capitalised at over £1 billion and the first Scottish business to make profits of more than £1 billion. The Bank of Scotland were furious with us!'

'Before Columbus, the bank had been all about measuring risk. Afterwards, bottom-line profitability was all that mattered and to hell with everything else,' laments one ex-senior manager at Royal Bank of Scotland. 'Yes the culture was too cosy before – yes it was wrong that every manager ran his own business and yes we needed a harder commercial edge, but I think we went too far the other way and became sales obsessed.'

4

Hanging on the telephone

Insurance company Direct Line was another of the profit drivers that enabled Royal Bank to survive the shocks of the early 1990s' recession. Founded in 1985 by Peter Wood from an office in Croydon, South London, Direct Line rewrote the rulebook for motor insurance. Before, the market was dominated by firms like Eagle Star, Norwich Union and General Accident, none of which sold directly to the public but, instead, traded through brokers. Direct Line smashed this clubby system apart by bypassing the middlemen and selling policies directly to the customer – first over the phone and then via the internet. At a meeting with Peter Wood in 1984, Royal Bank chief executive Charles Winter saw the potential and agreed to give Wood – a former computer programmer at merchant bank J Henry Schroder Wagg – the £20 million he needed to get the business off the ground. Thanks to its low cost-base, advanced use of telecoms and IT, use of call-centres and astute marketing, Direct Line soon became the dominant force in UK motor insurance.

An advertising campaign featuring a red phone on wheels presented Direct Line as a plucky consumer champion and was designed to show up the inadequacies of the existing insurance players. Together with First Direct, a similar direct-to-consumer brand launched by Midland Bank in October 1989, Direct Line heralded a revolution in UK financial services.

Its branchless and low-cost model enabled Direct Line to offer low premiums and have the lowest costs-to-premiums ratio in the sector. It also enjoyed a remarkably high average annual renewal rate of 80 per cent. But there was constant friction with its banking parent, especially when the bankers asked to sell their banking products to Direct Line's customers, something Wood strongly resisted. Royal Bank also found Wood's pay, which reached more than £17 million a year in 1994, a constant source of embarrassment. Wood said, 'Some of the old buffers at Royal Bank used to ask stupid questions. Frankly, I couldn't be bothered to answer them . . . They were pompous in some ways.'[1] RBS was rewarded in the early to mid 1990s when Direct Line started delivering impressive profits. These were £50 million in 1993 rising to £112 million in 1995 (more than one sixth of the RBS total). Customer numbers soared from 500,000 in 1991 to 2.5 million in 1995. Less than a decade after its launch, Direct Line had overtaken Eagle Star to become the number one seller of motor insurance in the UK. At a time when the bank was still recovering from the toxic soup of the late 1980s lending spree, this was a massive fillip. By 1993, the City was already valuing Direct Line at £1.2 billion and investors were urging Mathewson to sell it off. However, Mathewson insisted it was not for sale, describing it as a 'core part of the Royal Bank group looking forwards'.[2]

Rival insurers, including Eagle Star, jumped on the direct-to-consumer bandwagon in the mid 1990s. They managed to steal some of Direct Line's customers and its profits shrank to £26 million in 1996, the Royal Bank share price suffered and, in analyst parlance, the bank got 'de-rated'. Some analysts were pleased that RBS, which had been boasting that Direct Line was immune to the so-called 'insurance cycle' – a boom-and-bust cycle in the insurance sector – had got its comeuppance. In 1996, one analyst said, 'Direct Line turned out to be a typical, cyclical general insurer and, as soon as rates came off and claims went up, the P&L crunched from £126 million to £26 million in a year and RBS got de-rated again.'[3]

The bank's management, led by Mathewson, was reluctant to acknowledge any of this. Indeed it's fair to say bad habits set in around this time. The bank's board of directors developed a habit of treating investors' criticisms and recommendations – however legitimate – with disdain. Direct Line, which also suffered because of losses on its investment portfolio, sought to disguise the damage by diversifying into other types of insurance, including life and home insurance, as well as other financial services products.

When Wood walked away in 1997, the bank was obliged to buy him out for an additional £24 million, causing further criticism from unions, politicians, media etc. However, Wood argued that if he had created a business as successful as Direct Line in the United States he would be worth billions, not millions. The business remained an enduring part of the Royal Bank of Scotland Group for many years to come, with a proposed disposal in April 2008 scrapped after bids fell below Goodwin's £7-billion price target. The business was later sold off in tranches via a series of stock market flotations at the European Union's insistence.

Mathewson acknowledges that, without Direct Line, Royal Bank of Scotland would have had less breathing space to implement Columbus and might have gone under or been taken over in the early 1990s. Speaking at Wood's leaving do in 1997, he thanked Wood for helping the bank retain its independence.[3] Wood joked that the bank ought to erect a statue of him outside its registered office at 36 St Andrew Square. If that were to happen, Wood would be competing for space with the equestrian statue of the former Royal Bank of Scotland governor and Peninsular War hero, John Hope, 4th Earl of Hopetoun.

In 1995, Royal Bank of Scotland again showed that it was more willing to think outside the box than its larger, more staid banking peers when it formed a £40-million joint venture with Tesco, whose chief executive, Terry Leahy, had only just taken over after Tesco's earlier relationship with NatWest disintegrated. Tesco split with NatWest after the English bank refused to offer a full suite of financial products under the Tesco name for fear of cannibalising its own business. Given its own experience and understanding of multi-branding, RBS was less fearful about this sort of thing. Tesco Personal Finance was launched in July 1997. This came just five months after Sainsbury's Bank, a joint venture between Bank of Scotland and J Sainsbury, had become the UK's first supermarket bank when it launched in February 1997.

Inspired by *Foundations of Corporate Success*,[4] a 1993 book by John Kay, a professor at London Business School, Mathewson believed the bank should have an identifiable competitive advantage in everything it did. In the book, Kay argued that companies can derive competitive advantage from the creation and exploitation of distinctive capabilities.

Mathewson sought to put this into practice by turning RBS into a financial supermarket in its own right. By the mid to late 1990s, it was trading under a range of brand names, including Royal Bank of Scotland, Royal Scottish Assurance (an ill-fated joint venture with life insurers Scottish Equitable and Scottish Widows), RBS Advanta,

RoyScot, Direct Line, Tesco Personal Finance, Virgin Direct, Linea
Directa and Citizens. There were parallels with the detergents market,
where multinationals Procter & Gamble and Unilever have been slapping a range of brand names on similar formulations of soapsuds for
years. There are also parallels with how Volkswagen segments the car
market, selling vehicles with similar chassis and engines under different
marques, including VW, Audi, Seat and Skoda. Other bankers and sell-
side analysts were sceptical. To some, it smacked of opportunism – to
others, lack of focus. But Mathewson strongly believed a multi-brand
approach made sense partly because it enabled the group to win new
customers without alienating existing ones.

One ex-RBS insider says, 'One of George's principles was "competitive advantage" and one of his principles in retail banking was
to go for the soft underbelly of the big four banks. As a small newly
launched player like Virgin, Tesco or Direct Line, you can be in the
upper echelons of the best-buy tables. The multi-brand approach
enabled RBS to compete on the front book without cannibalising the
back book. If you're NatWest and Barclays there is no way you can
win enough new business to make up for the customer losses you'd
suffer.' A bank's 'back book' is its existing savers and borrowers who
are locked in to specific interest rates; its front book is its new customers
who can be lured in with 'teaser' rates. Mathewson also believed it
would be very presumptuous of the bank to impose the RBS brand
on people who had chosen to bank with acquired businesses. He used
to tell colleagues, 'There are darker forces at play here. We should let
the customers decide.' A multi-brand approach also enabled the group
to diversify its reputational risk – it meant that, if one brand became
tarnished for any reason, the damage might be contained.

The multi-brand approach was bearing fruit. In January 2000, the
bank confirmed that it had effectively doubled its personal customer
base in seven years, growing customer numbers from four million
in 1992, to eight million in 1999. Reminiscing about the glory days
of the 1990s in a valedictory interview with *The Herald* in April 2006,
Mathewson said, 'All of these things [Citizens, Direct Line, Tesco etc.]
contributed to us, for several years, being the fastest growing bank in
Britain from a situation where we were frankly in the crap. We got to
this point where we were making a billion pounds (in annual profits).
We were the first Scottish company to ever make a billion pounds.'[5]

5

Financial engineering

In presentations to the Royal Bank's board, still chaired by the patrician Sir Michael Herries, Mathewson proposed a change of strategy. Instead of transforming the group into 'one of Britain's most profitable banks, measured by return on equity, by 1997', he said the goal was to make it 'the most profitable bank, measured by return on equity, by 1997'. In a strategy paper issued in June 1991, the revised goals included: to 'capture the entire banking business of the typical personal customer'; to 'increase market share among sophisticated corporates'; to 'build market share, rather than maximise profitability, at Direct Line'; and to 'put in place the culture, internal structures and delivery channels to target and manage the relationships with corporate and personal customers'. Critically, he also said the bank would 'enhance the quality of the risk-assessing process and explicitly link this to the assessment of risk and reward'.[1]

Mathewson enlarged on these themes in a speech to a conference at the Royal Lancaster Hotel, London, in October 1991. He conceded that the banking sector was in dire straits but insisted that cost cutting alone was no route to salvation. He wanted the bank to focus on growing the profit it could earn from each individual customer through 'a more targeted definition of the customer base; a more intimate knowledge of the customer base; and a more careful monitoring of the customer base. These imply heavy investment in technology and "smarter" ways of working.' He added that essential ingredients in his turnaround strategy included 'an avoidance of the temptation [to be diverted from the long haul] by newly fashionable trends or apparent "sure things" – particularly when these seem to offer a large and apparently easy increase in the size of the loan book.'

The first division to put the new ethos to the test was the newly created Corporate and Institutional Banking Division (CIBD). This business was formed when the bank's existing corporate and institutional clients – those with annual turnover of in excess of £20 million – were lifted out of the branches and transferred to a new business unit centred in London but with operations in Manchester, Glasgow, Edinburgh, New York, Hong Kong and Singapore. In its first few months, CIBD was led by John Barclay. Barclay, who formerly ran the bank's New York office, hired Tim Goode from Midland Bank to bolster the bank's London-based treasury and capital markets business, taking it to over 100 people.[2] It wasn't long before Mathewson hired his own man, Iain Robertson – who had succeeded him as chief executive of the Scottish Development Agency – to run CIBD, with Barclay being shunted upstairs to the deputy chief executive role. The *Financial Times* said, 'Robertson is moving from County NatWest, where he is deputy chief executive and group finance director . . . This means that the Royal Bank will now have two former chief executives of the Scottish Development Agency in its top ranks.'[3] Mathewson and Robertson knew each other well, having collaborated in the 1980s, notably on an audacious public–private rescue of the Weir Group, which involved risking government funds to underwrite a rights issue for the troubled Cathcart-based pump maker.

After a law degree at Glasgow University and training as an accountant with Peat Marwick, Robertson joined the civil service in 1972, working in both the industry and energy departments in Whitehall. He returned to Scotland in 1978 to take a senior role in St Andrews House, the civil service headquarters in Edinburgh. Known as 'the Bald Eagle' by Scottish Office colleagues because of his pronounced cranium, Robertson became director of Glasgow-based Locate in Scotland, a public body that aimed to attract multinational corporations to 'Silicon Glen' or elsewhere in Scotland. He steered it through something of a purple patch in the mid 1980s, enabling successive Conservative Secretaries of State for Scotland – George Younger and Malcolm Rifkind – to trumpet a string of job-creation stories.[4] After a not entirely happy spell as Mathewson's successor as chief executive of the Scottish Development Agency between 1987 and 1990, Robertson moved to the City where he worked as finance director and deputy chief executive of County NatWest, a subsidiary of National Westminster

Bank. When he got the call from Mathewson, he was delighted to leave County NatWest as it was still traumatised by the fallout of the 'Blue Arrow' affair (a scandal involving the cover-up of a failed issue of new stock which happened before he arrived).

From CIBD's office in Birchin Court just behind the Bank of England, Robertson embarked on ambitious plans to reinvent the bank's approach to corporate banking. Soon after arriving, he conducted a survey of the bank's top 200 customers, with a view to establishing how profitable they were for the bank. Robertson recalls, 'The research showed that only about 40 or 50 of the top 200 customers (20–25 per cent) were profitable. The rest were either on the margin of profitability or loss-making.' The survey also revealed that RBS was seen as 'a plain vanilla bank' by corporate customers. This was an insult, meaning it was competent at providing basic needs like overdrafts and short-term loans but, unlike other banks such as Barclays, Chase Manhattan, Deutsche Bank or JPMorgan, it was not trusted to provide longer-term finance or complex financial engineering. 'We had some good people but were bereft of the products that customers actually wanted,' admits Robertson.[5]

Robertson and his colleagues pored over the balance sheets of major corporate customers in order to gain an understanding of their likely future financial needs. 'Over the next three years, we put in place a whole range of new products, we changed the whole way we operated, we retrained every relationship manager so they were better able to understand customers' needs,' said Robertson.[6] He also dramatically enlarged his division's product range by hiring additional talent to spearhead its growth in specific market niches. New joiners during the 1990s included: Brian Crowe, a small, slight, studious man who subsequently took holy orders, from Chase Manhattan (derivatives, treasury and market risk); Christopher Elliott from S.G. Warburg & Company (loan syndication); New Zealander Tom Hardy from Deutsche Bank (project finance); Iain Houston from Johnson Matthey and Charterhouse (structured finance); pugnacious, deal-making Scot Leith Robertson from Bank of Scotland (leveraged finance); and Johnny Cameron from Kleinwort Benson (fixed income). Leith Robertson, a high flyer in the growth market of funding private equity and management buyouts, stood out in that his arrival broke a centuries-old taboo on Bank of Scotland executives jumping ship to join RBS.

Robertson said the process of training them taught him a lot about CIBD's staff. 'We had a lot of bright people who were very competent but, when you trained them and gave them the new skills, you could see them flowering. We ended up providing a lot more financing to customers, we started offering more risk and interest-rate hedging products for the customer base and we became a lot more profitable very quickly.'[7] For Robertson, it was all about building relationships based on mutual trust.

The Corporate and Institutional Banking Division was less hide-bound by convention than many of the established banks and was not afraid to become involved in innovative ventures and partnerships. One example was Priority Sites, a joint venture with the government-backed urban regeneration quango, English Partnerships. Launched by Deputy Prime Minister John Prescott in October 1997, Priority Sites sought to develop speculative industrial and commercial floor space in more run-down areas that were shunned by traditional private sector property developers. The venture, which was 51 per cent owned by the bank and 49 per cent by the public sector, had completed 30,000 square metres of workspace across England by early 2001 and had a substantial ongoing programme of over 150,000 square metres of space in the pipeline. The bank initially injected £40 million.[8]

To aid transparency, team-building and cross-selling, RBS started to move all its corporate and institutional businesses into 175,000 square feet of modern office space at No. 2 Waterhouse Square in spring 1994. In a development behind the old Prudential Assurance Building, on Holborn, the new premises could house 1,200 staff and incorporated a 250-position dealing room. Robertson says, 'We brought five disparate parts of corporate banking and treasury all together in the one place and we actually found that people talked to each other. We did quite a lot of business on the back of that.'

The bank was aiming to ratchet up its position in treasury, including foreign exchange trading and derivatives, but only for the purposes of serving customers' needs. 'Our aim is to sell more treasury products into our well-established customer base who in the past may not automatically have turned to us for treasury services,' a Royal Bank spokesman told *FX Week*. 'It's an investment in the future.'[9]

One of the highlights of Robertson's year was an annual lunch, hosted by the bank's chairman George Younger in the RBS offices in Lombard Street and then Waterhouse Square, for around a dozen Greek shipping magnates. Royal Bank was also a major lender to the sector, mainly financing tankers and cargo ships. 'It normally ended in a major argument among the Greek ship owners. They just argue full stop. They would disagree on anything and everything,' recalls Robertson. 'And they weren't capable of quiet disagreement – there was always a lot of waving of arms and raising of voices. George Younger was brilliant at calming them down and telling them to get back to running their businesses.'

One corporate customer with whom Robertson enjoyed a good relationship was John Ritblat of the commercial property company British Land. 'He understood relationship banking better than most relationship bankers,' says Robertson. 'I probably met him twice a year and it was always a delight. He has such a breadth and depth of knowledge and experience, it was always intellectually challenging.'

A relationship with Enron, the Houston-based energy giant which went bust on 2 December 2001, was less fulfilling for the bank. Like dozens of other international banks, the Royal Bank of Scotland was enticed into Enron's financial hall of mirrors, in which nothing was quite what it seemed, by the prospect of turbocharged profits from a string of essentially bogus deals during the late 1990s. Between 1997 and 1998, RBS helped Enron facilitate fourteen structured-finance deals, three of which involved a power station in Teesside, that enabled Enron to conjure up fraudulent income and bury billions of dollars of debt. Royal's relationship with the Houston-based energy giant was, for a while, extremely lucrative, but it ended up costing the bank £200 million in bad debts – which, Robertson says, is the biggest loss he has ever made in his career – as well as a fortune in legal fees. Robertson claims that he had no idea that Enron's finance director, Andrew Fastow, who was later jailed for ten years, was a crook or that the structures to which RBS was lending were a sham. 'To be defrauded by someone like that, I just found it impossible to take. The behaviour was unsanctionable in 1,000 years. They basically had been lying for a long time,' Robertson said, adding, 'I met Fastow in London probably in about mid 2000. He wanted to come and see who the new people were because he had had a long relationship with NatWest and Gary Mulgrew, David Bermingham and Giles Darby [the so-called 'NatWest Three', investment bankers who were jailed in the USA for alleged fraud] who had left and he hoped the new people would actually meld in as well as those three had melded in.'[10]

Under Robertson, the bank also pulled out of asset management and investor services. In asset management, it sold its underperforming Capital House business to Newton Investment Management in stages between 1994 and 1998. In investor services, it sold RBS Trust Bank to the Bank of New York for up to £400 million in 1999. Richard Greensted, editor of *Scrip Issue*, the leading news, analysis and information website for the global investor services industry, says that RBS Trust Bank seems to have been a slapdash operation. 'They were pitching for new business, and talking up their operations, at the same time as breaching regulations left, right and centre.' The business received a string of fines from the Investment Management Regulatory Organisation (IMRO) in the late 1990s for what Greensted describes as a 'rather relaxed method of accounting for client assets'.[11]

Just as he was making an exit from fund management, Robertson was getting into railways. In December 1997, RBS acquired the train and rolling-stock leasing company Angel Trains from Guy Hands' Nomura Principal Finance Group, for £395 million. The government of Prime Minister John Major, who had won the 1992 election with the highest popular vote in British history, created three Rolling Stock Operating Companies (ROSCOs), as part of its privatisation of British Rail in 1994. The private equity arm of the Japanese bank Nomura had done very nicely out of Angel Trains – following some fancy financial footwork, it had extracted £440 million in profit in four years. 'We had a sense there were other things we should be doing and decided we should be doing more with asset finance. In my view, banks are properly designed for asset finance – done properly,' said Robertson.[12] 'We were up against NatWest in the bidding for it. We won because we were more nimble and were willing to work through a night and come to a conclusion. At the far end, I think RBS made well over £1 billion in profit when we sold Angel Trains five years ago. I still haven't got my bonus from that!!'[13]

Aside from the mishaps with Enron and the debacle in asset servicing, Robertson's CIBD – underpinned by a seriously enlarged treasury function – was a major success during the 1990s. Within 18 months of Robertson's arrival, CIBD was contributing half of Royal Bank of Scotland's group profits. Its profits surged from £67.7 million in 1992 to £129.7 million in 1993 (the RBS group profits rose from £0.4m to £253.8 million over the same period).[14] By 1996, the division was making at least £250 million of the wider group's pre-tax profits of £602 million. One of Robertson's goals on joining had been to ensure that, within five years, RBS was considered 'a top two relationship bank' by each and every one of its major corporate customers, and it was a goal RBS achieved. Robertson says, 'I strongly believe this was because we ensured the customer always came first. We weren't in the business of taking huge proprietary risk on our own book – full stop.'[15]

Wings spread

The first time the Royal Bank of Scotland chartered an executive jet was in mid December 1988. Four of its top brass – chief executive Charlie Winter, strategy and development director George Mathewson, group secretary Miller McLean and senior manager of group strategic planning Frank Kirwan – were crossing the Atlantic for a ceremonial dinner in Providence, Rhode Island. The event was to celebrate the completion of the purchase of New England-based bank Citizens Financial Group, the final flourish in a deal-making process that had started about 18 months earlier. It was to be the first of 30 acquisitions RBS made in the United States over the next 16 years.

As the executives ate their in-flight breakfast soon after leaving Edinburgh Airport, Winter, a modest man who would never normally have dreamed of travelling by corporate jet, joked, 'The question isn't whether we get one of these things – the question is what standard of in-flight catering we choose!' Being a relatively parsimonious and Calvinist Scottish bank, the plane they had chartered lacked the range to make it across the Atlantic Ocean in a single flight so they had to break their journey in Iceland to refuel. Winter lit up his first cigarette just after take-off and continued to chain-smoke all the way. He had difficulty getting back through security in Reykjavik Airport because the scanners kept picking up the silver foil in the many packets of cigarettes he had secreted away in his suit pockets. As they neared their destination, Providence's T.F. Green Memorial State Airport, the tiny jet passed through a powerful thunderstorm and had to divert to New York. During the tempest, Winter carried on chain-smoking inside the aircraft's tiny cabin and, when Kirwan, Mathewson and McLean disembarked, they were coughing and spluttering. 'We passively smoked our way across the Atlantic!' says one of the passengers. 'The first thing I did was take my suit to the dry cleaners.'[1]

In a speech given at a signing ceremony in Providence on 16 December, Mathewson said he saw great cultural similarities between Citizens and Royal Bank, 'We were attracted by what Citizens is – a financial organisation with an ethos and a thirst for controlled growth that matches our own.'

Winter first entered talks with Citizens chief executive George Graboys, described by one of the Royal Bank people as 'a risk-averse community banker', about a possible deal in June 1987. The planned takeover was formally announced on 29 April 1988, with Royal committing to pay $440 million (£235 million), in cash for Citizens which, at the time, had two branches in Rhode Island and 30 loan offices across New England. Citizens had grown its total assets by nearly 37 per cent over the previous two years, to $2.6 billion by the end of 1987. Its profits had not quite kept up, growing by 35 per cent over the same period to $43.6 million.

Royal Bank decided that it trusted Graboys and allowed him and the Citizens management team to run the bank pretty much as they saw fit, giving them a degree of autonomy that was surprising given the torrid experience other UK banks had had in America. In an interview with *The Providence Journal* four months after the deal was completed, Winter made it abundantly clear that the Royal Bank was giving Graboys a largely free hand. Only three RBS directors joined the Citizens board and they attended meetings in rotation. The most stringent form of oversight that was introduced by Royal Bank was the secondment of trusted bean counter Grahame Whitehead as Citizens' financial controller – his role was to ensure that the American bank's internal accounting processes were 'aligned' with those of the Royal Bank.

Haunted by memories of Midland Bank's disastrous takeover of Crocker National Bank and suspicions that Royal Bank was paying over the odds for an underwhelming US bank towards the fag end of a bull market, analysts made no secret of their displeasure. The job of the analysts, so-called 'City scribblers', is to scrutinise quoted firms – poring over balance sheets, assessing the figures, kicking tyres, being alert to banana skins and quizzing the management in an attempt to hold them to account. Employed by stockbroking firms, investment banks and asset management firms, they produce detailed research reports on quoted firms, giving investors reasons to 'buy', 'hold' or 'sell' the shares. Arguably, this relatively small group (no more than about 20 or 30 analysts follow the average company) have the power to make or break a management team.

And, in the late 1980s and early 1990s, the bank analysts were pretty sceptical about RBS. They didn't like the Citizens purchase much in the first place so, when Winter told them he was going to compound the error by buying additional banks in the US, they were reaching for the smelling salts. And Royal Bank rode roughshod over analysts' concerns. In May 1993, it was paid – yes, RBS was paid – $48.9 million to take ownership of New England Savings Bank, in New London, Connecticut, by Connecticut banking regulators. The previous month, Citizens paid $95 million to buy Boston Five Bancorp, which it had to shore up with $100 million of fresh capital. According to the Associated Press, Mathewson admitted that Royal had paid too much for Citizens at the top of the market and the Associated Press banking correspondent concluded that 'some bank analysts call the strategy brilliant, some call it stupid and others say they'll wait and see whether it works'.[2]

Between 1988 and 2000, Citizens Financial chief executives George Graboys and his successor, Lawrence K. Fish, who took the reins on 30 September 1992, bought 19 other American banks. These included: UST Corporation, Neworld Bancorp and Boston Five Bancorp (in Massachusetts); Old Stone and Bank of New England (in New England); Old Colony (in Rhode Island); First New Hampshire (in New Hampshire); and New England Savings (in Connecticut). The takeovers – which became easier following deregulatory changes in the United States that permitted American banks to open branches outside their home state from about 1996 – multiplied RBS's exposure to retail and commercial banking in the United States by a factor of ten. Royal Bank of Scotland added $21.24 billion in assets and 353 branches to the $2.6 billion in assets and 30 branches it had acquired with Citizens Financial in December 1988. Each was bolted on to, and rebranded as, Citizens.

RBS was a beneficiary of the savings and loan crisis of the late 1980s and early 1990s. In the USA, savings and loan (S&L) associations, also known as 'thrifts', are community-based organisations for savings and mortgages, which are similar to UK building societies. A relaxation of regulation under President Ronald Reagan in the 1980s, which was intended to make S&Ls more competitive, ended up nearly scuppering America's S&Ls. The sector became a cesspool of fraud, crime, corruption and fraudulent lending. The management of many S&Ls prioritised self-enrichment over sustainability. When the Federal Reserve chairman Paul Volcker raised US interest rates, the S&Ls' house of cards came tumbling down and 747 thrifts failed or needed to be bailed out. But RBS saw this as an opportunity. US bank valuations were bombed out in the early 1990s and Graboys and Fish used funds from RBS to become bottom fishers, picking up wounded US financial institutions on the cheap.

Analysts were displeased partly because, in the early 1990s, the return on equity from US banks was 10 per cent – much less than the 25 per cent that was available from the UK, where higher returns were largely the consequences of weaker competition and more apathetic and gullible consumers. The City would have far preferred that Royal focused on taking advantage of that than on Stateside adventurism in the early 1990s. They were also concerned about the bank's declining profitability – its profits (before exceptional items) dwindled from £336 million in 1989 to £241 million in 1990, to £76 million in 1991 and to £61 million in 1992 – mostly as a result of legacy issues from Royal's 1980s lending spree. To most analysts, RBS's American adventure did not just seem counter-intuitive – it seemed positively perverse.

According to Simon Samuels, a banking analyst at Barclays, who has followed the banking sector since the early 1990s at various securities brokerages including Salomon Smith Barney, RBS had offended analysts by completely ignoring their strategic preferences. In particular, their sensibilities were offended by Mathewson's refusal to pay any heed to the highly successful UK-centric approach favoured by Brian Pitman, the chief executive of Lloyds Bank. He said, 'The view in the early 1990s was that focused simple banking was a good thing and that sprawling empires around the world and exposure to corporate banking were a bad thing. But RBS was very much in an anti-Pitman mind-set. They believed in building an empire, they developed a US business out of nothing and they trumpeted and promoted their market share in corporate banking as a good thing. George Mathewson was a bit of a corporate buccaneer. He was the anti-Pitman banker.'[3]

Royal Bank's European strategy was less buccaneering but no less unpopular with the City scribblers. At heart, the bank wanted to ensure it was ahead of the pack when the single European market took effect on 1 January 1993. Europe planned to create a single borderless market of 325 million people across the 12-nation bloc, with the expectation that tax and labour laws would be harmonised and a single currency and European central bank created soon afterwards. Between 1988 and 1991, businessmen and financiers across the political bloc were salivating about the opportunities the new single market would throw up, while also being nervous of the risks if they stood still. It spawned a thousand conferences. In banking, the conventional wisdom was that '1992' would spark a frenzy of bank mergers, which would culminate in there being only seven large banks left in Europe. And Mathewson wanted RBS to be one of them.

Speaking in 1989, Mathewson said, 'The single European market is a potential force for the greater good for the wider world as well as for its own citizens. It should make Europeans wealthier, bigger consumers, and European companies more robust . . . [but] the internal evolution of the market must be along liberal competitive lines, rather than heavily regulated ones or many of the potential benefits will be frittered away.'[4] He also warned that if sterling were to stay out of single European currency the British currency would become an irrelevance and 'the consequences would be calamitous for the financial sector in Britain, in London and Edinburgh both'.[5]

In the hope of striding ahead of other banks as banking consolidated, RBS went in search of a European partner bank. Specifically, the board decided it wanted to do a deal with a long-term strategic partner that would be prepared to take ownership of the 16 per cent stake in RBS that was then owned by the Kuwait Investment Office (KIO). Having owned this stake since 1982, KIO wanted out and this was causing nervousness at the top. The board's fear was that if the KIO stake ended up in the wrong hands (say, of an aggressor like Lloyds Bank) Royal Bank would once again find itself vulnerable to takeover.

Instructed to focus on Spain, which had joined the EU two years earlier, senior manager of group strategic planning Frank Kirwan soon identified three banks – Banesto, Banco Popular and Banco Santander – as possible partners. But Santander got in touch with Royal Bank about a possible partnership before Kirwan had even picked up the phone. Kirwan and Mathewson hopped on a plane to Madrid for a meeting with Santander's executive vice-president Juan Rodríguez Inciarte. The meeting got off to a good start and, towards the end, Mathewson flagged up the possibility that some or all of the Kuwaiti stake might be available. Inciarte – who had joined Santander from Midland Bank España in 1985, having previously worked for Chase Manhattan in London – bounded across the table saying, 'Yes, yes we are interested – we should go and meet the chairman.' That evening, Mathewson and Kirwan met Emilio Botín, the third generation of Botíns to run Banco Santander, who had become chief executive only three years earlier. Again the chemistry seemed good and he was positive about the possibility of a deal.

On 3 October 1988, the Royal and Santander were ready to unveil their strategic alliance. The multifaceted deal included: cross-shareholdings between the two banks; directors of each bank sitting each other's board (RBS chairman George Younger and non-executive director Ian Grant on the Santander board, Emilio Botín and his brother Jaime on the RBS board); and a commitment to collaborate on joint ventures and other opportunities. While Santander bought a 9.9 per cent stake in the Royal Bank (which left the KIO with a 6.1 per cent stake), it granted all voting rights to the Royal – a major positive for the Scottish bank as it gave it some protection from takeover and lessened the chance of successful shareholder revolts. Meanwhile, RBS bought a 1 per cent stake in Santander. Unsurprisingly, the arrangement went down badly in the Square Mile. Investors and analysts saw it as cosy stitch-up that protected management and undermined shareholders' democratic rights.

Unveiling record half-year profits of £171 million, which were bolstered by a fair amount of reckless lending into the property and house bubble of the 'Lawson Boom', Winter enthused about the Santander alliance. On 3 May 1989, he told analysts that the two banks were already making 'impressive progress' on franchising links, cross-continent cash machines and joint corporate services.[6] However, Kirwan says that the alliance never really blossomed as Royal Bank had hoped. 'The ability of RBS customers to put their cards into Santander cash machines to get out pesetas was the most tangible achievement. But neither the joint venture into the Spanish mortgage market for ex-pats nor the notion of serving RBS clients from Santander branches ever really got off the ground.'[7] But the alliance did bring other benefits. It opened the eyes of the Edinburgh-based bankers, who had been somewhat cloistered in their St Andrew Square headquarters, to banking developments elsewhere. It gave them a sounding board. And it gave them a deep-pocketed and loyal partner which would team up with them on some major deals in the years ahead.

Simon Samuels believes that Royal Bank of Scotland drew the wrong conclusions from the success of its US and Spanish adventures. He says, 'A recurring theme at RBS was that it was a rebellious and contrarian bank. This was both the making and the breaking of it. By the late 1990s, RBS was beginning to get some credit for its contrarian strategy and that fuelled George's and Fred Goodwin's egos, tempting them to think that, whatever the City consensus was, they could do the exact opposite. They took it as proof that, if they were to bet black and everybody else had bet white, black would always come up.'[8] There was also an element of 'Wha's like us? Damn few and they're a' deid' creeping in at the top of Royal Bank in the 1990s, with some ex-insiders claiming the swaggering self-confidence was bolstered by the psychological effect that the film *Braveheart*, released in May 1995, had on the national psyche.

One former senior insider believes Mathewson paid insufficient attention to the extent to which the positive economic backdrop of the 1994–99 bull market had contributed to the Royal's success. 'In banking, there was a big following wind throughout the 1990s and this, arguably, bred some complacency. With hindsight, one of George's less brilliant ideas was to run the bank in a very highly geared way [that is with a weak capital base, a high degree of leverage and a dependence on wholesale funding markets]. George felt that all the Columbus changes in risk management had made the bank invulnerable.'

George's big ambition

The 1990s was a transformational decade for Britain's banks and building societies. For many years, the building societies, most of which could trace their origins to the Victorian era, had been locally focused, community-minded savings and loans organisations. Their model was simple and safe – they took in deposits from savers and then lent money to people who wanted to buy a house, within tightly defined geographical areas. Until the early 1980s, they were a protected species with a near monopoly of UK mortgage lending, with rates set centrally.

However, the freedoms introduced by the Thatcher government, enshrined in the Building Societies Act of 1986, changed all that. Building societies were suddenly able to do most of the things that banks could do – such as offering current accounts and a full range of personal financial services including tax-efficient savings vehicles called personal equity plans (PEPs) and tax exempt special savings accounts (TESSAs). In need of capital, building society bosses were tempted by the idea of demutualising then converting their institutions into joint-stock banks. Abbey National was the first to go down this route, in July 1989. As other large building societies pondered the future, banks were trawling the country, shark-like, in the hope of persuading building societies to sell to them instead. After all, it would remove their worries about capital and shield managements from the vicissitudes of the stock market, while enabling the banks to get their hands on savers' deposits and giving them a captive audience for the 'cross-selling' of financial products.

The Royal Bank of Scotland blew hot and cold about the idea of snapping up a building society throughout the 1990s. Speaking at a board meeting in 42 St Andrew Square on 14 March 1990, Winter said he had already lined up several societies as takeover targets. However, after Mathewson became deputy chief executive the following year, the plan was shelved. At a board meeting on 26 June 1991, Mathewson said that residential mortgages could be reached more cost effectively through 'aggressive marketing' of Direct Line insurance products. Mathewson predicted demand for residential mortgages would decline over the next ten years 'as a result of demographic trends'. He also warned that the 'difficulties of integrating a banking culture with a building society culture were greater than originally envisaged'.[1] So the plan was put on ice.

One positive spin-off from Royal Bank's strategic alliance with Banco Santander was that it provided an informal high-level forum at which Mathewson and colleagues, including successive strategy directors Frank Kirwan and Iain Allan (a qualified actuary who joined from UBS Phillips & Drew in December 1993), could compare notes and mull over strategic options with their Santander counterparts. The sessions were normally held in either Edinburgh or Madrid one day before a board meeting. Mathewson and colleagues became accustomed to sharing ideas with the Santander directors Juan Rodríguez Inciarte and Emilio Botín – both of whom were regular visitors to Edinburgh as a result of their roles as non-executive directors on Royal Bank's board. One consensual view that emerged from these sessions was that banking sector consolidation was going to accelerate and that any bank that failed to make acquisitions would become a takeover target itself. It was 'eat or be eaten', said one ex-RBS executive.

In September 1992, a small private bank, Adam & Company, established by a group of Edinburgh business people in 1983, admitted it had got itself into serious difficulties. A Nick Leeson-style 'rogue' trader in its London-based treasury department had covered up losses of £21 million following a string of disastrous dollar/Deutschmark foreign exchange bets. 'The dealer acted as a rather inexperienced gambler at a roulette table and continued to bet on the same outcome, backing the dollar against the Deutschmark, doubling up from time to time as the situation became more desperate', Adam's former chairman, Sir Charles Fraser, told *The Glasgow Herald*.[2] The losses wiped out the private bank's capital base and there was a real risk it would go down the tubes. The board responded by closing down the offending treasury unit, suspending the trader and arranging to meet the bank's largest shareholder, 75-year-old Mme Françoise Schlumberger Primat, in her Normandy chateau. Adam's chief executive, James Laurenson and director of banking, Ray Entwistle, flew to France and managed to persuade *La Grande Dame* and her advisors that it would be in her interests to rescue the bank with a cash injection of around £21 million.

The Glasgow Herald's Eric Baird wrote, 'In theatrical terms, Mme Primat was not just an investing "angel" but a whole host.'[3] Entwistle and Laurenson also managed to persuade the Bank of England to give the near-bust private bank some breathing space while they put it on a more even financial keel. After the foreign-exchange losses became public, the Royal Bank helped shore up Adam's finances by arranging sufficient facilities to safeguard it from the risk of a liquidity crisis arising from a possible run on the bank. The run never materialised but Adam was severely weakened and, in the teeth of vehement opposition from founder director Sir Iain Noble, its board agreed, in July 1993, to sell it to the Royal Bank for £10.5 million. Of that, £9.5 million went straight to Mme Schlumberger Primat, who chose to take the loss rather than wait for her convertible preference shares to be repaid over 20 years.[4] As the ink dried on the deal, Mathewson said: 'The purchase will enable us to offer Adam's private client fund management services to more people in Scotland. Adam will keep its own board and identity for the time being because that's what the customers want.'[5] In the end, Royal Bank of Scotland ran Adam – which had offices in Edinburgh, Glasgow, London and Guernsey and some 4,000 current account customers – in an arm's-length fashion for 17 years. It kept its own identity, information technology systems, customer service ethos, investment strategy and board of directors until 2010. However, in the wake of the debacle, chief executive James Laurenson left the bank and was replaced as chief executive by Ray Entwistle.

By 1994 it was clear the UK was emerging out of recession, and talk of a building society takeover was rekindled in 42 St Andrew Square. Over the next four years, Mathewson held tentative merger talks with a number of societies and other mutually owned financial institutions up and down the United Kingdom. He later told *The Scotsman*, 'I would expect some of the mortgage banks to go [be acquired or merge] over the next five years. I don't think they have the firepower to really be serious players.'[6]

One early paramour was the Cheltenham & Gloucester Building Society (C&G). But RBS's plan was stymied in April 1994 when Lloyds' chief executive Brian Pitman snatched the 140-year-old Cheltenham & Gloucester from under Royal Bank's nose. Terry Eccles, a northerner who headed up the financial institutions group at investment bank JPMorgan, was instrumental in advising Pitman on the deal. Lloyds became the first British bank to buy a building society and the deal put them ahead of the game. Apart from the carpetbaggers who had opened accounts within the previous two years, C&G's 800,000 members received windfalls of between £500 and £13,500 and, within a matter of months, C&G mortgages were being pumped hard through the Lloyds branch network.

John Major was into his third year as prime minister, his party was in a state of civil war over Europe and he was struggling to explain what the 'back to basics' policy actually meant. Disappointed that C&G had escaped his grasp, Mathewson turned his attention to the Trustee Savings Bank (TSB), founded in the 19th century for customers of modest means. As an amalgamation of UK savings banks, it had a much more populist, thrift-based tradition than Royal Bank. However, by the early 1990s the bank, whose slogan was 'the bank that likes to say yes', had lost its way. It had failed to settle on a viable strategy in the wake of its 1986 stock market flotation and was widely seen as a sitting duck for takeover. Its ill-timed £777-million acquisition of merchant bank Hill Samuel in October 1987 had exacerbated its plight. To Mathewson's chagrin, Lloyds again snatched TSB from under his nose and JPMorgan's Eccles was, once again, Lloyds' secret weapon.

Other mutuals that were eyed up by Mathewson during the 1990s included: the Woolwich (demutualised and floated in 1997 and swallowed up by Barclays in 2000); Halifax (demutualised and floated in 1997 and merged with Bank of Scotland in 2001); Nationwide (which retained its mutual status); and Scottish Widows (demutualised and swallowed up by Lloyds in 2000). So why did all these courtships end in rejection? One ex-RBS insider said, 'What we did was the equivalent of waving a little flag and, after no one paid any attention, we just hid.' Some ex-colleagues believe it was because Mathewson feared that a failed takeover would put Royal Bank 'in play' – that is, in City parlance, make it susceptible to takeover. One former colleague says,

'The pattern was George dreamed of the pretty girl but didn't quite have the guts to chase her because he was scared he'd end up with egg on his face.' There was also the issue of contacts. Mathewson lacked the connections of London-based bank chairmen like Lloyds Bank's Sir Jeremy Morse.

As several doors slammed in Mathewson's face, one opened. Hong Kong and Shanghai Banking Corporation (HSBC), which had been barred from acquiring Royal Bank of Scotland by the Monopolies and Mergers Commission in January 1982, had a second stab at taking it over in 1996, one year before Hong Kong, then a British colony, was handed back to China. HSBC's chairman and chief executive Sir William 'Willie' Purves, a revered Kelso-born banker, visited George Younger's London flat for discreet talks with the RBS top brass. Younger and Purves had both served in Scottish regiments during the Korean War and immediately hit it off. Younger was not averse to a deal so long as HSBC provided firm guarantees that it would retain the Royal Bank brand and preserve Scottish jobs. Mathewson was more sceptical – he still thought RBS's 'strategic options' strategy had plenty of mileage in it. HSBC volunteered to make some concessions if it would ease the path to a deal, including relocating its global headquarters from London (where they had been since 1993) to Edinburgh. In the end, however, the talks foundered over Mathewson's insistence that he should be chief executive of the merged group. This struck some members of the HSBC camp as ludicrous, given Mathewson's comparative lack of banking experience and the size difference between the two banks. Ex-colleagues say it was largely owing to Mathewson's intransigence on this score that another door was closed.[7]

In May 1997, Tony Blair won the general election after turning the Labour Party away from socialism and towards free markets and wealth creation. The British press had worked itself up into a lather of excitement about the 'gold rush' of windfalls – usually ranging from a few hundred to a few thousand pounds – available to members of building societies and mutual insurers that converted to banks. The renewed rush to demutualise presented the banks with some exciting acquisition opportunities. However, partly because of the collapse in profitability at Direct Line, which had weakened its share price, and the thinness of its capital layer, the Royal Bank was still considered vulnerable in banking circles. Eager to overturn this irksome assumption,

Mathewson decided to acquire the Wolverhampton-based building society Birmingham Midshires.

On 13 August 1997, Mathewson announced an agreed deal to buy Birmingham Midshires for between £605 and £630 million. Mathewson said the deal would double Royal Bank's residential mortgage book and increase its retail savings balances by 75 per cent. Ahead of the deal being made public, Mathewson was asked at an informal gathering of Royal Bank executives about his plans for the brand. The assumption among the RBS executives was that he would want to rebrand its operations under the Royal Bank of Scotland banner to raise RBS's profile south of the border. Instead, he declared that the Birmingham Midshires name would stay. 'We'll keep the name and run it as a separate division,' he said. People's surprise was understandable. Earlier acquisitions like National Commercial Bank of Scotland and Williams & Glyn's had been rebranded as RBS in recent years. Ex-insiders see it as the moment when the bank's unorthodox 'multi-brand' approach was born.

Mathewson resented investors' failure to recognise his success in turning round RBS over the past seven years. Even after the success of Nova Reda, Project Columbus and Direct Line, the unorthodox buy-and-build strategy of Citizens in the United States and the massive growth of the corporate division under Iain Robertson, many in the City were unconvinced by the bank that George had built. 'Analysts complained that he [Mathewson] ran the bank like a venture capital company,' wrote Caroline Merrell in *The Times*. 'Sir George, in turn, found it difficult to conceal his dislike of what he believed to be a short-sighted view of RBS by investors, which led to the shares being undervalued compared with those of its peers.'[8]

As Mathewson pondered how to escape from this bind, the nation was mourning the death of Diana, Princess of Wales. She was killed, aged 36, in a car crash in Paris on 31 August 1997. Meanwhile, New Labour were making all the right economic noises with Chancellor Gordon Brown saying the newly elected government was not going to try and build a 'New Jerusalem' on a 'mountain of debt'. Royal Bank directors found the remarks reassuring, especially given the fiscal ineptitude of most previous Labour governments.

In the end, Royal did not acquire Birmingham Midshires. After a vocal bunch of the society's members accused its board of selling the society on the cheap and Mathewson made clear that RBS was not willing to pay a penny more than £630 million, Halifax trumped Royal Bank's bid with a £780-million offer. The Yorkshire-based mortgage bank was hungry for deals in the wake of its conversion to joint-stock bank status the previous year. In the end, it secured its prey, triggering windfalls of £1,250 each for Birmingham Midshires customers, more than they would have got out of Mathewson's sporran.

Mathewson's failure to capture Birmingham Midshires caused mutterings in the Square Mile. The view was that if the Royal Bank of Scotland couldn't even buy a medium-sized UK building society, it had little chance of remaining independent. Mathewson rubbished such talk. In July 1998, he told a press conference in Edinburgh: 'I don't think either of the Scottish banks [Royal Bank of Scotland or Bank of Scotland] will be absorbed. We are both doing well enough. Our profits and share price would make it difficult for anyone. Also the synergies are not there – we don't have so much to shut.'9

Bridling at City scorn and desperate to ensure Royal Bank of Scotland didn't become somebody else's lunch, Mathewson pulled out all the stops in his attempts to make an acquisition south of the Border. And this time, rather than footling about with mere building societies, he wanted to shoot the lights out with the acquisition of a bank. With perfect timing, all hell broke loose at Barclays. On Friday 27 November 1998, the bank's reformist chief executive Martin Taylor, a former *Financial Times* journalist once described as 'the cleverest boss in Britain', resigned unexpectedly. Taylor wanted to sell or quarantine the risk of Barclays' 'casino' arm, Barclays de Zoete Wedd (BZW), after it lost £325 million on Russian bonds during the Rouble Crisis of August 1998. But a cabal of knights on the Barclays board was determined to keep BZW at any price, apparently seeing it as a patriotic duty for Barclays. Another flashpoint came over 'leaks' of boardroom papers to the *Sunday Telegraph* and the *Daily Telegraph*, apparently designed to undermine Taylor. There was also a disagreement between Taylor and Barclays' chairman, Andrew Buxton, after the latter allegedly reneged on promises he had made the chief executive. Some directors were also unhappy that Taylor – described in the media as a 'wunderkind', when he took over as Barclays' chief executive in November 1993 – had wasted time advising the New Labour government on a planned over-haul of National Insurance. They felt he should have been manning the pumps.[10] By October 1998, Taylor felt he had little choice other than to resign.

When the resignation announcement came, the City of London was stunned. On the same day, Barclays also warned that its 1998 profits would be £300 million less than the £2.2 billion analysts were expecting. This triggered an 8 per cent fall in Barclays' share price. In an interview with *Management Today*'s Andrew Davidson, Taylor said, 'The board was attached to this fantasy of a UK champion [in relation to the future of BZW]. It was absurd, absolutely absurd.' Taylor said there was a fundamental clash between the 'shareholder-value model' – meaning doing what is best for the share price – and the 'old-fashioned establishment model'.[11]

A company without a chief executive and whose strategy lies in tatters is 'in play' and RBS did not waste any time in targeting a takeover. Advised by JPMorgan's Terry Eccles and probably also egged on by new recruit Fred Goodwin, who joined from Clydesdale on 1 August 1998 (see chapter 8), Mathewson was less timid than in earlier courtships. He made a beeline for the Barclays board and sought to tell them that the Royal Bank of Scotland had a management team that was supremely well qualified to turn Barclays around, given Mathewson's leadership of 'change' programmes and Goodwin's reputation as a fearsome cost-cutter at Clydesdale Bank. But he said they were only prepared to come to the table if Barclays would agree to a 'reverse takeover' – City jargon for a deal in which a smaller institution takes over a larger one and its management takes the reins in the enlarged entity. One investment banker says, 'Eccles and his team at JPMorgan had a good sniff around. Royal Bank did all the sums and Mathewson tried to persuade Sir Peter Middleton, the Barclays chairman, to hear him out.' However, huge tranches of Barclays' shares remained in the ownership of the bank's very grand founding Quaker families (including the Bevans, Gurneys, Peases, Tukes, Trittons and Thomsons) who were reluctant to throw in their lot with an 'oik' and a 'Jock' like Mathewson. Even so, Middleton reluctantly agreed to a meeting to discuss the proposal and it was fixed for the second week of February.

A few days later Middleton called Mathewson to tell him the meeting was off since the bank had appointed a new chief executive to replace Taylor – Michael O'Neill, chief financial officer of Bank of America. O'Neill was due to start at Barclays' Lombard Street headquarters in April 1999. When O'Neill, a 52-year-old former US Marine, fell ill and was unable to take up the Barclays job, Mathewson saw it as an opportunity to have a second stab at a £22-billion reverse takeover of Barclays, which he believed would be an excellent swan-song to his seven years as RBS chief executive. Having dusted down its numbers from February, Royal Bank claimed it would be able to cut the enlarged group's costs by £500 million a year in the event of a merger. Michael Lever, banking analyst at HSBC, said that cost savings might be even higher. He said, 'A merged group would have total assets of £290 billion . . . the second largest in the banking sector. Cost savings of just under £850m pre-tax might be possible, with nearly 70 per cent of these coming from Barclays. There would also be potential for cross-selling based on complementary product strengths as well as an enhanced customer base and additional distribution channels.'[12]

The Scottish bank went as far as notifying the Takeover Panel, a non-statutory body which regulates mergers and acquisitions. 'George was going around the City saying, in his usual tactful way, that the best thing for Barclays would be to be taken over by Royal Bank,' said Peter Burt, the former chief executive Bank of Scotland.[13] However, the proposals remained anathema to the founding families and Middleton refused to be railroaded into a deal.

Mathewson eventually pinned Middleton down for a one-to-one meeting. The pair had lunch in the Savoy on London's Strand at some stage in April. The meeting did not go well. Mathewson told Middleton, 'I feel that we have the management, that we can take over Barclays and that that would be to the benefit of your shareholders.'[14] However, in the politest possible way, Middleton told Mathewson to get lost. Mathewson recalls, 'It was quite obvious he was not really interested.'[15] The RBS chief executive was 'quite crestfallen' on his return to St Andrew Square, according to former colleagues. Nevertheless, the feedback from the meeting was useful to the bank. It began to realise that Barclays had totemic significance in the City and was unlikely ever to be available for takeover. However, what also became apparent was that the City saw National Westminster Bank rather differently. RBS realised that investors in the Square Mile would welcome a takeover of the Lothbury-based institution, given that it was so scandal-plagued and poorly managed.

In the late 1990s, the stock market was rallying in what turned out to be the dying days of a long bull market. The FTSE-100 index hit an all-time high of 6,930 on 30 December 1999. Irrational exuberance, perhaps encapsulated by the New Labour 1997 election theme song D:Ream's 'Things Can Only Get Better', was the order of the day amid talk of the 'new economic paradigm' caused by the rise of the internet. Shares in internet – or dotcom – businesses, many of which turned out to be flaky and worthless, were being aggressively touted by financial intermediaries. And, with or without internet banking arms, 'bricks and mortar' banks were seeing their share prices go through the roof. Between the end of 1998 and mid April 1999, the share prices of both Royal Bank and Barclays surged by 40 per cent, with Royal Bank of Scotland hitting 1425p and Barclays 1999p.

Mathewson kept up the pressure on Barclays for most of May and June. In a sign it was feeling the heat, Barclays said it would cut 6,000 jobs or about 10 per cent of its UK workforce, saving £200 million a year. Mathewson asked his investment bank advisors at JPMorgan, Goldman Sachs and UBS to examine the possibility of 'going hostile' – going over the heads of Barclays' board and appealing directly to the English bank's shareholders. He had some champions in the media including Andrew Garfield, financial editor of *The Independent*, but, to his credit, Garfield leavened his cheerleading with criticism: 'At times, the degree of devotion Sir George has inspired in those closest to him can seem dangerously like hero-worship. Others, even within the bank, can find him insufferably arrogant and bemoan the fact that since Bob Spiers retired as finance director there is no one on the board to hold him in check . . . Critics accuse him of lacking clear strategic focus, and of simply buying anything that moves. Some say RBS, for a bank of its size, has its fingers in too many pies.'[16]

In Scotland, there was pride that a local player had parked its tanks on Barclays's front lawn. But there was also concern that a deal would see Royal Bank's centre of gravity drift south. Writing in the *Sunday Herald*, Alf Young commented, 'The nominal combined headquarters might well have been St Andrew Square, but Sir George and the others would have been London-bound five days a week, for months, perhaps years, to come.'[17] In a speech to his own bank's Corporate and Institutional Banking Division in June 1999, Mathewson insisted that a deal would be good for both sets of shareholders and 'a unique opportunity to create value'.[18]

But institutional investors refused to prod the Barclays board into giving Royal Bank of Scotland a hearing. RBS suspected they were closing ranks in order to protect one of their own. Mathewson had not gone out of his way to cultivate links with the City and many City-based investors regarded him as uncultured, aggressive and with an overinflated sense of his own worth. One financial editor wrote that his 'overtly Scottish separatist views go down like a lead balloon with the City establishment'.[19] At 59, he was due to retire in 2000 and his heir apparent, Fred Goodwin, had limited banking experience. One investment bank advisor to the Royal Bank thought the structure put together by Eccles was likely to short-change Barclays shareholders: 'It was in RBS paper [that is RBS shares rather than cash] and worth only 10 per cent more than the Barclays share price at the time. So it was only going to work if Royal Bank of Scotland's share price went up by 10 or 15 per cent on the announcement of the deal. I said to George, "This deal just isn't going to happen." The trouble is, like most Scots, he politely listened to your advice and then ignored it.'

The Bank of England governor Eddie George, a chain-smoking Cambridge-educated economist who was said to be 'as thick as thieves' with the Barclays chairman, decided it was time to call a halt to Mathewson's rough wooing. He had a word in the ear of RBS chairman George Younger, telling him Mathewson's behaviour simply was not on, and Mathewson's dream was finally shattered when, on 28 July 1999, Barclays announced the appointment of Matthew Barrett, the 54-year-old chairman of the Bank of Montreal, as its next chief executive. So, despite all the bluster, no hostile bid ever emerged. A senior Scottish banker said, 'Royal Bank needs to consummate. They walked away from Midshires, their courting of Halifax came to nothing and now Barclays, it would appear, have spurned them. There were others as well. Will they always be jilted?'

A year earlier, two even larger bank mega-mergers were consummated in the United States – NationsBank merged with BankAmerica to form Bank of America and Citicorp merged with Travelers to form Citigroup. The latter of these mega-mergers was technically illegal at the time and forced Washington's hand where banking regulation was concerned. The administration of President Bill Clinton, swayed by ex-Wall Streeters in its midst, believed it had no option other than to repeal large parts of the Glass–Steagall Act. The 1933 Act prevented deposit-taking retail banks from sharing the same ownership as securities broker-dealers and investment banks, thus limiting the chance that depositors' cash, which was subject to state guarantee, could be frittered away in the 'casino' of the financial markets. The unpicking of the Act in 1998 and 1999 sent a powerful and dangerous message to Wall Street and the banking industry that, if they lobbied sufficiently hard, they would get what they wanted.

'The most worrisome problem is that these new Goliaths will touch every American citizen and corporation, and will be so intertwined with major financial firms around the world that they will never be allowed to fail,' wrote Jeffrey E. Garten, dean of the Yale School of Management and a former Undersecretary of Commerce in the Clinton administration in September 1997.[20] 'Knowing that they cannot go belly-up, these firms may take even more risks than they now do. On the one hand, taxpayers may be called upon to shore them up when they get into big trouble.'[21] Garten, a former managing director of Lehman Brothers and the Blackstone Group, continued, '[F]inancial firms that are not disciplined by real threats of failure could create economic havoc by financing too much or too little and by exaggerating the already rising volatility in world stock markets and currencies . . . several factors could lead them into dangerous territory. They will be ferociously competing with one another and with their European and Asian rivals. The firms' top managements will be increasingly reliant on computers to assess investments precisely when human judgments about risk have never been more critical. In addition, our regulatory system . . . may be too fragmented to keep up with the new conglomerates.'[22] Every one of his predictions was to come true over the course of the next decade.

With the tide moving firmly towards less regulation, some remained determined to swim in the opposite direction. In 1998, Brooksley Born, chair of the Commodities Futures Trading Commission, a Washington-based regulator of derivatives trading, warned that unregulated derivatives markets with no constraints on the amount of borrowed money that could be used to buy derivatives could 'pose grave dangers to our economy'.[23] Born circulated a 13-page draft proposal putting forward questions about the evolution of the derivatives market and outlining possible new rules. Wall Street investment banks reacted furiously. The regulators alongside whom Born worked – Federal Reserve Chairman Alan Greenspan, Treasury Secretary Robert Rubin (a former co-chair and co-senior partner of Goldman Sachs) and US Securities and Exchange Commission Chairman Arthur Levitt – thought she was insane. They believed any further regulation of financial markets would be economically disastrous and that Born's proposal to regulate derivatives and force such trades onto regulated exchanges was perverse, since it would undermine the legality of trillions of dollars of existing derivative contracts, disrupt the free flow of finance and undermine US prosperity and economic supremacy. The Deputy Treasury Secretary Larry Summers called Born and said, 'I have thirteen bankers in my office, and they say if you go forward with this you will cause the worst financial crisis since World War II.'[24]

Derivatives – which include futures, swaps and options – are essentially bets on future prices. The key to understanding them is that those who buy them are betting on the future value of an asset. By enabling companies that are selling and distributing physical goods (BP delivering oil or an agribusiness selling grain, for example) to hedge against future price fluctuations, derivatives serve an essential economic function. Used sensibly, they are a pragmatic solution to the randomness that had characterised the global economy since President Richard Nixon unilaterally scrapped the Bretton Woods agreement in 1971. But derivatives – later dubbed 'financial weapons of mass destruction' by Warren Buffett, chairman of Nebraska-based insurance conglomerate Berkshire Hathaway – were increasingly being used by investment banks and other sophisticated investors for gambling. They were also being used by banks and other financial institutions to obfuscate and distort their balance sheets, subvert regulations, game the system and artificially boost both profitability and executives' bonuses. As business journalist Gillian Tett says, 'At the heart of the business is a dance with time . . . This new form of trade spread fast across Wall Street and the City of London, mutating into wildly complex deals that seemed to give bankers God-like powers. With derivatives they could dismember existing assets or contracts and write contracts that resurrected them in entirely new ways, earning huge fees.'[25]

In the end, Born's heresies were crushed and she lost her job. As the former IMF chief economist Simon Johnson and former McKinsey consultant James Kwak wrote, 'By 1998, when it came to questions of modern finance and financial regulation, Wall Street executives and lobbyists had many sympathetic ears in government, and important policymakers were inclined to follow their advice. Finance had become a complex, highly quantitative field that only the Wall Street bankers and their backers in academia (including multiple Nobel Prize winners) had mastered, and people who questioned them could be dismissed as ignorant Luddites.'[26]

The Fred and Johnny show

During the summer of 1997 George Mathewson was coming under pressure to find a successor. He had been Royal Bank of Scotland's chief executive for just over five years. He would turn 60 in May 2000 and Sir Iain Vallance and other non-executive directors wanted to ensure that he had a deputy in place who would be capable of taking the reins when the need arose. Mathewson had a chat with Iain Robertson, who had successfully built up RBS's corporate banking and treasury arm between 1992 and 1998 and was now chief executive of the Royal Bank of Scotland's UK Bank. But Robertson told him he wasn't interested. He was put off by the media relations and investor relations aspects of the job, which take up at least 25 per cent of the average chief executive's time. Mathewson also had an informal chat with Dumfries-born John McFarlane, who had recently stepped down as group executive director of Standard Chartered. However, nothing came of that either and, a few weeks later, McFarlane took a job as chief executive of Australian and New Zealand Banking Group (ANZ) in Melbourne. Headhunters retained by Royal Bank of Scotland scoured the world but failed to deliver a suitable successor.

The Asian crisis, which erupted in July 1997 after the collapse of the Thai baht, was a major concern to banks which had lent heavily to south-east Asian countries including Indonesia, Malaysia, the Philippines and South Korea. These so-called Asian Tiger economies went into sharp reverse in 1997–98. The Royal Bank of Scotland was less affected than banks like HSBC and Standard Chartered but there was no guarantee that the instability wouldn't be infectious. At the time, Mathewson was more preoccupied with things closer to home, including the imminent launch of the Virgin One account in partnership with Virgin founder Richard Branson, and the planned takeover of Birmingham Midshires.

Then Mathewson had a brainwave. He had come across Fred Goodwin, a gangly, bespectacled Paisley Buddy, who had been chief executive of Clydesdale Bank for just over a year, at meetings of the Committee of Scottish Clearing Bankers (CSCB), a trade body for the banking sector, in Edinburgh. Mathewson (RBS chief executive since 1992), Alastair Dempster (TSB Scotland chief executive since 1992), Peter Burt (Bank of Scotland chief executive since 1996) and Goodwin (Clydesdale Bank chief executive since March 1996) met every few months at the CSCB, where they tried to put their banks' common interests ahead of their normal competitive instincts.

Mathewson was impressed by Goodwin's intellect, grasp of detail and no-nonsense approach. He recalls, 'Fundamentally, I thought he was a very bright guy and everything he said at the meetings seemed to make sense. It struck me that here was somebody who could become finance director and who had the potential to be chief executive. Right here on our doorstep.'[1]

The finance director slot was available because RBS's then finance director, Bob Spiers, 61, who joined from property group Olympia & York Canary Wharf in July 1993, was due to retire. After a boardroom discussion about how the appointment might be pitched, Mathewson bumped into Goodwin at a cocktail party in the Scottish National Gallery on the Mound. Surrounded by idealised classical landscapes by Claude Lorrain and Nicolas Poussin, Mathewson popped the question. Would Goodwin, then 39, be interested in becoming Royal Bank of Scotland's finance director? He was thinking that, if Goodwin could be persuaded to leave Clydesdale at this point, he could become one of several internal candidates for the top job.

Goodwin told Mathewson he wasn't interested unless Mathewson could give him some sort of guarantee that he was his anointed successor. He also told Mathewson that he had agreed to go to Melbourne, Australia, on a six-month secondment with Clydesdale Bank's owners, National Australia Bank (NAB). Mathewson said he would consider Goodwin's request and that he was perfectly happy to await Goodwin's return. During his sojourn 'Down Under', Goodwin was also being 'groomed' to take over the reins from the Melbourne-based bank's cheif executive Don Argus, who had hired him for the Clydesdale role two years earlier and who was due to retire in 1999. While in Melbourne, Goodwin oversaw a reorganisation of NAB, including the 'streamlining' of its head office. One Australian banker who was at NAB at the time said, 'Fred was not well liked and his wife Joyce didn't like us colonials. We were very grateful to her when she encouraged him to return to Scotland.' Joyce Goodwin's desire to leave was not just fuelled by antipathy for the Lucky Country's inhabitants. She also had no desire to permanently transplant their two young children – John and Honor – 10,500 miles away from their friends and family. One ex-colleague says, 'The joke was that Fred didn't like the climate in Australia but I think genuinely Joyce missed Scotland.'

On his return from Melbourne in May, succession talks resumed. Eager to secure Goodwin, Mathewson caved in to most of the chartered accountant's demands. Goodwin ended up with a generous package, complete with a £90,000 'golden hello' and the title 'deputy chief executive' which implied he was the heir apparent from day one. The bank also agreed to allow Goodwin to join RBS's defined benefit pension scheme on the (fictional) basis that he had been with RBS since the age of twenty. The bank also agreed that, for the years of Goodwin's employment, his pension benefits would accrue at twice the usual rate, 2/60ths, of his pensionable earnings per year. Mathewson claims this was common practice at the time. However, it was this deal, hammered out in May–July 1998, that would later enable Goodwin to retire on two-thirds of his final salary from the age of 50, giving rise to one of the UK's biggest-ever business controversies. In exchange, Goodwin was prepared to throw in the benefits accrued from his Deloitte & Touche and Clydesdale Bank pensions. The bank's remuneration committee – then chaired by George Younger and with Iain Vallance, Angus Grossart, Robin Duthie and Bill Wilson as members – saw Goodwin as hot property and believed he deserved a generous package. One member recalls, 'We were keen to have him. We knew he was good enough and we wanted to have him – as George wanted to have him.' At a media conference to unveil the appointment on 7 July 1998, most journalists present were in no doubt that Goodwin was Mathewson's heir apparent, but Mathewson refused to confirm this. He added that, if Goodwin were ever to become the Royal Bank chief executive, he would earn a place in Scottish banking history. 'If – and I say if – Fred eventually gets my job, he will be unique in having signed the banknotes of the two banks.' Rival bankers were crowing about the appointment, saying it revealed that RBS was incapable of growing its own talent and smacked of desperation.

Aspects of Fred Goodwin's character, including his bizarre need to intimidate others and the 'Fred the Shred' moniker were well known in Scotland's business world at the time. In an article published on 8 July 1998, *The Herald*'s deputy business editor Ian McConnell wrote, 'The chartered accountant's decision to switch horses further depletes a Clydesdale top management team already hit by departures which have been attributed to his "autocratic" style.' McConnell added, 'Goodwin has earned the nickname "Fred the Shred" for the restructuring which he has effected at Clydesdale . . . But, attempting to dispel criticism of his management style yesterday, he said, "I am happy to be judged on my track record . . . I don't believe I do have an autocratic style. At the end of the day, individuals will characterise things differently, depending on how it has impacted on them." ' At Clydesdale Bank, where Goodwin was deeply unpopular after 15 months as chief executive, staff were delighted to see the back of him and cracked open the champagne on the news. Cameron McPhail, a former head of wealth management at RBS, told the BBC, 'My first hearing that Fred Goodwin was coming on board was a call from the Clydesdale Bank, where they said they had been celebrating his departure for three days now; and they wished us all the very best of luck.'[2]

Frederick Anderson Goodwin was born on 17 August 1958 and brought up in Ferguslie Park, a housing estate in north-west Paisley, Renfrewshire. He spent his first decade in a 'four-in-a-block' property, at 28 Tannahill Terrace. 'He came from the better-off end of Ferguslie – a police sergeant lived in his block and the Provost just across the road – and Goodwin would have seen potential and been hungry for success,' says retired driver Henry Lawrie who now lives in the Goodwin family's former home.[3] The suburb, located between Paisley town centre and the Rootes Group car plant at Linwood, where Hillman Imps were made, housed 13,500 people in 3,500 dwellings at its peak. Goodwin's father, also called Fred, was an electrical engineer with Kilpatrick & Son, which became part of the Balfour Beatty group, and is said to have had high hopes for his son. He has variously been described as 'a tyrant' and 'a complete bampot'. His mother's name is Mary Lynn (née Macintosh). Goodwin had a sister, Dale, and a brother, Andrew. Young Freddy, as he was known locally, once got into a fight with a boy named Dennis Taylor. When he lost, according to two contemporaries cited by the *Sunday Times*, Freddy's father came out and held Taylor down behind a lilac tree, while Goodwin punched him in the face. Goodwin has said he has no recollection of the incident.[4] At the age of eight, Young Freddy was badly injured after being struck down by a car as he walked home from school. His leg was in a cast for months and contemporaries claim that he was pampered after that. When he was about ten, his parents gave him a go-cart which came wrapped in brown paper and local kids were asked to come round to sing the US Navy song, 'Anchors Aweigh' as he unwrapped it.[5] Not long after that, the family moved house, leaving Ferguslie Park for the more affluent Paisley suburb of Ralston – also in Renfrewshire but closer to Glasgow city centre. Young Freddy got a place at Paisley Grammar School – a prestigious selective state school which took one in ten applicants and where parents were required to pay a modest fee.

Although not hugely gifted academically, Goodwin stood out. He played rugby instead of football, supported Rangers instead of St Mirren, his local football team, and he was the first of his peers to own his own car. This, a gold Rover 3500, was his pride and joy. When Goodwin and several of his Paisley Grammar School contemporaries went up to Glasgow University to read law in 1975, most continued to live with their parents in Paisley. Goodwin set up a car pool and became their chauffeur, giving four fellow students, including the brothers Ian and Alan Smart, a lift to and from university. At the end of each journey, Goodwin would carefully work out how much each passenger owed in petrol money, which alienated some. Alan Smart, a former head of broadcasting at the Scottish Parliament, who was a regular passenger in the Rover, says, 'Fred was always right-wing, I don't know about now but he was definitely a true blue Tory then. He was also a "no" voter in the 1979 devolution referendum.'[6] At university, where he was the first Goodwin from the family to receive higher education, Goodwin occasionally skipped lectures in order to play pinball. Smart says, 'For a while, we played every lunch time and you could see the competitive streak in him. Sometimes we would dodge lectures if we went on a good run and won a lot of bonus games.' Goodwin was narrowly beaten by Alan Smart in an unofficial championship played in the basement of

Glasgow University Union.[7] Goodwin recalls, 'Sometimes I would go home at night with my arms aching from working the flipper and I once won the top prize of £1 in a student competition. But it was great fun.'[8] According to Smart, Goodwin wasn't 'a big boozer' – just 'an unassuming nice guy who was good company'.[9]

After gaining his law degree in 1979, Goodwin chose not to use it. He turned instead to accountancy. This further distanced him from his law-class contemporaries, most of whom went straight into apprenticeships with Glasgow law firms. Goodwin joined Touche Ross, then the seventh-biggest accountancy firm in the UK. He qualified as a chartered accountant with the Institute of Chartered Accountants of Scotland in 1983 and, between 1985 and 1987, he helped turn the Thatcherite privatisation dream into reality. He led a team of consultants at Rosyth naval dockyard on the Firth of Forth whose role was to knock the yard into shape ahead of its privatisation. Militant dockers handed out leaflets urging resistance to Goodwin's proposals and 'a union leader warned him that "the [River] Forth will run red" if he pushed ahead'. But Goodwin would not be cowed. In 1988 he was appointed an executive director of Northern Ireland's largest industrial employer, the aerospace group Short Brothers, ahead of its 1989 privatisation. Goodwin once said he liked the access that auditing brings: 'People think auditing is deathly boring but I loved it. There are very few other positions where someone who's just left university can go into the managing director's office and ask, why did you do that like that?'

It was at this point that Goodwin met Joyce Elizabeth McLean. Around the same age as Fred and with an MBA from Strathclyde University, she had worked in commercial finance for Citibank and French group Compagnie Bancaire before co-founding Glasgow-based finance boutique LMS Mortgage Consultants. She quit in 1990, the year the couple married, and they settled in the Renfrewshire village of Kilmacolm, 15 miles west of Glasgow.

Goodwin's attention to detail and ability to get things done impressed his bosses at Touche Ross, especially the firm's UK managing partner John Connolly, who ensured he became their youngest-ever partner. In 1988 Goodwin's biggest claim to fame during his time with Touche Ross, which became known as Deloitte following a merger in 1990, was his involvement with the liquidation of Bank of Credit and Commerce International (BCCI).

The shadowy banking empire, which laundered money for Saddam Hussein and the Medellin drug cartel (run by the gangster Pablo Escobar) among others, had been exploiting loopholes in the global banking supervisory framework for years. The bank's founder, Agha Hasan Abedi of Pakistan, had deliberately organised its operations to avoid detection, putting key offices in tax secrecy jurisdictions including Luxembourg and the Cayman Islands. He then worked with a coterie of front men to conceal the baksheesh and the bank's hidden control of businesses. In a coordinated swoop, the Bank of England and regulators in other countries shut down its branches and seized the bank's assets on 5 July 1991. Majority-owned by Sheikh Zayed bin Sultan Al Nahyan of Abu Dhabi, BCCI claimed to have assets of $14 billion but most of this had simply melted away. Six of Deloitte's partners were appointed as liquidators in various jurisdictions to retrieve as much hidden loot as possible. Goodwin was not among them. What he did was run the global liquidation's back office, which meant he was responsible for deploying resources (up to 500 Deloitte staff worked full-time on the liquidation for nine years) ensuring the insolvency partners had the necessary software and hardware, paring costs, handling billing and overseeing litigation.

One Deloitte manager who worked with Goodwin on the liquidation was bemused by Goodwin's approach. 'I found him rude, abrupt, opinionated and secretive. It was huge relief when he left.' The source claims that, before he upped sticks to join Clydesdale Bank in 1995, Goodwin left former colleagues with a nasty surprise. Deloitte was being sued by BCCI Holdings (Luxembourg) SA and its joint liquidators, the Luxembourg lawyers Georges Baden and Julien Roden, in a dispute over some £100 million in fees. Baden and Roden claimed that Deloitte's bill was excessive. Just prior to leaving Deloitte, Goodwin unilaterally settled with the Luxembourg lawyers, agreeing to cut approximately £8 million from the bill. What perplexed some colleagues was that he did this without even consulting them. 'That was some parting gift!' said the ex-Deloitte manager. 'Nobody could understand how or why he'd done it. To this day I'm at a loss. He left us with a massive bill, while also undermining our ability to charge fees.' Others say that Goodwin's experience of the BCCI cesspool taught him enduring lessons about geopolitical risk. 'It left Goodwin deeply suspicious of any lending to the Far East. It may have changed his world view about where, and where not, to be in business.'

Goodwin consistently misrepresented his role in the BCCI winding-up exercise. The Edinburgh-based financier Peter de Vink recalls: 'The very first time I met Fred was at a dinner with Gerard Eadie [chairman of double-glazing firm CR Smith]. Before Fred arrived, I was told that, at a very young age, he had single-handedly led the BCCI liquidation. I expressed astonishment. When I asked Fred about it over dinner, he led us to believe that he was the sole partner in charge – and at no point did he acknowledge that he was part of a team. A few months later, I met Brian Smouha at a friend's house in London. Brian was introduced as the senior Deloitte's person on the BCCI liquidation. I said to Brian, "But I thought that Fred Goodwin led that." I'll never forget his face. Without saying a word, Brian conveyed the impression he'd never heard anything so ridiculous in all his life!'

Later on, while at RBS, Goodwin claimed to have been the 'chief operating officer of the worldwide liquidation of BCCI'. This claim also caused raised eyebrows among Goodwin's ex-colleagues at Deloitte. One said, 'Deloitte never used titles like that. You were either an insolvency partner or you were not. Fred was not.'

Goodwin did little to dispel the myth and, to this day, there are still people who believe Goodwin single-handedly led the global liquidation of BCCI. As recently as 2012, newspapers, including *The Guardian*, *Daily Mail*, *Mail on Sunday*, *Telegraph* and *The Times*, have claimed he led the liquidation. The myth was convenient for Goodwin, but to embellish your CV is a serious offence. The example which sprang to de Vink's mind was that of Jimmy Gulliver, the Scottish entrepreneur who was pushed out as chairman by the board of Argyll Group, owners of Safeway supermarkets, after falsely claiming to have an MBA from Harvard University.

Another banking client Goodwin advised when he was at Touche Ross was Melbourne-based National Australia Bank. He advised on its £472-million acquisition of Clydesdale Bank, Northern Bank and National Irish Bank in 1987 (the Australian bank bought all three banks as a job lot from the ailing Midland Bank). He also advised NAB on its £893-million purchase of Yorkshire Bank in 1990. NAB's acquisition spree was initiated by Don Argus before he became chief executive and carried on afterwards.[10] Arguably, if it had not happened, Goodwin would never have become a banker.

Before these takeovers went ahead, Argus wanted Goodwin to carry out due diligence of the targets, which meant sifting their loan books, looking out for irregularities and un-creditworthy borrowers. The thoroughness with which Goodwin carried out the task impressed Argus. In 1995, Argus plucked Goodwin from the obscurity of the world of bean counting and offered him the role of Clydesdale deputy chief executive, with the chance to become chief executive after interim Clydesdale CEO Frank Cicutto returned to Australia. It is possible that none of this would have happened if Charles Love, a career banker who was appointed chief executive of Clydesdale in 1992, had not died of a heart attack while on a skiing holiday in December 1993.

Speaking to *The Herald* about his new job on the day it was announced in early March 1995, Goodwin said, 'Whilst, for a number of years, my work has been very much involved with banks, this is the first time I will actually be part of the management team. I could not have chosen a more interesting point at which to move into banking, both in terms of change taking place in the sector and developments within the Clydesdale Bank itself.'[11]

However, within days of arriving at Clydesdale Bank's St Vincent Place headquarters in 1995, Goodwin had alienated almost the entire management team. His control-freakery came as a massive shock. They could not believe that Goodwin only allowed them the time it took him to peel and eat a banana to make internal pitches. They were shocked when he rejected their carefully worked-up business plans on a whim. One ex-Clydesdale senior manager says, 'A colleague and I had spent weeks working up a deal which had already been signed off by everyone in the bank. We walked in to meet him for the first time, expecting him to sign it off. He looked at us and then said, "We're not doing the deal . . . Now, would you like a cup of tea?" It was extraordinary behaviour.' The ex-senior manager went on to say, 'Fred was a micromanager and a deeply unpleasant individual. He is probably the most difficult and overbearing individual I've ever had to work with.'

Goodwin seemed to delight in tearing strips off colleagues and 'shredding' them in front of their colleagues. Even David Thorburn, who had been best man at Fred and Joyce's wedding in 1990 and studied law with Goodwin at Glasgow University, was not spared. Ex-Clydesdale insiders were stunned when Goodwin 'annihilated' Thorburn, then Clydesdale's regional manager for north-east Scotland, at an 'away day' in front of senior colleagues. Goodwin launched the verbal onslaught because Thorburn had moved one of the statues in Clydesdale's Aberdeen branch without permission. One ex-colleague recalls, 'Fred went mental. I had never seen anything like it. It was astonishing considering they were supposed to be personal friends.' It was also around this time that Goodwin told a newspaper that he had no time for 'cynics, spectators, or dead wood'.

Soon after being promoted to the top job on Cicutto's return to Australia in March 1996 – aged only 37 – Goodwin had a replica long-sword, similar to the one used by Mel Gibson in the movie *Braveheart*, hung on the wall behind his seat in the bank's board room. One former senior executive at Clydesdale says, 'I kept having this awful thought he was going to remove it from the wall and start brandishing it about – and maybe even slice someone's head off.'

Goodwin had long harboured ambitions to run the Clydesdale. He told the *Sunday Telegraph*, 'This'll sound corny but there was only one job I ever saw in my auditing days that I really fancied – chief executive of Clydesdale.'[12] Goodwin's contemporaries from Paisley Grammar and Glasgow University were astonished that 'Young Freddy' had climbed so high, so fast. They wondered whether this could be the same unassuming Goodwin they had known in their younger days. The business journalist Alf Young went to interview Goodwin in the bank's office at 30 St Vincent Place in Glasgow around this time and recalls there was a rack of leaflets with details of mortgage offers in the waiting room. Young asked Goodwin, 'Which of these deals, hand on heart, is the best deal over 10 years?' But Goodwin refused to answer. Young believes this typified how banking was evolving. 'It no longer had anything to do with customer service or giving people the best deal. His sole goal was to take this sleepy Scottish bank and make it a force to be reckoned with. He was convinced that he could deliver that for the Australians – make it a real force.'[13] Understanding the product and serving the customer had been sacrificed on the altars of growth and Goodwin's ego.

Goodwin's obsession with decor, appearance and tidiness was another surprise to Clydesdale's 5,500 staff. One day, he forced a group of senior managers onto their hands and knees to pluck weeds from the car park of the bank's Glasgow headquarters. And, in 1997, he ordered a mass tidy-up across the entire Clydesdale and Yorkshire Bank net-work, which stretched from the Midlands to the north of Scotland.

Fred's anti-litter crusade saw unsightly piles of paper removed from the group's 610 branches and notices taken off the walls. Sellotaped notices were a particular bugbear for Goodwin. On 17 July 1997, according to the author and columnist Iain Martin, divisional and district managers were ordered to appear in front of Goodwin to report on progress with the great clean-up. Martin wrote, 'Some appeared to be terrified; others struggled to keep a straight face.'[14] During the campaign, Goodwin was apprehended when taking photographs of the exterior of the branch in his home village of Bridge of Weir by Strathclyde Police. He felt the area around the cash machine was too scruffy and wanted evidence. The police officers refused to believe that the tall gangly young man with a camera could possibly be the banking group's chief executive. They arrested him and took him back to the police station for questioning, where he eventually persuaded them who he was.[15] Goodwin also had an obsession with knives, forks and spoons. After colleagues ordered a brand-new set of cutlery for the Clydesdale Bank Plaza, the bank's flagship business banking centre on Edinburgh's Lothian Road, Fred insisted this was junked and replaced with a silver service that was more to his taste.

Goodwin's strange obsessions with minutiae did not prevent him from delivering improved financial results. In his short time as chief executive of Clydesdale Bank, Goodwin managed to drive up profitability and drive down costs – which meant sacking a fair few people. He also commenced work on harmonising the IT systems of the NAB's four UK and Irish banks. However, critics claim it all came at a tremendous human cost. One said, 'Fred left the banks as hollowed-out shells.'

Fred's hobbies were largely solitary – rebuilding greenhouses, restoring his 1972 Triumph Stag and playing video games. However, he did play golf and took up one more social pursuit around this time – pheasant shooting – partly because he wanted to ingratiate himself with the upper echelons of Scottish society. In the 1990s, Goodwin was taught how to wield a 12-bore shotgun by Gerard Eadie, chairman of Dunfermline-based conservatories and double-glazing firm, CR Smith, at Eadie's estate near Kinross.

On learning Goodwin had taken up shooting, Peter de Vink decided to invite him to join a shooting party on the edge of the Moorfoot Hills in Midlothian. De Vink recalls, 'I realised Fred had only recently taken it up so I asked him if he'd like me to organise "a man" – an instruc-

tor to stand with him. He looked at me with disgust and said he was
perfectly capable and safe on his own. When Fred arrived dressed in an
immaculate tweed suit, the moment he took his gun out of its sleeve,
I could tell he was an absolute beginner and wished I had insisted on
him being supervised.' De Vink was concerned Fred would wipe out
one of his other guests. As with BCCI, Fred had been unable to resist
the temptation to exaggerate his skills.

After being poached for the Royal Bank of Scotland job and following his brief sojourn in Australia, Goodwin arrived for work at
42 St Andrew Square on 1 August 1998. In his first full year as the
Edinburgh-based bank's finance director and deputy chief executive,
he was paid a salary of £382,000 and a bonus of £190,000. Together
with certain other benefits this took his first year's pay to £592,000.

During August to September 1998 the Connecticut-based hedge
fund Long-Term Capital Management collapsed, creating jitters in the
financial markets and a precedent-setting $3.6-billion bailout supervised
by the US Federal Reserve. Goodwin was touring Royal Bank's various
outposts at this time and was very much in listening mode. One thing
that struck those who encountered him was his lack of interest in the
details of credit scoring or anything to do with the finance director role.
Given this was supposedly why Goodwin had come – after all, finance
director Bob Spiers was due to retire in October 1998 – Goodwin's
uninterestedness struck observers as strange. The assumption was that,
under a deal with Mathewson, he intended to delegate this part of the
job and, indeed, finance and risk director Grahame Whitehead did
fulfil many of the functions until the arrival of Fred Watt in September
2002. One ex-colleague said, 'In the 12 months prior to getting his teeth
into the NatWest takeover, Fred didn't actually seem to do anything.
In his first year, we were all bemused, wondering, "What's the point of
Fred and what is he here to do?" He was very poised but we weren't
sure what for.'

Goodwin was already displaying some decidedly odd behavioural
characteristics. One ex-colleague recalls: 'In his first few weeks at
Royal Bank, Fred's tactic was to unsettle people by being deliberately
confrontational. For example, he had my personal assistant in tears.
I remember having to calm her down afterwards and just thinking,
"What an arse." It was by no means an isolated incident. It was part
of a deliberate pattern of behaviour which, arguably, bordered on the

psychotic. My experience of Fred at a personal level was that he was utterly charming, very good company, good fun. But he had this weird capacity to switch between business and pleasure in the blink of an eye. For example, you might have had an excellent evening with Fred and then, the next morning, he would be demolishing you in front of colleagues for some minor transgression, without so much as a flicker.'

Goodwin soon developed a habit of verbally tearing people apart at morning meetings. Held every day between 9.30 a.m. and 10 a.m., these united a small group of top executives in Edinburgh, London and locations elsewhere via videoconferencing suites. The aim was to discuss and deal with urgent and day-to-day issues, ensuring decisions were made quickly. But Goodwin quickly turned them into a freak show. He would pick on one senior executive at each meeting and then eviscerate them in front of their colleagues. One ex-RBS senior insider says, 'Fred created a feeling of terror, which was hugely counterproductive for the bank. People were scared to speak up around him. Fred clinically destroyed people with his intellect. I remember one guy at a meeting who said something silly – he was trying to show off. And Fred just destroyed him in front of everyone. Fred then started to crack his fingers – one of his ways of intimidating people. The guy immediately left the bank!'

The meetings soon became known as 'morning beatings' and the executives waiting for Goodwin would play games of Hangman to see who might be 'strung up' next. Johnny Cameron was frequently on the receiving end of Fred's wrath. Ex-colleagues remember him 'absolutely quaking . . . shitting it'. Cameron was prepared to tolerate Goodwin's trashings and stood up to him more than most but he did find them irksome. One senior RBS source said, 'Fred was at his worst during the morning meetings. He enjoyed grandstanding in front of ten or so people. After a contretemps with one of us executives, Fred would stare at us fiercely, fiercely, fox-like – with thin eyes.'

An affable and well-spoken career banker, Cameron was frequently mocked by Fred over his unconventional attire. At one morning meeting in the winter, by videoconference, Cameron, who had long since given up wearing the company tie, was wearing a rather natty pullover. Goodwin's standard joke was: 'What's Johnny's woolly jersey today? What are they all wearing down in London these days?' He would also occasionally mock Cameron for being the son of a clan chief, for being landed gentry, for being an Old Harrovian and for having a posh accent.

John Alistair Nigel Cameron was at the opposite end of the social scale from Goodwin. An Old Harrovian, he is a 'Chelsea Highlander' to the extent that he has forsaken the Scottish glens for a home in Chelsea and his visits to Scotland are mainly limited to stalking, shooting and fishing on the family's 70,000-acre estate at Achnacarry, near Fort William. Ex-colleagues believe that 'the boy from Paisley' was jealous of Cameron's upper-class roots.

Cameron, appointed by Iain Robertson, joined RBS on a basic salary of £275,000 a couple of weeks before Goodwin. He was hired as number two to Robertson in what was then the bank's Corporate and Institutional Banking arm and agreed to take the job on the second approach from Robertson partly because he was led to believe he too would be in the running to succeed Mathewson. Born in Inverness in June 1954, Cameron is the second son of Col. Sir Donald Cameron of Lochiel, 26th chief of Clan Cameron, a chartered accountant who fought with the Lovat Scouts and the Cameron Highlanders in the Second World War. His mother is Margaret Gathorne-Hardy, a niece of the 3rd Earl of Cranbrook. Cameron *père* was on the board of the Royal Bank of Scotland for many years and was its vice-chairman from 1969 to 1980. Johnny's ancestor Sir Donald Cameron of Lochiel, 'Gentle' Lochiel, the 19th chief of Clan Cameron, is a Jacobite hero, having raised an army for Prince Charles Edward Stuart, the 'Young Pretender' in August 1745 ahead of the doomed '45 Rebellion. An accomplished rugby player in his youth, Johnny gained a 2:1 in politics, philosophy and economics from Christ Church College Oxford before moving to Hong Kong to work for the trading company Jardine Matheson from 1976 to 1980, whose controlling shareholders, the Keswick family, were longstanding family friends.

After spending 1980–81 studying management at MIT Sloan School of Management in Boston, Cameron made an abortive attempt at getting into the City but ended up working for McKinsey & Company between 1981 and 1983. Cameron did not particularly like management consultancy, finding spreadsheets and report writing tiresome and, after marrying Julia Wurtzburg, the daughter of Count Raymond Wurtzburg, in 1982, he moved to the niche investment bank, County NatWest, in 1983. Buoyed by the Lawson boom and the market liberalisation that came with 'Big Bang', County Bank, as it was then called, was going through a purple patch. It was ahead of the pack where innovative funding structures for commercial property deals were concerned. However, County had a pivotal role in the 'Blue Arrow' affair (the merchant bank was found to have duped investors into investing in a rights issue, or share sale, that became one of the biggest City scandals of the 1980s and culminated in three senior executives being sentenced to suspended jail terms which were quashed at the Court of Appeal in July 1992). Cameron had no involvement in the scandal. However, it caused a loss of nerve at County. The stigma of possible criminality, coupled with the stock market crash of October 1987, caused its parent, NatWest, to clamp down. Cameron left the following year and spent 1988 to 1998 at Kleinwort Benson, another City investment bank, where he survived its 1995 sale to Germany's Dresdner Bank – another big step in the so-called 'Wimbledonisation' of the Square Mile, when pukka British merchant banks and firms of stockbrokers sold out to overseas players eager to get a toehold in London. At Kleinwort Benson, Cameron is said to have exploited his easy charm and quasi-aristocratic status to the full. 'The mentality in the City at the time was very much churn them and burn them,' said one Square Mile insider. 'Johnny couldn't be more charming and hail-fellow-well-met, but his guile is well rehearsed.' The second son of Lochiel was arguably well suited to take on the role of 'super salesman' inside Robertson's burgeoning Corporate and Institutional Banking empire.

Norman McLuskie, deputy chief executive of Royal Bank of Scotland's UK Bank, was another target of Fred Goodwin's wrath. And, after company secretary Miller McLean had been subjected to a particularly vicious bruising, he was spotted wandering around St Andrew Square in a daze, having concluded his career was over. One reason Goodwin behaved in this manner was his supreme self-confidence. He thought he was the best lawyer, the best accountant, the best banker, the best PR person, the best economist. But the Paisley-born accountant also seems to have derived pleasure from humiliating people and may have seen it as a way of exerting authority, quashing dissent and suppressing rivals. One senior ex-colleague says, 'I think Fred was both evil and mad. He would punish, pulverise and beat people up. He was a sadist.'

Goodwin also frequently turned against people on credit committees (committees of senior bankers whose role is to approve larger
loans). Any bank manager who introduced a remotely flaky or poorly
presented proposal when Goodwin was there would be shredded.
Robertson says, 'I ended up spending a lot of time after meetings trying
to calm people down and working out how to deal with the customer
fallout. I think there was a degree of showboating to it but there really
isn't any room for that.' One senior manager on the corporate side
remembers Goodwin saying the bank should pull the rug out from one
of Edinburgh's largest businesses – apparently on a whim. Attending
a credit committee as part of his induction process in 1998, Goodwin
said, 'I don't like this business – I think we should sever this connection.' The corporate executive said the business was a long-standing
customer, wasn't in breach of covenant, had reasonable cash flow and
was asset-rich for the purposes of the bank's security. In the end, other
members of the credit committee including Mathewson overruled him
and the customer survived to trade another day. It was an early sign of
the tyrannical abuse of business borrowers – especially asset-rich ones.

Goodwin later insisted that Robert Taylor, the US-born head of
the private banking arm at NatWest subsidiary Coutts & Co, should
become his personal bank manager, even though this broke all the
internal rules – the head of private banking was not supposed to
manage individual accounts. One day, Taylor's personal assistant
opened a letter from Goodwin. It was a handwritten note, attached
to a letter that Taylor had earlier mailed to Goodwin. In the spidery,
sloping hand that was his trademark, Goodwin had written, 'Robert,
you may have thought you had a career at this bank. You can now
consider it over. Fred.' On reading this, Taylor's secretary burst into
tears. Distraught, she was thinking, 'Oh my God, what have I done?
I've lost Rob his job.' It seemed that Taylor was going to be fired – and
all because of her error. A few days earlier, she had mistakenly put a
draft (complete with corrections) of a letter to Goodwin folded inside
an envelope alongside the final, signed version of the letter. She went
up to Taylor and volunteered to resign as she thought she'd ruined his
career. But Taylor consoled her saying, 'Don't worry. This is a total
over-reaction on Fred's part. Sometimes he can be a bit of a psycho-
path. I'll deal with it.'

RBS's culture had been open and collegiate under Mathewson

but Goodwin's menacing behaviour was causing it to deteriorate fast. Desperate to avoid being singled out for the Fred treatment, people tended to keep their heads down. They might launch initiatives without telling Goodwin for fear of having them knocked back. The culture shifted from one that promoted creativity and entrepreneurialism to one that stifled it and in which internal audit function, which totted up the figures internally, became known as 'the Stasi'. Goodwin's strengths – which included a powerful intellect, superb memory and a willingness to confront difficult issues – were undermined by his Rottweiler-esque approach to managing people.

But Mathewson, still chief executive at this point, was relaxed about Goodwin's behaviour – where management styles were concerned, it seems he was catholic in his tastes. This is surprising given that, nearly a decade earlier in March 1991, Mathewson told Royal Bank of Scotland branch managers that 'counterproductive misfits must be decisively dealt with. Among the most damaging, in my opinion, are bullies – bullies to their subordinates, but sycophants to their superiors'[16] (*see* Chapter 2, p. 24). Mathewson says, 'Fred's style is not my style, OK? But I've always recognised that there's more than one way of skinning a cat. And you can look through all the management theory you like – theory X, theory Y etc. And I can come up with examples of any of these styles working.'[17] One ex-colleague says, 'George treated Fred like the prodigal son and was protective and supportive of him.' Mathewson also believed that, over time, Goodwin would mellow and mature. Like a young Bordeaux, he may have been a bit rough around the edges but he was sure to develop into one of the grand vintages.

In the nine months that followed Goodwin's arrival at the bank, Scotland was abuzz with excitement at the prospect of getting its parliament back after a gap of nearly three centuries. In September 1997, 74.3 per cent of Scots voted in favour of devolution and Blair's government passed the Scotland Act the following year. Following the Scottish parliamentary elections of 6 May 1999, a coalition government of Labour and the Liberal Democrats came into power. The parliament, initially located in the Assembly Hall of the General Assembly of the Church of Scotland on the Mound, opened for business on 12 May 1999. At the opening ceremony, the acting presiding officer Winnie Ewing MSP, said, 'The Scottish Parliament, adjourned on the 25th day of March in the year 1707, is hereby reconvened.'

Fred Goodwin – who voted 'no' in the March 1979 referendum on Scottish devolution – was sceptical and derisive about the new parliament and could see little point in the bank engaging with it. He just thought that Royal Bank of Scotland, as an emerging global player, was too big for that sort of thing and, in any case, the regulation of financial services was a 'reserved power' under the Scotland Act, meaning it would continue to be controlled by Westminster. In the end, however, he decided to outsource the bank's interaction with the new parliament to the Edinburgh-based industry lobby group, Scottish Financial Enterprise (SFE), then led by chief executive Ray Perman. Goodwin had wanted RBS to sever ties with SFE and, had the bank done so, as one of the biggest contributors to SFE's coffers, it would probably have caused the organisation to collapse. But Perman managed to persuade Goodwin that RBS would need to engage with the new Scottish parliament somehow and that SFE would be the perfect vehicle for doing this. But Goodwin still thought the Scottish parliament – which had voted itself out of existence in 1707 in a deal without which the Royal Bank of Scotland would not have come into being – a bit of a joke.

In early 1999 Mathewson had a brainwave. The Royal Bank was running out of space – the main head office buildings at 42 St Andrew Square, 38–52 West Register Street and Drummond House in South Gyle were becoming increasingly overcrowded and embarrassingly shabby. It needed a new head office. He arranged for the bank to buy New St Andrews House, a brutalist 240,000-square-foot office block, to the rear of the company's existing St Andrew Square head office. This concrete carbuncle of a building had lain empty for many years after the discovery of asbestos had forced the civil service to find alternative accommodation. The plan was to demolish it and build a 300,000-square-foot 'World Headquarters' for Royal Bank of Scotland in its place. Mathewson aimed to create an iconic building of which Edinburgh and Scotland could be proud. The plan was very well received locally by the media and politicians. Even conservation groups, delighted that the hideous New St Andrews House would face the wrecking ball, welcomed it. Further positives included that the scheme would help regenerate a relatively run-down part of Edinburgh and that the bank was showing its commitment to remaining in Edinburgh. During the design phase, Mathewson was a regular visitor to the

Forres Street offices of the Royal Bank's favoured architectural practice, Michael Laird Architects. The Lord Provost of Edinburgh, Eric
Milligan, was present at one of the coffee-fuelled design sessions. A
bank official told Milligan, 'You know, if you don't let us build this,
we'll be off!' It was a bullying approach that was later to reap rewards
for the bank.

But the project was beset with problems. These largely stemmed
from the fact that while the spatially-challenged bank had bought
New St Andrews House, it had failed to buy the 1970s shopping centre
underneath – the St James Centre. That was owned by Coal Pension
Properties and managed by LaSalle Investment Management, a subsidiary of Jones Lang LaSalle. LaSalle was concerned about possible
disruption to the shopping mall during the construction phase and
was looking for hefty indemnities from the bank. Meanwhile, RBS's
security chiefs were alarmed by the prospect of having an open access
retail mall directly underneath the head office. They feared this might
leave them vulnerable to bomb attack.

After taking the reins from Mathewson on 6 March 2000, Fred
Goodwin started to cool towards the project and it was not just because
it was Mathewson's baby. He found the demands of LaSalle's Scottish
director Stephen Spray tiresome and feared the project exposed the
bank to massive risk, including that the construction budget could be
overshot and completion be delayed. Other reasons for Goodwin's lack
of enthusiasm included that he personally wanted the head office to
be closer to Edinburgh Airport and he was hankering after something
that would make more of a statement about Royal Bank of Scotland,
something that would echo the ethos of the Silicon Valley technology
giants, which were increasingly monopolising the upper echelons of
the Fortune 500 rankings. He was impressed by – even jealous of – the
€480-million La Ciudad Financiera that Santander's chairman Emilio
Botín was constructing at Boadilla del Monte, 15 kilometres west of
Madrid. When complete, the sprawling Ciudad Financiera would
house all of Santander's 12,000 head office staff in nine office buildings,
while incorporating a kindergarten, a sports complex, an art gallery,
a 'university' or training centre and even an 18-hole golf course. If
Botín had one of these, Goodwin wanted one too. In October 2000,
Goodwin pulled the plug on the New St Andrews House project.

9

Bagging NatWest

By September 1999, NatWest was a beached whale of an institution with an unfortunate habit of lurching from one crisis to the next. In February 1997, six senior traders and managers in its investment banking division, NatWest Markets, were dismissed after covering up £92 million of losses resulting from bad bets on interest-rate options. The debacle led to NatWest and two of its former employees – trader Kyriacos Papouis and his boss, Neil Dodgson – being fined £375,000 by the Securities and Futures Authority (SFA).[1] Since 'Big Bang' in 1986, NatWest had been trying to build a serious global investment bank and had spent £550 million buying investment-banking boutiques Gleacher, Hambro Magan and Greenwich Capital. But it was failing miserably. NatWest Markets was accident-prone, suffered from a lack of management controls and had very high costs. After NatWest Markets lost £706 million in 1997, NatWest chief executive Derek Wanless accepted defeat and announced that the acquired businesses would be sold. For investors, it was a strategic U-turn too far.

NatWest – formed from the 1970 merger of Westminster Bank and National Provincial Bank – was a bank imbued with a civil-service ethos. One ex-NatWest senior manager says, 'NatWest was a big lumbering dinosaur, run by pale, male and stale executives who were so out of touch it was laughable. It suffered from labyrinthine bureaucracy and decision-making. It took one of my colleagues 17 signatures to get a message out to the branch network. It was an organisation that was dead from the neck up.' NatWest executive directors were pampered, with each reportedly having five secretaries and chauffeur-driven limousines at their beck and call. One director is said to have had three houses paid for by the bank – one in London, one in Paris and one in

Rome. Other senior executives were charging NatWest for domestic staff. When Sir Ian MacLaurin, the former chairman of Tesco, joined the bank's board in 1990, he was surprised to discover that, after board meetings, the directors sat down to a formal dinner with a liveried waiter behind each chair. One leading bank analyst said, 'NatWest, ShatWest, CrapWest, as everybody called it, was a joke of a bank. It was hugely underinvested, it had been badly managed for 20 years, its profitability had been structurally below everybody else's, there'd been some events around NatWest Markets as well. It was just a really bad bank.'

So when, on 3 September 1999, the bank the City loved to hate announced it was going to spend £10.7 billion on acquiring the insurance and fund management group Legal & General investors were incredulous. Wanless tried to sell the deal on the basis that it would bring scope for cross-selling insurance, investment and pensions products to his bank's six million customers (a model known as 'bancassurance'). Sir David Rowland, who had been NatWest chairman since April 1999, strongly believed in bancassurance and welcomed the deal, as it would also enable him to resolve succession issues at the bank. He wanted to squeeze Wanless out and bring in Legal & General chief executive David Prosser as Wanless's successor.

NatWest's investment bank advisors David Mayhew, of Cazenove, and Terry Eccles, of JPMorgan, had badly misjudged the mood of the City towards NatWest.[2] They had also overestimated investors' enthusiasm for bancassurance. Investors revolted by pushing NatWest's share price down by 25 per cent over the next two weeks. They had effectively put the bank 'into play' (made it vulnerable to takeover).

From his office in the Bank of Scotland's high-Victorian palazzo overlooking Edinburgh's Princes Street, Peter Burt was like Captain Ahab sharpening his harpoon. Nairobi-born Burt, a former Hewlett-Packard executive with a dry sense of humour, joined Bank of Scotland in 1975. He had first sought a friendly reverse takeover of NatWest in late 1997 but had been rebuffed. In the summer of 1999, Bank of Scotland tried a different route, plotting with Royal Bank of Scotland to launch a joint 'carve-up' bid for the wounded giant. However, the two Scottish banks failed to agree on dividing the spoils and the Royal Bank's enthusiasm was more muted than that of Bank of Scotland. In particular, Royal Bank's chairman George Younger is thought to have seen the proposal as a non-starter. After plans for a joint bid fell apart and NatWest announced its L&G takeover, RBS and its advisors considered making a stand-alone bid for NatWest but Mathewson vetoed the idea.

So it was left to Burt to act. Burt had suffered a loss of face earlier that year after Bank of Scotland had entered an unholy alliance with the rabidly right-wing and homophobic US television evangelist Pat Robertson. The deal had had to be unwound at a cost of £3 million to the bank after it met with fierce opposition in Scotland. He now had a tight window of opportunity as a result of the timetable laid down by the Takeover Panel, a self-regulatory body that referees City takeovers. Burt says, 'NatWest's September 3rd bid for Legal & General was to be approved at an extraordinary general meeting on October 6th. If it was approved by shareholders at that point, we knew we would have missed our chance, since a merged L&G and NatWest would be too big for us to acquire.'[3] He appointed the investment banks Morgan Stanley, Credit Suisse First Boston (CSFB) and Gleacher Partners (which had recently 'demerged' from NatWest) to advise on the takeover. Chief executive of the Bank of Scotland since 1996, Burt lives near North Berwick in East Lothian but he more or less moved in to CSFB's One Cabot Square head office in London's Docklands for the next three weeks. Together with Bank of Scotland colleagues George Mitchell and Gavin Masterton, and with input and advice from CSFB's Simon de Zoete and George Maddison, Gleacher's Eric Gleacher and Chas Phillips and Morgan Stanley's Donald Moore and Peter Stott, and in conditions of the utmost secrecy, Burt put together a detailed plan for a £22-billion hostile takeover offer for NatWest, to be paid in a mixture of Bank of Scotland shares and loan notes.

The audacious takeover offer was unveiled to the stock market at 7 a.m. on Friday, 24 September. One of the more remarkable things about it was that there had been no leaks. So, when he unveiled the bank's offer, pitched at a 19.5 per cent premium to NatWest's previous closing price, it came out of the blue. If stock markets can be 'stunned', the London one was stunned that autumn Friday morning. At 7 a.m., the BBC Radio Four *Today* programme broadcast the news but got the name of the bidding bank wrong, saying Royal Bank of Scotland was bidding for NatWest. At an analysts' conference later that morning, Burt spelt out the logic for his bid. He damned NatWest's proposed deal with L&G, lambasted NatWest's management as incompetent serial underperformers and promised to run the bank much better. He said, if Bank of Scotland were to take over NatWest, it would retain the NatWest brand and run it alongside its own, cut costs by £1 billion over three years, sell off non-core businesses and return cash to shareholders. On finishing the presentation, Burt was given a standing ovation by the analysts – an unheard-of occurrence in the City. One investment manager said, 'People were just so fed up with NatWest. That positive vibe almost carried Bank of Scotland through.' *The Economist* said, 'NatWest has been a limping, troubled, formerly great British institution for far too long. Which is why the great British bank auction is such good news.'[4]

Burt, then aged 55, spent the afternoon in offices of the PR firm Brunswick, on Lincoln's Inn Fields, outlining his plans to journalists. Most of the hacks (including me) were impressed by his audacity, and use of quotable adages like 'You don't have to own the cow to sell milk' to rubbish NatWest's planned merger with L&G. The fact that he had unleashed a full-blooded takeover battle, which would almost certainly draw in other banks, added a frisson to his bid. Burt's bid completely wrong-footed NatWest, which was forced to tear up its plans to merge with L&G and mount a defence that was not too dissimilar from Burt's attack, in that it revolved around disposing of assets, closing branches and cutting costs. Sir David Rowland manned the parapets, shouting that Burt's proposals were 'unwelcome and ill thought out'. He said he was determined to stop Bank of Scotland from acquiring NatWest Group on the cheap and later told the *Sunday Times*, 'They have got competent people. But there is a big difference between running a corner shop and running Tesco.'[5]

RBS chief executive George Mathewson was on a visit to the United States as the hullaballoo started. He was watching the first day of the Ryder Cup at the Country Club in Brookline, Massachusetts, where two Scottish players, Paul Lawrie and Colin Montgomerie, were performing well against the Americans, when someone called his mobile. The use of phones is banned at the Ryder Cup so Mathewson, then aged 59, dived behind a bush to take the call. The caller said, 'Bank of Scotland have just bid for NatWest. What should we be doing?' Mathewson, angry at being upstaged by the Bank of Scotland and whispering into the phone to avoid distracting nearby putters, knew he could not sit back and watch his cross-town rival treble its size by acquiring NatWest but he did not want to rush into anything. He flew back to the UK. In the meantime, RBS issued a holding statement saying it had been 'looking at the NatWest position for some time and was watching the situation closely'.

RBS promptly hired Andy Chisholm of Goldman Sachs and Matthew Greenburgh of Merrill Lynch – two of the biggest beasts in the investment banking jungle – as advisors. On 26 September, the bank plus its advisors met in the Fleet Street office of international law firm Freshfields. It was a Sunday morning and the City was deserted. Four people from RBS – Mathewson, deputy chief executive Fred Goodwin, strategy director Iain Allan and communications director Howard Moody – met Greenburgh and Chisholm as well as other investment bankers and corporate brokers. Greenburgh, the son of a lawyer, who joined Merrill Lynch in 1998 after working at Barings Bank, recommended that RBS should make a counter-bid as soon as possible. He said this would give the Edinburgh-based bank 'early-mover advantage'. However, Mathewson, keen to show who was boss, urged caution. He still had doubts about pursuing a takeover of NatWest, and didn't want to be rushed into anything. Strategy director Iain Allan agreed, suggesting that leaving Bank of Scotland to stew in its own juice would provide RBS with valuable information about its bid and the stock market's response. Chisholm, an experienced Canadian-born investment banker who had been with Goldman Sachs in London since 1987, also argued for a measured approach. By the end of the meeting, the thinking inside the RBS camp had gelled around four principles: (a) RBS would make a counter-bid for NatWest; (b) its preference was for a 'friendly' deal (that is, one that had the blessing of the NatWest board); (c) RBS would not rush into anything, preferring to draw things out to give itself time to put together detailed takeover and integration proposals, which would revolve around growth, not just slashing and burning; (d) RBS would be careful about its public utterances as the Takeover Panel has strict rules governing what putative bidders can say in such contests. Mathewson says, 'It was certainly my idea to stretch it out as long as possible.'[6] One former aide adds, 'George was quite nervous about getting Royal Bank into play and did not want to make a false move.'

One ex-advisor recalls there was also a strong anti-English flavour to the Royal Bank's battle plans, claiming that Goodwin saw himself as the reincarnation of Prince Charles Edward Stuart. He said, 'The mindset of both Mathewson and Goodwin was along the lines of "We're going to stuff those bastards in London." They thought Royal Bank was streets ahead of any of the English banks and wanted to prove it.' The source added that Goodwin – who was starting to come out from under Mathewson's wing around this time – was 'so self-confident it was almost scary'. The RBS top brass did have an Achilles heel – Mathewson's contempt for fund managers, the very people the bank had to woo in coming weeks. He also had an unfortunate habit of putting his foot in it. 'George had an arrogant view of investors. I remember hosting a lunch before the NatWest takeover with some of the bank's very important big shareholders – including about 12 fund managers and buy-side analysts from places like Mercury Asset Management. George explained why RBS had sold off its investment business, Capital House, saying, "Of course, I don't believe in active fund management. I think we're rapidly moving towards index-tracking and passive asset management. Active fund managers add absolutely nothing." Given the audience and his need for the support of such people, it was a major gaffe!'

For most of the next month, Bank of Scotland and NatWest slugged it out, with each bank hurling abuse at the other via the business pages, while it was an open secret that RBS was planning a counter-bid. Other large British banks were prevented from bidding by UK competition law but there was vague talk that former building societies, including Abbey National and Halifax, might toss their hats in the ring. When the Bank of Scotland released results for the six months to the end of August on Wednesday, 29 September, investors were impressed by the 12 per cent jump in interim pre-tax profits to £471 million and the 22 per cent rise in lending. But Rowland said the results demonstrated worrying underlying trends and accused the bank of 'buying market share' and 'storing problems for the future'.[7]

On 14 October, the Bank of Scotland elaborated on its offer with the release of a detailed takeover document. Then, two weeks later, NatWest fought back with a defence plan which seemed to steal some of Bank of Scotland's clothes. The *FT*'s 'Lex' column gave this six out of ten saying, 'NatWest has in no way demonstrated it deserves to stay independent, but it is beginning to strengthen its negotiating position.'[8]

Although still sitting on the sidelines, Royal Bank was far from inactive. Over the next five weeks, a ten-strong team inside the bank put together a 'playbook' – precise, fully costed proposals for taking over NatWest and for amalgamating the two banks' various businesses in ways that would provide a springboard for cost cutting and revenue growth. The project was led by Goodwin. Other team members were RBS strategy director Iain Allan, who played a critical role preparing investor presentations and doing the sums, Miller McLean, responsible for legal aspects, and Grahame Whitehead, who focused on finance and risk. Based in Royal Bank's London office at Waterhouse Square, Holborn, Allan and strategy colleague Steve Corbett prepared a 'top-down' analysis of the cost savings and revenue synergies that might arise from an RBS/NatWest merger. Mathewson says, 'Iain was very active all the way through getting the numbers. He is a human dynamo and intellectually very able.'[9]

In parallel, an Edinburgh-based team did a 'bottom-up' analysis of the financial benefits of amalgamating NatWest and RBS. This team, all recent émigrés from Clydesdale Bank, comprised 'Mr Integration Benefits' Bill Dickson, IT and systems guru John White and human resources director Neil Roden. They based their analysis on detailed discussions with executives in each of RBS's divisions. Though some had argued that it would make more sense to shift the entire enlarged group's IT on to the more sophisticated NatWest IT platform, it did not take Dickson and Goodwin long to reach a different conclusion. White, who formerly worked for IBM, recalls a meeting in Goodwin's office in 42 St Andrew Square. 'Fred and I had great debates about the use of IT in business from a business benefit point of view. He will be embarrassed to hear me say this but [he] is one of those leaders who is a very simple thinker . . . I remember one Tuesday evening in the third week of November 1999, at about 8 o'clock, Fred, myself and Bill Dickson were discussing [whether we] would . . . move on to the NatWest platform or . . . move NatWest on to Royal Bank. Then Fred asked a simple question, 'Who had the most cost-efficient set of business processes?'' [10]

Realising RBS had the upper hand where efficiency was concerned, with a cost-to-income ratio of 53 per cent compared to more than 70 per cent at NatWest, White says it took them 'three or four minutes' to decide to amalgamate both banks on to the RBS system in the event of their bid being successful. Overall, RBS's Edinburgh-based 'bottom-up' team identified more than 110 cost-saving initiatives, of which 70 were in processing and information technology. They also identified more than 40 revenue-boosting initiatives, mainly in corporate and retail banking. The creation of a shared 'manufacturing' division – to take care of all back-office functions including call centres, processing systems and information- technology – was pivotal to their plans. So, while RBS and NatWest would retain their own corporate iconography – branch decor, branding and chequebook design – all back-office and behind-the-scenes stuff including call centres would be crunched together to save money. That alone was slated to deliver three-quarters of the planned cost cuts and revenue enhancements envisaged by the RBS team. There were already rumours swirling around the stock market that RBS was aiming to deliver £300 million more per year in cost savings than Bank of Scotland.

During October and November of 1999, RBS's Edinburgh and London teams liaised daily via video links. When they had their first face-to-face meeting in mid November 1999, they were pleasantly surprised to discover that, even though they were approaching the task from opposite ends of the telescope, the benefits they had identified were broadly similar. 'There were some interesting discrepancies but a meeting that should have taken hours lasted only a few minutes,' said one ex-RBS senior insider.

In November 1999, a cache of leaked documents mysteriously showed up in the 'Grey Lubyanka', the offices of the *Daily Express*, on Blackfriars Bridge, outlining what was billed as RBS's 'kinder, gentler' approach to turning around NatWest. The *Express* said, 'The documents, described as a manifesto, showed that RBS's bid plans are highly advanced and reveal that the bank's strategy is to keep redundancies and branch closures to a minimum and avoid selling parts of the business.'[11] This was all part of a so-called Royal Bank charm offensive, designed to persuade investors (and NatWest's board) it would pursue a more emollient path than its 'slash and burn' rival.

Throughout this period, Mathewson's strong preference was for a 'friendly' merger with NatWest. However, Goodwin was not in favour of that – his preference was for a hostile bid since this would have put RBS in the driving seat. Soon after the Bank of Scotland's original bid, Sir David Rowland called Younger's wife, Diana, and asked if he could

have a one-to-one meeting with her husband. Rowland said, crypti-
cally, 'Just tell him it's hugs – nothing more than hugs.'[12] The pair met
in the Youngers' London home in Kennington and scoped out whether
there was any chance of a face-saving 'white knight' deal. The idea was
back on the table a month later, on Saturday, 28 October, when a group
from RBS got together with their counterparts from NatWest to discuss
a possible friendly tie-up between the two banks. The two sides met,
without advisors, at the Howard Hotel, overlooking the River Thames.
Mathewson did most of the talking, stressing that Royal Bank wanted
to create Britain's best bank for employees, customers and shareholders. However, according to one person present, his proposals were
cold-shouldered by NatWest.

NatWest and RBS had another meeting about a friendly deal on
Saturday, 27 November. This was held in the Fleet Street offices of law
firm Freshfields, which had been built on the site of the pre-Wapping
News of the World offices. Mathewson, Goodwin, McLean and Allan
were there for the Royal Bank with Rowland and Ron Sandler making
up the NatWest contingent. Rowland had recently brought in Sandler,
a chum and former colleague from his Lloyd's of London days, as chief
operating officer. Advisors present included Merrill Lynch's Matthew
Greenburgh and Goldman Sachs's Andy Chisholm (for RBS), and
Cazenove's David Mayhew, JPMorgan's Terry Eccles and Dresdner
Kleinwort Benson's Tim Shacklock (for NatWest). During the meeting, Rowland said that, in his view, if anything were to come of the
talks, it would really be a NatWest takeover of RBS. This wound up
Mathewson who insisted, 'Not from our point of view, it wouldn't!' It
seemed 'as though an icy blast had blown across the room', said one
advisor who described this as the gaffe that killed off the chance of a
friendly deal.

The talks also stumbled on price. NatWest was not keen on the
idea of being paid in RBS shares, fearing these would be debased the
moment a deal was announced. The fact that Bank of Scotland had
raised its bid to £25.6 billion the previous day and thrown in a special
dividend worth £2 billion on the sale of non-core businesses may also
have queered the pitch for Royal Bank. Plus Rowland had a vested
interest in allowing the two Scottish banks to fight each other for as
long as possible. The longer RBS and Bank of Scotland slugged it out,
he thought, the more he'd be able to sell NatWest for. The board of

NatWest formally rejected the RBS 'friendly' approach on the afternoon of Saturday, 27 November.

As soon as the Freshfields meeting was over, Mathewson pushed the button on plan 'B' – a £26-billion-plus hostile counter-bid for NatWest for which all the preparatory and paperwork had already been done. But, on the Sunday afternoon, Mathewson was getting cold feet. He was concerned that RBS was not ready to put its head above the parapet but one colleague told him they had crossed the Rubicon. He had not seen his wife for three months and told Mathewson there was no way he could now go home and tell her the bid was off.

At the time, I was financial editor at the *Sunday Herald*, and all that Saturday I awaited developments in the paper's 10 George Street newsroom in Edinburgh. Finally, at about 5 p.m., I was given word, couched in the enigmatic language of the City spin doctor, that talks about a 'friendly' deal had collapsed and that Royal Bank was likely to make a hostile bid for NatWest on either Monday or Tuesday. For a financial editor, this was manna from heaven. A hostile bidding war between Scotland's two largest companies for one of the largest companies in the FTSE-100 could be expected to provide endless scope for stories over many weeks. I bashed out a 950-word story for the news pages headlined 'Royal Bank to pounce on NatWest', which opened with the words 'Scotland's two biggest banks are locked in a fight to the death for the multi-million pound takeover of National Westminster Bank'.[13]

And luckily, the Royal Bank unveiled a £26.4-billion hostile takeover offer for NatWest at 7 a.m. on Monday, 29 November 1999. The two core messages it was eager to convey were: (1) RBS was a solid operator that could be trusted to run NatWest without disruption to customers or to financial stability; and (2) shareholders accepting its bid would make a ton of money. However, the counter-bid got off to a rocky start, with a 10 a.m. conference call ending before it had really started. About 30 journalists dialled in to hear Mathewson talk about RBS's bid. However one of the journalists had left their phone on speakerphone, which meant everyone on the call could hear clattering and shouting from that journalist's newsroom. Mathewson was furious, shouting, 'What's that f★★king noise? I can't hear you. What are you . . .' Two minutes into the conference, Mathewson picked up the conference call telephone, said, 'F★★k this!' and slammed it down. He then looked across to the adjacent glass room where investment bank advisors including Greenburgh were sitting. They were all mouthing the words 'What the f**k?' It was not the most auspicious of starts to the Royal Bank's attempts to woo the media.

At 11 a.m., RBS chairman George Younger, Mathewson and Goodwin presented an 81-slide presentation titled 'Creating a new force in banking' to analysts and investors. Younger said Royal Bank envisaged moving both banks on to a common technology platform within three years and promised cost savings of £1.18 billion and 18,000 job cuts over the same period. Goodwin said, 'The bulk of the cost savings relate to back-office processing, to head-office areas and so on. They don't relate to customer-facing staff.' Mathewson reminded the audience of some of his achievements at RBS and said a merged RBS–NatWest would be able to grow revenue by £390 million without disruption to customers or branch closures, while keeping both the NatWest and RBS brands alive. But, in the end, it was a damp squib. The initial RBS bid only valued each NatWest share at 1590p, just 13p a share above the Bank of Scotland's revised offer. Investors and analysts were underwhelmed. Investors were also surprised at RBS's reluctance to close NatWest branches. Most thought saving money by eliminating branches was the whole point of the exercise. In England, NatWest had 1,700 while Royal Bank had 308, so there must be some overlap, thought investors, especially in the north-west heartland of the former Williams & Glyn's. Analysts also fretted that the combined entity would have such a big share of the UK banking market, especially in business banking, that it would find growth difficult. In a research note, David Poutney, bank analyst at WestLB Panmure, said, 'Compared to Bank of Scotland's clinical assassination of NatWest's management, there is a feeling of johnny-come-lately about RBS's bid.' As analysts weighed up the merits of the two competing bids, anti-globalisation protestors brought the centre of Seattle to a standstill, forcing the closure of the opening ceremonies of the World Trade Organisation meetings.

Withering put-downs from NatWest's top brass soon followed. Sandler said, 'It's very easy to stand on a soapbox and promise completely un-realistic savings and performance targets.'[14] Over the course of the ensuing takeover battle, Rowland perfected a sarcastic tone towards his Scottish aggressors. In response to RBS's initial offer, he said it had overestimated the merger benefits and underestimated the risks of bolting a huge bank onto a relative minnow.

Royal Bank was already suffering from 'the winner's curse'. Even though the sparring banks had not changed their offers, the value of Bank of Scotland's offer had surged ahead of that of Royal Bank before the week was out. This was because investors presumed that, if RBS were to acquire NatWest, the Scottish bank's share price would tank, because it would find turning around NatWest such a gargantuan struggle. On 16 December, the Office of Fair Trading, which had already cleared Bank of Scotland's bid, cleared the Royal Bank's too. This fired the starting gun on a revised 60-day timetable under Takeover Panel rules. The critical dates were 31 January – the date by which final offers would have to be made – and 14 February – the date by which either RBS or Bank of Scotland was required to have secured majority support from NatWest's shareholders. If these dates were missed, the bids would lapse.

On a conference call with journalists on Tuesday, 30 November, Burt ignored the advice of his media minders, Brunswick, and launched personal attacks on Goodwin and Mathewson. First, he described Mathewson as 'prickly' and difficult to work with. Then, faking amnesia, Burt added, 'What is Fred Goodwin's nickname? Remind me. Fred the Shred? Fred the Impaler? Who would you rather do business with?'[15] Burt also lambasted RBS and its auditors PricewaterhouseCoopers for creative accountancy. Citing research from financial analyst Terry Smith, of stockbrokers Collins Stewart, he accused the bank of using a 'racy' approach to burnish its image and to understate its cost-to-income ratio – a critical yardstick of operational efficiency. Burt said his bank would 'walk away without a backward glance' if Royal Bank of Scotland was foolish enough to pay a 'silly price'. Royal Bank turned the other cheek, careful not to get sucked into a media slanging match.

Peter Burt's wry humour, self-deprecatory style, folksy metaphors and occasional willingness to put the knife into his opponents won him the support of journalists. By contrast, Goodwin rarely deigned to talk to journalists. And Mathewson had a tendency to rub journalists up the wrong way. At a dinner RBS held for journalists in the Savoy Hotel in mid January, Mathewson was rude to *The Times*' banking correspondent, Caroline Merrell. In a Q&A session, Merrell asked about the structure of Royal Bank's £22-billion offer, including whether there was a ceiling on Santander's investment. Mathewson responded by saying, 'That's a good question. You're not as stupid as you look.' RBS advisors were aghast. RBS insiders generally tried to keep Mathewson away from journalists after that. On the NatWest front, Rowland was accessible, succinct and sarcastic but Ron Sandler thought the relentless media coverage was a distraction that reduced the debate to sound bites.[16]

Investors and analysts were underwhelmed by the colour of the Scots' money. HSBC banking analyst Michael Lever said that, in the wake of RBS's parsimonious offer, 'there was a greater chance that NatWest would remain independent'.[17] He said both the Scots' offers undervalued the English bank, whose shares he believed to worth £17 on a 'stand-alone' basis.[18] Royal Bank had been expecting a more positive reception from the City but Iain Robertson put a brave face on things. When I interviewed him via video link from Waterhouse Square on the Friday, he said, 'We firmly believe the best way to improve an organisation is through growth. By all means get NatWest as efficient as you can, but make sure you have growth firmly in the minds of the management. Make yourself competitive – and aggressively competitive if need be. That's our way.'[19]

The pattern over the next few months was one of increased offers from the two squabbling Scottish banks, often accompanied by 'sweeteners' in the shape of innovative hybrid financial instruments that one investment banker calls 'funny money'. RBS also made much of the fact its deep-pocketed partner, Santander, was backing it with an unconditional offer to buy an additional £1.7 billion worth of Royal Bank's shares.

Each fresh offer from the Scots was met with scorn and derision from Rowland – his primary put-downs were that the bids were inadequate, targets for cost savings and revenue synergies were fanciful and integration proposals were risky. Rowland also continually highlighted the fact that a great many mergers between banks in the US had gone pear-shaped. He said RBS's revised bid of 17 December 'contains seeds of substantial shareholder destruction'[20] and took delight in mocking the Scottish banks' plans for IT. He also ridiculed the Bank of Scotland's treasurer and managing director Gavin Masterton as 'the invisible man', since the Dunfermline Athletic fan, who had squandered an estimated £200 million of his bank's money on loans to Scottish football clubs, was so rarely around.

In December, Rowland persuaded Gordon Pell to leave a board role at Lloyds TSB to become head of NatWest's corporate and retail banking divisions. Pell says, 'It was a very strange Christmas. After 29 years with Lloyds, my wife and I held hands and said, "Well, here we go!" and jumped off the cliff.'²¹ Pell joined NatWest on 8 January 2000. One ex-NatWest insider said, 'The interim management team of Rowland, Sandler and Pell injected the type of vitality and energy that had been lacking from the business for years.'

It was a gruelling few months for the big bankers involved. The very future of their organisations was on the line. Goodwin and his RBS colleagues and advisors focused relentlessly on getting their message across to investors. They presented to more than 70 fund management groups in England, Scotland, Continental Europe and the United States during the 20-week campaign, some on multiple occasions. The main objective was to convince NatWest shareholders that RBS could be trusted to deliver its cost savings and revenue growth promises. Younger was present at every presentation. 'He was always calm and he perhaps kept things on a more civilised level than they might otherwise have been,' says Mathewson. 'He enjoyed the process – he enjoyed it more than I did. It was more wearing on us.'²² What Mathewson did not know was that, all the way though the takeover battle, Younger was having to go daily at 8 a.m. to the Cromwell Hospital on Cromwell Road for radiotherapy treatment, as he had been diagnosed with prostate cancer and was reluctant to go under the knife since he did not believe the chairman could go off sick during such a critical takeover. It was a stoicism that contributed to Lord Younger's early demise three years later.

Greenburgh and Chisholm recognised that selling the virtues of the RBS takeover proposals came more naturally to Goodwin, who was due to become chief executive if the deal came off, than to Mathewson. He was more cool, calm and collected and had a greater mastery of the numbers. Politely, they suggested that Mathewson – who found making repeated presentations to investors much more gruelling than Goodwin – might want to take more of a back seat and let his protégé take the lead at investor and analyst presentations, even though he was not yet chief executive. This was a shrewd move as the investment community found Goodwin to be persuasive and beguiling. Even though no one fell in love with Goodwin as a person, they were full of admiration for his plan for NatWest and believed he could deliver it. Simon

Samuels, then an analyst at Salomon Smith Barney said, 'If you've ever seen [JPMorgan chief executive] Jamie Dimon present, Fred was like that – like a machine gun. Without having to look at a single note, he knew all the numbers, and he corrected people when they made factual mistakes. His memory, attention to detail and ability to assimilate information were phenomenal. Sometimes, chief executives just present their strategic vision but never see it through, and we suspected this might be true of Burt. With Goodwin you could be confident he would see it through.'[23]

In his determination to snatch the prize, Goodwin could also be brutal. The RBS advisors on the deal included Andy Chisholm and Richard Murley of Goldman Sachs, Matthew Greenburgh, Paul Thompson and James Agnew at Merrill Lynch, Oliver Pawle of UBS Warburg and George Welham and Nick Miles at Financial Dynamics. At one point, Goodwin became convinced that Merrill Lynch and Goldman Sachs were slacking. RBS was paying these firms the best part of £143 million to advise on its bid but Goodwin believed he was getting poor value for money. At one stage, he summoned the top bosses from Goldman Sachs and Merrill Lynch in New York to a meeting at his Edinburgh head office. Herbert Lurie, global head of financial institutions group, attended for Merrill and a senior representative of Goldman was there alongside Greenburgh and Chisholm and several senior RBS executives. Goodwin berated the American investment bankers for what he saw as Chisholm's and Greenburgh's underperformance and reminded them who was paying the bills. One ex-advisor said, 'Fred was very much of the view that no one was as good as he was. If he'd been able to complain to God, he'd have got him on the phone.' Ex-RBS executive director Iain Robertson recalls, 'We had meetings at 8 a.m. in Waterhouse Square for the best part of a year and, at some of these meetings, the blood actually came out under the door. Everyone was on the receiving end at one stage or another. If Fred felt that something hadn't been delivered on time or hadn't been delivered in the way he wanted it delivered, he wasn't one to pussyfoot around. What was surprising was that, by the end of the day, no one was bothering [about the earlier shouting matches]. People just got on with it.'[24]

There was intense rivalry between Merrill Lynch's Matthew Greenburgh and Goldman Sachs's Andy Chisholm throughout the takeover battle, with one ex-senior RBS insider saying, 'They were constantly bickering over fees.' Greenburgh had fewer blazing rows with Goodwin than Chisholm, which was partly down to the fact he was more compliant. Some describe Greenburgh as the Royal Bank's secret weapon during the takeover battle. 'He was the star on the investment banking side,' said one ex-RBS advisor, adding, 'Matthew is incredibly clever – very sharp. And he was also prepared to sail very close to the wind. He spent most of his evenings having his knuckles rapped by the Takeover Panel. He was actually quite brilliant and quite prepared to put his neck on the line.'

Most large investors in NatWest saw sitting on the fence as the best course of action. The view at the time was the longer that RBS and Bank of Scotland slugged it out, the higher the take-out price for NatWest. But Mathewson and Goodwin didn't seem to grasp this, and were infuriated by fund managers' indecisiveness. They were so confident in the superiority of their proposals that they just couldn't understand why asset management groups weren't flocking to publicly endorse their bid. Senior fund managers complained of being harassed on the telephone by Mathewson and Goodwin during the bid process. On 31 January 2000, the denouement was approaching. Both RBS and BoS put in their final offers. Even with sweeteners and 'funny money', neither delivered a knockout blow. NatWest rejected both on 1 February, dismissing them as 'inadequate and risky', adding that they largely comprised 'vulnerable' paper and would leave the bidders stretched if they succeeded. Also on 1 February, analysts at Salomon Smith Barney delighted the Royal Bank camp by declaring that it deserved to win. Simon Samuels said the Royal Bank's management team was 'stronger and with more integration experience' than that of BoS. He also wrote, 'Ultimately, we believe that it requires a seismic shock for NatWest – an underperforming business over the past decade – to fully extract value from its hidden franchise.'[25]

Mathewson, Goodwin and Greenburgh were not averse to the use of bullying to get their way. When Commerzbank analyst Alex Potter published a research note urging NatWest shareholders to reject both bids and expressing scepticism about RBS's proposals, Mathewson was furious. RBS sought to get the note withdrawn and even to get Potter fired. But Commerzbank held its ground. In early February 2000, Goodwin and Mathewson had dinner with HSBC's Michael Lever and sought to persuade him to publicly endorse their bid. But Lever – who

later complained of being 'bullied' by the RBS executives – ended
up issuing a 48-page report recommending that NatWest shareholders should reject the bids from both Scottish banks. Lever said they
presented 'unacceptable risks' and would be unable to deliver on their
promises.[26] One advisor to RBS said, 'George was under huge stress
and lost it in some of the meetings.'

On Friday, 4 February, Younger, Mathewson and Goodwin had a
meeting with the 'ice maiden' Carol Galley and Stephen Zimmerman,
co-chief executives of Mercury Asset Management (MAM), which,
with a 4.65 per cent stake in NatWest, was seen as capable of sway-
ing the outcome. Mercury was poised to lend its support to the Bank
of Scotland. Sources say it had based this decision on the fact that it
owned significant stakes in all three sparring banks but had its biggest
stake in RBS. The asset manager, bought by Merrill Lynch for £3.1
billion in 1997, believed that accepting BoS's offer would be in its own
customers' short-term interest since the reverse 'winner's curse' effect
would drive up the value of its RBS shares. One advisor to RBS, UBS
Warburg's Oliver Pawle, is understood to have 'read the riot act' to
Mercury's head of financials, Richard Milliken, advising him that
Mercury had a fiduciary duty to vote according to what was best for its
NatWest shareholding, not for its other interests. Milliken was warned
it would become a *cause célèbre* in the City if Mercury failed to vote
according to what would be best for its NatWest shareholding. At a
meeting at Mercury's offices in King William Street, Mathewson made
it clear to Galley and other Mercury executives that RBS would hold
her publicly accountable for her actions. The aim was to put the fear
of God into the ice maiden, in the hope that she would melt. MAM
also came under pressure from its owner Merrill Lynch, whose mergers
team led by Matthew Greenburgh was advising RBS on its bid.

On the Friday before the finishing line, brokers Cazenove, who were
retained by NatWest and still fighting to keep it independent, are reported
to have persuaded the business section of the *Sunday Times* to run a story
saying that Lloyds TSB was poised to mount a hostile takeover of RBS.
It was a deliberate spoiling tactic, designed to muddy the waters and
confuse the City but the takeover talk was soon discovered to be tosh.
Then, on Monday afternoon, UBS subsidiary Phillips & Drew Fund
Management (PDFM), a large City investment house which had a 2.3
per cent stake in NatWest, lent its support to the Bank of Scotland bid.

Next morning, Tuesday 8 February, there was euphoria in Bank of Scotland's London nerve centre in Cabot Square but despair in RBS's 'war room' in Waterhouse Square. Not only had the *Financial Times'* 'Lex' column endorsed the Bank of Scotland but it seemed PDFM's support was about to trigger a landslide victory for Bank of Scotland. It looked like Burt and his team had harpooned the whale after all. The Royal Bank team was at a low ebb. Mathewson is said to have been particularly scratchy and Younger 'a bit rattled'.[27] The winner's curse was reversed with RBS shares rising and Bank of Scotland's falling, presenting opportunities for hedge funds. But all was not lost for Royal Bank of Scotland. Later that day, Deutsche Asset Management, formerly Morgan Grenfell, which owned 1.4 per cent of NatWest, endorsed RBS. And then the so-called 'conditional acceptances' came flooding in. The previous day, after protracted negotiations between Greenburgh and the Takeover Panel, Merrill Lynch's Paul Thompson had faxed more than 15 asset-management firms that had stakes in NatWest, asking them for provisional support for the RBS bid. If enough could be persuaded, Greenburgh believed, it would break the investor logjam, 'We wanted to create a bandwagon effect and avoid a split vote,' says one advisor to RBS. 'We always knew that was pushing the boundaries of what is allowed by the Takeover Panel.' By lunchtime on Tuesday, 8 February, Greenburgh's brazen ploy seemed to have worked. Investors speaking for nearly 13 per cent of NatWest's shares pledged non-binding allegiance to RBS. The bank decided to bring forward a Regulatory News Service (RNS) announcement. It was headlined '12.88% of NatWest shares accept bid'. The signal worked its magic on the City's sheep-like investment community, flushing other coy investment groups out of the woodwork. At 6.43 p.m., Bloomberg and Reuters terminals flickered into life with the news that Schroders, one of NatWest's largest shareholders with a 3.33 per cent stake, was backing Royal Bank of Scotland. It was a watershed moment. Mathewson recalls, 'I remember sitting in Waterhouse Square that evening, when Mercury and Schroders were still deliberating. First of all Schroders came down for us. I was on the phone to Patience Wheatcroft at *The Times* at the time and then Fred put his head round the door and said, "MAM's come down for us too!" I said down the phone to Patience, "Wham, bam, thank you, MAM!" And that was the headline on her piece in *The Times* the next day. She never thanked me for that.'[28]

That evening, the RBS team of Mathewson, Goodwin, Robertson, Benny Higgins, Iain Allan and Howard Moody gathered to celebrate in a Holborn pub, just round the corner from Waterhouse Square. As they drank their pints, Mathewson told Higgins, a charmer with a colourful past and a passionate Celtic fan, that his team had just been thrashed 3–1 by Inverness Caledonian Thistle in the Scottish Cup (another David and Goliath contest that sparked one of football's most memorable headlines – 'Super Caley go ballistic, Celtic are atrocious'). Higgins, who had been a youth player for Celtic, reacted in disbelief, unable to accept that 'The Hoops' could possibly have lost to such a minnow. It was pretty much how many of NatWest's 64,400 staff would feel about being acquired by RBS.

Although other large shareholders in NatWest – including Prudential with 4.78 per cent, Legal & General with 2.97 per cent and Standard Life with 2.6 per cent – had yet to show their hands, a bandwagon was already rolling across the Square Mile. On Wednesday evening, an exhausted Burt retreated to Edinburgh while Goodwin and Mathewson headed to the Savoy Grill, where they tucked into two enormous Knickerbocker Glory ice creams.[29] That same evening, Younger met Rowland and made one last attempt at striking a 'friendly' deal. But there were no hugs from Rowland this time. No hugs at all.

Just after 6 a.m. on Thursday, 10 February, the BBC reported that RBS had won the largest banking takeover in British history – but still NatWest refused to formally admit defeat. Later that day, Phillips & Drew switched sides, saying it was going to vote for RBS. At 5 p.m., NatWest held a briefing for staff in the canteen at 41 Lothbury. A grinning Rowland claimed there were still some wild cards which might enable it to retain its independence but he was clutching at straws. The next morning, NatWest ran up the white flag. Investors speaking for more than half its equity had thrown in their lot with the Royal Bank. The English bank advised its remaining investors to accept the Scottish bank's bid. Rowland said, 'We congratulate Royal Bank of Scotland and look forward to helping them ensure the success of the new organisation.' Because of the fall in its share price, the Royal Bank's offer was now worth £20.987 billion. That compared to £27.6 billion for Bank of Scotland's second bid on 25 November 1999 – and £26.5 billion for Royal's initial offer, made three days later. Both of these had been rejected by Rowland as 'inadequate'.

The gyrations of the three banks' share prices during the takeover battle were telling. Between 23 September 1999, the day before Bank of Scotland's initial hostile bid, and 14 February 2000, when the takeover battle ended, Royal Bank of Scotland shares plunged by 29 per cent – falling from 1149p to 807p per share – and the bank's market capitalisation had tumbled from £10.2 billion to £7.2 billion. Bank of Scotland's shares slumped by 23.6 per cent over the same period, falling from 706p to 539p per share, causing its market value to slump from £8.6 billion to £6.7 billon. NatWest's shares rose 8 per cent over the 20-week period, increasing from 1046p to 1133p, inflating its market value from £17.4 billion to £18.9 billion.[30] The Scottish banks had sacrificed an awful lot of shareholder value in their pursuit of NatWest.

In Scotland, whose economy had been blighted by the acquisition of dozens of large companies by English and overseas concerns in recent decades, there was jubilation. Mathewson and Goodwin were seen as heroic figures who had slain a giant, come back with sacks of booty and put two fingers up at the Sassenachs in the process. In particular the takeover had been the making of Fred Goodwin. However, Tim Hindle, associate editor of *The Economist* and author of several books on banking, was less enthusiastic about the deal. He described RBS's £21-billion takeover of NatWest as a defensive manoeuvre designed to shore up an outmoded business model from the threat posed by e-banks like Prudential's Egg. I called him for his views on the deal on 11 February 2000 and he said, 'It smacks of the players in a mature and crowded market huddling together for warmth.' Aside from some clever financial engineering and promises of growth, it was hard to miss that the squabbling banks had, in essence, been competing over who could fire the most people at NatWest and who could extract the most value from its 6 million customers.

The champagne reception that Royal Bank of Scotland held to cele-brate its victory at Waterhouse Square on the Friday night was a subdued affair. 'Everyone was so exhausted – it was more of a wake than a celebration. All the adrenalin had been used up,' said one person who was there. Younger was painfully aware of the challenges that lay ahead. He told the gathering, 'What you've just done is the easy bit.' When I spoke to him on Saturday, 12 February, Younger told me that bank employees 'blanched a bit at that'.

Anglo-Scottish blend

With one bound, the Royal Bank of Scotland had transformed itself from a relatively insignificant provincial player to the seventh largest bank in Europe. It had gone from having 650 branches, 22,000 staff and total assets of £88.8 billion to having 2,400 branches, 94,000 staff, 15 million customers and total assets of £320 billion. It became the UK's third biggest bank – after HSBC and Lloyds TSB.

But Royal Bank's £21-billion takeover of National Westminster Bank left many of the latter bank's 64,400 employees in a state of shock. That the 166-year-old institution had lost its independence was bad enough, but the seemingly barbarous nature of the victors made it worse. Mathewson and Goodwin had committed themselves to dismembering NatWest's empire, amputating non-core divisions and firing 18,000 staff (27 per cent of the total). The trepidation was most intense in NatWest's head office at 41 Lothbury since RBS had made no secret of its intention to close down this palatial 156,600-square-foot building and transfer all the functions to Edinburgh.

In a diary he kept at the time, NatWest's director of purchasing, Peter Smith, captured the mood, 'After work [on Monday, 14 February], there was a celebration at Gibson Hall in the City, our grade one listed Victorian banking hall, with decent champagne, wonderful nibbly things to eat and the NatWest jazz band (whose existence I was not aware of). Much of the conversation with colleagues turned to personal situations. Will there be a role for us? Do you want to stay? Would you move to Edinburgh? Do you speak Gaelic?'[1]

For Smith, the humiliation was total when, three weeks later, Royal Bank of Scotland's 'daisywheel' logo and colour scheme popped up on the NatWest intranet site (an internal internet site for NatWest staff), replacing NatWest's more familiar 'three arrowheads' colour scheme and device. Writing in his diary, Smith said, 'Today [Monday, 6 March], is finally and absolutely the day. At around 10 a.m., the NatWest header on the intranet home page suddenly changes to the Royal Bank of Scotland Group. Messages appear from Lord Younger, RBS's chairman, and Fred Goodwin, its chief executive.' Smith added, 'Today feels like the ultimate let-down . . . In the short term, at least, I am significantly better off – and considerably more cynical about the nature of capitalism.'[2]

'I felt physically sick that day,' says one former senior NatWest executive, who quit soon after the bank was acquired. 'It was the end of an era, after 342 years.'

The cultural differences between the two institutions were striking – NatWest was large, plodding and bureaucratic whereas RBS was smaller, entrepreneurial, dynamic and quick to make decisions. One ex-insider said, 'Goodwin's mob used to tell NatWest's managers to eat a plate of red meat for breakfast to become more aggressive – it was that bad!' A former senior manager in NatWest Corporate, who prefers to remain nameless, remembers a period of intense uncertainty when RBS was focused on identifying people it wished to retain from within NatWest. 'We pretty much went into limbo from March to September 2000. Not much work got done that summer. People were honing their CVs and going for interviews while RBS started at the top and were working their way down through the organisation like a threshing machine – relentlessly, layer by layer, weeding out the people they didn't want . . . And unsurprisingly enough, it often turned out to be the RBS candidates that got the jobs!'

For many of those who survived, RBS was a breath of fresh air and a liberation. A former NatWest corporate banker says the two banks were like chalk and cheese. 'Johnny Cameron was impressive. He would walk around floor to floor, introducing himself, taking the temperature, fielding questions wherever he could. Just by being articulate, personable and looking relatively young, he was so different to what we were used to.'

A few weeks after the takeover, Goodwin was apprehensive about an invitation to attend the annual NatWest pensioners' lunch in the Royal Lancaster Hotel as guest of honour. Considering the number of people he was sacking at NatWest, he feared he would be booed, heckled or

worse so, when he entered the function suite, he was pleasantly surprised. Not only was the chairman of the NatWest pensioners' association, an Englishman, sporting a kilt in the Royal Bank boss's honour
but Goodwin was bagpiped into the room and, as he strode towards the
top table, the serried ranks of pensioners rose to their feet and gave him
a standing ovation. It was a hugely gratifying moment for Fred. One
of his ex-colleagues recalls, 'There was actually huge support for RBS
within the NatWest rank and file. There was a lot of frustration about
the mismanagement of NatWest throughout the 1990s.'

An unusually mild spring day, 6 March 2000 was the start of 'Year
Zero' for NatWest. Mathewson, who had been chief executive of RBS
for the past eight years, moved upstairs to the specially created role
of executive deputy chairman. Friends say that Mathewson was suffering from exhaustion and even depression following the gruelling
struggle for NatWest and was glad to take a few weeks off. On holiday
in the Caribbean in the wake of the deal, Mathewson is said to have
been lethargic and reluctant to go anywhere or do anything, which
concerned his wife, Sheila. Also, at some stage over the next 12 months,
Mathewson called George Younger and told him he wasn't sure he
wanted to be Royal Bank of Scotland's next chairman. 'Maybe he realised that dealing with Fred was going to be tricky – maybe he wondered
whether he'd have the energy for that,' said one source.

Goodwin, who became the youngest chief executive of a FTSE-100
company, was like a coiled spring. One executive recalls a 9.30 a.m.
'morning meeting' on Monday, 14 February 2000, the day the takeover
was officially in the bag. George Mathewson congratulated everyone
and told them that they deserved a decent rest. Goodwin replied, 'Oh,
no. There's no time for that.' And metaphorically he rolled up his
sleeves.

The merger faced massive risks, including the possibility that
botching the integration of the two banks' IT systems would lead to
the payments system falling over. There was also the possibility that
NatWest staff might be so disenchanted with the takeover they would
mutiny. And it didn't help that the integration was being played out
against a volatile financial backdrop. The dot.com bubble, a three-year
period during which investors became delusional about the prospects
for internet start-up companies, had burst just as RBS got the keys to
NatWest. On 10 March, four days after the completion of the deal,

the NASDAQ Composite index peaked at 5,132.52. Over the next two years, the technology-laden index shed about 70 per cent of its value, wiping $5 trillion off shares in technology companies. Even today, 14 years later, the NASDAQ has yet to regain those speculation-fuelled highs – at the time of writing, it was at 4,095. The Millennium Bug, also known as Y2K, had cost British banks about £1 billion to prepare for but had failed to produce the catastrophic consequences many had expected. The euro had become a non-physical currency on 1 January 1999 but the government of Tony Blair had chosen to retain sterling after an evaluation of Chancellor Gordon Brown's 'five tests'. And, on the very day the NatWest deal completed, Madonna's cover version of 'American Pie' was the number-one-selling single in the charts. To Goodwin, this was perhaps a good omen – the 1972 Don McLean original was one of his favourite songs and he could sing every word.

Speaking a few years later, Goodwin looked back fondly on the deal as if it were ancient history: 'In the year 2000, everything seemed so simple then; we had just taken over NatWest; we were up to our neck – indeed, some thought well over our head – in "opportunities" and "challenges". The priorities were simple, it required no thought whatsoever to identify that we had to go and deliver the transaction benefits which we'd promised to everyone – we had to keep the show on the road and at the same time deliver underlying income growth, and improving efficiency wouldn't be a bad idea either.'[3]

The first step was to hammer out a new organisational structure ('group architecture') along the lines of what had been presented to investors during the takeover battle. The second was to quickly select the executive teams to populate the new structure, starting with the head honchos and then moving swiftly down through the ranks.

The deal looked like a rout of NatWest when the first high-level appointments were made public. After Younger concluded that the NatWest board was 'useless', none of its members made any attempt to come forward with proposals between 14 February and 6 March. Goodwin kicked things off with a massive boardroom clear-out. In early March, thirteen NatWest directors, including four knights – Sir David Rowland, Sir Sydney Lipworth (a founder of Hambro Life-turned-lawyer), Sir Michael Angus (former chief executive of Unilever) and Sir Richard Evans (the chairman of BAE Systems) – and two lords – Lord Blyth (then chairman of Boots) and Lord Powell (former foreign policy advisor to Prime Minister Margaret Thatcher) – as well as chief operating officer Ron Sandler and the future City minister Paul Myners, were given their marching orders. One ex-RBS insider says, 'Fred just went in to Lothbury and, one by one, fired all the NatWest directors. He went in and just said, "Next – you're fired!" I think he got pleasure from that.' In the end, two directors – finance director Richard Delbridge (Fred was going to need to replace himself) and Gordon Pell, NatWest's chief executive of corporate and retail banking, who had only joined two months earlier after spending most of his career at Lloyds TSB – were selected to stay on as directors of the enlarged group.

He may not have thought much of its directors but Goodwin did take a shine to the furniture and *objets d'art* in the NatWest boardroom. Almost immediately the boardroom table, the chairs and some of the artwork were shipped north to Edinburgh, where they were installed on the ground floor of 42 St Andrew Square. Goodwin also had his eye on a David Hockney painting and a Regency clock in NatWest's Lothbury headquarters, both of which were also 'liberated' and put in his corner office on the first floor of the bank's St Andrew Square headquarters.

Goodwin intended to appoint Essex-born Richard Delbridge as finance director of the enlarged group. Delbridge had been NatWest finance director since 1996, having previously been a partner at Arthur Andersen and also a former finance director with HSBC. However, at some stage between Monday 6 March and Friday 17 March, Delbridge got cold feet, probably because he had decided that Goodwin would be an impossible boss. One former colleague of Delbridge says, 'Richard is solid, dependable, realistic and very strong on risk management but Goodwin is a risk taker who is also really pernickety about the stupidest things. I suspect Richard just decided it would be more trouble than it was worth. He'd already been through the trauma of an aggressive takeover when he agreed to stay on as finance director after HSBC acquired Midland in 1992.' On 17 March, the bank announced Delbridge wasn't coming after all. The RBS spin at the time was that, at the age of 57, he was too old to provide long-term leadership, always a convenient excuse.[4]

Whereas the entire NatWest board was cleared out, all 15 Royal Bank of Scotland directors kept their berths on the enlarged bank's board – and all also formally stepped on to the NatWest board.[5] Their total pay went through the roof. Overall, the pay and perks of RBS's 15 board directors increased by 162 per cent, from £4 million in 1999 to £10.5 million in 2000. The figures, which were net of the company's contributions to their pensions, were inflated by 'special' bonuses, which the bank's remuneration committee, chaired by Younger, awarded to four executive directors on 6 March 2000. This caused Goodwin's total package, excluding share options, to leap by 282 per cent from £592,000 to £2.3 million. Iain Robertson's ballooned by 210 per cent from £657,000 to £2 million. And Mathewson's rose by 165 per cent from £836,000 in 1999 to £2.2 million in 2000. Younger saw his pay rise 32 per cent from £285,000 to £379,000 – far more than he ever earned as a cabinet minister. Non-executive directors Sir Iain Vallance and Sir Angus Grossart saw their annual fees soar by 57 per cent from £56,000 to £88,000.[6]

'As the Royal Bank team reshaped British banking, they were also looking to do very well for themselves,' says Alf Young, one of Scotland's leading business and economics writers and a former policy editor of *The Herald*. 'That was never very far from George's thinking. He was always talking about the bloody share price and why wasn't it going up. All the time I knew him at RBS, every time I met him, he was moaning that the City doesn't understand what we're trying to do. I think George was quite into self-enrichment.'[7]

One former RBS executive director says, 'Quite a few people did very well out of the acquisition of NatWest, including me. I was promoted to a much bigger job. My pension pot immediately went up. But Fred was the biggest winner. He became the chief executive of a mega-bank and that made him worth a lot more in Hay MSL [a widely used proprietary system that grades jobs and levels of pay by size and responsibility] points.'

Having axed the NatWest board, Goodwin unveiled the seven-strong senior management team that would lead the combined group's biggest 'customer-facing divisions'. Of the seven individuals, five were from RBS and two from NatWest. From the Royal Bank side: Iain Robertson became chief executive of corporate banking and treasury; Norman McLuskie became chief executive of retail direct (which included credit cards and the joint ventures with Tesco and Virgin); Cameron McPhail became chief executive of wealth management (which included RBS International, Coutts & Co and Adam & Company);

Ian Chippendale remained chief executive of Direct Line Insurance; and Larry Fish remained as chairman, president and chief executive officer of Rhode Island-based Citizens. Only two divisional directors were from the NatWest side: Gordon Pell, who became chief executive of retail banking, and Martin Wilson, who remained chief executive of Ulster Bank. The Bank of England is said to have insisted that RBS appoint Pell to run the enlarged group's retail banking business. This was because the Bank's Silk Cut-smoking governor Eddie George did not believe anyone on the RBS side was up to the job.

When the next tier of senior appointments was unveiled on 17 March, it became clear that this was not a merger of equals but a massacre of NatWest by the marauding Scots. RBS man Grahame Whitehead, 48, a former partner at accountants Deloitte Haskins & Sells who had spent a few years in finance roles with Citizens in the US, became interim finance director in Delbridge's absence (he would become deputy finance director a few months later when Goodwin hired Fred Watt, former finance director of lighting firm Wassall, as group finance director). Miller McLean, 50, remained as group company secretary and group head of legal and regulatory affairs; Iain Allan, 53, remained as group director of strategy; Howard Moody, 50, remained as group director of communications; and Neil Roden, 43, remained as group director of human resources.

The sole NatWest executive who made the grade in this round of hirings was Mark Fisher. At the age of 39, the 'big blustery Yorkshireman' was already seen as a heavyweight. Born in Sheffield, he joined NatWest as a graduate trainee in 1981 armed with a first-class degree in mathematics from Bradford University and an MBA from the University of Warwick. Goodwin was clearly impressed by what Fisher had achieved at NatWest and it helped that the two men shared a passion for fast cars (just as they would both, according to former colleagues, later engage in office affairs). Goodwin appointed Fisher as chief executive of the enlarged group's 20,000-strong manufacturing division, which included all back-office functions, call centres, information technology, processing, administration, property management and procurement.

One ex-colleague says, 'Fred was Alexander the Great, leading the troops from the front. Mark Fisher loved him and loved the way Fred really knew the nitty-gritty of bank operations. At NatWest, Mark struggled to find any executive who had either the time or the inclination to discuss technicalities along the lines of "This is how we're going to do direct debits." They would all have thought that sort of stuff was beneath them. You also have to remember that Mark would have owed Fred some loyalty. When Fred plucked him out of NatWest, he told him that this would be the making of him.' The ex-RBS executive added, 'Mark was very smart, very hardworking, but was Fred's most loyal henchman in terms of exerting the brutal Fred doctrine.'

Fisher had been chief operating officer in NatWest's retail bank, where, with Tim Jones, he had been leading a five-year 'change management' programme that got under way in 1996. This programme, which entailed branch closures, the loss of 10,000 jobs and the introduction of new systems and processes, turned out to be essential to Goodwin's subsequent attempts to meld the two banks together. A former colleague of Fisher at NatWest said, 'All I would say is that Fred acquired his integrator . . . What Mark had done in the retail arm of NatWest, where we were processing 10 million transactions a day, was the equivalent of changing all four tyres on a car while doing 70mph in the outside lane of a motorway. There are not many people who can do that and RBS very definitely lacked the skills to do that in-house.' The two men who reported to Fisher in RBS's manufacturing division – Martin Webb and John White, both information technology specialists in their late 50s – came from the RBS side.

On 19 April, in a presentation to investors titled 'Delivering on our promises', Mathewson and Goodwin outlined their progress.[8] In their first month, they had applied the 'group architecture', made the key appointments, finalised detailed three-year plans for each retained division and aligned internal systems and controls. Or so they said. They had also evaluated the logic of disposing of units that had been earmarked for sale and reversed their decision to sell Connecticut-based Greenwich Capital.

To their pleasure, Goodwin and his RBS senior colleagues discovered that NatWest was in better shape than they had thought. This enabled them to raise their target for cost savings by more than £200 million to £1.34 billion through 121 cost-saving initiatives – 10 more than previously envisaged. With a sales blitz in mind, RBS also nearly doubled its forecast for annual revenue benefits to £595 million. Goodwin told the City the bank would axe 9,000 of the forecast

18,000 job cuts in year one. That impressed City analysts, who don't really care about the social consequences of deals as long as they make money. But it went down badly with the trade unions and, indeed, with the people concerned. Mathewson predicted the merged bank could achieve profits of £5 billion within three years, overtaking Lloyds TSB and nipping at the heels of HSBC. Mathewson added, 'Our aim is to create the pre-eminent banking group in Europe and, one month after doing the NatWest transaction, I am convinced that the group has the skills, resources and equipment to achieve that.'[9]

Ex-NatWest insiders were surprised by Goodwin's forensic focus on costs. Frances Coppola, then a senior business analyst and project manager on contract to NatWest, said, 'Fred was micro-managing the business. He was constantly nit-picking over expenses claims, office phone bills and department costs. He would carp at the managers concerned.'[10]

Gordon Pell first heard that Goodwin had singled him out to run the merged outfit's retail banking arm – which had 2,400 branches across the UK – on 5 March 2000. The pair lunched together in the City Rhodes restaurant on New Street Square, EC4. Restaurant critic Matthew Norman said the joint venture between celebrity chef Gary Rhodes and catering giant Sodexho was 'a miserable, moribund executive canteen', where 'the food itself almost surpasses the decor in drabness'.[11] There seems to have been a meeting of minds. Pell told me, 'I ran through what I was going to be doing with NatWest retail and he said, "Well, that's 99 per cent of what we're going to do with NatWest retail." '[12] Pell continued, 'NatWest retail had been the forgotten army of the NatWest empire. The whole emphasis had been on trying to keep the corporate bank under control – including the investment bankers. NatWest retail got the bit of attention and the bit of money that were left after everyone had dealt with that . . . There was a very clear view inside NatWest that retail banking was yesterday's business – dead – and that it was all about cost reduction. There had been a lot of very big programmes driven through to reduce costs. It had a superb franchise. This is what I found so bizarre – that they had reached the conclusion that a superb franchise was going nowhere.'[13]

Many RBS insiders were astonished by the absence of any sales process in NatWest's retail arm and that NatWest Group had used its retail business as a 'cash cow' to fund the growth of its corporate bank and treasury (paradoxically, RBS would fall in to the same trap later).

'They had embarked on a project called the retail transformation programme, that project had actually been proceeding quite well and quite a lot of its benefits became the Royal Bank's benefits,' Pell added before continuing: 'But the top management team had to be "excused" – to use an American usage. Eight out of eight. All done ethically and sensibly and all within three weeks of March 5. They had lost track of the fact that they were really managing a sales force and not a load of bank clerks and they were about nine or ten years out of date, actually.

'Having two brands made sense because there was so little overlap. I had managed a brand merger between Lloyds and TSB. In that case, the logic of bringing the two brands together was quite clear as 600 of the branches were literally within 100 yards of each other. With RBS/ NatWest, it was 100 [branches overlapping] if you pushed it. One of our great successes was in running both brands very strongly.'[14]

Within three months of the deal completing, RBS aimed to rejuvenate the NatWest brand and make a statement of intent with a £30-million advertising campaign using the slogan 'There is another way', developed by the agency, M&C Saatchi. Goodwin also visited several NatWest branches where he held 'town hall' sessions to meet staff and answer their questions. He believed these branch visits helped to build trust among NatWest employees and break down the power bases of branch leaders who were dragging their heels over integration. As part of its mission to keep staff abreast of developments, the bank hired BBC Newsnight presenter Kirsty Wark to make a film for Royal Bank's internal television station, RB-TV, outlining the human aspects of the merger. When Wark turned her Paxman-esque interview technique on Goodwin – asking him tough questions which were sourced directly from worried NatWest staff – he was satisfied with the results, though he later described the interview as 'a kind of Chinese water torture'. However, the feedback from NatWest's mostly English employees was less positive. One Royal Bank insider said, '[Wark] was too Scottish. Many employees were worried the merger was a Scottish takeover anyway. Combined with Fred, the overall impression was rather Scots-heavy.'[15] So the bank hired a new presenter, Sally Magnusson, for its next internal broadcast, aired in August 2000. Magnusson, the daughter of *Mastermind* host Magnus, presented the BBC's *Reporting Scotland*. Although she is also Scottish, her more dulcet tones were deemed less offensive to English ears.

Throughout the three-year integration programme, Fred Goodwin was relentlessly focused on ensuring that his executive team did not miss targets. In their 19 April 2000 presentation to investors, Mathewson and Goodwin had some fun by unveiling what they described as the 'good surprises' and 'bad surprises' arising out of the takeover. They said that 'good surprises' included Greenwich Capital Markets, a Connecticut-based bond-trading house founded as a two-man partnership by William Rainer and Edwin L. Knetzger III in 1981. The business, acquired by NatWest for $590 million (£385 million) in 1996, was one of 37 so-called 'primary dealers' authorised to trade in Treasuries – government bonds issued by Washington DC to fund its deficits. It was, therefore, able to underwrite debt for the United States government and to act as a trading partner to the Federal Reserve. Greenwich was also a rising star in 'structured finance' – which meant repackaging parcels of debt for onward sale to third-party investors.

During the takeover battle, the Royal Bank had told investors it would sell this business partly because Goodwin didn't particularly want to own a 'black box' financial operation – the sort that constructs complex and opaque financial products. The decision to sell was reversed after Iain Robertson visited the business's head office in Greenwich, Connecticut, in March 2000. Robertson was sufficiently impressed by the quality of Greenwich's management and risk management professionals that he recommended the business should be kept. Robertson said, 'In the time that I was at RBS, Greenwich was a very good corporate citizen – they worked very hard and I was happy with the decision to keep them. If we had sold Greenwich, we'd have sold it for about £200–250 million. In the first two years after the takeover of NatWest, it actually made more in profits than we were going to sell it for.'[16]

The new Corporate Banking and Financial Markets (CBFM) division combined all the corporate banking and financial markets businesses of both NatWest and RBS – including Greenwich. On the day it was formed, 6 March 2000, the new organisation became the largest corporate bank in the UK, with approximately 75,000 corporate customers and over 100 corporate banking offices in the UK, serving some 200 of the FTSE-250 companies.

Robertson says RBS and NatWest had markedly different approaches to corporate lending and it was the former's quicker and more customer-friendly approach that prevailed. 'The typical

NatWest way was that you bundled a file up [for credit approval] and it disappeared for four weeks and went through God only knows what mechanisms and then it emerged with a "Yes" or a "No", without any questions or anything else. The NatWest people really welcomed the change to our process. It liberated the people on the corporate banking side of NatWest – they felt that, if they put forward something that was sensible, that the customer wanted and it hung together properly, they could actually get it through and get it through quickly.'[17]

On the financial markets side of the business, some tough decisions were called for. The other two main units on the NatWest side were Greenwich Capital and Greenwich NatWest (which had recently been invented and was effectively an outpost of Greenwich Capital in London). Then there was NatWest Global Financial Markets, which focused on foreign exchange and treasury. The inter-divisional relations at NatWest had deteriorated to the extent that the Greenwich NatWest people called Global Financial Markets 'go f**k yourself!' Robertson and Cameron decided that the way to deal with the internecine strife was to get rid of most of the Greenwich NatWest people in London but to leave Greenwich Capital in Connecticut pretty much intact. David Bermingham, Giles Darby and Gary Mulgrew, the 'NatWest Three', who worked for Greenwich NatWest in London and who were later found guilty of a wire fraud related to Houston-based energy trading giant Enron, all resigned in 2000 to go and work for Royal Bank of Canada.

One early decision facing CBFM was which brand to use. Robertson says there was 'lots and lots of scratching of heads' about the issue which was discussed at length with George Mathewson, who had been elevated to executive deputy chairman. Robertson continued, 'In the first two or three weeks of just talking to customers, we discovered very few of the larger corporates had made a conscious decision to become NatWest or Royal Bank customers and, as long as they continued to get the right or better service, they didn't really care. And Royal Bank had a better name in the market than NatWest, so we thought, let's become Royal Bank of Scotland, and we did it, there was hardly an eyebrow raised.'[18]

However, CBFM kept both the Royal Bank of Scotland and NatWest brands alive for its small and mid-sized customers, whose bosses were seen as more susceptible to brand names. Soon afterwards,

CBFM landed upon a new advertising slogan – 'Make it Happen'. It was intended to encapsulate the division's 'can do' spirit and desire to help customers achieve their dreams. CBFM first used the slogan on advertisements published in the *Financial Times*, the *Daily Telegraph* and the *Glasgow Herald* in October and November 2000. But Goodwin and RBS's group director of communications Howard Moody so liked the slogan they purloined it for use across the wider group. Some senior figures, including Gordon Pell, had reservations, fearing the slogan could backfire. However, Goodwin and Moody pushed it through and, in a campaign codenamed 'Paint it Blue', the motto was soon being plastered on Heathrow Express trains and on gangways and terminal buildings at Edinburgh, Heathrow and John F. Kennedy International Airports. 'The sums being spent on that were extraordinary,' says one former Royal Bank of Scotland senior manager.

Robertson says CBFM delivered the promised merger benefits ahead of schedule. He said, 'Post-merger, the first thing we had to do was to deliver all the action plans that we had said we'd deliver. And we delivered them about six months early. And we delivered more income growth and more cost savings than had actually been in the plan. The second thing that we did was decide how and where to grow the business.'[19]

NatWest's chairman, Sir David Rowland, had warned that, if either of the two Scottish banks got their hands on NatWest, they would end up falling flat on their faces. Both RBS and BoS had proposed junking the NatWest system and migrating all of the enlarged group's IT onto their own platforms, which Rowland argued would lead to a systems meltdown. In the end, however, Fisher, Webb and White pulled off what looked like a textbook integration, transferring almost all of NatWest's IT operations on to RBS's smaller information technology platform ahead of schedule.

Even though RBS's IBM-based information technology platform was smaller than NatWest's, it had the advantage of being more flexible, in terms of both 'scalability' – it could handle more transactions – and 'adaptability' – it could be adapted to handle additional types of transaction.

John White commented, 'It's pleasing to say that we completed full integration – general ledger, accountancy systems, HR systems, risk systems, all the retail, all the corporate bank, all of the distributions channels – [and] we did all that in two years and seven months.' Describing the switchover weekend in October 2002, White said, 'We had 2,500 people working that weekend all over the place. We had the Financial Services Authority monitoring it every two hours. But, if we had failed, when you think of the damage it could have done to the UK monetary system – we have a significant part of the UK payment system – we have 5,500 ATMs, if we had not got all of them to work – think of the calamity in a country the size of the United Kingdom.' And he added, 'As we neared switch-off, I said to my colleague George Adams, "If this doesn't work out, George, you and I are in prison." And he smiled at me, he was a very quiet man, and said to me, "You know, success has many fathers. Failure has only one." It was a great time – we consumed something like 5,000 ice creams that weekend and a couple of hundred thousand sandwiches that were all brought in and I lost count of the number of pizzas.'[20] The migration was so seamless that it was a non-event as far as most customers were concerned.

Goodwin gave a couple of revealing interviews around this time. The first, in August 2000, was given to Doug Morrison, a business journalist with *Scotland on Sunday*. In the interview, Goodwin admitted that the 'Shred' nickname annoyed him but argued it had been more of an asset than a liability during the takeover battle. He said, 'The supreme irony is that, at Clydesdale, I grew income by more than I cut costs. However, on the basis that "Charming" and "Considerate" didn't rhyme with Fred, I guess we had to live with "Shred".'[21] He also said, 'I actually think – verging on the passionately – that what works is what's good for the shareholders, the customers and the staff. If you get a situation where something's good for the staff and customers but not good for the shareholders it's probably going to end in tears.'[22]

One of the other 'good surprises' that Mathewson and Goodwin chanced upon and which they also referred to in their 19 April 2000 presentation to analysts, was a wine cellar they discovered in a former bullion vault underneath NatWest's Lothbury headquarters. The cellar contained 2,209 bottles of classic French wine, including plentiful supplies of Château Lafite Rothschild, 1972 vintage. Goodwin joked at the time about it being 'so valuable that, for security purposes, I can't tell you where it is going'.[23] However, it has since emerged that, after handing a few of the more ordinary bottles to supportive analysts, Royal Bank had these liquid assets shipped north to Edinburgh more or less straight away. The bank also had a fair few bottles of Château Latour 1970 liberated from NatWest delivered to Preston Hall, a neoclassical country house in Midlothian about 12 miles south-east of Edinburgh. Here, triumphant Merrill Lynch deal-maker Matthew Greenburgh, together with Andy Chisholm of Goldman Sachs, who had both earned fat fees from the takeover battle, hosted a celebratory dinner for RBS in April 2000. At the dinner, Goodwin was presented with an Airfix kit of a model car and Merrill Lynch presented the Royal Bank team with engraved silver plates. But the house's late owner, Major Henry Callander, was surprised to see rare and expensive wines being trundled out of a delivery van at 7 p.m. on the night of the dinner. He saw that as bad form since such classic vintages need time to settle. It was a typical clash between old money and the nouveau riche. And the newly affluent were in the ascendancy.

In an interview with Ruth Sunderland published in the *Daily Mail* on 9 November 2000, Goodwin agreed he could come across as 'direct' and he also admitted to a fundamental problem that would dog his next eight years as RBS chief executive – how to sustain a growth rate that had been briefly turbocharged by what rivals bankers describe as 'the dripping roast' of a serendipitous acquisition.

However, when he unveiled profits of £6.45 billion for the year to December 2002, Goodwin sought to dispel fears that RBS was dependent on the positive benefits of acquiring NatWest for profits growth. He said, 'We have grown an Abbey National in the last three years in income size at least. We did a lot more than just integrate NatWest.' Goodwin then jokingly reassured everyone that it did not mean that the bank had created a toxic time bomb, like former building society Abbey had become.[24] As the *Telegraph*'s 'Questor' investment column reported, 'RBS has delivered on every target it set for itself when it acquired NatWest, plus more besides.'[25]

Even today, the £21-billion NatWest deal is spoken about in hushed tones and revered as the banking acquisition of the century. It made Goodwin's name as a banker, gave him the licence to do other deals and was the subject of an adulatory Harvard Business School case study titled 'Royal Bank of Scotland: Masters of Integration'. Some commentators and ex-insiders allege there was a degree of 'smoke and mirrors' about the integration, even suggesting it was a botched job. However, ex-RBS IT insiders have rubbished such claims, arguing the word 'integration' was a misnomer, since what really happened was the migration of all NatWest's data onto RBS's systems. One ex-insider who reported to RBS's head of payment operations, told me, 'I was in charge of the automated teller machine (ATM) migration. As with all the other migrations, a lot of hard work went into this over the best part of three years by many thousands of people, and the NatWest customer data and accounting was all successfully migrated. There were some pains for customers in the ATM area, for example we took away some of the functionality from NatWest ATMs, but then we also took away the notoriously long queues at NatWest ATMs. Many people thought the IT migration was a simple job; it was anything but. We were all extremely proud of what was achieved.'

Frances Coppola, then a consultant project manager at RBS, said that as far as group accounting was concerned, the integration actually gave rise to 'a fragmented financial systems architecture' which, crucially, lacked a central system for consolidating numbers from across the group and also opened the door to internal fraud.[26] One issue Coppola and members of her team had to contend with was that NatWest and Royal Bank had fundamentally different approaches to financial reporting. NatWest's former finance director, Richard Delbridge, had introduced a system that enabled finance staff to see an 'audit trail', meaning 'read through' access to underlying financial and operational information, which was the approach favoured by the Bank of England. However, the Royal Bank had a more rudimentary approach based around the manual keying-in of high-level data into a Microsoft Excel spreadsheet, meaning there was no audit trail. The RBS approach was much more susceptible to fudging and obfuscation.

Coppola says that, in its usual bolshie way, RBS was determined to stick to its inadequate 'spreadsheets' approach to group financial reporting – even after the Bank of England had told the bank this would not do. According to Coppola, the bank's Corporate Banking and Financial Markets business dragged its heels more than any part of the enlarged group. CBFM, she says, insisted on continuing to churn out bald data into which it was impossible for anyone to 'drill down'.[27] This meant there was no proper audit trail or access to underlying data. In August 2002, there was a showdown. Coppola prepared a report on the readiness of the various divisions to migrate to the new Bank of England-sanctioned approach. In it, she highlighted CBFM's refusal to cooperate with the initiative but, in typical RBS fashion, the report was suppressed and Coppola was dismissed. Coppola says, 'CBFM made no real effort to adapt their business model to suit the new architecture. From CBFM's point of view, it meant that the new systems didn't really support the business and they would be doing a lot more manual processing and fudges – which gave obvious opportunities for gaming the system and fraud.'[28]

One ex-RBS executive director said the myth of the NatWest takeover's success was based on two unrecognised features of the deal: firstly, the bank picked a misleading start date for its share performance comparisons – specifically, it used 800p as the starting share price, when the real price should have been up to 2100p, the value of RBS shares before the bank announced its intention to bid for NatWest; and, secondly, the media accepted this deliberate misrepresentation without question and the City was too embarrassed to admit it got its sums wrong. The former executive director said, 'Having been sucked into a bidding war by the Bank of Scotland, Goodwin overpaid for his prey. This meant that, irrespective of the success of the integration, the numbers were never going to work, even with a favourable economic wind.'

The wrong kind of growth

On 1 March 2001, the Royal Bank of Scotland delighted the markets with spectacular annual results for the 12 months to December 2000. The bank said profits had surged by 31 per cent to £4.401 billion on a pro forma basis. This caused the bank's share price to climb by 7 per cent to 1659p, taking Royal Bank of Scotland's market capitalisation to £44.4 billion and enabling it to comfortably leapfrog Lloyds TSB as the UK's second biggest bank.[1]

Goodwin played down suggestions that Royal Bank was going make a counter-bid for Abbey National, which was on the receiving end of a £19.8 billion hostile takeover offer from Lloyds TSB. However, at a press conference to announce the annual results, he said his bank would consider 'mercy killings' of smaller financial services players if the need arose. The integration of NatWest was ahead of schedule and winning plaudits. NatWest's branch closure programme, which had commenced under the *ancien régime*, had been halted. Instead, its branches were being spruced up in a £150-million makeover and it was doing customer-friendly things like opening branches on Saturdays and enabling customers to phone their branches rather than call centres. RBS was also lavishing £30 million on a high-profile advertising campaign plugging the NatWest brand, created by advertising agency M&C Saatchi. Television commercials, using the slogan 'There is another way', gleefully knocked rival banks for shutting their branches and claimed NatWest was not doing anything of the sort. The enlarged group was securing positive media coverage and its shares had more than doubled in value since the NatWest deal had been completed on 6 March 2000. Goodwin had attended a pre-election lunch with Tony Blair and other bankers at Chequers, the prime minister's country retreat in Buckinghamshire, cementing the impression that he had arrived.[2]

However, the biggest nuisance for Goodwin at the time was actually the UK government. In October 2000, the Competition Commission warned that the enlarged group might have a 'scale monopoly' in small business banking. The Commission's private warning followed the findings of a report that Chancellor Gordon Brown had commissioned from the bankers' *bête noire*, former telecoms regulator Don Cruickshank. In March 2000, Cruickshank had produced a report accusing British banks of ripping off their UK retail and small business customers to the tune of between £3 billion and £5 billion a year. Brown, still in his Calvinist, sceptical about bankers phase, was, at the time, determined to clip the banks' wings.

The Royal Bank could hardly have picked a worse time to reveal that it had paid £2.5 million in bonuses to four directors as a pat on the back for the NatWest deal – especially since the deal had reduced, not increased, competition. The information was disclosed in the directors' remuneration section of the RBS annual report, published in March 2001. The money had been shared by Goodwin, Mathewson, Robertson and McLuskie exactly a year earlier. As soon as this became known, the bank was subjected to a roasting in the media, as well as from politicians and investors. But then Mathewson poured petrol on the flames. In an interview with Simon Targett of the *Financial Times*, Mathewson claimed his £759,000 special bonus, together with those paid to Goodwin (£814,000), Robertson (£773,000), and McLuskie (£197,000) were so insignificant they 'wouldn't have given you bragging power in a Soho wine bar'. Asked by Targett if the bonuses had been cleared by shareholders, Mathewson said they hadn't. 'Frankly it [the award of the bonuses] was not worthwhile talking to shareholders about.'[3]

The comment ignited a blazing row that extended far beyond the media to politicians, investors and corporate governance watchdogs. Investors dislike 'transactional' bonuses since, in a worst-case scenario, they encourage empire building that has everything to do with the executives' desire for self-enrichment and vainglorius pursuit of scale for its own sake and nothing to do with long-term shareholder value. Alluding to the then political climate towards the banking sector, Patience Wheatcroft wrote, 'The bonus payment smacked of the crass insensitivity that has made the banks so unpopular, both in the high street and in high places . . . Just when the banks need allies, he [Mathewson] has succeeded in alienating his shareholders.'⁴

It was left to Royal Bank's outgoing chairman, George Younger, to pour oil on troubled waters. The National Association of Pension Funds (NAPF) and the Association of British Insurers, representing institutional investors, were determined to make the bank's directors feel the heat. They sought to have Sir Angus Grossart and Sir Iain Vallance removed from the board. Both men were on the remuneration committee that had signed off the bonuses. On 28 March, the bank managed to defuse the gathering storm when it wrote to the NAPF 'clarifying' that some of the money was being paid in RBS shares and it wasn't long before the shareholders' revolt fizzled out. It was left to private shareholder Miss Mary Mackenzie, a retired Edinburgh schoolteacher, to admonish Goodwin and Mathewson for their greed. Speaking at the bank's annual general meeting in the Edinburgh International Conference Centre on 11 April 2001, Miss Mackenzie, who was a fixture at the AGMs of the Scottish bank until her death in October 2012, said, 'One cannot admire people who need so many bonuses and financial inducements to do a day's work.' The retired schoolteacher and scourge of corporate greed added, 'One could mention camels and needles.'⁵

At the meeting – his last as chairman – Younger was suitably contrite. He said it was a 'great concern that some shareholders have felt unhappy about this. We do our damnedest all the time to act in the interest of the shareholders.' Younger had been unwavering in his support for Mathewson over the previous 12 years, but this episode tried his patience. Mathewson believes Younger made a very good chairman. He says, 'George was a very solid and balanced occupant of the chair and ran the board well. He had highly developed diplomatic skills. He was a much tougher man than many people realised. He was definitely of the aristocratic class, which is not a criticism but it could fool you into thinking that he was just a nice guy. Underneath there was a hint of steel.'⁶

From the late 1990s onwards, Mathewson, eager to become the first non-aristocrat to hold the post, made no secret of his desire to succeed Younger as chairman. However, the former Defence Secretary had reservations. In principle, he was against the idea of a chief executive becoming chairman because of the risk that such a person could become a back-seat driver and crowd out his successor as chief executive once in the chairman's role. He was also concerned about Mathewson's brusque style and lack of connections. Several existing non-executives at Royal Bank also wanted the job, including chairman of British Telecommunications, Sir Iain Vallance, who had been a vice-chairman of Royal Bank since 1994. But in the end, Younger acquiesced to having Mathewson as his successor on the tacit understanding that Mathewson would be a 'hands-off' chairman as Younger had been.

The UK's Combined Code of Corporate Governance didn't yet ban such appointments outright. But a revised code published a few years later, which incorporated the findings of the 'Higgs Review of the Role and Effectiveness of Non-Executive Directors', did. The revised code cited a number of reasons why promoting a chief executive to the chairmanship is a bad idea. These include that it can impede good governance, cause confusion between non-executives and executives, cause inadequate disclosure to the board and lead to tension between the chairman and chief executive.[7]

Mathewson formally stepped up to the RBS chairmanship at the bank's annual general meeting on 11 April 2001. With the benefit of hindsight, he admits he was so determined to avoid being seen as intrusive that he may have over-compensated and become too 'hands-off'. Ex-colleagues and friends of Mathewson believe that, either because of that or because he was 'somewhat in awe of Fred', Mathewson became 'semi-detached from the bank' and 'more absent than the chairman of a major company should be'. One former Royal Bank non-executive director remarked, 'George let Fred off the hook too early and I do blame George for that.' Ex-colleagues say Mathewson's laid-back approach enabled Goodwin to seize the levers of power and centralise more of the power on himself, even going as far as to usurp some of the functions of the chairman's role and running some of the bank's board meetings. One former senior colleague, who worked at the bank from the mid 1990s to about 2004, says, 'George liked to think that he could control Fred but he got that completely wrong. The truth was he couldn't. George is still in denial about this – at least he certainly still seemed to be in denial when he was interviewed by the BBC programme, "RBS: Inside the Bank that Ran Out of Money".[8] It's a real shame. George needs to be more honest with himself.'

Speaking about his working relationship prior to becoming chairman in April 2001, Mathewson says, 'Yes, there were differences of emphasis and obviously Fred's style is not my style, but it's important to realise just how effective Fred was at times. In running the retail business, he had a gift for plain communication down the line. All the staff knew where they were with Fred. Fred's problems were with his immediate reports, not further down the line. Yes, certainly our views could diverge on people but we didn't really diverge on anything significant.'9

Mathewson refuses to accept that his decision to hire Goodwin as his successor was a massive mistake. However, he does accept that the board should probably have pushed Goodwin out once the NatWest integration was complete in 2002. He says, 'Even before the NatWest takeover, Royal Bank was the number one in the UK for effectiveness, efficiency and customer service. After the NatWest takeover, we were still the number one and we had brought NatWest up to number two. That was a huge achievement and Fred never gets any credit for that at all. If you could rewrite history and do it right, you'd have got rid of Fred two years after the takeover. He had done what he was best at. And you would have kept Iain Robertson, which would have meant you would never have had the problems like you had under Johnny Cameron. But that's not how life works.'10

There are risks to having a semi-detached chairman and a control freak as chief executive. With too much power vested in the hands of one person, power can go to their head. There may be an absence of checks and balances since everyone reports to the chief executive. According to ex-insiders, it wasn't long before Goodwin had transformed Royal Bank of Scotland into something resembling a dictatorship, with Fred requiring absolute loyalty of staff – and naysayers banished to the Gulag. Senior executives began to believe that, if they wanted to retain their jobs, they were going to have suck up to Fred, play along with his games and shield him from bad news. One person with high-level knowledge of RBS said, 'Fred was the alpha male – he dominated everything at the bank. If you wanted to know whether or not you were going to get something through the board, it wasn't the chairman you went to – it was Fred. It was very much Fred's company – the Royal Bank of Fred.'

However, speaking to the Treasury Committee on 10 February 2009,

Goodwin disputed this was what RBS was like, saying, 'My manage-ment style is something that evolves and changes, depending on the circumstances, but I believe I have led the bank in a responsible fashion with my colleagues, and I have been equally receptive to bad news and good news. Of course, I wanted solutions rather than problems, but you cannot exist in a job like mine by ignoring problems, and I do not have a track record of ignoring problems or leaving problems undealt with.'

A former senior executive at RBS claims that Goodwin found ways of subverting the group's corporate governance processes, especially when it came to communications with the board. He said, 'While I was there, the work was always done amongst the group executive manage-ment committee, which Fred totally dominated, before anything could go to the board. They didn't take anything to the board unless they absolutely had to and they always timed it and packaged it so as to minimise the chance that the non-executives would interfere or change anything.'

The tone of an exchange of emails written on 25 March 2003, with the subject line 'Jet for the chairman', suggested Goodwin was firmly in the driving seat. The emails suggest that, despite being the bank's chairman, Mathewson almost had to plead with Goodwin to be allowed to use the Dassault Falcon 900EX private jet the bank had acquired in October 2002, for a trip to Catalonia, even though he was asking two months in advance in order to speak on behalf of the bank at a conference in Barcelona. When Goodwin did give his chairman permission to use the plane, his response was terse and grudging.

'After George Younger retired, the strains started to show,' remarked one former senior executive. Mathewson attended more and more meetings via a dedicated videoconferencing facility that was installed in his Perthshire home and became much more interested in external pursuits including, increasingly, his role as chairman of the fund-raising arm of the Royal Botanic Garden Edinburgh. In that role, Mathewson was instrumental in raising £10.7 million for the construction of the John Hope Gateway building, designed by Edward Cullinan Architects, which was completed in 2009.

Between 1998 and 2008, there was only a solitary woman on the RBS board. First, it was the retired civil servant Eileen Mackay, the wife of a former leader of the civil service in Scotland. On 1 January

2006, Mackay was replaced as the board's token woman by Janis Kong, boss of Heathrow Airport and a director of British Airports Authority. Following a few retirements and deaths, five new non-executive directors were appointed to the RBS board between January 2001 and June 2002. They were: the former Irish attorney general, Peter Sutherland; former Commercial General Norwich Union (CGNU) chief executive, Bob Scott; Second Permanent Secretary to the Treasury, Sir Steve Robson; former European Commission director general for the environment Jim Currie; and former Union Bank of Switzerland (UBS) investment banker Colin Buchan. On paper, they looked a fairly impressive bunch but senior bank insiders suggest that, since Fred Goodwin played a part in their selection, their independence was compromised. In April 2005, two longstanding boardroom fixtures, Edinburgh merchant banker Sir Angus Grossart and former BT chairman Sir Iain Vallance, were both eased out by activist investors who felt they had been there too long to be effective. Grossart, described as a staunch ally of Goodwin, had been a non-executive director for 19 years and Vallance for 12 years.

On 14 February 2000, three weeks before he took over as chief executive, Goodwin had a contretemps with the bank's longstanding auditors, PricewaterhouseCoopers (PwC). The PwC audit partner, Amyas Morse, now the UK's auditor general, refused to sign off a 'racy' accounting treatment related to the purchase of NatWest that would allegedly have flattered the enlarged group's profitability. Goodwin did not like it when people, even well-qualified professionals such as Morse, stood up to him and was furious. Ex-colleagues say that, on exiting a 'morning meeting' in which the matter was discussed, the bank's head of human resources Neil Roden said, 'Whoo-hoo, that's the end of PricewaterhouseCoopers!' A former executive director at RBS explained, 'Fred could tolerate some pushback but could not tolerate anyone who was fundamentally opposed to the direction of travel.' Not long afterwards – on 21 March 2000 – Goodwin is said to have unilaterally fired PwC as auditors. Rather than choose NatWest auditors KPMG, Goodwin appointed his 'alma mater' Deloitte without out a tender. Ex-RBS insiders allege that Goodwin's main reason for this was that he saw them as more biddable than PwC and so less likely to challenge him over accounting treatments. At the very least, there was scope for conflict of interest: Goodwin had worked at Deloitte for 16 years, from 1979 to 1995; he had been a partner there from 1988–95;

and the firm's UK managing partner John Connolly is widely considered to be Goodwin's mentor.

Connolly, a portly Mancunian who left school at sixteen and went
straight into accountancy, became a fixture at RBS annual general
meetings over the next eight years but he had a patchy track record.
He was reprimanded and fined £40,000 by the UK accountancy
profession's Joint Disciplinary Scheme (JDS) as a result of his role in
the 1988 Barlow Clowes fraud, which cost the government £150 million in compensation to the thousands of mainly elderly savers who
were ripped off. Peter Clowes, the architect of the scam, was jailed
for ten years. But, according to a JDS report published in July 1995,
Connolly rubber-stamped deceptive financial reporting and signed off
accounts containing 'fictitious income'. The disciplinary body said 'the
professional efficiency, conduct and competence of John Connolly fell
below the standard which should be displayed by, and may properly
be expected of, a Chartered Accountant'. Stewart Hamilton, emeri-
tus professor of finance at the Lausanne-based business school, the
International Institute for Management Development (IMD), says, 'In
my view, Connolly should have been struck off for that. Had he been
a small practitioner in Peterborough or Peterhead that would have
happened but the JDS went easy on the big firms.'[11] What surprised
observers was that, instead of drumming Connolly out of the firm,
Touche Ross partners voted him in as their UK managing partner.
Professor Hamilton believes this set the ethical tone for Touche Ross,
which became Deloitte in 1990.

At the time, Royal Bank of Scotland's official stance towards the
change of auditor was that it had little choice other than to dismiss
PwC (its own auditors) and KPMG (NatWest's) because of concerns
over conflicts of interest. PwC audited two of the UK's other big banks
– Lloyds TSB and Barclays – while KPMG audited both HSBC and
Halifax. Factors in Deloitte's favour included the quality of the work it
had done for RBS during the takeover battle, notably a partisan report
rubbishing NatWest's interpretation of the risks of banking takeovers.

According to the UK's corporate governance code, the firing of
auditors and the appointment of new ones are the responsibility of the
audit committee, a subcommittee of the board exclusively made up of
non-executive directors. However, the widespread view in the accounting profession is that Goodwin made the appointment and asked the

audit committee to approve it after the event. The RBS audit committee at the time had four members – Bill Wilson (the chairman, since
deceased), Angus Grossart, Eileen Mackay and Murray Stuart. IMD's
Hamilton says, 'It is my recollection that Royal Bank of Scotland did
not fully adhere to due process when replacing PwC with Deloitte. It
was probably the earliest indication that Fred was going to do his own
thing and would be unwilling to follow normal conventions. In an ideal
world, the chief executive should be utterly indifferent to who the auditors are and should have absolutely nothing to do with auditor selection. If the chief executive does have strong views on auditor selection,
the first question the audit committee should be asking themselves is
"Why?" '[12]

Royal Bank paid Deloitte £5 million for auditing its 2000 accounts,
signed off on 28 February 2001, and £5.1 million for non-audit work
in the same period. Former auditors PwC were paid £2.4 million for
auditing the 1999 accounts, signed off in December 1999, and £9.4 million for non-audit work. Both these sets of figures ought to have raised
alarm bells with investors since, whenever non-audit fees exceed audit
fees, there is a risk that the independence and integrity of the audit are
compromised. One former RBS executive director adds, 'The relationship between Fred Goodwin and Deloitte & Touche was inappropriate,
ineffective and incestuous. The FSA did not even bother to investigate
this, and we need to know why that was.' A former senior executive at
RBS believes Connolly was disinclined to challenge Goodwin on the
valuations of the bank's underlying assets, saying, 'If Fred had declared
that a CDO [collateralised debt obligation] was worth 90 cents in the
dollar, John Connolly wasn't going to dispute that and say it was worth
only 30 cents in the dollar. If he had done that, Fred would have lost
his job.' So, it seems, mutual back-scratching was the order of the day.

Perhaps the most egregious error that Royal Bank of Scotland made
in the aftermath of the NatWest acquisition was that it started to chase
the wrong kind of growth. During the 1990s, Royal Bank of Scotland's
strategy was broad-brush and flexible. It revolved around growing
income, improving efficiency (Project Columbus played a big part here)
and maintaining 'strategic options' for future growth. Underpinning
the approach was efficient balance-sheet management, which meant
sailing fairly close to the wind where capital and leverage were concerned. The approach enabled Royal Bank to outpace every other UK

bank, with the possible exception of Bank of Scotland from 1992 to 1998. But RBS did not even discuss changing its strategic approach in the wake of the NatWest deal. This was despite the fact that total assets grew from £37.4 billion in 1993 to £455.3 billion in 2003, which made it harder for it to duck and dive its way around the financial market place. The changes in the macroeconomic backdrop might also have sparked a strategic rethink. For most of the 1990s, a benign economic wind propelled the bank's growth. The economic conditions in the 2000s were altogether less stable, although Alan Greenspan's loose monetary policy following the 11 September 2001 terror attacks in the USA, imitated by other central bankers around the world, gave false comfort. With the benefit of hindsight, some of the bank's former executive directors concede they were foolish not to have reassessed the strategy.

Various people did try to persuade Goodwin to review the bank's strategy but he wasn't interested. He was using the NatWest integration as his avoidance mechanism. One ex-colleague said, 'That persisted for a couple of years and, once the integration was complete, he became an adrenalin-fuelled deal junky, always living on the edge. Fred tended to do things because they gave him a thrill, not because they made strategic sense.'

Asked about his strategy at a February 2004 meeting with investment analysts, Goodwin said, 'We try not to have a strategy; we just try to generate lots of options – at first blush that looks slightly eclectic . . . If the world changes and some of the things no longer work, we have the benefit of having lots of options. We move on. These are options, not promises.'[13] And one former NatWest executive said, 'When RBS took over NatWest we learned Fred's favourite book was *Five Frogs on a Log*, a practical guide to making acquisitions work and mercifully short. Johnny arrived and was brandishing the *Harvard Business Review* article by Amar Bhide, "Hustle as Strategy", which played well against the dominant thinking laid out by George Mathewson of "serial opportunism" – stay lean, be alert, watch your environment, move fast. My own view at the time was that this was good, old-fashioned, Scottish commercial pragmatism and I liked it. It worked.'

One consistent theme during Goodwin's tenure as chief executive was the dramatic growth of the investment bank – the financial markets part of Iain Robertson's CBFM. The NatWest deal had made the enlarged group the leading player in European debt capital markets.

As government and corporate borrowing went through the roof, these markets were on the cusp of a long boom. CBFM was also growing as a result of the expansion of its leveraged finance operations, led by Leith Robertson, who was poached from Bank of Scotland in 1993. 'Leith was a street fighter of a businessman. A deal maker to the tips of his fingers, he was pugnacious, energetic, fiercely Scottish, focused and capable,' says one former colleague. In the world of leveraged finance, he was to become a legend with the establishment of specialist outposts in Frankfurt, Madrid, Milan, Paris and Stockholm. The investment bank also grew by poaching, usually at great expense, teams of specialist bankers from rival financial institutions as well as through the rapid growth of Greenwich Capital Markets in Connecticut. Even as CBFM was mushrooming, Goodwin always sought to play down RBS's involvement in investment banking, perhaps because investors were of the view that UK clearing banks that branched out into this area invariably came a cropper. He also sought to downplay RBS's burgeoning involvement in investment banking by bundling the financial results for the investment banking arm with those of the UK corporate lending arm. Sometimes Goodwin seemed to be in denial that the investment bank even existed. The second consistent theme to RBS's non-strategic strategy was the enlargement of Citizens Financial through the acquisition and integration of other banks, mainly in the north-east of the United States. The third theme, closely allied to the first and second themes, was the accumulation of assets. One former director later said, 'Everywhere you looked, they were taking on assets – billions of dollars' worth of planes, billions of dollars of ships, commercial real estate across America and Britain. They were buying everything to meet Goodwin's targets and his targets were assets.'[14]

A fourth consistent theme, and one that both RBS's former head of retail banking, Brian Hartzer, and former chief executive Stephen Hester admitted to, was the use of the UK retail bank as a 'cash cow' to fund overseas empire building.[15] One executive director who left the bank in about 2002, said, 'When I left the bank, we were awash with deposits. Two years later, they had worked their way through the deposits and were having to rely on wholesale markets again. The shape of the balance sheet had completely changed in the space of about two years.'

Underlying it all was Goodwin's desire to overtake JPMorgan and turn Royal Bank of Scotland into a global financial services supermarket or global 'universal' bank – a sort of mini-me to the New York-based behemoth, Citigroup. But it was a quixotic dream even in the early 2000s. Just as Fred Goodwin set off on his mission to create a world-straddling financial services supermarket, financial commentators were already questioning the logic of such organisations. And this was largely because of the conflicts of interest that they threw up. In a September 2002 article, Anthony Bianco and Heather Timmons wrote, 'If ever there was a bank too big to fail, it is Citigroup, with its $1 trillion in assets and 270,000 employees in 100 countries . . . It's starting to look as though the very model of the financial conglomerate is fundamentally flawed. Sprawling institutions such as Citi, JPMorgan Chase, Merrill Lynch, and others are riddled with conflicts of interest, compounded by abuses by aggressive bankers.'[16]

One person who knows Goodwin well believes his obsession with growing the balance sheet through deals was largely driven by fear. Sources claim that Goodwin became convinced that either Barclays or RBS was going to be acquired by JPMorgan, Citigroup or Bank of America. One source said, 'He had made it his mission that RBS was not the one that got acquired.'

One of Goodwin's most transparent vanity purchases came in April 2002, when the noted petrol-head paid an astonishing £110 million for Doncaster-headquartered used-car dealership Dixon Motors. The deal netted the company's founder Paul Dixon and his son Simon over £8.8 million. The pair, together with two other directors, were also eligible for a bonus of £13.5 million if they achieved what Royal Bank claimed were 'extremely stretching' profitability targets by 2006.[17] Even though there was a marked lack of synergies between a chain of car retailers and a bank, RBS claimed that owning Dixon Motors made strategic sense. Unsurprisingly, it turned out to be a disaster for RBS, with a lot of money seemingly being siphoned out of the business. The bank made a partial exit from Dixon Motors in September 2005, ousting Paul and Simon Dixon and installing a new management team along with a revised ownership structure, in the hope of turning the place around.[18] But the business was already beyond repair and went bust in August 2007. Goodwin's dream of becoming an 'Arthur Daley' was in tatters and the bank had lost tens of millions of pounds because its board had nodded through a £110-million whim of the chief executive.

At Gleneagles Hotel in Perthshire, a few weeks after the NatWest deal was completed in March 2000, Fred Goodwin gave a presentation to senior colleagues who had been involved in the acquisition. Every slide had size or scale somewhere as its theme. One showed the size of RBS – which then had a market capitalisation of £23.9 billion – side by side with that of HSBC – whose market value was then £59.8 billion. Goodwin surprised colleagues by saying he saw no reason Royal Bank of Scotland shouldn't be bigger than HSBC. One RBS executive who was there says, 'I remember thinking to myself, "Oh, my God, Fred's getting a bit ahead of himself here." ' Another person who sat through Goodwin's Gleneagles talk said, 'I just thought, "Oh, Christ! This guy is on a mission to turn RBS into the biggest bank in the world!" ' These Gleneagles 'off-sites' for senior executives became a regular fixture on the RBS calendar and were invariably punctuated by at least one epic drinking session that went on into the small hours.

An obsession with scale and rapid growth characterised Goodwin's approach to every market in which RBS participated. In Scotland, he told corporate managers that they must regain the top slot as the biggest lender to Scottish business from HBOS and didn't seem to mind if this entailed taking on bad bets and companies spurned by other lenders. In Ireland, Goodwin pressurised his Ulster Bank operation, which was bought with NatWest, to go hell for leather for rapid lending growth despite a speculative frenzy in the country's housing market. In candid comments, RBS's current chairman Sir Philip Hampton said things got out of hand. 'We were lending to anyone with a pulse. We were taking on clients that other banks were rejecting.'[19] In America, Goodwin insisted Citizens' chief executive Larry Fish must do more and bigger deals to grow the Citizens' footprint beyond its New England heartland. And, in the Global Banking and Markets (GBM) division, the RBS investment bank, Goodwin and Cameron were obsessed by league tables and wanted GBM to be ranked one, two or three in the market segments in which they played. When GBM, including its RBS Greenwich Capital unit, became the world leader in the underwriting of asset-backed securities in 2006, Goodwin boasted about it in the annual report. (An asset-backed security is a security or bond whose interest payments are derived from a specific pool of assets. The pool of assets is usually illiquid. Bundling them into a financial instrument means they can be sold to other investors under a process known as

securitisation, and allows the risk of investing in the assets to be diversified because each security represents a fraction of the total value of the
diverse pool of the assets. The assets can include anything from the
income stream from credit cards, car loans and residential mortgages
to esoteric cash flows from aircraft leases, royalty payments and movie
revenues.)

Another error Goodwin made in the wake of the NatWest deal was
to chase quixotic financial goals. He had a hang-up about earnings-
per-share (EPS) growth and this formed a key part of the incentive
plan for all the executive directors. One bank analyst says, 'Fred used
to lead off all of his presentations with, "Oh, I'm sorry to have to show
you this slide again but I'm just going run this through quickly." And
it was what earnings-per-share had done over the last 25 years. And it
was just a bar chart that went up, sort of bottom left to top right. He
went, "Oh, and here's dividends as well." That was all he cared about.'
The trouble is that a focus on earnings-per-share tends to mean a blind
eye is turned to the quality of the assets being used to drive the growth.
UK corporate history is littered with examples of companies which
ended up as pale shadows of their former selves as a result of such
myopia – ICI and Trafalgar House are just two examples.

Another 'metric' used by RBS to incentivise its chief executive was
return on equity – net income divided by common shareholder equity
– but this, too, is a flawed metric. UK banks' obsession with return on
equity (RoE) since the 1990s has been hugely damaging. According to
Andy Haldane, the Bank of England's executive director for financial
stability, chasing RoE 'flattered returns, and hence compensation',
during the credit bubble years, since banks put risk ahead of return
and short-term ahead of long-term performance. 'Instead of adjusting
for risk, RoE is flattered by it. This is fine for short-term investors [like
hedge funds] which thrive on the bumps. But for longer-term investors
they are a road to nowhere, as recent experience has shown.' Haldane
added that chasing RoE created an alarming 'myopia loop' in which
both investors and management become increasingly short-termist.[20]

In *The Bankers' New Clothes*, the Stanford University professor Anat
Admati and her co-author, the German economist Martin Hellwig,
explained why, saying, 'If no account is taken of how much debt has
been taken to create leverage and, more generally, of the risk of the
equity per dollar invested, RoE is not a meaningful measure of perfor-

mance, nor does it measure shareholder value. If no account is taken of the market environment, such as market rates of interest, comparison of RoE with a given benchmark is not meaningful. Implying otherwise is another article of the bankers' new clothes.'[21] And, as Haldane observes, it wasn't just banks who were in the myopia loop – institutional investors were stuck in a very similar place. One senior City fund manager says: 'RBS was doing what most investors wanted banks to do at the time, which was efficient balance-sheet management, efficient capital management. In terms of its tier-1 capital, RBS was fairly innovative. There wasn't much in the way of traditional capital in there but there was a fair amount of preference shares and other assorted rubbish. They were an outlier in terms of how they used this to boost their return on equity but, at the time, we welcomed that. We saw it as a good thing. Looking back, one of the most ridiculous things that investors did was to tell companies in which they invested that gearing was good! We were saying it and we were saying it all the time.'

At RBS, the annual process of budget setting became a nightmare for each divisional head. They would work for weeks on plans to get costs and staff numbers down and profits up. Then Fred would tell them they were being hopelessly timid – costs would have to go much lower and profits higher. It didn't matter if they told him it was impossible. He would then come up with a phrase such as 'It's my way or the highway', 'Suck it up' or 'That's life in the big city'. The culture became one of the fast buck, but it was demoralising. As the political commentator Nick Cohen says, 'Anyone who raised doubts about the tiny amounts of capital backing lending, or the failure to invest in computer systems that could cope with the banks' trades, heard managers tell them in threatening voices that they were "Business Prevention Officers". Carry on getting in the way and the hierarchy would mark them as fifth columnists whose naysaying was destroying the bank's viability and the chance for bonuses for everyone working in it.'[22]

Size seemed to be all that mattered. But targeting size for its own sake and obsessing over short-term profits growth caused the bank to lose its moral compass. One former senior RBS corporate banker says, 'Under Fred Goodwin, there was only one way – his way. We completely lost our solid banking focus after Iain Robertson left. Royal Bank of Scotland became a hollow institution where nobody cared how you did things, as long as you got results.'

By July 2003, a minority of investment analysts was waking up to the risks inherent in RBS's approach. They sought to raise the alarm about the rapid growth in RBS's commercial property lending. But these analysts, who included Fox-Pitt Kelton's Mark Thomas and SG Securities' John Tyce, were largely ignored. And, by 2005, anxiety was more widespread with analysts and investors becoming increasingly concerned about the way Fred was running the bank. This was one reason the bank's share price was in the doldrums. It had increased for a couple of years after the completion of the NatWest deal, surging from about 800p in March 2000 to 2040p in May 2002. But the share price had since fallen back to 1600–1700p a share, which meant that RBS was dramatically underperforming compared to other UK banks. Investors were getting tetchy and fed up.

Goodwin resolutely refused to accept that he might be the cause of this. For example, when the *Sunday Times* journalist Peter Koenig asked him about the weakness of RBS shares in November 2003, Goodwin blamed investors for being paranoid. 'Some people say the share price has run down because of fears we're going to ask (shareholders for cash to finance a deal). Others say it's because we plan to return cash to shareholders via a buy-back, which they say means we've run out of ideas. So both ends of the paranoia scale are alive and well.'[23]

The fear culture

In April 2001, large tracts of Britain's countryside had become no-go areas as thousands of pigs, sheep and cattle were slaughtered by government edict, their corpses cremated on gigantic funeral pyres. However, some 120 of the Royal Bank of Scotland's most senior bankers and executives still managed to make it north to Gleneagles, an opulent 1920s hotel nestled in the Perthshire hills. As the Royal's boys – and they were largely male – settled in to the £325-a-night hotel and golf resort and the late-night drinking sessions that accompanied these events, the foot-and-mouth debacle was far from their minds.

Towards the end of the executive conference, Goodwin asked them to form 'break-out' groups and to jot down what they saw as the biggest problems facing the bank. On returning to the Gleneagles ballroom, the executives handed their sheets to Goodwin. And there was near unanimity – the number one problem facing RBS was, according to its most senior executives, a 'culture of fear'. One group said that 'it's impossible to be open and honest at RBS, there's so much paranoia about'. As the results were fed back to Goodwin, people feared the worst but, when the CEO took the stage, there was no shouting match, recriminations or abuse. Instead, according to several people present, the Paisley-born chartered accountant, then 43, quietly said: 'We should lock the doors because the people who make the decisions in this bank are all in this room. That is you, not me – so what are you going to do about it?' He added, 'Don't tell me you're frightened of little old me?' A silence descended on the room. One of the executives present said, 'You could have heard a pin drop after that.'

Goodwin believed the Royal Bank of Scotland had a better chance of increasing its profits if he could persuade its 100,000-plus employees to think more alike and, above all, to *believe* in RBS as much as he did. He wanted them to be more driven, more focused on sales and more focused on efficiency and the bottom line. 'Certainly in our organisation [RBS] growth is key,' said Goodwin at a Smith Institute seminar at 11 Downing Street in October 1999. 'Large numbers of our people, the vast majority of our people, are incentivised around targets of customer acquisition, growth, provision of products to customers.'[1] And Goodwin cared deeply about people's feelings, said Neil Roden, the bank's director of human resources and one of Goodwin's most loyal lieutenants. But not their feelings generally, just how they felt about the Royal Bank. Speaking to a PricewaterhouseCoopers publication, Roden claimed, 'How people feel about the organisation is very, very important to Fred.'[2]

Roden, a former disciple of Karl Marx who became an ardent neoliberal, was very close to Goodwin, according to people who know both men well. Ironically, however, he is said to have moved across to RBS from Clydesdale in 1997 in order to get away from Goodwin. But, after Goodwin followed him from St Vincent Place to St Andrew Square, Roden displayed unflinching loyalty. Soon after arriving at Royal Bank, Roden set about developing a 'performance management' system to replace the 'Max' system the bank had introduced during Project Columbus. RBS's new approach bore an uncanny resemblance to Jack Welch's vitality curve.

Welch, the former chief executive of General Electric, introduced the curve to the diversified industrial conglomerate in 1981. The curve aimed to get the best out of staff by grading them on an annual basis into top-performing As (20 per cent of the total), middle-ranking Bs (70 per cent) and underperforming Cs (10 per cent). General Electric would pull out all the stops to nurture and retain the As, showering them with rewards. Bs were, according to Welch, 'the heart of the company and critical to its operational success'.[3] They would be adequately rewarded and given tips on how they might transform themselves into As. Welch said Cs were people who 'can't get the job done and procrastinate rather than deliver'.[4] Everyone classed as a C was dismissed on an annual basis. There was a fair amount of *pour encourager les autres* to this.

At Fairfield, Connecticut-headquartered General Electric, which makes everything from aero engines to generators, the system worked. Using this performance management and a range of other procedures and rules of thumb, Welch transformed the fortunes of the company, boosting its market capitalisation from $12 billion in 1981 to $500 billion in 2001. Welch said, 'Our vitality curve works because we spent over a decade building a performance culture with candid feedback at every level. Candour and openness are the foundations of such a culture. I wouldn't want to inject a vitality curve cold turkey into an organization without a performance culture already in place.' But Welch's legacy is now looking ragged around the edges. The methods that delivered under Welch singularly failed to do so under his successor Jeffrey Immelt. Under Immelt, GE's share price has dwindled from $40 in 2001 to $26.56 at the time of writing.

Management experts have long argued that 'rank-and-yank' performance management programmes are counterproductive. As early as 1991, a decade before RBS's programme got into full swing, the American management thinker W. Edwards Deming said it was wasteful to 'rank people, teams, salesmen, divisions, with reward at the top, punishment at the bottom'. Deming added, 'Ranking . . . has led to the so-called annual appraisal of people. The result is conflict, demoralization, lower productivity, lower quality, suppression of innovation.'[5]

But this did not stop rank-and-yank programmes being widely adopted in the UK, across both the public and private sectors. At RBS, Goodwin and Roden started introducing theirs in 1999–2000. It sat atop a human resources framework that included offering a 10 per cent profit share, funded pension and 25 to 30 days holiday for full-time staff, plus the option of trading holidays for cash. Employees could also choose from a flexible menu of other benefits like discounted shopping vouchers, childcare facilities, discounted mortgages and discounted personal loans. 'Tough management, tough HR and good money – that was what you signed up to at RBS,' said one ex-senior manager.

There were four main elements to the RBS system. It was shaped like a triangle, with 'control' at the centre and the three points of the triangle being 'sales', 'people' and 'customer service'. But, whereas sales were measured daily, the other two were only measured weekly or monthly. Roden, an ardent believer in rank-and-yank, was named 'HR Director of the Year' on several occasions in the 2000s and he also received an honorary degree from Glasgow Caledonian University for 'exceptional contribution to human resources'. He was convinced that he had developed a reliable means of holding RBS managers accountable for their actions in areas including financial performance, customer service and people management. In early 2005, Roden took the system on to the next level when he launched a 'human capital toolkit'. This was a secure web-based system that collated data about individual employees and their performance and enabled RBS management to scrutinise individuals' output on a real-time basis. Even as the bank was starting to implode in 2007–08, Roden was still sure it all made sense.

As Roden dreamt of peering into the stuff of RBS people's very souls, the performance management system was causing a lot of grief internally. The cycle of pain started each autumn when Goodwin coerced senior managers into agreeing financial goals and other targets that they knew would be virtually impossible to achieve. If the executives exceeded these, they would be praised to the hills, ranked in the top 20 per cent (the As) and rewarded handsomely. However, if they missed the targets – even if this was the result of *force majeure* – they would be consigned to the C doghouse. If in senior roles, they would probably be frozen out by Goodwin and senior colleagues and openly mocked in front of their peers. Underperformers were derided as 'muppets' and 'bottom feeders'.

Workers, including counter staff and call-centre employees, were graded under the Performance Evaluation Framework (PEF). A score of five recognised 'shoot the lights out' performance, four was for 'strong performance' ahead of expectations, three was for 'just doing your job in line with expectations', two was for 'underperformance' and one was for 'unacceptable performance'. The scores were hugely important to every RBS worker – they dictated their chances of promotion, their chances of a bonus and their chances of retaining their jobs. People who were considered to be future leaders were put on to RBS's Leadership Excellence Profile (LEP), a more sophisticated template. To excel under LEP, mana-gers had to achieve demanding financial goals while also demonstrating qualities like 'Burning Drive for Results', 'Strategic Dexterity', 'Winning the Licence to Operate', 'Delivering through People' and 'Leading Others'. The gobbledegook was part of a supposedly democratic 'talent management' programme aimed at growing leaders from within.

In early 2013, Phil Taylor, professor of work and employment studies at the University of Strathclyde and assistant dean of Strathclyde

Business School, produced a 91-page research report, 'Performance Management and the New Workplace Tyranny', for the Scottish Trades Union Conference. It was based on extensive interviews with employees of Royal Bank and other financial services and telecoms firms in the UK. Taylor said that rank-and-yank systems are readily abused and create seriously dysfunctional internal cultures. He says the criteria used when appraising staff for performance management programmes are 'far more subjective and open to abuse than even the pseudo-scientific quantitative categories'.[6]

At RBS, the performance management system gave rise to a multitude of sins. These included dangerous groupthink, and the prioritisation of sales over anything else. Many ex-insiders say it had a deleterious effect on morale, was used as an instrument of oppression and caused untold stress, anxiety and even mental torture. One former senior manager says, 'It made it impossible for people to do their jobs properly. Both PEF and LEP encouraged people to focus on their personal output, based on a rigid set of behaviours and objectives imposed from on high, not on whether they were delivering service to customers.' In corporate banking, the performance management system drove managers effectively to fleece their customers. One ex-senior manager in corporate lending said, 'The system turned bankers into double-glazing salesmen. All that mattered was driving the numbers – delivering results, hitting short-term goals, sweating the assets. In corporate banking, we were increasingly run by number crunchers and we were encouraged to hit our customers with every additional charge that we thought we could get away with. That included making loans conditional on them taking out interest-rate swaps, even though we didn't really understand those products. The view from on high was it didn't really matter if one or two customers walked or if we were dogged with complaints. Reputational risk didn't get a look-in.' The worse people treated their business customers, the more kudos they got internally – so long as it resulted in higher revenues for the bank. Being soft on a business was seen as a disciplinary offence, especially if it meant less revenue for the bank.

In the branches and call centres, Rob MacGregor, national officer at Unite the Union, says RBS's version of rank-and-yank was 'deliberately designed to break down collectivism'. He said the system forced everybody to prioritise sales over ethics and ensured everyone looked after themselves – their own performance, their own sales, their own bonuses. MacGregor adds, 'It was shaped by Fred Goodwin's own personal ideology, which infected the culture of the entire group.'[7]

Goodwin had a particular obsession with RBS regaining its position as Scotland's number one corporate bank – a mantle which, in the early noughties, it had lost to Halifax Bank of Scotland (HBOS). New incentive programmes were introduced which rewarded business banking managers who hauled in the most new business, with the annual winners being rewarded with all-expenses-paid, five-day trips to places like the Old Course Hotel in St Andrews and to Lisbon. But the trouble was that, in actively seeking to woo customers away from banks such as HBOS, the bank ended up with a lot of Scotland's less creditworthy firms as borrowers – many of which it should never have taken on. Ex-insiders say the credit team 'were subconsciously getting sucked into the sales culture', meaning they were no longer assessing propositions on their merits but were focusing on the scope for future earnings from cross-selling to those clients. One former Scotland-based RBS business banking manager says, 'If HBOS were offering a business customer 3 per cent over base, we'd cut our margins and offer 2.5 per cent over base. Quite a lot of the customers we took over in this way I suspect have gone bust.'

Some individuals were driven to push the envelope with growth strat-egies that were too aggressive. One classic example was Donald Mackenzie, a manager in Royal Bank of Scotland's West End branch in Edinburgh. In the early 2000s, he was hailed internally as a hero. Repeatedly top-ranked by the performance management system, Mackenzie was named RBS business manager of the year three times. However, he turned out to be a crook who, in July 2006, was jailed for ten years for embezzling £21 million from the bank. David Burns QC, in defence of Mackenzie, cited the pressure that people such as his client were put under to meet sales and lending targets. In 2009, Mackenzie was released from Castle Huntly open prison near Dundee after serving only three years of his jail term and was last spotted working in an optician's shop in Dundee.[8] One ex-relationship manager in RBS business banking said, 'There was always pressure to sell more. If you look at the list of the top performers in RBS, three to six months down the line, you invariably found that, in about two out of ten cases, they had achieved that by doing something that was either silly or wrong.'

Even before Mackenzie was jailed, the FSA chairman Sir Callum McCarthy was seeking to root out flawed incentive schemes along these lines from British banks. Speaking at the British Bankers Association conference on 2 December 2003, McCarthy, a man once described as 'too nice to be a regulator', warned banks that the FSA would 'come down hard' if they continued to incentivise their sales forces to irresponsibly sell inappropriate or inadequate products to their customers.[9] However, the warning fell on deaf ears at the banks and McCarthy failed to follow through. Thanks to the stance taken by Tony Blair's government towards the banking sector, bankers were feeling pretty unassailable by 2003. Royal Bank continued to use its performance management frameworks PEF and LEP unchallenged for another decade or more.

Skewed incentives drove sharp practice across RBS's retail business. As early as 2001–02, the mis-selling of PPI was endemic across the group. The bank's Glasgow-based leasing arm Lombard Direct was creaming in £40 million a year in secret commissions from unwary borrowers. It was doing this by covertly cross-selling mainly redundant PPI policies to two-thirds of Lombard's personal borrowers. And 60 per cent of their premiums were going directly to Lombard as commission. According to a report in the *Mail on Sunday*, 'In 2001 and 2002, Lombard customers were persuaded to spend £85 million on cover. Of this, £53 million was commission for Lombard and about £10 million went to Lombard's insurance partner, Pinnacle. A mere £3 million was paid in claims.'[10]

Jayne-Anne Gadhia, a retail banking executive who ran the Virgin One brand at RBS, was dismayed when her bosses insisted on continuing to sell PPI policies even after they were aware that it was a rip-off for which they knew the bank would eventually be hauled over the coals. Gadhia told the Parliamentary Commission on Banking Standards that, in 2006, she spoke to a senior RBS colleague 'about the need to withdraw PPI at that time from our – from RBS's – marketing'. The reply was, 'Yes, it's clear that that should be withdrawn, but we can't be the first people to do it because we would be the ones who lose profit first.'[11] Gadhia believes all the UK banks knew that PPI was rotten but 'nobody was prepared to be the first mover to resolve it because they felt that their share price and profitability would be damaged first'.[12] Gadhia has also said that, by the time of her departure in late 2006, 'cracks were starting to show' at RBS and that being there 'just made [her] miserable'.[13]

The most invidious aspect of the rank-and-yank system was that staff's performances had to be 'managed to the curve', meaning that performance ratings given to individual workers within a given team or division often had to be manipulated up or down to ensure that they complied with a normal distribution or 'bell curve'. In cases where everyone in a particular team had excelled, for example, the managers were obliged to mark some people down just to ensure the distribution was acceptable to their bosses. One ex-RBS manager said, 'This was hugely damaging for morale. People were having their remuneration and career prospects harmed just so the bank could reach a pre-ordained statistical outcome.'

The RBS performance management was also widely used to 'manage people out of their jobs'. The union Unite claims this is still happening, with targeted individuals given artificially low grades so they can be 'performance managed out of the business', without a need for full redundancy compensation. Rob MacGregor says the process can take just 12 weeks from selection to departure and that employers like RBS commence the process by deliberately setting unrealistic and unattainable targets. Under the RBS performance measurement system, people were scared to speak their mind for fear of being labelled a troublemaker and marked down a couple of notches. That would lead to them being financially penalised and possibly thrown out of the bank. So rank-and-yank became an instrument of oppression that promoted groupthink and discouraged dissent.

Phil Taylor believes that performance management systems are counterproductive. In the conclusion of his 'Workplace Tyranny' report, Taylor wrote, 'An argument can be made that these performance management practices are not merely unjustifiable on grounds of welfare, decency, dignity and well-being, but that they may also be utterly counterproductive from a managerial perspective. They require enormous commitments of resource by middle and front-line management and serve merely to create a deep well of resentment and discontent amongst a highly pressurised workforce.'[14]

But surely morale cannot have been as low as Taylor is implying at the Royal Bank? Didn't its annual staff surveys, whose results the bank trumpeted at annual general meetings and in its annual report, reveal that between 80 and 90 per cent of the bank's 100,000-plus staff were happy, engaged and in love with their jobs? Well, the surveys were not quite what they seemed. Because people had moved from an environment where they were accustomed to having 'jobs for life' into one in which they believed they could be fired at a moment's notice, they were far too fearful of criticising the bank to be honest when completing the forms. Insiders say the annual survey was about as reflective of people's genuine views about their jobs as a Zimbabwean election – with managers also seemingly coercing, bullying or even bribing staff into completing it as positively as possible.

In 2010 the former Lloyds Bank chairman and chief executive Sir Brian Pitman said that 'incentives for sales targets have been a large part of the problem . . . It's a little short of crazy to incentivise people to maximise the number of loans they're going to grant.'[15] Yet at RBS no one dared challenge it. Ultimately, anyone who disliked rank-and-yank and the culture it engendered had little option but to leave. One former RBS corporate banking manager who left in 2008 told me that, in his last few years at the bank he found the culture to be diabolical. 'I spent 43 years with the Royal Bank of Scotland and I'm glad to be out of it. I feel better, I sleep better, there is much less stress and I feel rejuvenated. Latterly, we were just being pushed and pushed and pushed. We were having to bend over backwards to bring in new business. Fred was driving the market share. He was absolutely obsessed by that.'

For Ron Kerr, a lecturer at Newcastle University Business School, and Sarah Robinson, a lecturer at Leicester University School of Management, the bank was waging a campaign of economic violence against its own staff. Kerr and Robinson said, 'Within RBS itself, Goodwin's domination was maintained by economic violence. RBS's internal culture has been characterised as a culture of fear.'[16] They argue that the leadership culture at RBS was quasi-feudal, in that exploiting people's economic dependence and destroying their economic power lay at its heart.

Most British banks have altered the way they incentivise their customer services staff since the crisis, without totally abandoning rank-and-yank. According to *The Times*, RBS has changed its approach to the extent that people are rewarded for how well their branch as a whole has done, with a greater emphasis on customer service and sales performance only accounting for a 5 per cent weighting. In their 1982 book, *In Search of Excellence* – one of the first attempts to identify and explain the correlation between a positive corporate culture and strong performance – the ex-McKinsey consultants Tom Peters and Robert Waterman pointed out that 'poorer-performing companies often have strong cultures, too, but dysfunctional ones. They are usually focused on internal politics rather than on the customer, or they focus on "the numbers" rather than on the product and the people who make and sell it.'[17] That could almost have been written about Royal Bank of Scotland under Fred Goodwin. Making the numbers had become paramount – and it would have disastrous consequences.

Wall of silence

Overnight on 6 March 2000, the shutters came down at 42 St Andrew Square. Liaison with third parties was curtailed and contact with the outside world became much more controlled. Goodwin and his director of communications Howard Moody, another former Scottish Development Agency executive who joined the bank in 1996, exerted a tight grip on relations with key constituencies, including journalists, investment analysts, shareholders and rival banks. The use of external consultants such as McKinsey was outlawed unless personally authorised by Goodwin.

The bank moved away from the open, unstuffy, inclusive and collegiate culture that had been favoured by Mathewson to something more oppressive. Goodwin had made a conscious decision to emulate the approach of his mentor, Don Argus, former chief executive of National Australia Bank. Believing NAB possessed a unique set of skills and intellectual property, Argus feared these 'state secrets' would be diluted if shared. So he clamped down on interactions with the outside world, banning NAB executives from giving speeches, attending conferences or talking to the media. Michael Lafferty, a former *Financial Times* banking correspondent and founder of specialist financial publishing group Lafferty Group, says, 'Fred Goodwin brought the same oddball thinking across to Royal Bank of Scotland. Having decided he didn't want the outside world to know too much about what RBS was doing, Fred brought down a wall of silence around the bank. Whenever you see anything like that, it should ring alarm bells.'[1]

All external advisors to RBS were forced to sign unusually strict non-disclosure agreements or NDAs. If these were breached – if an affected party breathed a word about the bank's activities to the press, either off or on the record – they or their firms risked being summarily dismissed. In March 2002, Giles Barrie, former editor-in-chief of the magazine *Property Week*, was researching a feature on RBS's plans for its own property empire, which included buying up vast acreages of open-plan office space in the City of London and in UK regional centres such as Manchester and Glasgow, for its own occupancy. Barrie was taken aback by his usual sources' point-blank refusal to cooperate and discovered it was because of bloodcurdling threats the bank had issued to property consultants in a bid to dissuade them from speaking to journalists. Barrie said later, 'There were stories of advisors being fired for leaks and bizarre tales of Stasi-like witch-hunts. Everyone blamed Goodwin for this. He had imposed a fear culture, a blame culture and he was a terrible micromanager. It was all a bit creepy.'[2]

Only a handful of the bank's employees were authorised to speak to the media without the chief executive's permission. One was Jimmy Mclean, the bank's head of agricultural services; another was chief economist Jeremy Peat. Anyone who broke the rule or leaked things to the press risked severe repercussions. The bank didn't even trust its own media relations staff to speak to the media. One senior media relations executive was given a severe reprimand by Howard Moody for having the effrontery to talk to a journalist on the Scottish tabloid, the *Daily Record*. He was told never to talk to any journalist again without the express permission of either Moody or his sidekick Carolyn McAdam. The media relations executive considered this farcical and left the bank not long afterwards.

Most of the business and financial journalists I know regarded the Royal Bank of Scotland, at the group level, one of the worst companies to deal with. The default response of its media relations team to any question was to be uncooperative (for example, 'No comment' or 'We don't comment on market speculation'). Other responses ranged from the hypersensitive and prickly to the downright menacing. One London-based financial journalist said, 'Howard would come after you if you wrote anything vaguely critical. Companies that are sure of themselves don't really give a damn what you write about them. But Fred was the exact opposite. He was brittle and fragile, even during the period when RBS was on top.'

One of the issues was that Goodwin, for some reason, believed that Moody could 'control' what journalists wrote about the bank.

While wallowing in positive coverage and allowing this to go to his head, Goodwin went berserk whenever anything negative appeared, even if it was a negative phrase in an otherwise adulatory piece and especially if the negative coverage came without warning. Moody, the communications director, is said to have dreaded going to the 9.30 a.m. morning 'beatings' – especially the ones on Monday mornings. Iain Robertson recalls, 'At the Monday morning meeting, there would be a whole selection of Sunday newspapers. Fred didn't like surprises and one thing he hated with a passion was when things appeared in the Sunday newspapers that he did not know about in advance. Howard used to get absolutely flayed alive when that happened.'[3] In the event of negative press coverage appearing, Goodwin would ask, 'What have you done about it?' Moody, therefore, felt obliged to challenge the journalists responsible and reprimand them – if only to be able to report back to Goodwin that he had indeed done something. Other media relations staff also felt obliged to give 'bollockings' to journalists who had displeased Goodwin. 'Even if we just went through the motions, we had to do it,' says one former media relations executive.

A classic situation arose one Friday in September 2002 when I was researching an article about Royal Bank of Scotland from the *Sunday Herald*'s newsroom in Glasgow's Renfield Street. It was based on some research from ING Financial Markets' analyst Michael Helsby, which predicted the bank's profits would fall in 2004. Helsby said this was 'because, in its mature domestic markets, meaningful growth is not going to come via organic means' and as a result of mounting bad debts from lending to troubled corporate borrowers especially in the telecoms sector. I called Royal Bank's Carolyn McAdam for a response and she gave me some perfectly innocuous views which I wove into my piece and attributed to 'an RBS spokesperson'.[4] The article had gone 'off stone' (that is it had been subedited and was ready for printing) when, at about 10 p.m., Moody called. He said that all McAdam's quotes would have to be excised, as 'RBS doesn't comment on analysts' research'. I said, 'That's too bad, Howard, she already has commented and her quotes are in the piece!' But he just repeated the same sentence mantra-like over and over again, 'But, Ian, RBS doesn't comment on analysts' research.' I was reminded of the passage on 'blackwhite' in George Orwell's *1984* where it is explained that blackwhite means 'the ability to believe that black is white, and more, to know that black is white, and to forget that one has ever believed the contrary'.

Goodwin was notoriously litigious. In an article published on 18 May 2003, the *Sunday Herald*'s personal finance editor Teresa Hunter accused NatWest of making false claims in its television advertising. Specifically, she said that claims made in an M&C Saatchi TV commercial that NatWest was not closing any branches and that all calls to a NatWest branch were routed through to a branch were untrue. Hunter, who had full documentary evidence to prove her claims, wrote, 'While we are all allowed one mistake, two big whoppers start to look careless, not to say a trifle less than honest.'[5] Goodwin was apoplectic, especially after his initial lawyer's letter went missing as it was sent to the wrong address and he thought the newspaper was ignoring him. Finally, using his favoured lawyers Dundas & Wilson, he issued a £250,000 writ against publishers Newsquest, claiming they had defamed NatWest. The writ said, 'The statements made in the article were false and calumnious. The article falsely and calumniously imputed that National Westminster Bank PLC were incompetent, that they told untruths, that they were dishonest and that they sought knowingly to deceive or mislead customers. Each and all of these imputations are untrue and defamatory.' In the end, the matter was resolved after *Sunday Herald* business editor Kenny Kemp paid a visit to Howard Moody at his 36 St Andrew Square office. Kemp said the newspaper stood by the story but was willing to publish a 'clarification' explaining that the NatWest branches that were closing were not being closed by RBS but as a result of a closure programme initiated by the previous NatWest management. This went to Goodwin for approval, he accepted it and a 160-word 'clarification' was published in the *Sunday Herald* of 20 July 2003. Goodwin's ridiculous writ tainted many *Sunday Herald* journalists' view of his organisation.

Goodwin also blew a gasket after the *Sunday Times* ran a series of Prufrock diary pieces, written by Louise Armitstead between March and October 2004, which mocked his delusions of grandeur about the construction of the bank's Gogarburn head office. One alleged that 'the Laird of Gogarburn' had insisted on design features including 'a scallop kitchen' adjacent to his own office and a 'private road to the airport'. Armitstead also wrote that Goodwin had ordered 'a personal on-site cabin' to be built so he could keep track of progress on the building site in comfort. One of the pieces claimed he had tried and failed to pull rank when seeking to jump the ten-year waiting list for membership of the Bruntsfield Links golf club. Goodwin's first attempt at silencing the newspaper came when an aide threatened to withdraw all the RBS group's advertising from Rupert Murdoch's News International titles – which included the *Times*, the *Sunday Times*, *The Sun* and the *News of the World* – unless the *Sunday Times* published a retraction and an apology. News International chief executive Les Hinton said that Goodwin could 'get stuffed' and that there was no way he would bow down to a big advertiser throwing its weight about.[6] Further enraged, Goodwin then sued the newspaper for libel. A writ lodged at the High Court on 12 November 2004 claimed that the newspaper was 'engaged in a campaign to harass the executive [Goodwin] by repeatedly publishing in the *Sunday Times* false material about him calculated to expose him to ridicule'. The writ alleged that 'unless restrained', the newspaper would continue to make defamatory statements about Goodwin and the Royal Bank.

In early January 2005, two *Sunday Times* journalists, business editor Will Lewis and his colleague John Waples travelled north to Edinburgh in the hope of brokering a peace deal with Goodwin. After copious quantities of drink were taken, Goodwin agreed to withdraw the libel writ, on condition that the *Sunday Times* published a full-page interview in which he could rebut the Prufrock stories and extol the virtues of the Gogarburn campus. The resulting article – derided in journalistic circles as a 'puff' piece – was headlined 'Goodwin keeps building'. Its opening came straight out of the *Pravda* school of journalism: 'Since Goodwin stepped up to become chief executive six-and-a-half years ago, the group's market value has soared from £8.5 billion to £56.3 billion and its share price from 907p to 1,775p. In the process, RBS has pulled off a series of transformational deals that have changed the face of the multi-branded bank. It is now the world's sixth-largest bank, with 30 per cent of last year's £7.2 billion operating profit coming from America.'[7]

In the interview Goodwin rebutted Prufrock's claims that a bridge RBS had built across the A8 dual carriageway was part of a 'private road' to Edinburgh Airport, saying it was a requirement of planning permission. Some of the claims in the article, including the idea that Goodwin did not like to boast about the bank's success, stretched credulity but Lewis and Waples' recommendation that Fred ought to

try and become a little more approachable was spot on.[8] Fred's decision to withdraw the writ was also influenced by the RBS board, some
of whose members were uncomfortable with the idea that Goodwin
should use the company's resources to fund a personal libel action. His
chances of success were always slight, especially after a senior source
at Bruntsfield Links golf club vouched for the accuracy of one of the
stories.

Another bizarre instance of over-the-top litigation came in 2001,
when Goodwin sought to slap an injunction on Coal Pension Properties
and Balfour Beatty Construction, which were then in the process of
building the new Harvey Nichols department store on St Andrew
Square. Fred's reason was that their construction site was leaving
specks of dust on his Mercedes S600 parked nearby. One ex-colleague
of Goodwin said, 'Fred had his own litigation lawyer who had to deal
with that on a regular basis. Anything moved and Fred would try and
sue it – a bit like Jimmy Savile, Robert Maxwell and Rupert Murdoch.
There were many, many occasions on which Fred wanted to sue but
where Stephen [Pearson, RBS's litigation chief] persuaded him against
it.'

If the bank wanted to win friends and influence people in the media,
it certainly had an odd way of going about it. Goodwin's refusal to
give interviews, the unhelpfulness and obstreperousness of the press
office, the trigger-happy approach to litigation, the lack of accessibility
of other senior executives, the threats from Howard Moody when even
vaguely critical articles were being planned, plus the bank's inability
to be pro-active ensured that large sections of the Fourth Estate were
disinclined to give RBS an easy ride, even in the good times. After the
bank's failure, both Goodwin and the bank were subjected to a far
greater kicking by the media than they would otherwise have been, had
they made greater efforts cultivate the media on the way up.

Riding the Tiger

During 2002–03, Fred Goodwin turned his attention to Ireland. The country had become known as the 'Celtic Tiger' following a period of very strong economic growth. On the back of a turbo-charged property market and the attraction of foreign investors through the use of clever tax breaks, the country was buzzing. Gross domestic product had grown by between 7.6 and 10.9 per cent in the late 1990s and early 2000s. Population decline had gone into reverse, long-derelict sites were finally being built on, the Catholic Church was losing its grip and the country was sloughing off its deep-rooted fatalism.

As Goodwin looked across the Irish Sea, it was with a mixture of envy and disappointment. He wanted Royal Bank to have a bigger slice of the action but wasn't quite sure how to achieve it. Ulster Bank – the 167-year-old Belfast- and Dublin-based clearing bank he had acquired with NatWest – was well-run and the third largest bank in Ireland. Since RBS had acquired it in March 2000, certain changes had been made including the centralisation of processes previously carried out at branch level. This freed up branch staff to spend more time selling to customers. Also, as in the UK, corporate customers were stripped out of the branches and shifted into dedicated regional hubs. But, to Goodwin, something was missing. Under chief executive Martin Wilson, the bank seemed insufficiently hungry for growth. To make matters worse, the Royal Bank's arch rival, the Bank of Scotland, led by Peter Burt, had been making inroads into the Tiger economy since 1999.

Led locally by a young and dynamic former venture capitalist, Mark Duffy, Bank of Scotland (Ireland) (BoSI) had gone hell for leather into the Irish mortgage market, becoming a major irritant to stuffier institu-

tions such as Bank of Ireland, Allied Irish Banks (AIB) and Irish Life
& Permanent. In September 1999, BoSI threw down the gauntlet by
slashing the interest-rate margin on its mortgages to just 1 per cent –
half the level at other banks.

At just 2.5 per cent Irish interest rates were incredibly low, compared
to the prevailing rate of 5.25 per cent in the UK.[1] According to RTÉ
News, BoSI's bold initiative, which was accompanied by its launch of
Ireland's first tracker mortgage, 'triggered a mortgage price war' that
caused some real pain for existing lenders.[2] The former building society
First Active, for example, was forced to axe 175 jobs, saw a reduction in
profits and had to close down agencies. At the time Ireland's banking
system was widely regarded as a cartel. BoSI and Duffy were seen as
having done the Irish people a favour by helping blow this apart.

BoSI was not the only radical player in the market. Anglo-Irish
Bank, founded in Dublin 1964, was shaking things up in commercial property lending. Like Goodwin, Anglo's chief executive, Sean
'Seanie' Fitzpatrick, was not short of ego. Like Goodwin, he boasted
that his bank was light on process and able to make decisions quickly
and without a fuss. It was making good returns from generous loans
to the Republic's property developers. Against this backdrop, level-
headed bankers feared that remaining cautious and prudent would
cause their institutions to lose market share and their share prices to
tumble. Mike Soden, the Australian-born banker who quit as chief
executive of Bank of Ireland in 2004, said investors were largely
responsible for driving the more staid banks to hitch up their skirts.
He said, 'The big, international investors were constantly demanding
that Bank of Ireland change its approach, warning us they would
otherwise sell a percentage of their portfolios and move the funds
into Anglo-Irish.'[3]

Ulster Bank is actually two banks. Belfast-based Ulster Bank Ltd
comes under the jurisdiction of the United Kingdom and is regulated
by the FSA while the Dublin-headquartered Ulster Bank Ireland Ltd
operates in the Republic of Ireland and is supervised by the Central
Bank of Ireland. But the bank operated as a single entity, providing a
full range of retail and commercial banking services together with fund
management and stockbroking services to customers in the north and
the south. Founded in Belfast in 1836, its initial focus was serving the
needs of the north's blooming linen trade. Starting with a single office

in Belfast's Waring Street before opening a few others across the north, it first moved into the south in the 1860s, establishing branches in Sligo, Ardee and Dublin.[4] It was acquired by London-based Westminster Bank in 1917, five years ahead of partition. In Northern Ireland the bank became a bedrock of the Protestant, Unionist establishment and was the bank of choice for Loyalists down the generations, with the Catholic Nationalist community tending to favour Allied Irish Banks. Billy Abernethy, a senior executive at Ulster Bank, was chairman of a high-powered committee which co-ordinated the assassination of Catholics by Loyalist death squads, according to a book and a documentary programme made by the TV journalist Sean McPhilemy in 1991. the *Sunday Times* later claimed the programme was a hoax but McPhilemy sued the newspaper for libel and won.

By the time Royal Bank of Scotland took control of Ulster Bank in March 2000, Ulster had total assets of £9.2 billion (4.9 per cent of NatWest Group's total assets) and pre-tax profits of £165 million (7 per cent of NatWest Group's profit).[5] In 2000, it opened a new headquarters for Northern Ireland on Belfast's Donegall Square. And in 1998 it opened an impressive L-shaped edifice on George's Quay, just across the River Liffey from Dublin's burgeoning International Financial Services Centre (IFSC). Part of the façade was constructed from blocks of stone salvaged from the ruined Richmond House, a former seat of the Anglo-Irish Gason family, in Nenagh, County Tipperary.[6]

The IFSC, situated on the north bank of the Liffey east of Dublin's city centre, epitomised the Irish Republic's freewheeling approach to finance. A wasteland of disused shipyards was transformed into a modern business park stuffed with swanky new office buildings that housed the offshoots of some of the world's biggest banks, insurers, asset managers, asset servicing firms etc. and a subculture of accountants and lawyers. It was Bermuda-on-the-Liffey and Grand Cayman-on-the-Liffey rolled into the one and was channelling trillions of dollars of transactions for global financial services firms with little regulatory oversight and an unusually low rate of corporation tax.

Goodwin first met Cormac McCarthy, chief executive of Irish mortgage bank First Active, at a dinner in Dublin in late 2002. McCarthy, a chartered accountant, was charismatic and hugely ambitious. Goodwin famously would give himself five seconds to make important decisions and, using his 'five-second rule', he quickly concluded McCarthy was the man to help him solve his Irish problem.

'It wasn't as if [incumbent Ulster Bank chief executive] Martin Wilson was incompetent, lazy, hopeless or anything like that,' recalls one former Royal Bank of Scotland insider. 'It was just that he wasn't sufficiently ambitious or aspirational.' But McCarthy, then aged 39, had ambition and aspiration in spades. Raised in Nigeria and Zambia, McCarthy graduated from University College Dublin in 1983, before qualifying as an accountant with KPMG in Dublin in 1987.[7] He then moved to Woodchester, a small commercial leasing company, which was sold to GE Capital during his time as financial controller. While there, McCarthy relished the thrusting and somewhat brash American way of doing business. He joined First Active when it was still a humble building society in 1998 and helped steer it though its conversion to a publicly quoted company. After plans for a merger with Anglo-Irish Bank fell apart in early 2000, First Active was looking vulnerable but McCarthy effectively rescued it. Soon after becoming chief executive in August 2000, at the age of 37, he re-engineered FA. He put more emphasis on sales, set ambitious targets for each branch and toughened up the chasing of arrears. He also shut one-third of its branches, made 200 staff redundant, reduced commissions to investment brokers and exited unprofitable services, including credit cards and current accounts.[8] Other Irish bankers were impressed.

'At the time Cormac McCarthy was regarded as a very good banker and someone who knew the business well. He was very self-confident and Royal Bank clearly saw him as a rising star,' said Simon Carswell, finance correspondent of *The Irish Times* and author of two books on the recent history of Ireland's banking system.[9] 'I couldn't speak highly enough of him – he is a hell of a good operator,' said Johnny Ronan, co-founder of global property development group Treasury Holdings, which constructed First Active's headquarters in Dublin.[10] 'He is extremely able and very straight to deal with. He knew exactly what he wanted and just got on with it. The building society he was in charge of was a basket case and he sorted it out and modernised it. He did a hell of a job, and it seemed that the staff liked him a lot.'[11]

Goodwin had found his man and was willing to buy the whole of First Active to get him. 'In UK terms, it was the equivalent of Barclays taking over the whole of Northern Rock just to get Adam Applegarth as group chief executive,' said one Irish banking industry source. Others were less convinced of McCarthy's abilities. One former chief executive of a leading Irish bank said his institution considered buying First Active 'but we didn't because we couldn't make the numbers work'. He added, 'Cormac was an exceedingly good communicator but hadn't achieved that much.'

Under McCarthy's charismatic leadership, the ex-building society shook off its working-class roots and was feted as one of Ireland's most innovative and competitive financial players. Pre-tax profit rose from €41.1 million in 2000 to €66.1 million in 2002 – meaning that annual profits were growing by 30 per cent a year and driving up McCarthy's pay at the same time.[12] By June 2003, First Active had grown its total assets to €7.3 billion.

On 14 July 2003, a month after agreeing to buy the UK-based general insurer Churchill for £1.1 billion, Goodwin secretly flew to Dublin aboard G-RBSG, the company's private jet, for a discreet tête-à-tête with McCarthy. He drove around Dublin and met McCarthy in First Active's head office in Leopardstown, south of the city, to see if there was any scope for a deal. Again, the chemistry seemed right. The timing was good. In September, First Active was due to emerge from the five-year period of protective purdah which had followed its conversion to a PLC. Until then, no shareholder was allowed to own more than a 15 per cent stake in the company but afterwards all bets were off.

As negotiations proceeded in secrecy the Scottish bank, advised by investment banker Matthew Greenburgh of Merrill Lynch, made a surprising number of concessions to make the deal more attractive for First Active – which was being guided by veteran advisor Terry Eccles of JPMorgan. Goodwin dropped heavy hints that, if a deal could be reached, McCarthy would replace Wilson as Ulster Bank's chief executive. He also suggested First Active's finance director, Michael Torpey, would become finance director of the merged group. Roles would also be found for four of First Active's non-executive directors.[13] By early October, the two sides were ready to consummate and RBS trumpeted its €887-million (£620-million) takeover as the Irish Stock Exchange opened at 7.30 a.m. on Monday, 6 October 2003. The offer price, at a generous 33 per cent premium to First Active's closing share price the previous Friday, was pitched to block out possible counter-bidders and

to ensure there was no grumbling from the former building society's
army of small shareholders.

At an 11 a.m. press conference in Dublin, Goodwin insisted that both
brands would continue to trade under their own names and that two
separate branch networks would be maintained. The cost savings and
revenue-building benefits, he said, would come from pooling wholesale
funding, cheque processing, payment services, technology and other
core functions. Job losses would be 'in the low hundreds'. Across the
island of Ireland, the combined outfit would have 1.3 million customers, 263 branches and a 15 per cent share of the mortgage market.
Goodwin seemed confident this could be dramatically increased
through cross-selling. But the hype didn't wash with investment analysts. They were puzzled by Royal Bank's willingness to pay three times
'book value' – the total value of First Active's assets that shareholders
would theoretically receive if it were liquidated – for a little-known
Irish lender at a time when Ireland's property market was running out
of steam.

By October 2003, there had already been a few warnings that
the Irish property market was in trouble. One of the most startling
came from the Irish economist and broadcaster David McWilliams.
Speaking on RTÉ News's *Prime Time* programme on 16 October 2003,
just ten days after the takeover announcement, McWilliams said, 'The
Irish housing market is a scam. It is an enormous financial swindle that
could potentially confine an entire generation of young Irish workers
to years of bad debt. Far from being a reflection of economic vitality and fundamental demand, the housing bubble is, in the main, a
vacuous financial confidence trick that has been foisted upon us by an
alliance of banks and landowners.' He said that, averaging 10 times
the standard Irish salary, Irish house prices represented 'an economic
failure on a monumental scale' and that it was not demand that was
driving up house prices but 'excessive and irresponsible lending from
our financial institutions . . .' McWilliams added, 'If you throw loads
of money into an economy, there will be an asset price bubble . . . But,
if you're in a bubble and prospering from it, believing in it, it's normal
to dismiss sceptics as raving fools.'[14] And, this is exactly what the Irish
government, Irish regulators, central bankers, bankers and a great
many economists did. They hated the way McWilliams was raining on
Irish housing's parade and denounced him as beyond the pale.

Aged 45, Goodwin was enjoying the 'halo' effect of his NatWest triumph. He reassured the sceptics by reminding them of the NatWest formula – extracting cost savings and consolidating the back office, whilst keeping acquired brands alive. At the Dublin press conference, Goodwin also stressed that RBS wasn't just splashing out on First Active on a whim. 'We don't do acquisitions for fun. A bit like puppies, we don't buy them just for Christmas . . . We are not depending on the [Irish property] market to be as buoyant as it has been,' he said. 'The prognosis in Dublin is that the economy is still growing.' After the deal was completed on 5 January 2004, the centre of power at Ulster Bank gradually shifted south from Belfast to Dublin's George's Quay and it wasn't long before NatWest's 'three arrowheads' logo was removed from Ulster Bank's 185 branches across Ireland and replaced with Royal Bank of Scotland's 'daisywheel'.

With Goodwin's blessing, the Ulster Bank and First Active combination embarked on a 'Journey to One'. The destination? To overtake AIB and Bank of Ireland as Ireland's largest bank by 2012. It would be a huge challenge, not least because AIB and BoI had a joint market share of more than 70 per cent while Ulster Bank had a share of only 11 per cent. McCarthy thought that, with the 'power' of RBS behind Ulster and First Active, anything was possible. 'The mantra was that RBS was one of the best-capitalised banks in the world and that, thanks to the depth of RBS's pockets, we had a near limitless ability to lend,' recalls one Ulster Bank insider. 'The message was put about that RBS was like some giant oil tanker moored off the coast, stuffed to the gunwales with cash and that this was ready to be tapped.'

On a trip to the Republic in the mid 2000s, Goodwin attended a 'town hall' style meeting in an Ulster Bank branch. It was designed to whip up some enthusiasm among the staff for the journey ahead. A young female teller asked what Goodwin saw as the two biggest hurdles on the bank's Journey to One. His answer was terse: 'AIB and Bank of Ireland. Next question?'[15] As *The Irish Times*' Simon Carswell recalls, members of the audience were stunned by this response. They were left wondering, 'Is that it? Isn't he going to give us his thoughts on how the audacious goal might be achieved or the risks that might accompany it?' There were clear risks to the strategy. One was that Bank of Ireland was a moving target. It too was pursuing rapid growth. Both it and Allied Irish Banks were also liberally spraying money around at both ends of the property spectrum (in loans to property developers and speculators, fuelling construction and at the other end doling out generous mortgages to individuals).

Accompanied by razzmatazz and ritual, Ulster Bank's 'Journey to One' (J21, for short) gained a cult-like status inside the bank. According to one ex-insider, 'It was a form of brainwashing or indoctrination. They desperately wanted us believe that Ulster Bank could be the Number One bank of Ireland, that we could conquer the world.' She said, 'It was like they thought that, if we just put our minds to it, we could make it happen.' The fact that many grey-haired bankers were purged in redundancy rounds between 2000 and 2007 made it easier for new-fangled thinking to take root. One ex-Ulster Bank insider said, 'By 2007, Ulster Bank was, in terms of its age and experience profile, the very antithesis of what it had been before RBS took it over. This was a major contributor to what went wrong. Apart from anything else, it ensured few dared question whether McCarthy's mission made any sense.'

Ulster Bank was not averse to throwing money around as it sought to evangelise its 'Journey'. Each of its 6,500 staff went on two-day sojourns to hotels around Ireland to be told where their bank was heading. A video featuring Al Pacino was frequently shown at these J21 motivational sessions. Taken from the 1999 Oliver Stone film *Any Given Sunday*, this featured Pacino as a football coach, Tony D'Amato, attempting to persuade an American Football team that was down on its luck to have faith and to fight like tigers. The speech includes the words: 'We're in hell right now, gentlemen . . . We can climb outta hell . . . one inch at a time . . . On this team, we fight for that inch. On this team, we tear ourselves and everyone else around us to pieces for that inch. We claw with our fingernails for that inch.'[16] Some Ulster Bank staff found it nauseating to watch.

Ulster also paid an estimated €50,000 (£41,500) to Bob Geldof to speak at one motivational event. However, those present claim Geldof 'just took the piss', telling the bankers if Ulster were stupid enough to pay him that much just to show up they deserved everything they got. Where costs were concerned, there were two cultures inside Ulster Bank. There was a cost-conscious, Calvinist attitude inside Ulster Bank Limited (UBL) in the north but a more free-spending culture within Ulster Bank Ireland Limited (UBIL), the Dublin-registered business.

Gradually, the Presbyterian roundheads were losing out to the southern Cavaliers, partly because McCarthy was in the latter camp. 'Cormac McCarthy was a watershed between the two cultures, between the old-school and new-school banking,' said one ex-Ulster Bank insider. 'To many, Cormac McCarthy was the golden boy but others were getting the Alex Ferguson hairdryer treatment [being given verbal roastings].'

What Goodwin, McCarthy and others don't seem to have realised is that there was really only one way Ulster could achieve its goal of toppling Bank of Ireland as the island's largest bank. They would have to lend to businesses and individuals that saner bankers would not have touched with a barge-pole. They were going to have to lend at crazy multiples (in terms of loan-to-values on properties or multiples of annual earnings for corporate loans), on lax terms and on weak covenants. As one Irish property tycoon puts it, 'Achieving that goal would have depended solely on lending the most money – and lending money wasn't difficult at the time.'

As Ulster's 'Journey to One' gathered steam, the bank was desperate to blow its own trumpet and put itself on the map. An early publicity stunt came when it launched a £5 note to commemorate the Northern Irish football legend and noted dipsomaniac, George Best, who had died the previous year. On 12 July 2005 – a day which has gone down in Irish banking infamy – McCarthy launched Ireland's first-ever 100 per cent loan-to-value residential mortgage for first-time buyers. First Active leaflets were handed out to commuters on Dublin's bridges and the bank also sought to woo partygoers in the Irish capital's bars and nightclubs, by installing fluorescent light-boxes in the bars, on the dance floors and in the chill-out areas. The Irish government was, in the main, extraordinarily relaxed about the antics of banks and prop-erty developers, but this was too much. Irish housing minister Noel Ahern, the brother of former Taoiseach Bertie Ahern, said targeting young people while they were drinking and inebriated was simply not on. 'It's sending out the wrong message,' said Ahern. 'Mortgages are serious and this form of advertising is reckless.'[17]

Within a few weeks, all six Irish banks had copied First Active's move by launching 100 per cent-plus mortgages. The former chief executive of an Irish bank said, 'We didn't have any choice . . . These bankers in kilts came in with no long-term commitment to the market and destroyed a franchise that had been built up over 100 years. Both RBS and HBOS saw the opportunity to generate better returns in Ireland than in the UK, so they allocated a lot of capital to this market. But what they did was a bit like pouring petrol on a fire.' Before a year had passed, one third of first-time buyers in Ireland were borrowing 100 per cent of the value of their homes.[18] 'The effect was devastating,' said Shane Ross, an independent senator in Ireland's parliament and a former business editor of the *Sunday Independent*. 'And, by the way, it wasn't just 100 per cent mortgages – it was 110 per cent mortgages, it was 120 per cent mortgages in some cases. This was a sign of the banks going absolutely bananas.'[19] One Irish bank chief spoke to the head of financial regulation at the Irish Central Bank, Brian Patterson, and asked why it was allowing such loans, which only made sense for the banks if one believed that Irish house prices could never fall. Patterson replied, 'We're a principles-based regulator and can't interfere in the competitive market place.'

The banks sought to downplay claims that they were stoking up a catastrophe. They came up with other reasons for the buoyancy of Ireland's housing market while dismissing any suggestion it was due to them lending too much money on too easy terms. 'Soft landing' was the mantra of the day – bank economists believed any downturn in house prices would be mild and painless. Other warnings also fell on deaf ears. One of the most startling came from *The Economist*. In its 16 June 2005 edition, economics editor Pam Woodall wrote, 'The worldwide rise in house prices is the biggest bubble in history. Prepare for the economic pain when it stops.'[20] In an accompanying piece, the magazine said that because construction was such a big part of its economy Ireland was likely to be worse hit than any other country. In a research note dated 29 March 2006, Rossa White of Davy Stockbrokers warned that the market was getting dangerously overstretched. 'In the Dublin market, prices are now rising at an annualised 20 per cent lick, up from only 3 per cent less than a year ago . . . Investors must be extremely bullish about rental growth in order to justify the sort of record valuations ascribed to residential property in central Dublin. To us, this looks like boundless optimism.'[21]

On a visit to Larne, Galway, and other parts of Ireland in July 2006, my jaw dropped when I saw the prices in estate agents' windows and the glossy magazines. I saw a modest, 'two-up, two-down' Georgian townhouse in Dublin advertised at €3 million. Even compared to the

UK's bubble-territory prices, the prices seemed insane. But the likes of McCarthy just dug their heads deeper into the sand.

Indeed, McCarthy's positivity about Ulster Bank and the Irish economy knew no bounds. In a presentation to analysts in the City in November 2006, he said, 'Opportunities for growth are almost limitless in terms of the businesses we are in . . . we're seeing nothing in our business that would give any cause for concern . . . All the drivers of growth are there in abundance in our business and the opportunity is very, very significant.'[22]

More level-headed business people and financiers were slamming on the brakes. The Beatty and Doyle families, owners of the Jurys Doyle hotel empire, sensed the market was overheating and decided to offload some prime sites on the island of Ireland. Simon Carswell says, 'Effectively, they were taking their money off the table.'[23] News that they were selling a 4.85-acre site in Ballsbridge, an upmarket suburb of the Irish capital, triggered a frenzy of speculative interest from Irish banks and developers. The site included the Jurys Inn Custom House Hotel and the five-star Berkeley Court Hotel. The auction that followed – orchestrated by estate agents CB Richard Ellis (CBRE) – represented the pinnacle of Ireland's commercial property madness, with parallels with the Tulip Mania that gripped Holland in 1637. Sean Dunne, a County Carlow-born billionaire developer with strong Fianna Fáil connections, seemed desperate to get his hands on the site. Dunne knew all about lavishing money on objects of desire. In July 2004 he married the glamorous *Sunday Independent* gossip columnist Gayle Killilea. Their wedding, which reportedly cost €1.5 million, was held off the French and Italian Rivieras, on board the *Christina O*, a yacht formerly owned by Greek shipping billionaire Aristotle Onassis.[24]

Dunne was on holiday in Thailand when CBRE fired the starting gun for the Ballsbridge hustle.[25] As he lay in the Siamese sun, someone called to tell him that, if he wanted to buy the site, he would have to stump up €275 million within seven days. Dunne rushed back to Dublin and successfully arranged the necessary funding from two of his regular lenders, Bank of Ireland and Irish Nationwide. However, Ulster Bank's head of property finance, Paul McDonnell, was desperate to muscle in on the action. A report in the Cork-based *Irish Examiner* said, 'Ulster Bank was under huge pressure from its parent company, Royal Bank of Scotland, to grow profits in this country. Executives from the bank contacted Dunne about taking over from Bank of Ireland and Irish Nationwide in the landmark deal. Terms were agreed over a two-day period, including going through an RBS credit committee in London.'[26] The credit committee was made up of several members of RBS's Group Executive Management Committee, one of whom was allegedly Gordon Pell, RBS's chairman of Retail Markets.

'That Friday night, at nine o'clock, Ulster Bank walked through the door of my office,' Dunne later recalled. 'They produced a letter for the full purchase price.'[27] Ulster and RBS were so confident of Dunne's abilities and the site's potential, they lent him a further €130 million to purchase Hume House, a nine-storey office block adjacent to the main Ballsbridge site.[28] They also paid a further €207 million for the nearby head office of Allied Irish Banks. In the end, Dunne, or his bankers, forked out an eye-watering €379 million – an average price of €55 million per acre – for his corner of Ballsbridge.[29] Even though the site didn't even have planning permission, it briefly became the most expensive piece of real estate in the world. Although Ulster ultimately pumped €326.5 million into Sean Dunne's Ballsbridge dream, it did syndicate parts of the loan to Netherlands-based Rabobank (sum unknown) and to the now bust Icelandic bank Kaupthing (€84.1 million).[30] Having earned himself the title 'the Baron of Ballsbridge', Dunne's vision was to 'bring Knightsbridge to Ballsbridge' by erecting a 37-storey, 132-metre diamond-shaped residential skyscraper, alongside an array of expensive homes, boutiques and office buildings. But Dunne struggled to obtain planning permission and then the crisis intervened to turn Dunne's dream into a nightmare – he went bankrupt, pursued by creditors, including Ulster Bank, and is effectively now a fugitive from his creditors, living in Connecticut.

Ulster Bank's backing of the Ballsbridge project was far from the only error it made in the Irish commercial property market. With the blessing of the RBS group credit committee and based on a Panglossian view of the prospects for Ireland's economy, it also lent to numerous other Irish commercial property schemes that turned to dust. Many of these hare-brained schemes were to leave the bank nursing enormous bad debts when Ireland's property bubble burst and development sites shed more than three-quarters of their value. The Irish journalist and author Matt Cooper says, 'Ulster Bank concentrated heavily on lending to property developers who believed that retail spending would continue to rise and leisure spending would continue to soar, becoming a major lender to ubiquitous hotel developments.'[31]

Ulster Bank grew its total assets from £9.2 billion in 2000 to £54.8 billion in 2007 (a 495 per cent increase in seven years), while profits had grown at the more leisurely pace of 210 per cent – rising from £165 million in 2000 to £513 million in 2007. Residential mortgages, at £24.5 billion, accounted for half the total sum lent.[32] At a superficial level, Ulster Bank's 2007 numbers, incorporating those of First Active, looked good. Total assets were up 23 per cent on 2006, with profits up by 21.8 per cent and employee numbers rising to 6,400. The branch network had grown to 282 outlets. In the parent group's 2007 report and accounts, published in February 2008, RBS said Ulster Bank 'maintained its strong growth record and we have continued to invest in the good opportunities for future growth presented by the Irish market'. McCarthy was not inclined to slow the pace or change direction. As late as February 2007, Ulster Bank has sufficient faith in Ireland's future to embark on a further expansion drive.

Cormac McCarthy said he was opening seven new Ulster Bank branches in Munster, opening new business centres and opening a further seven First Active branches. First Active's managing director Colm Furlong said the firm remained 'proud' to have introduced 100 per cent mortgages for first-time buyers to the Irish market. Ulster Bank also allocated some €2 million a year to enlarging its Dublin headquarters on George's Quay, taking the lease on an adjacent building being vacated by the accountancy giant PwC.[33] However, in May 2007, it was rapped over the knuckles by UK regulators. After a two-year inquiry into Northern Ireland's current account banking market, the Competition Commission ordered Ulster Bank to drop certain opaque practices which, it said, were detrimental to its customers' wealth. It and three other banks in the province – Bank of Ireland, First Trust and Northern Bank (recently sold by National Australia Bank to Copenhagen-based Danske Bank) – were told they must be more explicit about charges and make it easier for customers to switch banks. A jubilant Steve Costello, chairman at the Consumer Council, said, 'This marks the start of a revolution in banking. The market is being transformed from being cosy and complacent for banks to being competitive and customer-focused.'[34] With the benefit of hindsight Costello's triumphant rhetoric seems farcical – especially when you consider the pure poison, in terms of toxic property loans, that was about to overwhelm the Irish banking system and topple the Irish economy. The Competition Commission's intervention was a classic case of UK regulators being unable to see the wood for the trees and barking up the wrong tree at the same time.

Royal Bank of Fred

Just before the Christmas break in 2002, Fred Goodwin learned that he had been named Forbes Global Businessman of the Year by *Forbes Magazine*. Sources close to the then 44-year-old believe that the award played a big part in inflating his ego, conceit and lust for power. The award had previously gone to corporate titans including Chris Gent, chief executive of Vodafone, and Jean-Martin Folz, boss of carmakers PSA Peugeot Citroën. But it wasn't just the trophy that mattered to Goodwin. *Forbes*'s accompanying article was unctuous. It was the sort of thing Goodwin had been trying to persuade communications director Howard Moody to get British journalists to write for years.

In the 2,127-word profile, written by *Forbes*'s European bureau chief Richard C. Morais, Goodwin was quoted as saying, 'I always work on the five-second rule . . . How a job offer makes you feel in the first five seconds when you hear the idea, before you spend ages agonizing, is what you should do.' Goodwin declared that, if RBS were ever to table an offer for Germany's Commerzbank, it would be time to 'send for the men with the white coats'. Defending RBS's decision to halt the NatWest branch closure programme and to permit customers to phone their branch, Goodwin said, 'If you're at war with your customers, you're living on borrowed time.' He also made it clear he did not believe in keeping branches open out of altruism alone, saying that interactions between customers and staff in branches provide greater opportunities for cross-selling than online or over the phone. Morais wrote, 'Goodwin's caustic challenges are frequently on the money, and they spur his team on to great achievements.' The article said Goodwin wanted Royal Bank of Scotland to be 'utterly stable', which was why he was steering clear of emerging markets. However, the article also highlighted analysts' concerns that the bank's corporate division was more exposed than that of any other bank to the economic downturn. Morais only quoted three external commentators – Northern Venture Managers' Michael Denny, Merrill Lynch's Matthew Greenburgh and Deloitte & Touche's John Connolly, all of whom had close links to the bank or had befriended Goodwin.[1]

Morais said, 'I did sense there was something imperial and hard-edged about him, but he seemed to be using that for a higher cause – delivering superior returns to the bank's shareholders.' Morais, who interviewed Goodwin in the boardroom of 42 St Andrew Square, says the PR people minders who were in attendance 'were very nervous'. Morais says that inside *Forbes*, the editorial team always used to wonder whether someone who was featured on the cover would succumb to the 'cover curse' – meaning they would start to believe their own PR, become hubristic and make bad business decisions.[2]

In the case of Goodwin, that transformation happened overnight. One former senior advisor to the Royal Bank of Scotland board says, 'Fred literally thought he was walking on water after that article. Before, people like me found him relatively easy to speak to; afterwards, he cut himself off. The real arrogance came in after that – he only wanted to mix with the most senior bankers, the governor of the Bank of England, prime ministers, presidents and members of the royal family. And, of course, the Scottish great and the good wanted to touch Fred's cloth.' But this was a dangerous frame of mind for the chief executive of a FTSE-100-listed firm, especially one with a semi-detached chairman and whose directors were in his thrall. There were early signs of a 'cult of Fred' developing inside the bank, with the messages and iconography honed to perfection by communications director Howard Moody. Fred was gradually being transformed from a gauche, bespectacled geek into a confident and assured global leader.

Goodwin became more high-handed with the trade union around this time. Rob MacGregor, the UNIFI rep, says that Fred took pleasure in giving both the union and the bank's rank-and-file staff 'a good kicking' whenever he could. MacGregor adds, 'But Fred kept himself above the fray. He was incredibly dismissive of anyone who disagreed with him.'[3] Once, after a negative article appeared in the *Mail on Sunday* slating the bank for its treatment of an RBS pensioner, Mrs Lightfoot, from whom the bank was trying to 'claw back' 79 per cent of her pension, MacGregor and Goodwin had a meeting. Goodwin threw a copy of the offending tabloid across the table at McGregor and shouted, 'Explain this!' MacGregor thought it decidedly odd, given he wasn't an RBS employee. Goodwin then said, 'I am not going to change my mind on this [pension clawbacks]. Why do you keep raising it? Which part of the word no do you not understand.'[4]

In autumn 1999, barely a year into Goodwin's Royal Bank of Scotland career, Sir Tom Shebbeare, chief executive of Prince Charles's flagship charity, the Prince's Trust, approached the 41-year-old Scot to see if he might be interested in becoming the chairman of the trust's fledgling Scottish arm, the Prince's Trust Scotland. Prince Charles founded the Prince's Trust in 1976 to assist young Britons aged 14–25 who were down on their luck to overcome obstacles and find gainful employment. As the prince put it, 'I wanted to offer a lifeline to those young people that society had left behind.'[5] Its main focus was on providing training, confidence-building courses, support and advice. Goodwin was considered a strong candidate given his position as a prominent and successful Scottish business leader who, thanks to his own upbringing in Paisley, ought to be able to empathise with disadvantaged young people. The trust, cash-strapped at the time, also hoped Goodwin would be able to use his influence to help fill its coffers. In October 1999, when he formally took up to the role, he was embroiled in Royal Bank's £21-billion bid for NatWest. However, his PA Mary McCallum stepped into the breach, handling some of the Prince's Trust and Prince's Scottish Youth Business Trust (PSYBT) administrative work while Goodwin found time to interview candidates for various roles within the merged trust. In May 2000, several new council members of the Prince's Trust Scotland were announced including the BBC broadcaster Kirsty Wark (who was already moonlighting as the presenter of internal broadcasts for Royal Bank of Scotland), double-glazing entrepreneur Gerard Eadie, ScottishPower chief executive Ian Russell and Kwik-Fit marketing director Peter Holmes. One council member of the Prince's Trust Scotland says they were hugely impressed by Goodwin's efficiency. 'Fred makes decisions so quickly, he didn't actually need to devote an awful lot of time to it. Whenever we had meetings with Fred, he would always say, "Okay let's do it". He would never say, "I've got to have a think about that." '

Within a year, the Royal Bank of Scotland had become the biggest corporate donor to the Prince's Trust. As part of a partnership programme, the bank pledged £11 million in donations and loans in August 2001 over a three-year period. In 2004, the Royal Bank unveiled a £5-million three-year extension to the programme and over 800 RBS employees volunteered to help the good cause. And, in July 2003, Goodwin was promoted to chairman of the Prince's Trust on a UK-wide basis. He succeeded Sir William Castell, a former president and chief executive of GE Healthcare. One former Prince's Trust insider says, 'There really was no question that Fred was the best candidate.'

Goodwin did such a good job of getting the Prince's Trust out of a financial hole that it endeared him to members of the royal household, including the Queen, who was delighted by his input. 'He got a lot of support from the Queen – she recognised what he had done to turn around her son's charity,' says one former council member. Indeed, the Queen or her minders were so impressed that they gave Goodwin an additional role as a trustee of the Queen's Silver Jubilee Trust, which distributes money to good causes. One source close to the royal family says, 'Everyone said what a great job Fred Goodwin did at the Prince's Trust. He was forceful. He was one of the few people who could stand up and talk about the situation of disadvantaged young people as if he really knew what he was talking about. He was shy at that time and not once did he show any signs of becoming a fantastically aggressive person who got things out of proportion as a result of giving up listening to people.'

Prince Charles regularly sang Fred's praises. He once said, 'Sir Fred Goodwin is another person I want to thank, because we could not do this without the aid of such a hardworking chairman. It is jolly useful having someone as chairman who also has an enormous headquarters that we can occasionally use for meetings! His contribution is quite remarkable.'[6]

However, some council members of the Prince's Trust believe that, in his role as UK chairman, Goodwin kept such a tight grip on the charity's finances that he stifled its creativity and adventurousness. Howard Williamson, professor of European youth policy at the University of Glamorgan, who sat on the trust's council for Wales says, 'In Wales, Sir Fred was a distant but omnipresent and controlling figure. The rain check on any idea put forward for development or consolidation was always "How would Sir Fred react?" And trying to second-guess that reaction always ended up at the bottom line.'[7]

It is possible Goodwin genuinely wanted to put something back into society. However, several of his former colleagues at Royal Bank of Scotland claim Goodwin's unspoken goals were to ingratiate himself with the royal family, enhance his social status and secure a 'gong' such as a knighthood down the road. A former senior executive at Coutts says a great many staff at the private banking arm 'worked their bollocks off' to meet volunteering and fund-raising targets for the Prince's Trust but never got a single word of thanks from Goodwin.

In August 2002 Goodwin did Prince Charles a favour by giving a berth to Sir Stephen Lamport, the prince's former private secretary and treasurer. The royal household was beset with scandal in 2002 as a result of the collapse of the trial of a former butler, Paul Burrell, who was alleged to have stolen items belonging to the late Princess Diana. The trial's collapse triggered a surge of lurid stories in the media, including allegations of gay sex in the palace and cover-ups. Lamport had come under fire for failing to tell the police and the Crown Prosecution Service that the practice of giving unwanted gifts to servants was endemic in Royal circles. The prince wanted a safer pair of hands and is said to have wanted Lamport out so that he could bring in Sir Michael Peat as private secretary in August 2002. Prince Charles was said to be extremely grateful when Goodwin created a new role – director of public policy and government affairs – for Lamport at the Royal Bank of Scotland. Ex-insiders claim Lamport was, in fact, little more than a glorified social secretary for the gauche and socially inept Goodwin. One former bank insider remembers Lamport one day asking, 'I don't want to trouble you but what do investment bankers do?' and another remembers that, having worked with Prince Charles for so long, he had adopted many of the prince's mannerisms. 'He walked like him, talked like him, thought like him.'

One of the duties of Lamport – who had worked as a diplomat, including serving as private secretary to Tory Foreign Secretaries Douglas Hurd and Malcolm Rifkind, before moving to St James's Palace in 1993 – was organising Goodwin's dinner parties. Held about once every three months from 2003 onwards, these brought members of the great and the good and the corporate elite together with Goodwin and senior members of his executive team in the plush surroundings of the executive suite on the eleventh floor of RBS's new London flagship office, 280 Bishopsgate. There tended to be about eight guests, with representatives of the bank including Johnny Cameron, Brian Crowe, Gordon Pell, Chris Sullivan, a former professional footballer who ran the bank's Retail Direct arm, and Jeremy Peat. Guests included Lord Robertson, the Secretary General of NATO, Digby Jones, Director General of the CBI, senior civil servants, politicians and the chief executives of many of the UK's largest companies.

While Goodwin was a bit stiff at these dinners, he was always polite and courteous. 'It was all about establishing Fred with the great and the good and trying to make him seem more human,' says one former RBS senior insider.

According to ex-colleagues and palace insiders, Goodwin gave Lamport a further task – 'Get me a f**king knighthood.' One senior source says, 'It was an unhappy arrangement. Sir Stephen was quite a gentle foreign office guy – not an action guy but a born diplomat.' Goodwin's knighthood was duly announced in the Queen's birthday honours on Saturday, 12 June 2004. While they were not specifically mentioned, Goodwin's role as chairman of the Prince's Trust and on the New Labour taskforces played a part. On the day of the announce- ment, Anne Shevas, a spokeswoman for Prime Minister Tony Blair, said Goodwin 'has undertaken many projects to the benefit of his bank and the good of Scotland as a whole'.[8] The idea that Goodwin, then only 45, merited a knighthood was initially put forward by Jack McConnell, First Minister of Scotland from 2001 to 2007 and an ardent Blairite. New Labour's bizarre love affair with the banking sector was such that more than 20 senior bankers were given peerages, knighthoods or other honours during New Labour's years in power. The award was welcomed by colleagues including Mathewson, who had accepted a knighthood himself 'for services to economic development in Scotland and Scottish Banking' in the New Year's Honours of January 1999. Afterwards, any journalist who referred to RBS's self-important chief executive as 'Mr' Fred Goodwin in articles received an earful from the RBS press office, who reminded them in no uncertain terms to remember that 'it's Sir Fred now'. It was clear how much it mattered to Fred. Others were less impressed. The Scottish Socialist leader Tommy Sheridan said, 'It's an absolute outrage that this man is to receive a knighthood for services to the community when all the community has received from him is low wages and unemployment.'⁹ Sheridan was referring to the sacking of 18,000 people during the NatWest integration and the sub-inflationary pay rises awarded to many of the bank's frontline staff. Lamport left the bank in 2007, in order to assist Prince Charles with the preparations for his own coronation.

Even though Goodwin was courteous and self-effacing when meeting Eddie George or Mervyn King, the successive governors of the Bank of England, he was remarkably rude about them behind their backs. With journalists, investment analysts and investors, Goodwin would be polite to their faces but disparaging behind their backs, often accusing them of cluelessness or idiocy. As with almost everyone he encountered, Goodwin assumed he knew more about their job than they did.

After the NatWest takeover, the Merrill Lynch investment banker Matthew Greenburgh – who earned a reputed £7-million bonus for his work on the deal – embarked on what rival investment bankers claim was 'a sustained campaign to ingratiate himself with Fred'. The schmoozing is said to have encompassed inviting and paying for Goodwin to participate in some of his favourite pursuits, including trips to Formula One Grands Prix and shooting excursions. One ex-senior source at Royal Bank said, 'It was a calculated campaign to suck up to Fred.' Greenburgh – whose nickname in the City of London is ELF (which is said *not* to stand for 'Erudite Likeable Fellow') was wooing Fred because he wanted Merrill Lynch to be the bank's preferred supplier of investment banking services on future deals. One ex-colleague of Greenburgh said, 'Matthew made it his business to, you know, pursue Fred.'

As part of this, Goodwin and Greenburgh travelled together to Modena, a town in the northern Italian region of Emilia-Romagna, where they paid a visit to the Maserati factory. There Greenburgh purchased a brand-new blue Maserati – a car that some claim he bought specifically to impress the noted 'petrol head' Fred Goodwin. He even bought it in RBS dark blue in honour of his favoured client. Asked if Greenburgh was constantly tempting Goodwin to do deals that would be good for Merrill Lynch but potentially bad for RBS, one rival investment banker said, 'I think Fred was probably prone to grandiose designs and Matthew would have indulged the fantasies, telling him that all things were possible. Matthew loves a deal.'

Laird of Gogarburn

Queen Margaret University, a former technical college founded in Edinburgh as a cookery school in 1875, was looking to amalgamate its operations at a single site and had been chosen as preferred bidder to buy the site of the Gogarburn Psychiatric Hospital, a recently closed 'home for mental defectives'. It was March 2001 and the National Health Service had put the 78-acre site on Edinburgh's western fringes on the market after the last of the patients had been moved out and into the care-in-the-community programme. Goodwin believed the site was perfect for the Royal Bank of Scotland headquarters. He then proceeded to infuriate Queen Margaret University's principal, Joan Stringer (whose winning bid is thought to have been between £12 million and £20 million), by gazumping her with an estimated £28-million offer. The university harrumphed and issued threats of legal action. However, in April 2001, the NHS bowed to commercial reality, revoked the college's preferred bidder status and said its offer no longer represented 'the best value the market could offer at this time'.

The bank completed the purchase on 5 June 2001 and made a detailed planning application to Edinburgh City Council seven months later. This was for one 350,000-square-foot 'world headquarters' office building, divided into six 'business houses' and one 'executive house', connected by a 280-metre glazed central street. The street would make up for the absence of local amenities by offering retail outlets including a small supermarket and a staff restaurant. Dotted around the site would be other buildings including a business school, conference centre and leisure centre with tennis courts and a swimming pool. The design was intended to promote 'transparency' and 'the exchange of ideas' between the 3,250 employees who would work there. However,

Edinburgh City Council planners were minded to reject the proposals since they encroached on the city's Green Belt. In the end, Lord Provost Eric Milligan and council leader Donald Anderson overruled the planners, arguing that it was essential that RBS stayed in Edinburgh and that rejection might well persuade the bank to move its headquarters elsewhere. In a later interview, Milligan admitted that the council 'fell over itself' to accommodate Goodwin's desires.[1] When permission was granted in September 2002, it was a significant breakthrough for Goodwin. A few weeks later, Goodwin paid a visit to former RBS chairman Lord Younger, who was dying of prostate cancer in Strathcarron Hospice near Denny in Stirlingshire. Goodwin arrived clutching two things – the architect's drawings for Gogarburn and a photograph of the bank's new private jet, a Dassault Falcon 900EX. Younger was polite, but after Goodwin had left, he turned to his daughter Joanna Davidson and said, 'It's when you see things like that you wonder if it's time to sell the shares.'[2]

Goodwin did not fully trust the bank's in-house property team to deliver the hugely ambitious Gogarburn project on time and on budget, and was desperate to avoid a fiasco like the Scottish Parliament building at Holyrood, which was ten times over budget and several years late. In a first for the bank, he outsourced project management to a specialist consultancy, Mace, which had recently completed out-of-town headquarters for British Airways and drugs firm GlaxoSmithKline (GSK). He appointed London-based architects Renton Howard Wood Levin (RHWL), who designed the GSK headquarters, to work alongside Michael Laird Architects (MLA). Goodwin immediately struck up a rapport with Mace and, at their suggestion, happily opted for a higher specification and raised the construction budget from £120 million to £180 million (the figure excludes site acquisition, landscaping, car parks, a road bridge across the A8, roads, sewers, waste-water treatment etc.). Mace did not do anything by halves and installed 60,000-square-foot of Portakabins at the Gogarburn site, providing four-storeys of air-conditioned office space for its 500-strong on-site team. They then drafted in an army of 6,500 construction workers from firms including Laing O'Rourke, Sir Robert McAlpine and WSP.

Professionals who worked on the project were astonished by how hands-on Goodwin was. He took an almost obsessional interest in everything from bus parking spaces, to the positioning of new trees in the

parkland, to the shape of the filing cabinets. At progress meetings with
RHWL and MLA, the architects were surprised by the extent to which
Fred had to win every argument. It was a pain for the architects and
project managers but Goodwin's hands-on involvement came as a relief
to his direct reports – including divisional heads like Benny Higgins,
who ran retail banking in the UK. Goodwin was so engrossed in the
minutiae of Gogarburn he was much less inclined to micromanage
their businesses for them.

With a view to expanding Gogarburn's acreage, Goodwin acquired
the Gogar Park Curling Club which was adjacent to the hospital site
– much to the chagrin of the curlers, who were furious at the loss of
their rink. He also tried to buy the Gogarburn Golf Club – many of
whose members were former psychiatric nurses at the hospital – which
adjoined the site to the west. He offered £4,000 to each of the golf
club's 450 members – the equivalent of £1.8 million for the 12-hole
course – but they refused to sell. 'We said no to Sir Fred Goodwin,' said
the club's treasurer, Moira Brown, punching the air in her clubhouse,
in an interview with Bloomberg. 'The mood was defiant. This is ours
and it wasn't for sale.'³ One member told *The Scotsman*, 'We have been
treated with contempt and sheer arrogance . . . We have 49 acres here,
and the bank have paid around £58 million for 78 acres next door.
That means, in those terms, our land is worth £35 million and we were
offered £2 million. Does that sound fair to you?'⁴

In the wake of Fred's abortive attempt to neutralise media criticism
with his libel writ against the *Sunday Times*, the bank sought to rustle
up more positive coverage by giving a carefully selected band of
journalists a sneak preview of the building site. The atrocious weather
and Somme-like mud at Gogarburn did little to dampen the spirits of
The Scotsman's reporter, who penned a story saying that Gogarburn is
'undeniably the most ambitious project by a company in Scotland in
living memory. For Sir Fred Goodwin, group chief executive, who has
been the butt of most of the criticism, it represents the crowning glory
for the Royal's rise to world recognition.'⁵

By July 2005, the building was complete. Goodwin took pride in the
fact it was six months ahead of schedule and on budget – as planned,
the total cost was reportedly £350 million. In early July, the first 2,000
of the roughly 3,250 RBS staff moved in from offices on St Andrew
Square and West Register Street. Goodwin, who was not formally

due to move in to his palatial new office until mid August, moved in early. This was because he wanted to avoid disruption from the 'Make Poverty History' march that was due to be held in Edinburgh on 2 July. Timed to coincide with the G8 summit at Gleneagles, the event saw 200,000 peaceful protestors march through the city centre but it later degenerated into violence and running battles on Princes Street.

On 14 September, the headquarters were officially opened by the Queen and the Duke of Edinburgh in an extravaganza also attended by Lord Provost of Edinburgh Lesley Hinds, Scotland's First Minister Jack McConnell, Secretary of State for Scotland Alistair Darling and Deputy First Minister Nicol Stephen. True to form, Prince Philip delivered one of his gaffes – after being shown a large open-plan office floor, he asked if it was a call centre. When told that it wasn't, he said, 'I suppose you've farmed that out to Bombay.'[6]

Goodwin pulled out the stops, spending a rumoured £1 million on the opening events. He organised a fly-past of four Tornados from RAF Leuchars in Fife, where the thrill-seeking Goodwin was well connected. He regularly visited the Fife air base in order to go for joy rides in one of 111 Squadron's Tornado F3 fighter jets. He got a Williams Formula One racing car, driven by Aussie driver Mark Webber, to career around the grounds at eye-watering speeds, terrifying some members of staff. He also unveiled a special RBS £50 note for the occasion. A small stage was erected about halfway down the central 'street' inside the Gogarburn building for speeches, from which Scottish First Minister Jack McConnell intoned, 'Building world-class Scottish companies that are competitive across global markets is a central part of our strategy for developing a modern and prosperous Scottish economy. The Royal Bank of Scotland is a perfect realisation of that ambition.'[7] In her speech, the Queen said, 'For many years, Scotland has had an enviable reputation for efficient financial management in a highly competitive market . . . The building is a fine tribute to the many generations of "canny" Scottish bankers who have made – and are still making – such a valuable contribution to the national economy.'[8]

Later, a master of ceremonies declared, 'And now, Ladies and Gentlemen, Your Chief Executive . . . Sir Fred Goodwin . . .' As Goodwin pranced up on to the stage in the manner of a minor celebrity or a pop star to give a brief peroration, some members of staff cringed. One recalls, 'I just thought, "Oh My God, this isn't how the

chief executive of a major company is supposed to behave." It just felt
so wrong. It was one of the most nauseating speeches I'd heard in my
life.' For the evening party, Goodwin had organised live music from the
ex-Spandau Ballet lead singer Tony Hadley, Go West's Peter Cox and
the inimitable Jools Holland. Among other things, they sang a cover
version of Thin Lizzy's 'The Boys Are Back in Town'. This required a
massive investment in a sound system with more than three kilometres
of 'low smoke' cable rigged up, out of view under the floor and in
a specially constructed duct above 'the street'. One guest said, 'The
whole thing was ridiculously over the top, nausea inducing. For me, that
was the moment that Fred started to lose the plot.'

According to the *Mail on Sunday*, Royal Bank staff were not particularly enthusiastic about the event or the opportunity to meet Her
Majesty. The newspaper said only 10 out of the 3,250 staff at Gogarburn
volunteered to meet her, which prompted the bank to 'round up staff
. . . to pose as enthusiastic "fillers" '.[9] The coverage doubtless enraged
Goodwin. He was more pleased with a report in the *Sunday Mail*, a
sister paper of the *Daily Record*. This painted a glowing picture of the
Gogarburn complex, with staff singing the praises of facilities such as
the crèche, leisure centre, gym, swimming pool and subsidised restau-
rants and cafés. Raj Morjaria, 24, who worked in internal communications, said, 'You can go to Starbucks and sit in lounge chairs and discuss
things over coffee. I'm probably more productive here.'[10] There were
disadvantages though. Unlike the old city centre offices, Gogarburn
was effectively a gated community, isolated from the outside world. 'It's
very Stepford Wives,' said one ex-executive director. Writing in *The
Guardian*, Simon Hattenstone described it as 'a private estate part San
Simeon, part *Truman Show*'.[11]

The bank had a tradition of 'Mess Dinners' for its top 25–30 executives four times a year. Generally, only one or two women attended
these black-tie events, which became more like *RBS's Got Talent* after
the move to Gogarburn in July 2005. At his flash new headquarters,
Goodwin had a state-of-the-art karaoke machine installed in the mess
dining room. From then on, each of the bank's top brass was expected
to perform a pop song of their choice, using the Japanese-developed
'empty orchestra', machine in front of colleagues as part of the post-
Mess dinner entertainment. Goodwin's right-hand man at these events
was the RBS tax advisor Graham Halstead, who was dubbed 'President

of the Mess'. Halstead was tasked with organising the table settings and the menus and ensuring the correct *grands crus* wines, carefully selected from the NatWest cellar, were served with each course.

After dessert, Ricardo, the bank's long-serving Italian-born maître d', brought in a bottle of sambuca, a rich Italian liqueur, and would pour some out for each guest. Goodwin would then ritually dip his thumb into his glass and ignite the spirit with a match, before passing on the flame to the colleague on his left. The flame and the pain were passed around the room from thumb to thumb, in a cult-ish way which Goodwin thought helped to 'bond' the bank's officer class. The bankers around the table were always nervous that they would be the one who broke the circle of fire and, if anyone chickened out, they would be branded a sissy. Many ended up with blisters on their thumbs the next day.

Once the flames had died out, the karaoke machine was cranked up and Goodwin often delivered a pitch-perfect rendition of Don McLean's 'American Pie', one of his favourite songs. Chief executive of retail banking Benny Higgins preferred to recite poetry. On one occasion, he is said to have recited, without notes, all five stanzas of the African American poet Maya Angelou's 1983 poem 'Caged Bird'. Other top RBS bankers performed karaoke songs of their own choice. At least two of the bankers who attended these dinners say they found them excruciating, likening them to the lavish dinner parties thrown by Russian leader Joseph Stalin. One former RBS executive said, 'The mess dinners got worse and worse, especially after the move to Gogarburn. They were pathetic really . . . I stopped going but you heard stories about people dressing up and sitting on each other's knees. If that had got into the papers, it wouldn't have looked too good.' At around midnight, pies were brought in from Goodwin's preferred pie butcher, Yorkes of Dundee, after which he and some of his cronies tended to go drinking elsewhere in Edinburgh until about two or three in the morning. One ex-senior RBS insider said, 'The big test was the next morning – you had to be in on time, fresh and working.'

Goodwin's obsession with interior decoration extended far beyond Gogarburn. In every major city in which the bank operated, he sought to consolidate the bank's operations into fewer and better quality offices. As part of this, he insisted that their interior decor was consistent with a template he had developed. In the City of London, the bank consolidated many of its employees in a brand-new 250,000-square-foot, 13-storey building at 280 Bishopsgate. In Birmingham, the bank took 350,000 square feet at the Brindleyplace canal-side development and, in Manchester, it took 500,000 square feet at Spinningfields. These were all brand-new, top-of-the-range city-centre offices. In the executive suites, including the opulent eleventh floor of 280 Bishopsgate, 'Executive House G' at Gogarburn and 'Fred's Pleasure Dome' at 35 St Andrew Square, Goodwin insisted that the deep and luxuriant carpets were a uniform shade of amber, that all tables, desks, filing cabinets and bookshelves were hand-crafted out of weathered sycamore and that armchairs were upholstered in the same shade of beige leather. Most of the furniture, including the new boardroom table and chairs, was handmade at huge expense at the Musselburgh workshops of Ben Dawson Ltd, which also produced the furniture for the Scottish parliament and the Welsh assembly buildings. Asked about the Paisley-born chartered account's eye for design, Dawson says Goodwin 'never accepted anything less than the best'.[12]

Whenever Goodwin inspected new bank premises, if he noticed anything that did not comply with his design and colour template, he insisted it was ripped out and replaced. Acres of recently laid thick-pile carpet were torn out of newly completed or refurbished offices in London, Edinburgh and elsewhere after Fred said it was a shade out. The man who bore the brunt of Fred's rages was RBS's head of property Ernest Sheavills, who sometimes quaked with fear ahead of their 'snagging reports'. At the Gleneagles off-site in 2003, Howard Moody was able to joke that Fred deserved an award for services to the British carpet industry.

Goodwin also ordered the construction of a vast $500-million building in Stamford, Connecticut. The project at 600 Washington Boulevard, formally announced on 20 September 2005, was intended to bring all RBS's North American investment banking and financial markets operations, including RBS Greenwich Capital, under one roof. The 12-storey, 1-million-square-foot derivatives factory would incorporate the world's second largest trading floor – with a floor plate of 95,000 square feet, it is large enough for 1,000 traders – but this too turned out to be a white elephant.[13]

In October 2002, the bank splashed out £20 million on a Dassault Falcon 900EX executive jet, which Goodwin subsequently used to travel to various outposts of his fast-growing empire. The three-engine 900EX was configured with eight seats and a bedroom for Fred at the back. It had a maximum range of 5,180 miles and a cruising speed of 590 mph, meaning it could comfortably fly non-stop from Edinburgh to Beijing and almost anywhere in the United States. *Flight* magazine described the plane as 'perhaps the premier large business jet on the market'.[14] The bank sought to keep the plane's existence hidden from its own shareholders and the media for the best part of two years. Even after Edward Simpkins, a journalist on the *Sunday Telegraph*, established the bank's ownership from official records, the bank tried to disguise its ownership of the plane. The *Sunday Telegraph* ran the numbers to prove that the plane made little financial sense. It estimated that a round trip from Edinburgh to New York in the Falcon would cost £140,910 – three times the cost of eight flexible first-class returns on scheduled flights.[15] Robert Peston said in the *Sunday Telegraph*:

> When we asked Royal Bank about all this [the purchase of the plane], it insisted that it leased the plane to lots of third parties, so the cost was lower than one might think. Oddly, it was unable to tell us how many hours have been flown by third parties – which didn't fill me with tremendous confidence in its financial controls . . .
>
> Then there's the nagging question of why the jet's home is Le Bourget, Paris, rather than closer to where RBS's executives are based, in Edinburgh. It's generous of Goodwin to pay for the flight crew's regular shuttles from France to Scotland. Can there have been a subconscious desire to hide the sleek plane from the envious eyes of RBS's shareholders? Unthinkable.[16]

It later emerged that in 2002–03 the bank and Goodwin had a serious ding-dong with the Inland Revenue over the plane's tax status. The revenue believed that use of the plane by Goodwin and his wife Joyce should be taxed as a 'benefit in kind'. This would have added many tens of thousands of pounds to their tax bills. To avoid this, ex-insiders claim the bank transferred ownership of the corporate jet from the Royal Bank of Scotland Group to RBS's Lombard Aviation leasing subsidiary. This gave the impression that the Falcon 900EX was not just a personal plaything and dedicated air taxi for the chief executive but was chartered out to third parties on a regular basis. What was surprising though was that, whenever interested parties rang the plane's 'gatekeeper' at Royal Bank of Scotland – 'Scary' Mary McCallum, Goodwin's PA – to ask if it was available for slots many months in advance, they were invariably told the plane was unavailable.[17] Some observers began to wonder whether the change of ownership was a ruse.

Most senior RBS executives dreaded going on the plane with Goodwin because of his lack of social skills. If asked to join Goodwin on the Falcon 900EX for a long-haul flight, many invented excuses and travelled on scheduled flights instead – which undermined the logic of owning the jet. Executives who did travel overnight with Goodwin were obliged to sit up all night while Fred reclined in regal splendour in his bedroom aft. The arrangement was a double inconvenience since, once Goodwin had gone to bed, the plane's only toilet became inaccessible because you had to pass through his private suite to reach it. 'We'd be sitting there cross-legged all night,' said one.

Goodwin felt the plane was not good enough for him and, two years after buying it, he ordered the next model up, the slightly larger Dassault Falcon 7X, a 'fly by wire' aircraft, costing $45 million. This had a larger cabin and a slightly longer range of 6,456 miles. The first Falcon 7X aircraft to come off Dassault's Bordeaux-Mérignac production line was bought by the French state for the use of President Nicolas Sarkozy. It was soon nicknamed 'Carla One' by the French press after his wife, the Italian pop singer Carla Bruni. The yet-to-be-fulfilled RBS order was cancelled soon after Goodwin was ousted on 13 October 2008.

Goodwin and his co-directors also had a fleet of 12 chauffeur-driven Mercedes S600 cars at their disposal 24 hours a day. At Goodwin's insistence, each of the top-of-the-range 5.5-litre 493-horsepower V12 limousines was painted in Pantone 281 – the shade of dark blue used in the bank's 'cow's arse' logo. Their leather seats were coloured Pantone 7409, the same amber as the office carpets. According to a *Sunday Times* whistle-blower, whose testimony has gone unchallenged, the bank spent £100,000 a month on part-time chauffeurs, which equates to £9.6 million for the duration of Goodwin's tenure as chief executive. One former insider said there were rumours that the sole reason that Goodwin asked BAA executive Janis Kong on to the RBS board was to organise so-called rapid access privileges at BAA's airports. Whether or not she played any part in it, Goodwin obtained such privileges at

BAA's Edinburgh Airport. His chauffeur-driven Mercedes could go straight through the security gates and on to the airport's apron, taking Fred directly to the steps of the Dassault Falcon 900EX plane, meaning that this titan of global finance could avoid having to do anything so plebeian as to wait in the departure lounge or pass through security scanners. The RBS chief executive is said to have got a particular thrill out of this and was the only person to be accorded such privileges.

RBS also paid for a permanent suite at the Savoy Hotel that Fred Goodwin used whenever he was in London. It came complete with a valet to look after his clothes, all at an estimated annual cost of £700,000. After kids got into his garden to play on the swings, he arranged for round-the-clock security at his home in Edinburgh's leafy Grange district, also at the bank's expense. Whenever he went for meetings outside the bank, Goodwin's flunkies would spend hours on the phone ahead of the event explaining what temperature King Fred liked his mineral water and what sort of snacks would be acceptable. It was said that, if 'rogue pink biscuits' were inadvertently included among the boardroom fare, there was all hell to pay.[18] Obsessed with the accoutrements of wealth and power, Goodwin was becoming increasingly detached from reality and, in playing along with his bizarre obsessions, his subordinates were making things worse.

The next stage on Goodwin's path to exaltation came when his bank unveiled a three-year sponsorship deal with the Williams Formula One motor sport team. The deal was supposed to be about building aware-ness of the RBS brand on the world stage but it also suited Goodwin, who was a noted petrol head. Mark Gallagher, ex-head of commercial affairs at Jaguar Racing, says he had a meeting with Howard Moody, RBS's communications director, and RBS's head of sponsorship David Webb at 280 Bishopsgate in September 2004. The goal was to establish whether the bank might be willing to sponsor Jaguar Racing. At the meeting Moody, who oversaw all public relations and sponsorship for the bank, was unequivocal. He more or less said the bank would only sponsor a Formula One team over his dead body. Gallagher did a double take on 6 January 2005, when he heard that Royal Bank was sponsoring the Williams team. Writing in the industry title *Pitpass*, Gallagher implied corporate governance failings, saying it was clear Goodwin had overruled one of his most senior lieutenants in whose expert view sponsoring F1 would be a waste of money. Gallagher wrote,

'[T]o quote RBS's own advertising campaign, clearly Sir Fred decided to "Make it Happen" and no one was going to stop it.'[19]

The bank unveiled its £28-million-a-year Williams deal at a press conference at 280 Bishopsgate on 6 January 2005. The team's wheelchair-using founder Sir Frank Williams told the conference, 'I'm very pleased. It's fantastic for us and shows that F1 still has a great deal to offer.' Williams added that his team would be under pressure to perform. 'RBS want to see a return on that investment, which means our car spending more time at the top of the grid.'[20] Over the next three and half years, Goodwin, Sir Jackie Stewart (who brokered the deal) and Williams – sporting tartan trews and white short-sleeved shirts emblazoned with the RBS logo – were fixtures at Grands Prix all over the world. As they hobnobbed with celebs and F1 bigwigs like Bernie Ecclestone, the bank's money was being spent like water.

And it wasn't just motor sport that Goodwin lavished RBS's money on. By 2007–08, the bank was spending a phenomenal £200 million a year sponsoring a string of other trophy events including the Six Nations rugby tournament, the NatWest series in cricket and the US and British Opens in golf, alongside its deal with Williams. It was also paying 'global ambassadors', such as the retired golfer Jack Nicklaus and Dunbartonshire-born retired racing driver Sir Jackie Stewart, a reported £3 million a year each to represent the bank at sporting events and be on call to spend time with Goodwin and RBS clients. Both Nicklaus and Stewart had been among his boyhood heroes and he had now effectively bought their friendship. Other 'ambassadors' included showjumper Zara Phillips (the Queen's granddaughter), tennis player Andy Murray and Indian cricketer Sachin Tendulkar. In each case, Goodwin entered into 'reckless' contracts to entertain clients.[21] Astonishingly, Goodwin continued to sign five-year contracts with sporting stars like Tendulkar in the weeks ahead of the bank's collapse. Goodwin also hired Peter Phillips, Zara's brother, in September 2005, to run the bank's sponsorship of the Williams Formula One team. Phillips, aged 27 when he joined the bank, moved to Asia to oversee arrangements at the Asian Grand Prix races. Every time the RBS circus rolled into Monaco for the Grand Prix, the bank spent a phenomenal £250,000 renting a vast apartment with trackside views, which it converted into a hospitality suite for guests on the day of the race.[22]

One former RBS insider said, 'The amounts of money that were wasted on Formula One were shocking. The bank spent about £28 million in the first year of the Williams sponsorship. There was no logic to it at all – it was just a vanity thing for Fred and because he liked motor sport. The tent that was erected for Fred to host a private lunch for five or six guests at the Monaco Grand Prix [in May 2006] cost the bank £37,000. It was just a private lunch that Fred had organised; that was just for the tent – before the food and drink or anything like that had arrived.'

In an opinion piece published on the specialist website Pitpass.com, Formula One expert Mike Lawrence fulminated about the corrosive effect that Goodwin was having on motor sport, turning it into a free-loader's paradise: 'None of the arguments put forward to support an outfit like RBS being in racing actually holds water. There is vague talk of making contacts and doing deals but . . . [a] business deal should make sense on paper, not because someone's had a good day at the races . . .'[23]

'Fred wanted to live like Aristotle Onassis on other people's money,' said one acquaintance. By the first half of 2005, a significant portion of investors in Royal Bank of Scotland had become concerned about Goodwin's megalomaniacal tendencies and were nervous he would blow their money on a deal with Bank of China. Some were also alarmed that the RBS board seemed content to allow Goodwin to run RBS as a personal fiefdom and even as a vanity project. Investors were also concerned about Mathewson's reluctance to engage with them, with some believing he was being insufficiently forceful in his dealings with Goodwin.

Fred was far from alone in liberally spraying shareholders' capital around. After he became chief executive of CBFM, Johnny Cameron had a massive, James Bond villain-style fish tank installed in his office on the first floor of 135 Bishopsgate. Ex-colleagues claim this cost £75,000. The tank became home to exotic fish from around the world, whose geographic origins were meant to reflect RBS's global reach. One ex-senior GBM executive says, 'The fish tank was a classic exam-ple of how Johnny had lost touch with reality. Johnny had no interest in fish at all, except the ones that you eat.' Cameron was afterwards jokingly referred to as 'Cod Cameron' inside 135 Bishopsgate. Some very expensive works of art, whose total value was reputedly £10 million, were also installed in the offices of Cameron, Brian Crowe and Leith Robertson. Robertson was wont to brag that there was a single painting in his office that was worth over £1 million. One ex-colleague said, 'Given Leith's complete lack of interest in art, it was the epitome of outrageous spend.' Cameron also had an executive coach, Christine Fitzpatrick, of PJR Executive Coaching, who ex-colleagues describe as 'ever present' at CBFM/GBM during 2004–07. Fitzpatrick drew from the teachings of the American psychologist Carl Rogers and Swiss psychiatrist Carl Jung to try to galvanise the second son of Cameron of Lochiel and senior members of his investment banking team into raising their game. On her website, Fitzpatrick says her goals are 'to inspire, to motivate and to foster creativity'.[24]

Enter the pharmacist

Under the bank's retirement policy, which had seen Younger remain as chairman until he was 70, Mathewson could theoretically have remained as RBS chairman until his 70th birthday in May 2010. However, the board decided to start casting around for a successor in late 2004, three years after Mathewson became chairman. The bank's non-executives were concerned about the deterioration in Mathewson's relationship with Goodwin. Sir Tom McKillop, the Ayrshire-born chief executive of global pharmaceutical company AstraZeneca, was identified as a strong candidate to succeed him. Born during a German air raid on Irvine in March 1943, McKillop is the son of a coal miner and was brought up in Dreghorn, an ancient village about two miles inland from Irvine. He was educated at Irvine Royal Academy, where he was 'dux', an award given to the most academically gifted pupil in the final year. After a degree and a PhD in chemistry from Glasgow University, McKillop did his post-doctoral studies in Paris, where he was 'exhilarated' to experience the revolutionary fervour of *les événements de 1968* at first hand.[1] He then joined ICI Petrochemicals and Polymers in Runcorn, before transferring to ICI Pharmaceuticals at Alderley Park in Cheshire in 1975, where he was soon managing large teams of pharmaceutical researchers. In 1994, McKillop became inaugural chief executive of Zeneca, after Imperial Chemical Industries demerged and renamed its pharmaceuticals business. He then led this into a merger with Swedish drugs firms Astra to create AstraZeneca in April 1999.

McKillop was due to retire from AstraZeneca during 2005 and was first publicly linked with the RBS chairman's role by *The Times* in February 2005. McKillop also sat on the boards of the oil giant BP, which was chaired by Peter Sutherland (a non-executive director of

RBS since January 2001) and Lloyds TSB. During the second half of 2004, Mathewson, who wanted his successor to be a Scot, approached McKillop to see if he might be interested in taking over as chairman from April 2006. McKillop was also favoured by Sutherland. Over dinner at McKillop's Chelsea flat, Mathewson popped the question, but McKillop told him he had no real interest in becoming the bank's chairman. McKillop had reservations since, after five years at Lloyds and a whole career in the pharmaceuticals business, he was keen to chair a company in a different sector. But Mathewson persevered and, in the end, McKillop was won over when Mathewson played the Scottish card. The Ayrshireman had left Scotland in his twenties and had not lived in or owned a house in Scotland since. His wife Elizabeth was also in favour of him taking the role for this reason. Mathewson said, 'Tom saw it as giving something back to Scotland. People who think Tom was not the right appointment are just being ridiculous. I have a very high regard for Tom – I think he is an outstanding man, I really do.'[2] However, ex-insiders claim that the reason Mathewson wanted McKillop to succeed him was that he was likely to protect his legacy. The other candidates for the role would be more inclined to institute radical change at Royal Bank.

Throughout June and July 2005, there was speculation that McKillop was being lined up for the job and, on 2 August 2005, the bank finally confirmed that the Scot was joining its board as a non-executive director and deputy chairman. The widespread assumption was that McKillop, then 62, would succeed Mathewson as chairman the following year. Despite his strong credentials and his successes at AstraZeneca, investors were far from bowled over. Many in the City snidely suggested that the only reason he had been appointed was because he was Scottish. *The Independent on Sunday*'s City editor Jason Nissé wrote that McKillop was 'low on the City's list of favourites since his company got its drugs pipeline in a twist at the end of last year. The legacy of Sir Tom [at AstraZeneca] may end up being a company that is superb at selling what it has but not great at safeguarding the future.'[3]

On 21 December 2005, RBS confirmed that McKillop would be taking over as the bank's chairman at the annual general meeting on 26 April 2006. In a comment piece published in the *Daily Telegraph* the next morning, business columnist Tom Stevenson summarised the City of London views at the time:

Ever since the former AstraZeneca boss spent a cool half million on RBS shares in September, there was little doubt where his day job would be. Investors will be glad to see the financial incentive because he [has] a serious job to restore RBS to favour in the City. Lionised as it built itself from regional player to global institution, the bank and its beleaguered chief executive Fred Goodwin are finding out how it feels to be yesterday's story . . . Having encouraged RBS in its acquisition-fuelled transformation via the ambitious takeover of NatWest in 2000 and then America's Citizens Financial and a string of 27 smaller deals, investors are now calling on the bank to rein in its growth plans or even to break itself up again . . . Prominent in the new boss's in-tray will be proving to the City that RBS is more than just a deal machine.[4]

18

Fundamentally supine

Senior people at Royal Bank of Scotland were nervous when, some eight years earlier, New Labour gained power in the UK. Memories of the economic chaos of the 1970s and the IMF bailout were hard-wired into some bankers' minds. But one former senior executive told colleagues not to worry. Blair was different. If his government did anything 'really stupid' such as impose a windfall tax on bank profits or raise the upper rate of income tax, it would be crucified by the markets. In a post-Bretton Woods world of free-floating currencies, the executive said, governments were constrained by market disciplines. If Labour introduced aggressively anti-business policies, they would risk an immediate sterling crisis. RBS executives were further reassured when, a year and a half after New Labour came to power, Trade and Industry Secretary Peter Mandelson said he was ' "intensely relaxed" about people getting filthy rich'.[1]

At the Mansion House dinner on 12 June 1997 – a lavish dinner for the City's great and the good – Chancellor Gordon Brown, wearing a lounge suit to emphasise his man-of-the-people credentials, was keen to ram home the message that the economy was in safe hands. He took great pleasure in declaring that the new government was giving the Bank of England its independence so it could set interest rates free from short-term political pressures.

The second announcement – retribution for the Bank of England's failure to forestall the collapses of BCCI, Johnson Matthew Bankers and Barings Bank – went down rather less well. This was that responsibility for bank supervision was being removed from the Bank and put into a new body called the Financial Services Authority. 'Steady' Eddie George, the central bank's governor since 1993, was delighted that the government was giving the Bank its independence but furious about this emasculation of its powers. The moves were formalised under the Bank of England Act 1998.

It had been a long journey for Brown. As an undergraduate at Edinburgh University between 1967 and 1972, he had been a firm believer in old-fashioned socialism, favouring wholesale nationalisation of all sectors of the economy, including banking. In the late '80s, Brown was still singing from the collectivist hymn sheet. In his 1989 book, *Where There Is Greed*, Brown denounced Thatcher's privatisation agenda, accusing her government of facilitating a massive transfer of resources from the poor to the rich. But the general election of 9 April 1992, which Labour leader Neil Kinnock lost to Conservative Prime Minister John Major, was a turning point for Brown and, like the Labour Party itself, he started to ditch his socialist dogma. He was part of a small group of radicals who were determined to refashion Labour as a party that was pro-business and pro-free markets, that invested in public services and which could be trusted to manage Britain in a fiscally prudent manner.

As part of their bid to modernise the party, Tony Blair and Gordon Brown visited Alan Greenspan. With them was Ed Balls, who had left the *Financial Times* to become Brown's economic advisor in 1994. Greenspan, a libertarian disciple of the Russian-born novelist and philosopher Ayn Rand and her philosophy of objectivism, had been chairman of the Federal Reserve since 1987. He welcomed the trio to the Fed in Washington in the autumn of 1994 and endorsed Balls' idea of giving the Bank of England its independence. He endorsed and promoted the notion that an independent central bank should make inflation-targeting the cornerstone of its monetary policy. The owlish Greenspan was impressed by Brown. In his autobiography, Greenspan wrote. 'Brown espoused globalization and free markets and did not seem interested in reversing much of what Thatcher had changed in Britain. The fact that he and Blair had arrived on the doorstep of a renowned defender of capitalism (namely, me) solidified my impressions.' He also reached a judgement on who wore the trousers between Blair and Brown. 'As we exchanged greetings, it appeared to me that Brown was the senior person. Blair stayed in the background while Brown did most of the talking about a "new" Labour.'[2]

Before 1997, British banks were loosely supervised by the UK's central bank, the Bank of England, which subjected them to rule by the 'Governor's eyebrow' (when the top man at the Bank – then the UK's leading financial regulator – raised one eyebrow, it supposedly put the fear of God into bankers). Other parts of the financial services sector were loosely regulated by a mishmash of government departments, commissions and boards, many of which had sprouted up around the time of 'Big Bang'. But by the late 1990s the City of London had changed enormously becoming much faster paced and more international. As Chris Skinner of the Financial Services Club explains: 'London was rocking, with many overseas banks basing themselves in London, the Eurocurrency markets were thriving and electronic trading was growing fast into programme trading, algorithmic trading and high frequency trading. Foreign exchange trading globally grew from half a trillion dollars a day to five trillion a day . . . none of this would have happened if the deregulation of the markets that took place in 1986 hadn't internationalised the London markets, and made them more open to overseas entry and automation.'[3]

Also, 'Big Bang' had given rise to financial conglomerates that straddled a range of financial and market disciplines. By the mid 1990s, RBS had joined their company. The boundaries between different types of financial activity were becoming blurred – securitisation, for example, had blurred the distinction between debt and equity while derivatives, such as credit default swaps, could be classified as either banking or insurance – giving rise to conflicts of interest and scope for regulatory arbitrage.

Brown and his advisors, including Ed Balls and Steve Robson in the Treasury, decided Thatcher's patchwork quilt of regulators would have to go. It had turned out to be a palimpsest of inadequacy, incapable of preventing scams, financial disasters and swindles such as the personal pensions and endowments mis-selling scandals, Robert Maxwell's pillaging of his company's pension funds, the Barlow Clowes affair, the BCCI collapse or the failure of Barings. New Labour wanted to sweep it away and replace it with a single consolidated regulator that would be more in tune with the post-'Big Bang' financial world. And they wanted the new regulator to be 'principles based', not 'rules based'. Step one came five months after the May 1997 election when the Securities and Investments Board was rebranded as the Financial Services Authority (FSA). In stages over the next few years, existing regulators had both their functions and their personnel transferred to the new regulator. In June 1998, the supervisory responsibilities of the Bank of England were transferred to the FSA. The UK Listing Authority, which regulates flotations and was part of the London Stock Exchange, followed in March 2000.

But, as New Labour's Financial Services and Markets Bill wended its way through parliament, concerted lobbying by banks and other financial players ensured that the new regulator had its wings clipped before it had even hatched. The emasculation was happening against a backdrop of widespread faith in the 'Greenspan doctrine', whose tenets included that bankers could be trusted, markets knew best, derivatives and securitisation eliminated risk, an abundance of credit was a necessary good and inflation-targeting by central banks limited volatility – and, of course, that it was impossible for central bankers to either spot or do anything about asset price bubbles.

The biggest bugbear for City types was that the proposed regulator would be too powerful, and accountable to no one. The Conservative peer Lord Jenkin, a former Secretary of State for Industry, complained that the FSA 'will be the most powerful institution created in peacetime Britain. It is in many respects legislator, investigator, prosecutor, judge, jury and executioner.'[4] Others were concerned that the regulator would be able to impose unlimited fines for broad-brush offences such as 'market abuse', opening the door to miscarriages of justice. Arup Daripa, Sandeep Kapur and Stephen Wright, economists at Birkbeck, University of London, wrote, 'In response, numerous amendments were made, essentially diluting the regulatory powers and also inserting checks and balances, arguably lightening further the already announced light touch of regulation.'[5]

The *Daily Telegraph* said the Financial Services and Markets Act (FSMA) was 'a truly baleful piece of legislation that ended up being so overrun with amendments (mostly to correct the Bill's own mistakes and idiocies) that there was no time for sensible debate'.[6] But the most baleful aspect of the FSMA was that it stipulated that the FSA 'must consider the international mobility of the financial business' before taking enforcement action and 'avoid damaging the UK's competitiveness'. As the journalist Nick Cohen has pointed out, this seemed to put bankers above the law. It was a straight line from the Financial Services and Markets Act 2000 being enacted to the FSA being given its statutory powers on 1 December 2001 (dubbed, for no apparent reason, 'N2'). The new agency had five simple objectives:

(a) to maintain confidence in the UK financial system;
(b) to protect and enhance financial stability in the UK;
(c) to promote public understanding of financial services;
(d) to provide appropriate levels of consumer protection;
(e) to reduce the scope for financial crime.

Within that, regulated firms were given eleven principles of business with which they must comply. They should:

(1)   conduct their business with integrity;
(2)   conduct their business with due skill, care, and diligence;
(3)   take reasonable care to organise and control their affairs responsibly with adequate risk-management systems;
(4)   maintain adequate financial resources;
(5)   observe proper standards of market conduct;
(6)   treat customers fairly;
(7)   communicate appropriate information to clients in a clear and fair manner;
(8)   manage conflicts of interest fairly;
(9)   take reasonable care to ensure the suitability of its advice to customers entitled to rely on its judgement;
(10) adequately protect clients' assets when responsible for them;
(11) deal with regulators in an open and cooperative manner.

The FSA was created as a body that was independent of government, whose staff were 'not to be regarded as Crown servants'[7] – a structure which conveniently enabled the government to wash its hands of it should anything go wrong.

Some of the regulator's five goals were contradictory – for example, just imagine if a large financial institution turned out to be riddled with money laundering and fraud. If it was deemed to be of systemic significance, the regulator might be tempted to turn a blind eye, for fear that rooting out the wrongdoing and punishing its perpetrators might harm 'market confidence' and 'financial stability'. Sadly the kneejerk response of the regulator, over its disastrous 14-year life, was invariably to prioritise these objectives over protecting consumers and fighting financial crime. When Rowan Bosworth-Davies, a former regulator who was then a consultant to Unisys, was asked by the Treasury to produce a report on how derivatives might be being abused by money launderers, one of the people he interviewed was a senior FSA official. Asked about the extent to which the FSA intended to use its enhanced prosecutorial powers, the official said, '[Y]ou should understand, because of the difficulties associated with obtaining convictions in the criminal courts, there is no unswerving acceptance of the need for wholesale prosecution powers . . . frankly, Howard Davies [the FSA's first chairman and CEO] has no intention of ending up with the sort of reputation which so bedevilled the SFO [Serious Fraud Office] in its early days. He refuses to be tarred with the same brush as [former SFO directors] Barbara Mills and George Staple.'[8] So, for a range of reasons – including fear of being mocked for failure, fear of destabilising the financial system, the desire to attract business from abroad, etc. – the FSA made an early and deliberate decision to keep the blinkers on.

According to former insiders, it did not help matters that Davies spent much of the early years of his tenure on international lecture tours extolling the virtues of the new 'super' regulator. Another weakness was that the FSA had not been given a competition remit. This was singled out for criticism by Don Cruickshank in his March 2000 review of the British banking sector. In an interview with the author, Cruickshank said New Labour's failure to give the new regulator any powers over competition 'beggars belief'. Actively regulating to prevent the formation of cartels, oligopolies and monopolies is one of the most reliable ways of ensuring that banks behave themselves and customers get a fair deal, Cruickshank said.

Another problem was that the relationships and boundaries between the new regulator, the Bank of England and the Treasury were ill-defined. In the end, important matters fell between the cracks. Sir Steve Robson, Second Permanent Secretary to the Treasury from 1997 to 2001, who was one of the main architects of the so-called tripartite approach, said it did not help that Brown had no real interest in financial regulation.[9] Because Brown ignored it, the best and brightest Treasury civil servants ignored it too.

There were initially high hopes for Brown's system of regulation.[10] In reality, however, even during its long gestation period from 1997 to 2001, the FSA was failing. It was wrong-footed by the collapses of the insurance firms Independent Insurance and Equitable Life. Likewise, after the Labour Transport Secretary Stephen Byers renationalised Railtrack in October 2001, leaving shareholders feeling robbed, the FSA seemed like a rabbit caught in the headlights.

During New Labour's first term in office, Brown brought in a number of policy changes – including slashing capital gains tax on business assets from 40 per cent to 10 per cent – which were welcomed by finance and the City. In April 2002, Brown said, 'Encouraging and democratising wealth creation was an essential driver behind a higher standard of living and the surest guarantee of better public services for all.'[11] Generally, the Labour government could hardly have been more supportive and accommodating of business and finance but there were also policies that went down badly with the financial sector. These included a £5.2 billion windfall tax on privatised utilities and the 'great pensions heist'. The latter involved the scrapping of tax relief on divi-dends paid into pension funds – also known as advanced corporation tax (ACT) relief. It is estimated to have cost £100 billion and is viewed as having killed off workplace pensions in the UK. Brown's decision to sell off the UK's gold reserves on the cheap made him seem particularly inept.

In the early days of the FSA's existence, Goodwin was exercised by the new regulator's anti-money-laundering regulations. At a seminar on social banking, he said, 'The notion that asking people to show pass-ports, gas bills, or anything else before you allow them to open a bank account prevents money laundering is fantasy, it's absolute fantasy.'[12] He stepped up his condemnation after anti-money-laundering legisla-tion was tightened up on both sides of the Atlantic in the wake of the 11 September 2001 terrorist attacks. Speaking at the British Bankers' Association conference in December 2003, he said the regulator was being far too stringent. Perhaps because of Goodwin's contempt for the regulations, RBS was to become a serial offender where inadequate anti-money-laundering controls were concerned, being fined £750,000 in December 2002, £5.6 million in August 2010 and £8.75 million in March 2012 – a total of £15.1 million over a decade. The FSA's March 2012 Final Notice was damning. It inferred that RBS's Coutts subsidi-ary turned a blind eye while drugs barons, deposed dictators, organised criminals and terrorists used the Queen's bank to scrub up their 'dirty' money. Describing Coutts's failings as 'significant, widespread and unacceptable', FSA enforcement director Tracey McDermott said the bank would have to strengthen its controls and ensure its money-laundering reporting officers (MLROs) had sufficient 'robustness' to challenge the firm's private bankers.[13]

Even though Brown made a big show of being pro-free market, he was, for his first five years as chancellor, sceptical about the banking sector. This was why he commissioned Don Cruickshank, the former telecoms regulator, to perform a review of banking services in the UK in November 1998. Cruickshank's hard-hitting report was published on 20 March 2000, three weeks after Royal Bank of Scotland completed its NatWest deal. The report levelled a number of powerful charges at the UK banking sector, the most serious of which was that it was operating a cosy cartel that ran counter to consumer interests. Cruickshank said that four banks – Barclays, HSBC, Lloyds and RBS/NatWest – were making 'super normal profits' of £3–£5 billion a year.[14]

Cruickshank pointed out that the most 'profound competition problems and inefficiencies' were in the area of payment systems.[15] He said there were strong parallels between the monopoly that the large banks enjoyed in payment systems and the gas, electricity or telecoms distribution networks. All were natural monopolies that formed an essential part of the national infrastructure. In the other utilities, however, a regulator monitored prices, service quality and investment, at the same time as ensuring fair access for new market entrants. Nothing like that existed in banking which, Cruickshank said, was wrong. He recommended the launch of a dedicated regulatory agency, Paycom.[16] Given the ability of modern computerised systems to carry out instantaneous transactions, he said it was absurd that banks still took three to five days to clear a cheque (helping themselves to the interest on the customer funds in the interim). He also identified numerous obstacles faced by customers wishing to switch banks.

Cruickshank's other main recommendations and proposals included:

- Banking for businesses was uncompetitive and needed radical change. Some banks should be forced to divest parts of their small-business banking operations, including Royal Bank of Scotland.
- The 'big four' banks' close links to the regulatory establishment raised the prospect of regulatory 'capture'. Changes were required

to ensure the FSA was sufficiently independent from government
and industry pressures.

- The Financial Services Authority should be required to promote
  competition over and above its existing five objectives.
- All too often, concerns about the safety of deposits and the
  soundness of banks were being translated into something close to
  a general decree that banks should not be allowed to fail. This was
  inappropriate.
- Emergency liquidity assistance should never be given to banks
  that are insolvent. A competitive market means banks should be
  allowed to fail.
- Banks needed to be more transparent on risk. The knowledge
  that a firm's regulatory capital-to-assets ratios would be published
  could act as a spur to more prudent management.

None of these proposals saw the light of day. Cruickshank accuses
Treasury civil servants of burying the proposals because they feared
they might interfere with the passage of the FSMA through parliament. And the civil servant Cruickshank has as good as blamed for
this dastardly deed was Sir Steve Robson, who joined the board of the
Royal Bank of Scotland in July 2001, just 16 months after the alleged
suppression of the report.[17] A conspiracy theorist might even argue
that the Edinburgh-based bank was rewarding him for something. The
only aspect of the Cruickshank Report that the government acted on
was that the small business banking market was a virtual monopoly.
It immediately referred this market to the Competition Commission.
Speaking to the Parliamentary Commission on Banking Standards in
October 2012, Cruickshank said the government's failure to act on his
recommendations for a payments regulator meant that a 'decade has
been wasted'. In an interview with the author, Cruickshank said, 'My
one regret is that I was not more strident.'

Two years later, on 14 March 2002, when the Competition
Commission came out with its report into business banking, it said
that the 'big four' banks operated a quasi-monopoly against the
public interest, although it added that the concentration was limited
to England and Wales and was not a problem in Scotland. However,
the Commission's cure – which was behavioural rather than structural
– was doomed to fail, according to Cruickshank. In an interview with

the author, Cruickshank said, 'The Competition Commission ducked the issue. They should have split up the regional and local monopolies.'

The commission's behavioural remedy was to force the 'big four' banks either to pay interest on small and medium-sized firms' current accounts in England and Wales (at Bank of England base rate minus 2.5 per cent) or else to provide small business customers with free banking. Brown said the commission's remedy was an interim measure and gave the banks six months to get their houses in order. He told MPs, 'While we are pro-profit, we are also pro-competition and cannot be on the side of any monopoly or any other behaviour that unfairly restricts competition in markets.'[18] It was one of the last times before October 2008 that he dared criticise the banks.

Even these modest measures were anathema to bankers. Gordon Pell, Royal Bank of Scotland's chief executive of retail banking, was furious. Indeed, he threatened the government with reprisals if it had the audacity to go ahead and impose 'price controls'. He said, 'We're hardly going to fall over ourselves to be helpful now. These extreme left-wing policies are more likely to restrict competition. Brown has had his one day in the sun. Now he'll pay the price as the banks' desire to assist him will be pretty minimal.'[19]

After several major US firms, including Enron and telecoms company WorldCom collapsed as a result of fraud and fraudulent accounting in 2001–02, the government of President George W. Bush reacted with a regulatory crackdown. Under the Sarbanes-Oxley Act, enacted in July 2002, directors who failed to adhere to stringent new accounting and control procedures faced jail. Blair and Brown saw this as an own-goal by the USA – and a fantastic opportunity for Britain. If they lowered the UK regulatory bar further and assured business people of a 'light touch' regime, London could win business from New York and other US centres, especially in areas like initial public offerings (IPOs). In November 2002, HM Treasury's financial sector director Robin Fellgett said that the Treasury saw Sarbanes-Oxley as 'a gift that will go on giving'.[20]

In March 2003, the Blair government indicated what sort of regulator it wanted when it announced that a former Barclays investment banker, Sir Callum McCarthy, was taking over as FSA chairman. To be an effective financial regulator, a degree of cynicism is required but McCarthy – a charming and diffident upper-middle-class former Manchester Grammar schoolboy – was no less bewitched by the finance sector's 'success' than Brown and Blair. The chances of him successfully challenging a top banker like RBS's Goodwin or Barclays' Bob Diamond on something such as the sustainability of their business model were almost zero. On his watch, the FSA succumbed to regulatory capture, not least with the appointment of James Crosby, chief executive of *über*-reckless and out-of-control Edinburgh-based bank HBOS, as a non-executive director in January 2004.

McCarthy and colleagues, like John Tiner, were so focused on making London the destination of choice for international banks and financial institutions and so proud of their 'light touch' approach, that they were blind to malpractice and risky behaviour in the UK banking and finance sector. Under McCarthy, who has barely been criticised for his role in the crisis, the FSA made a number of assumptions. One was that chief executives like Goodwin could be trusted to run their banks with integrity. A second was that it was OK to outsource regulation and responsibility for risk modelling to the banks – in other words, they should be allowed to mark their own homework – although, to an extent, the FSA had to do this because of the Basel capital adequacy regime first introduced in 1988. A third was the belief that guardians like accountants and rating agencies could be relied upon.

Goodwin was a frequent visitor to Ed Balls's Westminster office. He was eager to make sure that any adverse legislation or regulation, whether coming from Brussels or Westminster, would be watered down or seen off. 'Fred was a regular visitor,' Balls told the financial journalist Nick Kochan. 'He always wanted to ensure that we did the right thing for the banks. And he always came to see me rather than Gordon.'[21] Even though the FSA had lowered its guard, Blair and Balls considered it too interventionist. In a speech to the Institute for Public Policy Research in May 2005, Blair said, 'Something is seriously awry when . . . the Financial Services Authority, that was established to provide clear guidelines and rules for the financial services sector and to protect the consumer against the fraudulent, is seen as hugely inhibiting of efficient business by perfectly respectable companies that have never defrauded anyone.'[22] McCarthy leapt to the regulator's defence by boasting about just how lax it was. In a letter to Blair, he bragged about how enforcement proceedings had been cut by two-thirds since

2003. McCarthy also told the premier that the FSA had only six people regulating HSBC whereas there were 30 separate agencies regulating Citigroup in the US. McCarthy, who saw this as a positive, added, 'The thrust of our work in both the wholesale and the retail markets is to make the markets work effectively, and so avoid the need for regulatory intervention.'[23] Speaking in 2005, after a further watering down of its enforcement procedures, McCarthy clarified the position, saying, 'The FSA is not and will never be a disciplinary-led regulator.'[24] It was a slippery slope from adopting this hands-off approach, based on naive faith in the ability of 'the market' to guarantee good behaviour, to wilfully ignoring white-collar crime and high-level City fraud.

Regulators like McCarthy were so focused on enabling London to increase its share of the global market for corporate flotations that they turned a blind eye to the quality of the firms seeking a London listing. Even when oligarch-controlled firms from the former Soviet Union that were known to be dodgy or corrupt sought to sell shares on the London Stock Exchange, the FSA's UK Listing Authority didn't bat an eyelid. The *Guardian*'s financial editor, Nils Pratley, wrote, ' "Come to London, we have tracker funds that are obliged to buy your shares and our market authorities are toothless." That, one assumes, was not the pitch used by the London Stock Exchange and other commercially-minded City firms as they chased fees and flotations in the "Wild East" during the great mining boom. But it might as well have been.'[25] In the eyes of Blair, Brown, the regulators, City bigwigs and investment bankers, it didn't matter if UK-based investors in pension funds, tracker funds etc. were being taken for a ride. After all, drumming up business for the City of London and their fees were all that mattered, were they not?

Thanks to Blair's calculated lowering of the regulatory bar, London became a safe haven for some mind-numbing financial engineering and creative accounting, much of which would have spelt jail terms for its perpetrators in the US. In particular, London was attractive because its regulators permit (yes, they still allow it) infinite re-hypothecation. Theoretically, this means that a borrower such as a hedge fund or an opaque offshore investment vehicle can post the same collateral (physical assets) an infinite number of times as security to raise infinite amounts of borrowed money ('leverage') – and it does not even matter if the underlying assets aren't real. The possibilities are infinite and were a big draw for firms like BNP Paribas, Deutsche Bank, Lehman Brothers,

Merrill Lynch, JPMorgan and UBS when they chose to expand their operations in the City. It was also why London became the Mecca of the global hedge fund industry and the largely unregulated 'shadow' banking sector. Hedge fund assets under management in London's 'Hedge Fund Alley' – an area bordered by Curzon Street and Berkeley Square – grew at a rate of 63 per cent a year over the four years from 2002, reaching $300 billion in 2006.[26] As the financial website Zero Hedge put it, 'In essence, re-hypothecation . . . allows prime brokers to become de facto banks, only completely unregulated and using synthetic assets as collateral . . . In the UK, the epic failure of supervision allowed banks to become de facto monsters of infinite shadow banking fractional reserve leverage – every bank's wet dream!'[27]

Blair, Brown and regulators like McCarthy had created an environment in which financial firms such as RBS were pretty much above the law, where they could ignore financial gravity and swell their balance sheets on an endless tide of liquidity.

Another American firm that was persuaded to bulk up its operations in London was American International Group (AIG). It chose to locate and expand its AIG Financial Products (AIGFP) in London. The unit, led by Brooklyn-born Joe Cassano, was the poster child of excess in the global credit boom, issuing $2.7 trillion of credit-default swaps (a form of unregulated insurance on loans going sour) on humungous piles of American mortgage debt. The problem was AIGFP didn't really understand what it was doing and had insufficient collateral to honour its pledges after counterparties started to claim on their 'policies' when the US subprime market started to implode in October 2006. Whereas individual traders in individual banks, however risky or hare-brained their activities, would struggle to bring down the entire financial system, AIG – thanks partly to the negligence of the FSA and other supposed regulators – came close. Cassano and his greed-crazed colleagues put the global financial system in danger by taking risks they didn't understand and couldn't quantify. In the end, AIGFP's parent group AIG needed a $182-billion taxpayer-funded bailout in October 2008, without which many of its clients – mainly banks, including RBS – would have gone bust. It was little wonder the insurance giant became the subject of a protest song, by West Country 'acoustic roots' band Show of Hands, titled 'Arrogance, Ignorance and Greed'.

In a leaked memo, one former FSA senior executive revealed that, between 2003 and 2008, mid-ranking FSA staff were, for the most part, incompetent, poorly qualified and of too low a calibre to have any chance of properly regulating the financial services sector. Others were too lazy and complacent to bother checking up on what financial firms were doing. He said that none had the influence or the inclination to challenge the pervading 'light-touch laissez-faire regulation'. The ex-senior executive at the FSA wrote, 'Low calibre FSA management is perhaps the single biggest factor in this disaster . . . A culture of apathy and complacency marked the FSA in the period of its nadir, with anyone standing up against the official "light touch" policy criticized for rocking the boat and branded a troublemaker. In consequence many talented and conscientious people retired or left for the private sector. FSA supervision was hollowed out and its depleted ranks were staffed with mediocre people who cared little about the business of supervising firms.'[28]

However, the FSA wasn't wholly deaf, dumb and blind to City wrongdoing ahead of the crisis. The FSA division established in May 2004 to regulate the wholesale and institutional markets, initially led by former Credit Suisse investment banker Hector Sants, did sound the alarm about the accumulations of risk in both the hedge fund and private equity sectors between 2005 and 2007. It also sought to address insider trading by investment banks ahead of takeover announcements and sought to tackle so-called 'soft' commissions. Sants' division fined the hedge fund manager Philippe Jabre and his firm GLG Partners £750,000 each for market abuse, Deutsche Bank £6.4 million for misconduct in the handling of shares, Citigroup £13.9 million for a flawed bond trading strategy and Royal Dutch/Shell Group £17 million for overstating oil reserves. But there was a degree of tokenism to this. This was especially true when the FSA tried to stand up to the private equity juggernaut – at that point Sants seemed like the mouse that roared. And his division totally missed – or ignored – the widespread rigging of benchmarks and indices such as Libor until it was pushed into action as a result of an American inquiry.

In the retail space, the regulator's handling of the split-cap investment trust scandal of 2000–02 – which cost 50,000 investors some £700 million – was embarrassing. The FSA's retail division did fine Royal Scottish Assurance (RSA), a joint venture between Royal Bank and Edinburgh-based insurer Scottish Equitable, the then record sum of £2 million for 'serious deficiencies' in the handling of a flexible mortgage plan endowment policy between 1990 and 1994. The scandal prompted the *Daily Record* to delve into RSA chairman Benny Higgins's past. The Scottish tabloid newspaper came up with a story headlined 'Sex cheat insurance boss does to 30,000 customers what he did to his best mate; high-finance figure ran off with friend's wife'.[29] The FSA also fined RBS for breaches of anti-money-laundering regulations on three separate occasions.

During 2004, the regulator's records show it was concerned that Fred Goodwin was treating it in a high-handed and contemptuous manner. However, it failed to address the situation. The regulator's obsession with the peccadilloes of small-time intermediaries, such as brokers and independent financial advisors (IFAs), and with meaningless slogans such as 'treating customers fairly' was one reason it took its eye off the ball. Generally, it had a habit of raising the alarm about something – such as inadequate controls in HBOS corporate or a tyrannical boss at Royal Bank of Scotland or banks failing to segregate customers' assets from other assets in their treasury departments – but then failing to follow through.

Even when it was presented with irrevocable evidence of bankers' wrongdoing the FSA refused to act. When alerted to serious wrongdoing at banks like RBS and HBOS between 2004 and 2007, the FSA dismissed complaints by saying it 'did not investigate business models'. And clearly its top people remained delusional about the sort of people who were running the banks even after the crash had started. Speaking at an industry conference in November 2007, FSA chief executive Hector Sants said, 'I firmly believe the vast majority of firms are run by decent, honest people.'[30]

By the end of his tenure as chancellor, Brown was so besotted by the City – and the tax revenues it seemed capable of generating – that he had become blind to its flaws. (For the record, he claims to have been 'misled' by RBS.[31]) In his June 2005 Mansion House speech, Brown paid homage to a room full of black-tie-wearing City types, praising their 'unique innovative skills, [their] courage and steadfastness', before giving them heartfelt thanks 'for the outstanding, the invaluable contribution [they] make to the prosperity of Britain'. In his final Mansion House speech in June 2007, a few days before he succeeded Tony Blair as prime minister and even as the banking and financial world teetered on the brink of implosion, Brown positively genuflected to the bankers. He congratulated himself for 'resisting pressure' to toughen up the regulation of their activities. Thanks to the bankers' brilliant ingenuity and remarkable achievements, he said, Britain was living in 'an era that history will record as the beginning of a new Golden Age'. Economic Secretary to the Treasury Ed Balls was no less unctuous towards the banking fraternity. Speaking in 2006, Balls said it was 'essential' that banks should make turbocharged profits, adding, 'My starting point, as a Treasury minister, is this: "What more can I do – can we do together – to support and enhance the critical role that the banking industry plays in our economy?"'[32] Even as late as May 2007, Balls was championing the rights of bankers to do as they chose and insisting government's main role was to reduce regulatory interference even though it was already clear to many others that the fraud-based global credit bubble had burst. Speaking to a committee of the House of Lords that month, Balls praised the FSA from the rooftops for its lightness of touch, saying, 'It is very unusual . . . to be a government minister who is able to say with credibility on a public platform that the UK system of regulation is a substantial competitive advantage to the British economy, but you can absolutely say that in the case of the financial services industry.'[33] He added that the FSA's approach 'gives the financial services sector the ability to innovate and to be flexible [and] is a big competitive strength for us, but we always need to be mindful of the need to reduce the burdens where we can'.[34]

Tony Blair, described by some commentators as economically illiterate, went further even than Balls. He basically didn't see the point of financial regulation, believing bankers should be left to their own devices – which is pretty much what happened during his ten years in power. As long as tax revenues kept flowing into the Treasury's coffers, he didn't see the point in asking how it was made.[35] The political commentator Andrew Rawnsley recalls how Blair, when addressing some investment bankers towards the end of his premiership, said, 'I've taken the view all my time in office that you people should be left to get on with making money for yourselves.' Then, after a pause, he added, 'And the country.'[36] Having created a lax regulatory framework that was immensely favourable to banks, Blair's own reward included a £3.21-million-a-year part-time role as senior advisor to JPMorgan Chase chief executive Jamie Dimon six months after leaving 10 Downing Street.

To make matters worse, Bank of England governor Sir Mervyn King – more of an academic economist than a markets man – wasn't particularly interested in systemic risk, even though monitoring this was supposed to be the Bank's responsibility. In a revised memorandum of understanding (MoU) dated March 2006, responsibility for financial stability was passed from the Bank of England to a so-called 'Tripartite Standing Committee' made up of the chancellor, the Bank of England governor and the FSA chairman. King says, 'Many people feel that that wasn't terribly satisfactory as an arrangement, in large part because the tripartite had no direct responsibilities. Each of the players had their own responsibilities.'[37] After that, there was little chance of anyone in high office having a long hard look at the sustainability of the system. And, although maintaining financial stability was one of its objectives, the FSA turned a blind eye too. In its report into the collapse of RBS, the regulator said, 'It is noticeable that, during the period between January 2006 and July 2007, of the major topics discussed at the FSA board, only one out of 61 related in some way to bank prudential risks and issues.'[38]

The touchstone of New Labour's delusional thinking about banking and finance was the 'Greenspan doctrine' and the ideology had permeated every corner of the Bank of England, the Treasury, the FSA and Whitehall.

As Andrew Rawnsley writes, 'Not only had they [the bankers] convinced themselves that they were close to being gods, but their huge wealth and deceptive success dazzled politicians, who were beguiled by the myths of unrestrained markets, ever-rising asset prices and endless growth.'[40] Sir Nicholas Macpherson, a former employee of KPMG, one of the 'big four' firms of accountants, remains Permanent Secretary to the Treasury despite his role in fuelling the crisis. Speaking to the House of Commons Public Accounts Committee in September 2012, Macpherson admitted, 'There was a monumental collective failure of which the Treasury was part.'[41]

Three pillars of ignorance

Since 1930, Basel, on the banks of the Rhine in north-west Switzerland, has played host to the Bank for International Settlements (BIS), the so-called 'central bankers' central bank'. At first, BIS provided gold storage facilities and an international clearing house for war reparations but today its main aim is to underpin monetary and financial stability by fostering cooperation between the world's central banks. At the time of writing, Bank of England Governor Mark Carney and Deputy Governor Paul Tucker are both on its 19-strong board of directors, which is currently chaired by Banque de France Governor Christian Noyer. In the wake of the turbulence unleashed by the scrapping of Bretton Woods in 1971, the central banks of the Group of Ten nations decided to augment BIS by establishing a parallel organisation, the Basel Committee on Banking Supervision (BCBS), to set standards for bank supervision, risk-based capital and disclosure requirements for banks operating internationally. Established in 1974, the committee is made up of 42 governors of central banks and chief executives of financial regulators from 27 countries. It meets four times a year.

One of the committee's primary roles is to devise and promote the use of common standards and ratios of capital adequacy by banks and regulators worldwide in order to make banks safer. In particular, it crafts frameworks and formulae to ensure that banks have sufficient capital as a buffer to absorb losses in order to ensure they can survive an economic crisis, when borrowers are likely to default on their loans. For large international banks such as Royal Bank of Scotland, the Basel committee's deliberations are more important than virtually anything laid down by the FSA.

Despite the critical nature of its activities for global economic prosperity, the Basel committee operates like a conclave of cardinals in that its deliberations take place behind closed doors and outwith public scrutiny. Whereas news and media organisations will pore over the minutiae of, say, child benefit cuts in Westminster, the composition and the machinations of the Basel committee are rarely, if ever, mentioned – except by economics columnists and financial anoraks. Yet, between 1988 and 2008, this organisation introduced a series of policies that were highly favourable to the short-term interests of banks but disastrous for the rest of us.

You have to wind the clock back to the late 1980s to understand this. In 1988, the Basel committee introduced Basel I – also known as the Basel Accord – its first stab at putting together a framework for the capital adequacy of international banks. Basel I required banks to have a minimum capital-to-risk-weighted-assets ratio of 8 per cent – meaning that, for every $100 million of 'risk-weighted' loans, a bank needed to have at least $8 million of capital. Banks were expected to divide up their portfolios of loans into four 'risk buckets', each with a different 'risk weight'. The riskiest loans, including loans to corporates, were given a risk weight of 100 per cent – meaning the full value of the loan was considered to be risk-weighted. Mortgages were given a risk weight of 50 per cent or half of 8 per cent, which meant a $100-million portfolio required $4 million of capital. Supposedly risk-free assets, such as UK gilts or Thai or US government bonds, went into the 'risk-free' bucket and required no capital underpinning. The framework was gradually rolled out around the world to all countries with internationally active banks.

The Bank of England's executive director for financial stability, Andy Haldane, says that computing a regulatory capital ratio under Basel I 'involved little more than half a dozen calculations which could be conducted on the back of a small envelope by a competent clerk'.[1] He adds that the transparent and verifiable rules were easily applied with regulatory rules (Pillar I) providing a platform for supervisory discretion by regulators (Pillar II) and market discipline by investors (Pillar III). Haldane added, 'The Basel pillars were mutually reinforcing.'[2]

However, there were weaknesses – not least that the 'risk buckets' were so broad. *The Economist* explains, 'Banks [were] penalised no more for making loans to a fly-by-night software company in Thailand than to Microsoft; no more for loans to South Korea, bailed out by the IMF in 1998, than to Switzerland. In addition, bankers developed complex ways to distance themselves from the risk attached to the loans that they make.'[3] Basel I was having dangerous side effects – for example, it was persuading banks to lend in ways that reduced their capital requirement rather than because it made any business sense.

Since capital is expensive and having a lot of it is seen by some bankers as dampening profits and executive bonuses, the rules gave banks a powerful incentive to shift their riskier loans off their balance sheets and into opaque and barely-regulated off-balance-sheet vehicles like structured investment vehicles (SIVs), collateralised debt obligations (CDOs), collateralised loan obligations (CLOs), conduits etc. – a development which, by the way, only became possible thanks to the rise of powerful information technology. The Basel rules also gave banks an incentive to abuse derivatives and to shuffle assets between their banking books and trading books in order to bamboozle regulators and further minimise capital requirements.[4] The zero-risk weighting applied to certain assets also fuelled the madness of crowds, encouraging banks to pile into assets which were regarded as safe but which might readily be rendered unsafe by the sheer force of demand.

By the mid 1990s, banks were increasingly adopting a technique called Value at Risk (VaR) to give themselves a snapshot of how safe their portfolios of loans and other activities were. VaR models the historic correlations and volatilities of different assets in a portfolio, crunches the numbers and conveniently delivers a single number – for example, 99 per cent of the time, a given portfolio with $100 million of assets will have a maximum expected loss of $5 million over the course of a month. Despite known flaws, VaR became the touchstone for risk assessment in global banking. It caught on with bank managements and, indeed, regulators for four main reasons:

(1)   it was invented and promoted by JPMorgan, one of Wall Street's most respected names;
(2)   it was relatively simple to use;
(3)   it produced a maximum expected loss, expressed in dollar terms;
(4)   it provided a useful comfort blanket for bank chief risk officers, finance directors, chief executives and regulators.

The Basel committee was so impressed, it embedded the yardstick into the Basel I capital accord.

The committee's decision was surprising, not least because of the powerful voices that were ranged against it. In 1997, Nassim Nicholas Taleb, a Lebanese-American author, trader and financial risk expert, said VaR's weaknesses were legion and included the fact that it could not handle 'black swan' events (events that are completely unexpected at the time they occur), it gave false comfort to the directors of banks and it would be arbitraged by traders. Taleb said, 'Banks have the ingrained habit of plunging headlong into mistakes together where blame-minimizing managers appear to feel comfortable making blunders so long as their competitors are making the same ones . . . It can be safely pronounced plain charlatanism.'[5] Writing in 2001, members of the Financial Markets Group at the London School of Economics warned that dependence on VaR would 'destabilise and induce crashes when they would not otherwise occur'.[6]

Yves Smith, author of *ECONned* and a former executive at Goldman Sachs and McKinsey, says, 'This is classic drunk man under the street light behaviour . . . Despite its fundamental failings, VaR has become the lingua franca of risk management. It enables managers and regulators who are often not quantitatively very savvy to labour under the delusion that they have a handle on an organisation's exposures.'[7]

In view of the pace with which banking was evolving and particularly the emergence of diversified 'universal banks' and 'bulge bracket' firms during the mid to late 1990s, Basel I was becoming increasingly outmoded. US banks also favoured a revised Basel Accord that would make it easier for them to dominate the international stage. Yalman Onaran, a US-based senior writer at *Bloomberg News* and the author of *Zombie Banks*, says the committee was pushed to introduce the new rules by US banks eager to punch above their capital weight. 'Basel II, approved in 2004, was pushed by US lenders that wanted to expand further without having to worry about capital restrictions, according to bankers, lawyers, lobbyists and regulators involved in the discussions,' wrote Onaran. 'They persuaded the Fed that their own risk-management systems had become so sophisticated they could better determine themselves how much capital was needed.'[8] This was, of course, a massive and self-serving lie.

The revised Basel II capital adequacy framework was launched on

26 June 2004 and gradually rolled out around the world over the course of the next five years. It had three so-called pillars:

(1)   minimum capital requirements (which refined and expanded on the Basel I rules);
(2)   supervisory or regulatory review of banks' internal assessment process and capital adequacy;
(3)   effective use of disclosure to strengthen market discipline as a complement to supervisory efforts.

The hope was that three pillars would be stronger than one.

Under the Basel II framework, banks were still required to maintain capital equivalent to 8 per cent of their risk-weighted assets (so $8 of capital for every $100 worth of fully risk-weighted assets) but capital was divided into two tiers or layers. Tier-1 capital, the portion with the greatest loss absorbency, was intended to be a pre-insolvency buffer and could be made up of shareholders' funds topped up with retained earnings. Tier-2 capital – intended to be used to absorb losses in the event of a bank going bust or prior to depositors losing money – could basically be made up of any old rubbish. It could include a wider range of financial instruments, including preference shares, subordinated debt, hybrid instruments and even 'deferred tax assets'.[9] What the Basel committee failed to predict was that the value of some of these 'assets' would deteriorate sharply in a downturn. In the event of a financial crisis, they turned out to be about as much use as a chocolate teapot, fatally compromising some banks' ability to survive.

Even before the revised framework was introduced, powerful voices were warning it would lead to economic Armageddon. Charles Goodhart, Jon Danielsson and Hyun Song Shin of the London School of Economics, together with four other academics, published a paper in May 2001, warning that Basel II was too dependent on the opinions of credit rating agencies, which were unregulated and unreliable. They said, 'In so far as the purpose of financial regulation is to reduce the likelihood of systemic crisis, these proposals will actually tend to negate, not promote this useful purpose.'[10]

Royal Bank of Scotland's chairman George Mathewson also sounded the alarm before Basel II was published. In a speech to an industry conference in Brussels in March 2003, Mathewson said Basel

II was an accident waiting to happen and that its very complexity would restrict the ability of banks to manage their risks, the ability of supervisors to supervise and the capacity of markets to evolve and adapt. 'These are not trivial flaws,' he said.[11] He warned that 'Basel II would tempt unscrupulous banks to fiddle their internal estimates, especially if their commercial ambitions were constrained by tight ratios'.[12] He also warned that regulators would struggle to police the new system. Mathewson said the banking industry and the regulators should go back to the drawing board. Mathewson said, 'The root cause of our concerns lies in the complexity of the proposals. We believe those concerns are widely shared amongst our supervisory colleagues . . . In summary Basel II risks being too much, too fast. Adopting a more evolutionary approach is in all of our interests.'[13] But the Basel committee had passed the point of no return.

Long before June 2003, banks were finding ways around the new capital framework by transferring the ownership of their higher risk loans – including corporate loans, credit card loans, car loans, equity release loans and residential mortgages – to off-balance-sheet vehicles domiciled in tax havens. Basel was spurring banks to move into a fast-moving world of 'originate and distribute', securitisation and shadow banking in which the reduction of perceived credit risk and the avoidance of tax came to be seen as the keys to banking success. Bankers were also piling into credit insurance, via things like credit default swaps, to 'credit enhance' really stinky loans and make them look like good ones. The goal was to minimise the amount of regulatory capital they needed to maintain, thereby leveraging their balance sheet, bolstering profitability and maximising executive bonuses. The trouble was, though, that the credit risk was being pushed out to institutions that barely understood it. 'Bank regulators patted themselves on the back and said, "Look – we've made banks safer." But they've only done so by making other parts of the system weaker,' says Avinash Persaud, chairman of London-based liquidity advisory firm Intelligence Capital.[14]

The Bank of England's Haldane says Basel II's second and third pillars – supervisory oversight and investor oversight – effectively fell over on day one because everything was so opaque. 'To illustrate, consider the position of a large, representative bank using an advanced internal set of models to calibrate capital. Its number of risk buckets has increased from around seven under Basel I to, on a conservative estimate, over 200,000 under Basel II. To determine the regulatory capital ratio of this bank, the number of calculations has risen from single figures to over 200 million. The quant and the computer have displaced the clerk and the envelope. At one level, this is technical progress; it is the appliance of science to risk management. But there are costs. Given such complexity, it has become increasingly difficult for regulators and market participants to vouch for the accuracy of reported capital ratios. They are no longer easily verifiable or transparent. . . . For what the market cannot observe, it is unlikely to be able to exercise discipline over. And what the regulator cannot verify, it is unlikely to be able to exercise supervision over.'[15]

To their delight, bankers had created a system that enabled them to deploy sophisticated arrays of smoke and mirrors to deceive investors, regulators, depositors, politicians and just about everyone else.

The author of the UK's 2000 review into the banking sector, Don Cruickshank, believes that Basel II was the prime cause of the global financial crisis and that it was a dereliction of duty for politicians to allow the bankers to write their own rules. 'In Basel II, we effectively let the banks decide what risk meant, and their balance sheets broadly doubled in about six years,' said Cruickshank. 'I have not dug into the process; all I would observe is that the rules that emerged from that process were written in a way that enabled banks to deliver the very high leverage ratios which brought about the collapse of banks including RBS and HBOS in 2008.'[16]

All-American boy

In April 2000, Larry Fish flew from New England to Edinburgh for a board meeting. Inside his attaché case, the 55-year-old American banker had the details of a plan to acquire yet another US bank. He was seeking board approval for the deal and assumed this would be a formality. In the eight years he'd been with RBS, during which he had been buying up banks at the pace of about two a year, he had enjoyed an unusual amount of autonomy and had never been challenged over a deal. He was, therefore, taken aback when Goodwin, who had just taken over as chief executive, said, 'I don't like it.' Fred's response may have been motivated by a desire to bring Fish, a man not known for his humility, down a peg or two. After an embarrassed silence, the room emptied, leaving Goodwin and the American alone in the conference room. After some time, they re-emerged, having agreed to a revised structure. Fish then went back to the US to renegotiate the acquisition on Fred's terms.

When he first joined Citizens Financial in April 1992, three years after RBS bought it, Fish negotiated a wildly generous pay package. It included a long-term phantom share options scheme, a cash-based long-term incentive plan, a short-term discretionary annual bonus, three different defined-benefit pension plans, a plain vanilla share options scheme and, of course, an additional value shares scheme. This delivered a jackpot for Fish in 2000. The chairman, president and chief executive of Citizens Financial was paid a total of £17 million that year. Although modest compared to the pay of some American bank bosses, it was eight times Goodwin's annual pay of £2 million and was causing ructions internally. In his early days at the bank, before the NatWest takeover, colleagues told Goodwin that something was going to have to be done about Fish's pay – given that their divisions were generating more profit, it was just wrong that he was earning up to eight times what they were. Goodwin told colleagues, 'Leave this to me. I'll sort it out.' And he promptly flew to New England to pressure Fish into taking a pay cut. But Fish ran rings around the deputy chief executive. One ex-colleague said, 'It was an abject failure. Fred came back having given away even more of the ranch.'

Under Fish's predecessor, George Graboys, Citizens had been a small-scale consolidator of other thrifts and was reasonably effective at acquisition-led growth. Paying largely in cash from the Royal Bank of Scotland's own reserves, Fish pursued a similar policy, taking over fifteen other banks in eight years. These included the branch banking business of Boston-based State Street, Massachusetts-based UST and Manchester-based New Hampshire. In each case, the acquired bank was quickly rebranded as Citizens, with its back-office functions (cheque clearing, information technology etc.) stripped out into centralised processing centres across the north-east of the United States.

Fish, born in Chicago in 1944, originally intended to become a journalist. His first job in banking was with Bank of Boston in Brazil in 1974. From 1978, he ran Bank of Boston's Japanese operations. While in Japan, he met Japanese-born Atsuko Toko on a blind date. They fell in love and the couple later married. Fish returned to the Bank of Boston's head office in 1983, eventually reaching board level and running all of Bank of Boston's banking operations across New England. He followed this with a somewhat inglorious stint as president of the Los Angeles-based Columbia Savings and Loan (CS&L), which collapsed in the early 1990s. Fish was president and chief operating officer of Columbia Savings and Loan for 17 months until he resigned in August 1989. Fifteen months after Fish's departure, CS&L had to be rescued by the American government's Office of Thrift Supervision.

Fish moved on to become chief executive of another struggling institution, Boston-based Bank of New England, which was near bust as a result of reckless lending to the commercial real estate sector. He hacked down the balance sheet by disposing of several businesses, including one banking subsidiary – Rhode Island-based Old Colony – that was sold to Citizens. In spite of Fish's attempts to turn the Bank of New England around, it ended up being rescued by the Federal Deposit Insurance Corporation in January 1991. An uncharitable view would be that Fish had presided over two bank failures in the three years before being hired by Graboys and Mathewson. A more charitable one would be that Fish was a company doctor whose patients were too far gone before his arrival. One ex-RBS insider says, 'At the very least, that raises questions about his competence. The fact that he airbrushed the Columbia Savings and Loan role from his CV raises a few questions.'

Bank takeovers, especially so-called 'friendly' deals, are an advanced form of courtship. They can take months, if not years, of delicate manoeuvring to reach a climax. They require a fair amount of patience, guile, tact and diplomacy, particularly from the suitor institution. Given the egotism and volatility of many bank chief executives, the process can resemble walking on eggshells. Citizens' $2.1-billion (£1.4-billion) acquisition of the retail banking operations of Mellon Financial was no exception. Fish first approached Martin ('Marty') McGuinn, chief executive of Pittsburgh-based Mellon about a possible deal in 1999, not long after Mellon acquired RBS's asset-management business. Fish was persistent, calling McGuinn every three or four months and saying 'I'm still here'. On 26 May 2001, McGuinn took the hint and travelled north to Fish's Boston office to discuss a possible deal. He said that as long as Fish would take all of Mellon's 345 branches (which were in Pennsylvania, Delaware, New Jersey and Virginia), and all their customers and staff and paid a reasonable price, he would have a deal – and McGuinn would eschew touting the package around other potential purchasers. One of the advantages of an 'exclusive' deal was secrecy – it was less likely to leak out before it was ready and would, therefore, be less destabilising to customers and staff. However, attempts at keeping the deal under wraps failed and *The Boston Globe*, broke the story on 6 July 2001. The news sent RBS shares down 6.5 per cent to 1504p – indicating investors were sceptical. When the deal was confirmed via official announcements from RBS and Citizens on 18 July, rival banks were quick to knock it. Pittsburgh-based PNC Financial Services even ran ads featuring Scotsmen in kilts headlined 'You're better off at PNC', accompanied by a yellow badge reading 'Mellon customers click here'. The ads asked, 'Do Pennsylvanians want to have their loans approved in Edinburgh?'

RBS's investment banks, Merrill Lynch and UBS Warburg, ran a record-breaking 'book-running' exercise, codenamed 'Monet', in which 250 equity sales staff from the two banks persuaded existing RBS investors to throw $2.1 billion into the bank's shares. Thanks to the 'halo effect' arising from NatWest takeover, plus strong 2000 results, RBS was, at the time, seen as a bank that could do no wrong. Merrill Lynch's Rupert Hume-Kendall said, 'For a company that is as careful and scrutinising as RBS, the accelerated tender was a swashbuckling structure.'[1] Fish was no slouch – he was a schmoozer, a consummate networker and a major donor to the Democrats. One of Fish's greatest talents was that he successfully combined growth by acquisition with a deft marketing touch that enabled Citizens to retain the look and feel of a local community institution. Within weeks of taking over another bank, Fish aimed to have purged it of its former identity, rebranded its branches as Citizens Bank and introduced Citizens' iron-fist-in-a-velvet-glove sales ethos.

According to Peter Panepento, writing in the *Erie Times-News*, the difference between Mellon Bank and Citizens could be measured in lollipops and dog biscuits. 'Citizens' tellers handed out about 5.1 million suckers and 288,800 dog treats to customers at its 330 New England bank branches in 2000, according to its annual report. Mellon's total during the same time period? Zero.'[2] Fish's approach to wooing customers worked in the four states it entered through the Mellon deal. According to *The Philadelphia Inquirer*, the bank 'waged a canny, relentless, but low-key ad campaign portraying its products as simple alternatives to the bewildering menu that confronted borrowers at other large banks. Citizens gained market share . . . to become the region's second-largest bank ranked by deposits . . . Most spectacular, Citizens pledged $95 million, over the next 25 years, for naming rights and advertising guarantees to the Phillies' new stadium in South Philadelphia.'[3]

Fish's track record for acquiring and integrating banks was so strong the bank's Edinburgh head office just let him get on with it. One former RBS executive director said, 'Larry was likeable enough, a genial person, but he was full of bullshit. He took American-ism to an extreme.' In its annual report, Citizens Financial outlined its ethos as: 'Hug the customer. Smile. Say thank you. Return phone calls and e-mails in a timely manner. Do whatever you can every day, in every way, to provide world-class service. Consistently exceed customer expectations. Always honor our commitment to customers . . . The environment will be extraordinarily caring, like an extension of your own family.'[4]

After Mellon, rapid expansion in the United States bordered on an obsession for Goodwin. He no longer wanted Fish to just do small-scale 'buy-and-build' deals. He wanted big deals along the lines of Mellon – large regional franchises that took Citizens beyond its New England heartland. Goodwin had a number of reasons for prioritising US growth. One was that on 10 July 2001, Labour's Trade and Industry Secretary, Patricia Hewitt, blocked Lloyds TSB's attempts to make an £18-billion takeover of Abbey National. This killed off the prospect of large mergers and acquisitions in UK banking. Secondly, Goodwin recognised that the acquisition of a large continental European bank like Commerzbank would be a non-starter, partly because European labour laws meant that compensating sacked workers was prohibitively expensive and 'synergies' would be minimal. Thirdly, the City's voracious demands for earnings-per-share growth meant the RBS board thought acquisition-led growth was the only realistic option. A fourth reason was the scale of the consolidation opportunity. The American banking market was highly fragmented compared to most European banking markets, with thousands of local players and only a handful of national brands. Fifthly, acquiring banks in the United States was relatively painless from a regulatory perspective, and sacking people was relatively easy. Sixthly, Goodwin loved the United States. In an interview with Bloomberg, Goodwin said, 'It's large, it's well-ordered, there's prosperity. And we speak the same language – or almost.'[5] He liked its classlessness and the way that financial success was fêted.

One former senior colleague recalls how Goodwin became increasingly obsessed by America: 'Fred was dazzled by the US and the business opportunities he saw there. I remember him talking about the amount of money that people earn in the States. And there was a time when, if a big US bank had approached him, I believe he would have gone off and joined it.' Whenever Goodwin visited the US, Fish stroked Fred's ego and kept him busy. One ex-colleague said: 'Larry was forever blowing smoke up Fred's arse. Larry would avoid having Fred participate in deep and meaningful budget review meetings by fixing up for him to meet the Mayor of Chicago or showing him how wonderful the Citizens branches were. Fred really enjoyed it.' Citizens executives had been warned that Goodwin was cold, aloof and not very nice so they were surprised that, when he came to America, he was generally friendly and open.

Yet, even though Fred, Joyce, John and Honor Goodwin spent a three-week summer holiday in Cape Cod – where Larry and Atsuko Fish had a holiday home – Fish's relations with Goodwin were never as good as they had been with Mathewson. One source of disquiet was that Fred thought Citizens was too autonomous. Another was that Goodwin wanted the US arm to sport RBS's dark blue livery and 'daisywheel' logo while Fish preferred to stick with the well-known Citizens 'C' on a green background. He knew that overtly foreign banks are mistrusted in the US. Another difference of opinion was over corporate banking. Having had his fingers burnt with corporate and commercial property loans at Bank of New England, Fish preferred to give corporate banking a wide berth. This made it hard for Goodwin and colleagues like Iain Robertson to build a corporate banking business in the United States. Fish was also renowned for his arrogance.

The Citizens Financial board had seven non-executive directors on it. During a board meeting some time during 2005, Fish sent the other executive directors, including Tom Hollister, Brad Kopp and Stephen Steinour, out of the room, claiming he wanted to have a deep and meaningful discussion with the non-executives, who included Fred Goodwin and Edmond English, former chief executive of the TJX Companies. According to an RBS non-executive director who was present, Fish then told the non-executives, 'There's this really important matter that I would like your advice on. What do you think I should do when everything is going so well? I mean everything's going fantastically well at the moment and this is a matter of concern to me – what do you think I should be doing differently?' There was a long pause and muffled sniggers among the non-executive directors. Eventually one of them said, 'The most important thing, Larry, is that you *show some humility.*' Fish purposefully got out a pencil and wrote 'HUMILITY' on his pad. He then said, 'Thank you very, very much – that's extremely helpful of you. I think we could have the executives back now.'

Tempted by the spectacular financial rewards that running a larger bank would bring and shielded from direct shareholder scrutiny, Fish developed some bad habits. One was overpaying for deals. Richard 'Dick' Bove, an analyst at the San Francisco-based investment bank Hoefer & Arnett, said Royal Bank of Scotland was, in 2003, willing to buy anything that moved. Bove told *CFO Europe* magazine that the bank would buy 'almost any bank in the whole of the north-eastern portion of the country'.[6] And, according to figures from SNL Financial, Citizens' takeovers of the retail banking arms of State Street, in May 1999, and Mellon Financial, in July 2001, were two of the US's three most expensive bank takeovers, in terms of price-to-'book value', in the five years to 2003.[7]

Fish was eyeing an $8-billion takeover of Boston-based Sovereign Bancorp during the autumn of 2003. Rumours about a deal along these lines sparked investor unease since such an acquisition could have massacred the RBS share price. In the end, the bank escaped his clutches. This was just as well because Sovereign had some serious corporate governance 'issues'. To the deal-mad Goodwin, Fish's seeming inability to do big deals was a source of deep frustration. Fish was goaded into spending $1.2 billion on five smaller banks and one insurer in the fifteen months from June 2002 to September 2003. He paid $273 million for Massachusetts-based Medford Bancorp, $450 million for Pennsylvania-based Commonwealth Bancorp, $285 million for Massachusetts-based Port Financial Corp, $116 million for Pennsylvania-based Community Bancorp, $136 million for Pennsylvania-based Thistle Group Holdings and an undisclosed sum for Massachusetts-based Feitelberg Insurance.

Under pressure to do deals, Fish seemed willing to pay over the odds. The $450-million (£290-million) price tag for Commonwealth Bancorp represented a 65 per cent premium to the company's closing share price the previous Friday – and 18 times the bank's estimated 2002 cash earnings. Goodwin insisted he detected 'many opportunities to strip out costs'.[8] However, the price raised eyebrows among bank analysts. Richard Weiss, analyst at Philadelphia-based Janney Montgomery Scott, said, 'They paid more for [Commonwealth] than anyone around here would have considered.'[9]

Rather than ask questions about Fish's flashness with the Royal's cash, Goodwin was driving him on by, for example, showing him lists of large banks he wanted to acquire. Goodwin wanted to leapfrog the Mid-Atlantic states and create a beach-head in the Midwest, whose major cities include Chicago, Detroit, Cincinnati, Minneapolis–St Paul and St Louis. In particular, Goodwin coveted a bank in Chicago. There were other factors driving Goodwin. Firstly, with the NatWest integration complete, he had more time on his hands. Secondly, in November 2002, HSBC's $14.2-billion acquisition of Illinois-based subprime lender Household International raised the bar for US bank takeovers – even though it was recognised as an astonishingly bad deal. Thirdly, it was a time of bank consolidation in the United States. In October 2003, Bank of America announced the $47-billion acquisition of FleetBoston and, in January 2004, JPMorgan Chase announced the $58-billion takeover of Chicago-based Bank One. Fourthly, it seemed a good time from a currency perspective, as sterling was strong against the US dollar. In their eagerness to achieve rapid growth in the Midwest, Goodwin and Fish set up 'camp' in downtown Chicago and – a bit like a medieval monarch and his jester reviewing possible suitors for the hand of the king's daughter – they then proceeded to invite all the local investment bankers to introduce them to regional banks that might be looking for a well-endowed partner. According to a leading analyst, Fred said something like, 'I've got a week to buy something – bring me whatever is worth seeing.'

The gung-ho stance was in marked contrast to Goodwin's public statements. As he unveiled profits of £7.1 billion for 2003, Goodwin sought to dampen speculation that a big US deal was imminent. He said RBS would expect a return of 12 per cent from any acquisition and added, 'If the right acquisitions are not available, we will not make any.'[10]

KeyCorp, a financial services conglomerate based in Cleveland, Ohio, about 300 miles east of the Windy City on the southern shores of Lake Erie, emerged as one of the most interesting candidates for takeover. With $84 billion in assets (compared to Citizens' $77 billion), it was bigger than Citizens. However, KeyCorp's profits had stalled. They fell to $903 million in 2003, down from $976 million the previous year. By contrast, Citizens' profits had surged by 22 per cent to $1.4 billion in 2003. Goodwin and Fish saw KeyCorp as an excellent fit and an institution they could revive. Negotiations with KeyCorp's chairman, president and chief executive officer Henry L. Meyer III reached an advanced stage. But they stalled after the two banks failed to agree on a price and on who should get the top jobs – it seemed Meyer wanted to stay in charge. Throughout the talks, each of the two banks had another iron in the fire. They were both poring over possible deals with KeyCorp's cross-town rival Charter One. By April 2004, Charter One had 616 branches, 1.7 million customers, 7,843 employees and assets of $42.6 billion across six states – Illinois, Ohio, Indiana, Michigan, New

York and Vermont. About a quarter of the branches, 160, were in-store branches, located inside Wal-Mart and other supermarket outlets.

Charles John 'Bud' Koch, grandson of the Charter One's founder, needed a buyer as the bank's dynastic approach to succession was hard to reconcile with Sarbanes-Oxley. There was also an issue with anti-quated IT systems that were not up to speed with the new 'know your customer' anti-money laundering laws that the US had rushed through after the 9/11 terror attacks.

Charter One was founded as the First Federal Savings & Loan Association in 1933 to provide savings accounts and mortgages to Cleveland's growing Czech community. The name was changed to First Federal Savings Bank after the company demutualised and floated on the US stock market in 1988. The name was changed again, to Charter One, in 1992. After that, the rise of government-sponsored enterprises, Fannie Mae and Freddie Mac, which pool mortgages and sell them on secondary markets, started eating into the profits it could derive from selling home loans. Koch's survival strategy was to go on an acquisition spree. Speaking in March 1997, Koch said, 'There has been a once-in-a-career opportunity for a lot of us to make a huge amount of money by consolidating weaker players.'[11] In the early 2000s, Charter One sustained a reasonable level of profit by deploying its sales force to lure customers in with free chequing accounts and then cross-selling other products including credit cards, mortgages and home-equity lines of credit. Prime Time Tuesday, a marketing initiative that included extended opening hours, brought in $1 billion of deposits over a six-month period, according to *Forbes* magazine. Each Charter One branch was opening an average 1,300 chequing accounts a year – 30 per cent more than the average US bank.[12] In banking, however, 'bought' business tends to be remarkably promiscuous, melting away as soon as 'teaser' rates expire.

Fish called Koch in mid April 2004. According to one ex-Citizens insider, Koch told Fish, 'Well, if you're interested, you had better hurry because I have something else in the works.' In a bizarre three-way love triangle, Koch was also talking to Meyer about a $6–8-billion sale of Charter One to KeyCorp. To Goodwin, this was anathema. A merger between KeyCorp and Charter One would curtail Citizens' expansion plans and block its western advance. Most of the other big banks in the region which might be available had already been snapped up.

On the RBS side, the talks were led by Fish and Brad Kopp, Citizen's executive vice-president of strategy and development. In an interesting twist, Kopp worked for Lehman Brothers in its financial institutions group from 1981–93, the same investment bank that was now advising Charter One. RBS believed it could justify paying a generous premium for Charter One since it thought its network of retail branches could be used as a launch pad for a corporate banking business in the Midwest. One former senior RBS insider said, 'Under Bud Koch, Charter One had only three corporate relationship managers for the whole of Chicago! The prize for Fred was to create a massive corporate bank at a time when the US economy was booming.'

When Koch learned that RBS might pay as much as $10.5 billion for Charter One, he could not believe his luck. He and his family members owned about 10 per cent of Charter One's equity, meaning they would walk away $105 million better off since RBS intended to pay entirely in cash. The icing on the cake was that the Scottish bank seemed to want Koch to have a seat on the RBS board. As the talks progressed, sources suggest that Koch spent hours on the telephone to yacht brokers as he contemplated how he might spend his $105-million windfall. Charter One also negotiated generous golden parachutes for any executives who lost their jobs following completion.[13]

The talks were getting warmer by Monday, 19 April 2004. Due diligence was then compressed into three or four business days either side of the weekend of 24 and 25 April 2004. A group of about 145 executives from RBS and Citizens plus their advisors took over an entire hotel in the city, not far from the Charter One headquarters. Owing to the need for absolute secrecy, they checked in under the name Carlson Wagonlit Travel and pretended they were in town for a travel industry conference. The goal was to trawl through Charter One's loan book, pore over ledgers and check out as many as possible of its 616 branches, with the overall aim of ensuring the bank had nothing to hide and that RBS shareholders were not getting taken for a ride.

One former RBS compliance executive, who remained in the bank's St Andrew Square office at the time, said, 'Some of the messages we were getting back from the due diligence weekend were pretty alarming. I remember phone calls from people who had been deposited in rather scary places where the taxi driver was reluctant to even let them out. The message I got back from the finance guys who went out there was this was "not a typical Citizens' due diligence exercise". In banking speak, they were warning us that the asset quality wasn't as good as one might have expected.' One London-based RBS senior executive happened to be in Houston, Texas, at around the same time. The manager of RBS's Houston office introduced him to a couple of Charter One executives who were visiting the Lone Star State and their general demeanour convinced him RBS was buying a 'hick' bank. 'They were absolute cowboys. They thought they had died and gone to heaven, because suddenly they had got the backing of the RBS balance sheet to do whatever they wanted. They made out they had nobody supervising them at all.'

Royal Bank proudly unveiled its $10.5-billion takeover offer after the US market closed on Tuesday, 4 May 2004. It was the largest cash transaction in the history of US banking. RBS was offering $44.50 per share to Charter One shareholders, even though the Cleveland-headquartered institution shares had been changing hands for $35.95 the previous day. In the analyst conference, Goodwin sought to allay fears he had overpaid by saying the deal 'gets us across to the right side of the gulf which I think will open up and it gets us into the survivor pool of significant US retail banks'. The *Boston Globe* columnist Steven Syre wrote that, for RBS, the deal was a 'land grab rivalling the Louisiana Purchase'.[14] In a conference call with journalists, Goodwin talked up the prospect of further deals in the US. 'There are a lot of acquisitions still to make,' he said, adding that there could be 'a couple of thousand' attractive takeover targets in the US, 'versus almost none in Europe'. This put the fear of God into the analyst and investor community, who suspected Goodwin had paid over the odds for a bank which was, at best, mediocre. The idea of further such deals terrified them.

Some analysts talked up the deal. Nick Lord, banking sector analyst at Deutsche Bank, reiterated his 'buy' rating on Royal Bank of Scotland's shares and his 2050p price target, saying the $10.5 billion deal made sense. Lord told clients in a note, 'Charter One is a retail-oriented regional bank operating in nine mid-west and north-east US states. It is profitable, efficient and has shown good earnings growth in the past. In addition, it offers RBoS the opportunity to expand their Citizens franchise further into the fragmented US market.' But others were dismayed – disgusted even – by the deal. This was partly down to the suspicion that Charter One was what one analyst calls 'a pretty

crappy American bank stuffed to the gunwales with subprime lending and related dodginess' but also because RBS was carrying out a
£2.5-billion share-placing in order to fund it.

RBS's shares slumped 5 per cent to touch 1626p on 5 May, the day
after the deal was announced. One fund manager said, 'It was obviously a bad deal. A lot of the numbers were based on cost savings and
revenue growth that never materialised.' RBS significantly overpaid
and it was probably out of desperation. 'Investors were horrified,' said
one senior City source. Mercury Asset Management, one of the City's
leading asset management firms and one of RBS's largest shareholders, had a row with the bank over the deal.

As the deal completed on 31 August, Fish appointed Citizens'
senior executive Tom Hollister as president and chief executive of
Charter One to drive through the promised cost savings and revenue
enhancements. A veteran of numerous earlier Citizens' integration
programmes, Hollister, together with a number of other Citizens
executives, relocated to Cleveland, a city sometimes derided as 'The
Mistake on the Lake'. After they started forensically evaluating exactly
what RBS had bought, it wasn't long before they realised it was a bit of
a dog. Over the ensuing weeks and months, awareness of the scale of
the problem percolated up the bank but the main board does not seem
to have been fully informed. According to a number of former Royal
Bank of Scotland, Citizens and Charter One insiders, the following, in
no particular order, were their biggest problems:

- RBS had overpaid.
- The Midwestern banking market was fiercely competitive.
- As an institution, Charter One had no track record or ability in
  building long-term relationships with customers or long-term
  value.
- Charter One was not particularly adept at cross-selling products.
  Instead, it tended to blitz the market with heavyweight advertising
  to promote free chequing accounts and then make its money by
  hitting people who went overdrawn with punitive charges – some-
  thing for which Charter One and the wider Citizens Financial
  Group were later heavily fined by US regulators.
- Charter One had a disloyal and promiscuous customer base.
  Many of the customers who had been attracted to the bank by

generous offers in the build-up to the takeover melted away once their short-term deals expired.

- Citizens was unable to rebrand the 122 Charter One branches in Michigan, as the Citizens trademark belonged to Flint-based Citizens Republic Bancorp in that state. This led to the curious halfway house in which Charter One branches in New York State and Vermont were rebranded as Citizens but those in the Midwestern states were not. Using two brand names added to costs.

- Under Koch, Charter One had made no effort to comply with the anti-money-laundering legislation introduced with the Patriot Act 2002 (the US government's response to 9/11). Citizens had to pick up the tab for making the bank Patriot Act compliant and ran the risk of massive regulatory and individual penalties.

- Even though Charter One was not technically involved in the origination of subprime mortgages (it closed down the Charter One Credit Corp in April 2002, following legislation passed by Cleveland City Council), it was engaged in reckless lending to less affluent consumers across the 'Rust Belt' states. This mainly took the form of home equity lines of credit (HELOC), variably rated loans secured on customers' homes.

- The fact that Koch was ballooning Charter One's HELOC business, in the weeks prior to selling out, suggests he may have been 'dressing up' Charter One for a sale.

In a presentation to analysts, Fish claimed that, by July 2005, the conversion of Charter One was complete, with all technology and processing transferred to the Citizens platform. A few months later, Fish was looking for a scapegoat for the problems at Charter One – where return on capital had fallen short of the 12 per cent that Goodwin had promised investors – and ex-insiders allege he alighted on Hollister. When challenged on Charter One's underperformance by Goodwin, Fish allegedly told Goodwin, 'It's Tom. He is not getting the job done.' In the end, Hollister left the bank in late 2005 and joined energy firm Global Partner as chief financial officer in May 2006.

One non-executive director of RBS was unhappy with the way the deal was presented to the board. He says, 'It was "strike now or don't strike at all" kind of thing. The deal was rushed through within a few weeks and the board of RBS had no real chance to debate it.' The fallout reached the highest levels in the bank. Mathewson recognised the inadequacy of the Charter One deal and asked Goodwin to take action by, for example, apologising to investors for squandering their money on such a poor deal. But Goodwin refused. He had a pathological inability ever to admit to his own mistakes. Mathewson says, 'Fred will always, I suspect to his dying day, say it was a good deal.' Asked who was to blame for the transaction, Mathewson says, 'Well, Larry Fish played a large part in that. He wanted a bigger bang and he wanted, I presume, the financial rewards that would flow from it. Fred was far too soft on Larry.' Mathewson adds, 'The board could have said no but Larry and Fred had done 20 to 30 deals, all of them reasonable deals, so you tend to trust them . . . Larry really wanted to do the deal. He said to me, "This is better than the deal we didn't get [KeyCorp]." It wasn't.'[15]

It wasn't long before Goodwin's reluctance to divulge the truth about Charter One drove a wedge between himself and Mathewson. One ex-advisor to the Royal Bank of Scotland says, 'George basically fell out with Fred soon after Charter One. George started publicly criticising Fred for having done the deal – he was telling analysts and investors he understood why they were unhappy with it – he understood why the RBS share price had gone down the toilet. Afterwards, George basically was saying things had become too difficult [in terms of his relations with Goodwin]. I don't think he really wanted to have anything more to do with the bank after that.'

Simon Samuels, head of European bank equity research at Barclays, says Charter One was a turning point – the point at which RBS ceased to be trusted by investors. 'That was a deal about which people thought it was showing complete, cavalier disregard for shareholders,' says Samuels. 'When that one came out, we struggled to make the numbers work and had to believe in revenue synergies – which is generally a bad sign as they do not always comes through and are normally the icing on the cake. The cost savings were not enough to justify the transaction. That was when it all started to go wrong for RBS.'[16]

It took RBS until February 2009, four months after Goodwin was ousted, to confirm that Charter One had been a bad deal. In the footnotes to Royal Bank of Scotland's 'Annual Report 2008', the bank said it had taken a £4.382-billion goodwill write-down on Charter One. It was acknowledging that it had massively overpaid for the Cleveland-based bank – in fact, it had paid nearly £4.4 billion too much. So, with the benefit of hindsight, a bank for which RBS had paid £5.8 billion was perhaps worth only £1.4 billion! The investment bankers who advised RBS and Fred Goodwin on the deal – Matthew Greenburgh of Merrill Lynch and Andy Chisholm of Goldman Sachs – do not appear to have given very good advice on this occasion. However it is probably too late to claw back their bonuses.

No more deals

Some investors were so dismayed by the Royal Bank of Scotland's purchase of Charter One they started to agitate for change. Investors' prime concerns were that Goodwin had overpaid, that the deal would undermine rather than enhance the value of their Royal Bank shares and that Goodwin was burning a hole in the bank's capital base. There was also concern that the RBS board did not appear to give a damn. Many investors believed a period of 'cold turkey' was long overdue.

One issue the bank faced was that, being an Edinburgh-based institution that was proud of its Scottishness and with a dearth of directors on its board with serious City experience, the board failed to grasp the dynamics of the City. And it didn't help that Goodwin had, since *Forbes*' eulogy, cut himself off from some of the key advisors who were best placed to read this for him. Colin McLean, chief executive of SVM Asset Management, says, 'Fred just failed to grasp the way in which the City operates. He failed to appreciate the way the City sort of votes with its feet, which gives rise to the quote: "If the phone doesn't ring you'll know it's me." I doubt anyone was actually telling him they were pissed off with him or that they were worried about further share issues. Instead, they would have just melted away [that is they quietly sold their shares].' McLean adds, 'If the City thinks you're going to carry on issuing more and more shares, it'll just wait to buy them in the future. They won't feel any great compulsion to make a long-term investment at the current share price.'[1]

Three of the bank's non-executive directors – Mathewson, Sutherland and Robson – were more aware to investors' concerns than most of their colleagues. Sir George Mathewson had begun to publicly disparage his chief executive by openly talking of a 'Fred discount'. In

financial circles, this is a highly pejorative phrase. It implied George
believed Fred had become a negative for the bank – that his presence as
chief executive was suppressing the share price. RBS's shares had been
trapped in the 1500p to 1600p range for over two years, having tumbled
from an all-time high of nearly £21 in early May 2002. Rival banks
which were less obsessed with global domination, including Alliance &
Leicester, Barclays, Bradford & Bingley, HBOS, HSBC, Lloyds TSB,
Northern Rock and Standard Chartered, had seen their share prices
increase over the same time frame.

There was a school of thought among some board members that it
didn't matter if Goodwin had paid over the odds for Charter One since
RBS would be able to make up for it by cutting costs and channelling
more products – especially corporate loans – through Charter One's
branch network. People in this camp, the 'Fred believers', included
two Scottish knights – Sir Angus Grossart and Sir Iain Vallance – the
Australian senior independent director Bob Scott and South African-
Scot Colin Buchan. There were other factors bearing down on the
RBS share price. One was that most UK-based institutional investors
were 'overweight the stock' (that is they held proportionately more
RBS shares than they should have done, relative to the bank's weight
in the FTSE-100 index) and that RBS and its house broker had been
struggling to build a market for the shares among US-based investors.

Determined to establish how Goodwin and the bank were perceived
in the City of London, non-executive director Peter Sutherland commissioned City PR firm Brunswick to canvass analysts and investors
for their views on the bank, its strategy, its management team, its communications with investors etc.

Sutherland, a former attorney general of Ireland, was a busy man.
A non-executive director of RBS since January 2001, he also sat on the
RBS chairman's advisory group and its nominations committee. For
his RBS roles, he was paid £53,000 in 2004, £60,000 in 2005, £88,000
in 2006 and £97,000 in 2007. Sutherland was also a financial advisor
to the Vatican – where he was about to live through the succession
from Pope John Paul II to Pope Benedict XVI – chairman of Goldman
Sachs International, from which he netted a shares windfall worth
£145 million when Goldman Sachs was floated in 1999, and chairman
of oil giant BP. In the latter role, investors and analysts accuse him
of failing to rein in the 'Sun King', Sir John Browne, who was chief

executive until May 2007. The Irishman has also been accused of not doing enough to reverse the culture of cost cutting that contributed to calamities such as the Texas City Refinery explosion of March 2005 and the Deepwater Horizon oil spill of April 2010. In commissioning what became known as the 'Brunswick Report', Sutherland wanted to ensure he got a proper handle on the nature of the difficulties facing RBS.

City mistrust about Goodwin's inability to kick his deal-making habit suffused every results presentation from 2004 onwards. On Thursday, 24 February 2005, as he unveiled record pre-tax profits of £6.9 billion for the year to December 2004, Goodwin stressed that, since the acquisition of NatWest, nearly two-thirds of the growth in RBS's income had been 'organic'. He said, 'Our reputation for buying lots of things is simply not warranted. The underlying need for acquisitions is at a low ebb.' However James Eden, an analyst at Dresdner Kleinwort, remained unconvinced. 'RBS made comforting noises [but] the acquisition risk surrounding the shares is still there.' And he was right to be sceptical – as Goodwin was proclaiming his abstinence from deal making, his bank was in talks about buying a 15 to 20 per cent stake in the Bank of China!

Many investors were aghast when they got wind of this after a leak to the *South China Morning Post* in April 2005. China's banking sector had long been plagued by corruption, bad loans to poorly performing state-owned enterprises, embezzlement and poor governance. However, the Chinese government wanted western banks to buy minority stakes in the country's banks so the western players could help to transform the Chinese ones. Paradoxically, China thought its banks could improve risk management, corporate governance and marketing by learning from their western peers. The idea was that the then state-owned institutions could then be IPO'ed. As RBS's management team had zero experience of the Chinese market (and could therefore be easily hoodwinked), there were fears of a disaster even greater than that of Charter One. And it's worth bearing in mind that RBS's record was less glittering than its cheerleaders made out. Analysts at Deutsche Bank ran the numbers on the 21 acquisitions that RBS had made since 1997 and only a handful had matched their cost of capital. But Goodwin was not prepared to be thwarted by cautious shareholders. Speaking ahead of the RBS annual general meeting in April 2005, and partially confirming the *South China Morning Post* story, he said it would be 'remiss' of the Edinburgh-based bank not to look at possible deals in Asia.[2]

The Brunswick Report commissioned by Sutherland was ready by June 2005. It was a devastating indictment of Goodwin. A limited number of copies were distributed to RBS board directors and members of its group executive management committee (GEMC) in advance of their meeting at Gleneagles in June 2005. This gave Sutherland time to go through the report and highlight sections that were most critical of Goodwin. In his smooth Dublin lilt, Sutherland read out excerpts of the report to some 25 senior executives, executive directors and non-executive directors of the bank in the opulent 1920s railway hotel. The ones he read out included: 'Fred is out of touch'; 'Fred is arrogant'; 'Fred doesn't listen to shareholders'; 'Fred treats all shareholders like they're idiots'; and 'Fred is a megalomaniac'. As Sutherland read out these and further passages, other RBS senior executives and directors were furiously leafing through their copies, trying to keep up. At one stage, Sutherland said, 'Well, hang on – we haven't looked at page 48 yet. That's where it says that you're "a complete c*nt". Fred, what have you got to say about that?'[3]

'The report tore Fred to shreds – it was pretty devastating stuff,' said an RBS director who was present. ' "Arrogance" was probably the word that appeared the most. "Not listening to people", "not listening to investors", "being out of touch" also appeared a lot. There was scarcely anything positive about Fred in the report.' Another source said it was the only time in their life that they felt sorry for Goodwin. Asked how Goodwin responded, the source said, 'Fred remained calm. All I could see was the back of his neck, which just went redder and redder.' One other RBS director who was present said, 'You could say it was a very difficult moment for Fred.'

Following the debacle, RBS's board laid down the law, insisting that Goodwin changed his approach. He agreed not to do any more deals, to consider disposals (including a possible sale of Citizens), to prioritise consolidation of existing operations and organic growth, to consider share buy-backs and to improve his relations with the City. As part of the last pledge, the board said that divisional chief executives – including Johnny Cameron (Global Banking and Markets), Gordon Pell (Retail Markets), Larry Fish (Citizens Financial), Mark Fisher

(Manufacturing), Annette Court (Insurance) and Cormac McCarthy (Ulster Bank) – should increasingly be wheeled out to talk to investors. The board was determined to convey the message that the bank was capable of organic growth and that it had a depth of management expertise.

One former advisor to the bank said, 'What happened after that was that – in theory at least – Fred was a new man. He had taken all the criticism on board, he was not going to do any more deals and he was going to buy back some shares when the time came. Fred was like a reborn Christian. And Guy Whittaker came in as finance director in February 2006, and so everything was fine and dandy, or so it was thought.' The giveaway is perhaps contained in the four words 'in theory at least'.

And Fred still had supporters in the City. Asked whether investors lost faith in Fred following the Charter One deal, a leading City fund manager says: 'It would be an overstatement to say that people lost faith. If that had been the case, I suspect Fred would have been out the door. Yes, investors didn't like Charter One and that was largely because he overpaid, because it was dilutive and because he brought in the dreaded Goldman to advise. But what you have to bear in mind is that any deal in financial services post-2001 was a bad deal – because of the financial bubble and the bubble in property prices. To put it in perspective, Rio Tinto's $38-billion takeover of Alcan, on which Rio took $14 billion of write-downs, was a far worse deal. You also have to bear in mind that Fred Goodwin had rescued one of the worst banks ever [NatWest]. It was rotten to the core before he took it over and turned it around. Everyone was very grateful for that. That's why nobody felt they could touch him.'

A few days after being humiliated at Gleneagles, Goodwin let off steam by tearing around the racetrack at the Goodwood Festival of Speed in a £195,000 Lamborghini Murciélago, a 580bhp Italian super-car. A speed freak, he frequently also took his own Ferraris for a burn around the Knockhill racing circuit, near Dunfermline in Fife. But, at Goodwood, Goodwin misjudged a corner and careered into a crash barrier. The brand-new Lamborghini ended up on its roof, causing £60,000 of damage. Goodwin was reportedly unhurt, though ex-RBS insiders claim that he had to spend one night in hospital. The *Daily Mirror*, which broke the story, said, 'The brand-new Italian supercar, which accelerates from nought to 60mph in 3.5 seconds and has a top speed of 205mph, was left in a mangled heap ... But embarrassed UK Lamborghini bosses ordered staff to keep the prang quiet to spare his blushes.' Darren Pearce, former sales manager at Lamborghini's Manchester showroom, said: 'The boss of Lamborghini London was very keen no one should find out about Sir Fred. He said we shouldn't talk about it to anyone. Obviously, it was very embarrassing for everyone involved.'⁴ The crash was also hushed up by RBS and the organisers of the Goodwood Festival of Speed, where Goodwin and favoured corporate clients had become a fixture. Goodwin rapidly recovered his poise and few colleagues even learned about the crash.

A shiny, new, born-again Goodwin descended on the City with missionary zeal – though investors were never told of the enforced nature of his conversion. He kept making public pledges along the lines of 'I see no need for any further acquisitions' and 'I'm perfectly happy to grow RBS organically'. To prove he meant business, he vowed to hand back cash, which might otherwise have gone on deals, to investors, through mechanisms that included a £1-billion share buy-back programme and increased dividends. But investors remained sceptical. Some suspected that, at heart, Goodwin remained a deal junkie.

On 4 August 2005, five weeks after the car crash, RBS released its half-year results, audited as usual by Deloitte. At an analysts' conference in 280 Bishopsgate, Goodwin defended deals like Churchill Insurance, First Active and Charter One, insisting they would come good eventually. He also said, 'We're not actually planning to make any further acquisitions at this point. And guess what that means? We will not be seeking to issue any equity.' (This turned out to be a typical 'Fred-ism'. The Bank of China deal, then in its final stages of negotiation, was announced two weeks later.) But James Eden, an analyst at investment bank Dresdner Kleinwort Wasserstein, punctured the mood with an incendiary couple of questions. Eden asked, 'Do you agree that there's a management discount or can you think of another reason why your shares are so cheap?' There were nervous titters on the podium before Goodwin replied, 'I think there are a number of, a variety of, quite lurid rumours going about, about things that we are thinking about doing or have done or are about to do. I'm keen to close that industry down. I think if you look back to what management actually says and what management actually does, I'm happy to stand by that and be judged by it. As I'm happy to stand and be judged by the results we've delivered to date.' The bank's outgoing finance director Fred Watt then asked Eden to clarify what he meant by 'management discount'. Eden's clarification contained a killer phrase which made the headlines the next day. 'Well, I think there's a perception among some investors that Fred Goodwin is a megalomaniac who pursues size over shareholder value, and that that's the reason why Royal Bank trades on eight times 2007 earnings, whereas some of your peers trade on earnings multiples much higher than that.'

'It was as though he was saying the emperor has no clothes,' one senior RBS director recalled.[5] Goodwin was hurt and sought to put a brave face on it, while fumbling around for an adequate response. He said: 'I really don't think it stands a lot of scrutiny in terms of what we've actually done. I think the results you're seeing today demonstrate delivery against a quite clear, coherent strategy, and one which we've executed with, I think, considerable internal discipline. But I don't enjoy the rumours that go about any more than you do. I don't enjoy our shares having a discount any more than you do, and I'm very anxious to dispel rumours or concerns of that nature and that's why it's always been very important to me to maintain an open dialogue. And I've got the scars on my back from ticks and crosses charts in the past, but I think it was better to try to outline what we're doing and give people a flavour of it than just to spring things on you by surprise. And I think that has borne fruit. But I think we move on now into a different style and different form of dialogue.'[6]

The James Eden incident – perhaps the most extraordinary exchange between an analyst and a FTSE-100 chief executive to have happened in the UK – concentrated the minds of RBS's non-executive directors. One former ex-City advisor to RBS said, 'Eden's remarks caused a lot of heat at the time. Investors could hardly have made it more clear that they didn't want Fred to do anything there. They felt it [Bank of China] would be yet another vanity project on Fred's part and symptomatic of his desire to conquer the world.'

Since February 2004, RBS strategy director Iain Allan and Bank of China executive vice-president Dr Zhu Min had been engaged in secret on–off talks about a deal between the two banks. The idea was that RBS would enter several joint ventures with the Beijing-based bank in areas including credit cards, wealth management and corporate banking – gaining RBS an entrée to the Chinese market and enabling Bank of China to learn from its new partner. To cement the arrangement, the Edinburgh-based bank would buy a stake of around 10 or 15 per cent in its partner, at a cost of up to $5 billion, ahead of its 2006 flotation. Allan made several clandestine visits to Beijing, while Zhu had made several such visits to the Scottish capital, latterly accompanied by a group of some 25 Bank of China employees who came to conduct due diligence and were taken on tours of Edinburgh Castle, the Palace of Holyroodhouse and the grave of enlightenment economist Adam Smith in Canongate Kirkyard. Goodwin made several visits to Beijing on board G-RBSG during the 17 months of negotiations – sometimes accompanied by Allan and his RBS executive assistant Kerry McGuire.

Founded in Shanghai in 1912, Bank of China had $464 billion of assets, 238,000 employees and 11,307 branches in mainland China. According to Bloomberg, only five of the bank's domestic branches were connected by computer to its Beijing headquarters, while, during August 2005, the former head of its Hong Kong operation was given a suspended death sentence for corruption.[7] But this did not deter Goodwin, who believed that, since the bank was due to be privatised in 2006 via an initial public offering, RBS should be able to 'flip' its stake for a profit. But Goodwin also wanted to gain a foothold in the fast-growing China market and get his hands on some of the country's $1.65 trillion of deposits.

During the protracted negotiations, Goodwin occasionally became impatient and despondent, wondering whether a deal might ever be reached. This prompted the Bank of China's executive chairman, Xiao Gang, to write him a cryptic letter. In it, Xiao said, 'By a long road one knows a horse's true strength.' At first, Goodwin was bemused. But eventually he worked out that Xiao was telling him that he was being put through his paces and if he stayed the course he would prove his worth. As part of the elaborate pre-nuptial manoeuvrings, Goodwin and Xiao spent several evenings drinking shots of the Chinese alcoholic drink, Maotai, until the wee small hours.

But the less somnambulant RBS non-executives, including Robson and Sutherland, told Goodwin the deal he was initially proposing was not going to wash with investors. Goodwin asked Merrill Lynch to find some 'passive' partners to buy half of the 10 per cent stake RBS had pledged at short notice. The investment bank came up trumps, bringing in Hong Kong-based tycoon Li Ka-shing, Asia's richest man, whose business empire, Cheung Kong Holdings, is the world's largest operator of container terminals, and buying the residue itself.

When the deal was finally announced on 18 August, Goodwin toasted the agreement to take the Edinburgh-based bank into China with a glass of vintage local (Chinese) champagne. 'It had been a sweaty night of talks,' he said on a subsequent visit to the Chinese capital. 'The champagne tasted good.'[8] RBS was effectively taking control of a 10 per cent stake in the Bank of China and gaining a seat on its board, even though it was only buying 5.16 per cent of its equity. RBS was paying $1.6 billion. Li, well known to the Chinese and to Xiao, bought a 2.4 per cent stake for $750 million. And Merrill took the remaining 2.44 per cent stake.

RBS further calmed investors' nerves by saying it was selling its stake in Santander for £900 million in order to fund the deal, which meant that, contrary to expectations, it would not need to issue any new shares to fund the deal. The bank also sought to ease investors' concerns by claiming it had negotiated 'appropriate warranties and protections' to safeguard investors' interests. The fact that this was a less bad outcome than many investors had feared caused RBS shares to rebound slightly. They climbed 2.5 per cent on 18 August to close at 1647p. Richard Staite, an analyst at SG Securities, said the deal was positive for RBS, 'I'm pleased to see that it's a smaller amount than had been rumoured. I feel that the opportunities there are going to be interesting in the long-term. The announcement today also removes a big uncertainty that had been weighing on the share price.'[9]

At the signing, Xiao said, 'With its experienced management, outstanding business strengths, well-established internal control mechanisms and prudent management style, RBS is an ideal partner.'[10] However, because of communications difficulties, Goodwin acknowledged that the joint ventures were taking longer than anticipated to get off the ground. It also turned out that Goodwin's due diligence had been wanting. The brand name RBS intended to use for its wealth-management joint venture in China – Coutts – was a non-starter. In Mandarin, it sounded exactly the same as the word for 'trousers'.[11]

On 2 November 2005, Goodwin was given a hard time by investors and analysts in the question-and-answer session after his presentation to the Merrill Lynch banking conference in New York. Not only did the assembled analysts lay into him over his bank's over-leveraged balance sheet, they also criticised him for the lack of diversity on the RBS board, the absence of share buy-backs and a lack of management depth. The 'reborn' Goodwin was parroting his new mantra of no more deals and stressing he saw 'no strategic need for further acquisitions' and that his priorities were now 'to grow income, improve efficiency and improve return on equity'. But it all sounded a bit hollow after the Bank of China volte-face. He insisted he had behaved sensibly and ethically over the previous half decade. 'And so against that 2000–05 list of strategic objectives, I think we're happy that we clearly delivered the NatWest benefits, we kept the show on the road, we kept the organic growth moving forward strongly, we managed to improve our efficiency and we did it all whilst maintaining stable credit quality throughout the organisation, and we have addressed the other strategic priorities . . . it was not a case of pursuing the strategy at all cost, regardless of its impact on our shareholders.'[12] He also claimed RBS was making strong progress in investment banking, saying, 'We've truly, I think, transformed our financial markets business and have got ourselves to a place where we are top ten in all of the activities that we take part in around the world.'[13]

That evening, Goodwin was able to take him mind off banking when he and his wife Joyce had dinner at the White House with President George W. Bush and the First Lady Laura Bush. It was a black-tie affair in honour of Prince Charles and his new bride, Camilla, Duchess of Cornwall. Other members of Bush's neo-Liberal administration – including Vice-President Dick Cheney, Secretary of State Condoleezza Rice and Defense Secretary Donald Rumsfeld – were present, as were the professional golfer Tom Watson, NBC News anchorman Tom Brokaw and the fashion designer Oscar de la Renta. British ambassador David Manning, former president George H. W. Bush and his wife Barbara Bush, KPMG boss Mike Rake and leveraged buyout king Henry Kravis of Kohlberg Kravis Roberts were also present.[14] The 130 guests in the White House's state dining room were treated to celery and shrimp soup, buffalo medallions, petits fours cake and chartreuse ice cream. Entertainment was provided by the cellist Yo-Yo Ma.[15]

As Goodwin was extolling his own achievements in New York, in London the industry magazine *The Banker* was putting the knife in.

Geraldine Lambe, the magazine's capital markets editor, produced a long feature article reflecting investors' exasperation and trashing Goodwin's stewardship of the bank. She accused the Paisley-born accountant of turning a 'darling into a demon'. Lambe wrote, 'Where once they lauded Sir Fred as emperor in all his finery, now shareholders behave as if he has no clothes.'[16] In the weeks after his dinner with Charles and Camilla in Washington, Goodwin came close to throwing in the towel. On 20 November 2005, *The Independent on Sunday* reported that he was poised to quit, citing 'sources close to the board of Royal Bank of Scotland'. The article said Goodwin felt he was missing out on opportunities because of the low rating of RBS's shares and a frosty relationship with investors. The newspaper pointed out that the bank's shares, worth 1683p on 18 November, were the same price as they had been in early 2001. Something was awry. Over the same five-year period, Royal Bank's profits had more than doubled.[17]

Fred Watt, the bank's low-key finance director since September 2000, resigned in June 2005, claiming he wanted to spend more time with wife and three-year-old twins, James and Charlotte. However, Watt was actually sick and tired of having to work with Fred on a daily basis. Ever since Watt's surprise resignation, investors had been demanding that the bank appoint someone with real backbone, capable standing up to Goodwin, as Watt's successor. Chris Hughes, writing in *BreakingViews*, said, 'Goodwin is excessively dominant on the RBS board. If he really wants to close the discount, he needs to find a top-notch finance director to replace the departing Fred Watt and to attract some big names into the RBS boardroom.'[18]

The pleas fell on deaf ears at Gogarburn. In December, the bank announced that it had hired Guy Whittaker, a former foreign exchange trader, as Watt's replacement. A Cambridge graduate, Whittaker had been head of foreign exchange trading and currency derivatives at Citicorp in London during the 1990s, before moving to New York as Citigroup's group treasurer. But the Englishman was not a trained accountant, had never been a finance director and, although he was appointed by the board and not by Goodwin, he was never going to be capable of standing up to the chief executive. According to one banking expert, Whittaker's main achievement at Citi had been the installation of 'the world's worst information technology system, which was jointly developed with [Indian computer group] Infosys, for credit derivatives, which they expressly designed to bury toxicity and risk'. Yet RBS was so eager to persuade Whittaker to re-cross the Atlantic that they handed him a £4.5-million 'golden hello' in guaranteed compensation over several years, in order to buy him out of his Citigroup 'golden handcuffs'. Whittaker started as group finance director on 1 February 2006 in an office adjacent to those of Goodwin and Mathewson in Executive House G at Gogarburn. But, despite high hopes from the board, he turned out to be a disaster.

Goodwin missed out on a £1.4-million bonus in 2005 as a direct result of the weakness of the bank's share price. The money might have been paid out under a medium-term incentive scheme introduced for senior RBS executives in April 2001. However, the bank's share price performance was so dire that targets were missed. Goodwin was hardly going to go hungry (he still earned £2.893 million in 2005). However, the RBS remuneration committee – which was chaired by Bob Scott, the former chief executive of insurance firm CGNU, and which had the former eurocrat Jim Currie and ex-UBS investment banker Colin Buchan as members – responded oddly. Instead of cracking open the champagne and saying, 'Isn't it great that executive directors are being denied some potential rewards as a direct result of their own underperformance?', they skewed the system by splitting the targets to make it easier for them to be met. *The Economist* said the revised incentive plan looked suspiciously like it was 'designed to give managers an easier path to the trough'.[19]

Goodwin had a crisis of confidence over Christmas 2005, taking a six-week break to consider his position. He is understood to have come close to throwing in the towel. In the end, however, he decided to stay. He came back, raring to go, in early 2006.[20]

Failed alchemists

Throughout the 1990s, banks were looking for ever more creative ways of gaming the Basel rules by shifting credit risk off their balance sheets. One of the best ways they found was to create and market tradable securities, usually bonds, out of loans and other assets – so-called 'asset-backed' securities (ABSs). ABSs essentially pool thousands of existing loans and package them into a new legal structure that is capable of issuing securities which can be bought and sold by third-party investors. The alchemy was at first reserved for larger loans, such as leveraged loans, corporate loans, commercial property loans and aviation loans. It was welcomed by regulators and central banks, who were jaded by past bank failures. They regarded ABSs as a sensible means for banks to distribute risk to those more able to bear it.

Fannie Mae and Freddie Mac issued the world's first mortgage-backed security (MBS) – a tradable bond-based bundle of home loans – in 1970. Fannie and Freddie are two government-sponsored enterprises, created by the US government in 1938 and 1970 respectively to provide liquidity to the US mortgage market. They traditionally did this by buying mortgages from private-sector lenders, making it easier for the issuing banks to lend more to American homeowners, with a view to helping low- and middle-income Americans to get on to the housing ladder. Salomon Brothers and Bank of America pioneered private mortgage-backed securities in 1977.

During the 1990s, other Wall Street investment banks got on the bandwagon, creating MBSs in competition with those churned out by Fannie and Freddie. These investment banks often threw some higher-risk loans – so-called 'subprime' loans – into the mix. Subprime is a euphemistic term introduced in the early 1990s to describe lending to poorer Americans on low salaries with bad credit histories. The catalyst for this new type of lending was the 1993 Community Reinvestment Act, part of the Clinton administration's bid to enlarge US home ownership. The inclusion of subprime loans, an option that was not open to Fannie and Freddie, meant that the securities generated higher yields (they provided investors with a higher annual return) but it also meant they carried higher risk. From 2003 onwards, this method of blending subprime debt with less risky debt fuelled explosive growth in the US subprime mortgage market – and the housing market generally. When bank 'quants' – experts in quantitative analysis – crunched their numbers, they were able to say with some confidence that the correlation risk was minimal and the loans were safe. They turned out to be wildly wrong. The situation was exacerbated by the failure of America's regulators to notice the degree of fraud that was creeping in to the US housing market after the millennium or that this was being fuelled by new dynamics, including that mortgage originators were more concerned about whether they could on-sell the loans they issued than about their quality. As the American investor and newspaper columnist Barry Ritholtz says, 'The Federal Reserve failed to use its supervisory and regulatory authority over banks, mortgage underwriters and other lenders, who abandoned such standards as employment history, income, down payments, credit rating, assets, property loan-to-value ratio and debt-servicing ability. The borrower's ability to repay these mortgages was replaced with the lender's ability to securitize and repackage them.'[1]

Banks and professional advisors suddenly realised they could make a fortune by slicing and dicing debt and jumbling it around. The opaque vehicles they created, usually registered in tax havens, had the advantage of enabling them to substantially reduce their tax burdens and helping other market players to do the same – a fringe benefit that eventually became the tail that was driving the securitisation dog. Collateralised debt obligations (CDOs), invented by Michael Milken's investment bank Drexel Burnham Lambert in 1987, gathered momentum in 1997 when JPMorgan created one by packaging and selling bundles of corporate loans. Then, in 1999, JPMorgan was asked by Munich-based Bayerische Landesbank to package $14 billion of mortgages and other US consumer debt into a CDO structure. It was the first time a CDO had been used for mortgages. Gillian Tett, in her book *Fool's Gold*, notes that, initially, JPMorgan had reservations about this but eventually went ahead and created the first mortgage-backed CDO.[2] The innovative deal lit the blue touchpaper, turning the US housing market into a Ponzi scheme.

CDOs were divided into slices or 'tranches' on which investors' claims on cash flows would be met in pre-agreed levels of seniority in the event of default. The first to be met would be so-called 'super-senior' tranche, while the last – the 'first loss' or 'equity' tranche – would only be honoured if any money was left in the pot once more senior creditors had been paid off. Owners of the lower tranches were compensated for a greater risk of losing everything with higher returns ('yields') on their investment. The issuers of a CDO paid credit rating agencies to produce a separate credit rating for each tranche of the CDO. This was a fantastic business for rating agencies like Standard & Poor's (S&P) and Moody's, who would give the senior tranches the highest rating – typically AAA – while giving the equity tranches much lower ratings or even no rating. A great many people in banking and the financial markets did not recognise that credit rating agencies were being overgenerous with AAA ratings and therefore believed the AAA-rated super-senior tranches to be bullet proof. The senior tranches were often bought by insurance companies which, in a low-yield environment, were attracted to supposedly safe long-term assets that delivered marginally higher yields than sovereign debt. From 2000 to 2007, Moody's rated nearly 45,000 such securities as AAA and 83 per cent of securities given that rating in 2006 were ultimately downgraded.[3]

There was concern about CDOs as early as 2002 after it emerged that Barclays Capital was abusing them to palm off 'doomed to default' aircraft lease securitisations on gullible Italian and German banks in the aftermath of 9/11.[4] The FSA chairman and chief executive Howard Davies raised the alarm in January 2002. However, the regulator did little to follow up on his concerns.

In July 2002, RBS launched a new structured credit group specifically to develop a CDO business. The new group was run jointly by David Littlewood and David Henriques, previously co-heads of the bank's risk finance group. Steve Lyons and Anthony Lee, senior members of the credit derivatives team, joined the new group following the bank's expectation that credit derivatives would become a major source of future profit. Australian-born Symon Drake-Brockman,

RBS's global head of Capital Markets, was quoted as saying, 'Building a managed CDO business is an important initiative for the Royal Bank of Scotland.'[5] One former colleague said, 'Symon was a young, handsome, ambitious and super-capable banker who joined from ING Baring the previous year to build up the debt capital markets business. He turned a rather dull part of the business into a rather big, very credible and exciting bit of the business.'

However, there were some early voices of dissent. In September 2002, Ron den Braber, a Dutch-born structured-credit-pricing expert at the bank who had recently completed a PhD in the pricing of structured credit at Imperial College, produced an evaluation of the model RBS was proposing to use for its CDOs. The report, delivered to Royal Bank's heads of market risk, argued that the model was fundamentally flawed and might even bring down the bank. The report said, 'There is model risk in the David Li model[6] . . . The multivariate normal assumption probably over-prices first-to-default and under-prices last-to-default tranches using the same correlation inputs . . . This distribution very significantly under-estimates correlations and especially tail correlations.'[7] Although couched in opaque financial jargon, these were explosive findings. In effect, den Braber was saying that the valuations of Royal Bank's CDOs could only be maintained if there was little or no correlation between mortgage defaults in different regions of the United States. Den Braber describes his findings in stark terms, 'It was my job to write a detailed report stating everything that was wrong with the model, which is what I did. In the report, I said, "Watch out, don't do it this way. This is mispricing risk – it's extremely unreliable." – more or less predicting everything that happened – all the $30 billion they would later lose in one month.'[8]

Amsterdam-based den Braber, an outspoken maths geek who is now an independent risk consultant at QuantRisk, adds, 'What their model assumed was that, if someone defaulted on a mortgage in California, it would not impact on a mortgage borrower in Florida. But, of course, these things are mathematically dependent, as we found out during the crisis. Normally, if a model is 0.1 per cent out, that is just about acceptable but here we had a model in which something you believed to be worth 100 could become worth 20 if the circumstances changed.'[9]

Few others inside RBS seemed to care. As far as they were concerned, the model was just a black box that they fed numbers into and they just accepted the answers it spat out without question. Braber adds, 'When you put a new model in front of people, all the documentation should be there but I think there was just a spreadsheet. There was a lack of documentation when they introduced the model so what I did was to write the documentation – this is the model, this is the map, etc. – and then I pointed out all the errors, all the things that could go wrong, all the places where the model fell down.'

Using a flawed model to price CDOs was bad enough at a time when volumes were low but, once they began to climb to the skies between 2005 and 2007, it became a death trap for banks that bought and traded CDOs. Because the model RBS was using, the one that den Braber had sought to kill off, did not price correlation risk correctly, CDO valuations were seriously exposed to adverse changes in economic conditions. As den Braber remarks, 'The minute the economy deteriorated, it was bound to go from AAA to a junk bond in about ten seconds.'[10]

Like others who criticised the way in which RBS was doing things and warned of problems to come, den Braber was effectively eased out for his pains and he claims that, rather than being escalated up the management tree and brought to the attention of the likes of Drake-Brockman, Crowe and Cameron, his report was suppressed. He commented, 'It is amazing that, when a bank hires an expert in credit risk pricing models, they fire him when they don't like the answers he gives them.'[11]

RBS's decision to persevere with a model it had been warned was defective stemmed from the greed of its traders, management's obsession with making a fast buck and risk managers' inability to fight these powerful forces. RBS traders favoured the flawed CDO model as it could be relied upon to deliver them six- or seven-figure bonuses year in, and year out. And, if it led to the destruction of a 275-year-old bank further down the line, why should they care? They'd almost certainly have moved on within a couple of years anyway. At a conference at the University of Edinburgh in June 2012, both the Bank of England executive director for financial stability, Andy Haldane, and Edinburgh University professor Donald MacKenzie said the price-modelling and risk-modelling methodologies which underpinned RBS's CDO model remain 'canonical' inside investment banks even though they have long been known to be flawed. MacKenzie said this is because they enable

'Day One P&L' to be booked – meaning all the profit from a trade is taken on the day of the sale. In turn, this enables traders to enjoy immediate bonuses.

RBS greatly expanded its CDO business from 2002 onwards. Robertson – who was not told of the den Braber report – had reservations of his own and a credit committee that he chaired rejected one of their early CDO deals, some time around 2003. Robertson said, 'Greenwich Capital got one of the shocks of their lives when they put one of these deals though our credit committee and it got bounced back, exactly because I was not prepared to have it sitting in our books under any circumstances for any period of time. It was a packaging of mortgages. Of course some of the mortgage originators were less strict in the application of their own criteria as to what they were originating than they told people around them.'[12] Robertson retired from executive duties in June 2003, handing over the reins to Cameron and Crowe, who seemed much less inclined to challenge Jay Levine and Ben Carpenter, the co-heads of RBS Greenwich Capital from 2000 to 2007.

Thanks to the banking and financial reforms introduced by President Franklin D. Roosevelt in 1933, the US had not had a housing market crash for 74 years, which marked it out from the UK where the housing boom-and-bust cycle was all too familiar. This meant US property lending and the securities derived from it were regarded as ultra-safe and accepted as prime collateral in the funding markets.

Iain Robertson had been impressed by Greenwich Capital's risk management when he visited the firm's headquarters in the scenic Connecticut fishing port of Greenwich in March 2000 but RBS bosses ought to have been more wary of their new toy. The firm had helped to bankrupt its previous owners, Tokyo-based Long-Term Credit Bank (LTCB) of Japan. LTCB acquired Greenwich in June 1988, at a time when Japanese banks were strutting their stuff on the world stage on the back of a domestic property boom. Just like RBS a decade later, LTCB had grandiose plans for world domination. It saw swallowing Greenwich as a stepping stone on the path to transforming itself into an 'international wholesale bank headquartered in Tokyo'.[13] The *Financial Times* journalist Gillian Tett said, 'I interviewed Greenwich Capital in the 2000s and asked what it was like being owned by the Japanese. They said that it was fantastic because the Japanese came with pots of cheap capital and, although they did not know much about what

Greenwich Capital was doing, they [the Japanese] said, "Here's all this cheap money; go and build a business." So they did. That business made a number of the Greenwich Capital traders pretty rich. Of course, things went horribly wrong because the Greenwich Capital traders made bets on really dumb things and LTCB went bust.'[14]

Greenwich Capital was based at 600 Steamboat Road, Greenwich, Connecticut, in the former offices of collapsed hedge fund Long-Term Capital Management (LTCM). LTCM employed Nobel Prize-winning economists, leveraged itself to the hilt, used sophisticated computer models and . . . went spectacularly bust in September 1998. It then needed a $3.6-billion bailout from 14 Wall Street institutions, coordinated by the Federal Reserve. As a consequence, the LTCM diaspora joined Wall Street banks like Lehman Brothers where they introduced similar hubristic thinking.

From the outset, RBS gave Jay Levine and Ben Carpenter, whom it had retained to run Greenwich Capital, a remarkable degree of autonomy. Levine, who had learned his craft as a bond salesman under Wall Street's 'godfather of mortgage finance' Lewis Ranieri, was born in Los Angeles, the son of a Democratic-leaning banker. He did a bachelor's degree in economics at University of California Davis, before spending 1983–84 studying economics at the University of Leeds in England. Contemporaries at Leeds remember Levine as 'loudmouthed, very class conscious, immature and with a penchant for brightly coloured Benetton jumpers'. They were surprised by his ardent support for Margaret Thatcher and hatred of trade unions. One contemporary at Leeds remembers Levine struggling with his economics modules because, unlike his British contemporaries, he had not done calculus at high school. Levine returned to the States to join Freddie Mac in 1985 and then spent 1986 to 1993 at the Wall Street bond-trading powerhouse Salomon Brothers, latterly as head of non-agency mortgage trading. One trader who worked with Levine at Salomon describes him as 'a hustler more than anything else'. The ex-colleague added that, at Greenwich, 'Jay had control of his own balance sheet – that was a matter of pride for Jay. He liked to keep the RBS board in the dark.'

Levine's co-chief executive, Ben Carpenter, was a preppier and more unassuming character. Educated at the Hotchkiss School, a prestigious independent boarding school in Lakeville, Connecticut,

Carpenter was a member of the New England establishment. His 1985 wedding to public relations executive Leigh Worcester was covered by the *New York Times*. Prior to joining Greenwich in the 1990s, he worked for the Wall Street firms Bankers Trust and Morgan Stanley. He was Greenwich Capital's chief operating officer, which meant he oversaw the trading floor and proprietary trading, before being promoted to co-chief executive in early 2000.

In early 2004, Levine and Carpenter declared their intention to transform Greenwich Capital into one of the leading US players in debt capital markets by poaching two of 'the biggest swinging dicks' on Wall Street – John Walsh and Ben Cohen of Credit Suisse First Boston.[15] Walsh, hailed by the *Sunday Times* as one of the most powerful Brits in the US, joined on a package worth a reported $20 million a year in March 2004. The *Sunday Times* said, 'One of the most success-ful international bond bankers of the past 20 years, he is now using RBS's formidable balance sheet to win over Wall Street clients.'[16] Walsh rapidly hired a further 80 bankers in trading, bond origination, syndication and derivatives.

Meanwhile, Levine and Carpenter were content to exploit the RBS balance sheet without allowing their parent firm to have much in the way of access or oversight. Their refusal to engage with the rest of the RBS group was a 'running sore' and 'a constant source of irritation', according to one former GBM executive, which, he said, gave rise both to missed opportunities and to control issues.

Traditionally, trading government bonds and mortgage-backed securities was a comparatively unglamorous sector of the financial markets. However, as the credit bubble inflated, the market for MBSs and CDOs exploded just as mortgage-underwriting standards went through the floor. RBS Greenwich Capital surged up the 'league tables' of underwriters and bundlers of debt, regularly appearing among the top three players. The 600-strong team of traders at Steamboat Road grew to one of over 1,000, with most earning fabulous sums. Traders based in GBM's Bishopsgate office were jealous of their counterparts in Steamboat Road, largely because the latter were on generous fixed commissions. One said, 'Roughly, they were getting 10–14 per cent of each deal. So an ordinary sales person there would be paid several million dollars a year. The equivalent people in the London-based structured finance business would be getting £300,000–400,000. They were paid the best in the market. Jay Levine was paid more than anyone else in banking and that trickled down through all the various levels.'

By 2005, Greenwich Capital had become a vertically integrated debt factory. It was originating mortgage-backed securities and CDOs which were laced with subprime loans. It was then distributing these, taking them on to its own books and trading them. Daniel Gross, the *Newsweek* and *Slate* columnist says, 'They had a different culture – they were not in Manhattan. They were hard-working but they were less stiff than the bulge-bracket firms. They were less client centred. They didn't work to committee. Jay is a very nice, outgoing guy – high energy. They partied hard. They had the image of crazy parties. They had a Christmas holiday with a talent show. They went on trips. As they got more corporate, they became less vulgar, with more women entering the fray.'[17]

In an October 2005 interview with *The Banker*, Levine said, 'Ten years ago I was reluctant to say I was a mortgage trader; now suddenly it's in vogue. We were in the right place.'[18] Greenwich Capital prided itself on being meritocratic. Levine said, 'It's a very easy place, it's a very relaxed place, it's an apolitical place, it's a place where performance really matters and other things don't.'[19] He added, 'There's a consolidation going on among global players, and there's talk about who is going to survive. Well, RBS is going to be around. The resources it takes to compete today are huge, the clients are expecting major commitments, there's trading scale – on any given day, we're clearing $100 billion–$150 billion of bonds. For that you need a significant balance sheet and a significant parent.'[20] The Californian-born trader took home a phenomenal $60 million to $70 million in pay and bonuses between 2005 and 2007.

In June 2005, the trade body the International Swaps and Derivatives Association (ISDA) gave the CDO market fresh impetus by introducing the 'pay-as-you-go' credit default swap. The innovation meant that credit default swaps – quasi insurance policies against borrowers defaulting that are often used for speculation – could be written on asset-backed securities. The result was that, for the first time, the various moving parts of CDOs could be separately insured and effectively gambled upon. The move gave rise to a new phenomenon – the 'synthetic' CDO. These were more liquid – more tradable – than the standard kind and intensified the speculative frenzy in housing finance.

The arrival of the synthetic CDO enabled players in this market to ignore the elephant in its room – that the raw material of newly issued home loans was drying up. As Gillian Tett put it in *Fool's Gold*, 'The big dirty secret of the securitization world was that there was such a frenetic appetite for more and more subprime loans to package into CDOs that the supply of mortgage loans had started to lag behind demand.'[21]

Greenwich seemed blind to the dangers. In early 2006, it boasted that it had become a market leader in the origination, sales and trading of ABS. According to the industry publication, *Inside Mortgage Finance*, it underwrote $188 billion of subprime mortgage-backed securities from 2003 to 2007. It was vying for top slot with Bear Stearns, Lehman Brothers, Merrill Lynch, Citigroup, Credit Suisse and UBS. Having securitised less than $1 billion of US residential mortgages in 2000, it securitised $30.4 billion in 2004. This surged to a peak of $47.9 billion in 2005, before falling marginally to $40 billion in 2006.[22]

The RBS board was relaxed about allowing Greenwich to shoot for the stars. Back in London, Johnny Cameron, who was meant to be overseeing all this activity alongside his colleague Brian Crowe, was promoted to the RBS main board in early 2006 – to the dismay of some non-executive directors including Peter Sutherland. Cameron was getting into a hocus-pocus world all of his own. In a presentation to City analysts in October 2005, the Oxford-educated Old Harrovian said, 'We talk about being insurgent . . . the insurgent incumbent. We talk about restless success; we may be successful but we're still restless. We talk about keeping the magic, it is another phrase. There's something magical, there is some magic, about what we have got in [GBM], about our culture. We need to retain that even while growing into this international business.'[23] Cameron was eager to convey that, despite its transformation into a world-straddling investment bank, GBM could cling to its entrepreneurialism and 'make it happen' ethos. But, to some of the analysts in the room, it seemed like gobbledegook. It was around this time that Goodwin took the anchors off GBM, giving it access to the full RBS balance sheet, and allowed Cameron to do his first media interviews.

Cameron and Crowe made some very expensive hirings in London. In March 2004, they poached Frenchman Vincent Dahinden – a man described as Merrill Lynch's 'top dog' in the area by *Institutional*

Investor magazine – from Merrill Lynch to head up its global structured credit products business. Before Merrill Lynch, Dahinden had been European head of CDOs at Credit Suisse First Boston. The appointment was meant to put RBS on the map. Asked about how the market for CDOs was evolving, Dahinden, also a restaurateur with a stake in Club Gascon in Smithfield (a Michelin-starred restaurant famous for serving pâté de foie gras in seven different ways), commented, 'We're investment bankers, we don't care what happens in five years.'[24] In 11 words, he had summarised the 'devil take the hindmost' attitude of his social group. It was an attitude which, more than anything else, fuelled the gathering storm in global finance.

Dahinden may not have cared about what happened to RBS but he did care about how much tax he paid. A couple of years later, alongside his GBM colleagues Simon Drake-Brockman and Peter Nielsen, he joined an aggressive tax avoidance scheme, Eclipse Film Partners No. 35. Other investors in this wheeze included hedge fund managers, other bankers and the football managers Sir Alex Ferguson and Sven-Göran Eriksson. Eclipse's 289 members piled £50 million into Eclipse 35 in the hope of cutting their personal tax bills by £117 million. But Her Majesty's Revenue and Customs won a landmark court case against the film partnership in 2012, blocking it from receiving any tax relief and thereby undermining its *raison d'être*. Bill Dodwell, head of tax policy at Deloitte, said the Eclipse scheme was 'the closest case I've seen to a legal sham'.[25] After an appeal was defeated in December 2013, investors were saddled with losses of £1 million each, and some were bankrupted.

The derivatives and structured credit markets had become a gold rush. Activity was reaching fever pitch, massively enriching the executives dealing in them as well as their bosses. Many of the executives involved have since claimed that there were no opposing voices – nobody was warning them that the rich seam might soon collapse or even explode. But, in fact, there were a fair few.

On 4 March 2003, Warren Buffett, chairman of insurance firm Berkshire Hathaway, described derivatives as 'time bombs' and 'weapons of mass destruction, carrying dangers that, while now latent, are potentially lethal'.[26] He said they were concentrating, rather than spreading, risk and 'Large amounts of risk, particularly credit risk, have become concentrated in the hands of relatively few derivatives dealers, who, in addition, trade extensively with one another. The troubles of one could quickly infect the others.'[27] Buffett warned that parties involved in derivatives often have 'enormous incentives' to cheat in the accounting of them (in other words, commit fraud) and said contracts involving multiple reference items and distant settlement dates increased the scope for 'fanciful assumptions'.[28] Buffett warned that mark-to-market – which means assigning a current market value to derivative positions – could all too easily become 'mark-to-myth' and that derivatives abuse might well cause a systemic financial crisis.[29]

And, in June 2003, the Bank for International Settlements (BIS) (the central bankers' central bank) warned of a 'rising preponderance' of lending to commercial property and highlighted the massive growth in credit-risk transfer – the shifting of risk from banks onto sometimes gullible third parties and sellers of credit insurance. BIS noted that credit transfer had grown from a few billion dollars in the early 1990s to $2 trillion in 2002. BIS warned of the serious risks wrapped up in this frenetic and opaque game of pass the parcel. The central bankers' central bank said, 'With large firms increasingly trading among themselves, perceived difficulties with one counterparty might very quickly involve others. Moreover, large players can move markets in ways that could affect the cost and availability of needed hedging . . . idiosyncratic shocks could conceivably turn systemic.'[30]

BIS issued a further warning in January 2005, suggesting that the ratings that credit rating agencies were slapping on CDOs were unreliable. BIS urged players in these markets to do more of their own vetting whilst also recommending that they check whether sellers of credit protection, such as AIG, had the wherewithal to provide the promised cover. BIS also warned of so-called 'model risks' – exactly as den Braber had done two years earlier.[31]

Another stern warning came from Raghuram Rajan, then the chief economist at the IMF. Speaking to the elite of global central banking and neoclassical economics at Jackson Hole, Wyoming, in August 2005, Rajan warned that banking might be headed for 'catastrophic meltdown'. He blamed a number of 'perverse behaviours' in the markets.[32] For the gaggle of central bankers and economists at the Jackson Hole event – which was largely a 'love-in' for Alan Greenspan, who was retiring in January 2006 – this was heresy. Disciples of the 'Greenspan doctrine' and RBS bankers preferred their blindness to be wilful.

There were signs the UK's property bubble was stretching when, in October 2003, the BBC's *Money Programme* revealed that HBOS was actively encouraging its mortgage borrowers to lie about their incomes. The Bank of England chief economist Charlie Bean warned of asset price bubbles in July 2003 and the central bank's November 2003 inflation report said that the UK house price growth was unsustainable. These warnings were followed by further red flags about the UK's overheating property market from journalists including Patrick Hosking. Writing in *New Statesman* in April 2004, Hosking complained about estate agents and mortgage lenders who 'seem to think that each price increase adds another brick in the wall of evidence proving that property is somehow immune from the laws of economics. The truth is surely the exact opposite. Every price rise makes an eventual reversal all the more likely.'[33]

Very few people inside RBS seemed to be cognisant of any of these dangers, however.

Having recognised that more acquisitions were out of the question Royal Bank of Scotland was desperate to find other avenues to growth. At an 'off-site' at Gleneagles Hotel in June 2006, McKillop's first as chairman, the board and group executive management committee made the fateful decision to push for further rapid growth in investment banking. In particular, the board wanted GBM to aggressively pursue organic growth in leveraged finance, US mortgages and structured credit. In an email sent to Johnny Cameron, Leith Robertson and David Coleman (the group chief credit officer), Brian Crowe wrote, 'The board has been very bullish in the last 24 hours across all the GBM business in avoiding the defensiveness in approach that we tend to adopt, and to be more aggressive and ambitious.'[34]

But RBS was launching this renewed push just as cannier Wall Street banks, notably Goldman Sachs and JPMorgan, were withdrawing from the casino, and seeking to 'de-risk' their balance sheets by selling off as much of their mortgage-related financial instruments as possible to naive and gullible investors before it was too late. Warnings of an overheating US property market started to sound within weeks of RBS's fateful decision to pump up the volume, notably one from Nouriel Roubini, professor of economics at New York University's Stern School of Business. On 23 August 2006, Roubini said America's housing market was already collapsing and would bring down the US economy. Roubini said, 'Every housing indicator is in free fall, including now housing prices . . . This is the tipping point for the US consumer and the effects will be ugly.'[35]

In October 2006, the JPMorgan chief executive Jamie Dimon telephoned Bill King, head of the New York-based bank's mortgages 'pipeline' and instructed him to start offloading JPMorgan's inventory of subprime-linked assets before it was too late. Dimon said, 'Billy, I want you to watch out for subprime. We need to sell a lot of our positions. I have seen it all before. This stuff could go up in smoke!'[36]

Johnny Cameron and Brian Crowe, the GBM senior management team, only became aware that the US subprime mortgage market was deteriorating in late 2006. Thinking the problem would be short-lived, they remained gung-ho and signed off on Greenwich's appointment of Richard Caplan, head of Citigroup's North American CDO division, in October 2006. Caplan was another veteran of the Salomon Brothers derivatives team, where he had had a role in establishing some of the offshore shell companies that enabled Houston-based energy trading company Enron to cook its books. Caplan was asked to expand Greenwich's presence in the synthetic and cash CDO arena and almost doubled the number of $3m-a-year traders on the firm's CDO trading desk to 25. Despite RBS's concerted push into the repackaging of US subprime debt, Goodwin told the Merrill Lynch banking conference in October 2006, that RBS was steering clear of . . . subprime lending. 'The first overall observation: we don't do subprime credit. We have no subprime credits in our book.'

Asked for his view about potential slowdowns in the US and UK and the risk that, given widespread over-indebtedness, things could 'fall off a cliff' at the same conference, Goodwin said, 'There has been a sort of overhang of people waiting for things to fall out-of-bed and I think it is showing some signs of perhaps not falling out-of-bed at anything like the rate people anticipated. [In the UK there is] I think a palpable sense, and a sense which we would share, that we may – touch wood! – be passing the worst . . . GDP growth in the US still looks like being a number for next year that will begin with a "3" [. . .] If it does fall out-of-bed, which I hope it doesn't, but if it does then I think we [RBS] would be better placed than many.'[37]

In January 2007, when RBS's group risk committee expressed concern about the US subprime market, Greenwich was preparing several

CDO issues backed by warehoused mortgages and was worried that, if it backed out of these, it would end up making big losses on fire-sales of the contents of the warehouse – meaning individual mortgage loans and MBSs – which would have hurt staff bonuses. So it decided to issue the CDOs anyway, selling the junior tranches and making the fateful decision to hold on to the 'super-senior' tranches, which left items of dubious value sitting on the RBS balance sheet.

RBS did not see this as particularly risky – in fact, having loads of AAA-rated assets seemed to improve the bank's capital position. Cameron and others strongly believed that the 'liquidity squeeze' would be a temporary phenomenon. One former senior executive at GBM said, 'They represented £6 billion of assets in a balance sheet of £1000 billion and they were rated AAA-plus. Why would we have looked at those? They were AAA-rated and no one brought them to our attention and said "you really need to worry about these".'

On 6 October 2006, James Grant wrote in *Grant's Interest Rate Observer* that a 10 per cent fall in US house prices would completely wipe out investors in tranches rated AA or below. At the European CDO Summit in Monte Carlo in October 2006, the European financial industry – expecting a forum where they could learn 'new techniques for maximising profits' – was told by Sam DeRosa-Farag, president of hedge fund Ore Hill Partners, that the global CDO party had ended. He said, '[T]here are significant signs of a storm approaching.' And, within weeks, the storm hit. In February 2007, HSBC, Europe's largest bank, admitted that delinquencies on risky US mortgages had risen to a four-year high. Issuing the first profits warning in HSBC's 142-year history, chief executive Michael Geoghegan said the bank, which had tried and failed to acquire RBS twice, had made the mistake of 'going for volume' in the mortgage market.[38]

By March 2007, US house prices were falling sharply, as were the numbers of house sales. This prompted Cameron to launch what it calls a 'drains-up' look at the bank's US subprime exposure and what it might mean for the bank. But, he says, '[U]nfortunately no significant problems were identified, though we did establish a dashboard or a "watch list" of things to keep an eye on. It all looked fine.'

In an interview with the FSA, Cameron said he could not recall when he first became aware that the value of super-senior CDOs might fall as a result of developments in the subprime market. 'I don't think, even at that point, I fully . . . I had enough information. Brian may have thought I understood more than I did . . . And it's around this time [May 2007] that I became clearer on what CDOs were, but it's probably later.'39 Many seasoned investment bankers are stunned by these remarks. Before Cameron sanctioned Greenwich's aggressive bid to expand its presence in the structured credit sector and make audacious bets on CDOs, one might have thought he would have done some homework.

In June 2007, Cameron and colleagues were still hoping that the structured credit market would come roaring back by September. They saw a collapse similar to the one of the 1930s as unlikely. To avoid locking in losses on their super-senior CDO tranches, they decided against hedging their exposures fully. In the end, they only bought $250 million of hedges against their super-senior positions. Cameron told the FSA that this 'optimistic' approach was typical of Goodwin: 'He is and was an optimist and he tended to take an optimistic view of what was likely to happen and had often in his life been proved right . . . He genuinely did not believe that house prices could possibly decline as much as other people thought, and held that view strongly.'40

Bad leveraged bets

In an unprecedented orgy of speculation, debt and equity players were churning commercial property assets for short-term gain, having seemingly convinced themselves that the sector's boom-and-bust cycle was a thing of the past. Innovative deal structures such as so-called 'opco-propco' deals had become flavour of the month. An opco-propco deal is one where a property-heavy company such as Tesco separates into an operating company – the 'opco' – which runs the stores and a property company – the 'propco' – which owns the retail units and leases them back to the opco. Some prime properties were changing hands several times a year, giving rise to rich pickings for loan arrangers like RBS and commercial real estate lawyers.

Under its head of commercial real estate lending Stephen Eighteen, who reported to Leith Robertson, RBS Global Banking and Markets was one of the most prolific lenders to what seemed a burgeoning market. Spurred on by rivalry with old enemy HBOS but also by the arrival of aggressive Irish banks such as Anglo-Irish Bank, Allied Irish Banks and Bank of Ireland in the British market, Eighteen's team was lending prodigious sums to property entrepreneurs and tycoons of all shapes and sizes. However, sensing a commercial property crash might be imminent, other British banks, such as Barclays, Lloyds TSB and HSBC, were drawing back from the market.

Giles Barrie, former editor-in-chief of *Property Week*, says he found RBS's behaviour in this market almost impossible to believe. He says, 'RBS was making really, really rubbish commercial property loans in the UK, Ireland, Germany, Eurozone, South America and Australasia.' He was particularly puzzled by the bank's largesse to UK property tycoon Glenn Maud. With RBS backing him all the way, Maud, a former Sheffield lawyer, built a £4.5-billion commercial property portfolio in the six years between 2002 in 2008. Alongside the Irish property tycoon Derek Quinlan, he purchased 'trophy' assets including Citigroup's 45-storey regional headquarters in Canary Wharf and Ciudad Financiera, Santander's sprawling global headquarters near Madrid. The two global banks finalised the sale-and-leaseback deals, jointly worth £2.6 billion, just as the commercial property bubble was bursting. So RBS was being the mug, outsmarted by its erstwhile ally Santander. The bank was lending huge sums to other property speculators including: the 'Baron of Ballsbridge' Sean Dunne (*see* Chapter 14); Sir John Ritblat, founder and chairman of British Land; the Iranian-born property and retail tycoon Robert Tchenguiz (it lent him £350 million to buy the Welcome Break chain of motorway service stations); and Ulster-based housebuilder brothers Michael and John Taggart. RBS was also lending like there was no tomorrow in continental Europe, including underwriting the €7.57 billion (£5.2 billion) of debt that Spanish property giant Metrovacesa used to fund its ill-timed purchase of its French rival Gecina. Metrovacesa was bust by December 2008 and survived only thanks to a debt-for-equity swap.

One former Global Banking and Markets insider says credit approvals became 'lax' from 2007 onwards. He says, 'While Leith Robertson [the GBM deputy chief executive who oversaw all lending to commercial property and leveraged finance] did not personally sign off loans, he and Johnny could usually sway the credit approval process.' During 2007 and early 2008, the ex-insider said that the process was becoming 'lax and prone to short-circuiting'. Credit committees became much more perfunctory, without anyone asking hard questions. The ex-insider said, 'I challenged Johnny and Leith about this but they defended it, saying the sheer volume of business flow meant that we needed a faster committee process.'

In December 2006, in an interview with *International Financing Review* (*IFR*), Stephen Eighteen outlined plans to expand RBS's global reach further by chasing property tycoons around the world with truck loads of money. He said, 'Over the past ten years real estate has become increasingly global [...] Nowadays, the global opportunity funds and more sophisticated investors take a global approach, so we organise ourselves to service their requirements across the globe, often working with the same client in six or seven different markets.' Seemingly oblivious to the fact that the market for MBSs and CDOs had become polluted and diseased, Eighteen said RBS intended to turbocharge its global commercial property lending through greater use of securitisation and by setting up 'conduits'. Earlier, Alan Dickinson, the bank's chief executive of UK corporate banking, expressed dismay to colleagues about the apparent recklessness that characterised the market for leveraged loans, commercial property loans and some project finance loans during 2005 – a recklessness that was fuelled by the encroachment of trigger-happy Irish banks like Anglo-Irish Bank into the UK. A source said that Dickinson told colleagues, 'I can't wait for this to crash. When it crashes, people will get found out.'

Things were no less out of control in leveraged finance – another area overseen by Leith Robertson. In the heyday of the 'originate and distribute' model of banking, broadly between 2004 and 2007, GBM took the lead in this market in the UK and Europe, lending tens of billions, often at crazy multiples, to leveraged buyouts. And, since leveraged finance bankers were able to palm off this debt so easily onto third parties in the so-called shadow banking system, they became increasingly uninterested in the quality of the underlying loans.

A classic case occurred in November 2006 when RBS and Lehman Brothers lent $2.7 billion (£1.7 billion) to Formula One even though they seemed clueless about the future risks the business faced, including that all the Grand Prix teams looked poised to start racing under a new umbrella body. The money was needed to refinance F1's existing debt by owners CVC Capital Partners. However, according to one of CVC's co-founders, the valuation slapped on the Bernie Ecclestone-run empire was both 'pie in the sky' and 'ridiculous'.

In a court case of November 2013, Donald Mackenzie, co-founder and co-chairman of CVC, claimed RBS and Lehman were 'extremely careless' with regard to the $2.7-billion loan. Mackenzie alleged that the two banks requested that Ernst & Young put a £3.6-billion price tag on the F1 business even though the accountants were supposed to be carrying out an 'independent review'. Mackenzie claimed neither the banks nor E&Y were aware that a 'Concorde' agreement between F1 and the F1 teams had only a year to run and that no successor contract was in place. There was only a non-binding memorandum of understanding, and the team had itchy tyres. Under cross-examination by Philip Marshall QC, Mackenzie said, 'The banks were at the height of a banking boom. They didn't read the MoU properly. They didn't quite work out that it wasn't a Concorde, and they lent money against something that turned out to be very flimsy.' Mackenzie said the fact the teams could have walked away at any time highlighted the lack of security that RBS and Lehman Brothers had for their loan. 'It still surprises me, to this day, that they . . . really had nothing to rely on. And I'm sure they were extremely shocked and worried when, in 2009, it all started to unwind . . . But by that time it was too late, they'd lent the money.'[1]

A similar story was repeated thousands of times at RBS. By 2006–07, its bankers were throwing caution to the wind. Many were only too willing to turn a blind eye to the flakiness of borrowers' business plans and the flimsiness of their collateral and to effectively instruct professional advisers to produce 'stretch' valuations on often worthless assets, just so they could shovel money out the door and earn themselves spectacular bonuses.

At an industry conference in Paris on 14 November 2006, RBS's co-head of leveraged finance in France, François Guichot-Pèrere, boasted that 'for the first time in the French market in 2006 we have been above the eight [debt-to-EBITDA (earnings before interest, taxes, depreciation and amortisation) ratio].' He meant the bank was lending more than eight times a borrowing company's annual earnings and he was proud of it. He also said the number of parties funding each deal had nearly doubled. He said that, in 2002, the average leveraged buyout underwritten by RBS had 130 'debt providers'. By 2006, that had risen to between 220 and 225. He said these debt providers included banks, hedge funds, collateralised loan obligations (CLOs) and collateralised debt obligations (CDOs). Guichot-Pèrere said, 'It's cheaper, there are more bullets . . . And we accept more and more refinancing risk.' So the bank was willing to lend more recklessly and to take on more risk for a few extra sous.

The next speaker at the Parisian event, Richard Collins, managing partner in Indigo Capital, expressed astonishment at the Frenchman's remarks. He warned the assembled debt junkies that the edifice of re-cycled debt that they were building was at risk of implosion since so many of them were 'cutting corners' in pursuit of a fast buck. But Guichot-Pèrere brushed off the criticism, insisting that, if anything did go wrong, the landing would be 'soft'.[2]

Writing six months later in the *Financial Times,* John Plender said that lending standards had collapsed just as risks had escalated and financial returns were being competed away. He said some of the practices in the private equity sector were 'an abomination' that threatened stability and would have 'systemic consequences'.[3]

Cocooned in their Gogarburn bonhomie and satisfied with the profits GBM was creating, the RBS board was oblivious to the gathering storm.

24

I'm a-shattered, shattered!

Despite the mess his bank was already in, Goodwin was tantalised by the possibility of taking over ABN AMRO. He had the first of several discreet tête-à-têtes with the chairman of its management board, Rijkman Groenink, in February 2005. At the time, ABN had a market value of around €35 billion (£24 billion), less than half that of its Edinburgh-based rival, whose market capitalisation was then £56 billion. They met, without advisors, in a café at Heathrow Airport. As they sipped their cappuccinos, the imperious Scotsman and the bespectacled Dutchman discussed the consolidation in European banking, including Santander's recent purchase of Abbey National. However, Goodwin was forced to admit he was unable to do any deals at that time, as his capital ratios were too stretched and his shareholders too small-minded. However, if the situation changed, he said, there was one part of ABN AMRO he really wanted to buy – its Chicago-based subsidiary, LaSalle Bank. Goodwin believed that merging this with Citizens Financial would enable him to mask the weaknesses at Charter One. As he boarded the plane back to Schiphol, Groenink, nine years Goodwin's senior, thought Fred was a man he might be able to do business with.

Like NatWest in 1999, ABN AMRO was a national icon that had lost its way. Formed from the 1991 merger of Algemene Bank Nederland (ABN) and AMRO Bank, it could trace its origins to 1824, when the Netherlands Trading Society was established in The Hague under royal charter by King Willem I. On becoming chairman of the Amsterdam-based bank's management board – the equivalent of chief executive in a UK company – in May 2000, Rijkman Groenink vowed to grow the bank by expanding its wholesale banking arm, which includes lending to corporations and so-called 'casino' activities. The Dutchman, born in the naval port of Den Helder in August 1949, also made a commitment to focus on total shareholder return. He streamlined the lumbering Dutch giant into three global business units – corporate banking and financial markets (wholesale), retail and commercial banking (consumers) and private clients and asset management.

But Groenink's plan failed to deliver for shareholders. So, he embarked on a different strategy of serving mid-sized corporates in the 50 or so countries in which it operated. But this too failed to deliver the earnings per share demanded by investors. Investors then became tetchy when Groenink started making ill-considered international acquisitions. In particular, they disliked his 2006 purchase of Banca Antonveneta, based in Padua, Italy, and his attempted takeover of another Italian bank, Rome-based Capitalia. There was also concern about breaches of money-laundering laws by ABN AMRO's US operations. One analyst says, 'At a time when almost the most incompetent bank in the world could make double-digit returns on equity and stonking profits year after year, ABN AMRO was consistently under-performing.' And Jeroen Smit, the author of *The Perfect Prey*, wrote, 'ABN AMRO had become dysfunctional . . . It was fat, overweight, lazy, blind, arrogant, and consistently under-performing. It was like a wounded elephant that was bleeding from behind. It was the perfect prey.'[1]

Suspecting deal activity might be imminent and still eyeing LaSalle, Goodwin wrote to Groenink on 31 October 2006, asking if they could meet again. The two bankers agreed to meet at ABN's Gustav Mahlerlaan head office in Amsterdam on Tuesday, 9 January. London-based hedge funds began to scent blood. They believed that, if they could load up on ABN shares when they were depressed in value, they would clean up in the event of a contested takeover for ABN, which would almost certainly cause its shares to surge in value. The first to take a big chunk of ABN shares was Toscafund, a specialist hedge run by former Crédit Lyonnais banking analyst Martin Hughes. George Mathewson, who retired as RBS's chairman in April 2006, was chairman of the holding company that owned Toscafund and is thought to have favoured a takeover of Santander by RBS.

After Christmas 2006, Andrea Orcel, an Italian-French senior M&A executive at Merrill Lynch, who was always trying to engineer mergers and acquisitions in the European banking market, had a brainwave. It seemed obvious that ABN AMRO was going to be sold and, if it was, Orcel wanted to be sure that Merrill Lynch had a piece of the action. He was close to Santander's septuagenarian chairman Emilio Botín and knew Botín wanted to get his hands on ABN AMRO's Brazilian subsidiary Banco Real (which ABN had acquired in 1998) and maybe also its Italian subsidiary, Padua-based Banca Antonveneta (which the Dutch bank acquired during 2005–06). Separately, Orcel had heard from his colleague Matthew Greenburgh that Royal Bank of Scotland was gagging for a takeover of LaSalle.

Since Groenink was refusing to sell off these subsidiaries piecemeal, Orcel thought he might persuade RBS and Santander to mount a joint, carve-up bid for the whole of ABN AMRO. The scope for cost savings and synergies would mean that the Spanish and Scottish banks would be able to pay more than any single bidder. At first, Orcel, described as 'a consummate banker, known for his international reach and golden Rolodex',[2] thought, 'No, that's just too crazy. It'll never fly.' But, after mulling things over for a bit, he thought that Merrill Lynch might be able to make a carve-up work.

Born in Italy in 1963, Orcel grew up in Rome. He had worked at Goldman Sachs and Boston Consulting Group before joining Merrill Lynch in 1992. At the investment bank, he focused on M&A, often using his persuasive abilities to talk banks and other financial institutions into doing deals they later regretted.

Gradually, the consortium idea gelled. On Saturday, 6 January, Goodwin called Botín, whose strategic alliance with RBS had been unwound more than two years earlier, and asked him what he thought. The Spaniard was immediately enthusiastic saying that by happenstance he was looking for deals in Italy and Brazil. Botín had also done his homework and he told Goodwin that, for Real and Antonveneta, Santander should pay €17 billion. That was only two billion euros short of what it ended up paying.[3]

Santander and RBS made separate last-ditch attempts to persuade Groenink to sell them the parts of ABN they wanted but the Dutchman was not playing ball. When, as arranged, Goodwin took the Dassault Falcon 900EX to Amsterdam on 9 January to enquire about LaSalle, Groenink gave him short shrift, telling him the Chicago-based bank was not for sale, but promising to let the Scot know should it become available. On the flight home, RBS's director of strategy Iain Allan told Goodwin that he ought to be relieved. He said, even if Groenink had offered them ABN AMRO wrapped up as a Christmas present with a pretty bow, RBS should have rejected it. He warned the Paisley-born accountant that ABN was a sprawling and incoherent series of businesses which were largely sub-scale and lacking in competitive advantage. Allan was later to be sidelined as a result of his lack of enthusiasm for the deal. Soon afterwards McKillop called Goodwin to ask if there was any substance to the rumours that the Paisley Buddy was plotting a takeover of ABN AMRO. Goodwin was relaxed, saying, 'Groenink? Oh, I've been talking to him for ages and keeping the door open in case we can arrange something.' However, he did tell McKillop he thought that certain parts of the Amsterdam-based bank would be a perfect fit for RBS. McKillop was sceptical, not least because RBS had lately been promising it would do no more big deals.

Unbeknown to either Santander or RBS at this stage, ABN was by now deep in talks with its Dutch rival ING Groep about a merger that would have formed a Dutch 'national champion' – a deal that met with the approval of Nout Wellink, president of De Nederlandsche Bank (DNB), the Dutch central bank. The talks had been under way since early December 2006. It was the sort of cosy and shareholder-unfriendly deal that most Anglo-Saxon investors and hedge funds hated and they were seeking to derail it by pushing up ABN's share price and pushing down that of ING. On 10 January, the day after Goodwin's visit, Chris Hohn, the abrasive Surrey-born founder of London-based hedge fund The Children's Investment Fund (TCI), which had by now amassed a reported 2 per cent stake in ABN AMRO, had a meeting with Groenink in Amsterdam. He brought Davide Serra, an Italian-born hedge fund manager who had formerly worked as a banking analyst at Morgan Stanley.

Hohn and Serra did not mince their words. They told Groenink that his time was running out, that ABN AMRO's financial performance was dismal and that, if he had not turned around the bank's performance by June, they would force a break-up. Groenink was appalled. He suspected they were acting as a Trojan horse for Santander and RBS. The suspicion intensified when, the next day, Merrill Lynch's European banks analyst Stuart Graham issued a research note savaging Groenink for his performance as chairman and saying that the sum-of-the-parts valuation of ABN AMRO was higher than the bank's valuation as a single entity. As a result of this, ABN AMRO was now considered to be firmly 'in play' (vulnerable to takeover).

In the UK, as in the US, the authorities are relaxed about hedge funds and private equity firms picking off and ripping apart underperforming companies and firing thousands of workers. On the Continent, such behaviour is seen in a less favourable light. Hohn, the son of a Jamaican car mechanic, saw no merit in the Continental approach. He believed activist hedge funds such as TCI were a force for the good – they held complacent elites to account, boosted efficiency, and provided investors, including pension funds, with better returns. By now, a number of leading hedge funds had built up sizeable positions in ABN's shares. They included:

- **Algebris Investments** – founded in 2006 by Davide Serra, a former Morgan Stanley analyst who first presented Hohn with a break-up case for ABN in summer 2006. In October 2006, Hohn provided Serra with seed capital to set up the fund.[4]
- **Atticus Capital** – founded in 1995 by Tim Barakett. Nathaniel Rothschild, son of Lord Rothschild, was a London-based partner. In 2007, Atticus sought to bully Barclays' chairman, Marcus Agius, into dropping plans to merge with ABN AMRO.[5]
- **The Children's Investment Fund (TCI)** – founded in 2003 by Chris Hohn and Patrick Degorce. One of the hedge-fund world's most combative financiers, Hohn prides himself on giving a percentage of the fund's profits to charity.
- **J.C. Flowers & Co.** – founded in 2001 by California-born former Goldman Sachs partner J. Christopher Flowers, who is close to Jacob Rothschild. Ex-ABN CEO Jan Kalff was acting on behalf of the fund in autumn 2006. He approached Groenink to say, if ABN were to make any disposals, J.C. Flowers was be interested in buying them.
- **RIT Capital Partners** – founded as an investment trust in 1961 by Lord (Jacob) Rothschild. TCI's Hohn stepped down as a non-executive director in June 2007 'to remove any wrong impression of conflict of interest'. RIT acquired an undisclosed number of ABN shares between 21 February and 22 May 2007.
- **Toscafund** – founded by Martin Hughes in 2000, Toscafund is a long/short financial services sector fund. Ex-Royal Bank chair-

man George Mathewson is chairman of holding company Old Oak Holdings, where ex-RBS finance director Fred Watt was a non-executive. Hughes is a former banking analyst at Crédit Lyonnais, house brokers to RBS.[6]

European businessmen who had been on the receiving end of the Hohn treatment describe him as a very nasty piece of work. Werner Seifert, former chief executive of the German stock exchange Deutsche Börse, had had a bruising encounter with him a couple of years earlier. In a book he wrote about the experience, Seifert described Hohn's style as 'poison'.[7]

The situation became bruising for Groenink on 20 February, when TCI sent Groenink a highly aggressive letter. Written by TCI's Patrick Degorce, this berated him for his management of the bank and demanded that ABN push ahead with 'a spin-off, sale or merger of its various businesses'. It also said ABN must desist from any further acquisitions. The letter laid down a five-point action which TCI said must be presented and voted on at ABN's annual general meeting, due to be held in Amsterdam on 26 April.[8]

For brass neck, it took some beating. Groenink, then aged 57, was horrified, not least because Degorce and Hohn had already leaked the letter to Bloomberg News. He went to see Nout Wellink, president of De Nederlandsche Bank, the central bank. Wellink's biggest concern was that the hedge funds would scupper plans to form a Dutch 'national champion' through the merger of ABN AMRO and ING. Wellink, who had previously worked in the Dutch finance ministry, was so anxious he barely slept that night.

Speaking to the Dutch newspaper *NRC Handelsblad* a couple of days later, Wellink accused TCI of being 'close to reckless' and criticised its demand that ABN should 'work out what bits the bank should sell, and send the proceeds to us', saying this was 'a bridge too far'.[9] He hoped that publicly denigrating TCI as reckless would help ensure it was reined in, but voices from outside Holland clipped his wings by accusing him of protectionism. A spokesman for the European commissioner for internal market and services, Charlie McCreevy, declared that Wellink had no right to block 'legitimate capital-market activity'.[10] Wellink later stressed that he was being neither xenophobic nor protectionist. He just doubted whether it was wise to let hedge funds, with ultra-short-term agendas, dictate the policy of systemically important banks.[11]

Groenink suspected that hedge funds, including TCI and Toscafund, had formed a concert party to destabilise his bank and open the door to a hostile takeover from RBS and Santander. He was so concerned about this he persuaded the Dutch financial markets regulator *Autoriteit Financiële Markten* (AFM) to mount an official probe into the activities of TCI and other hedge funds. But AFM eventually closed its probe having found no evidence of malpractice.

At RBS's results presentation on 1 March 2007, the *FT*'s Peter Thal Larsen asked Goodwin if the buccaneering Scot considered himself 'out of the sin-bin' where acquisitions were concerned and whether he was doing or planning any further acquisitions.[12] Goodwin declared himself out of the sin-bin but insisted he was unaware of any possible deals at the time. 'I can't think there is anything out there at the moment that seems desirable, doable or affordable.'[13] That was a massive distortion of the truth – Goodwin had been busily plotting a takeover of ABN AMRO for two months and met Groenink about a possible alliance seven weeks earlier. RBS had gone as far as allocating secret code names to the parties involved: Santander was 'Sand', RBS was 'Rock' and their Dutch quarry was 'Arran', while the venture itself was dubbed 'Project Arran'. However, to be fair to Goodwin, FTSE-100 chief executives are often obliged to tell white lies when asked about market-sensitive plans that aren't yet in the public domain.

At the event, RBS unveiled pre-tax profits for 2006 of £6.5 billion, up 17 per cent on the previous year. Most of the growth was coming from Cameron's investment bank and Goodwin admitted that, during 2006, gathering deposits had been a 'difficult gig' for Citizens. Overall he claimed the results 'demonstrate that our model and our risk appetite has kept us away from some of the landmines. In unsecured consumer finance, we haven't had some of the shocks others have had [and] the fact we don't get involved in subprime lending has been another landmine we've kept away from.' Affronted by suggestions the US business was involved in subprime, Citizens' Larry Fish said, 'We don't do subprime, we have never done subprime, we have no plans to do subprime – subprime brings with it operational risks, regulatory risks and, of course, credit risks.'[14]

The City liked the results, especially the confirmation that subprime lending and big takeovers were off the agenda, and the 25 per cent hike in the dividend, and sent RBS shares up 60p to 2,069p.

On Friday 16 March, Groenink and the chairman of ABN AMRO's supervisory board, the former Sears, Roebuck chairman Arthur Martinez, had a meeting with TCI's Hohn and Degorce in London. They discussed TCI's letter of 20 February. Martinez and Groenink sought to persuade the hedge fund managers to drop their campaign to introduce resolutions at the bank's forthcoming AGM. But Hohn and Degorce refused to back down and the meeting ended in stalemate.

Meanwhile ABN's plan to form a 'national champion' by merging with ING was unravelling fast. It was largely because ING chief executive Michel Tilmant was never going to offer more than €31 per ABN share. There was no way the hedge funds were going to accept that. By 13 March, ABN's supervisory board dropped the proposed ING tie-up.

Desperate to avoid ABN falling into what he saw as the wrong hands, Groenink immediately resuscitated talks with Barclays. He had already met John Varley, the English bank's urbane chief executive, three times to discuss a possible merger between their two banks – in the spring of 2006, the autumn of 2006 and, most recently, at a meeting in Geneva in February 2007. They had already sketched out a five-point plan which would see Barclays make a string of concessions to assuage Dutch pride. These included that the merged bank should be headquartered in Amsterdam and that Groenink should be chairman of its supervisory board. Groenink called Varley in his head office at 1 Churchill Place, Canary Wharf, and said, 'We've closed the other file and we've made our decision. We are now ready to enter talks with you.' Varley – a strong believer in cross-border consolidation who harboured a dream of turning Barclays into a European version of Citigroup – was immediately enthusiastic. He replied, 'Fantastic – let's talk on Monday.' Barclays' chief executive of retail and commercial banking, Frits Seegers, a Dutchman, was no less buoyed up by the prospect of a deal. Seegers knew the Benelux market well and was on a mission to rapidly transform Barclays into a global force in retail banking.

When someone in the Barclays camp leaked the fact that Barclays was in merger talks with ABN to the *Sunday Times*, Groenink was furious. He saw it as a crass ploy designed to railroad him into exclusive talks. On Sunday, 18 March 2007, the newspaper's business section splashed with a story headlined 'Barclays in £80-billion offer to ABN AMRO'.[15] The article, written by Grant Ringshaw, presented Barclays as ABN's 'white knight', adding 'a deal would also be the biggest-ever cross-border banking transaction in Europe, creating a group with 47 million customers and more than 220,000 staff'.[16] By Monday, Groenink's anger had dissipated and the two banks felt able to jointly issue a brief stock exchange announcement confirming that they were in 'exclusive preliminary discussions' concerning a merger.[17]

Fred Goodwin was appalled. He had long feared that either Royal Bank or Barclays would end up being snapped up by JPMorgan Chase or Citigroup. Now that Barclays was poised to merge with ABN AMRO, he was concerned RBS would be the one that got gobbled up. One person who knows Goodwin well said, 'On hearing about the Barclays–ABN merger, Fred would have thought, "F★★k, it's us! Barclays is making itself bid-proof!"'

Deciding attack was the best form of defence, Goodwin activated plans for a 'carve-up' takeover of ABN AMRO – though he was mindful of the need to structure the deal in a way that would be acceptable to RBS's board and its shareholders. If the deal was going to fly, Santander and RBS were going to have to rustle up a third European bank to support their bid by buying ABN's Benelux branch network – which neither RBS nor Santander wanted.

Orcel came up trumps when he identified a willing buyer: Count Maurice Lippens, then 64, a Belgian aristocrat who had recently been ranked as the second most influential person in Belgium and had been chairman of the Belgo-Dutch bancassurer Fortis since its formation.

Orcel also sold the idea to Fortis's chief executive, another Belgian, named Jean-Paul Votron, then 56. Votron was a former Unilever, Citigroup and ABN AMRO marketer. It helped that both Lippens and Votron bore long-term grudges against Groenink. Votron had never forgiven the Dutchman for failing to appoint him to the ABN management board when they were both at the Amsterdam-based bank in the early 2000s. Lippens still resented the way in which the Dutchman almost thwarted his acquisition of Brussels-based Générale de Banque, in 1998.

Fortis had been eyeing up ABN's European branch network for some time – indeed it had been working alongside Citigroup on a joint bid for ABN. But the New York-based giant, worried about its subprime exposure, had recently pulled out. So, when Merrill Lynch's Orcel and Scholten came knocking at Fortis's Brussels headquarters, they were pushing at an open door. 'They [Lippens and Votron] were thrilled to be given the chance to play at banking's top table,' said one investment banker. The Belgians had no idea that Orcel was acting for Santander and that they were being drafted in as the fall guys.

With Fortis in the bag, Orcel believed the consortium could offer more than €35 a share for ABN, trumping Barclays' offer, which was expected to be in the region of €32. He also believed the hedge funds could be relied upon to exert pressure on the ABN board.

The RBS board met in London on 28 March. As the meeting opened, the mood was despondent. Some directors were concerned that Varley was pole-vaulting over their heads, thumbing his nose at them as he flew through the air. Not only did it look like he would walk off with ABN AMRO, it also looked like RBS would be incapable of doing anything about it. Then Goodwin, in a calculatedly low-key way, told them RBS might be able to buy ABN as part of a three-way consortium with Santander and perhaps also Fortis. The consortium would be able to pay €36 per ABN share, blowing Varley and Barclays out of the water. 'It was as if Fred had pulled a rabbit out of his hat,' said one RBS director. 'And the trump card was the involvement of Botín.' If the wily Spaniard, still hugely respected by the RBS board, was going to be part of this, it had to be a good idea. 'Fred played a blinder,' said one former RBS director who was present. He made a great show of just putting it forward as an idea. But we all knew he really wanted to do it. It seemed so brilliant. Matthew Greenburgh was key to all this and he was shuffling around in the background.' In order to ensure that the thing got through, Goodwin and Greenburgh had pre-briefed Tom McKillop on the proposal and he had sold it in advance to certain influential non-executive directors of RBS, including Peter Sutherland. That helped ensure the entire board voted in favour.

The only non-executive director who raised serious objections was Sir Steve Robson. However, his concerns related more to the complexity of what was being proposed than its wisdom. The most enthusiastic board member was RBS chairman Sir Tom McKillop, who told the meeting that the consortium banks would have to offer in excess of €36 per ABN AMRO share to be sure of victory. One area of excitement was that, in combining ABN AMRO's investment banking business with that of RBS, the merged outfit would dominate the rankings and league tables in many of the categories of investment banking, especially in the US. The RBS board then got so mired in a discussion about the practicalities of a consortium bid that they did not even discuss whether a three-way carve-up bid made any sense.

All the while, Groenink and Varley and their back-up teams were ploughing ahead with merger talks. They were aiming to tie the knot as soon as possible in order to pre-empt any rival bids.

Goodwin's Dassault Falcon touched down in Brussels on Friday, 30 March. He had come to charm his new Belgian friends, Count Lippens, whose grandfather had been governor general of the Belgian Congo, and the former Unilever marketer Votron. The two Belgians were still pinching themselves that, finally, they had been given the chance to play at banking's top table. When Goodwin lunched with Lippens in Fortis's magnificent Haussmann-esque corporate headquarters in the centre of Brussels, the Count 'fell immediately for the charm of Fred Goodwin'.[18] The pair saw eye to eye on how to carve up ABN and Goodwin and Votron also hit it off, especially after Matthew Greenburgh alerted Fred to their shared enthusiasm for fast cars and jets. On 11 April 2007, RBS's eight-man 'chairman's advisory group' – whose members were Colin Buchan, Fred Goodwin, Archie Hunter, Tom McKillop, Miller McLean, Bob Scott, Peter Sutherland and Guy Whittaker – gave the RBS chief executive the green light he craved. It was all systems go.

The following day, 12 April, RBS, Santander and Fortis congregated at the *belle époque* Four Seasons Hotel des Bergues, overlooking Lake Geneva. Even though this was where the League of Nations first met in 1920, these 'three amigos' hadn't come to make peace but war. Goodwin was accompanied by the RBS finance director Guy Whittaker, Merrill Lynch's Matthew Greenburgh and a handful of bank corporate finance and strategy staff. He had sidelined the man who customarily advised on deals, RBS director of strategy Iain Allan, because of his lack of enthusiasm for the planned acquisition. The principal negotiators for the other two banks were Lippens and Votron for Fortis, and Botín and Juan Rodríguez Inciarte, for Santander. A graduate in economics from the Universidad Autónoma of Madrid, Inciarte, then 54, had been involved with all Santander's deals since 1985. The banks had booked the entire suite of opulent, Louis-Philippe-style meeting rooms on the hotel's first floor.

One priority for the consortium banks was to ensure that their offer was pitched at a level that would be sufficiently generous to ABN shareholders to blow Barclays out of the water. Other priorities included agreeing how to carve up ABN AMRO and settling how much money each bank should pay.

Botín and Inciarte outsmarted their consortium partners that day. 'Neither Lippens nor Goodwin had done their homework. Compared to the Spaniards, they were woefully underprepared,' said one advisor to the consortium. Inciarte played a critical role and one of those who was present described him as 'a slippery character who ran rings around Fred and Guy, who were both very much in his thrall'. Another banker who was present said, 'Throughout the process, Emilio played Fred like a Stradivarius. He would put his arm around Fred and say, "Fred, you're the best bank CEO in the world – you're amazing!" But at the same time, he'd be picking his back pocket.' But Botín did grant one concession to Goodwin. He asked him to take care of the day-to-day management of the bid process.

One investment banker said that letting Botín get his way at the Hotel des Bergues meeting was among Goodwin's biggest mistakes. He said, 'Fred was a sucker. He signed up to an agreement that was legally binding for the rest of the acquisition process. He's been living with the consequences ever since.'

By 8 o'clock in the evening, it was agreed. Goodwin would take Chicago-based LaSalle, ABN's Asian banking operations, investment banking in Europe and the United States and the global transaction services business. Botín would get São Paulo-based Banco Real, the fourth-largest non-government-owned bank in Brazil, and Italy's Banca Antonveneta. Fortis would get branch banking in Benelux and a hodgepodge of wealth-management and asset-management businesses. In terms of price, the three amigos calculated that Barclays might offer as much as €36 per share so they decided to offer in the region of €39 per share. They agreed that 'Rock' (RBS) would pay 38 per cent of the total price, 'Fire' (Fortis) 34 per cent and 'Sand' (Santander) 28 per cent.

Before celebrating their accord with a glass of champagne, the three amigos sent a letter to Groenink letting him know of their intention to bid. It was hand-delivered to Groenink's office in Amsterdam next morning. The letter, the equivalent to a declaration of war, told of the amigos' 'strong interest' in acquiring ABN and insisted their offer would give the Dutch bank's shareholders 'immediate and superior value at a materially higher level than Barclays'. They said that, as a matter of urgency, they wanted to meet the ABN AMRO board to discuss their scheme. When Groenink opened the letter on Friday, 13 April, he was appalled. Even though he found it 'emotionally insufferable', he was reasonably confident that regulators in Holland, Belgium and the UK would block it. He says, 'My conviction was that what they were proposing was physically impossible – and I turned out to be pretty much right.'[19]

Goodwin's Dassault Falcon 900EX touched down at Schiphol Airport at about 5 p.m. on Sunday, 22 April. He had managed to persuade Groenink and other members of the ABN AMRO board to meet the amigos to hear their proposals at a meeting scheduled for 11.30 a.m. on Monday, 23 April. Goodwin had booked himself and his friends into the €600-per-night Amstel Hotel, which overlooks the Amstel River not far from the city centre. The hotel is a favoured haunt of the Rolling Stones when they are on tour in Holland. But Goodwin might well have mimed the Stones' 1978 song 'Shattered' ('Look at me, I'm in tatters! I'm a-shattered, shattered!') when three bombshells landed over the next few hours.

The first came on Sunday afternoon, before he was even airborne, when he learned that ABN and Barclays had consummated their deal and were poised to make a formal merger announcement on the Monday or Tuesday. Barclays would effectively be acquiring ABN for €67 billion – or a higher-than-expected €36.25 per ABN share – after having bent over backwards to accommodate Dutch regulators and assuage Dutch national pride. The second item of bad news came later on the Sunday. Groenink was selling LaSalle for the eye-watering sum of $21 billion to Bank of America. The record-breaking deal, described as 'poison pill' defence in that it made ABN less attractive to RBS, had been organised by the Dutch bank's patrician head of investment banking, Wilco Jiskoot. A third bombshell came at about 8.30 a.m. on Monday and, for Goodwin, it was the most devastating. Groenink's personal assistant called to say their meeting was off. Groenink had 'other engagements'. These included press conferences to trumpet the ABN and Barclays tie-up in London and Amsterdam.[20] Fred found the triple snubbing – no Groenink and therefore no meeting, no LaSalle, no ABN merger – infuriating in the extreme. He vowed revenge. One ex-colleague said, 'For Fred it became personal. He was telling us he wanted to "get Rijkman". At the time, it seemed like he'd stop at nothing to take him down.'

Goodwin's next move was to summon Groenink to Edinburgh for a meeting. Groenink offered to come on Tuesday, 24 April but Goodwin said that was impossible since he would be preparing for RBS's annual general meeting that day. Then the three amigos clarified their plans at a crowded press conference in Edinburgh on Wednesday, 25 April. The event, attended by journalists, photographers and film crews from all over Europe, was a slightly odd affair, as a result of Goodwin's insistence that the consortium was not making a bid or an offer for ABN and because the faltering English of Botín and Votron meant they could not understand journalists' questions. When Goodwin was asked by a Dutch journalist from *De Telegraaf* how the consortium would raise the €50 billion in cash it needed to fund its putative bid, he was evasive and just said, 'I think most people will think we are good for it. We've got the cash.'[21] In answer to a question about due diligence, Goodwin admitted he felt that cursory due diligence would suffice. He said, 'I think due diligence-lite would be what we'd be really wanting to do.'[22] Asked whether he would consider bidding for Banco Real on his own in the event of the consortium falling apart, Botín said, 'We are very, very happy to have Royal Bank and Fortis in this deal. This deal will be very good for everybody – for the shareholders of our three banks and also for the shareholders of the ABN bank.'[23]

The three amigos finally got a chance to talk to Groenink on the phone at 7 p.m. that evening. Dialling from his conference room on the 21st floor of ABN's Gustav Mahlerlaan head office, Groenink was accompanied by four other bankers, including advisors Donald Moore of Morgan Stanley and John Cryan of UBS. Goodwin started by demanding to know why the Dutchman was not taking the consortium more seriously. Groenink said, 'I'm terribly sorry, Fred, your letter of interest is too vague and too insubstantial for us to take seriously.' Goodwin then resorted to legalistic bullying, saying that, unless ABN AMRO started to treat the consortium with the seriousness he felt it deserved, he would sue them. Groenink put the speakerphone on mute and he and his colleagues and advisers had a good laugh at Fred's expense. Groenink then repeatedly asked Goodwin (a) to explain how the consortium intended to source the cash portion of its bid and (b) to provide more details on the consortium's plans for individual business units in the event that it was successful. Goodwin shouted back, 'It's none of your bloody business. I'm not here to be cross-examined.' Things were not getting off to a very good start.

Next, Goodwin had a shouting match with Cryan. The RBS chief accused Cryan, co-head of UBS's financial institutions group, of having betrayed him. This was because UBS had been instrumental in orchestrating the $21-billion sale of LaSalle to Bank of America even though, as 'house broker', UBS was also a longstanding advisor to RBS. But his jibes were a source of further hilarity in Gustav Mahlerlaan. The Dutch were wondering whether the Scot was losing the plot. Yet Goodwin had sympathisers in the City of London, many of whom accused Groenink of failing to look after the interests of ABN shareholders. 'It seems remarkable to me that they [the ABN board] want to recommend a paper deal at a lower price against a largely cash deal at €39. How that is not an abuse of fiduciary duty is a mystery to me,' said Alex Potter, an analyst at the stockbrokers Collins Stewart.[24]

When VEB, a Dutch shareholders' association, took ABN to court over its failure to allow investors to vote on the LaSalle sale, the battle took on a surreal quality. At ABN AMRO's annual general meeting, held in The Hague on Thursday 26 April, VEB's director Peter Paul de Vries, who was convinced that Groenink was acting against shareholders' interests in not taking Goodwin's consortium more seriously, stormed the stage and ended up being escorted out of the building by security guards. Shareholders had turned against the Dutch bank and were showing little faith in its management. Seventy per cent of them voted that the bank should either be sold or broken up.

On Friday 27 April, ABN agreed to provide the consortium with limited access to due diligence material. It was a minor coup for Goodwin but he still faced massive obstacles. These included Groenink's entrenched preference for Barclays as well as bloodcurdling threats from Bank of America chief executive Ken Lewis that he would use the might of the law to destroy any bank or individual that sought to scupper BofA's acquisition of LaSalle.

Goodwin was cheered when, on 3 May 2007, the Enterprise Chamber of the Amsterdam Appellate Court halted the sale of LaSalle, saying ABN AMRO would, after all, need to obtain shareholder approval if it wanted to sell the division. Staff in Gogarburn were astonished when Goodwin came out of his office clutching a Bloomberg story on the court ruling – and actually smiling. 'As a member of staff, you never saw Fred Goodwin smile,' one commented.

In one critical passage in the FSA's December 2011 report into RBS's failure, the regulator highlighted that the skimpy due diligence material that ABN had grudgingly handed over – which the regulator famously described as only 'two lever arch files and a CD-ROM' – was not made fully available to the RBS board.[25]

By this time, relations between the consortium and ABN AMRO had hit an all-time low. When Goodwin, Lippens, Votron, Martinez and Groenink had dinner together in the Amstel Hotel – the same fancy establishment where Goodwin had thrown a wobbly two weeks earlier – on Friday, 4 May, the atmosphere was glacial. Over the course of the meal, it became clear to the three amigos that Groenink would stop at nothing to escape their clutches. And it was also plain that Votron and Groenink still hated each other's guts. Before the hors d'oeuvres arrived at about 7.50 p.m., the bankers were surprised to hear bells tolling in the Amsterdam streets. Jeroen Smit said, 'The bankers were just sitting down to a glass of wine when bells began to toll. They looked at each other. Lippens realised that it was the signal to stand in memory of the fallen of the Second World War. He told Goodwin and Martinez that it was the tradition in Holland for everyone to stand for two minutes' silence and he proposed that they should honour the custom. The Belgian banker stood and the American and Scottish bankers, impressed by the solemnity of the occasion, did likewise. Votron and Groenink, despite being locked in bitter dispute, sulkily followed suit. For a short while silence was observed. Martinez felt that these were the best moments of the meeting.'[26]

On Sunday, 6 May, a day on which news of the disappearance of three-year-old Madeleine McCann from the Portuguese resort of Praia da Luz dominated the headlines, ABN AMRO's advisors, Morgan Stanley and UBS, submitted 31 questions to the consortium. They said they needed answers to assess whether the consortium's proposals were of any merit. At 5.45 p.m. on that day, Greenburgh fired off a response from his Blackberry, saying, '[W]e have provided sufficient informa-tion for you to be able to determine that our acquisition proposal is superior, subject only to confirmatory due diligence.' He added that some of the vendor's finer points could be taken up by the consortium's lawyers, Linklaters. On Monday, 7 May 2007, ABN AMRO formally rejected the consortium's $24.5-billion offer for LaSalle, claiming the conditions, which included that the consortium would have immunity from any litigation emanating from Bank of America, made it inferior to the Bank of America's $21-billion offer. The battle for ABN was becoming a field day for £1,000-an-hour 'magic circle' solicitors but hardly a barrel of laughs for others.

When they heard ABN had spurned their offer for LaSalle, senior RBS insiders, including Iain Allan and Miller McLean, were delighted. They assumed this meant the madness was over – that the three-bank consortium could be disbanded and Fred and other senior RBS figures could get back to their day jobs of running the bank (where there were some important issues to attend to, including subprime exposure in the US). Fred had repeatedly said LaSalle was the only really desirable part of ABN. If it wasn't available, the takeover plan clearly made no sense. The RBS executives were therefore incredulous when, following an RBS board meeting in Gogarburn and a consortium meeting in St Andrews, they learned that RBS was continuing to pursue its prey.

And once again, there were no dissenters on the RBS board. According to Gordon Pell, 'We went round the table and we voted and there was not a single dissenter.'²⁷ The process of finalising the offer document began in earnest.

In May, ABN AMRO allowed 50 Royal Bank employees a cursory look at its operations for due diligence purposes. They spent a day visiting their opposite numbers at ABN AMRO's head office and in other offices around the world. According to the FSA report, a few anomalies, including flaws in ABN's financial-market risk-management processes, were discovered but were ignored by RBS. 'Nevertheless, [RBS] executive management concluded from the due diligence that they had found nothing that should dissuade RBS from proceeding with the acquisition.'²⁸

Strangely, this contradicts another section of the FSA report, where Cameron is quoted as saying, 'One of the things that went wrong for RBS was that, and I say this to many people, we bought NatWest as a hostile acquisition. We did no due diligence. We couldn't because it was hostile. After we bought NatWest, we had lots of surprises, but almost all of them were pleasant. And I think that lulled us into a sense of complacency around that. The fact is that the acquisition of ABN was also hostile. We got bits and pieces of information but fundamentally it was hostile. There's this issue of "did we do sufficient due diligence". Absolutely not. We were not able to do due diligence . . . that was part of doing a hostile acquisition.'[29]

Despite the potential disaster that loomed if the deal went wrong, Goodwin still found time to spend the weekend of 26–27 May at the Monaco Grand Prix, where he was spotted on Monday 28 May cavorting with motor sports legends whose lifestyles RBS was massively subsidising, including the RBS global ambassador Sir Jackie Stewart. According to one report, Goodwin's decision to attend the Grand Prix in the swanky Mediterranean tax haven caused the consortium's offer for ABN AMRO to be delayed for a day, a story RBS's press office denied at the time.[30]

Goodwin flew back to London on Monday night and, first thing on Tuesday 29 May, he and his amigos, having restructured the bid to take account of the LaSalle situation, had another day in the glare of camera flashes and television lights as they unveiled their record-breaking €71.1-billion offer for the whole of the Dutch bank, conditional on LaSalle not being sold. The amigos were in generous mood, stumping up €38.40 per ABN share, with the cash portion lifted to a very generous 79 per cent, a move intended to satisfy their friends in the hedge-fund world.

The consortium claimed it would be able to make cost savings of €4.2 billion a year and generate extra annual profits of €1.2 billion if its proposals came to fruition. The three consortium banks planned to lay off 23,600 ABN staff, which was fewer than Barclays envisaged. At the analysts' conference, Goodwin was chipper. He said, 'We feel better about it than we did a month ago. We've had a chance to do more work, to gain more insight into ABN AMRO – and the numbers work. When you've got a compelling industrial logic . . . you can expect satisfactory returns.'[31] He rejected suggestions that the businesses Royal Bank was targeting were second rate and rubbished the idea that he was only interested in size and scale. With his trademark indignant sarcasm, he said, 'Goals around purely size are not particularly wonderful.'[32] When asked about RBS's stretched capital ratios, he sneered 'the principal arbiters [of capital ratios] would tend to be the ratings agencies who have expressed comfort with what's being proposed, so we're not losing any sleep over that one either'.[33] Goodwin got his comeuppance the next day when Moody's placed RBS on negative watch – meaning it was considering marking down its credit rating. Moody's said this was as a result of RBS's weak capital position and the 'execution risks' associated with its ABN bid. Goodwin added, 'It's been a long-running saga to question the financing, but there's even more cash in the deal now than before, so financing has not been an issue.'[34]

The Economist magazine was distinctly iffy about the proposals, writing, 'Taking over a banking group sprawled over 53 countries is hard enough. Splitting its businesses three ways is an even bigger task.'[35] Rival bankers were wondering if Goodwin had lost the plot, while central banker Mervyn King quietly got out his red flag and waved it about a bit. But there were plenty cheering for Fred too. Alex Salmond, who had been voted in as Scotland's First Minister on 16 May, wrote to Fred saying:

Dear Fred,
I wanted you to know that I am watching events closely on the ABN front. It is in the Scottish interest for RBS to be successful, and I would like to offer any assistance my office can provide. Good luck with the bid.
Yours for Scotland,
Alex[36]

Salmond was gung-ho for a deal but sources close to the First Minister stress that, at the time, he was labouring under the misapprehension that that regulators, including the FSA and De Nederlandsche Bank, were doing their jobs properly. When he wrote the letter, the First Minister assumed the FSA would not allow RBS to take over ABN AMRO if it put the Edinburgh-based bank's future at risk.

That Border Collie feeling

As he pursued his dream of acquiring ABN AMRO, Fred Goodwin was driven by three main things. The first was that he wanted to 'stop Barclays'. He feared that if Barclays was successful it would make itself bid-proof and RBS would find itself vulnerable to takeover. Secondly he wanted to 'get Rijkman'. He was furious with the chairman of ABN AMRO's managing board because he had made a fool of Goodwin early in the proceedings and because of his failure to honour a commitment over LaSalle. Thirdly, Goodwin had a binding legal agreement with his consortium partners. Under the terms of the so-called 'Geneva Convention' (the deal to which he had signed up at the Hotel des Bergues overlooking Lake Geneva), the three banks had agreed to emulate Alexandre Dumas' three musketeers' 'All for one, one for all' commitment in their fight for ABN AMRO. But the Geneva Convention also meant that the Royal Bank was obliged to see the deal through, even if the ground shifted under its feet. The fourth reason, the public one, was that Goodwin still believed that ABN AMRO was the deal of the century – it was simply too good to miss.

And, publicly, Goodwin remained upbeat about the deal. One RBS executive director said he did not once detect Fred Goodwin's enthusiasm waning at any stage during the six-month takeover battle – not even after obstacles like the absence of LaSalle or the first intimations of the credit crisis appeared. And, in a 27 June filing with the US Securities and Exchange Commission, Goodwin said that missing the chance to bid for ABN AMRO was 'unthinkable', adding, 'We certainly have been criticized for making acquisitions and putting growth ahead of short-term returns. But I think that it is my job and it is the board's job to put the welfare of the organization ahead of short-term returns.'[1]

But it was not all beer and skittles for Goodwin. On Friday, 13 July, the Dutch Supreme Court definitively confirmed that ABN AMRO *was* allowed to sell its Chicago-based arm, LaSalle Bank, to Bank of America without the need for a shareholder vote – a ruling which overturned the Enterprise Chamber of the Amsterdam Appellate Court's injunction from May. The part of ABN on which the idea of the take-over was founded and which Goodwin cherished more than any other part of ABN – LaSalle – had now, very definitely, escaped Goodwin's clutches. Instead, it ended up as part of Ken Lewis's Bank of America, an institution which the *Rolling Stone* financial reporter Matt Taibbi later described as 'a hyper-gluttonous ward of the state whose limitless fraud and criminal conspiracies we'll all be paying for until the end of time'.[2] McKillop was unconcerned, apparently having convinced himself that, because of the quality of other ABN businesses, including global transaction services, and because Bank of America's $21-billion cash payment would come straight into RBS's coffers on completion, the deal worked better without LaSalle. However, some senior RBS insiders thought this deranged.

Senior banking sources are adamant that Goodwin tried to pull out on or around 13 July (and possibly also during May). In a meeting with Botín, the RBS chief executive is alleged to have said that, without LaSalle, the deal no longer stacked up for RBS and that he wanted to call it a day. But Botín told him that was out of the question and reminded Goodwin that they had signed a binding agreement in Geneva and, if the Royal Bank withdrew, then both Santander and Fortis would 'recover their losses'. He also reminded the Scot of how Santander had helped RBS during the NatWest takeover – now, he said, it was RBS's turn to repay the favour. If this version of events is accurate, it would have been a bruising encounter for Goodwin, especially since relations with Botín had been cordial for many years. Merrill Lynch's Orcel also, reportedly, heaped the pressure on the RBS board to ensure that the Edinburgh-based bank did not get cold feet. There was, of course, a lot at stake for Merrill Lynch, given it was effectively underwriting the deal, meaning it could have been lumbered with the whole of ABN if the consortium scrapped its bid. Writing in *The Perfect Prey*, Jeroen Smit said that Fortis chairman Count Lippens was ner-vous the Scottish bank was poised to withdraw after the Supreme Court judgement went ABN's way. 'Behind the scenes, hard work had been done for quite some time to keep RBS on board, with Merrill Lynch banker Andrea Orcel playing an important role. Lippens was especially grateful for the support of Emilio Botín.'[3] However, sources close to Merrill Lynch insist that Goodwin never went to Botín to plead for an exit and that Orcel never had any contact with the RBS board.

Iain Robertson, the former chief executive of RBS Corporate Banking and Financial Markets who left the bank in 2005, believes Goodwin should have just accepted there might be litigation, taken it as a contingent liability and told Botín to get stuffed. 'There was supposedly a penalty clause – but my goodness, would £2 billion, £3 billion, £4 billion have not seemed terribly cheap compared to the carnage and horror that came about? That's probably where egos overtook sense.'[4]

One senior City insider said he bumped into RBS chairman Sir Tom McKillop during July 2007, after the consortium made its second bid, and remembers telling him, 'Tom, you've got to find a way out of this, you've got to pull your bid, get out of it, because the institutions don't want this takeover.' Oddly, McKillop didn't even reply. The City insider added, 'The message I got back, and the message I got from Merrill Lynch, was that the deal they had committed to could not be broken. And the *force majeure* didn't have any teeth. The value of wholesale banks had fallen by 15 per cent that month alone.'

Others suggest that Goodwin and the RBS board were also pressured by the swarm of hedge funds that had bought large stakes in ABN, notably Chris Hohn's TCI, in the belief that an RBS-led consortium would pay over the odds for it. If the Gogarburn-based bank had pulled out, the hedge funds would have ended up losing a significant portion of the approximately €50 billion they had invested in ABN shares, as its share price would have collapsed. Using legal and other threats, they are understood to have bullied Goodwin into pursuing his offer.

Cowed by such pressure in the wake of the Supreme Court ruling, the RBS board of directors never got around to having a deep or meaningful debate about the merits of buying ABN *sans* LaSalle. According to the FSA report into RBS's failure, the only forum at which it was formally discussed was a session of the chairman's advisory committee, with most members attending via teleconferencing facility, on Sunday 15 July. Once again there was unanimity. Early the next day, the consortium pushed the button on a revised offer which valued ABN at €71.1 billion (or €38.40 per ABN share). On the assumption that RBS would receive the proceeds of the LaSalle sale, the consortium said it was able to raise the cash portion of its offer from an already high 79 per cent to 93 per cent. The news sent ABN shares soaring. They rose by 3.5 per cent to hit €37.12 during Monday morning trading. At the media call on 16 July, Goodwin seemed to be relishing the battle, as he sought to win back the initiative. He insisted that it had never crossed his or anyone else's mind that the bid should be scrapped. He said, 'It was attractive to buy these businesses last week, it's attractive to buy them this week and that's the basis on which we're going forward. We never got near thinking of pulling out.' The vehement denial was, to some observers who knew Fred well, a giveaway.

The mantra of RBS directors throughout the bid process was that there was nothing to fear since they were dab hands at large-scale bank integrations and would be able to substantially reduce the cost-to-income ratio at ABN's hopelessly inefficient investment banking arm. They kept reminding investors and journalists of their achievements with NatWest where all the targets were beaten. At the 16 July press conference, Goodwin said that he expected RBS to be able to wring out annual cost and revenue benefits of €2 billion from all the ABN businesses it was buying by 2010, up from the just over €1.8 billion estimated before, excluding LaSalle. The sweetened bid was laid out in an offer document published on Friday, 20 July 2007. The gaps between Barclays' mainly share-based offer, then languishing at €64 billion as a result of falls in the Barclays share price, and RBS's 93 per cent cash-based offer had widened and the market assumed Barclays would have to raise its game. On 20 July, McKillop conceded that RBS 'would have preferred' to have been able to acquire LaSalle but he argued that, even without it, the deal seemed enticing. Goodwin did not speak to the media that day as he had gone to watch a spot of golf. He had rented an AugustaWestland A109 helicopter to take RBS ambassadors Sir Jackie Stewart and Jack Nicklaus to attend the second day of the British Open golf championship at Carnoustie in Angus, won that year by Irishman Pádraig Harrington.

On the Monday after the Open, three days after the consortium published its revised offer, Barclays raised its offer for ABN to €67.5 billion, which was still €3.6 billion shy of what the consortium was offering. It sweetened it by boosting the cash portion to 37 per cent. Barclays had only been able to do this after soliciting €13 billion from the China Development Bank and Singapore's Temasek Holdings. Barclays' chief executive John Varley made it clear that this was his final offer. 'We've put an enticing cream cake on the table for ABN shareholders. We are not going to top it up with cream.'⁵ But the cake didn't tempt investors and Barclays' shares slumped by 7 per cent over the next week. Out of desperation, Barclays then made a subversive attempt to collapse the consortium by 'taking out' Fortis. One source said, 'Barclays Capital was trying to persuade hedge funds to short [short-sell] Fortis, as part of a campaign to weaken its share price and kill its planned €13.5 billion rights issue.' However, since most hedge funds were 'long' on ABN AMRO shares, they didn't want to damage the consortium and did not play along with Barclays' plot.

In mid to late July, Groenink was coming under mounting pressure from the ABN AMRO board, especially the chairman of the supervisory board Arthur Martinez, to cease his love-in with Barclays and become more even-handed in his treatment of the bidding parties. Goodwin was also piling on the pressure for ABN AMRO to 'clear a pathway' to more constructive dialogue between ABN and the consortium. Martinez feared ABN would open itself up to lawsuits from investors, including hedge funds, if it continued to favour Barclays' much lower bid. But Groenink still strongly favoured Barclays and had a visceral mistrust of the consortium. Also, he differed from other ABN directors in that he did not believe that share price was everything. In the end, he came close to resigning as chairman of the management board but decided to stay on, although co-director Wilco Jiskoot, the head of ABN's investment banking arm, took responsibility for day-to-day negotiations with bidders. At a strategy session of the supervisory and management boards on Friday 27 July, ABN decided against recommending either offer. The boards felt that, although there was a 'strategic benefit' in keeping ABN intact, the Barclays offer was too low, while the consortium's was too risky from an execution perspective, given Goodwin's continuing refusal to answer basic questions.

In the UK, voices raised against the takeover were reaching a crescendo. In an opinion piece published on 28 July, the *Daily Telegraph*'s Damian Reece wrote, 'Of all the deals we've heard about potentially collapsing because of these jittery markets, surely the pursuit of ABN

AMRO should be at the top . . . It seems extraordinary that Barclays and RBS are so desperate to buy this second division bank at such a massive premium when the world's best banks, such as Goldman Sachs and Morgan Stanley, are off 14 per cent and 27 per cent respectively in the past month. Without the bid interest ABN shares would probably plummet 40 per cent . . . they [Barclays' and the consortium's bids] are looking wildly expensive and will need renegotiating, otherwise they both face collapse.'[6] Reece also questioned the strength of the RBS board's oversight and interrogation of what Goodwin was doing. This prompted McKillop to call Reece and say, 'The buck stops with me.'[7]

Most RBS staff were completely taken in by the internal hype about the takeover and still maintained a cult-like faith in Goodwin. Describing the internal response to the bidding, Roger Hunt, a human resources manager at the bank, said, 'I will never forget the positive feeling running right through RBS. You could almost touch it. We all had implicit faith in the executives and Fred Goodwin in particular. Despite adverse commentary in the press, we utterly believed that Sir Fred would land the deal of the decade and create a global platform for RBS to continue its unbelievable expansions in size, income and reputation . . . Throughout the months [of the bid], the lunch time chats in the corridor and the "street" were about our growing confidence that Fred would once again deliver the goods.'[8]

Yet there were numerous explicit public warnings of the coming collapse: Moody's downgraded masses of residential mortgage-backed securities on 10 July; the British mortgage bank Northern Rock issued a profits warning on 25 July; two Bear Stearns hedge funds with exposure to subprime assets collapsed on 31 July; and Jochen Sanio, president of German banking supervisory body, *Bundesanstalt für Finanzdienstleistungsaufsicht* (BaFin), said the world faced a systemic financial crisis, 'the worst since 1931'. However the biggest jolt came on 9 August, when the French bank BNP Paribas suspended three funds which were heavily exposed to US subprime debt. The fact that BNP blocked redemptions triggered a market panic, as investors feared they would be unable to retrieve cash from exotic instruments. On Thursday 10 August, the European Central Bank, led by its president Jean-Claude Trichet, sought to stem the market rout by pumping a phenomenal €94.8 billion of liquidity into the European banking system. Lehman Brothers' global strategist Matthew Rothman said, 'Events that models only predicted would happen once in 10,000 years happened every day for three days' between 8 and 10 August.[9]

But the consortium banks ploughed on. Each had to put their revised offers for ABN to their own shareholders for approval at extraordinary general meetings. At meetings in Utrecht and Brussels on 6 August, 90 per cent of Fortis's shareholders said they backed the deal. Lippens said this was 'fantastic news' and a strong sign that sharcholders had 'total trust' in the bank's management and board of directors.[10]

RBS held its shareholder meeting in the Edinburgh International Conference Centre on 10 August. That day, the FTSE-100 experienced its biggest fall in four years yet 94.5 per cent of Royal Bank share-holders voted in favour of proceeding. Only one major asset manager, Co-operative Asset Management, voted against while one, Royal London Asset Management, abstained.[11] At the meeting, McKillop was bullish, saying, 'We believe ABN is a very responsibly run bank and we have no reason to believe they have any undue exposure.'[12] Colin McLean, chief executive of SVM Asset Management, said that even though many investors hated the deal – 'They were overpaying for a load of old rubbish, really'[13] – they felt obliged to vote in favour. 'If the vote had gone against the bank, the entire RBS board would have felt compelled to resign,' says McLean, adding, 'But RBS should definitely have withdrawn.'[14]

RBS took advantage of the fact that ABN's share price had been weakened by the market turmoil by buying €2-billion worth of its shares (3 per cent of the Dutch bank's equity) at a discount to the offer price (€34 per share instead of €38.40 a share) on Monday 13 August. Barclays, meanwhile, was pushing on with its more diplomatic thrust, securing approval for its shares-based 'merger' from the Dutch finance ministry and the central bank, DNB.

The DNB was still dragging its heels on giving the green light to the consortium's more generous offer, which enraged Goodwin and his bidding partners. The DNB's main concern was whether the consortium banks – and especially Fortis – would be able to raise the money they needed to buy ABN. *The Times*' financial editor Patrick Hosking wrote, 'The battle lines are starkly drawn: RBS has the cash, Barclays has the connections.'[15] However, TCI's Chris Hohn didn't believe in diplomacy. He preferred the blunderbuss and, on 15 August, he sought to burst the logjam of regulatory opposition by firing off a letter to

DNB president Nout Wellink and Dutch finance minister Wouter Bos, which was copied to the European competition commissioner Neelie Kroes. The letter warned that, unless they lifted their objections, TCI 'will not hesitate to resort to every legal means to recoup our damages. These damages could amount to €10 billion.'[16]

On the Glorious Twelfth of August, Fred Goodwin took some time out from the battle when he attended a star-studded shooting party at Auchterhouse, north of Dundee. He brought along some amigos from the consortium banks, including Santander's Inciarte and Botín. Goodwin was photographed wearing a natty tweed jacket, red Santander tie and beige slacks while wielding an uncocked 12-bore shotgun at the annual charity clay-pigeon shoot. Between the bangs, Midlothian-based financier Peter de Vink met Goodwin and asked him, only half-jokingly, 'How is your Dutch, Fred?' Goodwin just wrinkled his nose and said, 'There would be no point in me learning Dutch. You all speak excellent English, don't you?' However, de Vink warned him that, even though English is the official language of ABN AMRO, its executives use Dutch as their 'secret language' to plot against foreigners they dislike. De Vink told Goodwin this was why the Barclays's chief executive John Varley had recently attended a three-week immersion course in the Dutch language in a Dutch nunnery, run by the Sisters of the Holy Order of St Augustine in Vught. De Vink went on to urge Goodwin to pull out of bidding, as RBS was paying in cash not shares and the banking sector was on the slide. But Goodwin just said, 'You know nothing!' and turned away. De Vink recalls, 'Goodwin's body language said it all. His dismissal of my suggestion that he should learn Dutch showed that he was just an inexperienced Paisley boy who had not seen much of the world. He was really unfit to take on something like ABN AMRO. How was it possible that no one on the board rebelled against the ABN takeover? I can only imagine that he simply was a great hypnotist who was simply knocking them all out!'[17]

On Friday 17 August, the *Daily Telegraph*'s finance columnist Jeremy Warner made clear the severity of the crisis that had gripped financial markets when he wrote, 'As turbulence in stock markets descends into a fully-blown rout . . . Nobody is going to risk a penny while the present state of uncertainty as to mortgage-backed security losses and the effect of the present credit squeeze on the real economy persists.'[18] Nobody, that is, apart from Fred Goodwin, Maurice Lippens, Emilio Botín and others at the top of their banks – as well as the majority of their investors.

Concerned about the way the ground was shifting beneath his feet, Groenink travelled to Edinburgh on Monday 20 August. In a private meeting in Goodwin's vast office at Gogarburn, he said that he and other members of the ABN AMRO management board would be willing to stay on for a transitional period of several months to provide some consistency and stability, if the consortium emerged triumphant. But Goodwin said, 'Thank you very much – we'll take that into consideration.'[19] Groenink also asked Goodwin if there was any way the Scot could scrap the idea of a consortium bid so that RBS could, instead, purchase the whole of ABN AMRO. Goodwin said, 'I am afraid it is too late for that.'[20]

In late August, McKillop revealed he wasn't completely blind to the worsening financial picture. He convened a meeting at Gogarburn, with Cameron dialling in from holiday. McKillop wanted Cameron to quantify the bank's exposure to CDOs and financial instruments. At the meeting, it was decided that RBS's total exposure amounted to £200 million to £400 million, a tiny fraction of the bank's overall balance sheet.[21] It was at around this time that the RBS board considered invoking the 'material adverse change' (MAC) clause in its offer document, which would have permitted it to lower its offer or pull out. The bank sought advice from its lawyers Linklaters on this topic in August but the One Silk Place-based solicitors concluded there was no legal justification for withdrawing. As I said earlier, the board also feared that invoking MAC would unleash a torrent of litigation, from both RBS's consortium partners and ABN AMRO shareholders. It also feared it would reopen the door to Barclays.

There was a serious rift on the board of Fortis – two of whose members, Richard Delbridge and Ron Sandler, were former NatWest directors. At a board meeting on 20 September, two of the bank's Flemish non-executive directors, Piet Van Waeyenberge and Jan-Michiel Hessels, pressed for the bank to invoke the material adverse change clause and either reduce or scrap its bid for ABN AMRO. At the meeting Waeyenberge said, 'That would be worth our while, even though there would probably be some damage in terms of reputation, as well as a risk of litigation from ABN AMRO shareholders.' But fearing loss of face, Lippens and Votron were determined to plough ahead.[22]

Votron's tone became increasingly brittle, according to colleagues. He threatened to resign unless Fortis pursued the deal. And Lippens was no less committed to continuing.

When ABN AMRO's works council schlepped across to RBS's Gogarburn office in September, they were stunned by how little work the Edinburgh-based bank had done to get ready for the integration. At a joint meeting with Royal Bank's executive committee, at which Goodwin was present, Hans Westerhuis, chairman of ABN's works council, asked RBS managers what their integration and growth plans were for the ABN businesses they were absorbing. To Westerhuis's astonishment, not one member of the RBS executive committee could provide satisfactory answers.[23]

The market 'correction' was turning into a rout. Global investors were petrified about the black holes that were opening up on the balance sheets of banks like RBS. The share prices of most banks began to tumble. By Tuesday 4 September, Barclays's offer for ABN was under water. The bank's shares had slumped to 614p, which meant the value of its offer had sunk to €60.5 billion, nearly five per cent below ABN's then €63.6-billion market value – and €10.5 billion short of the consortium's bid. Journalist Grant Ringshaw wrote, 'After a brutal few weeks Varley and Diamond will be hoping there are no more shocks in store. But their bid for ABN may already be beyond redemption.'[24]

By mid September, Newcastle-based lender Northern Rock was teetering on the brink of collapse. But Goodwin was so obsessed with winning ABN that signs of imminent crisis passed him by. He may also have been distracted by the clandestine affair he had recently embarked upon with a senior RBS colleague, who worked alongside Neil Roden in the bank's human resources department, but whom I am unable to name for legal reasons. To keep the liaison secret, Goodwin got himself a personal mobile phone, distinct from the RBS company mobile he traditionally relied on.[25] On Sunday, 9 September 2007, clad in his usual dark glasses, RBS tartan trews and branded white short-sleeved shirt, perhaps feeling he needed a short break from the complexities of the takeover battle, Goodwin was in the paddock at the Italian Grand Prix, in Monza, Italy.[26] Ominously, the Formula One race was won by a Spaniard, Fernando Alonso, driving a McLaren-Mercedes. The two drivers in the team that RBS was sponsoring, the German Nico Rosberg and the Austrian Alexander Wurz, came sixth and thirteenth respectively. And the Scottish driver David Coulthard, driving a car sponsored by energy drink Red Bull, careered off the track at 170 mph on the Curva Grande, tearing through an advertising hoarding for Dutch bank ING Groep. There might have been a message in that somewhere.

Some people in the City struggled to comprehend Goodwin's refusal to withdraw or lower his offer for ABN AMRO. Peter Meinertzhagen, chairman of the brokers Hoare Govett, which was part of ABN AMRO, tried to speak to Fred Goodwin on the telephone to persuade him against proceeding, largely on the strength of the horrors which he knew lurked on the ABN balance sheet. Mary McCallum, Goodwin's PA, initially told him that Fred would be very interested in such a meeting and that she would set it up. But, ten minutes later, she called Meinertzhagen back and embarrassedly told him that Fred had no desire to meet Meinertzhagen, one of the most trusted men in the City. One top-ten RBS investor was quoted in the *Mail on Sunday* saying that ABN's markets business (a key component of what RBS was getting) was now worthless. He said, 'We would rather RBS did not go through with this deal at all.'[27] The investor disquiet, coupled with rumours that Barclays had privately accepted defeat, unsettled ABN investors and its share price fell 2 per cent to €33.10.

The Northern Rock debacle was gathering momentum. The Newcastle-based lender, which had lent at crazy multiples into the UK's house price bubble and whose balance sheet was massively over-leveraged, had to go cap in hand to the Bank of England for liquidity support after an attempt to merge with Lloyds TSB failed. News of the emergency loan leaked to BBC business editor Robert Peston, who ran the story on Thursday 13 September. This triggered a run on the Rock, with long queues of depositors forming outside its branches. The government and the tripartite authorities seemed powerless to act, though the Labour Chancellor Alistair Darling did eventually offer to guarantee people's deposits on Monday 17 September. The governor of the Bank of England, Mervyn King, said television images of queuing depositors had unsettled wholesale funders. He said, 'After the run on Northern Rock, and the impact of the television pictures, it became evident that many of the funders of British banks around the world were no longer willing to fund British banks.'[28]

On Monday, 17 September 2007, the board of RBS made another

fatal error. They took a trading statement issued by ABN AMRO as if it were the gospel truth. The outlook statement, overseen by ABN's finance director Huibert Boumeester, who later committed suicide, and auditors Ernst & Young, said, 'Based on the results as per August year-to-date, we are on track to deliver an earnings per share of approximately €2.30 on an adjusted basis, notwithstanding the impact of the current turmoil in financial markets on our Global Markets results and continued disappointing performance of Antonveneta . . . We are pleased to report that current market circumstances have not resulted in a revision of our loan loss provision forecast . . . ABN AMRO has a very limited exposure to the subprime segment.'[29]

But of course ABN AMRO had a vested interest in putting a positive gloss on things. Too much honesty might have caused its suitors to drop their price or walk away. Speaking to the Treasury Select Committee in February 2009, Goodwin said, 'We got to 17 September 2007 and ABN AMRO reconfirmed their earnings estimates for 2007 and specifically stated that credit market markdowns had not affected them. They specifically stated that their credit portfolio and credit outlook were good. Again, that may seem hard to believe now, but at the time that fitted into the context.'[30]

At around this time, other banks, including Bear Stearns, Morgan Stanley, Lehman Brothers and Deutsche Bank, were taking markdowns on their credit portfolios (tradable loans). However, some banks, including Goldman Sachs and Lehman Brothers, were unveiling surprisingly strong third-quarter results. Plenty of market participants and commentators were confident that the 'liquidity squeeze' would be a temporary phenomenon. Goodwin was further reassured when RBS went into the market to raise funds for its portion of the ABN AMRO purchase in late September. He told the Treasury committee, 'We raised funds for the ABN AMRO transaction in late September; they were eight times oversubscribed. So [that was] the view at the time, and we could only work based on the view at the time.'[31]

RBS was further reassured by a report put together by its advisors Merrill Lynch in August 2007, which was calming about the state of the markets and ABN AMRO's wholesale banking business. If the board of RBS did rely on this report, it was not a particularly intelligent thing to do. Given the hundreds of millions in fees Merrill Lynch stood to earn if the deal completed, it wasn't exactly an objective observer. It was hardly going to tell RBS that the market turmoil could intensify or that ABN AMRO's markets business – which included a huge credit derivative business and some reckless leveraged loans to Russian oligarchs – was a ticking time bomb that was poorly wired and liable to explode at any time, even if it had known. So Merrill Lynch concluded that, at that time and based on public information, it could see no immediate impact from the market deterioration on ABN AMRO's liquidity or credit position and, therefore, no immediate impact on its asset quality.[32]

As Barclays' share price tumbled, its chances of winning ABN AMRO were subsiding. On 17 September, the Dutch authorities, led by Wellink, finally gave the consortium's bid the green light but with onerous conditions attached. They included that RBS must take responsibility for the whole of ABN AMRO as the bank was dismantled and that the Scottish bank must obtain regulatory clearance every step of the way, which hugely added to the executional risk of the transaction.

At this point, some were beginning to openly question Goodwin's sanity. the *Financial Times*'s European M&A correspondent Lina Saigol said the RBS boss and his bidding partners were 'driven by ego, conceit and a deep-seated need for power'. Saigol added, 'In the same way AOL's [takeover of Time Warner] came to symbolise the irrational exuberance of the dotcom era, the ABN transaction could well epitomise all that has gone wrong during this debt-fuelled boom.'[33] Three days after Saigol's piece, Johnny Cameron was talking up the deal in an interview with her paper and boasted that it would give RBS 'a whole new box of tricks to offer our clients'.[34]

Barclays finally threw in the towel on Friday 5 October, having secured only 0.2 per cent of acceptances, which meant the consortium had ABN AMRO in the bag. Varley denied that his bank was vulnerable or that he would have to resign. He also accused the consortium of paying too much.

Goodwin found the time to fit in another Grand Prix, visiting the Chinese Grand Prix in Shanghai with Jackie Stewart where he was wearing his customary motor-sport uniform including tartan trews, white short-sleeved shirt embossed with the bank's crest and wraparound shades. The Spanish driver Fernando Alonso, in a McLaren-Mercedes decked out in Santander colours did much better than either of the two Williams drivers – Nico Rosberg and Alexander Wurz –

whose cars and clothes were emblazoned with the RBS logo. Still, at least Scottish driver David Coulthard didn't crash this time. Driving a Red Bull-Renault, he came fifth.

RBS, Santander and Fortis had won ABN but they did not see this as a cause for celebration. On 8 October, Bloomberg News highlighted the level of investor discontent with the deal. Robert Talbut, chief investment officer at Royal London Asset Management, was quoted as saying, 'The Royal Bank-led offer is a very expensive transaction. The risk–reward doesn't add up.'[35] Other investors said they had put Goodwin on notice to demonstrate the deal stacked up over the next 12 to 18 months.

Others, impressed by the scale of the deal and the executional skills with which it was carried out, were more positive. The *Financial Times* banking editor Peter Thal Larsen wrote, 'The deal is a triumph for Sir Fred Goodwin, RBS's chief executive, who persisted in spite of the turmoil in the credit markets . . . However, separating ABN's Dutch retail and wholesale banking activities is complex and could take several years.'[36]

And for RBS to have acquired one of the largest companies in Holland plus an international network that stretched to 53 countries worldwide was, at first sight, a huge achievement. The editor of the *Times*'s Scottish edition, Magnus Linklater, wrote a eulogy to Fred, adding, 'You don't have to be an ardent capitalist to welcome this kind of success.'[37] Melanie Reid, a columnist on the same newspaper, wrote a column headlined 'Is this man the world's greatest banker?'[38]

The real winner, though, was Santander. On 10 October 2007, its chief executive Alfredo Sáenz (who has since left the bank as a result of a criminal conviction) gave a victory presentation to 700 of the bank's most senior executives. About 350 were with him in the theatre at Ciudad Financiera, the Spanish bank's headquarters, and another 350 or so were watching via video links from the bank's operations around the world. That included scores of senior executives in Abbey National's Triton Square headquarters in London. Sáenz was gloating and telling them how clever Santander had been. He talked the executive group through the merits of owning Banco Real and Banca Antonveneta (Santander 'flipped' the Italian bank to Banca Monte dei Paschi di Siena for €9 billion two months later). The gist of what he said was: 'We have got the best bits of ABN AMRO; we got the best

'Incomparably the handsomest townhouse we ever saw': the Palladian villa at 36 St Andrew Square, built for Sir Lawrence Dundas in 1774, was RBS's head office from 1828 until 1969. It is now a branch. (Royal Bank of Scotland)

RBS chief executive Fred Goodwin was mocked by the Sunday Times *over the construction of RBS's 'world headquarters' at Gogarburn, near Edinburgh. The complex is now headquarters in name alone.* (© RCAHMS. Licensor www.scran.ac.uk)

Fred Goodwin speaking at an anti-fraud conference in Beijing on 2 November 2006. He became a regular visitor to China after RBS bought a 5.16 per cent stake in Bank of China, which gave him a seat on its board. (Press Association)

United against NatWest: Santander and RBS directors unveil RBS's £26.4 billion takeover offer for NatWest. Clockwise from left: Bob Scott, Fred Goodwin, George Mathewson, Emilio Botín, George Younger and José María Amusátegui. (PA)

World domination: (left to right) Fred Watt, George Mathewson, George Younger and Fred Goodwin in the bank's Waterhouse Square London HQ in March 2001. Unveiling a 31 per cent rise in profits to £4.4 billion, Goodwin said he was not averse to 'mercy killings' of other financial players. (PA)

NatWest bounce: RBS's George Mathewson, Fred Watt and Fred Goodwin are upbeat as they unveil record pre-tax profits of £6.45 billion for the year to December 2002. (PA)

The enemy: Barclays' chief executive John Varley moved the English bank's headquarters from the City to a 32-storey tower in Canary Wharf in May 2005. He quietly entered talks with ABN AMRO about a merger the following year. (PA)

At a packed press conference in the Edinburgh International Conference Centre on 25 April 2007, Fortis's Jean-Paul Votron, RBS's Goodwin and Santander's Emilio Botín unveil plans for a three-way takeover of ABN AMRO. (PA)

Rijkman Groenink of ABN AMRO on his way to an Amsterdam courtroom on 2 August 2007. He was defending a claim from shareholders who were seeking a probe into alleged mismanagement at the Dutch bank. (PA)

No real contrition: Sir Tom McKillop gives evidence to the Treasury committee on 10 February 2009, a week after being dumped as RBS's chairman. McKillop admitted the ABN AMRO deal had been a 'bad mistake'. (PA)

McKillop and Goodwin leave the Treasury committee on 10 February 2009. Asked by MPs about their role in RBS's collapse, they effectively said, 'We're sorry, but we're not to blame'. (PA)

Two months after being parachuted in as RBS chairman, Sir Philip Hampton is driven away from the bank's annual general meeting in Edinburgh on 3 April 2009. At the meeting, Hampton called for an end to the 'public flogging' of RBS. (PA)

At a G20 meeting on 5 September 2009, Prime Minister Gordon Brown knocked back French and German proposals to cap bankers' bonuses. He was accompanied by Chancellor Alistair Darling and Bank of England governor Mervyn King. (PA)

Speaking to the Treasury committee in June 2011, RBS chief executive Stephen Hester expresses scepticism about plans for a 'ring fence' separating banks' investment banking and retail banking arms. The idea was proposed in an interim report of the Independent Commission on Banking. (PA)

Last of the 'big swinging dicks': Bob Diamond is mobbed by protestors as he emerges from Portcullis House after being grilled by the Treasury committee on 4 July 2012. MPs were incredulous when Diamond, who was fired as Barclays CEO the previous day, denied any knowledge of LIBOR rigging. (PA)

New Zealander Ross McEwan, who became RBS's CEO on 2 October 2013, wants to make it the UK's most trusted bank by 2020. McEwan, who earlier spent a year running RBS's retail arm and previously worked for Commonwealth Bank of Australia, has his work cut out. (Royal Bank of Scotland)

meat from the kill. We are the only ones coming out smiling. We have got the better of [or 'shafted' according to some translations] our consortium partners.' Abbey executives watching via the webcast in Triton Square were horrified. One recalled, 'It contrasted with the undying loyalty and solidarity we had heard so much about during the takeover battle. Now we knew that was just a hollow façade. He seemed so proud of behaving dishonourably. It was nauseating to watch.' Interestingly enough, RBS sources claim that Botín refused to take Goodwin's calls after 9 October. Perhaps the gangly Scot had now served his purpose?

At a victory press conference in London on Wednesday 10 October, Goodwin was asked if RBS had paid too much. The answer was a petulant: 'Yes, the people who win do pay more than the people who don't win and that is certainly the case here. But the gap between our offer and Barclays' wasn't much.'[39] He was asked if he had made a clandestine commitment (in Geneva) to proceed come what may and whether he had considered pulling out once LaSalle became unavailable. Goodwin did not deny either suggestion. Instead, he said, 'I think the transaction stands up strongly and La Salle is really ancient history.' He also insisted that ABN AMRO had superb risk management and controls. 'One of the things we recognise is that ABN AMRO has a world-class risk-management function and, as the world becomes an increasingly complex place, this is critically important.'[40] Privately, however, Fred recognised it was a Pyrrhic victory. That may explain why he did not wish any fanfare, either internally or externally. Goodwin told colleagues around this time that he felt like a Border Collie that has been chasing cars all its life on a single-track Hebridean road. After years of diverting but fruitless pursuit, for the first time in its life, it has caught a car. And, with the vehicle's rear bumper jammed between its jaws and the car still moving forward, the sheepdog doesn't quite know what to do. Wishing it had stuck to rounding up sheep, it can feel its body being dragged across the tarmac at speed.

On Thursday 11 October, Goodwin attended a long-scheduled meeting at the Oyster Club, an Edinburgh drinking club founded in the 1770s of which he was a member. Unusually, the club was holding the get-together in a mezzanine space in RBS's Gogarburn headquarters and a full complement of about 85 members had turned up to gawk at the building. As the diners prepared to tuck into a banquet of molluscs, Fred was nowhere to be seen. However, a small band of disconsolate-looking Dutch people was milling around aimlessly. An Oyster Club member asked them what they were doing and one of the Dutchmen replied, somewhat pathetically, 'We've come to be indoctrinated.' They were already finding being owned by RBS a harrowing experience. Then in strode Goodwin followed by a retinue of what looked like more senior 'prisoners-of-war'. Peter de Vink, a member of the Oyster Club recalls, 'It was quite extraordinary. Fred was acting like a victorious Roman emperor showing off the soldiers and officials he'd captured. The speech that Fred gave was awful – he made it clear these poor guys would have to adapt to the regime of King Fred or else lose their jobs. It was in bad taste and hugely embarrassing for all that attended.'[41] De Vink chatted to the ABN AMRO people after Fred had finished speaking and observed that Fred was a real *klootzak*, a derogatory term in Dutch. De Vink added, 'They were surprised I was using such language given the setting, but made clear they wholeheartedly agreed with me on this point. They just seemed so petrified by the whole experience.'[42]

The Economist said the ABN AMRO deal was 'a spectacularly cack-handed' attempt by RBS to grow its investment bank and international presence.[43] When one takes into account the shocking timing of the deal, the quality of the businesses and assets that RBS was taking on, the way in which the deal was funded, the high price (fixed before the financial crisis had started) and the culture clashes that would later mire the post-deal integration, it added up to an appalling error of judgement.

Asked if he regretted anything that had happened, Rijkman Groenink said, 'Yes, I regret a lot. There was a concentration of extremely negative things at the same time. The hubris of Fred Goodwin; the financial power of the hedge funds; the stupidity and vengefulness of the Fortis people; the extraordinary liquidity in the market; the whole perception – especially in the EU – that shareholders' rights were paramount; and the way in which the Dutch courts adjudged a number of cases in favour of raw shareholder power: in my view, such a poisonous cocktail, especially in a small country, with a weak government, and with a weak central bank was disastrous.'[44]

Speaking to the Treasury Select Committee in February 2009, Goodwin said, 'I think that, as we currently sit here today, I can only say that it was a bad decision. Who knows in years to come, but right here and right now it was certainly mistimed and I think that, if we knew then what we know now, we would not have taken the risk of finding out . . . It is a reality in business that you have to make judgments, you have to try and predict the future and you do not always get it right.'[45]

However, former RBS chairman Sir George Mathewson takes a different view. He says, 'Rijkman Groenink was very aggressive, very self-focused, thought he was the greatest thing since sliced bread and he ended up selling a dud bank for a great price. He ended up doing a great deal for his shareholders. It would be interesting to note the position of the Dutch regulators. For the regulators to say breaking it up would cause financial instability – for goodness sake, the business was dud, bust. I think Rijkman was either delusional or, indeed, just playing to get a bigger sum. In selling that business, you have to say, he did a wonderful job.'[46]

Explosions at ABN

At an investor lunch in Edinburgh's New Club, the favoured watering hole of the Scottish establishment, Colin McLean, chief executive of SVM Asset Management, questioned Goodwin's strategy. To most investors around the table, Goodwin was a local hero. He had transformed RBS into a global force and was putting Scotland on the map as a financial centre to rival London, Paris, Frankfurt and Geneva. To criticise him, at that point – it was 13 November, just a month after the ABN victory had been proclaimed – was heresy. There was polite disbelief around the table. The chief executive of another Edinburgh-based asset-management firm rubbished McLean's views. He said, 'If there was anything wrong with RBS, Fred would have told us.' But McLean, known for his skills as a short-seller of financial stocks, told the assembled company of investment professionals that, in his view, RBS was overstretched. McLean said, 'Superficially, RBS's capital ratios may look good [but] they're backed by a lot of "rubbish".' Asked to elaborate, McLean said, 'Royal Bank does not have enough tangible assets in its core tier-1 capital – there's too much goodwill and funny paper – and Fred keeps diluting the balance sheet through acquisitions.'[1] He then delivered his coup de grâce, saying that the bank would probably be unable to pay a dividend. 'There was a stunned silence for 30 seconds,' recalls McLean.[2]

McLean, of course, was right. The RBS balance sheet was stuffed with rubbish and it was severely overstretched, due to the difficulties of funding two giant banks that were overdependent on a diminishing commodity – wholesale interbank finance. On top of this, it was also being pushed into a corner by De Nederlandsche Bank (DNB). The Dutch central bank was insisting that RBS took regulatory and man-

agement control of the whole of ABN AMRO, whilst including the
entire bank – which, at the time, had total assets of €1.025 trillion – on
its balance sheet. That meant RBS would have to take responsibility
for the whole of ABN for months, if not years, while various limbs
were amputated and handed over to its consortium partners, Fortis and
Santander. This would turn out to be another ticking time bomb for
RBS.

On 11 October, Goodwin unveiled a new top management team for
the Dutch bank. He appointed trusted lieutenant Mark Fisher as chairman of ABN's management board, which meant the Yorkshireman
was effectively taking the reins from Rijkman Groenink. City scribblers
welcomed the appointment since Fisher was seen as a superb 'nuts and
bolts' integrator who had done an excellent job on NatWest. Brian
Crowe, who was suffering from a kidney-related illness, was replaced
as deputy head of GBM by RBS's leveraged-buyout chief Leith
Robertson, his deputy, on an interim basis. This freed up Crowe to
take the reins at ABN AMRO's global markets business from Piero
Overmars, who continued to run Asia and Europe, while the chain-
smoking ABN executive Wilco Jiskoot handed over control of global
clients. Both Jiskoot and Overmars agreed to remain on the ABN
managing board for the duration of the integration.

A former senior executive in Global Banking and Markets said: 'I
was absolutely gobsmacked when Fred made Mark Fisher chairman
of ABN AMRO. Here was a bank that needed intense scrutiny from
a banking and financial perspective but Fred appointed an operations
and IT guy as chairman. Brian Crowe was taken out of his role as
chief executive of capital markets and tasked with bringing the capital
markets businesses of ABN and RBS together. This led to some severe
management stretch at RBS capital markets. Brian's deputy Leith
Robertson stepped up to become acting chief executive of capital
markets. So ABN AMRO had an executive chairman who was not
grounded in analytical banking, the person charged with bringing
together the two capital markets business was suffering from a serious
illness and RBS's capital markets business was being run by a guy who
had presided over some of the most jaw-dropping decisions to invest
in deals.'

It was a recipe for disaster. Goodwin also wanted to appoint John
Hourican, chief operating officer of GBM, as chief financial officer

of ABN AMRO. But Hourican, an amiable Irishman and a former PricewaterhouseCoopers accountant who had been with the bank since 1997, was reluctant to go Dutch. Goodwin asked him three times before Hourican agreed. On the last try, Goodwin pleaded with the Dublin-born 37-year-old, saying, 'You won't be in the bastards' box if you don't do it but I really want you to do it.' Hourican relented and, on moving to Amsterdam, the Irishman bought the former home of Wim Duisenberg, the ex-president of the European Central Bank, for a cool €4.9 million. Aside from the departing Groenink, most other members of the ABN's management board remained in post for a transition period of a few months. The American former Sears, Roebuck & Co. executive Arthur Martinez remained as chairman of ABN's supervisory board but he was joined on that board by three amigos – Goodwin, Juan Rodríguez Inciarte (from Santander) and Jean-Paul Votron (from Fortis). Five of ABN's supervisory board members, including David Baron de Rothschild, stood down at an extraordinary general meeting on 1 November.

Hourican says the first post-acquisition meeting of the management board at ABN AMRO was polite but frosty. The meeting took place in Gustav Mahlerlaan on Friday, 12 October 2007 and was attended by three RBS-nominated directors – himself, Fisher and Crowe. Nearly all the ABN management board members were still there. Hourican says, 'They behaved very professionally, although there was a slight belligerence bubbling under the surface. I hold them in high esteem.'[3] Hourican adds: 'It took me a while to get the head office working effectively for us. They were initially resistant to everything we wanted to do. I think they had thought the sale of LaSalle would save them. They couldn't believe it when Fred Goodwin carried on [after LaSalle was sold]. But, once we were in there, they got on and did the job. They just didn't have a particularly good bank. The key weaknesses included a global network that basically didn't pay; a bloated cost base; an out-of-touch management team; a financial markets business that was strong in Netherlands but nowhere else; [and] an equities and M&A business that never made money. From an RBS perspective, the timing of the purchase could not have been worse. There was some very hairy stuff there.'[4] However, despite these criticisms, ABN AMRO's claimed net interest margin for 2007 was 2.34 per cent, 25 basis points ahead of RBS's 2.09 per cent.

In an interview with *Financial News*, published in mid October, Johnny Cameron was putting a brave face on things. In describing the task of crunching together the two wholesale banks, the Harrow- and Oxford-educated son of a clan chief resorted to cliché. 'There is no great magic or alchemy to it. It's all about attitude, accountability and culture. We have a straightforward approach to getting things done at RBS. No excuses – make it happen and get it done through sheer hard graft.'[5] Cameron told *Financial News* he had drawn up a list of 118 initiatives to ensure rapid integration. Each had cost and revenue targets attached and strict timelines, and each spanned ABN's wholesale operations in up to 53 countries. He seemed confident that the DNB would have given the break-up plan clearance by January 2008. Cameron told *FN*'s David Rothnie he was determined to start cross-selling RBS products to ABN's corporate clients as soon as possible. He said, 'We will start in January with a new box of tricks – a hugely expanded client and product base and a much bigger geographic footprint, particularly in Asia.'[6] Meanwhile, Crowe was making presentations to staff at the headquarters of ABN AMRO's investment bank, housed in an angular, 11-storey, 247,000-square-foot building at 250 Bishopsgate, next door to Fred's office at 280 Bishopsgate.

Within the parts of the Dutch bank it was getting, RBS had said that, by 2010, it was aiming to axe 19,000 jobs, make total cost cuts of €1.32 billion, and see a €481-million rise in additional income. It had also promised shareholders to slash the cost-to-income ratio on ABN AMRO's global wholesale business from 89 per cent in 2006 to 65 per cent by 2010. But the goals turned out to be hopelessly optimistic. Six of the eighteen Royal Bank directors took advantage of falls in the RBS share price to buy £2.5-million worth of the shares at prices between 400p and 500p in early October. On 17 October, Goodwin purchased £1.44-million worth of RBS shares at a reduced 'options' rate, more than doubling his holding to 694,443 shares.[7] On 9 November 2007, Tom McKillop piled £500,000 into RBS shares.[8] Non-executive directors Bill Friedrich (£200,000), Joe MacHale (£168,500), Charles 'Bud' Koch (£127,000) and Janis Kong (£21,500) also added to their stashes of RBS shares.[9] There were rumours too that north-west England entrepreneur Trevor Hemmings filled his boots by buying a 1 per cent stake in the Royal Bank of Scotland on 13 November.

In the build-up to the deal, Goodwin and other RBS executives had repeatedly argued that integrating ABN would be a doddle. After all, they had been described as 'masters of integration' by no less an authority than Harvard Business School following their integration of NatWest. However, in his haste to thwart Barclays and avenge Groenink, Goodwin had blinded himself to some fairly obvious differences between the two deals. These included:

- NatWest was a largely UK-based retail and commercial bank. ABN AMRO was a sprawling, global, universal bank with operations in 53 countries.
- RBS had no experience or knowledge of many of the markets where ABN had operations.
- RBS had bought NatWest on its own but was part of a consortium of three global banks when it bought ABN. Disentangling and dividing up the pieces between the three banks whilst ensuring ABN's vital organs continued to function would be challenging.
- RBS carried out the NatWest integration against a relatively benign economic backdrop. ABN was bought during a credit crisis and was integrated in the worst economic crisis since the 1930s.
- ABN's structured credit activities and leveraged finance businesses, mainly based in 250 Bishopsgate, were even more untamed than NatWest's markets activities.
- Unlike with NatWest, RBS was woefully underprepared.
- Goodwin was constantly jetting off to Grands Prix and golf tournaments during the takeover battle with Barclays. He and several senior RBS executives were less focused on the task at hand than during the NatWest integration.
- The due diligence on ABN AMRO was much skimpier than that on NatWest. Goodwin described it as 'due diligence-lite'.
- The 102,556 ABN AMRO staff were, as a general rule, pretty hostile to RBS's 'barbarians', unlike NatWest staff who generally welcomed their arrival.
- RBS was constantly coming up against significant linguistic and cultural barriers. Perhaps Goodwin should have taken Peter de Vink's advice and learnt Dutch after all?
- Laying people off in the UK is quicker, cheaper and easier than it is in Holland. RBS failed to take account of differences in employ-

ment law which, in the Netherlands, gives stronger protection to employees.

Other issues that meant the integration went much less smoothly than that of NatWest included:

- The targets for cost savings and revenues synergies were drawn up before the credit crisis erupted and would have been ambitious at the best of times. Against the backdrop of market mayhem that had taken root by October 2007, they were impossible to achieve.
- RBS needed to raise €22.6 billion in cash to pay its share of the deal, which meant massive short-term borrowings at a time when credit was becoming scarcer and more expensive.
- There were delays in getting the proceeds from the sale of LaSalle (which in the end never arrived) and the sale of Banca Antonveneta which Santander's Botín 'flipped' to Banca Monte dei Paschi di Siena.
- As the crisis intensified, rival banks were seeking to take advantage of the uncertainty surrounding RBS and ABN AMRO to pick off their clients and poach their staff.[10]
- The process of dismantling ABN was constantly delayed or held up by the DNB's requirement that RBS and its consortium partners obtain regulatory approval every step of the way.
- The DNB surprised RBS by refusing to grant Internal Ratings Based (IRB) status to ABN AMRO in January 2008. This meant it was unable to do its own risk modelling, which led to the Dutch bank needing to maintain a higher capital ratio than would have been necessary under IRB.
- RBS was unable to make any job cuts before the DNB approved its transition plan and, once the plan was approved, it had to enter a three-month consultation with Dutch workers' councils, unions and regulators.

One of the underlying problems was that, when the credit crisis became apparent in July 2007, RBS assumed this would be a 'blip'. It also assumed that its share of the LaSalle proceeds would be received quickly from Bank of America. On the strength of these assumptions, the Edinburgh-based bank decided to fund the lion's share of the cost of acquiring ABN with some €22.6 billion of borrowed money. This was in marked contrast to Santander, which had been quietly raising capital since May by, for example, doing a sale-and-leaseback of its headquarters campus near Madrid (paradoxically, to the RBS-backed property tycoon Glenn Maud) and Fortis, which had tapped shareholders for €13.5 billion in a rights issue during the second half of 2007. Of the €22.6 billion RBS borrowed, some €12.3 billion – more than half – had to be repaid in a year or less. But what really punctured the bank's maths was that it never actually received the €10.9 billion cash it was expecting in 'LaSalle proceeds'. FSA records suggest that the proceeds were 'eventually absorbed by losses made by ABN AMRO in the Netherlands, rather than transferred to RBS in the UK'.[11] It all added up to what the FSA described as 'a risky financing strategy' and left RBS perilously exposed as the credit crisis intensified.[12]

From the Dutch perspective, there was disbelief about the arrogance and naivety of the RBS executives who came over to expedite the integration. During the takeover battle, Mark Fisher had a meeting with members of the Dutch bank's staff council. The latter group were astonished by the flakiness of RBS's plans for ABN's wholesale bank. The staff council members, who included a couple of investment bankers, were surprised by the 'blasé attitude of senior RBS managers to the complexity of integrating a bank like ABN'.[13] When Fisher told the group 'it normally takes 30 days but, because this is a more complex deal, we will give ourselves 45 days', the ABN bankers just laughed.[14] That meeting set the agenda for many that followed.

ABN executives were stunned by the crassness of some of the policies RBS was trying to force through and by RBS executives' ignorance of international banking. They were also shocked when they discovered the extent to which Goodwin micromanaged RBS. Kilian Wawoe, a former vice-president of human resources at ABN AMRO, now an Amsterdam-based organisational psychologist, said: 'It seemed to us that RBS was a "Fredo-cracy". The RBS people would say things like "Fred doesn't like this", as if all decisions inside the bank were based on what Goodwin did and did not like. In one office that had recently been redecorated, Goodwin ordered the carpets to be replaced within 24 hours as they weren't the correct RBS colour. It was insane. The centralised way in which RBS was run was wholly at odds with the way ABN AMRO was run. They would come into our office and tell us,

"If you don't want to buy into our success story, then please feel free to leave." There wasn't much trust between the two banks. For example, if we told them that a particular course of action was impossible because of local legislation, the RBS people would check with independent lawyers that we were telling the truth.'[15]

Another ex-ABN insider said, 'The RBS guys were hopelessly out of their depth. They were full of shit, really.'

Initially, the senior investment bank executives who joined the executive committee of the enlarged group's investment bank – including Alexandra Cook-Schaapveld, Michiel de Jong, and Piero Overmars – continued to live in Amsterdam. But this angered Johnny Cameron, who made it plain that the merged business was headquartered in London. When the likes of Cook-Schaapveld sought to participate in meetings via video-links, Cameron said, 'Haven't you got the message yet? Our head office is in London. Why are you still in Amsterdam?'

The process of selecting which executives should be retained in the merged RBS and ABN investment bank caused serious internal ructions. Goodwin insisted it was being done fairly and on the basis of merit. Speaking in December 2007, he said, 'One of the most important things we've been doing is looking at management structures. One of the things we did after NatWest – and it slows things down a little bit but it's critically important in making all the management appointments – is to go through an interview process and we involve external consultants in the process, to ensure fairness and also to ensure an appearance of fairness. Once the senior appointments have been made, it removes a lot of uncertainty.'[16]

However, senior executives in the merged investment bank remember it as a time of anything but 'fairness'. Rather, they remember it as a time of vicious backstabbing and jockeying for position as staffing decisions were rolled out across the enlarged investment bank. One said, 'The atmosphere was horrible. People were cutting deals left, right and centre.' Ex-ABN insiders believe the selection process was unfair and suggest it was also so laborious and time-consuming that other important matters, such as whether the merged bank was solvent and whether it could survive a protracted economic downturn, were sidelined or ignored. One ex-ABN investment banker said the enlarged bank began to suffer 'death by PowerPoint'. He said that 'one set of RBS bankers would be presenting to another set of RBS bankers and it all got mixed up. It stultified debate. Both organisations became more and more inward looking.'

Royal Bank of Scotland people remember Fred Goodwin making impossible demands on them and ABN staff being obstructive. They claim that the convoluted legal and organisational structures within ABN AMRO created all sorts of problems. One ex-GBM insider said, 'ABN AMRO was a vipers' nest of political intrigue, personal manoeuvring and regulatory complexity. The labyrinthine internal structures meant RBS's management style – of quickly reviewing situations and making quick decisions – just would not work. It also meant some of the toxic stuff was well hidden. The irresistible force of RBS's pragmatic and open approach met the immovable object of ABN's avoidance culture.'

The nasty surprises lurking inside ABN AMRO included the $725 million ABN had invested with the US fraudster Bernard Madoff's Ponzi scheme, the way in which it had shouldered $840 million of risk on Goldman Sachs' Abacus 2007-AC1 synthetic CDO (which the Securities and Exchange Commission settlement later revealed Goldman to have pump-primed to explode) and eye-watering loans worth tens of billions of dollars to the Russian oligarchs Leonard Blavatnik and Oleg Deripaska, some of which would never be repaid.

Goodwin initially tended to blow his top when told of such 'bombs' going off inside ABN or elsewhere in RBS. One ex-RBS senior executive said, 'In December 2007 and January 2008, mines were going off all over the shop, in the shape of unhappy discoveries inside ABN – there was the Abacus deal with Goldman Sachs, there were loads of things that had not been properly accounted for. It was a nightmare. It was the exact opposite of NatWest. Plus the world was going to hell in a hand basket and the CDO problem was blowing up. So bombs were going off all over the place.'

'We had an on-the-beaches attitude at the time,' said John Hourican, 'But the problems we were finding were large and continuous . . . A lot of the stuff on the balance sheet was becoming very illiquid and hard to value.' One former senior GBM executive said, 'From quarter three of 2007 onwards, Johnny, Brian and Leith were in damage-limitation mode. Their private conversations were all about when to sack people and how many people to sack.' He recalls a meeting in October or November 2007, when Cameron, Crowe and Robertson were saying things like ' "Shall we take all the pain in the current year [2007] or phase the redundancies over time? Do we do the big bad investment banker thing or do we behave like pathetic clearing bankers?" That was the nature of the discussions they were having. Unlike everyone else, they had seen the numbers and they were aware of the scale of the thing. I remember them discussing this round a big table at 135 Bishopsgate. Johnny had his back to the window. I remember Leith saying it wasn't the RBS way to just sack everyone because of some bad results.'

By March 2008, Goodwin was becoming impatient over the time it was taking to sort out the mess. Ex-colleagues recall that Goodwin would 'jump on our heads' and demand answers for the delays. At meetings with executives, he would say, 'Surely we've had enough of these things? Surely you have got to grips with these things by now?' A bit like Adolf Hitler in his Führerbunker in Berlin in the final months of the Second World War, Goodwin seemed to veer between delusion and despair as his empire crumbled around him. He was in denial about the severity of the crisis and blamed subordinates, particularly Cameron.

The single biggest obstacle to a successful integration was ABN's Byzantine legal structures but the culture clash between the Scottish and the Dutch banks came second. Fons Trompenaars, a Netherlands-based management consultant RBS brought in to advise on the merger, believed there were misunderstandings on both sides. Trompenaars said RBS's biggest mistake was to assume that decisions made in the UK would be lapped up 'with a great hallelujah' by ABN staff in Holland and elsewhere. He said the Dutch bankers regarded their new Scots overlords as 'ethnocentric' and seemingly incapable of adjusting their approach to the sensitivities of Dutch corporate culture, where consensus building and internal discussion are a prerequisite for action. Trompenaars added, 'RBS needed ABN AMRO in order to interna- tionalize, but it was never going to achieve internationalization with the narrow mindset of "we know best".'[17]

After a while, Goodwin no longer wished to be told of the multiple explosions going off inside ABN. One ex-colleague said, 'To an extent, he had become semi-detached from the business and was living in a fantasy world by that time.' After weeks of flying off the handle when told of bad news about the integration, Goodwin became 'philosophi- cal' – a frame of mind subordinates found even more disturbing. His response on being told of yet another crisis inside ABN was to say, 'I'm not interested – just get on with it. As far as I'm concerned it's done.' So his team took to pretending that certain of the 118 integration initiatives had been completed even when they had not been started, just for a quiet life. The managers responsible would then rename the project and complete it under a different name, beneath Goodwin's radar screen.

One former senior executive inside GBM said, 'Fred was genuinely an optimist. As I said earlier, if he said black is white often enough, somehow his chaps would fix it so that black turned out to be white. In the first three or four months of getting ABN, he did not give it the same focus as he had given to NatWest. It was a much, much harder integration.'

Cameron was not making any concessions to the Dutch way of doing things. Indeed, he seems to have been getting desperate. The message he gave to the 150 newly appointed top executives in the merged RBS and ABN Global Banking and Markets business was stark. He told them, 'Everyone's got to be accountable – no excuses. You've got your budget figures – do it.' In an interview with *Financial News*, he said, 'I want RBS' culture to prevail; that is our concepts of accountability and our focus on getting the job done. I see the RBS culture like a virus and I want to make sure it gets into the veins of ABN AMRO.' That may have been why, of the 18 people selected to be on the merged investment bank's executive team, only five came from ABN AMRO.[18]

Ex-ABN insiders resent the subsequent tendency of UK politicians, bankers and commentators to blame all RBS's problems on ABN, as though it was a uniquely terrible bank and everything else about RBS smelt of roses. They admit there were problems within ABN AMRO but insist that any organisation that acquires a complex company with operations in 50-plus countries without doing any due diligence is bound to discover unexpected issues – especially if it buys it as a financial crisis erupts. One former senior ABN executive said, 'It was not that ABN was an absolute can of worms and the more they opened it up the worse it looked. If you looked inside any bank at that time, you would have found a whole bunch of things – including wildly optimistic valuations being put on certain structures. That wasn't a situation that was specific to ABN AMRO. It was a situation you would have found in any bank.'

Drink the Kool-Aid

Even though RBS was ranked in the top three underwriters and bundlers of US housing debt in 2005 to 2007, Goodwin was adamant that the bank did not 'do' subprime. Speaking to analysts on 1 March 2007, he said, 'We don't get involved in subprime lending.' And, on 5 June 2007, he said, 'We don't do subprime, so we have not perhaps been exposed to some of the more boisterous elements of the market that others have.'[1]

Asked about the bank's exposure to this market at the analysts' conference on 3 August 2007, a time when the board was focused on ABN, Goodwin had slightly changed his tune. He said, 'The short answer is we are one step removed. We have never lent directly to people who are the customers in subprime so we stand back from that . . . It's affecting a market in which we operate but it's not impacting on us in a direct way as it is impacting on some of the others.' And, at the same event, McKillop added, 'Six months ago, there was a lot of speculation ahead of our annual results presentation that we were going to be very adversely affected by the subprime situation. It just didn't happen – we said it wouldn't happen and you've seen it again today. We are not operating in that direct space.'

Both McKillop and Goodwin were, of course, lying. Much of the raw material in the multi-billion dollar market for repackaged US home loans from which RBS was profiting so handsomely was subprime lending and, without frenetic wholesalers like Greenwich Capital, the market would have dried up overnight. The Securities and Exchange Commission said, 'RBS was very active in the subprime market. RBS sponsored residential mortgage-backed securities for subprime mortgage lenders (such as Option One). RBS and/or its affiliates also purchased pools of loans from subprime lenders and offered residential mortgage-backed securities, as well as financed residential loans by subprime lenders.'²

By the summer of 2007, most Wall Street firms had recognised that the market for securitised US mortgage debt was an accident waiting to happen as borrowers increasingly defaulted on their loans and an absence of buyers meant the production line was becoming clogged with unwanted bundles of home loans which were unlikely ever to be shifted or repaid in full. Banks were also suddenly obliged to value securities and other financial instruments manufactured from the sliced-and-diced debt of US home owners more realistically thanks to new 'mark-to-market' accounting rules. Having previously been able to mark them to 'par' (face value), owners of CDOs now had to mark them to market (what they could sell them for if they were to have sold them that day). Goodwin, however, was so focused on his battle with Barclays over ABN AMRO, that he was paying scant attention to the brewing meltdown in the US mortgages market. He also trusted the AAA ratings Moody's and Standard & Poor's gave to super-senior tranches for even the worst CDOs and believed his auditors Deloitte when they said they considered these investments to be safe.

Also, if RBS had admitted that its vast holdings of subprime US mortgage debt had lost value or might lose value, it would, of course, have scuppered its planned takeover of ABN AMRO. Just like that of RBS, the Dutch bank's balance sheet was riddled with reconstituted subprime loans. To have acknowledged that such 'assets' were at risk would have rendered RBS's €71.1 billion offer for ABN not just impossible to finance but impossible to justify.

RBS effectively got caught with its trousers around its ankles when the market for asset-backed commercial paper (ABCP) froze up in August 2007. As investors sought to retrieve their cash, the ABCP seizure caused havoc for many banks and other financial organisations, which relied on this particular type of paper to provide short-term funding to their off-balance-sheet vehicles, including conduits and structured investment vehicles (SIVs).

ABCP was largely funded by American savers via so-called 'money-market funds', which were marketed as being as safe as deposit accounts. The ABCP reversal caused the French bank BNP Paribas to shut down two funds that invested in subprime mortgage debt on 9 August 2007.

This triggered panic in the credit markets as investors feared that other funds would also draw down the shutters. According to the New York Federal Reserve, it triggered a run on over 100 investor programmes, not all of them directly connected with subprime, amounting to a third of the entire ABCP market.

The ABCP seizure made itself felt in almost every corner of the financial markets and played a key part in the Northern Rock debacle. It forced banks to bring their off-balance-sheet vehicles back on to their balance sheets and start funding them themselves. This meant areas which were benefiting from bank funding suddenly found that facilities were removed. It was one of the reasons that, from July 2007 onwards, RBS slashed its lending to the real economy and started to persecute borrowers on whom a few weeks previously it had been lavishing new loans.

RBS Greenwich Capital axed just under a third of its CDO trading desk on 29 August. In total seven of the twenty-four-strong team left. Casualties included Rick Caplan, co-head of the CDO business, who had only joined in October 2006. Other banks were also laying off traders. However, the banks were, for the most part, still assuming that the market would come back.

On 18 October 2007, Citigroup's fixed-income research team warned that a great many CDOs were facing imminent default. According to *The Economist*, super-senior tranches of mezzanine CDOs were trading at between 20:00 and 50:00 (that is between 20 and 50 cents in the dollar) by late October, compared to the 100:00 they had been trading at since their 2004–06 launches.[3] A slew of negative research notes from Wall Street firms added to the banks' agony. At Merrill Lynch and Citigroup, the losses were so immense that the chief executives of both banks fell on their swords. Merrill Lynch's Stan O'Neal 'resigned' on 28 October after the firm racked up losses of $2.3 billion for the third quarter of 2007, as well as an $8.4-billion exceptional charge for subprime losses. On Sunday, 4 November 2007, Charles 'Chuck' Prince, who had been Citi's CEO since October 2003 and was famous for saying 'we're still dancing' in July 2007, was ousted after he declared initial subprime losses of up to $11 billion.[4] 'Prince, a lawyer by trade, was in over his head, just hopelessly inept when it came to understanding what an investment bank does,' said Jim Cramer, host of CNBC's *Mad Money* and co-founder of TheStreet.com.[5] In a further kick in the teeth for investors, Prince jumped from Citibank with a \$95 million 'golden parachute', while Stan O'Neal's rewards for failure at Merrill Lynch were \$159 million. Christopher T. Mahoney, a former vice-chairman of Moody's, said that, at banks like Merrill, Citi, Lehman Brothers, Bear Stearns and RBS, 'the big mistake, the original sin at the firms that crashed, was allowing their securitization operation to warehouse subprime mortgage-related assets that they couldn't sell'.[6]

Every assumption that had underpinned a \$650-billion market had turned out to be fundamentally flawed – as Ron den Braber had predicted in 2002.

The likes of JPMorgan, Goldman Sachs and New York-based hedge fund group Paulson & Co., realised this as early as 2005–06 and found ways of making money from the coming collapse, for example by 'shorting' subprime-related instruments, which, of course, accelerated their plunges in value. Mike Burry, a neurologist who also ran a hedge fund called Scion Capital, became convinced that subprime loans, especially those with 'teaser' rates, would start to shed value as soon as the 'teaser' rates expired. Increasingly convinced that the US housing market would collapse, Burry managed to persuade Goldman Sachs to sell him credit default swaps against subprime deals he thought would be vulnerable. As Michael Lewis wrote in *The Big Short*, 'Once again they shocked and delighted him: Goldman Sachs e-mailed him a great long list of crappy mortgage bonds to choose from. "This was shocking to me, actually," he says . . . He could pick from the list without alerting them to the depth of his knowledge. It was as if you could buy flood insurance on the house in the valley for the same price as flood insurance on the house on the mountaintop.'[7]

Even as Burry, Paulson and Goldman Sachs came to recognise that the market was bound to crash, others insisted on sticking their heads in the sand. And RBS Greenwich Capital – effectively run by joint CEOs Jay Levine and Ben Carpenter, together with chief financial officer Carol Mathis – was one of the biggest ostriches of all.

One senior executive who did try to persuade the firm to pull its head out of the sand was Victor Hong. As structured finance markets plunged, RBS Greenwich Capital's head of market risk, Bruce Jin, hired Hong as managing director of risk management and head of fixed-income independent price verification. Hong had earlier helped other Wall Street names, including Kidder Peabody, Credit Suisse and

JPMorgan, to avoid banana skins.[8] In his previous job at JPMorgan, he was instrumental in persuading the firm's chief executive, Jamie Dimon, to wind down holdings of super-senior tranches of CDOs before the crisis struck. On arrival at Greenwich Capital in late September 2007, Hong sought to instil similar discipline and a more realistic approach to the pricing of CDOs that remained stuck in the Steamboat Road-based firm's warehouses and on its trading book. According to his LinkedIn entry, Hong 'conducted strategic risk review for the chief executive officer [Jay Levine] and chief financial officer [former PwC accountant Carol Mathis][9] on housing-sensitive businesses, like super-senior ABS CDOs, subordinate ABS/RMBS, and floating-rate commercial loans. [He] alerted top global management in 2007 to critical risks, per special UK report ['The Failure of Royal Bank of Scotland', FSA Board Report].'[10]

However, Hong's warnings went unheeded. In one email exchange on 1 October 2007, Hong advised Greenwich's market risk group that its super-senior tranches of high-grade CDOs ought to be marked no higher than 60:00 (60 cents in the dollar), as opposed to 90:00. At around the same time, Henry Asare, a member of the market risk group, confirmed that the firm had been overstating the valuations on super-senior tranches of CDOs since April–May 2007. Asare said, 'I have been telling them this for 5–6 months but they don't want to hear.' Asare also noted that 'Citi and UBS are taking massive write-downs this quarter'.[11] Essentially, Hong had discovered that Greenwich Capital's traders had covered up their losses. But nobody at RBS seemed to want to know and he was prevented from raising his concerns with the bank's auditors, Deloitte.

Four weeks later, GBM chairman Johnny Cameron sent risk managers in RBS's markets group an email asking why 'the super-senior position end result is so sensitive to changes in the underlying assumptions'. But the email responses from three senior risk managers in GBM – Gareth Brown, Riccardo Rebonato and Bruce Jin – focused on the flaws in RBS's credit-loss models and were expressed in dense and illogical language which seemed designed to bamboozle.[12] One ex-GBM insider said, 'Those emails were gobbledegook. The credit risk models they were talking about were riddled with ridiculous assumptions – including that "principal" losses could not go above ten per cent.' The source added that GBM and RBS Greenwich Capital

were ignoring research from other Wall Street firms and 'were behaving like the management of a restaurant who, witnessing a room full of
diners choking on their food, insists there's nothing wrong'.

Amid the tsunami of subprime defaults predicted by Burry, analysts
at JPMorgan issued a spine-chilling research note on 2 November.
Head of global structured finance research Chris Flanagan said the US
had entered 'housing Armageddon' as all financial instruments linked
to the US housing market were starting to implode. In the 276-page
paper, he said, '[W]e estimate average super-senior recoveries of 33:00
given an asset liquidation.'[13] Around the same time, Citigroup analyst
Simon Samuels published a research note saying that RBS had the
weakest capital position of any bank in Europe.[14] On the same day, a
London-based analyst with RBS, Bob Janjuah, said that many banks
were being unrealistic about the valuations of the instruments on which
they had gorged. He predicted banks would lose between $250 billion
and $500 billion as a result of their ownership of such things.[15]

Against this backdrop, investors had good reason to be fearful about
RBS. Given the volume of CDOs and other subprime assets they
suspected it had on its books, they believed it would soon be owning up
to massive losses and would be forced to replenish its capital via a rights
issue. A rights issue is a way in which a company can sell new shares
in order to raise capital. Shares are offered to existing shareholders in
proportion to their original holding. In an information vacuum and as
the stricken bank was increasingly targeted by short-sellers and hedge
funds, RBS shares went on a downward spiral.

Having lost his battle to persuade his superiors at RBS Greenwich
Capital and the GBM finance team in London to accurately mark the
CDO book to market and after being blocked from raising his concerns
with Deloitte, Hong tendered his resignation. His resignation letter,
dated 8 November, was attached to an email sent to Johnny Cameron
and Chris Kyle in GBM in London. In it, Hong wrote, 'My expected
oversight and sign off responsibilities for monthly price verification would
be intolerable, based upon persistent discrepancies between trader marks
and analytical fair market values.' From the tone of the letter, it's clear
Hong was concerned that signing off false or deceptive numbers might
leave him vulnerable to prosecution or enforcement action in future.

Greenwich Capital's managing director of CDOs, Fred Matera,
resigned on the same day. Apparently fearing the timing might look

bad, Greenwich's head of human resources, David MacWilliams, sought to persuade Hong and Matera to stay or at least to delay their departures. Undeterred, Ian Gaskell, a veteran of NatWest Markets who moved to RBS Greenwich Capital in May 2007 to head up structured products, also made it clear he was uncomfortable with the firm's potentially fraudulent approach to CDO pricing. On 9 November 2007 (the day after Hong's and Matera's resignations), he sent an email to RBS's financial markets risk team, making it clear that he felt the valuations Greenwich was ascribing to its CDOs was far too high, given the collapse in ABX indices that tracked market prices. He said, 'I cannot comprehend how, in a falling ABX market, our inventory has done anything other than also fall in value.'[16]

In the build-up to the bank's critical pre-close trading update on 6 December 2007, Goodwin spoke to some senior RBS colleagues. Director of Strategy Iain Allan tried to explain that, even if the super-senior tranches were on the books at 100:00 and worth, say, 70:00 on a fair-value, market-to-model basis, they could readily lose all their value and become worthless in the very near future. Goodwin refused to accept this and said, 'The auditors are happy, the board is happy, the FSA is happy. What's your problem?' Also, according to one former RBS director, when the bank was deliberating on its CDO mark-downs, RBS finance director Guy Whittaker 'presented a paper showing three possible approaches to CDO valuations'.

One former GBM executive believes that Goodwin must have been aware that the bank was in dire straits from November 2007 onwards. 'Our capital adequacy was coming under severe pressure. The market no longer trusted us. Our share price was lagging behind the wider banking sector by about 50 per cent. Then there was all the data from across the Atlantic about subprime, with significant write-downs on subprime-related assets, and there was a suspicion there would be a domino effect. At the same time, from about November 2007, Fred was getting all these dire toxic messages from other areas of the bank, especially from Leith Robertson's area of leveraged finance and parts of ABN AMRO. Whether he was already having a sexual relationship with a member of staff at that time, I don't know, and whether he then started to think, "Oh shit!", I don't know. But I am one hundred per cent convinced that, from November 2007 onwards, Fred knew the bank was in serious trouble.'

If he did know, Fred Goodwin was showing little sign of it on 6 December 2007. In fact, he was oozing self-confidence. In its eagerly awaited pre-close trading update, RBS said profit and earnings per share for the full year ended 31 December would be 'well ahead of consensus', the capital ratios would be 'comfortably within the target ranges' and the integration of ABN AMRO was 'progressing well'. Goodwin added, 'The acquisition of ABN AMRO has rarely seemed more attractive.' Investors breathed a huge sigh of relief when the bank told them that the anticipated sea of red ink from the CDO area would be more like a puddle. Antony Broadbent, an analyst at Sanford Bernstein, said the disclosures 'apparently eliminate the perceived risk of a capital shortfall precipitating a rights issue, dividend cut, or both'.[17] The City breathed a sigh of relief, and Royal Bank's share price rebounded by 10 per cent that morning.

RBS and ABN said they were taking a £1.25-billion write-down after what was described as a £250-million improvement in the carrying value of RBS's debt. Super-senior tranches of high-grade CDOs were being marked down to 90:00 and super-senior tranches of mezzanine CDOs were being marked down to 70:00. £218 million of ungraded subprime inventory – essentially subprime mortgages stuck in a 'warehouse' which had not yet been repackaged – was marked down to 46:00. The news caused uproar on RBS's trading floors in London, Singapore and Greenwich, where traders knew the figures were fanciful. They feared jibes from traders at rival banks, most of which appeared to have been more honest about CDO write-downs. One ex-Greenwich executive said, 'Johnny, Guy and Fred were using models to distract investors. Their claims about Greenwich's CDOs being "better quality", "more diversified" or of a "better vintage" were such bullshit. There was no such thing as a "good" US mortgage by that time. Reserving a cabin in every class of the *Titanic* didn't save you from drowning when the ship went down.'

Some analysts were sceptical of the rosy picture Fred was painting. At the analysts' meeting on 6 December, Citigroup analyst Tom Rayner asked Goodwin, 'I just wondered how conservative you think you've been, or are you limited by auditors, etcetera, in exactly how much you can write down these exposures?' Goodwin said, 'We feel these [write-downs] are pretty conservative. That's not to say it's impossible that they could go up.' Goodwin also sought to reassure the analysts that RBS's vast commercial property loan book was safe and sound, with a loan-to-value ratio of 60 per cent and only 2 per cent of total advances going towards speculative developments. Goodwin said, 'It does feel as if we are quite conservative.' He may have believed it at the time, but approximately £68.5 billion of RBS's commercial real estate loans were of such poor quality that they ended up having to be put in the government's asset protection scheme (APS).[18]

Several senior ex-RBS sources believe that the reason Greenwich Capital's top brass opted for shallow markdowns was because they did not want to jeopardise their 2007 bonuses – if its CDO and subprime inventory had been accurately priced, the losses would have precluded any bonuses. On a wider level, Fred's reign of terror had created a culture of paranoia and secrecy across the bank that encouraged people to misrepresent the truth. And it remains unclear whether RBS management, including group finance director Guy Whittaker, played along with the charade because they did not want to undermine the RBS share price at a sensitive time for the bank or whether they were actually taken in themselves. And it is worth bearing in mind that there are subtly different methodologies for valuing such assets on either side of the Atlantic. RBS was permitted by the FSA to use its own 'internal models' to value them, especially where the effect of hedges is concerned, and this may have enabled it legitimately to take a more sanguine stance. In 2009, the Tory MP Sir Peter Viggers (he of 'floating duck island' fame in the MPs' expenses scandal) asked Goodwin at the Treasury Select Committee whether he understood 'the full complexity' of 'these vehicles that [his] clever young men were creating'. Goodwin's reply was breathtaking. He told the MPs, 'No, I would not. That is part of the secret of how you risk-manage it.'[19]

The mood inside RBS Greenwich Capital was turning ugly. Jay Levine had effectively been fired and was replaced by RBS's head of capital markets, the Australian-born Symon Drake-Brockman, who relocated from London to Greenwich in January 2008. Drake-Brockman said he found the place demoralised and infused with back-biting and sniping over money. In a speech to traders he said, 'All I've heard in recent years is that this is the very best place to be in RBS, that Greenwich is the jewel in the crown. Well, I don't think I've run into a more whiny, sappy group of individuals. You should be embarrassed. I'm embarrassed for you. Things are going to change.'[20]

Not everyone fell for Fred's spin. On 13 December 2007, JPMorgan Cazenove speculated that Royal Bank of Scotland might have to mount a £5.8-billion rights issue, a prediction which caused the shares to fall 10.75p to 462.5p. A flurry of sceptical comments appeared underneath the *FT* Alphaville story that itemised the bank's credit losses. One commenter, 'Hedgehog', said, 'RBS seem to have rose-tinted glasses when it comes to marking their own CDOs. There will be further write-downs to come in due course.'[21] He was right. There would be a further £5.9 billion of market write-downs four months later. Colin McLean of SVM Asset Management said, 'I think Fred did deceive the market. The issue for Fred is not so much that he should have known the risks and the scale of the problems and so should the Royal Bank of Scotland board, but that he actually seemed to be disingenuous about it. And I mean whenever he was asked about subprime exposure in 2006, 2007 and up to February 2008 he just kept denying the scale of it.'[22] McLean added, 'His approach went beyond ignorance into being disingenuous. And he kept this up till quite late in the day. I would question whether traders could have hidden it from him.'[23] However, in a statement, issued in February 2013, RBS said, 'We have previously stated with the FSA that the CDO valuations in 2007 were reasonable given the prevailing market conditions and consistent also with the general approach taken by peer banks.'[24]

Goodwin was more concerned than he was letting on. Two weeks later, on Saturday 22 December, he paid a private visit to the Morningside home of Chancellor Alistair Darling, who was then embroiled in a protracted debate about what the government should do with collapsed lender Northern Rock. Goodwin came alone, bearing a gift-wrapped panettone. Darling says: 'I could see that he was exceedingly tense. Fred doesn't do small talk and so we sat down and got straight to the point. I could see him becoming increasingly anxious, although this wasn't new – I'd noted that the more I spoke to bankers around this time, the more anxious they became. His message for me was clear: unless the Bank of England put more liquidity into the system, quickly, it would seize up, inevitably leading to another bank failure. By now, the Federal Reserve and the ECB [European Central Bank] had been flooding their systems with cash. I knew that there had been a meeting between the CEOs of the banks and Mervyn King [governor of the Bank of England] earlier that month, at which they'd asked him to take the same action.'[25]

King was concerned about 'moral hazard': if the Bank of England rescued the banks from the consequences of their own folly with unrestricted cheap lending, they would just go back to being mad again. Unusually for a twenty-first-century central banker, King still subscribed to the views of Walter Bagehot, the Victorian journalist and *Economist* editor who, in 1873, said that, during credit crises, the central bank or 'lender of last resort' should lend early and freely ('without limit') – but only to solvent banks, only against good collateral and only at 'penal' rates of interest.[26] Because Labour had given the Bank of England its independence in 1997, there was nothing Darling could do to make King change his mind. At the meeting in the chancellor's home, the RBS chief executive told Darling that King had not grasped the scale of the problem and that the crisis had 'moved beyond moral hazard'. Darling wrote, 'I had a great deal of sympathy with what Fred Goodwin was saying, but I asked the question: why were the markets singling out RBS for particular concern? His answer was that they felt RBS didn't have sufficient capital. I asked whether he was comfortable that RBS did have sufficient capital, and his response was that he felt that it did. And yet I was worried. It occurred to me that Sir Fred had not come just as a shop steward for his colleagues. He would not admit it, but I sensed that RBS . . . was in more trouble than we had thought.'[27]

Goodwin's disingenuousness and U-turns were eroding investors' trust. And providers of liquidity, including other large banks, were becoming more and more chary of RBS. They had similar suspicions about ABN AMRO, whose entire €1-trillion balance sheet had been consolidated with RBS's. RBS now had a £1.9-trillion balance sheet and, not only did this eclipse that of any other bank in the world, it was also 136 per cent of the UK's £1.4-trillion gross domestic product. The bank's 154 per cent loan-to-deposit ratio was another disincentive to other banks considering entrusting a few hundred million to the Edinburgh-based bank on the inter-bank lending market. In short, RBS was becoming more and more repellent to providers of wholesale funding who increasingly saw it as a bad bet. One ex-RBS senior executive said: 'Other big banks with interbank money to deposit would previously [before the ABN deal completed in October 2007] have given some to ABN AMRO and some to us. It might have been $50 million for us and $50 million for ABN. But once the two were combined, they were thinking, "We can't give $100 million to the combination, so we're only going to give it a total of $60 million." Even in a benign wholesale market, that would have happened. They would have had a prudential limit on any single institution – let's say $60 million. And, because of the state of the markets as we went into 2008, they were being even more prudent. There was just this constant shortage of wholesale deposits. It was like we were having to run up the down escalator. The people who were coming down were saying, "Sorry, we love you dearly but we're going to have to cut our lines a bit." '

Goodwin was also having trouble on the branding front. On 8 January 2008, he learned that his attempts to block furniture retailer MFI from registering his cherished 'Make it Happen' catchphrase as a trademark had failed. In a final appeal ruling, the UK's Comptroller-General of Patents, Designs and Trade Marks ruled against Royal Bank of Scotland and in favour of MFI. The comptroller-general was sniffily dismissive of RBS, saying, '[I]t is a relatively banal expression and one that is likely to require considerable use and education of the public before it will be regarded as distinctive of one particular trader.' Goodwin's earlier attempts to block MFI from using the slogan through the European Union's trademarks office had failed a year earlier. For once, Goodwin had come up against regulators with backbone – and he didn't like the experience. Paradoxically, the slogan – which the bank had been plastering all over America in the hope of making itself 'famous' with America's 'c-suite' (bosses with the word 'chief ' in their job titles) – didn't do much good for either company. Faced with competition from better managed rivals such as Stockholm-based IKEA, MFI collapsed into administration in November 2008 (just a few weeks after RBS's effective insolvency).

During January, McKillop was trawling around the bank's major institutional investors to gauge their views on the most appropriate way of raising capital. He said, 'I went out on a very deliberate programme across all the major institutions to take their views on, "If we need to increase our capital, what mechanisms would you prefer? Asset disposal, rights issues and so on." I was having those kinds of discussions and feeding all of that into the board so that we could frame options, but even then you would have a very wide diversification of views.'[28]

I personally had a long chat with Goodwin at a champagne reception he hosted in 'Fred's Pleasure Dome', the Grade-A listed Georgian townhouse that he spent £5.3 million refurbishing. As Sir Fred, as he then was, chatted animatedly to guests including Scotland's finance minister John Swinney and Scottish Labour Party leader Wendy Alexander, he seemed remarkably chipper and relaxed. Earlier that day, Monday, 21 January 2008, the FTSE-100 had crashed by 5.5 per cent because of uncertainty about the US economy. RBS's shares had plunged by 8 per cent to 342p but Goodwin was ostentatiously self-confident. I asked him why the bank had not invoked the 'material adverse change' clause in its offer for ABN AMRO in order to lower the price or even scrap its bid. He responded by saying, 'Ian, if you have an offer accepted for a house and there happened to be housing market correction in between your offer being accepted and the missives being concluded, you wouldn't pull out . . . would you?' He said there were parallels with the ABN situation and that to renege on the commitment he had made to buy ABN would be dishonourable. At the time, I thought it was quite an impressive response but, with the benefit of hindsight and reading between the lines, it chimes with the theory that RBS ploughed ahead with the deal for fear of being sued by investors in ABN. Goodwin also insisted the markdowns on the bank's portfolio of structured credit products unveiled six weeks earlier were sufficient. He implied that that had been a 'kitchen sink' exercise and more write-downs would only be necessary if there were a further deterioration in the US housing market. At the time, Goodwin's manner was reassuring.

The board believed it could address the bank's capital shortfall by making disposals. Assets it considered putting on the block included Angel Trains and the Bank of China stake. Goodwin also examined other ways of raising cash, including tapping Middle Eastern sovereign wealth funds (state-owned investment vehicles usually deployed by resource-rich countries to reinvest and protect the proceeds of oil and gas extraction). Talks with the Qatar Investment Agency proved abortive after existing investors in RBS rebelled, fearing a deal with Doha would limit their pre-emptive rights. Some institutional investors were actively pressurising the board to launch a rights issue – even if this meant that Goodwin left the bank. It is said that two RBS non-executive directors – Sir Steve Robson and Peter Sutherland – were also pushing for a rights issue

On 28 February 2008, at its annual results presentation, RBS reassured many investors when it revealed that profits for the year to

December 2007 had risen 9 per cent to £10.3 billion. In a display of bravura and despite ample evidence that the worst of the credit crisis was yet to come, it also raised its dividend by 10 per cent. Steve Slater of Reuters wrote that the results presentation had 'calmed investor nerves – even as [RBS] widened a write-down on risky assets'.[29] Goodwin said, 'We enter 2008 with real momentum behind our organic growth and with our product range, distribution capabilities and customer franchises materially enhanced.'[30] In response to suggestions that RBS had paid over the odds for ABN, Goodwin said, 'I don't have a lot of things that are 9 per cent earnings accretive pass over my desk. I don't often get the chance to get one of the best transaction services businesses in the world. I don't often get the chance to get into India. We're very pleased to have won that business.'[31]

He told investors that he was raising the expected synergies arising from the ABN deal from €1.7 billion to €2.3 billion. Goodwin claimed that progress with assimilating ABN, including liaison with the Dutch regulator DNB, was very good. The results were also flattered by the bank's sale of its stake in water company Southern Water. RBS had sold its 49 per cent stake in the privatised water business – which owned and operated approximately 100 water treatment works and 370 sewage treatment works across southern England – to a consortium led by Australia's Challenger Infrastructure Fund and JPMorgan Asset Management in October 2007. Altogether, the bank had raised £1.2 billion from asset sales during 2007, with the other main ones being the sale of its stakes in the London Stock Exchange and MasterCard.

The bad news, which was casually slipped in, was a marginal increase in write-downs on toxic US mortgage debt. In addition to the write-downs of 6 December, RBS said it was taking further write-downs of £659 million on CDOs, £495 million in traded securities, £456 million on assets guaranteed by bond insurers and £285 million on leveraged loan assets. There was also a £978 million write-off on the value of ABN's credit-related assets. The bank added that Citizens had seen an 88 per cent surge in bad loans in 2007, which caused the US arm's pre-tax profit to fall by 17 per cent. Clutching at straws perhaps, Goodwin declared the credit markets were seeing 'a trickle' of business but that recovery felt 'fragile' and might not gather momentum until the second half. He said, 'We need a healing period without bumps and loud noises.'[32]

Goodwin seemed unusually nervous and skittish that day – especially when analysts grilled him about the bank's capital ratios. At the analysts' briefing, Citi's Simon Samuels asked the directors what RBS's core equity tier-1 ratio was 'on a look-through basis, excluding the pieces of ABN that you did not own'. He added, 'Are you saying it's a number that you know and you don't want to share with us, or that it's unknowable?' Finance director Guy Whittaker was vague in response, just saying it started with a 'four' and a 'seven'. McKillop was patronising and condescending saying, 'It's a pretty theoretical kind of number but you can calculate it.' Goodwin came across like a petulant schoolboy. He said, 'We have our capital ratio, Simon, and we talk about the capital ratios as calculated in accordance with Basel and all the rest of it.' Before adding, '*If you want to calculate other ratios as people have historically, then feel free but it's not a ratio that we stand behind* [my italics].'[33] They were hardly the most reassuring of responses. The reality was that RBS's balance sheet was so stretched that its core tier-1 ratio had fallen below the regulatory minimum of 4 per cent. This meant it had less than £4 of capital to cover every £100 of risk-adjusted exposure on its balance sheet. By April, the ratio would fall to as low as 3.6 per cent, something the bank told a select group of 'insiders', institutional investors thought to have included Standard Life, Legal and General and Universities Superannuation Scheme.

Lehman Brothers' analyst Robert Law pinned Goodwin down on whether the bank needed a rights issue. Goodwin replied, 'There are no plans for any inorganic capital raisings or anything of the sort.' It was a claim that would come back to haunt him. Law then said, 'Can I ask what the attributable goodwill is on the balance sheet to the ABN AMRO businesses that you are retaining, so that we can actually work out what the tangible book value per share is for yourself?' Whittaker memorably responded, 'Ahhh, dudum, dudum, dudum, dudum. I want to say it's about eight [He meant about £8 billion] . . . Eight I believe is a pretty good number but I will confirm that to you.'[34] Trust was breaking down. RBS shares closed down 2 per cent at 402p.

In the middle of March, Cameron told Goodwin that the forecasts were looking terrible across the RBS/ABN investment banking and corporate banking operations and that they were getting worse. It was after this and after other means of raising capital (disposals and selling shares to Middle Eastern sovereign wealth funds) proved abortive that senior insiders recognised a rights issue would be necessary after all. One former RBS non-executive director said that valuations of a lot of the assets that RBS was holding 'just collapsed, particularly in March 2008. March was a desperate month.'

At the time, it was an open secret inside the bank that a rights issue would be required and that, if one was required, Goodwin would have to go. The pressure was getting to Goodwin. That month, the bank held an executive 'off-site' meeting in Edinburgh. In the evening, there was a dinner at the Edinburgh International Conference Centre (EICC) on Morrison Street. Well after midnight, after the comedian Michael McIntyre had done some stand-up comedy as post-dinner entertainment, a group of senior RBS executives – Goodwin, Cameron, Crowe, Whittaker and Fisher – were drinking single Highland malt whiskies by the bar. Someone from RBS's equity capital markets unit who had had one too many made a beeline for Fred. His boss, seeing the situation unfolding, tried to intervene but was too late. The executive said, 'Look Fred, you do realise that, if the ABN deal doesn't work, you're f★★ked?' The well-oiled executive added this would mean a capital raising and that Goodwin would have to resign. Goodwin turned to the person's boss, another GBM executive, and said, 'Look this [ABN] was a deal that was done for GBM, by GBM.' Goodwin then started to jab the GBM executive in the chest, saying, 'It's all you guys' fault – it's you who have f★★ked everything up. I suggest you get back to that old money-making machine of yours and get it working again, before you come bleating over here to me and asking me for new capital.'

According to the FSA report, '[B]y March 2008, there was increasing FSA involvement at the most senior level, with the FSA pressing RBS to acknowledge the need for a large rights issue.'[35] But Goodwin remained in denial. Yet again, and despite the views of some of his co-directors, he thought he'd be able to busk it.

The global financial crisis took a turn for the worse over the weekend of 15 and 16 March. A crisis of confidence at New York-based investment bank Bear Stearns caused leading clients to flee and lenders to pull overnight funding. The bank had got caught with too many toxic bundles of debt on its books when the securitisation sausage machine seized up and a classic 'run' ensued. In a deal brokered by the US Federal Reserve, which threw in $30 billion of funding to underpin Bear's most rancid assets, the 85-year-old Wall Street institution succumbed to a rescue takeover by JPMorgan. The deal caused *Financial Times* chief economics commentator Martin Wolf to write that 'the dream of free-market capitalism' had just died. Bear's chief executive, James E. 'Jimmy' Cayne, dubbed the 'dope-smoking megalomaniac' by boardroom colleagues, had been as disastrous a chief executive as Goodwin and was no less clueless about repackaged debt. As *The Economist* noted, 'Bear's crash marked the moment when a delirious Wall Street was knocked to its senses. As one executive put it at the time, in terms that Mr Cayne might appreciate: "You can't fly like the eagles and poop like a canary." '[36]

The collapse of Bear sparked fears of a domino effect. the *Financial Times*' 'Lex' column said that panicked institutional investors were now screening their bank holdings according to three criteria: (1) Does the bank have sufficient liquidity to remain solvent? (2) Does it have sufficient tier-1 capital to remain solvent? (3) How good is its asset quality? Lex said there was particular concern about RBS.[37] 'That was a period of constant stress,' says Cameron.[38]

On 20 March, Goodwin and other bankers went to Threadneedle Street to see the governor of the Bank of England. HBOS's Andy Hornby, Barclays's John Varley, HSBC's Stuart Gulliver and Goodwin all pleaded for the Bank of England to help them out by injecting more liquidity into the market. One commercial bank insider told *The Times*, 'The British central bank has done far less than its counterparts to address the issue of liquidity and the money markets and has a much tighter definition of the collateral that it will accept.' The bankers were becoming exasperated by King and his hang-ups about 'moral hazard'.

On a visit to the *Financial Times* offices at One Southwark Bridge Road, in March, McKillop and Goodwin were blaming their misfortune on mark-to-market accounting rules. One ex-*FT* insider said, 'They were both very exercised about mark-to-market rules, saying these might trigger a further downward spiral – in which assets were marked down further which, in turn, would further undermine their capital position, which would precipitate losses, which would then further undermine confidence and asset prices.'

Fred Goodwin managed to put his travails behind him when he flew to Bahrain for the Bahrain Grand Prix on 5 and 6 April. He was spotted sharing wise-cracks with Vodafone's chief executive Arun Sarin and Formula One Svengali Bernie Ecclestone 'in the paddock' at the three-year-old Sakhir Grand Prix track. The plight of Fédération Internationale de l'Automobile (FIA) president Max Mosley, whom the *News of the World* alleged had taken part in Nazi-style orgies, appears to have been a major topic of conversation. The Williams F1 Team's website later reported, 'The tartan terrors are back with AT&T Williams this weekend. Sir Fred Goodwin, chief executive of the Royal Bank of Scotland Group, Sir Jackie Stewart and Peter Phillips are all wearing the RBS tartan trews – in a team owned by two Englishmen.' Again, the two Williams racing cars, driven by Nico Rosberg and Kazuki Nakajima, trailed the field coming eighth and fourteenth respectively. The 57-lap, 191-mile race was won by the Brazilian driver Felipe Massa in a Ferrari.

Soon after jetting back from the Persian Gulf in the bank's Dassault Falcon 900EX, Goodwin had a rude awakening. On 9 April, he had a meeting with Hector Sants, the chief executive of the FSA, who was laying down the law. Clive Briault, the FSA's director of retail supervision, who is alleged to have handled Goodwin and RBS with kid gloves, had left the FSA two days earlier, on 7 April. Sants, who had done his homework by having sent a supervision team to visit RBS's American operations to check capital adequacy across the bank, was in no mood to take any flimflam from Goodwin. He may have been galvanised by a comment from a senior FSA banking supervisor, Clive Adamson. In an earlier FSA internal meeting, Adamson had commented that RBS's Basel II-mandated disclosures were 'a pack of lies', an allegation for which he was rebuked by one unnamed colleague.[39] At his meeting with Goodwin, Sants ordered the Paisley-born accountant and RBS to do three things: (a) raise capital; (b) raise as much capital as they could; (c) do it via a rights issue. He also told Goodwin that the bank's board must confirm their intention to do these things in writing.

Speaking to the Treasury Select Committee in January 2012, Sants recalled: 'I have no doubt that he would not have had a rights issue of that size without my personal intervention . . . We pressed them to raise as much capital as they possibly could.' At the meeting, Goodwin professed ignorance of the bank's exact capital position. He said, 'I am not sure about the exact ratio numbers', whilst acknowledging that the position was 'likely to be a breach [of individual capital guidance] in March and very tight for April'. Goodwin, perhaps post-rationalising the meeting with Sants, came to believe that a rights issue was now the only way he could save the bank. (And sources close to Goodwin claim the bank had, since 28 March, been working on plans for a £4-billion rights issue which, when combined with the sale of the insurance division, would raise some £8 billion of capital.) Goodwin cancelled meetings with institutional investors to work on the capital raising. By Monday 14 April, advisors Goldman Sachs and Merrill Lynch were working full steam ahead. However, Goodwin never told his non-executive directors of Sants' intervention. One said, 'If Hector Sants did tell Fred, Fred never passed the message on.'

On Tuesday 15 April, a collection of top-of-the-range limousines, including Goodwin's dark blue Mercedes-Benz S600, purred into Downing Street. Bankers, including HSBC's Michael Geoghegan, HBOS's Andy Hornby, Lloyds TSB's Eric Daniels, Barclays' John Varley and Goodwin, had come for a 7.15 a.m. breakfast meeting with Gordon Brown. The Prime Minister had intended to use the meeting to pick the bankers' brains ahead of his forthcoming visit to the US but capital strength was also discussed. One of the attendees, US-born investment banker Bruce Wasserstein, boss of Lazard, told Brown that all Britain's high-street banks were 'woefully undercapitalised'. Wasserstein's warning prompted some furious scribbling by Downing Street aides but a stony silence from the bank bosses. Goodwin, whose bank was the most dangerously undercapitalised of the five, did not breathe a word of his capital-raising plans.[40]

Goodwin had agreed to pay Goldman Sachs and Merrill Lynch a fee of 2.25 per cent – comprising a basic 2 per cent fee, plus a success fee of 25 basis points – of the sum raised in the rights issue or a total of £270 million between them. To the RBS board, these seemed excessively generous terms – as if Fred saw the rights issue as a means of rewarding his friends in the City. On 18 April, they told him that he'd have to go back to Goldman Sachs and Merrill Lynch and get them to reduce their fees. Whittaker later managed to persuade Greenburgh and Chisholm to trim their fees to 1.9 per cent plus a 25 basis points success fee. However, even this was steep compared to what other banks, including UBS, were being charged for the underwriting of a rights issue at the time. In the end, the two investment banks accepted a fee of 1.5 per cent and a success fee of 25 basis points. The board had managed to slash the total fees by £60 million – they were now £210 million – if the thing flew.

In the week commencing 14 April, there was growing speculation that RBS was poised to launch a deeply discounted rights issue of up to £13 billion – meaning shareholders would be offered newly minted RBS shares for a price well below the current share price – and that this would be unveiled on Tuesday, 22 April. Even though it was obvious that Goodwin would take a lot of flak – given this would represent a massive U-turn on his remarks in February – there was also a view that he would benefit from a 'halo effect' for jumping in first, and would also be more likely to raise the full amount than other UK banks that needed to raise money in this way. On Friday 18 April, the RBS share price actually jumped by 5 per cent to 384p. Investors were piling back into bank stocks on the assumption that RBS's move would lift the entire sector.

Goodwin had, it turned out, made a Faustian pact with the tripartite authorities. Under the terms of the unwritten agreement, the Bank of England had promised to provide the liquidity he craved as long as he made shareholders feel some of the pain by tapping them for capital. On Sunday 20 April, McKillop convened a conference call involving the bank's entire board, at which the directors signed off the £12-billion rights issue, including the revised fees for the underwriters. And on Monday 21 April, the Bank of England announced details of an ambitious £50-billion plan designed to help hard-pressed banks by letting them swap risky mortgage debt for more secure government bonds. The so-called 'Special Liquidity Scheme' (SLS) was King's most significant response yet to the credit crisis and a sign that the Old Lady of Threadneedle Street was allowing principles to be overtaken by pragmatism. Under the SLS, the banks would be allowed to trade in assets of a dubious and illiquid nature in exchange for gilt-edged bonds for periods of up to three years. It would be very useful to the banks since it would give them more collateral against which to borrow.[41] Darling and a Treasury team had been working on the scheme for months and put a great deal of effort into getting King and the Bank of England to agree to it.[42]

RBS announced its £12-billion rights issue, the proceeds of which it would not get its hands on until June, as part of its interim pre-close trading update on Tuesday 22 April. In addition to the rights issue, the bank said it intended to raise some £4 billion by selling its general insurance businesses – Direct Line, Churchill, Privilege and Green

Flag – and it also said it was taking massive additional write-downs on its portfolio of subprime-related securities (including CDOs, subprime inventory and monoline exposures) to £5.9 billion. This was five times what RBS had admitted to on 6 December 2007 but this part of the announcement was largely buried by the brouhaha surrounding the rights issue. Investors were stunned that a bank which had told them it had no need raise capital on 28 February – a day on which it had announced record profits of £10.3 billion and raised its dividend – had depleted its capital to the extent that it needed to raise £12 billion. Something just didn't add up.[43] Fitch, the credit ratings agency, downgraded RBS with immediate effect and Moody's put it on review for a possible downgrade. A ratings downgrade is serious for a bank. It makes it more expensive for the bank to borrow money and influences which types of institutions are able to place money with the bank. As the market digested the seriousness of the situation, the bank's shares slid by a further 4 per cent to close on Tuesday at 345p. Sandy Chen, analyst at Panmure Gordon said, 'RBS, especially post-ABN and post-rights, is destroying value on a grand scale.'[44]

At a seminal analysts' conference that morning, a nervous-looking Goodwin claimed the rights issue was 'about the wellbeing of the bank. I can well understand that this isn't easy for shareholders. It's not easy for me either.' Asked if this was his worst day as RBS chief executive, he said 'I certainly hope so.'[45] On the terms of the issue, RBS said it was issuing 11 new shares for every existing 18 shares and these would be priced at 200p each. That represented a 46 per cent discount to the bank's closing share price of 372.5p on Monday 21 April. Four members of the RBS board – Goodwin, McKillop, Cameron and Whittaker – were facing investment analysts in the 280 Bishopsgate auditorium. The performances were even less convincing than those of 28 February. For a start, the directors insisted that launching a rights issue was entirely their own decision – even though many of the analysts knew they had been told to do it by the regulator. McKillop denied it saying, 'We have to be very, very clear . . . there was no explicit request from anyone to strengthen our base.' Goodwin said, 'I completely agree with that – no request to increase the capital base.' To many who were present, these seemed like bare-faced lies. Citi's Simon Samuels asked the four RBS directors about RBS's leverage ratio. Whittaker answered, 'A number of you rightly estimated ratios of around sort of 1.5, 1.4 [per cent] towards the end of last year.'[46] Whittaker was referring to the equity-to-asset ratio favoured by US banking analysts and regulators when judging banks' solvency. Crucially, it's a ratio that strips out goodwill – the value that a company ascribes to its acquisitions. As the writer and finance expert Nicholas Dunbar wrote, 'In other words, if you stripped out what RBS thought ABN was worth based on an inflated price, then the merged bank was leveraged sixty or seventy times . . . If RBS was a US bank [that] would have forced the FDIC [Federal Deposit Insurance Corporation] to shut it down immediately. Even a well-run bank in a benign economy could not be trusted to protect depositors with sixty times leverage.'[47] Pretending ABN was worth more than it was was a vital crutch for Goodwin at the time, and part of what appears to have been the web of deceit surrounding RBS.

Asked by HSBC analyst Peter Toeman if the board accepted culpability for failing to withdraw from the ABN deal and failing to renegotiate its price, McKillop seemed incapable of providing a straight answer, saying, 'Looking back, we purchased ABN at a point when bank valuations were way higher than they are today. That is very unfortunate, you could call it misjudgement, but that is a matter of judgement.'[48] With this trite remark and others including his opening comment ('This has been a tricky time for banks and we all have much to learn') together with his unconvincing denials that the regulator had forced RBS's hand over the rights issue, McKillop lost the faith of many investors. One buy-side analyst later said that McKillop came across as clueless and out of his depth at this analysts' conference, adding, 'At the end of the meeting, McKillop said, "Look, I don't need this job, I don't need all this aggro, I could be off." It was a disgrace. He was trying to collect £750,000 a year for being RBS chairman without taking any responsibility for what happened to the bank.'[49]

During a separate conference call with US analysts held later that day – 22 April – Goodwin confirmed that the bank was making innocent customers pay for its own *folie de grandeur*, Goodwin said, 'What we're seeing is customer recognition that they're going to have to pay more for money than they would've paid a year ago . . . The trick will be, as we put our hurdle rates up, to put them up enough to get proper rewards so that we force proper rewards for the risks that we are taking and the funding that we are providing without losing market share and becoming uncompetitive.'[50]

The next day, Wednesday, 23 April 2008, the bank's board faced more than 300 angry shareholders at its annual general meeting at the Edinburgh International Conference Centre. The session opened with a brand-new, sumptuously produced, four-minute 'a day in the life' corporate video which flaunted RBS's post-ABN AMRO international reach. The *Gladiator* soundtrack that had previously been used to introduce sessions like this had been replaced with a bespoke choral/orchestral piece specifically recorded for the bank using a full orchestra in Prague. Sitting at the centre of a politburo-style dais, McKillop confirmed the bank was seeking to raise £12 billion and that it needed the money to strengthen its balance sheet. Humility is not a trait that comes naturally to Goodwin, so he let McKillop do almost all of the talking. McKillop insisted that 'the time has come to rebase the capital. We're convinced the actions announced yesterday were in the best interests of shareholders.'[51] Asked by one shareholder about whether the mute Goodwin would have to go, McKillop said the entire board and not just Goodwin was responsible for RBS's situation. He said, 'There is no single individual responsible for all these events. To look for a sacrificial lamb just misses the whole point. This is an extremely strong board. There are no patsies on this board.'[52]

I have never been to a corporate AGM where the shareholders have been more incensed – and I've been to many AGMs. Fred Lawson, a shareholder from Musselburgh, told McKillop: 'I have to say that I am finding very little confidence in you. In the Northern Rock situation, it was stated that the chairman and chief executive had no qualifications and knowledge of banking and I see your background is as a pharmacist . . . I'm finding you just a little bit like PC Plod rearranging the deckchairs on the *Titanic*.' To applause and the sound of murmured 'Hear! Hear!', another shareholder, John Stein, questioned the level of directors' pay: 'You guys were paid as though you were superhuman and it is very clear that you are not.'[53] One big shareholder later told *The Times*'s Patrick Hosking, 'Of course he [Fred] should go. He is a megalomaniac. He got one thing right – NatWest. Everything else he has done has been catastrophic.'[54]

Many other RBS investors, particularly those based south of the border, shared that view. In Scotland, however, many were backing Fred. Speaking on the fringes of the shareholder meeting, the bank's former chairman, George Mathewson, said, 'This is not the day for throwing out the baby with the bathwater.'[55] He claimed it would be 'meaningless' and 'fanciful' to set a timetable for replacing Goodwin while RBS still had not completed the assimilation of ABN AMRO. Other Scottish-based financial types were equally supportive of Goodwin. Willie Watt, chief executive of fund manager Martin Currie, said, 'Fred has experience of the BCCI [Bank of Credit and Commerce International] workout and the integration of NatWest and RBS – there aren't that many people with that level of experience around.'[56]

For a no-holds-barred view of the destruction that Goodwin had wrought and investors' inability to punish him for it, you had to look to the American press. *Fortune*'s senior writer Colin Barr let rip: 'Even in the pathetic pantheon of subprime mortgage losers, Royal Bank of Scotland stands out . . . in a bizarre break with the Merrill-Citi-UBS model, in which top execs who oversaw disastrous mortgage invest- ments were forced to resign, RBS is standing behind the management team that led the firm into this morass . . . Last year, RBS belatedly began cutting back on the CDO business, bidding adieu to co-CDO head Rick Caplan and scaling back the size of the unit. But by then, CDOs backed by billions of dollars in souring loans were already out the door and blowing holes in the balance sheets of investors around the world.'[57]

Interestingly, the Federal Housing Finance Agency (FHFA), acting as conservator for Fannie Mae and Freddie Mac – which exist to boost home-ownership in America, taking on mortgages sold by other firms to ease bank balance sheets and keep credit flowing – is suing RBS and RBS Greenwich Capital. The suit, dated September 2011, claims the RBS division routinely breached its own mortgage-lending rules and bullied surveyors into wildly inflating the valuations of American prop- erties in the run-up to the crisis. The FHFA also claims that Greenwich was so desperate to ratchet up fees and bonuses before the subprime market collapsed that employees repeatedly made false statements to clients. The FHFA's suit is one of 17 such suits made against a number of leading banks, including Barclays and HSBC. The suit against RBS and RBS Greenwich Capital alleges that executive bonuses were so geared towards writing high-risk business that they rushed deals through without due diligence. Sometimes, 'owner occupancy data was materially false', the FHFA alleges. The suit alleges that RBS 'furnished appraisals that they understood were inaccurate and that they knew bore no reasonable relationships to the actual value of the underlying properties', displaying 'systematic disregard of their own underwriting guidelines'. If RBS were to lose the case, which it has said it will contest, legal experts believe it could be liable to pay damages of at least $6 billion.[58]

RBS's accounts for the year ended 31 December 2007 show the bank was still valuing its CDOs at 84.00 for high grade and 70.00 for mezzanine. By the time of RBS's interim update, published on 22 April 2008 at the time of the rights issue announcement, the bank had marked down the super-senior tranches of CDOs to 52:00 and 20:00. And on 24 October 2008, in the run-up to its nationalisation, RBS finally announced serious losses on super-senior ABS CDO tranches. The final write-down came in November 2008, when RBS marked down the super-senior tranches of high-grade and mezzanine ABS CDOs to 52:00 and 16:00, respectively. Even that may have been too high, according to some calculations. The delayed acknowledgement of losses, which Hong had urged the bank to recognise in October 2007, served little purpose other than to enrich a few of Greenwich Capital's traders and managers with outrageous bonuses for the 12 months ended 31 December 2007. The corollary was that investors had the wool pulled over their eyes. If the bank had displayed the same level of honesty about its CDO and MBS mark-to-market losses as some other Wall Street banks in the second half of 2007 – which was what Victor Hong wanted it to do – its problems would have come to light sooner. Everything could have been very different both for RBS and its investors.

Some believe that, in the months following the beginning of the credit crunch in July 2007, Goodwin and senior colleagues may genuinely have believed that the crisis would be a short lived affair, a 'blip' or temporary squall from which markets and the bank would rapidly recover. In such a scenario, they may thought that severe asset price mark-downs were unnecessary, and that battening down the hatches would be a waste of time. Clark McGinn, former director of asset finance at RBS global banking and markets, says: 'They thought that, in facing economic stress, they could be like Evel Knievel and, by speeding up, carry over the yawning chasm. They turned out to be Eddie the Eagle.'[59]

The crash

Having sat through the annual general meeting on 23 April 2008 with 'the look of a man about to climb the gallows', Goodwin was spared the noose.[1] He and his co-directors spent most of the next few weeks trying to persuade investors – many of whom were absolutely furious with the bank – to support the rights issue. He was hoping that, at the very least, he and McKillop might cling on for 12 to 18 months, by which time they would be able to leave with at least some dignity, preferably once ABN AMRO had been dismantled and assimilated.

Analysts and investors were obsessing about RBS's capital, liquidity, asset quality and provisioning policy but Goodwin preferred not to talk about such things. Still having an affair with a senior human resources professional from inside the bank, he almost seemed to be living in a bubble. When challenged, he refused to engage. One fund manager said, 'Meetings with Fred were very difficult because, if you pushed too much, he would just become aggressive and then clam up. So you'd end up skirting around some issues. He did come out with some of the most ludicrous remarks, one of which was "Capital doesn't matter. We are so profitable that capital doesn't matter."

On Friday, 25 April, two days after the annual general meeting, Goodwin, McKillop and the bank's head of investor relations Richard O'Connor headed along the road to Aegon Asset Management, which owned about 30 million RBS shares, worth about £110 million at the time. They met at the Dutch-owned asset manager's offices, at 3 Lochside Crescent in Edinburgh Park. Goodwin spent the first fifteen minutes of the meeting in silence and was happy to let O'Connor do all the talking. When one fund manager made clear that either Goodwin or McKillop would have to go, Goodwin did speak. He said, 'If that's

what you think, why don't I leave the room while you deliberate?'
Asked about the bank's commercial property exposure, McKillop
claimed he had been 'all over the commercial-property book'. But,
when asked about what proportion of the book was at a loan-to-value
ratio of 80 per cent or more, the chairman didn't know, which the fund
managers present believed suggested the chairman was, once again,
talking through his hat. Throughout this period analysts and investors
were surprised by the optimism that Goodwin and other bankers still
had about the UK economy. 'They seemed delusional,' said one asset
manager. 'By 2008, it was fairly clear to most of us that Northern Rock
was the canary in the mine and things were going to get fairly horrific.
Yet the bankers just seemed incapable of recognising this.'

Goodwin's biggest challenges were to finalise the rights issue prospectus and, if possible, complete the disposal of the insurance division, a process which had kicked off in February. By law, a rights issue
prospectus must reflect a company's true reasons for raising capital,
present an accurate picture of its financial state and offer an accurate
picture of its future prospects. This prospectus also had to be sufficiently enticing to investors to persuade them to stump up £12 billion
in cash. For RBS, it was going to be a delicate balancing act.

Over the next few days Goodwin worked alongside finance director
Guy Whittaker, in-house lawyers Miller McLean and Chris Campbell,
others from within the bank and external solicitors including Matthew
Middleditch, a partner at Linklaters, to dot the i's and cross the t's on
the prospectus. Also in the rights issue team were Matthew Greenburgh
and Rupert Hume-Kendall of Merrill Lynch, Andy Chisholm and
Matthew Westerman of Goldman Sachs and Jim Renwick at UBS, plus
others from accountants Deloitte and lawyers Freshfields Bruckhaus
Deringer. The bank also engaged the services of former UBS investment banker Oliver Pawle as consultant and worked alongside the UK
Listing Authority (UKLA), a part of the FSA, to ensure the document
was not in breach of the regulations.

The 147-page document was ready to be distributed to RBS's
200,000 shareholders on Wednesday 30 April. It included a nine-page
letter from McKillop, in which RBS's embattled chairman said, 'With
reinforced capital ratios, the group will be in a stronger position to
navigate through an economic environment that remains uncertain,
and well placed to take advantage of the growth opportunities avail-

able to it. To the extent permitted, each of the directors intends to take up his or her rights to subscribe for new shares under the rights issue.' However, on page eight of his letter, he also added the rider, 'The outlook is inevitably clouded by the disruption to markets, as a result of which volumes are likely to be significantly lower in some areas of global banking and markets.'[2]

Normally, a rights issue or IPO prospectus also includes a long list of things that could go wrong – so-called 'risk factors'. RBS's prospectus devoted six pages to risk factors, including that: 'earnings may be affected by general business and geopolitical conditions'; 'RBS's borrowing costs and access to the debt capital markets depend significantly on its credit ratings'; 'the value or effectiveness of any credit protection which RBS has purchased from monoline insurers may fluctuate depending on the financial condition of the insurer'; and 'proposals for the restructuring of ABN AMRO are complex and may not realise the anticipated benefits for RBS'.

RBS stated that, once it had raised the £12 billion, it would not run out of working capital for at least another 12 months. With the benefit of hindsight the document was, at best, disingenuous. For example, it made no reference to the fact that the FSA had ordered the rights issue.[3] Nor did it mention that, by the time it was published on 30 April, the bank was making use of $11.9 billion of clandestine emergency loans from the US Federal Reserve (it would later make even greater use of these covert facilities, whose existence the Fed only admitted to following a Freedom of Information request from *Bloomberg*). If these two facts had been spelt out in the prospectus, investors would have been much more wary of handing over £12,300,000,000.

According to subsequent investor lawsuits, other errors of omission or commission in the prospectus included:

- it understated RBS's exposure to exotic credit derivatives;
- it understated RBS's short-term funding requirement;
- it neglected to mention that the €10.9 billion cash payment from the sale of LaSalle had been delayed;
- it neglected to mention that RBS's core tier-1 capital had fallen as low as 3.6 per cent by 30 April 2008;
- it neglected to mention the bank had breached or was close to breaching its individual capital guidance (ICG);[4]

- it played down problems with the ABN integration;
- it failed to acknowledge ABN was overvalued on RBS's books;
- it failed to admit the inadequacies of RBS's 'back office', risk management and controls;
- it failed to admit that RBS had incomplete knowledge of its own financial position.

The vast majority of institutional investors, retail investors and RBS staff were willing to suspend their disbelief and allow themselves (and those whose savings they were supposed to be looking after) to be led over a cliff. There was a 'halo effect' based on the trust the bank had built up over three centuries and Goodwin's perceived achievements over the past nine years. So, when the bank claimed it needed to 'rebase its capital position', investors believed this was the goal and were happy to reach into their pockets. Gordon Brown, who replaced Tony Blair as Prime Minister on 24 June 2007, recalled in his memoirs, 'I thought that finally the banks were coming clean and we had at least a fighting chance of the losses being declared and a restoration of the markets.'[5]

Investors also considered the rights issue share price of 200p – 47 per cent below the 372p pre-rights price – a bargain. Many less sophisticated investors were also swayed by the blue chip names on the cover of the prospectus – Merrill Lynch, Goldman Sachs and UBS. Fear played a part too. Some investors were concerned that, if they didn't take up their rights, the bank would fail. One City investment manager says, 'There certainly was a feeling that, by supporting these rights issues, we were helping out our investors by preventing the collapse of the financial system. That is definitely what we felt.'

Asset management firms and institutional investors with considerable holdings of RBS shares that did not participate in the rights issue included Baillie Gifford (one of the biggest investors in RBS with about 94.5 million shares before the rights issue), Goldman Sachs International (59.3 million), GMO Woolley (20.5 million) and T Rowe Price (18.5 million). Interestingly, Baillie Gifford dumped 10.8 million RBS shares between 1 June and 31 August 2008, with Goldman Sachs offloading 12 million shares over the same period.[6] So, while one part of Goldman Sachs was earning millions in fees by underwriting the RBS rights issue, other parts of the Wall Street bank suspected that, however brilliantly it was spun, Royal Bank's rights issue was the equivalent of putting a Band-Aid on a burst artery.

In Scotland, patriotism also came into it. Even though RBS had been downplaying its Scottishness over the previous couple of years (for example, switching from its full name to the initials RBS), it still had a corporate tartan, printed its own uniquely Scottish banknotes and sponsored arts, cultural and sports events north of the Border, including the Edinburgh Festival Fringe. It had helped to put Scotland on the map as a serious financial centre. Both the bank and Goodwin himself were used to being lionised by the Scottish media. *Scotland on Sunday* named him top dog in its 'Power 100' for four consecutive years between 2003 and 2006. And many middle-aged and older Scots had done very well by holding shares in the bank since the 1980s or 1990s. If RBS had hit a sticky patch and needed some extra cash, many Scots felt obliged to stick their hands in their pockets. On the back of such thinking, many shareholders borrowed money to ensure they could take up their maximum rights of 11 new shares for every 18 they already owned. Mathewson, the former chairman, was one of the biggest enthusiasts, advising friends to 'fill their boots'. He finally lost more than £5 million on RBS shares after the bank imploded.

Goodwin and McKillop also persuaded tens of thousands of their own employees to participate in the rights issue. In late 2007 and early 2008, as the crisis intensified, employees of RBS and NatWest were subjected to a barrage of propaganda telling them RBS would be immune from the market mayhem. 'It was a very well-polished machine. There was constant spin telling us not to worry, that everything was fine,' said one Gogarburn-based employee. 'Almost every other day there was an audio conference or a town hall-style meeting. The more senior people were telling us to "just keep drinking the Kool-Aid".'

Many employees had such faith in the bank that they had put their entire life savings into RBS shares – through share options, employee share ownership plans (ESOPs) and save-as-you-earn (SAYE) schemes. When McKillop sent an intranet message appearing to urge them to buy the shares, they were reassured. One ex-manager in corporate lending said, 'They were urging us to borrow money, telling us to remortgage our homes to go out and buy as many shares as possible. It was like a religion or a cult at RBS. People had tied up their whole lives and savings with the one institution.'

One senior executive spoke to Goodwin soon after the prospectus was published, saying, 'This is one hell of a rights issue, Fred.' Goodwin wasn't keen to discuss the matter but eventually said, 'Everything is fine. We're going on to even greater things.' Later that day, the same executive bumped into Cameron in RBS's 135 Bishopsgate office. He asked the son of the clan chief, 'Johnny, what about the rights issue? Will it do it for us?' Cameron's reply was: 'Bang on. We're fine, absolutely, absolutely!' The GBM executive said, 'When your CEO and your head of your division say those sorts of things, it gives you some confidence. So I wrote a cheque for £250,000.' Goodwin kept a list of executives who were not participating. And, at the annual NatWest pensioners' lunch at the Lancaster Gate Hotel in April 2008, Goodwin advised some 1,000 NatWest pensioners to put as much money as they could in to the rights issue. 'He was very charismatic and knew how to work an audience,' said NatWest pensioner Peter Hoare. 'He was very bullish about ABN AMRO and told us we should stick with him.' Hoare ended up losing £90,000.

Goodwin used unusual tactics to try to persuade some of the biggest individual investors in RBS to take up their rights. At a lunch at the stockbrokers Brewin Dolphin in May 2008, there was a large bottle of Tabasco sauce sitting on the sideboard. Goodwin picked up the bottle and told representatives of one of the UK's wealthiest entrepreneurs, 'I'll drink the entire contents of this if anyone loses out by investing in this rights issue.' The entrepreneur, already a major investor in the bank, was persuaded to invest £400 million, buying 200 million of the discounted shares. After the bank's failure, he was furious with Goodwin – though history does not relate whether he held Goodwin to drinking a giant bottle of the spicy peppery sauce.

While most traditional 'long only' investors seemed blind to the perilousness of RBS's position, hedge funds were more alert. John Paulson, founder and president of New York-based hedge fund Paulson & Co., could scarcely believe that UK regulators had allowed the bank to become as much as 70 times leveraged. In the expectation that the bank would fail, he borrowed 144 million RBS shares, or 0.87 per cent of its equity, with a view to selling it short and profiting from what he expected would be RBS's demise. In May, RBS discovered that Goldman Sachs, supposedly a trusted advisor and one of the two main underwriters on the £12-billion capital raising, was seeking to undermine the rights issue. The New York-based investment bank was 'passing on' shares it was supposed to be under-writing and 'sub-under-writing' them to a bunch of hedge funds, thought to include Paulson's, which were short-selling the shares. 'It was despicable behaviour and, yes, they were caught red handed,' said one investment banker. City sources say Goldman Sachs was doing this 'in order to offset its posi-tion' as it was taking a gloomier view of financial markets than many of its peers. The activity could readily have pushed the RBS share price below the 200p level and might even have caused the rights issue to flop. Goldman Sachs is also alleged to have given £500-million-worth of new RBS shares to HSBC without telling its client or anyone else. One source said, 'What Goldman was doing was an absolute disgrace. Not only was it incredibly disloyal, it was also in breach of the FSA rules about treating customers fairly.' On finding out, Goodwin got on the phone to Goldman Sachs's Andy Chisholm and gave him a piece of his mind. Sources claim Chisholm said, 'This is the most embarrassing moment of my professional career.' Some members of the RBS team wanted to report Goldman to the FSA but that never happened. In the end, RBS's chairman Tom McKillop called Goldman Sachs's New York-based chief executive Lloyd Blankfein to complain. According to a senior investment banker, as a result of that call, Goldman Sachs's co-chief executive of investment banking Richard Gnodde 'went down on his hands and knees' and apologised for his bank's behaviour.

It was impossible for RBS to penalise Goldman during the rights issue as it would have disrupted the process but the Wall Street-based firm was punished once the fund-raising was complete on 6 June. RBS withheld the firm's 25 basis point success fee which meant Goldman Sachs's total fees were docked by some £15 million. A spokesperson for Goldman Sachs said, 'This version of events contains characterisations which we reject. RBS remains an important client of the firm.' Despite all this, one RBS advisor claims that the rights issue was 'a triumph' largely because, by the time it closed on 6 June, investors had taken up 5.8 billion new shares at a value of 200p each, meaning the bank had raised nearly all of the £12.3 billion it sought. It was an achievement that marked RBS out from rival banks. Both Bradford & Bingley (B&B) and HBOS also staged rights issues that spring. But theirs were flops which left underwriting banks holding up to 92 per cent of the offered shares. B&B's £300-million rights issue had a take-up rate of just 28 per cent. And after investors saw through the spin of its chairman, Lord Stevenson, and chief executive, Andy Hornby, the take-up rate on HBOS's £4-billion rights issue was a disastrous 8.29 per cent.

It was not all *Schadenfreude* and joy at Gogarburn and Bishopsgate. RBS's shares fell 5 per cent to close at 234p the day the rights issue was completed. Already, one of investors' expectations – that RBS shares would rebound – had been dashed.

One might have thought a company that had just gone cap in hand to its investors for £12,300,000,000 in order to stave off financial collapse might afterwards rein in its own spending. Yet, just a month after announcing the rights issue, Goodwin blew hundreds of thousands of pounds at the Monaco Grand Prix, a harbour-side carnival of glitz and glamour that remains the extravagant pinnacle of the Formula One season. The bank reportedly picked up the €10,000-a-night tab for Jackie Stewart and his wife Helen to spend four nights in their regular suite at Monte Carlo's Hotel de Paris. At a Coutts reception at the Hotel de Paris, the bank unveiled a triptych portrait of Jackie and Helen Stewart commissioned from the Scottish artist Jack Vettriano. RBS's spring, summer and autumn seasons of corporate entertainment at the UK's leading sporting events – Wimbledon, Six Nations rugby matches, Grands Prix and golf tournaments – continued as if nothing had changed. According to a leaked email, it spent £300,000 during the Wimbledon tennis fortnight alone. Among other things, that gave RBS and its guests around-the-clock use of an 'entertainment suite' for more than 42 guests on each of the tournament's 13 days.[7] The bank also lavished £12,000 on tickets for senior executives to attend a talk given by former US President Bill Clinton at Aberdeen's Exhibition & Conference Centre. The event, scheduled for 15 June 2008, two weeks after RBS banked the £12.3 billion proceeds of its rights issue, was cancelled at the last minute after Clinton pulled out. Event organisers PB Events went into administration, leaving RBS and others with little or nothing to show for their cash. 'Goodwin and his cronies saw the bank as their own personal cash machine,' says one Scottish businessman familiar with its lavish spending on corporate hospitality. 'Even after they'd driven it into the ground and become dependent on the generosity of shareholders for their continued existence, they carried on feathering their own nests as if nothing had changed!'

Goodwin and McKillop were nowhere near out of the woods.

There were continued muffled calls for one or the other to resign. Many investors were surprised by the extent to which McKillop was shielding Goodwin from blame, feeling this undermined his credibility as chairman. (McKillop was insisting that only Fred could pull off the ABN integration so he should stay until that was complete.) One group of investors was so disillusioned with McKillop they sought to depose him as chairman and replace him with Sir Philip Hampton, a former Lazard investment banker who had been chairman of J Sainsbury since 2003. Meanwhile, McKillop was belatedly seeking to strengthen the board with the appointment of three strong non-executive directors who were not Scottish and had solid banking credentials. He put head-hunters Whitehead Mann on the case.[8] McKillop was also looking to refresh the management team and had spent January to March trying to persuade the JPMorgan investment banker Bill Winters to jump ship to RBS. Winters had a reputation for having 'saved JPMorgan countless billions of dollars when he refused to let his group join the structured-product gold rush'.[9] McKillop's thinking was that Winters could initially replace Cameron as head of RBS's investment bank, before replacing Goodwin in due course. But it was not to be. Winters was surprised that the RBS board was unable to provide him with adequate risk numbers, and no less surprised when Peter Sutherland told him that, if he did become Cameron's successor at the top of the investment bank, there was no guarantee he would subsequently replace Goodwin. Winters was told that they were very happy with Fred. The American decided to give the bank a wide berth. One City source said, 'Bill had no real desire to be left sitting there when it went wrong.'

Another plank in Goodwin's attempts to bolster the bank's crumbling capital base – his attempt to sell the insurance businesses Direct Line, Churchill, Privilege and Green Flag – was turning to dust after prospective buyers realised that RBS had been running them as 'cash cows' for years and also that the rise of price comparison websites jeopardised their future. Goodwin had been warned by head of insurance Chris Sullivan in 2007 that the businesses needed something in the region of £300 million to £800 million spent on their IT systems to remain viable but he refused to invest. In January 2008, Warren Buffett, also known as the 'Sage of Omaha', made an opportunistic offer of around £5–6 billion for the entire RBS insurance division. The

Nebraska-based investor told Goodwin that, if there were to be a deal, it was conditional on Berkshire Hathaway being given exclusive bidder status. However, Goodwin rejected the offer, believing that, if Buffett was willing to offer as much as £6 billion, the insurance businesses could easily command more in an open auction. It was another grave misjudgement on Goodwin's part.

On 22 April the bank confirmed it was seeking offers for the insurance division. Unusually, it ruled out private equity buyers, believing they would struggle to raise funds, which meant the bidding was largely limited to other insurance companies. However, when Switzerland-based Zurich Financial Services pulled out on 11 June, only Germany's Allianz and US-based Allstate were left in the race. By June, they too had melted away and the sale was pulled.

By the summer, things were getting desperate inside Cameron's sprawling Global Banking and Markets division. In June, Cameron was being driven to watch the races at Ascot in Berkshire when finance director Guy Whittaker called. Whittaker, who contrary to expectations had turned out to be a lackey of Goodwin, asked him to justify his gloomy outlook. Dissatisfied with the prognosis he was hearing from Cameron, Whittaker put Goodwin on the line. 'There are going to be more losses, Fred,' Cameron warned the chief executive, who was reluctant to accept things could possibly be as bad as Cameron was suggesting. Cameron realised that the funding of the wholesale business was becoming ever more critical. Over the summer, he put most of the division's product sales staff on deposit-gathering duties, with bottles of champagne handed out to those who landed large deposits. 'We literally had a taskforce out there trying to convince corporates not to take their money away,' says one former senior RBS investment banker.[10]

GBM was in turmoil. Having gone through what insiders called 'the internal madness of the ABN AMRO acquisition', people in Cameron's division had been hoping for a quieter time. But now they were having to contend with the collapse of Bear Stearns, the intensifying credit crisis, a share price which was going through the floor, further stress in structured credit, the beginnings of a 'silent' run on the bank and the slow-motion culture clash with their ABN AMRO counterparts. Every week something new, difficult and challenging would rear its head. One ex-GBM insider says, 'The weekly meetings became ever more focused on capital requirements with instructions from the highest level for capital usage to be limited where possible. In some businesses, good deals were deferred or even declined. In others, less attractive deals seemed to garner support. This became known on the street, which further closed off the funding markets. The credit write-downs of April 2008 were quickly followed by rumours that more would be required. By March–April, the commercial real estate finance and leveraged finance books were coming under serious strain as underlying valuations plunged. And the bonanza we'd been expecting from ABN AMRO just never materialised. People were increasingly recognising that we should never have done that deal.'

The omni-shambles was exacerbated by a vacuum at the top. Brian Crowe – the supposedly 'safe pair of hands' sometimes described as 'Johnny's brain' – went off sick in June 2008 with kidney disease and he ended up requiring a transplant. Cameron's eye was off the ball as a result of an affair he was having with the wife of a close friend, a relationship that is thought to have started during the ABN takeover battle. 'Johnny had gone all doe-eyed,' said one ex-colleague. 'One day he bounded up to me and told me "I'm in love".' Another ex-colleague says, 'In late 2007 and early 2008, Johnny was absent without leave. His crotch was ruling his head. He was there but there were no lights on.' Things are said to have come to a head early in 2008, when Cameron's 26-year marriage to Julia messily unravelled.

At the June strategy 'off-site' at Gleneagles, Alan Dickinson, who now ran the UK bank, said he had not experienced anything like the then market turmoil in all his years as a banker. He told senior colleagues he believed the UK was heading for a serious recession, which was going to cause RBS real pain.[11]

There was an unusual blast of honesty from Goodwin at the RBS trading update on Wednesday 11 June. 'There is clearly more bad news than good news but we're not looking at the end of the world,' Goodwin told analysts at a conference in Bishopsgate. 'It is almost exclusively bad news. The risk environment is changing.'[12] The shares plunged by 9 per cent to 212.25p, their lowest level since the NatWest takeover. They had collapsed by 44 per cent in six months, while the index of UK banking shares had fallen by only 26 per cent. There was marginally better news on Friday 13 June, when Goodwin said Royal Bank had sold its train-leasing arm, Angel Trains, to Babcock & Brown for £3.6 billion. The following month, he said the bank was selling its half stake in Tesco personal finance to Tesco – for £950 million.

The bank's madcap expansion over the previous decade was going into reverse, with the proceeds from disposals going towards filling capital holes. Another RBS employee gave a remarkably candid appraisal of the state of the markets. Speaking on 18 June, RBS's chief market strategist Bob Janjuah declared there would be a fully-fledged financial crash over the next three months, as major central banks would be paralysed by inflation. 'A very nasty period is soon to be upon us – be prepared,' said Janjuah.[13] And, on 27 June, the bank found it even harder to persuade funders to entrust their money to it after Moody's Investors Service stripped the bank of its AAA credit rating. Moody's warned that the bank faced more volatile earnings, a weaker economy and the possibility of further write-downs. On 1 July 2008, the shares closed at 199p – a penny below the rights issue price.

The summer of 2008 was marked out by atrocious weather, Chris Hoy's three gold medals at the Beijing Olympics, Amy Winehouse singing 'Love Is a Losing Game' at pop festivals around the UK, Russia's war in Ossetia . . . and a calm before the storm for the bankers. Shutting the stable door five years after the horse had bolted, Chancellor Alistair Darling unveiled a few legislative changes in his speech at the Mansion House on 18 June. Darling said that responsibility for financial stability would be restored to the Bank of England, which would also take charge of a new 'resolution regime' for failing banks. Darling also said that a new Financial Stability Committee (FSC) would be set up within the Bank, drawing on independent City expertise. It also emerged that Sir John Gieve – who had taken a lot of flak over the authorities' cackhanded response to the crisis – would step down as deputy governor in early 2009.

On 8 August 2008, the day the Olympics opened, RBS unveiled a pre-tax loss of £691 million for the first half of the year, the second-biggest loss in British banking history. Goodwin told the assembled analysts, 'I am very disappointed. I am numbed by it. I am also galvanised by it.'[14] One of the few straws Goodwin could cling to was that the analysts' consensus had been for even worse losses. The bank said it was pulling in its horns in the UK market through removing facilities and weaning clients off credit by tightening up terms and conditions on loans etc. – a tightening of the screw that was already causing pain for a great many corporate and commercial borrowers. Goodwin seemed blasé about the harm this might cause, saying, 'After initial squeals of pain from the customer-facing colleagues as we start down this path, actually we are managing this now [*sic*] in a less painful manner and will see these gains and improvements continuing into the second half as we further de-leverage the balance sheet.'[15] That was banker-speak for 'We don't care if customers are made to suffer, as long as we save our skins.'

At the presentation on 8 August, Goodwin boasted to analysts that sales of interest-rate swaps had soared 59 per cent in the first half of 2008 vis-à-vis the first half of 2007. The bank embarked on a concerted push to sell these complex over-the-counter derivatives to its existing SME customers in 2005. It did this by exploiting business customers' trust in the bank and lack of financial acumen. Interest-rate swaps were highly attractive products from the bank's perspective since the economy was slowing and each product's lifetime profits could be booked on day one, boosting short-term profitability and bonuses. However, many of the SME customers who bought them ended up being ruined when interest rates fell (as I explain in Chapter 33). At the time, the Libor rate was already well known to be unreliable and 'dishonest' – suggestions banks were lying about the rate had been aired by the *Wall Street Journal*, the *Financial Times*, *Bloomberg News* and Bloomberg Television. The suspicion was that Libor panel banks, which included RBS, were submitting false Libor numbers either to cheat derivatives counterparties or reduce their own borrowing costs.

Officials at the Bank of England and the Treasury were relaxed, aware that downward pressure on Libor would give banks some breathing space as the crisis intensified, as it gave the impression they were able to borrow money at lower interest rates than they were actually borrowing at, and made them seem stronger than they were, in the hope that it would reduce the need for state aid. Libor got only a cursory mention at RBS's session with analysts in Bishopsgate on 8 August, when Cameron acknowledged it was getting a bit squiffy. He said, 'There are a lot of strange things going on in the money markets, as you know, in the Libor and the Libor fixings and so on . . .'[16] At the same session, Goodwin boasted about putting greater numbers of business borrowers into the bank's specialised lending services (SLS) unit, a centralised repository for borrowers considered to be delinquent or in default. He told the analysts that, in terms of the 'levers' that RBS was able to pull in order to minimise bad debts, the bank was now 'incentivising' its relationship managers to transfer corporate borrowers into SLS by giving them an 'amnesty' if they did so. Goodwin said, 'They get immunised from it if it goes into the centre.'[17]

James Alexander, an analyst with M&G Investments, asked why, in view of RBS's 'well-known appetite for risky leveraged property transactions around Europe', its provisions for bad debts were not higher. He said, 'A German bank did announce a rather large provision a couple of days ago for, I think, a transaction that you were co-leading with them in. They announced €250 million and you don't seem to have announced anything of that size.' Cameron, wearing a rather natty pair of reading glasses with yellow stems, said: 'Well, the answer to the first part is, first of all, I don't accept the premise about we are only doing all the risky lending in Europe, if I can just park that point! Secondly, the definition of non-performing loans and potential problem loans is run by risk they bring forward, and that's the number and that is the trend. Again, it might reflect the de-risking point. I don't know whether that is why it hasn't gone up as much as you would expect, but that is the number produced by the independent risk department. And thirdly Spanish property: yes, a difficult market. We are working with some of our customers there; we are appropriately provisioned today and very comfortable with that, but who knows looking forward!'[18]

Cameron's final sentence, a rare expression of candour from a leading UK banker, was hardly reassuring.

However, Goodwin was adamant the bank would be profitable in the full year to December 2008, claiming it had more than replaced the £5.9 billion lost in credit market write-downs. Horribly mangling the pronunciation of the word masochist, McKillop said, 'Maybe you have to be a bit of a masochist [Gordon Pell turned away, with a pained look on his face at this point] but it's when things are tough that you really, really do see organisations perform . . . I'm a great believer in adversity sorting out who the long-term winners are going to be.'[19] Little did McKillop realise how wrong he was at this point.

At a press conference that day, *Schadenfreude* at RBS's misfortune was palpable. Andrew Johnson, deputy City editor of the *Daily Express*, asked Goodwin why, after the string of failures on his watch, he still considered himself to be the right person to lead the bank. Goodwin

said, 'It's not me solely that runs the bank. There are a team of people.'
Goodwin also said, 'I won't do this job forever but, right now, you find
me extremely galvanised to the task at hand.'[20] It was in the wake of
this that Gordon Pell, RBS's chief executive of Retail Markets, who
had long harboured dreams of succeeding Goodwin, said to one RBS
employee in a corridor of the Bishopsgate office, 'At this rate, there's
going to be one of two Gordons running the bank – it's either going to
be me or Gordon Brown.'

Having reluctantly nationalised Northern Rock, Brown's government was loath to nationalise any other banks. Rather than tackling the
disease – the banks' rotten cultures, precarious business models, capital
and liquidity shortfalls – he preferred to try to address the symptoms.
In particular he wanted to find ways of 'unblocking the mortgage
market'.[21] He asked his friend, the former HBOS chief executive Sir
James Crosby, to lead a review of the mortgage market in April 2008.
But Crosby, who is today seen as one of the most incompetent bank
chief executives of his generation, came back with a proposal (a state
guarantee for mortgage-backed securities) that the Treasury saw as
woefully inadequate.

At the time, the Treasury, the FSA and the Bank of England were
much more concerned about the difficulties being faced by mortgage
banks like HBOS, Bradford & Bingley and Alliance & Leicester than
they were about Royal Bank of Scotland. The Treasury put HBOS
on its 'watch list' after September 2007 and Darling says 'alarm bells'
started to ring about the other Edinburgh-based bank in July 2008.
Darling said, 'HBOS was becoming increasingly desperate. There was
whiff of death surrounding the whole operation.'[22] Under its flibberti-
gibbet of a chairman, Lord Dennis Stevenson, HBOS had driven itself
into the ground largely as a result of astonishingly reckless lending in
the UK, Ireland and Australasia. In its half-year results at the end of
July, the bank said profits for the first half had collapsed by 72 per cent
to £848 million. It slashed its dividend and told investors they would
be paid in shares not cash. Just like RBS, the bank was punishing once-
loyal customers in a desperate bid to stay afloat.

HBOS's chief executive Andy Hornby, who was becoming increasingly stressed out by summer of 2008, sidled up to a stronger partner in
the shape of Lloyds TSB in the hope that it might rescue HBOS from
the consequences of its own folly. On 15 August 2008, the 41-year-old

Bristolian had 'a quiet drink' with Lloyds TSB chief executive Eric Daniels with a view to selling the bank to Lloyds.[23] A deal would be cemented the following month, after Gordon Brown 'got into a huddle' with Blank at a Citigroup event in Spencer House in St James and agreed to waive competition law if Lloyds would rescue HBOS.[24]

Brown was becoming increasingly anxious about the state of the banking sector. He asked his protégé, Shriti Vadera, a former UBS Warburg investment banker, to find ways of resolving the crisis. Vadera had come to Britain aged fifteen, five years after her family was expelled from Uganda by the country's dictator Idi Amin, and had been a minister in the Department for Business, Enterprise and Regulatory Reform since January 2008. She cancelled her summer holiday and, working alongside Treasury official Tom Scholar, set about finding ways of unblocking the plumbing of the UK financial system. Talking as they strode across Trafalgar Square one August afternoon, Vadera and Scholar concluded that a complete recapitalisation of the British banking system was the only answer. As they passed beneath Nelson's Column, Vadera turned to Scholar and asked, 'Are you thinking what I'm thinking?' Scholar was. In view of the three abortive bank rights issues of spring 2008, it seemed there was only one source of capital left – the government. In a series of email exchanges under the title 'Is it capital?', they fine-tuned their thinking.[25] Brown and Darling agreed with the approach. The Bank of England – whose special liquidity scheme was due to expire on 11 September – had independently reached a similar conclusion.

At the end of August, Darling gave a remarkably candid interview to *The Guardian*'s Decca Aitkenhead at his dynastic croft on Great Bernara, an island off the Isle of Lewis. The chancellor said the economic times 'are arguably the worst they've been in 60 years'. He also said, 'And I think it's going to be more profound and long-lasting than people thought.'[26] Darling's gloomy assessment was accurate but it infuriated Brown. The prime minister was about to try to relaunch his premiership with a range of economic programmes and, on his return flight from the Beijing Olympics on 25 August, he told journalists he believed the UK economy would have recovered within six months! He also argued Britain was better able to withstand a global recession than other countries. Though polite to Darling in person, Brown sent his media 'attack dogs', including his notorious special advisor Damian

McBride, to rubbish his chancellor's views. The whole Westminster village went into a collective swoon. In his book *Power Trip*, McBride said, '[Darling] was either catastrophically inept or misguided when it came to his public interventions with the press . . . If relationships and trust between the Brown and Darling teams were already fairly strained before that day, they were pretty much broken thereafter.'[27] Writing in *Back from Brink*, Darling said, 'The fact that what I had said was true did not seem to enter their minds. No one wanted to acknowledge that we were heading for an extremely serious downturn.'[28]

Two weeks later, it was clear that it was Darling, not Brown, who was right. On the weekend of 13 and 14 September, Lehman Brothers, the New York-based investment bank whose London office Gordon Brown had opened four years earlier, went bankrupt. When the bank declared a quarterly loss of $3.9 billion on 10 September, its shares went into freefall. The previous week, the government of President George W. Bush had been widely accused of 'turning Communist' after fully nationalising the mortgage giants Fannie Mae and Freddie Mac, so it had little appetite for further nationalisations. Bush also feared that rescuing Wall Street firms from the consequences of their own reckless-ness and greed would not look good politically.

Over the weekend of 13 and 14 September, it looked like either Bank of America or Barclays might mount a rescue takeover. Barclays was only stopped by FSA chairman Sir Callum McCarthy and Chancellor Alistair Darling after it emerged that, unlike with Bear Stearns, the US government was not prepared to guarantee Lehman's $60 billion of toxic assets. For once, the UK authorities made a good call about finance. Bank of America and Barclays both slunk away – the voracious BofA was anyway preoccupied with an opportunistic takeover of the crippled Merrill Lynch – which meant it was curtains for Lehman. On Sunday, 14 September 2008, the 10 o'clock news bulletins on both BBC and ITV carried the news that Lehman Brothers had been 'allowed to fail'.

Later on Sunday, Bank of America secured its takeover of Merrill Lynch but AIG, the giant insurer whose health was pivotal to the structured credit markets and therefore to RBS's survival, also seemed to be teetering on the brink of collapse. After playing hardball with Lehman, the US government went soft on the insurer and handed it a $182 billion bailout. Surviving investment banks Goldman Sachs and Morgan Stanley changed their status to 'bank holding companies' in order to save their skins, at the same time as seeking infusions of capital from Warren Buffett's Berkshire Hathaway and Tokyo-based Mitsubishi UFJ Financial Group.

Lehman Brothers' failure, which saw 5,000 bewildered London staff turfed out on to the streets of Canary Wharf carrying their possessions in cardboard boxes, gave rise to fears that other over-leveraged and reckless banks would also be pushed into insolvency. As Rachel Johnson put it in the *Sunday Times*, 'There's no doubt. For those who work in the City, last week was their 9/11. The assault on the twin towers of greed and capitalism looks like felling hundreds of thousands of workers in the months ahead, in a Trollopian saga that gets twistier and blacker by the day. Notting Hill . . . is in the eye of the money storm for it's right here, in these storeyed terraces and crescents, and in these stuccoed mansions, that the big swinging dicks brought their millions in bonuses and – bankers went the neighbourhood.'[29]

At executive director level, the mood inside RBS turned from one of detachment to black humour. The collapse of Lehman and a downgrade in AIG's credit rating sent shares in both RBS and HBOS into freefall on Monday 15 and Tuesday 16 September. On the Tuesday, RBS shares slid a further 16 per cent to 177.6p. HBOS's plummeted 40 per cent to 139.4p. *Credit Writedowns'* Edward Harrison commented, 'With the equity and capital raising markets closed, RBS's options are effectively limited . . . Whether HBOS and RBS remain going concerns depends heavily on the measures they and the UK monetary and regulatory authorities take to bolster a jittery market.'[30]

On Tuesday 16 September, senior members of the Edinburgh fund-management community congregated at RBS's Gogarburn headquarters for a scheduled get-together with RBS's executive directors. One investor says he was struck by the 'demeanour, body language and use of gallows humour of the executive directors'. Those present included Goodwin, Cameron, Fisher and Whittaker. The directors sought to divert the fund managers' attention by speculating about what might happen to the doomed HBOS and AIG. 'You could sense they knew the game was up,' said one investor who was present.

Meanwhile, treasurers at rival banks, unsettled by RBS's widening overnight borrowing requirement, were pulling billions out of the bank. Unable to persuade anyone to lend it money for more than twenty-four hours, RBS had become dependent on overnight funding to fill the hole. And, according to Libor numbers, the rate at which banks were borrowing overnight funds had risen to 7.5 per cent, possibly higher for RBS. 'We had a meeting internally about pulling back our risk limits on RBS because there was clearly something going horribly wrong,' said the head of treasury at a major UK bank.'[31]

Despite the unprecedented 'silent' bank run on RBS, Goodwin still found time to appoint another 'global ambassador' on a package of around £3 million a year. This time it was the Indian cricketer Sachin Tendulkar, known as the 'Little Master'. Goodwin also paid a visit to ABN AMRO's office at 250 Bishopsgate, which had been rebranded in RBS colours nine months earlier. Ahead of his state visit on Friday 19 September, there was a flurry of memos notifying traders they must tidy up their desks before the arrival of King Fred and insisting that all ABN-branded research reports had to be binned or hidden. One memo heralding the visit said, 'Dear All, Sir Fred will be visiting 250 Bishopsgate on Friday between the hours of 2pm until 4.30pm. I cannot stress how important it is that your floors/areas are tidy and clutter free . . . Please get rid of your newspapers, put away mugs and plates, tidy up paper piles.'[32]

On 23 September, eight days after Lehman Brothers collapsed, Stephen Hester attended his first RBS board meeting as a non-executive director. He says the board was more preoccupied with what had gone wrong with RBS's ABN AMRO acquisition than the implications of the Lehman collapse. 'Nothing was thought to be life-threatening,' Hester told *The Guardian*. Two days later, on 25 September, Goodwin put in another call in to the chancellor. He told Alistair Darling that conditions were very bad and that RBS had been considering whether to stop lending to customers. Darling asked Goodwin what would resolve the situation and Goodwin said 'long-term funding'.[33]

Goodwin did not have his troubles to seek. On 30 September, the Irish government, nervous about a run on the country's *über*-reckless banking sector, said it was providing a 100 per cent guarantee to depositors and other creditors of Irish-owned banks. The move, which the Irish rushed through without consulting Jean-Claude Trichet, president of the European Central Bank, infuriated other European leaders. It meant Ireland was effectively underwriting its banking sector to an extent no other country had done. It sparked an unprecedented capital

Death's Head

There's something incongruous about a Labour prime minister seeking economic advice from the princes of Wall Street. However, this is just what happened on Wednesday, 24 September 2008, when Gordon Brown went on a fact-finding mission to New York City. Brown recognised that continuing with a piecemeal, fire-fighting approach to the crisis was failing. So far, the government had nationalised Northern Rock, persuaded the Bank of England to be more lenient, waived competition law so Lloyds TSB could buy HBOS and banned the short-selling of financial stocks, but now Brown wanted a more comprehensive solution. With other banks in peril, he was veering towards a state-funded recapitalisation of the entire banking sector – but he didn't want Britain to go it alone. Ideally, he wanted to persuade other countries – especially the US – to follow suit.

At the start of his two-day visit to the United States, Brown had a 'power breakfast' with 17 leading Wall Street financiers at the Waldorf Astoria on Park Avenue. Guests included Tim Geithner, president of the New York Federal Reserve, the currency speculator and philanthropist George Soros – also known as 'the man who broke the Bank of England' – and Steve Schwarzman, private equity king and co-founder of the Blackstone Group. Others present included the Bank of New York Mellon chief executive Bob Kelly and Goldman Sachs chief operating officer Marc Spilker.[1] According to Shriti Vadera, who also attended the breakfast, the Wall Street players were sceptical about the Bush administration's planned Troubled Asset Relief Program (TARP), which would allow America's banks to dump their toxic assets on the taxpayer, doubting whether it would unblock finance's clogged arteries. Vadera was careful not to divulge what the British government flight in Europe, as depositors in banks whose governments were not providing such a safety blanket – like the UK – withdrew billions of euros and transferred the funds to the suddenly 'safer' banks of Ireland. Goodwin was doubly furious since foreign-owned banks – even those with a significant presence in Ireland, like Ulster Bank – were ineligible for the guarantee. Over the course of the next four days, £732 million was removed from Ulster Bank.[34] Goodwin decided it was time for some serious string-pulling. He made 'two dramatic protests' – first to Prime Minister Gordon Brown and then to heir to the British throne, Prince Charles. He also spoke to Darling. He demanded they telephone the Irish Taoiseach Brian Cowen and order him to extend the guarantees to the subsidiaries of foreign banks in Ireland.[35] Eventually, on 9 October, the Irish government obliged but, by then, it was too late.

was planning, as it was market-sensitive, but she did gain the impression that American investors saw recapitalisation as a good idea and recognised that the government was the only possible source of fresh capital.

Brown was eager to evangelise his mission to the US Treasury Secretary Hank Paulson and other world leaders who would listen. But Paulson, a former chief executive of Goldman Sachs, snubbed him. He was too busy working on the $700-billion TARP proposal, on which Congress was due to vote the following Monday. Next day, Friday 26 September, Brown gained an audience with President George W. Bush in the Oval Office, in front of hordes of cameramen, photographers and journalists. With his characteristic lack of chit-chat, the Fifer asked the president if he believed TARP would be sufficient to resolve the crisis and whether it would be passed by Congress. Bush reassured him, saying, 'I believe it is big enough to make a difference and I believe it is going to be passed.' Brown then told the president that, in his view, the real problem was capital – the banks were running dangerously low on it. The US president told him that the exhausted Hank Paulson was doing everything possible to get TARP through Congress. The notion of handing billions of taxpayers' money to US banks was not something Paulson and Bush would be likely to consider. Brown thought this stemmed from distrust of state intervention – especially given the roasting they had been given for nationalising Fannie Mae and Freddie Mac and bailing out AIG.[2] In an anteroom to the Oval Office, Vadera and Brown took a call from Darling, who told them that Bradford & Bingley, the buy-to-let lender, was bust and would have to be nationalised that weekend.

On the flight back to London, Brown was feeling isolated. He was handed a fax. It was an early-stage blueprint for saving the financial system, pieced together over the previous few weeks in the corridors of Whitehall, the City and Canary Wharf. Its authors included Darling, Scholar, Treasury official John Kingman, Vadera and a gaggle of senior bankers and investment bankers from Standard Chartered, UBS and JPMorgan Cazenove. Brown liked what he saw but fear was gnawing away at him. He says, 'We were now sure that at least two of the world's biggest banks could collapse within days – and soon others could come tumbling down. The UK economy would face a depression if RBS and HBOS both failed. The choice was clear: either we had to accept all the associated risks, or simply leave the free-market banking system to collapse . . . As we debated, I had come to a settled view: we needed a comprehensive plan centred on capital and, if necessary, Britain would have to go it alone. On that overnight flight, I knew that the path we were choosing could be a lonely one.'[3]

By happy coincidence Bank of England governor Mervyn King, FSA chairman Adair Turner (a fearsomely intelligent former McKinsey & Co. consultant and former vice chairman of Merrill Lynch Europe who had started as FSA chairman six days earlier) and Darling were coming round to the same view. King had in fact been thinking along these lines for a while. At a lunch with American diplomats on 17 March 2008, King had proposed a comprehensive government-funded recapitalisation programme for the banks.[4] Now he favoured putting such a plan into action and hosing the banks with new capital. Darling and Turner provisionally agreed. However, according to Darling, the Treasury, led by Permanent Secretary Nicholas Macpherson, was much more sceptical and, in some quarters, downright hostile. Darling instructed Treasury officials to overcome their reservations – this was a national emergency and the clock was ticking fast. He told them to accelerate their work on a comprehensive recapitalisation plan and to do so in lockstep with the FSA and the Bank of England. Macpherson and his mandarins reluctantly agreed and worked around the clock for the next two weeks. Unlike with Paulson's TARP, none of this frenetic UK planning was public knowledge at the time – and the secrecy of the approach would be a double-edged sword over the next few days.

On Sunday 28 September, I had the 'splashes' on both the front and the back pages of the *Sunday Herald*. The front-page lead was headlined 'RBS will get "billions" in US bailout of economy' and focused on how RBS stood to benefit from TARP. The main story on the back page was headlined, 'Call to sack HBOS directors'. In the first, I wrote, 'There is also a head of steam developing behind the idea of a UK version of the US lifeboat, with large banks lobbying chancellor Alistair Darling and Bank of England governor Mervyn King on a near daily basis. "There is a severe crisis in the money markets," said Neil MacKinnon, chief economist at ECU Group. "The UK should take a leaf out of the US book and look at a government-backed rescue." '[5] The bankers didn't know it but, over the same weekend, Darling and Treasury officials were frantically putting together a 'comprehensive rescue strategy' for the banking sector – and it would be a belt-and-braces approach giving them liquidity, credit guarantees and recapitalisation.[6]

On 29 September, the US House of Representatives rejected the initial version of the TARP bill, voting it down by 228 to 204. Many Republican and Democrat politicians just couldn't understand why 'Main Street' should pick up the tab for Wall Street's failures. For Paulson and Bush – who had assumed that Congress would approve the $700-billion scheme on the strength of a flimsy three-page document – it was a major humiliation. It sent global markets into a tailspin and further weakened British banks. The Standard & Poor's (S&P) 500 index fell by 8.8 per cent, its worst one-day fall since 'Black Monday' (19 October 1987). Even before the news that TARP had been rejected, the FTSE-100 tumbled 5.3 per cent, closing at 4,818.77 points, after the Treasury announced the nationalisation of Bradford & Bingley. The failures of several US and European banks – including Wachovia, Fortis, Bradford & Bingley, Hypo Real Estate – was hardly filling investors with confidence. On Tuesday 30 September, RBS shares sank another 5 per cent to 172p on fears it would have to write down the value of the goodwill associated with its ABN AMRO acquisition in the wake of Fortis's collapse and that it would continue haemorrhaging deposits to Irish banks.

That Tuesday, Darling held the first of several *Death's Head* meetings in his room in the Treasury. He says, 'At that time, hanging on the wall in my room was a huge canvas painted by the late Scottish artist John Bellany. Its title was *Death's Head* and its deathly centrepiece was right above the middle seat at the conference table. I am sure it was simply coincidence that Sir Fred Goodwin chose to sit there that day. Over the next seven days, other chief executives and their chairmen would take it in turns to sit on that seat, entirely by chance. Curiously, not one of the bank directors who chose that particular seat survived the crisis.'[7] Others who were present included Lord Myners, a former Gartmore fund manager and former Marks & Spencer chairman, whose appointment as a City minister was about to be announced,[8] Lord Turner, Sir Mervyn King and the Treasury officials Sir Nicholas Macpherson and John Kingman. Aside from Goodwin, the bankers included Barclays' John Varley, Lloyds TSB's Eric Daniels, Santander's António Horta-Osório, HSBC's Dyfrig John and Standard Chartered's Peter Sands. Goodwin assumed the role of spokesman for the bankers. He told the government and tripartite authorities that banks, including RBS, were dependent on overnight funding and needed to be sure that facilities would be available. When King proposed a government-funded recapitalisation of the banking sector, the bankers pooh-poohed the idea. Goodwin insisted RBS didn't need capital (funds that banks hold in reserve to support their business) – it needed liquidity (access to cash, short-term borrowings). As the Bank of England's deputy governor Sir John Gieve later remarked, for the bankers to admit they needed fresh capital was tantamount to acknowledging that 'their strategy was in tatters'.[9] Darling recalls, 'As they trooped out of the room, my thought was this had been a less than satisfactory meeting.'[10] He was frustrated because he felt unable to divulge, or even hint at, what the government was planning until the plan was fully formed. This need for secrecy would cause some frayed nerves over the next few days.

The US Congress approved a revised version of the TARP legislation on Thursday 2 October, though only after the bill was sweetened to placate Democrats and Republicans who had opposed the original version. The US government duly started to buy toxic assets from banks and financial institutions, alleviating the crisis on Wall Street. But confidence in RBS was evaporating fast. On 3 October, the bank's very short-term wholesale funding gap widened to £100 billion. That day, RBS told the FSA that a Korean newspaper had run an article claiming it had such severe liquidity problems that two major UK bank counterparties had felt the need to carry out credit checks before lending to it overnight. On the same day, there was a tug of war over Fortis, RBS's erstwhile partner on 'Project Arran'. Now bust, the Belgo-Dutch bancassurer, whose chief executive Votron had been forced out in July 2008, was being torn into pieces by various governments. Gillian Tett says, 'Several different governments grabbed its assets at the same time and pledged them as collateral, partly because when it ran into problems it was not clear who owned it or how it would be wound down.'[11] Johnny Cameron was spending virtually every day inside the Bank of England, keeping the 'lender of last resort' au fait with RBS's struggle to replace lost deposits and stay afloat. Cameron said, 'These were days that I never, ever thought would happen. There we were, saying, "We're not sure if we can fund ourselves tomorrow." '[12]

Over the weekend of 4 and 5 October, there was intense speculation about the bailout Brown's government was plotting – or, indeed, whether it was plotting one at all. Both Brown and Darling wanted their rescue package to have a degree of 'shock and awe'. That element would be missing if everybody knew in advance. So they were frustrated when Shadow Chancellor George Osborne, reputedly tipped off by King, appeared to give the game away on the BBC's *The Andrew Marr Show*. The German government moved to save troubled lender Hypo Real Estate with a €50-billion rescue plan and Chancellor Angela Merkel announced that Germany would explicitly guarantee bank deposits. By Monday 6 October, a consensus was forming that Brown was poised to announce a recapitalisation of Britain's entire banking sector, which the *Financial Times* hoped would be in exchange for preference shares or warrants – warrants were a device for ensuring that taxpayers would benefit in the event that rescued banks' share prices recovered – rather than common equity.

When Darling stood up to address MPs at 3.29 p.m. on Monday, 6 October, City traders were on tenterhooks, hoping for news of the rumoured bailouts, but all they got from Darling were hollow platitudes, along the lines of 'the government stands ready to do whatever is necessary' to ensure systemic stability. Traders assumed this meant his rescue plan was either half-baked or weeks away, by which time Britain might not have any banks. It triggered a massive sell-off, with the FTSE-100 index closing down 391.1 points, 7.85 per cent, its largest single-day points fall since it was launched in 1984. RBS shares collapsed by 20.5 per cent to close at 146p. The slide accelerated after Standard & Poor's cut its credit rating on RBS for the first time since December 1998. One senior figure in GBM says the downgrade was the tipping point for the Edinburgh-based bank and, 'after that, there was a run. It switched like a light.'

That evening Darling hosted another *Death's Head* meeting with bankers including Goodwin. The bankers were hoping for news of a fully worked-up plan but, as the meeting progressed, it became clear it might be weeks away. Instead, they were treated to a theoretical discussion and, as the *Financial Times* reported, 'Little sense of urgency was evident.'[13] Barclays' chief executive John Varley was the most vocal in pressing the chancellor to get his act together and deliver something useable. Scared of leaks, Darling was reluctant to divulge too much until the government's 'once-and-for-all' solution was ready. However, one of the bankers is understood to have leaked news of the meeting to the BBC business editor, Robert Peston, within a few minutes of leaving the Treasury building, possibly in an attempt to chivvy the chancellor along. And, sure enough, an item on the bankers' frustration with Darling appeared on the BBC's 10 o'clock news that night. In a blog published at 7 a.m. next morning, Peston wrote that RBS, Lloyds TSB and Barclays had made it clear to the chancellor that they would 'like to see the colour of the taxpayer's money rather quicker than he might have expected'.[14] The story made it clear that (a) the banks were desperate and (b) the government was in disarray. RBS shareholders, already panicky, panicked even more.

On the morning of Tuesday, 7 October 2008, the Icelandic government declared a national emergency, passing new laws to protect personal savings and its domestic banking system and agreeing a $5.4-billion bailout loan from Russia. Reykjavik also seized control of its second-largest bank, Landsbanki, fired its board and put the bank into receivership. As Fred Goodwin stood up to address some of RBS's biggest investors at the annual Merrill Lynch banking conference in the grand ballroom of the Landmark Hotel, near Marylebone, at 8.45 a.m., he sought to put a brave face on RBS's travails, highlighting its 'strong franchise', 'opportunities for growth', 'operational effectiveness' and geographic spread of businesses. He claimed the integration of ABN AMRO was 'ahead of plan'. He wound up by insisting that the bank would meet profit and revenue targets for the full year and 'had the flexibility to respond to organic opportunities as they emerge'.[15] Goodwin then invited questions.

The first came from an investor who asked Goodwin whether he was aware that the RBS share price had plunged by 35 per cent during the half hour he had been speaking. Goodwin mumbled an answer and went pale. He cancelled some meetings scheduled around the conference and sped back to 280 Bishopsgate. Confidence in the bank had evaporated. The shares had sunk to 95p, their lowest point since the early 1990s recession. The bank's market capitalisation had shrivelled from £75 billion in May 2007 to £16 billion. 'In the early hours of Tuesday morning, we thought we had time to polish the plan. By 9.30 a.m., we didn't,' says David Soanes, head of capital markets at UBS, one of seven external advisors to the Treasury. 'The drop in confidence in some of the banks accelerated that morning and it was contagious.'[16] The culture at RBS was one of denial. Insiders sought to blame anyone but themselves for the bank's collapsing share price. The BBC's Robert Peston was, for a time, their favoured scapegoat. One former senior insider says, 'It surprises me that Peston hasn't been charged with some form of insider dealing or criminal conspiracy. He was effectively the guy who brought RBS down.'

Darling landed in Luxembourg at 7.15 a.m. on Tuesday 7 October for a meeting with other EU finance ministers, including France's Christine Lagarde. But the chancellor had only been in the meeting for a few minutes when his special advisor, Geoffrey Spence, called him out. He told Darling that RBS's shares were in freefall and had already been suspended twice that morning. Darling says, 'I knew the bank was finished . . . The game was up. If the markets could give up on RBS, one of the largest banks in the world, all bets on Britain's and the world's financial system were off.'[17] At 11.30 a.m. that day, the *Daily Telegraph*'s banking editor Philip Aldrick ran an online article which said, 'What has really sparked concerns is speculation that RBS needs another £15bn of capital – on top of the £12bn raised earlier this year – and is prepared to let the Government part-nationalise the bank to secure the cash. Such a move smacks of desperation.'[18]

Darling went back into the finance ministers' meeting, only to be called back out an hour later. RBS chairman Sir Tom McKillop was on the line. Darling, who was looking out over a rain-swept industrial estate, says, 'He sounded shell-shocked. I asked him how long the bank could keep going. His answer was chilling: "A couple of hours, maybe."'[19] Providers of dollar funding were giving the Edinburgh-based bank a wide berth because of fears it might fail. Corporate and wholesale depositors, including a large oil firm, removed an astonishing £6 billion in deposits on the Tuesday alone.[20] Overall, big companies pulled £35 billion of deposits out of the bank in the wake of the Lehman collapse. This was more than ten times the £3 billion that depositors had withdrawn from Northern Rock 13 months earlier. It looked as if RBS – with 'assets' of £1.9 trillion and 170,000 plus staff – might fail before the day was out. McKillop told Darling he 'wanted to know what the government was going to do'.[21] This sent a chill down Darling's spine. He believed that, if the government were to allow RBS to fail, it would be a financial Hiroshima.

In an interview with the *Mail on Sunday*, Darling said, 'The thing about a collapse of the banks is that it wouldn't just have been the banks in ruins, it would have been complete economic and therefore social collapse. People without money can do nothing – you can't buy your petrol, you can't buy your food, anything. It was rather like a nuclear war, you know you think it will never happen. And then someone tells you that a missile's been launched. It was very scary. That moment will stick with me for the rest of my days.'²²

Darling called Macpherson at the Treasury and told him to call King at the Bank of England, and ask him to open the monetary taps. Darling authorised King to 'put as much money into RBS as was necessary to keep it afloat that day'. Darling later wrote, '*We would stand behind the bank even if it meant using every last penny we had* [my italics]. If RBS closed its doors, the banking system would freeze, not just in the UK but around the globe.'²³

Darling flew back to London on a private jet, arriving mid afternoon. Then – weeks earlier than originally envisaged – he and Brown pushed the button on their comprehensive bank rescue plan. He also called Bill Winters, co-chief executive of JPMorgan Chase's investment bank, to check that the New York-based bank would keep clearing for RBS to ensure the bank could limp on for the rest of the day. Winters chose his words carefully. He said, 'We can clear for them still, if you say we can.'²⁴ He meant JPMorgan would continue to clear as long as the government promised not to allow the Edinburgh bank to fail. Darling assured him they wouldn't. At 11 a.m., Downing Street was still refusing to confirm the timetable for a recapitalisation plan, warning against 'irresponsibility' in dealing with market-sensitive information – a veiled reference to Peston's stories. The prime minister's official spokesman said, 'As and when the Treasury are in a position to say more, they will say more but we are not going to speculate prematurely.'²⁵

The name given to the huge covert loans that the central bank made to RBS was 'Emergency Liquidity Assistance' (ELA). It was a desperate holding measure. Without it, RBS and HBOS, which had received the clandestine emergency funding six days earlier, would almost certainly have gone bust. Within days, RBS was making use of an astonishing £36.6 billion of ELA money. The government and the Bank of England kept the ELA secret, only revealing its existence in November 2009.

By market close on 7 October, RBS's shares had tumbled 39 per cent in a single day to close at 90p. HBOS's were down 41.5 per cent to just half the level at which Lloyds TSB's rescue takeover had been pitched. Barclays' shares had dived by 22 per cent, closing at 285p. As the *New York Times* said, reports of a government rescue package, when combined with the lack of any firm announcement from the government, had left investors with little to do but punish UK bank shares. The banks' fate was in the government's hands. 'There is no such thing as a safe bank now,' said Willem Buiter, a political economist at the London School of Economics. 'They are only as safe as the authorities make them.'[26] The once swaggering proponents of unfettered free markets – who have no hesitation in closing down customers who show the slightest sign of breaching covenants or defaulting on their loans – were bust. With their usual sense of entitlement, the bankers were looking to the state to save them and, in this instance, the UK state could hardly have been more obliging.

At the Treasury, it was all systems go. Darling and Brown aimed to have the rescue ready to announce to markets and media at 7 a.m. on 8 October. At about 5 p.m. on the Tuesday evening, the bank chief executives had a preliminary conference call to see if they could form a united front ahead of crunch talks with the government. Several banks, including HSBC, Standard Chartered and Santander saw no need for taxpayer-funded capital but were willing to participate in bailouts if it would stabilise the system. Others, including Lloyds, HBOS and RBS, wanted the package to be agreed and wanted it now. By 6 p.m., the bankers were back at the Treasury. The chancellor was flanked by Myners, Treasury officials, an array of advisors from investment banks UBS and JPMorgan Cazenove and lawyers from Slaughter and May, as well as Michael Klein, an ex-Citibank investment banker. According to the *Sunday Times*, Barclays' John Varley told Darling that the time for dithering was over and the time for action was now. He was backed up by HSBC's Michael Geoghegan, Lloyds TSB's Eric Daniels and HBOS's Andy Hornby. But Goodwin was unusually quiet.[27] He remained adamant RBS did not need any more capital. He told the meeting, 'We don't have a capital problem. We have a liquidity problem. All we need is short-term cash.' After he had said this, the *Death's Head* room went quiet. Then one of the other bank chief executives said, 'Everyone knows it [capital] is your problem.'[28]

After the meeting, Goodwin and his finance director Guy Whittaker were ushered into an anteroom for a private meeting with Myners and civil servant Tom Scholar, without any other bankers present. Goodwin was no less adamant that RBS had no need of capital. He told Myners, 'It's a subtle issue, but we have the wrong kind of capital.' He insisted RBS's problems were no worse than those of any other bank. If the government could provide some short-term cash, everything would be fine. Myners, however, was not taking any of Fred's nonsense. He told Goodwin and Whittaker that RBS needed to be recapitalised – the government was requiring it to do so in order to restore confidence in the banking system. The government was aware that large corporate depositors were removing billions of pounds' worth of deposits from RBS, but was offering to stand behind the bank. During this private meeting, Goodwin also insisted that ABN would turn out to be a good deal. In small talk, Myners asked Goodwin how many RBS staff were paid more than him (Goodwin's pay at the time was £4.19 million). Goodwin replied it was probably closer to 200 than 100.[29]

By 7.30 p.m., Darling was back at 11 Downing Street for a council of war with Brown, King and Turner. The 54-year-old chancellor led the negotiations in his second-floor office. Then back at the Treasury, Goodwin and the other bank chief executives arrived for another *Death's Head* meeting. Darling was accompanied by Shriti Vadera and Yvette Cooper, the Chief Secretary in the Treasury, as well as civil servants Macpherson, Kingman and Scholar. On the bankers' side of the table, the usual suspects, Daniels, Varley, Hornby and Goodwin, were accompanied by HSBC finance director Douglas Flint, Abbey chief executive António Horta-Osório, Standard Chartered finance director Richard Meddings and Graham Beale, chief executive of the Nationwide Building Society. Mervyn Davies was also present, in two roles – as chairman of Standard Chartered and as a long-standing government advisor. The meeting was tense as the chief executives of HSBC, Abbey National and Standard Chartered bank insisted their banks did not require bailouts, though they were willing to endorse the plan. In the talks, the bankers were fussing over conditions that ministers sought to attach to the bailouts, with much haggling over issues like the terms of access to the loan guarantee.[30]

Unlike Paulson's $700-billion toxic-waste dump or the Irish government's 100 per cent depositor guarantee, the British scheme sought to tackle three of the issues that had dogged the banking sector since September 2007 – lack of capital, lack of liquidity and lack of funding.

The government's core proposals included a £50-billion capital injection through the use of preference shares, an extra £200 billion injection into the money markets and guarantees on £250 billion of bank debt issuance to make it easier for banks to refinance their short-term funding. However, the bankers in the room were telling Darling they wanted the second two, without the first. He made it very plain this would not be possible – they would have no access to liquidity or guarantees unless they raised capital. Goodwin argued that, if the government were to declare the banks needed £50 billion in capital, people would think the situation was far worse than it was. He claimed that RBS did not need anything like the £20 billion proposed, which he said was based on erroneous calculations by the FSA. The bankers were also fretting about what their shareholders would think. But Brown and Darling were sticking to their guns, telling the bankers the deal was final.

Darling was exasperated by what he saw as the bankers' ingratitude, and says, 'It crossed my mind not only that the banks had failed to appreciate that there could be no negotiation, but also that they might be daft enough to take up the option of suicide – and I simply couldn't afford a row of dead banks in the morning.'[31] In a breakout session, Myners and Vadera made it clear that, while the detail might be debatable, the main deal was not open to negotiation. By 10 p.m., it seemed like the bankers had capitulated and Gordon Brown, looking ravaged, felt able to retire to bed. But the prime minister still had grave doubts the plan would work. He confided in his personal spin doctor, Damian McBride, 'We've just got to get ourselves ready in case it goes wrong tomorrow. And I mean really wrong.'[32]

After an Indian takeaway was brought in – which was why this meeting was later dubbed the 'Balti Bailout' – Darling was struck by Goodwin's calmness. During a break in proceedings, 'Sir Fred, ever cool, strolled out as if he were off for a game of golf', whereas HBOS's Hornby 'wore his heart on his sleeve: he looked as if he might explode'.[33] The erstwhile Masters of the Universe, bludgeoned into submission, retired to bed at about 2 a.m., just after Darling turned in at 1.45 a.m. Numerous officials and professional advisors, including lawyers and accountants, stayed up all night putting the finishing touches to the rescue plan. Brown was kept informed by phone and was consulted at 5.28 a.m. when Darling and the banks signed off the deal. Everything had to be ready for the markets opening at 7 a.m. At

9.20 a.m., on Wednesday, 8 October 2008, Brown and Darling spelt out what was being proposed at a press conference in No. 10. The principal ingredient was £50 billion of equity capital support, backed up by the launch of a £250-billion credit guarantee scheme and an extended £200-billion special liquidity scheme.

Participating banks would only be eligible for the goodies they really wanted – guarantees and state-sponsored liquidity – if they could prove they had sufficient capital first and the FSA had embarked on a series of stress tests to assess whether they met the required 9 per cent threshold. If they needed to strengthen their capital, they were given the choice of either participating in the government's recapitalisation scheme, which would supposedly mean restraints on their behaviour, including a ban on paying dividends, or raising it from private-sector sources, which would leave them with greater freedom of manoeuvre. But the precise terms and conditions still had to be ironed out bank by bank. Vadera was paranoid as to how the package would be received by the markets. She said, 'For me, that was the scariest moment because we had no idea who was going to follow, no idea what the markets would think, no idea what the public would think, no idea whether it would boost confidence.'[34] Brown's next challenge was to get through Prime Minister's Questions in the House of Commons. He was fortunate to have an ace up his sleeve. The Bank of England had brought forward its interest rate decision and was cutting the UK base rate to 4.75 per cent as part of a globally coordinated package of rate cuts, orchestrated by King. The opposition Conservatives backed the plan, although they did call it 'a desperate, last-ditch attempt to prevent catastrophe'.[35]

Initially, the markets responded favourably – though some analysts doubted whether it was enough to kick-start the moribund inter-bank lending markets. In a leader column published the next morning, the *Financial Times* referred to the need for tough conditions and expressed concern about the programme's impact on the national accounts at a time when, thanks to Brown's poor stewardship of the economy, Britain faced a large and growing budget deficit. 'Government rescue proposals turn a problem of liquidity and solvency in banks into risk for taxpayers ... if the government buys holdings in these financial institutions, it must also exercise sufficient control of them to make sure that the banks neither abuse the competitive advantage of state backing nor take undue risks.'[36]

While Vadera was attempting to snatch 20 minutes' sleep that afternoon on a sofa in her office, Goodwin telephoned her. In a U-turn on his stance the previous day, the Paisley accountant declared that his bank was in urgent need of capital from the government. 'You'll be shocked by the number,' said Goodwin to Vadera. 'It's ten billion!' This from a man who had spent the previous days insisting that liquidity was the bank's only problem. 'I am shocked,' Vadera responded. 'That's quite small. I think you need a lot more than that.'[37] [38]

Goodwin later told the Treasury committee, 'Of necessity, this was all happening at an extremely rapid rate . . . The rate of deterioration . . . by the time we got through into that week, Monday 6 October, the 6th and 7th saw a collapse in bank share price, a collapse in our price, a collapse in the FTSE and a real collapse in confidence.'[39]

On the Wednesday morning, the *Daily Telegraph* ran a story, written by business editor Jeff Randall, saying that both Goodwin and McKillop were being fired and would quit their roles before the day was out, to be replaced by Stephen Hester and Philip Hampton respectively. Goodwin was enraged when he read this. His flunkies demanded an immediate retraction and an apology from the newspaper, which is owned by the brothers Sir David and Sir Frederick Barclay. When other media sought to follow up on the story, the bank's media relations executives told them Goodwin and McKillop were staying put. An RBS spokeswoman told the *Daily Mail*, 'The board has been completely focused on fixing things, and these issues have not even been discussed.'[40] But Randall's source turned out to be spot on – he was just a few days early. Brown and Darling had already made it clear to government colleagues that, unless Goodwin and McKillop went, there would be no bailout. RBS non-executive director and former Treasury mandarin Sir Steve Robson had been discreetly informed of this.

In articles published that day, some Scottish journalists argued that the collapses of HBOS and RBS had reduced Scotland's chances of becoming independent. The *Daily Telegraph*'s Scottish political editor Alan Cochrane wrote that the failure of the two national icons would 'prove to be another nail in the separatists' coffin'. He also said Goodwin and other bankers had shattered the traditional image of probity and integrity that Scottish bankers had built up over centuries and that the 'old maid' had been 'exposed as a harlot'.[41]

Unfortunately, the shock and awe of Wednesday morning's

announcement was not enough to reverse the silent run on RBS and HBOS. Billions of dollars, pounds, yen, euros and Swiss francs were flooding out of the banks. Quite large institutions – including central banks, large corporates and other institutional investors – were so terrified the two large Scottish banks would fail they were willing to pay large penalties to extricate themselves. Lord Myners says, 'We not only knew how much money was going out, we had a waterfall chart of large deposits maturing and were able to see how, if this process didn't stop, the bank would be dead by the following week.' He immediately realised that the RBS and HBOS bailouts which had been formally announced on the Wednesday morning would have to be brought forward to Monday. 'We had hoped that the announcement that we made at 7 a.m. on the 8 October would buy us time,' says Myners. 'We expected to have at least a week in which to finalise and implement the rescue package. However, all the intelligence that we were getting on 9 October suggested we had less than a week.'[42]

At a 3 p.m. meeting on Thursday 9 October, John Kingman, the 39-year-old Second Permanent Secretary to the Treasury, told advisors from Credit Suisse that, unless the bailout was agreed and finalised by 7 a.m. on Monday morning, RBS would go bankrupt. The Credit Suisse team was stunned. If RBS collapsed, Kingman continued, a third of payments would stop, wages would go missing, bills would go unpaid and savings would disappear. It would cause an earthquake of global proportions that would make Northern Rock and Lehman Brothers seem like minor tremors. It would be no good just bailing out RBS, argued the Credit Suisse team, led by James Leigh-Pemberton, the son of a former Bank of England governor. Doing that would simply move the spotlight to other British banks, especially HBOS and Barclays. But Kingman – a former *Financial Times* journalist, who had taken the lead role at the Treasury because Scholar had been called abroad – told them just to focus on RBS. Other advisors were working on other banks. For the next three days, the offices, meeting rooms and corridors of the second and third floors of the Treasury building would be crammed with bankers, lawyers and civil servants working around the clock to try to stave off Armageddon.

RBS was coming under further relentless pressure on Friday 10 October. That day, its shares lost 25 per cent of their value, closing at 71.7p. Stock markets around the world were in meltdown, with

investors in panic mode. Japan's Nikkei-225 index plunged 9.6 per cent
to 8,276.43, dragging other indices down. The FTSE-100 index plummeted by 8.9 per cent, to close at 3,932.06. By the afternoon, rumours
were swirling around London's trading floors that RBS was already
bust. That evening, the Treasury called Goodwin and the other bank
chiefs to yet another meeting in the Treasury to let them know that the
rescue plan had been brought forward and needed to be finalised and
agreed by 7 a.m. on Monday morning. Each bank was asked to ensure
that its chairman, chief executive and finance director were available
for meetings at the Treasury at any time of day or night throughout
the coming weekend. In the case of banks where the government
was insisting on the departure of the chairman and chief executive
(HBOS and RBS), the banks were also asked to ensure their senior
independent directors were available and on call. Late on Friday, the
RBS nominations committee, pre-empting the government, decided
Goodwin would have to go but there still seemed to be some confusion
over the status of McKillop.

The endgame for RBS was approaching fast. On Saturday, 11
October, Myners chaired a meeting in Room 301 at the Treasury, a
corner room overlooking Birdcage Walk. RBS directors McKillop,
Goodwin, Whittaker and Bob Scott were present for the bank, as well
as the bank's own advisors, who included Merrill Lynch's Matthew
Greenburgh. The government delegation was led by City minister
Lord Myners, the Second Permanent Secretary to the Treasury John
Kingman, the FSA's Clive Adamson and others from the FSA and
Bank of England, as well as the Slaughter & May partner Charles
Randell. Altogether some 20 people were in the room. The Treasury,
the FSA and the Bank of England had earlier carried out a detailed
assessment of RBS's capital needs. As they dictated the terms of the
bailout to McKillop and his cronies, 'McKillop looked ashen-faced. He
looked completely shocked by where he was,' according to Myners.[43]
RBS was being required to sell the government £20 billion of equity
and, in a change since the Balti Bailout, £15 billion of that would be in
the shape of ordinary shares with only £5 billion in preference shares
bearing a 12 per cent interest rate. The £20 billion was almost double
the bank's shrunken market capitalisation of £10.9 billion. Conditions
included: that the bank would be banned from paying a dividend until
the preference shares had been redeemed; that senior directors would

be ineligible for cash bonuses in 2008; and that the future bonuses would have to be paid in shares and more closely tied to the bank's long-term performance. At Brown's insistence, a further condition was that the bank must maintain its lending to small businesses and mortgages at 2007 levels and at competitive interest rates. Given RBS's desperate need to de-leverage and the fact that 2007 had been the peak year for credit issuance, it was an odd criterion to insist on but, for Brown, maintaining pre-crisis lending levels was a *sine qua non*.

Most of the RBS board directors had been kept in the dark about the fate that awaited the bank and were dumbfounded when told what was in store during an impromptu board meeting that started at 11 p.m. on the Saturday night. McKillop was in 280 Bishopsgate but most of the other directors participated via conference calls from their homes. One ex-executive director of RBS said, 'When I was told of the nature of the deal during that 11 p.m. board meeting, it came as a bolt from the blue. We were all completely gobsmacked and there was a certain sense of "they can't do this to us" and McKillop was saying, "Yes they can and they have." '

Some directors doubted whether the government's programme would resolve the wider capital and liquidity issues facing the market. One source close to the RBS board said, 'The manner in which we were being treated was fairly unpleasant. The government and the authorities were intransigent. Either we accepted their terms or the whole board had to resign – which we did not believe would be in the interests of the bank or the country.'

Even as their ship was sliding beneath the waves RBS directors were extraordinarily preoccupied with feathering each other's nests. Myners felt it would be wrong to discuss the details of Goodwin's termination in the full meeting in Room 301. So he asked McKillop and RBS senior independent director Bob Scott to join him and the Slaughter & May partner Randell for a side meeting in the room next door. Myners then told the RBS chairman that the rescue was conditional on both him and Goodwin stepping down. Myners recalls, 'Tom McKillop said there would be no problem with Fred Goodwin going, saying, "We've already handled that." '[44] However, McKillop was refusing to step down himself. He insisted that he would remain in place until RBS's next annual general meeting. Bob Scott backed McKillop on this, warning Myners that the entire RBS board would resign en masse if the government were to force the chairman out too. Darling says, 'McKillop saw no reason to go . . . the bank's board seemed to be behind him. They seemed to have no sense of responsibility for what had happened at RBS and were more concerned about saving face.'[45]

Myners said, 'I said the government would wish to be assured that there's nothing that might appear to be a reward for failure; that we would expect you to seek the best possible deal for the bank in your termination talks with Goodwin; and thirdly, within that, we would not oblige them to abrogate any contractual obligations that they had. McKillop did not dissent.'[46] What McKillop neglected to tell Myners was that, earlier on the Saturday, McKillop, Scott and other RBS directors had exercised 'discretion' by categorising Goodwin as a 'good leaver' (someone who is asked to leave but departs without causing a fuss). By this simple step, they ensured that Goodwin was eligible to take his full, undiscounted pension from the age of 50. It meant his annual pension entitlement was effectively doubled to £703,000 a year – something that would later become the subject of huge controversy. Some in the Treasury thought the RBS board, which devoted many hours to perfecting a generous exit package full of bells and whistles for Goodwin, had its priorities wrong. If they had been this fastidious about risk management, then perhaps the bank would not have failed. According to Colin McLean, chief executive of SVM Asset Management, the pension arrangement was, in itself, in breach of the UK's corporate governance code. McLean said, 'Much of it was an unapproved scheme, with money just being bunged in. It should have all been handed to an independent remuneration committee; instead that remuneration committee left the final decisions to the board on which Fred sat.'[47]

It is fair to say, though, that Myners' mind was focused on bigger issues that night – including whether Britain would have any banks the following week. Arguably, he didn't have the time or the inclination to pore over the minutiae of the employment contracts of departing executives. He was also reassured when McKillop and Scott confirmed there was nothing in Goodwin's termination agreement that would contravene the government's 'rewards for failure' principles. However, one source close to the RBS board accuses Myners of 'spinning a web of lies to cover himself' and that Bob Scott did spell out the details of the pension to Myners. In a letter to the Treasury committee, McKillop said, 'Lord Myners was told at that meeting [on Saturday 11 October] that Sir Fred's pension benefit would be the sensitive issue and that it would be "enormous" . . . full disclosure was made to the government of the position, as was necessary at the time. There was no concealment of any relevant matter.'[48]

Treasury sources say Goodwin handled the situation with confidence and dignity, unlike McKillop who seemed a broken man. However, at some stage over the weekend, Goodwin did quip that he wasn't happy with the government's handling of things, telling Myners, 'This isn't a negotiation – it's a drive-by shooting.'[49] The choice of words suggested he remained firmly in denial about his role in the RBS collapse. Goodwin was showing zero gratitude to those who were going out of their way to save his bank.

In the end, Barclays narrowly escaped the government's clutches by pledging to raise £6.5 billion of capital from private-sector sources. After saving £2 billion by scrapping its dividend, it cemented a deal whereby Sheikh Mansour bin Zayed Al Nahyan, a member of the royal family of Abu Dhabi, and Qatar Holding would inject £7.3 billion of fresh capital in November 2008. But the deals, which involved the payment of up to £300 million in alleged 'kickbacks' to Mansour, Qatar Holding and Challenger (an investment vehicle of Sheikh Hamad bin Jassim bin Jabr Al Thani (the prime minister of Qatar) and his family), would come back to haunt Barclays. The alleged bribes which intermediary Amanda Staveley claims she knew nothing about are now the subject of Serious Fraud Office and Financial Conduct Authority (FCA, one of the two successor bodies to the FSA) inquiries.

The government had lined up two possible candidates to replace Fred Goodwin – the American-born JPMorgan investment banker, Bill Winters, and the British Land chief executive Stephen Hester, who had joined RBS as a non-executive on 27 August. Winters had turned down the chance to move to RBS eight months earlier. The second time around, he was no more enthusiastic and probably saw the task of turning around the damaged lender, with the government breathing down his neck, as a poisoned chalice. It was also recognised that, if RBS were to buy out Winters' JPMorgan share options, it would be a PR disaster for the bank and the government. Hester, the former head of fixed income at Credit Suisse First Boston, who was admired for the way he had turned around Abbey National, was called to 11 Downing

Street on the Saturday afternoon. He came fresh from killing a few pheasants at a shoot at his Oxfordshire estate, Broughton Grange, still wearing his shooting gear. To avoid drawing attention to himself, the 47-year-old investment banker parked his Bentley around the corner from Downing Street and walked the short distance to the chancellor's office at No. 11. Yorkshireman Hester was interested but only if he could get what he considered to be a fair rate of pay. He ended up with a package worth up to £9.6 million a year, as neither Darling nor Myners was willing to risk losing him for the sake of a few million. On the Monday morning, Hester's appointment was officially announced and the Goodwin era was over.[50] Darling said, 'If we were to salvage anything from RBS, I needed to get the best candidate and to pay him what was needed. As it happens I think he was the right choice.'[51]

As the exhausted officials, lawyers and politicians drifted off to bed in the early hours of Monday, 13 October 2008, a row broke out at 3 a.m. between two advisors. According to *The Times*, Merrill Lynch's Matthew Greenburgh, now advising Lloyds TSB, violently disagreed with Simon Robey at Morgan Stanley. The Black Horse was seeking to lower the price of its takeover of the crippled HBOS, whose share price had collapsed since the deal was announced on 17 September. With less than four hours to go before the comprehensive bailout had to be announced to the market at 7 a.m., Myners wondered whether he would have to wake up Brown and Darling and tell them that catastrophe loomed and because of a private spat. Myners decided to leave the two pugilists to fight it out in a corridor of the Treasury. Finally, at 6 a.m. – with the fate of the world's financial system hanging in the balance – Greenburgh, who sources suggest was frazzled by the lengthy pre-bailout negotiations, backed down. A so-called 'compromise agreement', essentially the cosy terms of Goodwin's departure, was thrashed out by the RBS chairman's committee in the early hours of Monday morning. In a meeting held largely by conference call between 12.40 a.m. and 3 a.m., according to the minutes, 'the Directors agreed that Sir Fred Goodwin would step down as Group Chief Executive and be replaced by Mr Stephen Hester. Sir Fred would continue for a short period as Chief Executive until Mr Hester was released from British Land to allow a smooth handover at both companies. At the appropriate time, Sir Fred would cease to undertake the role of Group Chief Executive.'[52] Goodwin was in attendance at 280 Bishopsgate, accompanied by loyal human resources director Neil Roden and representatives of law firm Maclay Murray & Spens LLP to agree an exit package and sign relevant documents. Towards the end of the process, the departing chief executive's mask finally slipped and he became overwrought and visibly upset about being flung out of the bank.

Brown and Darling unveiled their make-or-break deal aimed at saving the UK and, indeed, the wider world, from financial Armageddon at a press conference in 10 Downing Street on Monday 13 October. Brown said, 'The action we are taking is unprecedented, but essential for all of us . . . In extraordinary times, with financial markets ceasing to work, the government cannot just leave people on their own to be buffeted about . . . we must, in an uncertain and unstable world, be the rock of stability on which the British people can depend.' Describing the capital injections into three of Britain's largest banks, Brown said, 'We have agreed to make a series of commercial investments amounting to £37 billion of public money in a number of UK banks.' The government also made it clear that it had no intention of becoming a permanent owner of stakes in banks. Rather, it wanted to unwind its ownership, for a profit, over time. It also emphasised it had no desire to run RBS, HBOS or Lloyds directly, preferring to run them at arm's length via the new quango, UK Financial Investments (UKFI). Darling said he thought it appropriate for government-nominated directors to join the boards of both RBS (which would be 60 per cent government owned) and Lloyds/HBOS (which would be 43.5 per cent government owned). 'Ministers aren't going to get involved in the day-to-day running,' he said. Brown was adamant the government would no longer tolerate 'rewards for failure'.

Investors reacted positively, with the FTSE-100 recovering almost half of the previous week's losses. It closed 8.3 per cent higher, up 325 points at 4,256.9 – the index's second-biggest daily percentage rise ever. In the US, the Dow Jones closed up 935 points or 11.1 per cent – its largest daily jump in percentage terms since 1933. RBS staff, however, were shell-shocked. Not only had their once-swashbuckling institution become a ward of state but three of its directors – McKillop, Goodwin and Cameron – were being forced out and any savings they had had in RBS shares had been rendered worthless. One senior manager says, 'We just could not believe it. There was disappointment, anger, frustration. We had been proud to be Royal Bank and now, all of a sudden, we were a pariah.'

Ex-insiders say the message that Goodwin put out on the bank's intranet on Monday 13 October was comically inadequate. The Paisley-born accountant showed no sign of humility or contrition. One staff member says, 'We had been vaguely expecting some sort of apology. But there wasn't even an acknowledgement that we should not have gone for ABN AMRO. He just talked about leadership style and how his was more suited to building, creating, growing . . . and then he said he felt it was the right time for [him] to step aside!' Former RBS chairman George Mathewson told BBC Scotland that day was the 'direst and worst day for a long time. I obviously welcome the stability introduced to the banking system but it is deeply regrettable that we have, effectively, government ownership of a large part of the banking system.'[53] With all four bank bosses who had sat underneath John Bellany's *Death's Head* – Hornby, Stevenson, Goodwin and McKillop – now either gone or going, new blood was required to rebuild what was left of the banking system they had trashed. Much was resting on the shoulders of Hester and Eric Daniels, the 57-year-old Marlboro-smoking, Montana-born chief executive of LloydsTSB.

The Nobel Prize-winning economist Paul Krugman said that Brown and Darling had raised the bar for other world leaders who still needed to rescue their banking sectors. Writing in the *New York Times*, Krugman praised both men for their boldness. 'Has Gordon Brown saved the world financial system?' wrote Krugman. 'Mr. Brown and Alistair Darling . . . have defined the character of the worldwide rescue effort . . . the British government went straight to the heart of the problem – and moved to address it with stunning speed . . . They may have shown us the way through this crisis.'[54]

But there were already concerns about the lack of firm conditions attached to the bailouts. On Tuesday, 14 October, Liberal Democrat Treasury spokesman Vince Cable said the government should force the bailed-out banks to shut down all their subsidiaries in tax havens. Cable said, 'It seems totally inappropriate for banks funded by the taxpayer to be systematically avoiding British tax or helping customers to do so.'[55] At the time, RBS had an astonishing 393 subsidiaries in tax havens, including RBS International in Jersey, Zurich-based RBS Coutts, which handles the accounts of wealthy customers and operates in Jersey, the Cayman Islands and the Isle of Man; and Jersey-based Arran Funding, through which the bank channelled billions of pounds worth of UK securitised mortgages and credit-card loans.

And there is no doubt that RBS had been behaving badly where tax was concerned. In a report published on 13 March 2009, *The Guardian* revealed that RBS Global Banking and Markets had established 13 transatlantic structured finance schemes, varying from £1 billion and £6 billion in size, whose raison d'être was tax avoidance. In an interview, *The Guardian*'s investigations editor David Leigh said RBS used the vehicles 'to spin money around, so that the tax losses ended up offshore in the Cayman Islands. RBS would then do a deal with an American bank, so that the US bank got the benefit of the tax losses, as well as the British bank. They were getting benefit of the tax loss twice – it's called double-dipping.' The bank's partners in the tax ruse included AIG, Fortis, Swiss Re, Morgan Stanley, Merrill Lynch and Goldman Sachs. Overall, according to *The Guardian*, RBS had parked £25 billion in the schemes, costing British and US Treasuries more than £500 million in lost revenues, though the US Treasury appeared to have been a bigger loser than the UK's. The bank insisted that the structured finance department responsible had been disbanded and that it had called time on the practice. An RBS spokesman told *The Guardian*, 'The idea that we could take support from the Treasury with one hand and somehow pick their pocket with the other would be wrong on every level. We have always sought to avoid this sort of stance and that's more important now than ever. It's not a sustainable way to do business.'[56]

Fred found out

For years, Royal Bank of Scotland bankers had been strutting their stuff on the financial stage, puffed up with braggadocio and inflating debt bubbles wherever they turned. The internal mantra had been that RBS was one of the 'largest and best capitalised banks in the world'. However, just like other claims including 'we don't do subprime', 'we don't do investment banking', 'we won't be making any takeovers', 'we don't need inorganic capital-raising of any kind', it was a distortion of the truth. Goodwin had built the bank on a wafer-thin layer of often-shaky capital. Even after tapping its own investors for £12 billion in June 2008 and the government for £20 billion in October 2008, the bank remained undercapitalised. Now on taxpayer-provided life support, it was a deeply traumatised institution. Internally, many of the bank's 170,000-plus staff had hero-worshipped Fred Goodwin. So they struggled to come to terms with the idea that he had been busking it all along. One Gogarburn-based relationship director said, 'Even after the crash, I was still quite loyal to Fred Goodwin and my initial view was that we should have kept the bastard on – if only to make him work for his money. When I found out how clueless he had been about what was going on inside the bank, I was dumbfounded.'

Another issue for staff was that many had had such faith in the bank they had invested the bulk of their savings in its shares, with many being bullied by the bank into borrowing money to buy shares in the rights issue. Given the shares had sunk to 10p at one point, it did not instil a particularly positive attitude towards their employer. Initially, many insiders preferred to blame others for the bank's plight. Favoured bogeymen included BBC business editor Robert Peston, Prime Minister Gordon Brown, Chancellor Alistair Darling, Bank of

England Governor Mervyn King, the non-executive directors (considered by some insiders to be a bunch of freeloading 'yes' men who had failed to look after shareholders' interests), the ratings agencies, the auditors and, of course, customers who had borrowed too much. When I asked someone who was on the RBS board until February 2009 who was to blame for the collapse, he said, 'The fundamental causes of the collapse were the huge indebtedness of Western governments and subprime policies encouraged by the US government . . . It's fundamentally governments who caused the financial collapse.'

By mid January 2009, it was clear the bank remained in crisis, and Brown was waking up to the fact that it was in a far worse state than he had thought, with far greater quantities of toxic loans and bad debts on its books than its board and auditors had admitted to. It was still not lending and, even after the £32 billion of fresh capital since June 2008, it was struggling to stay solvent. It was becoming obvious that Brown had oversold the 13 October 2008 bailouts. They had cauterised some of the bank's self-inflicted wounds but further bailouts would be required. Secondly, given the recent downward trajectory of the RBS share price, it was looking like Brown's government had significantly overpaid for its 60 per cent stake. And, finally, nursing the banks back to health would take far longer than envisaged. That was going to be a marathon, not a sprint, with no chance of a quick 'flip' for capital gain.

Friday, 16 January 2009 was a bloody day for bank stocks. Bank of America Merrill Lynch (BoAML) had been formed the previous month when Bank of America rescued Merrill Lynch by buying it for $50 billion but, that Friday, shares in the merged BoAML and in Citigroup tumbled as they declared aggregate losses of $25 billion (£17 billion) for the three months to December. The news hit Barclays hard because of fears that it was hiding losses. Its shares slumped by a remarkable 25 per cent in a frenetic hour of trading between 3.30 p.m. and 4.30 p.m. RBS shares plunged a further 13 per cent to 34.7p. The Brown government was forced to acknowledge that its rescue had failed and that another one would be required.

Darling, Myners, Treasury officials and their advisors spent another weekend holed up in the Treasury for emergency talks with leading bankers. Darling says, '[T]he position at RBS was far worse than anyone had imagined.'[1] According to Paul Myners, there were now only three options left for RBS: (1) full nationalisation combined with a restructuring into a 'good bank' and a 'bad bank'; (2) the injection of further government-funded capital; and (3) the launch of an 'asset protection scheme' to insure the bank's dodgiest assets. Brown had an absolute phobia of nationalisation. He dreaded accusations from the Tory opposition that he had reverted to Socialism. Nor was the idea of incorporating RBS's near £2-trillion balance sheet into the UK national accounts of much appeal. So option one was ruled out. Option two, further capital injections, risked crowding out the remaining private-sector shareholders and might cause RBS to struggle to remain as a listed entity. The insurance option was beginning to look more and more attractive. The idea, based on clever financial engineering, had been developed by the Credit Suisse investment bankers led by James Leigh-Pemberton. Philip Aldrick wrote, 'The idea quickly caught on. By leaving all the bad assets with the banks, it was simpler to implement than [an alternative proposal from the FSA]. Most importantly, it was entirely unfunded – the "contingent liability" would not affect the public debt.'[2]

The government unveiled the asset protection scheme, although only in vague terms, at a press conference on Monday 19 January. It also unveiled a raft of other asset-purchase and credit-guarantee schemes designed to shore up RBS and the British banking system. The government also said it would raise its stake in RBS to 70 per cent by converting its £5 billion of preference shares into ordinary ones. With large bags under his eyes, Brown looked shattered as he struggled to sell the package to a room full of journalists. Despite their best efforts to get him to admit it, he refused to acknowledge that the measures he was announcing that day meant the much-vaunted October 2008 bailout had been a failure. He just said these were 'comprehensive measures' to get the banks lending again, emphasising that they were designed to help people and companies, not to enable fat-cat bankers boost their lifestyles. Somewhat theatrically, he said he was 'angry' with RBS. He slammed the bank for its investments in subprime US mortgages and its acquisition of ABN AMRO. 'These are irresponsible risks that were taken by a bank with people's money in the UK.' But he was not sufficiently angry to even comment on whether the bank's pre-crisis behaviour would be investigated.[3] The biggest frustration for Darling and other ministers was that the bailout announcement got drowned out by dire news from the bank itself which, much to their annoyance, Hester had insisted on announcing the same day.

When Hester and finance director Guy Whittaker were going through RBS's books over the previous few days, they realised that the bank was in a far worse state than they had been told by the previous management. The fact that Whittaker had suddenly became aware of losses he previously didn't know about begs one or two questions about his fitness to be the bank's finance director. RBS was going to have to declare a loss of up to £28 billion for the year to December 2008 and, under stock exchange rules, the discovery of the losses was 'market-sensitive'. The bank was, therefore, required to issue a Regulatory News Service announcement. So, on the Monday morning, RBS made the largest profits warning in history. It said it was going to lose £7–8 billion for the year to December 2008 and would also have to take a goodwill write-down of £15–20 billion on acquisitions including those of First Active, Charter One and ABN AMRO – a sign that it *had* paid way over the odds for these companies. Hester also felt obliged to warn that the size and timing of future credit losses were unpredictable. The doom-laden announcement panicked investors and caused RBS shares to nosedive by a record-breaking 67 per cent that day. At one point they touched a low of 10p, a fifth of the level at which Brown's government had part-nationalised the bank four months earlier and 95 per cent below the rights issue price. However, they rebounded a little to close the day at 11.5p. At one stage during the day, Hester called Darling to reassure him there was no need to be panicked into full nationalisation. 'It's just the market trying to find its level,' the Yorkshireman told the chancellor.[4] Darling was rattled and, that evening, asked Treasury officials 'to draw up contingency plans in case RBS were to fail. For the first time, we had to consider full nationalisation. The implications were considerable. The remaining shareholders would be wiped out and it would have a huge impact on confidence in the UK.'[5]

RBS did not have its troubles to seek that month. On 18 January 2009, it emerged that Ian Hamilton QC, who as a student had been part of the group who repatriated the Stone of Destiny from Westminster Abbey, was suing RBS in Oban Sheriff Court. In a small claims action, Hamilton, an RBS customer for 60 years, claimed that he and his wife had been 'fraudulently induced' into buying £1,282 worth of shares in the rights issue. He accused the bank of concealing its true financial position and misrepresenting itself as solvent. Hamilton, then 83, said RBS directors would be called to the court to give evidence. He said, 'It is a remarkable state of affairs that the defenders of a great company can run it into the ground without answering in court for their behaviour.'[6] RBS said it would defend the action 'vigorously'. The *Sunday Times* columnist Gillian Bowditch said, 'What is absolutely petrifying is that Hamilton may be our best – if not our only – hope of getting to the bottom of what went on.'[7] After the bank insisted the action be transferred to a higher court, Hamilton withdrew for fear of crippling costs.

At the end of January, the Nobel prize-winning economist, Professor Joseph Stiglitz said that Brown's government ought to have allowed RBS to fail. Speaking at the World Economic Forum in Davos, Stiglitz said, 'The UK has been hit because the banks took on enormously large liabilities in foreign currencies. Should British taxpayers have to lower their standard of living for 20 years to pay off mistakes that benefited a small elite? There is an argument for letting the banks go bust. It may cause turmoil but it will be a cheaper way to deal with this in the end. The British parliament never offered a blanket guarantee for all liabilities and derivative positions of these banks.' Stiglitz said the government should have underwritten all deposits to protect the UK's domestic financial system, and used the skeletons of the old banks to build a healthier structure. 'The new banks will be more credible once they no longer have these liabilities on their back.'[8]

Between October and December 2008 four of RBS's directors walked out or were thrown out – Goodwin and Cameron both left soon after the first bailout, while Mark Fisher and Larry Fish went in November and December respectively. Fisher, the hero of the NatWest integration and Goodwin's most loyal lieutenant, joined the newly merged Lloyds/HBOS operation, where integration skills were in short supply, while Fish 'retired' with a £1.4 million-a-year pension (£26,923 per week), the largest ever awarded by a British company. In the wake of the bank's £28-billion profits warning and disillusioned with its board, given their apparent failure to spot these losses, the government decided it was time for a more comprehensive boardroom clear-out. First out the door was Sir Tom McKillop, chairman since May 2006. He left on Tuesday 3 February bringing what Peter Thal Larsen called 'an abrupt end to his disastrous three-year tenure as RBS's chairman'.[9]

He was widely seen as having been far too close to Goodwin, to have rubber-stamped catastrophic policies, and to have egged Fred on to do the fatal ABN deal. The man the government chose to replace him was Sir Philip Hampton. Seen in Whitehall as a safe pair of hands, he was appointed as non-executive director and chairman-designate of RBS on 19 January. He became its chairman on 3 February, which meant he had to hand over his role as chairman of UK Financial Investments to the former Fidelity Investments fund manager Glen Moreno. Bizarrely, given the circumstances, Hampton was a strong advocate of 'light-touch' regulation. He remained as chairman of the supermarket group J Sainsbury until a successor was found on 1 November 2009.

Two days after Hampton – whose glittering career had included advising on mergers and acquisitions at Lazard and serving as finance director at British Steel, British Gas, BG Group, British Telecom and Lloyds TSB – took over as chairman, he made his presence felt with 'a night of the long knives'. On Thursday 5 February, seven RBS non-executive directors from the Goodwin era were turfed out: Bob Scott, a director since January 2001; Peter Sutherland, a director since January 2001; Sir Steve Robson, a director since July 2001; Jim Currie, a director since November 2001; Bud Koch, a director since September 2004; Janis Long, a director since January 2006; and Bill Friedrich, a director since March 2006. To ensure the Edinburgh-based bank's collective memory was not completely wiped out, Hampton retained three non-execs: Colin Buchan, who'd been there since June 2002; Archie Hunter, September 2004; and Joe McHale, September 2004. The RBS company secretary, Miller McLean, who had been in that role since 1994 and was, therefore, one of the few to know where all the bodies were buried, also kept his position. And two executive directors – the finance director Guy Whittaker and chairman of retail markets Gordon Pell – stayed on as well. The latter was promoted to deputy chief executive on 2 March. Hampton made it all seem routine, saying, 'With several directors completing two or more terms or otherwise wishing to retire, now is the right time to reduce the size of the board, whilst ensuring an appropriate level of continuity in its key committees.'[10]

The bloodletting followed the revelation earlier that day, via a leak to *The Times*, that RBS was poised to hand hundreds of millions in bonuses to executives and traders, despite the losses and the need for unprecedented taxpayer support. To some members of the cabinet, including Deputy Prime Minister Harriet Harman, this was outrageous and had to be stopped. But other government ministers were relaxed and argued that ripping up contractual agreements that RBS had with staff (some of these were the guaranteed bonuses that had been proferred to Scott Eichel's 50-strong team of former Bear Stearns mortgage traders), would send the wrong signal to the markets. Brown was fence-sitting and so the government made no firm decision about how to respond. Andrew Rawnsley says this meant 'the Labour government put itself on the wrong side of a populist wave'.[11]

Public anger intensified after the so-called 'unfab four' – Goodwin, McKillop, Hornby and Stevenson – appeared before the Treasury Select Committee on 10 February 2009. Their excuses and apologies came across as lame, partial and insincere. And this seemed more true of Goodwin than the other three. He did not apologise for anything he had done but only for the 'distress' the bank's troubles may have caused. 'I apologised in full and am happy to do so again . . . There is a profound and unqualified apology for all of the distress that has been caused and I would not wish there to be any doubt about that whatsoever.' In answer to a question to Nick Ainger MP, Goodwin, bridling at being singled out for blame, said, '[I]t is just too simple . . . to blame it all on me. If you want to blame it all on me and close the book, that will get the job done very quickly, but it does not go anywhere close to the cause of all of this.'[12] He was, once again, trying to characterise himself as the innocent victim of circumstances beyond his control. He was trying to tell the world 'It wisnae me!'

Some commentators were stunned by the economic illiteracy and bizarre views on risk management displayed by Goodwin during the hearing, which was to be his last public appearance. The Edinburgh-based banking consultant Robert McDowell says, 'Goodwin said he was shocked by the speed of the market collapse. This showed his total economic naiveté and lack of cyclical awareness. Without awareness and understanding of the economic cycle, a person cannot be considered professionally competent to accept regulatory or fiduciary responsibilities.'[13]

Appearing before the same committee the following day, Hester explained that getting RBS back to stand-alone health was going to be 'a really huge job' that could take three to five years. He added that 'frankly, the risk-management systems at Royal Bank of Scotland need a lot of change'. Asked about bonuses, Hester said, 'I do think banking pay in some areas of the industry is way too high and needs to come down and I intend us to lead that process.'[14]

In late January, Simon Hattenstone, a *Guardian* journalist, turned up on the doorstep of the south Glasgow bungalow belonging to Fred Goodwin's parents-in-law, Norman and Nessie McLean, where the Goodwins had taken refuge from journalists. Hattenstone had brought a megaphone. He stood on the pavement outside the bungalow and, amplifying his voice through the loudhailer, invited Fred to apologise for trashing RBS. Hattenstone said, 'I have a series of questions to ask you. One: would you like to apologise to the public for the state of the RBS? Two: would you like to thank the public for bailing you out? Three: would you like to give back your bonuses?'[15] But Goodwin refused to come out. He is said to have been so traumatised by Hattenstone's kerbside performance that he and his family decided to flee to France. In February, he and Joyce took their children, John and Honor, out of their Edinburgh schools and they moved to Cannes. Goodwin's friend and shooting partner, Sir Fraser Morrison, a construction and architecture magnate to whom he had lent money when at Clydesdale Bank, had offered to lend the family his £4-million luxury chateau, in the hills above the resort. Fred and family were to stay there under the Mediterranean sun until August.

The bonus situation was embarrassing enough for Brown's government. But the next discovery was incendiary. While Treasury officials were leafing through a draft version of the RBS 2008 accounts, they spotted that Goodwin had a pension entitlement of £703,000 a year – a discretionary entitlement that had been nodded through by McKillop and the RBS board on Monday 13 October 2008. It seemed that Goodwin would be eligible for the money from his 50th birthday, which had fallen in August 2008.

Treasury officials immediately recognised this could become a *cause célèbre*. Myners tried to defuse the situation by calling Goodwin in France and trying to persuade the Paisley-born accountant to make a 'gesture of goodwill' by handing back at least some of the money. Goodwin refused and later accused Myners of trying to bully him, alleging that the City minister had hinted at dire consequences if Goodwin didn't comply. The Treasury is then thought to have leaked news of Goodwin's pension to Robert Peston. The BBC business editor's 25

February 2009 scoop on the infamous pension, including news of the doubling of his pension pot to £16 million and ministers' determination to claw some back, unleashed a media and political storm that diverted many people's attention away from the wider crisis at RBS.[16]

In his public utterances at the time, Brown insisted that the failure of much of Britain's banking system was entirely America's fault. He began to retreat into what Rawnsley calls his 'mental bunker'.[17] Darling, for one, was astonished that it was another two years before Ed Balls and Gordon Brown acknowledged that the regulatory near-vacuum they had created might have had anything to do with it.

The public mood was turning ugly. Sources close to the government, thought to include the government spin doctor Damian McBride, and Media House, a PR firm retained by RBS, were working hard to spread as much ordure as possible on the head of Fred. From late February to May, there was a steady drip-feed of leaks about Goodwin to papers from the *Mirror* to the *Sunday Times*. Stories tended to highlight some of his worst excesses and egotistical tendencies – including the obsession with ripping out new carpets, the upbraiding of staff over 'rogue biscuits' and the fact that he employed a man to make sure only banknotes bearing his signature were dispensed by the cash machine at Gogarburn. Newspaper editors up and down the land were asking reporters to look out for 'dirt' on Goodwin and other high-profile bank executives.

On 25 March, while Goodwin and family were ensconced in the Côte d'Azur, a group calling itself 'Bank Bosses Are Criminals' smashed three of the windows at their vacant £3-million home in Edinburgh's Oswald Road as well as two of the windows of his £120,000 Mercedes-Benz S600 coupé. In a statement emailed to the Edinburgh *Evening News*, the group said: 'We are angry that rich people, like him [Goodwin], are paying themselves a huge amount of money and living in luxury, while ordinary people are made unemployed, destitute and homeless. Bank bosses should be jailed. This is just the beginning.'[18] Neighbours interviewed on STV News had little sympathy for Fred. The historian David Starkey fuelled the public anger by saying, 'All the arguments about reward for risk are spurious when there is no penalty for failure. In Tudor times, Fred Goodwin's head would have been chopped off, parboiled and placed on a pike.'[19] A week later, at the G20 summit in London, an effigy of Goodwin was hanged by protesters outside the

Bank of England. And, as Brown grandiloquently sought to persuade world leaders of the need for a coordinated response to the crisis, protesters stormed and ransacked a branch of Royal Bank of Scotland in Threadneedle Street.[20] Then, on 17 June, effigies of the severed heads of Goodwin and McKillop were skewered on pikes on London Bridge. The effigies – made of clay, wax, hair and the severed necks of sheep by artist David Fryer – formed part of the Two Degrees Festival of 'theatre, art and activism that confronts climate change head on'. The next day, Goodwin, still in his Côte d'Azur hideaway, volunteered to reduce his pension to about £342,500. But he retained a £5-million tax-free lump sum and past bonuses. In a press release, Hampton said, 'On any measure this represents a very substantial reduction to Fred's pension . . . I am very pleased that we have resolved a situation that has been a difficult and unhappy one for all the parties involved, and it is to Fred's credit that he has done this on a voluntary basis.' Hampton said that the RBS board would now be able to focus on restoring the bank to health.[21] It was a sensible gesture on Goodwin's part but, in the end, it was too little too late. He remained, and remains, a pariah.

As a coda to the pension saga, it's worth pointing out that two former colleagues of Goodwin retired with even bigger pensions than he did. As I said earlier, Larry Fish, ex-chief executive of Citizens Financial, broke UK records by leaving the wreckage of RBS with a pension pot of £16.88 million. RBS's ex-chairman of retail markets Gordon Pell, who left the bank in March 2010, retired with a pension pot of £9.83 million, giving him an annual pension of £517,000 (or £9,942 per week). Goodwin is having to make do on £6,586 a week. Yet neither Fish nor Pell has been demonised.

Defibrillation and despair

Stephen Hester grew up in North Yorkshire, the son of a chemistry professor and a psychotherapist, and was educated at Easingwold School, a comprehensive 12 miles north of York, followed by Lady Margaret Hall, Oxford University, where he gained a first-class degree in Philosophy, Politics and Economics and was chairman of the Tory Reform Group. Hester joined investment bank Credit Suisse First Boston straight after leaving university, eventually running its fixed-income division from New York. He was forced out by chief executive John Mack 'The Knife', reportedly after guaranteeing bond traders multimillion-pound bonuses, irrespective of their performances. Hester then spent two years, between 2002 and 2004, at Abbey National, a troubled bank which he cut down to size before selling it to Santander for £9.3 billion in November 2004. He then joined the property group British Land, where his open management style and bluntness are said to have shocked some property industry insiders. The Labour government asked him to become non-executive deputy chairman of the newly nationalised Northern Rock in February 2008 and he remained on its board until becoming RBS chief executive in November 2008. Hester has expensive tastes, including passions for skiing, gourmet cuisine and horticulture. He has built an 80-acre garden that one newspaper has described as 'his very own Versailles' at his 350-acre Oxfordshire estate, Broughton Grange, where he employs six full-time gardeners.[1] He also owns a jumbo ski chalet in Verbier, in south-west Switzerland.

Hester spent most of his first six months at RBS fire-fighting. In a BBC programme called 'Rebooting RBS', Hester made it clear what sort of culture he wished to see at RBS. He said, 'I have set out to drive very clearly a spirit of openness, transparency, disclosure, of blunt-speaking, thoughtfulness, and empowerment . . . and of course changing cultures takes years not months.'[2]

One former RBS executive said, 'I think he was very courageous to take on the job. He seemed to listen and didn't come across as being as arrogant as Fred – which wasn't difficult.' Staff found him a less complicated person to deal with than his predecessor. One senior bank insider said, 'Fred was revered within the bank . . . and we all wasted a lot of time and energy discussing how to manage him and trying to second-guess how he would react to things. There is no need to do that with Hester: he is transparent in his management style and leaves people in no doubt what is expected of them.'

Within days of taking the reins, Hester asked consultants McKinsey & Company to conduct a thorough review of the Royal Bank of Scotland Group and help develop a new strategy. No consultancy had been allowed to set foot in the bank since 2000, when Goodwin had imposed a group-wide ban. The McKinsey team, led by Pat Butler, an Irishman who, ironically, had also worked on Project Columbus before Goodwin's ban took effect, was told there were no sacred cows. The McKinsey consultants spent the next three months thoroughly evaluating the bank, division by division. Managers in each of RBS's business units were asked to submit multiple business plans outlining proposals for cutting costs and boosting profitability – and the units that came up with the weakest plans were seen as candidates for the axe.

Having been rubber-stamped by the RBS board, UK Financial Investments and the Treasury, the final strategy was unveiled alongside RBS's annual results on 26 February 2009. The bank would: continue to operate internationally, albeit in fewer countries; continue to be a major player in investment banking, albeit with a trimmed down balance sheet that employed 45 per cent less capital; and continue to run a major retail, commercial and corporate bank in the United States. The document plainly stated, '*Our aspiration is that RBS should again become one of the world's premier financial institutions, anchored in the UK but serving individual and institutional customers here and globally, and doing it well* [my italics].'[3] The plan was essentially predicated on a 'back to business as usual' mindset and the notion that the bank could use its 'casino' arm to trade itself out of its difficulties. At the time, Reuters columnist Alexander Smith thought the plan disastrous. 'You might have expected the British government, which now owns 70 per cent, to put pressure on RBS to pull out of investment banking. After all, it is hardly in the taxpayer's interest to insure risky and unprofitable investment banking activities. But the state seems reluctant to exercise its ownership rights – fearing it will be accused of back seat driving.'[4]

It was a gamble that failed to pay off. Even though McKinsey had considered a worst-case scenario known internally as 'Nuclear Winter' – involving a deterioration of the global economy and RBS losing market share – the consultants had not predicted the depth and length of the economic downturn or the European sovereign debt crisis.[5] Nor had they taken into account the urgent need for cultural change inside the bank.

To avoid accusations that it was micromanaging RBS, Lloyds and other rescued institutions, Brown's government outsourced the management of its stakes in them to a specially created government agency called UK Financial Investments (UKFI), which was launched on 3 November 2008. However, UKFI, initially run by John Kingman, followed by Robin Budenberg, Jim O'Neil and James Leigh-Pemberton, was peopled by superannuated investment bankers who had little or no interest in implementing real reform – their main goals as bankers had been ensuring that they were paid king-size bonuses. Kingman, Budenberg and O'Neil were so focused on RBS's profitability and its share price that they seemed happy to nod through any policy, no matter how deleterious it might be to the interests of customers or the environment. Their own ingrained belief in bankers' rights to bonuses meant they invariably sided with the bank's management – including with the bank's remuneration committee – on pay. Indeed, it recently emerged that UKFI had overruled Chancellor George Osborne when he sought to rein in egregious pay awards at the bank. In a blog published in July 2010, I wrote, 'Watching Budenberg and his colleague Sam Woods at the [House of Commons Environmental Audit] committee hearing was a deeply depressing experience. The pair seem to be throwbacks to the Friedman-esque 1980s, before awareness of corporate and social responsibility even existed – and short-term financial performance was all that mattered. The people who run UKFI and the UK government are desperately clinging to the wreckage of the myopic value system that got us into this mess in the first place.'[6]

On Thursday 26 February the bank declared losses of £24.1 billion which, although the biggest in UK corporate history, were less than feared. The government also re-announced the asset protection scheme (APS) – this time with some flesh on the bones. The scheme was essentially a gigantic taxpayer-provided insurance policy designed to ring-fence £325 billion of the bank's flakiest assets. By its sheer scale, the scheme was testimony to the profligacy, recklessness and greed of the Goodwin years. Benefits of the scheme, from the bank's perspective, included that it enabled RBS to shrink its balance sheet, reducing 'risk-weighted' assets from £578 billion to £434 billion; in turn, this enabled the bank to bolster its core tier-1 capital ratio. From the government's perspective, it allowed the bank to limp on as an ostensibly independent company without the need for full nationalisation. Myners says, 'I think the asset protection scheme was an extraordinary piece of financial engineering. It involved the Treasury taking on probably the largest, in terms of nominal value, contractual obligation in the history of the country.'[7] However, not everyone was overjoyed. On 26 February, the economist Willem Buiter published a blog examining the economics of the scheme headlined, 'A taxpayer rip-off of surprising boldness'. Buiter said the government could have made taxpayers' lives much less wretched by simply putting RBS out of its misery.[8]

The third announcement on 26 February was that the government would inject a further £13 billion of capital into RBS – this time in the form of B-shares (a class of shares with fewer voting rights than A-shares), with the option to inject £6 billion more if need be, though the government's voting stake would be capped at 75 per cent. The bank also made a commitment to lend up to £25 billion in each of the next two years to British companies and individuals. Other announcements included that the bank was scrapping its sponsorship deal with Williams Formula One, closing the curtain on another of Fred's follies. The bank also unobtrusively announced it would drastically scale back activity in structured real estate and leveraged and project finance, areas where billions of pounds of losses had been made. Leith Robertson, the man who oversaw these areas, had made himself scarce six days earlier.

Last but not least, Hester unveiled a five-year recovery plan for the bank based around McKinsey's proposals. Hester said the restructuring would leave no part of the bank untouched, with every business being set new revenue growth and cost-cutting targets. He aimed to cut costs by £2.5 billion a year within three years. Hester refused to provide any specifics on job losses but did not disagree when analysts suggested 20,000 might go. Goals included returning the bank to profitability by 2012 and enabling the government to sell its stake by the same date. Hester insisted he wanted RBS to remain a 'universal' bank offering a range of services including retail, commercial, corporate and investment banking. Hester also declared the bank's commitment to retaining GBM, which made a stunning operating profit of £4.87 billion in the first half of 2009, as he saw it as 'the engine of the group's recovery'. Rocket fuel was being provided by post-crisis stimulus measures introduced by governments around the world and by the strong performance of the bank's rates and currencies businesses – which specialise in trading swaps and other derivatives linked to interest rates and foreign exchange. Only later did it emerge that, in some of these areas, the bank's strong performance depended, at least in part, on 'cheating' – the bank had been profiting at counterparties' expense through the falsification of Libor rates and, allegedly, also through the manipulation of currency benchmarks etc. Another key part of Hester's strategy was an internal good bank/bad bank split. This meant the RBS balance sheet would be split in two, with the creation of a new 'non-core division' which would have its own management team. It would take responsibility for £240 billion of the group's assets, including £145 billion of derivative balances and £155 billion of risk-weighted assets which would be run off or liquidated over the next three to five years. In the new 'bad bank', 90 per cent of assets would come from Johnny Cameron's GBM. As part of the retrenchment, the bank would be exiting 36 of the 54 countries in which it did business. Critically, the strategic plan was signed off and approved by UKFI and Alistair Darling's Treasury. For the first time since 2008, a modicum of confidence returned to the bank and its shares rose 5.9 per cent to 29p that day.

What the plan did not include, however, was any obvious commitment to changing RBS's culture, rooting out malpractice or upgrading its increasingly decrepit IT infrastructure. One executive said the most stunning statistic that came out of a strategy session held at Gogarburn business school in spring 2009 was that RBS's cash machines had an average age of 20 years. 'Their biggest problem, bar none, is they have crap data processing and piss-poor knowledge management. There was no evidence that Hester was addressing these issues.'

In early March, John Hourican, who took over the GBM reins from Cameron in October 2008, gave a rousing speech to GBM staff in the former ABN AMRO headquarters in Amsterdam. He declared it was time to '[re]invent the business and invent the future'. Hourican claimed that management had spent 14 weeks 'absolutely ripping the bank apart', going through its assets and modelling the risks of those assets against various economic scenarios. Hourican said the £300 billion of assets that were being dumped into the UK taxpayer-insured internal 'bad bank' were ones that had 'some issues' and had been earmarked for sale or wind-down. He said Hester had purchased a 'catastrophe cover piece of insurance' from the UK government which, he claimed, was good enough to ensure the bank could survive Armageddon. He said he was confident that the GBM 'engine room', where he was now chief engineer, was capable of pumping out revenues of £10 billion a year and a return on equity of 20 per cent. 'We should be able to do that without dramatically driving for growth.' Hourican stressed that the government and UKFI were backing the bank to the hilt, despite 80 per cent of GBM's balance sheet being denominated in currencies other than sterling.

Hourican was candid (for a banker) about what had caused RBS's failure. He highlighted woeful risk management and 'awful' back-office systems. He admitted the bank had 'got a little bit complacent in how we manage our risk' and that it was wrong that RBS management had been kept in the dark about certain risks to which the bank had exposed itself. He also said the bank had concentrated its lending on too few individual and corporate borrowers. 'We have, in GBM, 606 names with over £350 million of exposure [each] and we have over 100 names of over £1 billion of exposure [each].'

Hourican said it was totally unacceptable that 1,000 of GBM's 10,000 back-office staff spent their working lives doing nothing other than 'data clean-up and reconciliation' – which sounded horribly like they were airbrushing data to suit their masters' needs. He added, 'You do not want "I was a data cleaner" on your gravestone. It must be one of the most soul-destroying things to do. We have to rescue our people from that shit.' He said the bank was investing £600 million in an IT upgrade in order to reduce the amount of data cleaning the bank needed to do. The Irishman was basically implying that the systems and controls in RBS's investment bank were woefully inadequate. This was confirmed by two subsequent events.

On 24 July 2013, the Financial Conduct Authority fined RBS £5.6 million for shocking lapses in its internal record keeping. The FCA said the investment banking arm had failed to properly report 44.8 million trades between November 2007 and February 2013 and failed altogether to report 804,000 transactions between November 2007 and February 2012. The FCA's director of enforcement, Tracey McDermott, said the failures made effective enforcement all but impossible, adding that they had been aggravated by the bank's acquisition of ABN, which had left RBS with an astonishing mishmash of 38 transaction-recording systems.[9] Further evidence of the inadequacy of GBM's systems and controls emerged a few days later, when it transpired that an unqualified imposter had infiltrated RBS's investment bank and posed as a bond salesman. KK Ho managed to slip through security to attend senior meetings, speak to RBS customers and wander the trading floor. The *Daily Telegraph* said Ho did this through 'duping senior managers by boasting of relationships with wealthy clients and handing out forged business cards'. A former manager in RBS's property services arm, Ho had been laid off by the bank and given a temporary desk so he could look for a new role but he took the opportunity to reinvent himself as a 'big swinging dick'. His deception and continued presence on RBS's Bishopsgate trading floor were only discovered by human resources staff after managers began to question his identity. It was a matter of huge embarrassment to the bank.[10]

In his Gustav Mahlerlaan peroration, Hourican insisted that he wanted to see 'a clearly defined trading mentality' right across GBM. He told employees their underlying assumption should be that everything in RBS was for sale – including business units, loans, portfolios of loans and risk. The unspoken corollary was that clients would get trampled on.

Hourican said staff should ignore the bank's bombed-out share price – 'It just puts you in a bad mood' – and focus instead on its credit default swaps, which he described as a more accurate indicator of its position. He said Hester was 'doing a great job' in keeping UKFI at bay, leaving him free to run the investment bank without too much interference and allowing him to pay people as much as he chose. 'Stephen's job is to deal with the shareholder . . . My job is to run the division and get us as much space to run the division as possible . . . so I am not too often down at Whitehall, and have not met Gordon Brown, thank

God!' Hourican said, unlike Lehman Brothers, RBS was regarded by
the politicians as intrinsic to the global economy – in other words, 'too
big to fail'. He proudly said that the bank had been 'singled out by the
actions of regulators and governments to survive'. He suggested one of
the minor quid pro quos required by the UK government at the time
of the bailouts – that bonuses must be deferred and not paid in cash
– coupled with the more negative light in which bankers were viewed,
had been hard for some bankers to accept. 'We need to stop thinking of
ourselves as having replaced prisoners, prostitutes and politicians at the
bottom of the social order.'[11]

In a gift to the investor groups suing the bank for allegedly misleading them into pumping £12.3 billion into the pre-crash rights issue,
Hourican admitted this fund raising had been 'a reaction to an urgent
need to raise capital'. This implied it was an emergency Band-Aid,
which was at odds with the sales patter of Goodwin and McKillop the
previous April.

Despite having said that bankers' pay was too high and needed
to come down, Hester was willing to throw vast sums at supposedly
talented staff. In August, it emerged the bank was splashing out £7 million in guaranteed bonuses to poach Antonio Polverino, an aggressive
bond salesman, from Merrill Lynch, and new finance director Bruce
Van Saun was expected to be paid an annual package of £5.4 million
similar to his last full-year salary at Bank of New York Mellon. But the
'golden hello' paid to Polverino, one of the largest paid by any bank in
2009, did not inspire much loyalty in the Italian. Once the £7-million,
two-year guaranteed bonus had expired in March 2012, he walked.
Hester argued that the bank was having to pay more to attract and
retain top-performing bankers, after an exodus of staff as a result of its
near-collapse. He also hired Brian Hartzer, 42, the former chief executive of the Australian operations of Australia & New Zealand Banking
Group (ANZ), to take over from Gordon Pell as head of retail, wealth
and Ulster Bank, handing him a £2.2-million, share-based 'golden
hello' on arrival. It also emerged that the head of the investment bank,
John Hourican, was paid a total of £7.5 million in salary and perks,
in 2011. Hester insisted that British taxpayers had a vested interest in
paying for the best employees in order to get RBS back on its feet and
off the government's hands.

Nor was Hester leading by example where high pay was concerned.

On or around 18 June, UKFI signed off a package worth up to £9.6 million a year for Hester. However, it would only deliver this bonanza if the RBS share price, which was languishing at 37p in late June, rose above 70p by 2012. Reports suggested he would receive £6.4 million in long-term incentives and a further £1.6 million in non-cash bonuses over and above his £1.2-million basic salary. He would also receive £420,000 a year pension contribution in lieu of a company pension. Graham Goddard, deputy general secretary of Unite the Union, said Hester's package would be met with 'absolute disbelief' by bank workers. 'Over the last few months, thousands of RBS staff have lost the jobs which gave them just a fraction of Hester's pay. For these workers and their families, the suggestion that the RBS chief executive will be awarded such a bumper pay package will leave a foul taste in their mouths.' However, UKFI defended the package, insisting that its pay awards were based on 'long-term, sustainable performance which rebuilds the businesses of the banks'.

The bank was facing trouble from abroad. Banco Santander, which had dramatically grown its UK business through the acquisitions of Abbey National in 2004 and parts of Bradford & Bingley and Alliance & Leicester in 2008, had, since January 2009, been lobbying European Competition Commissioner Neelie Kroes to launch a 'state-aid' investigation into both RBS and Lloyds. Botín, then 74, wanted Kroes to force a break-up of both RBS and Lloyds so he could cherry-pick the best bits at fire-sale prices and bolt these on to his existing Abbey operation, run by António Horta-Osório. Fresh from driving through a tough restructuring of two German banks that had also benefited from state aid, Kroes, a diminutive 68-year-old Dutchwoman, launched a tirade against complacent UK politicians who were content to leave RBS in its current form. She told the 300 or so delegates at the British Bankers Association (BBA) conference in Merchant Taylors Hall on 30 June there was a better way: '[RBS] is not a bank with a sustainable business approach. It is not possible to deny the need for change in such a bank or the system that supervised it. This bank was not merely too big to fail, it was: too big to supervise; too big to operate; too complex to understand and highly dangerous to the European Single Market . . .

'For me, a win–win situation means: the banks are viable without state support; the taxpayers escape a huge bill; non-aided banks are not punished because of aid given; the bank [RBS] has a business model

that reduces systemic risk. So we will be working with the UK government to achieve this . . . I appeal again to your self-interest. There can't
be a second bailout.'[12]

Kroes' intervention threw a spanner in the works for Darling. His
vision, if he had one, was to keep 'too big to fail' banks like RBS and
Lloyds intact and just sort of hope they kind of recovered. The MP
for Edinburgh South-West seemed to think this could be achieved by
hiring investment bankers to run them and letting them return to the
'casino' with chips from the taxpayer. Kroes' intervention was also
a slap in the face for the BBA's chief executive Angela Knight, who
opposed break-ups. Many British bankers seemed ignorant of the EU's
state-aid remedies and that Kroes had enforced some 100 restructurings on bailed-out European banks over the previous nine months. For
many British taxpayers, however, Kroes's intervention came as a breath
of fresh air. At last, someone seemed to be willing to stand up to the
banks instead of just handing them billions and mollycoddling them.

Kroes spent from June to October 2009 in talks with the UK Treasury
about which parts of RBS's busted empire should be earmarked for
sale. Leading the talks for the government were Permanent Secretary to
the Treasury Nicholas Macpherson and Second Permanent Secretary
Tom Scholar. Hester was perplexed that the Treasury, which had given
its blessing to a five-year strategic plan that was predicated on the
retention of GBM and Citizens in February, was now going behind his
back to tell Kroes these were the government's favoured disposals. The
Treasury's U-turn was based on political, not commercial, considera-
tions. Darling's department had decided that continued ownership of
GBM and Citizens would become a running sore, not least because of
the bonuses they insisted on doling out, which cabinet ministers such
as Deputy Leader Harriet Harman regarded as an aberration. Hester
saw the Treasury as treacherous. One former RBS insider said, 'Rather
than defending the man that he had appointed and the strategy he had
signed off in January, Darling saw the [state-aid remedies] process as a
means of orchestrating a break-up of RBS by the back door – which
they could then blame on Europe.'

At a bruising encounter in Brussels on Friday 30 October, Kroes told
Hester that RBS would have to dispose of Citizens, the private banking
arm Coutts & Co. and Global Transaction Services (the best business
the Edinburgh-based bank had acquired with ABN), as well as large

chunks of GBM. But Hester accused Kroes of enforcing 'pound of flesh' remedies that would derail his recovery plan, cause 'a £9-billion loss of value in RBS' and hurt UK taxpayers. He reminded her that the bank was shrinking its balance sheet by some 40 per cent and that, under a scheme called 'Project Rainbow', it was prepared to sell 318 of its UK branches – a move that would be far more positive for competition in UK banking than the Treasury proposals she was fronting. In desperation, towards the end of the meeting, he offered to throw in RBS's insurance businesses – Direct Line, Churchill and Green Flag – for luck. But Kroes refused to budge.

Returning from the Belgian capital on Eurostar, a dejected Hester bumped into Jon Cunliffe, head of Gordon Brown's European and Global Issues Secretariat. He discovered that, by a stroke of luck, Brown was also on board, returning from an EU summit. Hester walked up the train to Brown's carriage. He told the prime minister of his frustration and disappointment with the Treasury's behaviour. He reminded him that his government had signed off a five-year strategy for RBS in February before warning Brown that the remedies Kroes was trying to force through with Treasury backing would destabilise the bank and prevent taxpayers from getting a return on their investment, and would do nothing to increase competition in the UK. Brown told Hester not to worry – he would deal with it.

Brown did intervene, overruling Macpherson, Scholar and Darling and insisting the assets on Kroes's 'sacrifice table' be switched before anyone got out a knife. So Hester won the battle – RBS was allowed to keep the businesses it wanted and, instead, it would be sacrificing the energy-trading business Sempra, the 318 former Williams & Glyn's branches and its insurance businesses including Direct Line. Kroes warned that if RBS failed to meet the EU's targets for balance sheet reductions it would be required to make further disposals.[13] In a later House of Commons debate on the banking sector, the Liberal Democrat Vince Cable said he welcomed the enforced disposals as he believed it would 'stop the process by which banks have long been ripping off their customers'.[14]

The economic backdrop was dire. The main index of UK commercial property prices plunged 44 per cent between June 2007 and July 2009. In Ireland, commercial property valuations fell by between 70 and 80 per cent. This was wreaking havoc with RBS's viability since so much of its lending had been to the commercial real-estate sector. The British economy was mired in its longest recession on record, with a surprise 0.4 per cent drop in gross domestic product in the third quarter of 2009. And the picture was even bleaker in Ireland, where RBS's lending had, if anything, been even worse.

By autumn 2009 the government was yet again forced to admit that the bank was in an even worse state than it had thought. On 3 November, the government poured a further £39 billion into Royal Bank of Scotland through a new programme dubbed 'Financial Stability Measures', £25.5 billion of which was intravenously injected as fresh capital. This took the total amount of capital that taxpayers had put into RBS to £45.5 billion, making RBS the most expensive bank in the world to bail out. The government had increased its stake to 84 per cent, making the fiction of RBS's independence harder to sustain. The government also pledged to put a further £8 billion of capital into the bank if necessary and unveiled some modifications to the asset protection scheme – without which it would have been categorised as a state subsidy under EU rules. The first year's premium was set at £700 million and the pool of assets insured was reduced to £282 billion. Lloyds, which had intended to sign up to the APS in January, managed to exit the scheme but only after paying a penalty fee and promising further capital raisings. In a bid to quell further rows over bonuses, the Treasury required both Lloyds and RBS to pledge not to pay discretionary cash bonuses to any staff earning above £39,000 in 2009 and to defer all bonuses until 2012. This drove some RBS investment bankers to dust down their CVs.

Following this third bailout of RBS, the Labour MP Michael Meacher asked Darling in the House of Commons, 'Why is my right honourable Friend so enamoured of this busted, out-of-control, casino-market model of banking which costs the taxpayer such gargantuan sums?' Darling, still eager to feed the monster that RBS had become, and perhaps naive about banks and banking, said he thought that having 'a properly functioning commercial banking system is quite a good thing'.[15]

False dawn

Initially, everything seemed to go swimmingly for Stephen Hester. In the year to December 2009, his first full year as chief executive, Global Banking and Markets turned in a profit of £5.7 billion and a return on equity of 30 per cent. It was a Lazarus-like performance, given that the unit had notched up an operating loss of £11 billion in 2008. The £5.7 billion – five times more than the profits made by RBS's UK retail bank – also represented a racing start for John Hourican, who took GBM's reins in October 2008. Hourican was renowned inside the bank for his samba dancing skills – he had shown these off at RBS's leveraged finance team Christmas party in 2000, where he drew plaudits for his dance with two semi-clad female Brazilian dancers. Now he was showing similar prowess as head of the investment bank. But there were other significant factors at play – and the board may have made the mistake of confusing genius with a bull market. A fair amount of GBM's turbocharged performance was being driven by the Bank of England's quantitative easing programme, the fact that other central banks worldwide had also been flooding the markets with liquidity and also, especially in rates and currencies, that some of its traders were cheating. GBM's performance was also flattered since it had been able to toss many of its toxic deals into the newly created 'non-core' division where they would cease to be a drag on perceived performance.

Hester said that 'the heavy lifting' was being done in the 'non-core' division and that this enabled the bank's core businesses to support customers despite the de-leveraging of the group. With the benefit of hindsight, Hester's turnaround strategy was naive. It depended on a number of assumptions about banking and economics in a post-financial crisis world, all of which were wrong. The assumptions seemed to include:

(1)   that there would be a 'V-shaped recovery' – the sharp decline that the UK and global economies suffered would be followed by a rapid recovery from the crisis;

(2)   that the government, after a brief period of accommodating the bailed-out banks including RBS in a state-sponsored intensive care ward, would be able to rapidly 'flip' them back into the private sector at a profit;

(3)   that financial regulators would not dramatically clamp down on banks' trading or other activities post-crisis – for example, by demanding that banks set more capital against trading activities;

(4)   that the EU state-aid remedies would somehow not apply to banks the UK government had rescued;[1]

(5)   that it would be possible for a gigantic investment banking operation, with its trading mindset, penchant for risk-taking and self-serving bonus culture, to exist under public ownership.

Hester's defence of the 'universal' model became trickier after the Independent Commission on Banking (ICB) hammered several nails in its coffin. The commission was launched by Prime Minister David Cameron in June 2010 so that he could kick the increasingly contentious issue of bank reform into the long grass while the coalition found its feet. The commission – led by economics professor and warden of All Souls College, Oxford University, Sir John Vickers – deliberated for 15 months. During this time, Cameron was able to deflect questions about banking by citing the fact that a commission was under way. It also meant the government allowed Hester to run RBS as he saw fit. Senior RBS insiders refer to May 2010 through to October 2011 as 'the period of maximum laissez-faire'.

The honeymoon of non-interventionism ended on 12 October when Vickers' commission produced a series of recommendations including that universal banks such as RBS, HSBC and Barclays should, at least in the UK, split themselves in two by erecting a 'ring fence' between their investment banking arms and their retail banking activities. Another was that they should maintain higher core tier-1 capital ratios

– 10 per cent – than those recommended by Basel III – 7 per cent. The reforms were accepted by Chancellor George Osborne and a version of them was implemented in the UK's Financial Services (Banking Reform) Act 2013, enacted in December 2013. Even after this became government policy, Hester huffily refused to go along with it. He criticised the proposals on BBC One's *The Andrew Marr Show*, arguing that a ring fence would undermine RBS's value and harm stakeholders' interests without actually making the bank any safer. Politicians and regulators were taken aback. They had assumed Hester would fall into line and be supportive of the ring-fence idea and take it as his cue to exit investment banking. A senior RBS insider said, 'Unlike António Horta-Osório [chief executive of Lloyds Banking Group], Stephen wasn't prepared to be malleable – that was a turning point in terms of relations with the government.'

The eurozone crisis further queered Hester's pitch. It started in October 2009 when Greece upwardly revised its budget deficit from 3.7 per cent of gross domestic product to 12.5 per cent of GDP. This put the country at risk of defaulting on its bonds and triggered a €110-billion bailout from the International Monetary Fund, the European Central Bank and the European Union, a grouping which later became known as 'the troika', in May 2010. In sharp contrast to Gordon Brown's banking bailouts, the rescue package came with harsh conditions attached, including an austerity programme. The next eurozone dominoes to fall were Ireland (which needed an €85-billion troika bailout in November 2010), Portugal (€78 billion, May 2011), Greece (a second bailout of €130 billion in March 2012), Spain (a banking bailout of €39.5 billion in December 2012) and Cyprus (€10 billion, May 2013). The crisis, which at its height became an existential one for the euro currency, also morphed into a banking crisis, while giving the lie to the notion that European nations would never default on their debts. One side effect of the crisis was it made British regulators much, much more wary of sprawling financial conglomerates like RBS.

With €68.7 billion of eurozone sovereign debt on its books, RBS was the bank with the third largest exposure in Europe.[2] In February 2012, the bank revealed it had a £1.45-billion portfolio of Greek government bonds, acquired with ABN AMRO. RBS could have offloaded these for a reasonable sum in the early stages of the crisis. However, it held on to them and sat idly by as their value plunged by 79 per cent.[3] Traders at rival banks claim RBS was writing large amounts of credit default swaps on Greek sovereign debt 'on a bogus theory that it could "never trigger" '.[4] It was around this time that Hester said, in an interview, 'We've got our tin hats on' in readiness for further fall-out from the eurozone crisis and regulatory reforms.[5] Speaking in his New Jersey drawl in February 2012, RBS's finance director Bruce Van Saun admitted things were far worse than the bank had anticipated when it finalised its recovery plan. He said, 'The drag from Europe and some of the tightening that's required in the UK to put it back on a firm fiscal position is leading to a slower recovery, and a lower interest rate environment than we expected going into the plan.'[6]

But then, on 26 July 2012, the president of the European Central Bank, former Goldman Sachs executive Mario Draghi, came to RBS's rescue. He said he was prepared to do whatever it took to save the collapsing euro. The rhetoric, coupled with some tweaking of whether the ECB was permitted to buy the sovereign bonds of EU member states, worked and gave markets and near-bust 'zombie' banks across Europe a new lease of life. However, the attitude of regulators – particularly the Bank of England's Mervyn King and the FSA's Andrew Bailey, a former chief cashier at the Bank of England who is now chief executive of the Prudential Regulation Authority (PRA) – was hardening towards RBS, amid concerns it was being less than candid about the valuations of its commercial property loans and other assets on its balance sheet. In a major blow for Hester, the Financial Policy Committee of the Bank of England told RBS in December 2011 that it must reduce the total risk-weighted assets in its investment bank by at least a third. The pressure to shrink the markets business was also channelled by George Osborne, the Treasury and UKFI. On 19 December 2011, Osborne told the Commons that the bank had made significant changes since 2008, including halving the size of its investment bank. However, he added, '[B]ut I believe RBS needs to go further . . . We believe RBS's future is as a major UK bank, with the majority of its business in the UK and in personal, SME and corporate banking . . . RBS will make further significant reductions in the investment bank, scaling back riskier activities that are heavy users of capital or funding.'[7] At the time, senior people in RBS, the FSA and the Bank of England would have been aware of an ongoing regulatory probe into Libor rigging by the bank.

Hester, conscious he was losing his battle to keep RBS as a universal bank, responded by axing more than half of the 20,000 jobs in RBS's investment banking arm over the next 18 months. This prompted the US publication *Dealbreaker* to run a story saying, 'Pretty ugly over there [RBS Securities in Stamford]. The Queen's Bitches are being slaughtered'.[8] ('Queen's Bitches' was apparently a nickname given to the bank's Connecticut-based investment bankers and traders.) There were few takers for units and divisions that he sought to sell. The enforced dismantling started in February 2012 with the 'sale' of corporate brokers Hoare Govett, which had come into the RBS fold with ABN AMRO, to the US brokerage Jefferies. But it wasn't really a sale – it was more of a giveaway, with the City stockbroker reportedly sold for £1. RBS also tried to sell its cash equities business but failed to find a buyer and the business was closed in February 2012, causing 300 redundancies. RBS had more luck with its Asian equities business, which employed roughly 400 people, selling this to the Malaysian bank CIMB Group in April 2012. The Edinburgh-based bank also sold its 70-strong equity capital markets and deals advisory business in Holland back to the bank it had bought five years earlier, ABN AMRO, parts of which had reverted to Dutch ownership following the collapse of Fortis. The next stage came in December 2012 when, after failing to find any takers, RBS closed its UK-based mergers and acquisitions advisory business. Its total earnings had plummeted from $436 million in 2007 to $74 million in 2012 and so RBS's 40 M&A bankers were made redundant. On Thursday, 13 June 2013, in response to further pressure from the PRA, the bank said it would shed a further 2,000 investment banking jobs over the next 18 months as it was exiting equity derivatives and retail structured products, while running down peripheral eurozone government bond market making. Many of these were fairly capital-intensive areas. The goal was to refocus on fixed income across foreign exchange rates, debt capital markets and credit- and asset-backed securities.

RBS's rump investment bank, whose name was changed to Markets & International Banking (M&IB) in February 2012, had become a pale shadow of its former self, even though it now also included Global Transaction Services, formerly part of ABN. It had become a pretty miserable place to work, with the regular purges being accompanied by backbiting, recrimination and sometimes high emotion. At times 'open civil war' broke out inside its 280 and 250 Bishopsgate offices, complete with fist fights and police raids. Managers felt let down by Hester, accusing him of becoming a puppet of the government. 'He has always said to us that none of this is being driven by the political agenda, but he is not really believed,' said one insider.[9]

The co-chief executives of RBS M&IB, Peter Nielsen and Suneel Kamlani, sought to put a brave face on the enforced shrinkage of their division, saying, 'We have every intention of maintaining our presence as a global flow powerhouse.'[10] The bank also said it was concentrating risk management in four trading hubs – London, Stamford, Singapore and Tokyo. Nielsen and Kamlani added that the markets unit would be further reducing its balance sheet, with a target of £80 billion by the end of 2014.[11]

International Financing Review's editor-at-large, Keith Mullin, said, 'I do wonder about the future of the division, though. Through the restructuring, the proportion of group assets accounted for by markets has been slashed from 56 per cent to 22 per cent as the group exited products and sold businesses . . . Has the markets division been prepped for sale? People discount a break-up of the group but I'm not so sure.'[12]

The number of staff employed by the investment bank collapsed from more than 20,000 at its swaggering peak to below 9,000. Overall the government wanted Hester to render the division safe by forcing it to focus on providing add-on services to RBS's corporate banking customers and blocking it from proprietary trading (trading on its own account). 'Our goal from these changes is to be more focused for customers, more conservatively funded, more efficient and with better, more stable returns for shareholders overall,' said Hester.[13]

As chancellor, George Osborne opposed the idea that a single penny of UK taxpayer-provided capital should go to support Citizens Financial. In December 2011, he told the House of Commons, that he wanted RBS to sell the Rhode Island-based lender and to do it quickly. UKFI, however, managed to persuade him against quick sale, believing the unit would command a better price if a sale were delayed until the US economy had recovered. In September 2012, a compromise agreement was reached. In a plan endorsed by the PRA and UKFI, RBS announced it would be offloading Citizens through an initial public offering in 2014 or 2015. The Rhode Island-based lender was expected to be worth in the region of $9–15 billion (£5.6–9.3 billion) but after Citizens failed a US Federal Reserve 'stress test' in March 2014, such

a valuation looks like pie-in-the-sky. Battles with the Treasury, UKFI
and the Prudential Regulation Authority were beginning to wear
Hester down. He was particularly irritated when, in August 2012,
Business Secretary Vince Cable, a senior Liberal Democrat member
of the UK's coalition government, said he wanted to see RBS fully
nationalised. Cable argued this was the only way to ensure the bank
lent to the enfeebled UK economy, especially to small and medium-
sized firms. Former Liberal Democrat Treasury spokesperson Lord
Oakeshott backed him, saying, 'If RBS, the worst non-lender by far,
won't do its basic job, we must nationalise it – it's not Marxism, just
common sense.'[14] But Osborne opposed such a move and a Treasury
spokesman said, 'The government's policy has always been to return
RBS to the private sector but only when it delivers value for money for
the taxpayer.'[15]

Hester's reasons for defending the universal banking model were
wearing even thinner after RBS was found to have engaged in a long-
running campaign to rig the London Interbank Offered Rate (Libor) –
a crucial interest rate on which the price of $350 trillion of derivatives
and other financial instruments is based – as part of a wider conspiracy
involving other global banks and interdealer brokers. Libor is set by a
panel of around 20 large global banks. Each day at 11 a.m., they are
supposed to submit the rates at which they are able to borrow money
from other banks – for a range of currencies and time spans – to the
Libor panel at the British Bankers Association, which then knocks out
the top two and bottom two numbers before averaging out the rest
to create the rate. But a bunch of sleazy and bonus-crazed traders at
RBS found ways of manipulating the rate by putting in false submissions in collusion with their peers at other banks, using brokerages as
Trojan horses, in order to flatter profits and turbocharge bonuses. At
RBS, the markets division was prospering on the back of rigged rates
for at least half a decade. According to regulators, the main period
when the crimes occurred was from January 2006 to November 2010.
Alleged perpetrators, such as Neil Danziger, were sitting at the heart
of RBS's investment banking arm, in its rates division and on trading
floors in London, Singapore, Tokyo and elsewhere. Danziger's trades
generated rich pickings for the brokers, who entertained him lavishly
in exchange, according to the *Wall Street Journal*. He was allegedly taken
to strip clubs and spent long weekends with them in Las Vegas. *WSJ*

European banking editor David Enrich says, 'Traders and brokers have always enjoyed chummy, symbiotic relationships. But ... efforts to curry favour escalated from expense-account meals and night-time carousing to more legally questionable activities ... Brokers have paid for traders to spend weekends in the Alps and Saint-Tropez, and on occasion, have even bought them cocaine or prostitutes.'[16] Danziger, a 38-year-old born in South Africa, has not been charged with any wrongdoing.

The anonymised regulatory documents from the FSA, Commodities Futures Trading Commission (CFTC) and US Department of Justice (DoJ) provide countless examples of malpractice by RBS personnel. According to the FSA, 'Improper requests took place over a number of years, were widespread, and involved three benchmark rates and at least 21 derivatives traders and primary submitters located primarily in London and Tokyo but also in the United States and Singapore.'[17] Other current and former RBS traders and submitters who have been named as having had some involvement in the scandal include Brent Davies, Tom Hayes and Paul White. At the time of writing, only Hayes has been charged – with eight criminal counts of conspiracy to defraud – though some of the 21 others with whom he is alleged to have conspired have been indicted by the court. The trial of Hayes, who worked at RBS from 2001–03, and is thought to have learnt some of his benchmark rigging skills there, is due to commence in 2015.

The day of reckoning for RBS came on 6 February 2013. After a two-year investigation, the CFTC, DOJ and the FSA whacked the bank with record fines of $612 million (£390 million). 'We are holding RBS accountable for a stunning abuse of trust,' said assistant US attorney general Lanny Breuer. 'Our message is clear: no financial institution is above the law.'[18]

The regulators released a slew of embarrassing emails and instant messages from RBS traders. In response to messages from traders from 'Bank A' and 'Bank B', on 20 August 2007, one RBS senior yen trader wrote: 'Yes[,] he always led usd in my mkt[,] the jpy libor is a cartel now ... its just amazing how libor fixing can make you that much money ... Its a cartel now in london[.]'[19]

Managers within RBS Global Banking and Markets were aware of and condoned the multi-bank conspiracy to defraud. The CFTC concluded, for example, that 'the manager responsible for RBS's global yen derivatives trading was not only aware of improper requests for false submissions by others, but also personally asked . . . traders . . . to submit rates to benefit his positions.'[20]

Embarrassingly for Hester, Libor-rigging was found to have gone on for nearly as long under his stewardship – two years and one month – as it had done under Goodwin's – two years and ten months. And, even more embarrassingly for Hester, RBS traders continued to rig yen Libor and Swiss franc Libor, even after the CFTC asked the bank to conduct an internal investigation of its Libor-setting practices in April 2010. The traders carried on regardless, seeking to cover their tracks by sending each other fewer instant messages.

Also, in what some regard as an attempted cover-up, an unnamed senior manager in RBS wrote back to the FSA after it requested written evidence that the bank's systems and controls relating to Libor submissions were up to scratch. In a letter dated 21 March 2011, the senior manager claimed, 'Group Internal Audit has conducted a review of the Libor setting process and the issues raised are being addressed to their satisfaction. Thus, on that basis I confirm that RBS has in place adequate systems and controls for the determination and submissions of its Libor rates.'[21] This was either misleading or a deliberate lie. RBS's systems and controls for Libor submission were still inadequate. All of this enraged the regulators and reinforced the impression that RBS was a rogue institution.

Bill Black, a former senior regulator in the US who is now an associate professor of economics and law at the University of Missouri-Kansas City, said, 'This is the biggest scandal, the biggest anti-trust felony, in the history of the world, and it continued for years. Even after the investigation became public knowledge, the felony continued, and it continued with greater efforts being made to cover it up.'[22] There was renewed clamour for prosecutions. In a debate in the Commons, Labour MP John McDonnell said, 'My constituents now look on the City of London as a fetid swamp of corruption. They see only people forgoing bonuses but no one being imprisoned for the swindles that have taken place.'[23]

At 7 p.m. that night Hester told Channel 4 News's Krishnan Guru-Murthy he saw no need to resign.[24] The government and the bank had already let it be known that the chief executive of M&IB, John Hourican, would be resigning – a move designed to take the heat off Hester. Speaking to the Parliamentary Commission on Banking Standards a few days later, Hampton ominously hinted that Libor was not a one-off. 'We have a major programme of control, remediation and improvement right across the group, but specifically concentrated in the markets business. Libor is an egregious example, but it is not the only example of control failings in that business.'[25] In an interview with John Humphrys on BBC Radio 4's *Today* programme in August 2012, Hester admitted that banks had become 'detached from society' and needed to reconnect with their customers. He said that the sector was 'coming down to earth with a bump' following the spate of scandals. Regarding the possibility of banks discovering additional problems, he said, 'Of course there is still a risk that you turn over rocks and find new things [that you have to clean up].'[26]

The fallout from the Libor scandal is far from over. In addition to Hayes, three former employees of UK brokers ICAP – Darrell Read, Daniel Wilkinson and Colin Goodman – are facing trial in the US. If found guilty, they could face jail terms of up to 30 years. ICAP has already been fined $87 million (£54 million) for its part in the Libor scandal and other bankers and brokers are also likely to face criminal charges. However, the senior bankers whose divisional success and personal bonuses were inflated by the fraud are expected to be let off the hook by continuing to plead ignorance, to scapegoat their minions and argue that 'it wisnae us'. On 4 December 2013, RBS shareholders had to shell out a further €391 million (£324 million) after a European Commission probe found the bank had formed a cartel with supposed rivals, including Société Générale, JPMorgan, Citigroup and Deutsche Bank, to rig both yen Libor and Euribor (the euro currency's equivalent of Libor). RBS chose to settle with Brussels to ensure a reduced fine. Barclays and UBS escaped fines altogether because they blew the whistle on their co-conspirators and co-operated with the EU authorities. In a statement, Sir Philip Hampton said, 'We acknowledged back in February that there were serious shortcomings in our systems and controls on this issue, but also in the integrity of a very small number of our employees. Today is another sobering reminder of those past failings and nobody should be in any doubt about how seriously we have taken this issue.'[27]

Numerous other official regulatory probes into RBS's rigging of Libor and related benchmarks are still under way, including ones in

Japan, Singapore and Switzerland. The bank may also be on the hook to pay up to £80 billion in compensation to investors, including pension funds, US cities, public sector entities and other financial market participants, who lost money as a result of its rigging of Libor and related benchmarks. RBS has already been named as a defendant in scores of Libor-related lawsuits in the US.[28] One of the latest came from Fannie Mae, which is suing RBS and eight other banks over the $800 million of losses it claimed were incurred as a result of the banks' rigging of benchmark rates, including Libor.

Some analysts see Libor as banking's 'tobacco moment'. In March 1997, the tide turned for the tobacco industry. After years of denial and as part of a settlement of lawsuits in 22 US states, the maker of Chesterfield cigarettes, Liggett & Company, admitted that its products caused cancer. It was a breakthrough that changed the tobacco industry forever and culminated in companies having to pay out compensation over many years and the industry becoming a pariah. The Libor settlements of 2012–13, in which banks including RBS have admitted to criminal wrongdoing, may have similar painful consequences for the banking sector.

Despite the pain of the Libor settlement and the government's insistence that it should wind down its increasingly toxic investment bank, RBS persists with some fairly high-risk activities. Back in August 2008, long after it was evident that the US mortgage market was rotten to the core, Symon Drake-Brockman, by then promoted to chief executive of RBS Global Banking and Markets in the Americas, hired a 50-strong mortgage team from Bear Stearns, led by Scott Eichel and Dave Cannon. The legacy mortgage-backed securities and CDOs were reassigned to the bank's non-core division. Eichel and Cannon and their team arrived at RBS Greenwich Capital at a time when the price of mortgage assets was at rock bottom but they started running a trading-oriented structured mortgage and structured credit business. Their performance has been stellar ever since, thanks to the quantitative easing programme (QE) of Ben Bernanke, who succeeded Greenspan as chairman of the US Federal Reserve in February 2006. QE, also known as 'money printing', was a monetary policy introduced by the Bernanke's Federal Reserve in December 2008 and the Bank of England in March 2009. The aim was to boost consumer spending and economic activity at a time when the effects of conventional monetary policy – lowering or raising interest rates – were blunted by ultra-low interest rates. Under QE, the central bank creates new money which it uses to buy government bonds and mortgage-backed securities from private banks. This floods the banks and financial institutions with liquidity, giving them a greater incentive to lend and invest, thereby promoting economic activity. That's the theory anyway.

One ex-senior executive from GBM said: 'Scott Eichel and the ex-Bear mortgage traders are running huge and complex risks and, if the takeaway from the crisis was that people did not want banks to do that sort of stuff any more, well, GBM are still doing it in spades. In fact, it's been one of their big drivers!

'The one lesson of the crisis was supposed to be, "don't let a strong P&L blind you to how that P&L is being made". People like Hester and the audit committee chairman Brendan Nelson just avert their gaze and just accept that making huge profits is all that matters!

'Culturally these are supposed "rock-star" traders. The board is just not asking any questions and ignoring the risk factors. If Vince Cable understood that an 83 per cent government-owned institution was making over £1 billion a year for the past couple of years just from that one team of mortgage traders, on what might be deemed an extreme form of "casino banking", I suspect he'd be horrified. It's the sort of thing we were supposed to have got rid of post-crisis.'

Scott Eichel, now RBS's global head of asset-backed products and credit trading, last year insisted his unit has been taking a more risk-averse approach. In an emailed statement dated 30 July 2013, Eichel said that, across Wall Street, 'business models are changing due to the regulatory environment, which has led to higher capital ratios, lower liquidity and the shift to more electronic trading'.[29] In April 2014, RBS's head of securitised credit trading, Adam Siegel, who reports to Eichel, was placed on leave. This was linked to a widening US government probe of the fraudulent sale of asset-backed securities by banks to Washington's Public-Private Investment Programme.[30]

Though Hester comes across as a decent guy and was an accomplished performer in front of critical panels such as the Treasury Select Committee, he never fully grasped the extent to which the public mood towards bankers had changed as a result of the bailouts and crisis. He was always going to be on a hiding to nothing with his desire to maintain RBS as a global universal bank. 'Hester has never acknowledged that the rules have changed since he came up with the strategy,' said one City grandee. 'It's very difficult to make money in investment banking now.'[31] And one of Hester's failures was his apparent tolerance of systemic wrongdoing in large areas of the bank.

33

Hester's ledger

Was Stephen Hester a success or a failure in his five years as Royal Bank of Scotland chief executive? And was he even the right man for the job? In order to answer these questions, it is necessary to break down his performance into a number of areas. I have chosen to focus on four: financial performance; shrinking the bank; the battle over bonuses; and conduct, culture and ethics. Hester's relations with the government and regulators are mainly covered in Chapter 36.

Financial performance

Through asset sales and some fancy hedging footwork, Hester managed to halve the RBS balance sheet to £806 billion by his final day as chief executive, 30 September 2013. Risk-weighted assets had been reduced to £410 billion. The bank's loan-to-deposit ratio fell from 154 per cent in 2008 to 94 per cent on the same autumn day, meaning RBS was covering its lending with its own deposits. The group's liquidity portfolio – cash or assets that can readily be sold for cash – had risen from £90 billion in December 2008 to £151 billion on 30 September 2013. Hester also managed to cut the bank's dependence on short-term wholesale funding from £297 billion to £35 billion as of 30 September 2013 and reduced its leverage ratio to 3.6 per cent. Under Hester, the bank also repaid £500 billion of emergency loans and guarantees received from the Bank of England at the height of the crisis. RBS's core tier-1 capital ratio was boosted from just 4 per cent under the old Basel II definition to 11.6 per cent on 30 September 2013 under the more stringent Basel 2.5 rules (a halfway house between Basel II and Basel III which, at the time of writing, hadn't become effective yet). Taken together, that is no mean feat.

However, one must be wary of some of the figures. For example, it emerged in June 2013 that a tenth of RBS's core tier-1 capital was made up of deferred promises not to have to pay corporation tax for years. The bank believed it could treat the deferred tax as an asset because, under conventional accounting standards, the losses RBS had racked up since 2008 could be booked against future profits for the purposes of corporation tax.[1]

In terms of share-price performance, Hester was a disaster. For mainly cosmetic reasons, he carried out a ten-for-one share split in May 2012. A shareholder with 10 shares worth 20p each at the time would instead have found themselves the proud owner of a single share worth £2. This deceptive ploy was rubber-stamped by shareholders at the bank's annual general meeting in Gogarburn on 31 May 2012 but it could not mask the fact that the value of RBS shares halved during Hester's five years as chief executive. They were down from 655p on 13 October 2008, the day he was announced as Goodwin's successor, to 327p at the time of writing.

Between 2008 and 2013, RBS declared total losses of nearly £46 billion, partly as a consequence of asset price write-downs, revaluation of its own debt and the huge costs of mopping up the consequences of rampant wrongdoing before and after the bailout. For the year ended December 2012, the bank's declared losses climbed to £5.2 billion, up from £2 billion in 2011. The huge loss was incurred even though operating profits from its core business grew to £6.341 billion. In the year to December 2013 losses rose to £8.24 billion. In keeping with other results under Hester, a respectable operating performance was wiped out by exceptional items, goodwill write-downs (because Fred kept paying way over the odds for acquisitions), provisions for bad debts and provisions to cover the escalating cost of litigation and redress, with seemingly perverse accounting requirements relating to the cost of the bank's own debt thrown in. The bank was doing the financial equivalent of running up the down escalator. Even five years after Goodwin was thrown out the door, the sins of the past keep coming back to floor it. And that will continue to happen for many years to come.

The biggest consistent thorn in the bank's side was Ulster Bank. Under blue-eyed boy Cormac McCarthy, Ulster Bank abandoned Presbyterian probity and engaged in some extraordinarily cavalier financial debauchery. It opened the lending taps and lent reckless

billions into Ireland's stretched property bubble as part of its insane
Journey2One strategy. And the losses on those loans keep washing
in year after year. For 2013, Ulster Bank declared losses of over £1.5
billion, up from £1 billion in 2012. Presenting the 2012 results, New
Jersey-born finance director Bruce Van Saun said, 'We also have been
losing our shirt in Ireland.' And RBS will keep losing it for some years
to come and is currently looking at ways of ridding itself of the Ulster
operations in the Republic.

Despite the injection of an astonishing £15 billion of capital since
the crisis – nearly half the total sum that was injected into RBS by
British taxpayers in 2008–9 – and even after £18 billion of the bank's
most radioactive assets had been transferred to RBS's non-core division
– that is nearly half the assets accumulated on McCarthy's disastrous
watch, Ulster remains a basket case.

In the UK, Royal Bank's core business, which includes NatWest,
has been suffering from the double bind of high funding costs and
reduced income from lending. During 2012, the stagnant UK economy
and already high levels of personal indebtedness slowed new lending
as heavily indebted borrowers were reluctant to borrow more and preferred to pay off their existing borrowings, while the high costs of funding coupled with low interest rates on pre-existing lending squeezed the
bank's interest margins. The introduction of the government's Funding
for Lending Scheme (FLS) in July 2012 may have eased the funding
pressure but it did little to encourage lending – RBS reduced its overall
lending by £2.35 billion in the second half of 2012 despite obtaining £750 million in cheap funding from the FLS scheme. The bank
has faced repeated and justifiable criticism over its lending to SMEs.
According to a report written by the former Bank of England deputy
governor Sir Andrew Large, RBS's share of SME lending fell from 42
per cent of net lending before October 2008 to 27 per cent five years
later. That was partly because the bank reduced the length of time it
was prepared to lend for and imposed much more onerous conditions
on business loans as it sought to deleverage itself. The Large Report,
described as 'independent' even though it was commissioned by the
bank, added that 'risk aversion' among RBS bankers and cumbersome
internal structures meant credit-worthy business customers were being
turned away.

Nearly six years on from its near-demise, RBS has made some

impressive progress, but has not yet turned the corner. RBS was riddled with bad lending, bad business practices, bad culture and bad management. The strategy of splitting it in two and gradually running down legacy assets left it too weak to lend productively which, for a bank of such significance, had atrocious economic consequences, especially in Scotland, where RBS and Lloyds Banking Group have more than 70 per cent of the market between them.

Honey, I shrank the bank

Bloomberg called it 'the world's worst bank' and said it was run by 'a silver-haired Scot' from a fifth-floor office overlooking Liverpool Street Station.[2] The wire service was referring to RBS's non-core division which Hester created in 2009. In his BBC interview with Andrew Marr on Sunday, 8 February 2012, Hester explained that one of his three main tasks at RBS was to defuse the 'biggest time bomb ever put on a bank balance sheet and dismantle it safely'.[3] He was referring to £258 billion of less attractive assets which the bank had separated out and placed in its internal 'bad bank'. While the *Financial Times* described the process of getting rid of these assets as 'among the most dramatic shrinkages of any bank in the world',[4] critics have claimed that the bank sold off the 'easier stuff' – the more attractive of these assets – first and often at fire-sale prices. The paucity of buyers at the height of the global downturn meant some of these assets were given away. However, the scale of the challenge and the speed with which it was carried out – all but £28 billion of the original £258 billion of non-core assets had been disposed of by the time of writing – marked it out as a big success for Hester.

Hester turned to Rory Cullinan to lead the new non-core division. Before returning to RBS in 2009, Cullinan was co-managing partner of the Moscow-based investment bank Renaissance Capital, in whose employ he roamed Africa and Russia in search of deals. Before that the Scot was RBS's head of equity finance under Fred Goodwin between 2001 and 2005. This meant he was selling off some of the stuff he had bought.

Cullinan put together a team of more than 600 bankers, traders and analysts to offload the unwanted assets. According to *Bloomberg Markets Magazine*, they 'spent 2009 determining the intrinsic value of every mortgage security, loan and asset in his bulging portfolio'.[5] The team got off to a strong start. In one week in June 2010, they sold the bank's Argentina branch network to Banco Comafi, RBS Pakistan to Faysal Bank and RBS UAE to Abu Dhabi Commercial Bank. They flogged off the bulk of RBS's retail and commercial businesses in Hong Kong, Singapore, Taiwan and Indonesia, with investment banking in Taiwan, Philippines and Vietnam going to Australia's ANZ Bank. The majority of these operations had come into the fold as a result of RBS's disastrous acquisition of ABN AMRO. RBS's Kazakhstan retail business was sold to HSBC, while the Korea Development Bank took on the bank's retail operations in Uzbekistan. As one failed empire builder retrenched back to native soil, stronger Asian and emerging market players were feasting on the scraps as they embarked on empire building of their own.

On 17 November 2010, Cullinan announced a deal to sell RBS's portfolio of infrastructure projects to the Bank of Tokyo-Mitsubishi (BTMU) for about £3.9 billion. The assets that changed hands included debt and equity stakes in PPP and PFI schemes including the Edinburgh Royal Infirmary, the Addiewell, Peterborough and Ashford prisons, a rail-freight tunnel through the Pyrenees, the Muurla–Lohja motorway in Finland and oil and gas infrastructure projects in Europe. The deal spanned 21 countries, 240 separate clients and involved 60,000 documents being stored in a data room, with about 2,000 questions asked during the process. Having rejected lower offers, Cullinan's team also sold RBS Aviation Capital, a finance company that leased commercial aircraft and which had owned Fred's corporate jet until it was sold in October 2008. The business was bought by another Japanese bank, Sumitomo Mitsui Financial Group, for $7.3 billion – a 4 per cent premium to book. RBS also sold WorldPay, the payment processing business, to the private equity groups Bain Capital and Advent International in 2010. They paid £2 billion for the business, which is the second largest operator of automated teller machines (ATMs) in the US, in 2010, but margins in the processing sector are coming under pressure and Bain and Advent have since struggled with the business.

In many cases, the bank lent the purchasers the funds with which they bought these assets. For example the bank sold a £1.4-billion portfolio of commercial mortgages to New York-based private equity firm Blackstone but provided as much as £600 million of debt to fund the deal. In September 2011, it provided debt funding to enable Patron Capital to purchase the 24 UK hotels that the bank seized after Jarvis Hotels defaulted on loans.[6] The Grosvenor House Hotel on London's Park Lane went to the Indian conglomerate Sahara India Pariwar for £470 million. The luggage company Samsonite was floated. RBS's Sempra commodities business, which had to be sold as part of the bank's state-aid agreement with the European Commission, was split between JPMorgan, Noble Securities and Société Générale. The sale of the bank's insurance businesses – Direct Line, Churchill, Privilege and Green Flag – another state-aid requirement, commenced via an initial public offering (IPO) in October 2012 and was completed via a so-called 'bookbuild' on 26 February 2014. The price suggests RBS sold the business for between £2.6 billion and £3 billion, half the £6 billion that Warren Buffett's Berkshire Hathaway had offered in early 2008.

There were a few failures on Cullinan's part. A planned sale of RBS's Indian retail and commercial banking operations to HSBC, announced in July 2010, was a flop. After two and half years of talks, the deal was blocked by the Indian regulators and, instead, RBS ended up axing 1,000 staff and closing 23 of its 31 Indian branches. It kept eight branches, mainly located in big cities including in Delhi, Mumbai, Chennai, Kolkata and Hyderabad to serve corporate and private clients. In August 2013, RBS announced a separate deal to sell its business banking, credit card and mortgage units in India to Ratnakar Bank, which was founded in 1943 and is headquartered in Kolhapur in southern Maharashtra. The fact no price was disclosed suggest this was another giveaway fire-sale.

Another big disposal that fell through was the 'Project Rainbow' deal to sell 318 branches (mainly the RBS-branded branches in England and the NatWest-branded branches in Scotland) to Spanish bank Banco Santander. The idea had been worked up by Hester to appease the European Union and sidestep the need to offload RBS's investment bank in October 2009. By August 2010, Santander, which offered £1.65 billion for the Rainbow branches – which are predominantly in the north-west of England and are strong in the small business market – was the only serious bidder. However, the transaction was complex and unwieldy, as it involved trying to create a bank within a bank so that 5,500 staff, 1.8 million retail customers, 250,000 business customers and £22.2 billion in deposits could be seamlessly transferred to a new owner. In October 2012 Ana Botín, chief executive of Santander UK and daughter of the group's chairman Emilio Botín, told Hester the deal was off. The *Daily Telegraph* claimed Santander took fright when it became aware of the 'medieval' nature of RBS's IT platform – the one that caused the systems meltdown in June and July 2012.[7]

RBS eventually opted for a curious arrangement that involved two US private equity firms getting into bed with the Church of England to buy the 'Rainbow' branches. The deal, announced on 27 September 2013, saw Corsair Capital and Centerbridge Partners lead a consortium of investors that paid an initial £600 million for a 49 per cent stake in the reborn Williams & Glyn's. The consortium acquired its stake via a bond that is programmed to convert into equity as soon as the 'Rainbow' operation is floated on the stock market. If an IPO does happen, the consortium will then pay RBS an additional £200 million, depending on Williams & Glyn's post-IPO share price performance. As with many similar RBS disposals, the bank lent the buyers some of the money they needed to acquire the asset – in this case £270 million. RIT Capital Partners, an investment trust chaired by Lord Rothschild, and the Church Commissioners, a body of 33 clergy and lay-people who oversee the Church of England's finances, are also part of the Corsair Capital consortium. One of the current Church commissioners is Andreas Whittam Smith, founder of *The Independent*, who insists that the new spin-out bank will uphold 'the highest ethical standards'.[8] RBS and the Treasury had to seek an extension to the deadline for completing the disposal from the EU (the original deadline of December 2013 has already been missed). In the interim, the Corsair-led consortium is already running the 314-branch operation in partnership with RBS, preparing to separate out its technology platform, staff and customer accounts and to rebrand the unit. At the time of writing, it has yet to obtain a separate banking licence from the Bank of England.

After four years of marathon deal-making, Cullinan's non-core division has whacked a £258-billion financial 'heap of junk' down to £28 billion and eased pressure on RBS's balance sheet. 'RBS was obviously bankrupt, and there was a lot of tension, a lot of chaos, and I was living in here,' Cullinan told *Bloomberg Markets Magazine*, referring to the bank's Bishopsgate office. 'Now, it's a paragon of calm.'[9]

The battle over bonuses

Hester did himself few favours with his huffy insistence that bonuses must be paid at all costs – even when the bank was massively loss-making and was paying no dividends and the rest of the country was enduring austerity as a consequence of its failure. But Hester won a few back by waiving his own bonus on several occasions. Asked whether he could run the bank without paying bonuses by Channel 4 News's Jon Snow, Hester said, 'It is an experiment that I think would fail.' In his five years at the helm, the bonus issue was the most visible flashpoint between himself, his government owners and UK citizens.

In mid February 2009, it emerged that RBS intended to pay cash bonuses to some staff. Beneficiaries included Scott Eichel's ex-Bear Stearns team of structured-credit bankers, who were on guaranteed bonuses. There was an immediate media and political storm, with shadow Business Secretary Ken Clarke suggesting the government should have imposed a £2,000 cap on bonuses as a condition of the bailout. He said, 'If someone came and told me there were legally-binding bonuses which we had to pay regardless of performance and even though the company has gone bust . . . I would have said well sue and be damned and challenged on it.'[10]

Chancellor Alistair Darling, reluctant to put Clarke's idea to the test, wound up sanctioning the legally binding cash payouts but wanted to prevent RBS from being too generous where discretionary bonuses were concerned. He said the Edinburgh-based bank would slash its total bonus pool from £2.5 billion in 2008 to £340 million in 2009 and that future bonuses would be paid in shares, not cash. This was too much for the bank to bear. In November 2009, just after Hester had won his battle over the future shape of the bank, the bank started to lobby against the restrictions the government was imposing, arguing they were driving away staff. 'This requirement may adversely impact RBS's ability to attract and retain senior managers and other key employees and thereby place RBS at a significant competitive disadvantage,' the bank said in a 27 November report to shareholders. But Gordon Brown was determined to persevere with his crackdown. On 2 December his spokesman Simon Lewis said, 'The old bonus culture – short term, completely unrestricted – was inappropriate.' Lewis said the bank had entered a commitment from 2010 to 2013 to ensure it would be 'at the leading edge of implementing the G20 principles, the FSA Remuneration Code and any remuneration proposals from the Walker Review that are implemented.'[11]

Some of the bank's tactics bordered on extortion. In early 2010, RBS said it would suffer a mass exodus of investment bankers if it was prevented from paying a total of £1.5 billion in bonuses for 2009. When that didn't work, the bank's board threatened to resign en masse unless it got its way. Yet again, Brown's government gave the bank an inch and it took a mile. Despite a clause in the asset protection scheme agreement permitting him to block RBS bonus payments, Darling didn't use it and waved through a marginally reduced £1.3-billion bonus pool for 2009. This prompted the singer Billy Bragg to launch a Facebook campaign, NoBonus4RBS, urging people to withhold their income tax over RBS's behaviour. The campaign attracted 30,000 followers but was like water off a duck's back for the bank and UKFI, which always backed Hester to the hilt on anything bonus-related. There was another outcry in February 2011 when it emerged that, despite annual losses of £1.1 billion, the bank intended to shell out £950 million in bonuses, including £2.04 million for Hester. The bank insisted that cash bonuses would be capped at £2,000, with the rest being paid in shares.

On 8 March 2011, *The Guardian* revealed that more than 100 RBS bankers would be paid more than £1 million each in shares for 2010. Five people shared £26 million, including Hester, who was billed as collecting £7.7 million thanks to the onset of a long-term incentive plan.[12] The situation was worsened by the fact that on 17 January 2011, Hampton had talked of a 'gangmaster culture' among traders and investment bankers, implying they were holding a gun to management's head in order to extort undeserved financial rewards from the bank.[13] Their seemingly insatiable appetite for bonuses – even though these incentives played such a key part in fuelling the crisis, and even though the bank remained loss-making and incapable of paying dividends – was incomprehensible to many. Their sense of entitlement seemed to outweigh everything else, including public perceptions of their institution, their 'profession' and whether their employer had a future.

At the bank's annual general meetings, the board was, year after year, lambasted by furious ordinary shareholders who could not understand why a bank that had impoverished them was still insisting on showering senior bankers with massive pay and bonus packages, while freezing the pay of ordinary workers. At the April 2011 meeting, shareholder Tom Weir said the bonuses the bank was paying were 'really obscene to the degree of greed and corporate theft'. Under pressure, Hampton admitted that he found the payment of bonuses 'hard to justify'. But, resolutely ignoring the need for cultural change, he insisted the bank had to keep paying them or risk seeing an exodus of talent.

The issue flared up yet again on 25 January 2012, when Hester was in his jumbo ski chalet in the Swiss ski resort of Verbier. And this time the barbs were much more personal. The board leaked information that Hester would be getting a bonus of nearly £1 million, over and above his £1.22-million salary for 2011. The board apparently thought he deserved it despite some very poor performances in 2011 and had convinced themselves they would get it past the public and the politicians, as it was half the £2.04-milllion bonus awarded to Hester the previous year. Cameron's government originally sought to block the deal but caved in after the RBS board – where the former Standard Life chief executive and Creative Scotland chairman Sandy Crombie had sat as senior independent director since June 2009 – again pressed the nuclear button and threatened to resign en masse. Ridiculous histrionics by a species that Business Secretary Vince Cable called the 'Pinstripe Scargills' had become the order of the day. This time, a major row was brewing. The *Daily Mail* went for the jugular, running a piece detailing Hester's separation from his first wife, Barbara Abt, and his affluent lifestyle. It was headlined 'The £8m mansion RBS chief Stephen Hester gave to his ex-wife . . . while he rents £4m apartment'. Much to Hester's chagrin the piece was illustrated with a picture of him in full hunting regalia – a photo he particularly hated.[14] The riots of 6–10 August 2011, after which a 23-year-old college student, Nicolas Robinson, was jailed for six months for stealing a £3.50 case of water from a Lidl supermarket in Brixton, were fresh in many people's minds, and the *Telegraph* columnist Peter Oborne drew parallels between Hester's greed and the decline in the morals of young people:

[I]t is outrageous and insulting that Mr Hester should insist on such a huge salary, and beyond belief that he should be insisting on a bonus. Furthermore, it is important to bear in mind that he is by no means the hungriest RBS employee. His colleague John Hourican, the head of RBS's calamitous investment banking division, is reportedly demanding more than £4 million. Consider this: supposing that Mr Hourican gets his bonus, it will pay him approximately £11,000 every single day – as a state employee. In just three days, it would surpass the amount that a young corporal, risking life and limb in Afghanistan, gets in an entire year. Just as much as young people who think it is OK to lie and cheat, the Hesters and Houricans of this world are proof that something has gone horribly wrong with the British system of values.[15]

With impeccable timing, Labour leader Ed Miliband cleverly organised a vote on Hester's bonus in the House of Commons for the following week. Had this gone ahead, the vote would almost certainly have gone against the government and the RBS board, which would have been hugely embarrassing and disruptive to both. So Prime Minister David Cameron called Hester at home at 11 p.m. on Sunday 29 January and told him the game was up – he would have to renounce the bonus. The bank confirmed his decision on the morning of Monday 30 January and tried to present it as a magnanimous move on the ruddy-cheeked Yorshireman's part, even though he had quite clearly been backed into a corner.

Some financial commentators were appalled that the government had caved in to the mob. William Wright, a columnist for *Financial News*, told the BBC that it was taking political meddling in RBS's affairs to 'what some people may consider to be intolerable levels'.[16] Hester was angry with Sir Philip Hampton, believing the RBS chairman should have done more to stand up for him and not just acceded to the government's will. From February 2012 until Hester's departure in September 2013, relations between the two men are said to have become so strained Hester was calling Hampton 'the great deceiver' behind his back, and the two men were barely on speaking terms. After five years at the bank, Hampton, Hester and other board directors remained out of touch, taking taxpayer support for granted. Their detachment from the real world came across during an exchange on 11 February 2013, five days after the bank paid fines of £390 million for the manipulation of Libor. Hampton told members of the Parliamentary Commission on Banking Standards that he believed Hester's pay – which could have been as high as £6.8 million that year – was 'modest' and 'well below the market rate of people working in banking'.

Despite waiving his bonus for three out of his five years as RBS's chief executive, Hester still earned £14 million in his time there, including a 'golden parachute' worth £5.6 million due to being forced out. That added up to £2.8 million a year which, when compared to most people's salaries or wages, is an obscene amount. However, when compared to the total pay of the chief executives of other similarly sized banks, it is, in fact, quite modest. He took more flak for it than anything else he did and would almost certainly have won more kudos if he had sought to lead by example on pay.

Culture, conduct and ethics

In his testimony to the Parliamentary Commission on Banking Standards in February 2013, Stephen Hester said, 'At RBS, one of the very first things I did – in fact, I think it was literally the first statement I ever made as incoming chief executive – was about refocusing the company around customer-driven activity . . . I have not made one single statement to shareholders, who may be thought to be interested in profits, without saying that customers come first.'[17] The intentions were noble but sadly, Hester and the Hester regime failed to walk the talk.

Where small businesses and medium-sized business customers were concerned, the bank's main priority was to increase the margins on their loans and hit them with as many additional fees and charges as possible. A great many business borrowers were tipped over the edge and saw the bank seize their business and personal assets after the bank mis-sold them interest rate swaps.

Under Fred Goodwin, RBS was the UK's biggest peddler of these derivatives, which Barclays chairman Sir David Walker believes should never have been sold to small businesses.[18] In a mis-selling spree that peaked in 2005 to 2008, ex-insiders suggest the bank targeted SME borrowers who were in a 'vulnerable' position – perhaps they were refinancing or extending their borrowings at the time – and who also had property assets worth a multiple of their total borrowings. The bank used a set methodology to cajole selected commercial customers into buying the swaps, also known as interest rate hedging products (IRHPs), which, in more than 90 per cent of cases, were neither requested nor desired by the customers. The sequence went roughly as follows:

(1) The bank assessed how well-informed each customer was about interest rates by asking questions such as 'could your business cope if rates rose to 12 per cent?'.

(2) The bank would sell the customer a 'vanilla' loan or loan extension.

(3) The bank would agree this loan in principle which, in many cases, prompted the customer to increase expenditure on the assumption the loan would be forthcoming.

(4) The bank's relationship manager would introduce the customer to commission-based salespeople from GBM's derivatives desk but these people would be presented to the customer as objective 'advisors'.

(5) The relationship manager would casually warn the customer that interest rates were historically low and likely to rise.

(6) In a presentation, 'advisors' would bamboozle the customer with graphs and pie-charts showing the trajectory of UK interest rates over three decades (UK rates had risen from 3.75 per cent in February 2003 to 5.75 per cent in July 2007 and customers were led to believe they would go higher).

(7) The relationship manager would express concern that, when rates rose, the customer would struggle to service their borrowings.

(8) The relationship manager would then suddenly spring news on the customer that the promised loans were conditional on them taking out an interest rate swap or related hedge.

(9) Business customers who had been deemed 'muppets' (gullible and clueless about rates) in step one would be sold a 10-year hedging product, which would generate tens of thousands in commission payments for bankers and the bank, even if the business person was about to retire and even if maturities on underlying loans were far shorter than 10 years.

(10) The 'advisors' would celebrate by pre-spending their bonuses in the bars and clubs of the City. There are reports that, on at least one occasion, swap salesmen were seen high-fiving colleagues in the pub and boasting of having 'raped' a small business customer.

When interest rates fell from 5.75 per cent to 0.5 per cent in the aftermath of the bank bailouts, many small businesses that had bought such products found that as a result of their IRHPs they were being hit with massive, punitive monthly payments that neither their relationship managers nor the super-slick salesmen had warned them about. They also learned the bank would demand exorbitant break fees if they wanted to extricate themselves from their swap early. When business customers complained to RBS, the bank stonewalled them or insisted it had done nothing wrong or found ways of persecuting the customer. If business customers threatened legal action against the bank, the bank's officials told them they would not succeed. This was pretty much RBS's stance during the first four years of Hester's reign – and it was hardly customer-friendly.

The swap sales team at RBS's 135 Bishopsgate building was particularly callous in its handling of customer complaints. One banker who worked there and who has since left the sector in disgust says, 'They thought they were untouchable. One SME owner – a woman who was of Indian or Pakistani origin – contacted us in August 2012 about her interest-rate swap. When her hand-written complaint was passed around internally, the attitude was "What a f**king joke – ha, ha, ha – read this! She's clueless. She doesn't even know what mark-to-market or breakage costs are!!" When she called, the team gathered around the phone, put it on mute and were laughing their heads off at this poor woman whose business they'd destroyed.'

James Ducker, a former derivatives salesman at Lloyds TSB and HBOS-turned-whistle-blower, tried to alert the FSA to the scale and severity of the crisis in March 2011 but he too was given the cold shoulder. In an email he sent to the regulator on 7 March 2011 he warned that 'national, industry-wide mis-selling took place, was accepted and indeed encouraged'. But Roger Breavington, of the FSA's financial crime and intelligence division, replied that the FSA 'does not become involved in a single dispute between an individual customer and a financial service provider'. Ducker wrote back to the FSA on 26 October 2011, saying, 'Not only have there been systemic, bank-wide mis-selling practices, but all banks are now dismissing the complaints even when they have merit. This is further breaching rules and regulations.'[19] However, still the regulator took no action.

It was only after intense pressure from small firms, the campaigning group Bully Banks, politicians and the media that the FSA changed its tune. In June 2012, the regulator introduced a 'redress' scheme it

had cobbled together with the UK's four biggest mis-sellers of swaps –
RBS, Lloyds Banking Group, Barclays and HSBC. It was an imperfect
outcome since the scheme gave the banks latitude to decide whether
or not they had swindled their own customers and to decide which
complainants were 'unsophisticated' enough to be eligible for compensation. But, for many affected firms, it was better than nothing. The
review confirmed that RBS was the biggest mis-seller of the products,
with a total 10,528 cases of mis-selling recognised by the review team.
Even the opposition leader Ed Miliband has admitted to being unable
to get his head around hedging products. Speaking to Sky News in July
2012, Miliband said, 'I visited a guy called Alan who runs a signage
company in Putney. He was in tears. It's a chilling story about what
the banks are doing to people. He has lost about a £1m because of the
banks. He got sold a "dual interest rate swap". I have a master's degree
in economics and I can't understand it.'[20]

Having pretended the swaps crisis was immaterial and stonewalled
customer complaints for over 12 months, RBS eventually acknowledged its bottom line would be affected in February 2013, when it
took a £750-million provision to cover compensation costs, a figure
which many observers believed to be farcically low. It threw in a further
£500-million provision for IHRP mis-selling in its surprise trading
update of 27 January 2014 – taking the total to £1.25 billion. Experts
think even this is still too low, with some arguing that the Edinburgh-
based bank will ultimately have to stump up at least £5 billion to right
this wrong.

On 25 November 2013, the Yorkshire-based entrepreneur Lawrence
Tomlinson unleashed a bombshell of a report outlining even more
egregious behaviour by RBS. He said the bank was purposefully 'engineering' financial distress and defaults in its own small business customers, in order to profit from their demise.[21] Tomlinson is the founder
and chairman of Leeds-based LNT Group, which employs 2,000
people and whose operations include care homes, climate protection
equipment and the manufacture of Ginetta sports cars. He researched
and wrote the report in his capacity as 'entrepreneur in residence'
at the Department for Business, Innovation & Skills (BIS), where he
was working one day a week as an unpaid adviser, alongside Business
Secretary Vince Cable, ministers and civil servants.

Clearly, in a major downturn, many businesses will struggle – especially if they're poorly managed and heavily indebted and have taken speculative bets that turned sour. In such instances, banks are perfectly entitled to seek to retrieve funds but what Tomlinson unearthed at RBS was much more disturbing. His report alleged that RBS is tripping up perfectly viable businesses in order to transfer them to a separate 'turnaround' unit of the bank called the Global Restructuring Group (GRG). Tomlinson said the bank was engineering defaults through mechanisms including the sudden withdrawal of funding and/or overdrafts, arbitrary changes to the terms and conditions of loans and the use of 'tame' firms of chartered surveyors to produce ultra-low valuations on commercial property assets that would put customers in breach of covenant. Other triggers included the mis-sale by the bank of swaps or IRHPs, whose servicing costs became crippling after the Bank of England slashed UK interest rates to 0.5 per cent, and even, in some cases, simply the fact that turnover had fallen 10 per cent short of a plan or that financial reports had been filed a day or two late.

Once in GRG, where Tomlinson says managers were 'incentivised to asset strip', the businesses are saddled with massive additional rates, fees and charges, including having to pay tens of thousands of pounds for 'Independent Business Reviews' produced by accountancy firms appointed by the bank.[22] Their owner/managers are then asked to provide personal guarantees over their borrowings and made to jump through a further series of Kafka-esque hoops. RBS likes to present GRG as a recovery or turnaround unit – a cuddly sort of place where businesses that are in financial difficulties are nurtured back to health, along the lines of an intensive care ward or the A&E unit of a hospital. However, most business people with experience of GRG see it rather differently. They have variously described it as being 'mugged by a hit squad', being 'driven into an abattoir or butchery', being put through 'a mincer' and even being 'dropped into the 10th circle of Dante's Hell'. In his report, Tomlinson said RBS's reaction once a business customer is in distress is 'utterly disproportionate at best and manipulative and conspiring at worst'.[23]

After months of this sort of treatment, during which time the bank continues to suck cash flow out of the business, companies are allowed to limp along until they can safely be put into administration, often with accountancy firms, like KPMG and PwC, that are closely aligned to the bank serving as administrators. In many of the cases highlighted by Tomlinson, the bank then sought to profit from the firms' collapse. A separate division of RBS, West Register, would sometimes jump in to snap up the targeted firms' property assets on the cheap, with higher offers from other bidders being ignored. Many RBS customers to whom this happened were not even told or aware that West Register is a division of the bank – they were led to believe it was an independent property developer! Tomlinson said, 'They trust [RBS] all the way down the line. Usually, by the time they realise what's going on, it's too late.'[24]

In his report Tomlinson said, '[I]t became very clear, very quickly that this process is systematic and institutional.'[25] An ex-Ulster Bank insider seemed to confirm this. In an interview with Ireland's *Sunday Independent*, the whistle-blower said, 'If Ulster Bank saw an opportunity to enforce a default which it could profit from, it did it . . . It was simply outrageous what went on.'[26] Another RBS whistleblower said that, halfway through 2008, managers told GRG staff the 'turnaround' unit's ethos had to change. He said the unit was, overnight, expected to be much more aggressive towards distressed firms, taking larger fees, seizing equity stakes and insisting on new terms and agreements. Asked by Siobhan Kennedy of Channel 4 News what the fees were for, the whistleblower said, 'Nothing really. The fees were just there to make sure [firms] were pushed to the brink. And we were often asked why we weren't putting more fees on these companies.' The whistleblower told Channel 4 News that shifting customers' assets into West Register was firmly on the bank's agenda. He said, 'It verged on illegal. But morally it was bankrupt.' The whistleblower confirmed that GRG had complete control over customers' accounts and was not answerable to any other part of the bank.[27] Tomlinson told the Treasury Select Committee he was frustrated with the widespread belief that banks such as RBS have been keeping too many 'zombie' firms afloat.[28] He said the reality was that many firms were falling victim to banks that were using 'vampire practices'.[29]

Before writing his report, Tomlinson examined 200 examples of firms to which this sort of thing happened. In the report, he made reference to 23 cases, 20 of which involved RBS. Because of the culture of fear that permeates RBS's Global Restructuring Group and the firms that are languishing within it, Tomlinson had to be very careful to redact his report to ensure their identities were obscured. Tomlinson said, 'This

is a huge scandal. It's about stealing people's businesses, people's livelihoods, it's about people with cancer being chased for debts the bank
has created, sometimes without the customer's knowledge; it's about
the bank creating situations that put people into a corner where they
can hit them with outrageous fees and transform them into zombie
companies, companies that would in many cases never have become
zombie companies if the bank hadn't increased its margins and fees. As
far as RBS is concerned, zombie businesses are the perfect result: it's
an excellent fee opportunity. Once the owners have been milked for all
that can be had, the business can be put into administration.'[30]

The Global Restructuring Group scandal owes its origins to the
bank's response to the crisis of 1990–92, which was when the bank first
turned its restructuring and recovery division into a profit centre (*see*
Chapter 3) and secondly to the crisis of 2008–12. The group became
more rapacious in August 2008, and its treatment of business customers became even more shocking after the bail-out.

In February 2009, the government of Gordon Brown and UKFI
laid down a short-sighted strategy for the part-nationalised bank. The
immediate priorities were firstly to maximise short-term profitability
and secondly to maximise short-term shareholder value, with a view
to the bank trading itself out of its difficulties and being 'flipped' back
into the private sector at profit by 2012.

In leaked internal strategy papers dated May 2009, the bank said
it would 'strengthen the level of resourcing available to support the
buy-in activity', which means it would allocate funds to West Register
and related units to buy customers' commercial property assets on the
cheap.[31] And an email leaked to the *Sunday Times* suggests that, around
this time, West Register developed 'an appetite' for certain types of
property.[32] The May 2009 strategy document revealed these to include
offices, retail and industrial premises, pubs, hotels, nursing homes, car
dealerships and hospitals.

Tomlinson referred to the 'culture of fear' that permeates GRG.
This and the bully-boy tactics of its operatives mean that customers
whose businesses are transferred there are often too terrified to speak
publicly about the way they are being treated for fear of even worse
treatment afterwards. This was why Tomlinson felt obliged to mask the
identities of the 23 case studies in his report. In turn, this enabled RBS
chairman Sir Philip Hampton, when seeking to rubbish the report in a

BBC interview on 25 November, to dismiss Tomlinson's allegations as 'unsubstantiated' and 'anecdotal'. Hampton also told Robert Peston that the bank had dealt with vast numbers of customers in distress since the crisis. He said 'tens of thousands' of business customers have been transferred to GRG since the crisis and that at its peak the value of these firms was £90 billion. 'If there are facts that show we have behaved in the wrong way then we will take appropriate action.' He acknowledged the bank may have been 'too heavy' in some instances.[33] Within days, RBS referred the matter to 'magic circle' law firm Clifford Chance for what it said would be an 'independent' investigation. As a member of RBS's 'panel' of law firms, Clifford Chance reportedly earned £6 million from RBS in 2013, and, although major law firms are adept at constructing 'Chinese Walls', it is somewhat surprising that RBS did not instruct a firm where there was no possibility of any conflict of interest arising.

Two days after the Tomlinson Report came out, the pressure was mounting on RBS. The *Financial Times* revealed that the Serious Fraud Office was considering an investigation into the bank's alleged abuses.[34] At the time of writing this had become a fully-fledged criminal probe, under which the SFO's principal intelligence officer, Colin Croucher, is examining hundreds of claims.

On Friday 29 November the Financial Conduct Authority said it was launching a 'skilled persons report' into the alleged malpractice, under section 166 of the Financial Services and Markets Act (FSMA) 2000. This triggered a surge in correspondence from aggrieved business customers of RBS and NatWest to the Canary Wharf-based regulator. One FCA insider joked, 'We may have to open a second mail room to deal with the volume of claims.' In January, the FCA declared the probe was being outsourced to the Washington DC-headquartered Promontory Financial Group – a firm which, disturbingly, is reported as having a history of 'whitewashing' financial crimes on behalf of regulators and banks – and the mid-tier accountancy firm, Mazars.[35] However, unlike most section 166 probes, control of this particular investigation will remain with the FCA and not with the institution being investigated. Asked how he believed regulators might react to what they find, Tomlinson told MPs, 'I think they'll be shocked at the treatment of the businesses, I think they'll be shocked at the lives ruined.'[36]

Since July 2012, I have been contacted by owners and managers of hundreds of businesses that claim to have been treated in the most despicable way by RBS. Some are deeply traumatised by the experience, having lost everything and been financially ruined by the bank. They struggle to understand how a once-trusted institution and business partner turned into a rapacious and kleptocratic monster that treats them with brutality and contempt and seems hell-bent on their destruction.

There are parallels with the HBOS Reading scandal of 2002–08, which I have also written about and which saw up to 200 companies needlessly destroyed after Bank of Scotland forced them to use the services of a turnaround consultancy, Quayside Corporate Services, which did not always have their best interests at heart. For years Lloyds and HBOS sought to deny they had done anything wrong but a police inquiry, Operation Hornet, led to two former HBOS executives and eight of their associates, including Quayside personnel, lawyers and accountants, being charged with fraud, fraudulent trading, blackmail and related offences. The trial is due to be heard at Southwark Crown Court in 2016.[37]

An RBS spokesman said, 'The vast majority of businesses that have gone through GRG have had a positive outcome, either returned to the main bank, re-banked or paid their debt back, with only a minority facing insolvency. These are serious allegations that have done damage to RBS's reputation and the independent review by Clifford Chance we have commissioned will examine these. It is important to note that the most serious allegation that has been made is that RBS conducted a "systematic" effort to profit on the back of our customers when they were in financial distress. We do not believe that this is the case and no evidence has been provided for that allegation to the bank.'[38]

I first became aware of the activities of RBS's Global Restructuring Group in November 2010 as a result of the outcome of a lawsuit brought against the bank by Hamilton-based property developer Derek Carlyle. In August 2008 the bank reneged on a pledge to lend Carlyle the additional £700,000 it had promised him to complete a residential development near Gleneagles Hotel in Perthshire. After withholding the promised funds, the bank sued Carlyle for the £1.4 million he had already borrowed, pursuing him for so-called personal guarantees. The bank then set about trying to 'destroy' Carlyle financially and psychologically, using bully-boy tactics, harassment and persecution of his family, intimidation of his solicitors and playing a part in getting him sequestrated over a minor £4,000 debt. The Scottish judge Lord Glennie found in Carlyle's favour, on 13 January 2010, ruling that the bank had created a 'collateral warranty obligation' when one of its officials agreed to the additional funds over the telephone and that its failure to honour this commitment meant it was firmly in the wrong. Glennie censured the bank, accusing it of 'a lack of candour' in its handling of the case – a phrase normally used by the judiciary to describe lying.

A few weeks later Carlyle's MP, Jim Hood, told a stunned House of Commons, 'RBS personnel seem to believe they are above the law and not accountable for their actions . . . they had the power to bully and destroy – and to hide when caught . . . When I came to this debate, I hoped that we were dealing with rogue managers and rogue directors at RBS, but from the interventions that I have taken [from MPs across the UK] I suspect that it is even more serious. It is not rogue people: it may be institutionalised.'³⁹ RBS sought to get the judgement quashed at an appeal hearing of the Court of Session in July 2013. After a three-day hearing, three judges found in the bank's favour, saying that, despite its withdrawal of promised funding at the eleventh hour, the bank had done nothing wrong. Carlyle responded to the judgement by saying, 'I take from these points that businesses in Scotland should now be aware that they should not expect trust or morals from their bank.'⁴⁰ However, in a judgment dated 11 March 2015, which followed a hearing in November 2014, the UK Supreme Court overturned the Appeal Court's ruling. The five Supreme Court judges unanimously ruled that Lord Glennie's original assessment of five years earlier was correct; in other words that, when a bank official confirmed the loan by telephone, it represented a legally binding contract. The judgment left RBS in an awkward position. Not only was it potentially liable for Carlyle's £3 million counter-claim for damages, it was also liable for legal costs of at least £1 million. Carlyle told the *Herald*: 'I hope that this [will] stop RBS from persecuting myself, and other customers, in personal vendettas, and that Ross McEwan will be the man who stands tall and pays for the needless destruction caused to myself and my family over the past seven years.' Though the bank accepted the Supreme Court judgment, it has yet to settle with Carlyle, or even, at the time of writing, to discuss a settlement.⁴¹

The story of an alleged crime spree by RBS gained traction in September 2012, when it emerged that City of London Police had launched a criminal probe into the alleged theft, by West Register, of a conference hotel in Sittingbourne, Kent. The police are seeking to establish whether the bank committed a crime when it forced Chris Richardson and Innes 'Ernie' Berntsen's hotel business into administration following the withholding of funds and the reassignment of the hotel's ownership to West Register.

One of the most high-profile cases where the bank placed a customer's properties into administration before transferring their ownership to West Register involved Charters, a luxury residential development of 34 flats at Sunningdale, near Windsor. Fifteen apartments were sold off-plan before the economic downturn in 2005 and 2006. Having already lent £37 million to the project, RBS refused to continue to support it and, in May 2009, placed the developers in administration, with PwC acting as administrators. At the time, John Morris, one of the property developer's directors who was backed by investment bank Investec, offered to pay £32 million to buy the scheme back. RBS rejected the offer saying, 'We're not attracted to accepting a discount on the full amount due.'[42] A year later, the bank accepted a £16.2-million offer for Charters from West Register.

Addressing Hester and the rest of the RBS board at the bank's annual general meeting on 19 April 2011, shareholder and former SME customer Nigel Henderson said, 'The jackboot culture is alive and kicking – literally as well as metaphorically – within your bank, despite your pious statements.' Henderson alleges the bank misappropriated the Portree Hotel, on the Isle of Skye, and the £800,000 from the sale of the Park Hotel, in Montrose, from him. Henderson, having built a business worth £2 million making profits of £400,000, became an RBS customer in July 1997. He says, 'Before signing two personal loan agreements for £400,000, I made it clear to the bank that we intended to redeem the proposed loans early. The bank assured us that this would be fine, that the maximum penalty would be three months' interest, and that the loan documents would be drawn up accordingly. In November 1998 we deposited more than £800,000 with RBS, intimating we wished to exercise early redemption, as agreed. But they demanded £240,000, seized our cash and refused to allow us to exit the loans. They had embarked on a conscious process of deceit to engineer

our total financial destruction.' In early 2014, RBS headed off a Police
Scotland inquiry into the matter by refusing to provide detectives with
requested paperwork, and on 30 April 2014, an executive assistant of
Sir Philip Hampton wrote to Henderson saying, 'The bank's position
remains that it does not accept the allegations you continue to assert.'

At the annual general meeting on 30 May 2012, Neil Mitchell, a
former chief executive of Torex Retail, accused Hester and the
board of 'behaving like [Russian president] Vladimir Putin and the
Central Bank of Russia in Moscow'. The Torex case is a complex one.
Mitchell alleges that, after he blew the whistle on fraudulent activity at Torex, an AIM-listed company specialising in software for the
retail trade, he took the company to GRG, which he believed to be
a genuine business support unit. He did so on Monday, 20 January
2007. However, Mitchell soon realised that GRG did not have the best
interests of Torex Retail's shareholders, bondholders or other creditors
at heart. This was confirmed on 19 June 2007, when RBS put Torex
Retail into administration, with KPMG as administrators. On the
same day, GRG sold the business, shorn of its liabilities, to favoured
private equity buyer, Cerberus Capital Management, for £204 million,
even though credible offers of £390 million or more had been tabled
by other buyers. In doing so, Mitchell alleges that RBS and KPMG
defrauded Torex Retail's bondholders and shareholders. Speaking at
the RBS annual general meeting, Mitchell said, 'You are refusing to
ever investigate legitimate complaints.' He said that the bank's preference, when faced with complaints and allegations of wrongdoing, was
to seek to persuade aggrieved parties to 'issue them with writs' so that
such matters could be 'kicked into the legal quagmire'. Rather than
open a dialogue, Mitchell said the bank's standard response was 'deny,
dilute, delay, divide'.

The bank has repeatedly sought to kick Mitchell's complaint, which
goes beyond Torex Retail to encompass allegations of a broad-based
'systemic institutionalised fraud' by RBS involving a dozen large corporate borrowers, into the long grass. On 6 September 2012, Mitchell and
his general counsel Carlo Colombotti met Hampton in a pokey little
meeting room on the eleventh floor of RBS's swish Bishopsgate head
office. Mitchell says Hampton 'seemed very exercised'.[43] At the meeting, also attended by RBS general counsel William Luker, the RBS
chairman told Mitchell, 'We do not understand the locus of the claim

being with the bank. You do not have a claim. If you think you have a claim, you should take it to other parties such as KPMG.'[44] Hampton also claimed that the bank had never received a single complaint or allegation of malpractice by GRG and that Mitchell must, therefore, be talking nonsense when he spoke of a 'system of abuse'.[45] Mitchell says, 'He raised his voice, he pointed at me, and told me I needed to understand how business and banking were done. He insisted that what had happened was not criminal, "only very sharp business practice", and that it was, therefore, OK. He was behaving more like a stressed-out middle manager than the chairman of one of the world's largest banks.'[46]

Mitchell, a former executive manager at BAE Systems, who has advised multinational corporations in the film, media and technology sectors and has also worked as an IBM management consultant, added, 'Even though commercial lending is not a regulated area, they should have flagged up my original complaint to the FSA since there were possible systemic failings.'[47] In a letter to Colombotti dated 8 November 2012, RBS's Luker reiterated the bank's stance, writing, 'We are firmly of the view that there is no merit in your client's claims.'[48]

RBS's former chairman George Mathewson doubts whether Stephen Hester and Ross McEwan, the New Zealand-born finance executive who succeeded Hester as chief executive in October 2013, really know what was going on inside the business. He says, 'What I do know is this. The bank's relationships with small corporates at the front end are now disastrous – and this is true throughout the banking industry. I believe the loss of confidence between bankers and customers is a huge economic blow to the United Kingdom. It's difficult to explain to people. A friend in the property sector says, "We used to be on the same side of the table and looking for ways to make money for us both – now we're on opposite sides of the table and they're trying to make money from us."'

Business people who claim to have lost everything as a result of GRG's activities, and who previously suffered alone and in silence, were hugely heartened by Tomlinson's report. Not only did it make them realise they were not alone; it also gave them a voice. Many are now confident they will be able to obtain some form of justice and compensation from their oppressor. One senior business person who alleges that his company – his life's work – was effectively wiped out

and its assets stolen by GRG and West Register, emailed me on 4
March 2014 to say:

> Lawrence Tomlinson has changed everything. We feel like we have
> survived in a concentration camp and are finally able to speak about
> our experiences. I think RBS is behaving a bit like the Nazis during
> World War Two: they know the war is turning against them, but
> they're still shooting the prisoners until the last day. It won't be long
> before they take off their uniforms and try to blend into the crowds.[49]

Then just after 11.30 a.m. on 17 April 2014, one day before the Easter
break, Royal Bank of Scotland unveiled the findings of Clifford
Chance's 'independent' review of Tomlinson's allegations which, to
the dismay of affected individuals, seemed to exonerate the bank. Most
British and overseas media ran with the Edinburgh-based bank's own
PR line that it had been 'cleared' of wrongdoing. The headlines carried by the *Yorkshire Post* ('Review finds no evidence that RBS set out to
defraud its business customers') and the *Daily Telegraph* (' "No evidence"
RBS put SMEs out of business') were fairly typical.

However, a closer reading of the 60-page Clifford Chance report, for
which RBS paid £1.5 million, suggested the headlines were misleading.
A key contention of Tomlinson and the thousands of businesses that
have suffered at GRG's expense is that the fees charged by the so-called
'grim reaper group' can be so extortionate they put customer firms at
risk. So when Clifford Chance admitted it had not bothered to examine
GRG's fees, as it found them 'difficult to understand', it suggested a
massive lacuna in the report.

The Clifford Chance report also confirmed Tomlinson's allegation
that RBS uses non-compliant 'internal' valuations when valuing customers' commercial property assets and that these are often based on
the assumption of a 'short marketing period' (i.e. that assets would be
sold at 'fire sale' prices). The law firm, which does some £6 million of
work a year for RBS, said in its report that, 'internal valuations were
not carried out to the standard of the [Royal Institution of Chartered
Surveyors'] Red Book'.

Such 'back-of-a-fag packet, desktop valuations' are at the core of the
GRG scandal since they can enable the bank to manipulate valuations
up or down to suit its own ends – and there are instances where it has

used artificially low valuations to put business customers into default. However, Clifford Chance's report said, 'We have seen no evidence that the bank deliberately manipulated valuations to procure a customer's transfer to [GRG]. In our review we did not test the accuracy of the bank's valuation methodology.'[50]

Responding to the Clifford Chance report, Tomlinson said he was puzzled by the bank's decision to claim it had been cleared of a 'central allegation' that he had not actually made ('systematic fraud'), but welcomed its endorsement of several of his core claims. He also welcomed the bank's announcement, made on the day the Clifford Chance report was published, that it would close down controversial property unit West Register; waive default interest for 90 days; and introduce greater transparency over fees and charges to distressed firms. As Tomlinson pointed out, such changes give RBS less of an incentive to transfer viable firms to GRG. Others saw them as a tacit admission from the bank that something was indeed rotten in the state of Denmark.[51]

The bank has an extraordinarily high-handed approach to litigation. On 11 April 2013, the Court of Appeal found against RBS in a long-running dispute with the Texas-based hedge fund, Highland Capital Management. Highland claimed it lost $100 million when the bank terminated a $668-million CDO offering at the height of the crisis in 2008 and then seized the underlying loans. The bank then switched these assets from its trading book to its banking book following a 'sham' auction. That was part of a concerted exercise by the bank to shift billions of pounds' worth of assets off its trading book (where they needed to be 'marked to market') to its banking book (where they didn't). The bank seems to have considered the charade essential, as it enabled it to give the impression that its assets were worth more than they were. Three judges of the Court of Appeal in London overturned two earlier judgements that had been in RBS's favour after concluding that the bank had secured these outcomes through deceit. Lord Justice Aikens said, 'In my view the liability judgment was obtained by the fraud of RBS through the misstatement and concealment of facts by SG [former RBS senior employee Sam Griffiths].'[52] And the bank's reward to Griffiths for being mendacious on its behalf? He was given a formal warning, promoted to managing director and awarded a £500,000 bonus according to Robert Jones, a barrister at LexLaw. Jones added, 'It strikes us as surprising that RBS do not consider lying under oath to be a sackable offence.' He also said, 'This judgment must raise grave doubts about the culture of RBS and its approach to litiga-tion.'⁵³ The feuding parties settled out of court in September 2013.⁵⁴

In a candid interview for in-house magazine *RBS Business Agenda*, published in September 2012, Hester insisted that any episodes of criminality at RBS were relatively isolated incidents. 'Often reputa-tional hits are caused by small numbers of wrongdoers who are not illustrative of the wider base of staff.'⁵⁵

Hester axed 41,000 jobs during his time at RBS and his treatment of some was brutal. One ex-RBS executive, who left the bank in 2012, said, 'The corporate culture at RBS started off being not very good but it massively deteriorated after Hester took over. The corporate culture was poisonous under Hester – it was horrible. Their attitude was, if they could get away with something, they would do it.' The executive recalled how the bank wanted to make a member of his team, a senior investment banker with 30 years of service, redundant. This would require paying out quite a large redundancy settlement. The executive said, 'Things of that size have to go to Stephen and Stephen's response was "I am sick and tired of having to pay these huge redundancy set-tlements – pay him the legal minimum and let him sue."'

The culture has deteriorated among middle-ranking members of staff too. One Manchester-based RBS relationship manager said, 'The culture has become horrible here. We're facing relentless pressure to get the margins up, which means we're having to squeeze more and more money out of our corporate customers. We don't like having to do this. But we've got no choice.' The person said having to effectively 'extort' money out of longstanding contacts was making many bankers at RBS and NatWest deeply miserable and causing them to want to leave. 'But we've all got final salary pensions and so walking away would be very financially difficult. We're kind of trapped.'

Retail banking staff, who earn average annual salaries of £15,500, faced a 'continuous onslaught' during Hester's five-year reign, with tens of thousands of job losses from this area of the bank, according to officials at Unite the Union. Surviving staff are in 'a permanent state of fear' because of continuous restructurings, and the 'iniquitous and unfair performance management system', according to Unite national officer John Nolan. He said the bank's damaging rank-and-yank system is alive and well and has only been marginally tweaked in the past five years. 'During 2012, there were 31,000 RBS employees who never got a pay rise – and that was just based on the strength of low performance management scores,' added Nolan. 'And a few hundred staff are "performance managed" out of the bank each year. RBS is abusing staff and treating them shabbily – you would have thought the banks would have learnt their lessons, but they haven't.'[56] Speaking to the House of Commons Scottish Affairs Committee, Unite national officer Rob MacGregor said, 'I cannot recall a time when the morale of bank workers has been at such a low ebb.'[57]

There is also frustration inside the bank that, despite its 2008 failure, the managers who are below executive level – the ones who executed the policies that destroyed the bank, who cajoled their minions into putting all their spare cash into the 2008 rights issue, causing them tremendous financial hardship – are still in situ.

Under Fred Goodwin, RBS did not believe in the offshoring of UK-based jobs to India but that has now changed. This is partly because, as part of its ABN AMRO acquisition, RBS inherited a business process outsourcing (BPO) operation in Chennai (formerly known as Madras). With a staff of 7,000 when RBS took it over, the bank retained and expanded it so that today RBS employs roughly 11,000 people in India – more than the 9,000 that it has left in Scotland. The bank also set up an Indian datacentre in Mumbai to which it started to transfer jobs from the UK. In 2011 it was hiring experienced software people in the subcontinent on annual pay of £9,000 to £11,000 in Hyderabad – less than a quarter of what an equivalent worker could expect to be paid in Britain. It then transferred many of these inexpensive employees to the UK using Intra Company Transfers, a loophole that permits multinationals to bring overseas workers to the United Kingdom without a visa. This enabled RBS to fire more expensive experienced UK-based IT staff who were more au fait with the idiosyncrasies of the bank's 1960s' vintage mainframe computers in Edinburgh and Southend-on-Sea – sometimes with disastrous results. MacGregor said, 'Hester has achieved something quite remarkable – he inherited a thoroughly demoralised workforce, battered by job cuts, performance targets and chronic low pay . . . and he actually managed to make them feel even worse about the organisation which employs them.'[58]

34

Et tu, George?

The rift between the government and Stephen Hester was widening. The government and the regulatory authorities wanted Royal Bank of Scotland to abandon pretensions of global scale, accelerate the wind-down of the investment bank and refocus on lending to businesses and individuals in the UK. They wanted the bank to become a 'me-too' of Lloyds Banking Group, in other words. The coalition government and the regulatory elite now saw this as the only way the bank could be reprivatised within a reasonable time frame. Much to their annoyance, however, Stephen Hester was persisting with a lonely battle – albeit supported by a few City analysts and institutional investors – to keep RBS as a global 'universal' bank. 'Stephen's view was always that RBS would never be an attractive proposition for shareholders unless it retained a sufficient spread of business lines and retained geographic diversity. But the government wanted it to become much more UK-orientated,' a senior RBS insider said. It was to be a source of continuous friction to the extent that, by spring 2013, 'both regulators and government were becoming increasingly fed up with Stephen', according to one senior RBS insider. UKFI, the agency Gordon Brown set up to ensure that the state-owned banks were independently managed, was about as useful as a chocolate teapot in this debate. In its final report, the Parliamentary Commission on Banking Standards described it as a 'fig leaf to disguise the reality of direct government control'.[1]

Before accepting the RBS job in October 2008, Hester told the then chancellor, Alistair Darling, he would only accept the job on two conditions. One was that his pay was in line with that of equivalent banking jobs and the other that the government undertook to be a hands-off owner that allowed him to run RBS along commercial lines.

Darling and Gordon Brown had both agreed, and Hester had taken them at their word. According to Iain Dey at the *Sunday Times*, Hester was intensely irritated when the promises were broken.[2]

One reason the Treasury, the Bank of England and the FSA were eager to force the bank to pull in its horns was because they were scared. They feared that if RBS was allowed to persist with Goodwin-esque *folie de grandeur* it would end in tears, which would require yet another bailout – which might have caused a revolution in the United Kingdom. As the eurozone sovereign debt crisis unfolded between 2009 and 2012, they feared a 'nightmare scenario', based on several potential threats that:

(1) the valuations RBS was placing on non-core assets were ridiculously high;

(2) Hester's post-crisis repair job was only skin-deep;

(3) a major exogenous shock, such as a sovereign default in the eurozone, would expose the bank to financially crippling losses;

(4) the cost of righting past wrongs (so-called 'redress') would erode the bank's capital base.

As the authorities were aware, there were already multiple regulatory probes in numerous jurisdictions into RBS – into Libor rigging, woefully inadequate transaction reporting at GBM, feeble money-laundering controls at Coutts and Citizens Financial, the mis-selling of mortgage-backed securities to wholesale clients in the US and the mis-selling of interest rate swaps to SMEs in the UK. In the corridors of power, there was a suspicion that Hester was not taking some of these probes seriously enough, especially where provisioning (setting aside money to pay fines and compensate consumers) was concerned. Given that RBS remained one of the world's largest and most complex banks, with 1,161 legal entities spread over 16 countries and total assets of £1.313 trillion, some top regulators, including Andy Haldane at the Bank of England, were increasingly taking the view first expressed by Neelie Kroes in June 2009 – that it remained a danger both to society and to itself.[3]

When he gave his evidence to the Parliamentary Commission on Banking Standards on 6 March 2013, Mervyn King trashed Hester's performance over the past four and a half years, as well as that of the government. He referred to the government's handling of RBS as 'nonsense'. The governor told the commission there was concern about the coherence of the bank in its current shape, saying, 'RBS has a portfolio of different activities which do not sit well enough together to make the market willing to bid for it.'[4] He said the time had come to fully nationalise RBS, then break it up. King said the government could then seek to reprivatise the 'good' pieces to recoup as much as possible of the bailout costs and create a bank which was capable of fulfilling its purpose of lending to the UK economy and leave a so-called 'bad bank', which would be saddled with RBS's toxic assets, in public ownership in the hope that their value might increase over time.

'We should simply accept the reality today that it is worth less than we thought and should find a way to get an RBS that can be useful to the UK economy,' said King. He added, 'The whole idea of a bank being 82 per cent owned by the taxpayer and run at arm's length from the government is nonsense.'[5] There could hardly have been a more damning indictment of the way in which Brown and Darling had rescued RBS or a more powerful vote of no confidence in Hester's regime. King also hinted that any further intransigence from Hester would not be tolerated – that he was at risk of similar treatment to that which was meted out to the former Barclays chief executive, Bob Diamond, after he stood up to the Bank of England in early July 2012. (Diamond is widely considered to have been fired by King's diktat.) King went on to devote much of his last six months as governor to lobbying the government and others for a break-up of RBS along the lines he had outlined to the parliamentary commission. Hester was clearly living on borrowed time. On 1 July, King handed over the governorship of the Bank of England to the Canadian Mark Carney. As a former governor of the Bank of Canada and ex-Goldman-ite, bankers generally saw Carney as a softer touch.

When Osborne appeared before the commission nine days before King, on Monday, 25 February 2013, he had been much more supportive of Hester. He argued that British banks needed to maintain their scale and range of services in order to cater to global corporations. He agreed with Hester that the RBS should be kept intact. The chancellor also infuriated the commissioners by telling them their conclusions would make no difference to the Financial Services (Banking Reform) bill.

Lord Lawson, chancellor under Margaret Thatcher and a member of the commission, asked Osborne for his views on a 'good bank'/'bad bank' split at RBS, adding that, in his view, such a move could enhance the bank's ability to lend and eventually make it easier to privatise parts of the bank. Osborne said his preference was to let Hester finish the job and that there would be 'very considerable obstacles' to nationalising RBS and splitting the bank into 'good' and 'bad' parts. Osborne said that a break-up would require the injection of a further £10 billion or so of taxpayer funds to buy up the portion of the bank that the government did not already own, adding that the government was unwilling to throw any more money at the bailed-out bank. Osborne admitted that the slow recovery of the banking sector was a 'drag' on the UK economy and, true to his laissez-faire credentials, he refused to intervene on bankers' pay. Taking his cue from Hester and Hampton, Osborne told the commission that RBS could be reprivatised before the May 2015 general election.[6]

Hester was quietly livid with King. He was also feeling unloved, privately complaining to friends that he felt underpaid and under-appreciated. He also thought that Hampton was too aligned with the politicians and the regulators and was not doing enough to protect the RBS chief executive's interests. Relations between the two men had been souring for a year but hit rock bottom from March 2013 onwards. On at least three previous occasions, Hester threatened to resign, according to Whitehall sources, usually over concerns about political interference. 'Stephen has always been like this,' one City veteran told the *Sunday Times*. 'He gets exasperated, he blows up, then he gets back to work.'[7] One ex-colleague sympathises. 'Overall, I think Stephen did a very good job and, in some ways, it's amazing he didn't leave earlier. Hampton was not doing nearly enough to support him.'

Osborne had a Damascene conversion (or maybe he succumbed to pressure from King) in the weeks following his appearance before the parliamentary commission. From the end of March 2013, he was four-square behind Andrew Bailey at the Prudential Regulation Authority and King at the Bank of England. Presenting a united front, the Treasury, Bank of England and PRA sought to force Hester's hand, basically telling him he had to make further deep cuts in RBS's Markets and International Banking (M&IB) business, the renamed GBM – or else. They told the Yorkshireman that he was going to have to exit equity derivatives and retail structured products, while running down peripheral eurozone government bond market making – all areas which are quite hungry for capital. Hester sought to resist. He argued that if he were to do what they wanted RBS would lose credibility in international financial markets. The *Daily Mail's* Alex Brummer says, 'It was after this that the Treasury contacted Hampton and made it plain that the UK government – by far RBS's biggest investor with an 81 per cent stake – no longer believed that Hester was the right man for the job.'[8] If Hester was going to have to be dragged kicking and screaming into every single decision, there was no way that Osborne and the regulators were going to be able to work with him on the path to reprivatisation. It was time to get rid of this turbulent banker.

The notion that RBS should be split into a 'good bank'/'bad bank', what King was still pushing for, was anathema to Hester. A split along such lines, which the Brown government had considered and dropped in 2009, would imply he had been a failure as RBS's chief executive. However, the resolve in Westminster and Whitehall strengthened after the PRA calculated that, despite Hampton's and Hester's assertions that the bank was 'sorted', it actually had a capital black hole of between £12.5 billion and £25 billion. The fact that the bank was still not prioritising lending to UK SMEs and was treating many existing SME and corporate customers shabbily was seeping into the Westminster consciousness. Politicians also knew the bank had an IT system that was held together with Sellotape and pieces of string which was at risk of blowing up again at any time. They also recognised that RBS's markets division was far from reformed despite the Libor fines. Other obstacles to rapid reprivatisation included the bank's bombed-out share price, the huge costs of compensating ripped-off customers and its recent financial under-performance.

Confidence in the integrity of RBS's investment banking arm, M&IB, was further shattered in the second half of 2013, when it emerged that it was being probed by multiple regulators around the world, including the Financial Conduct Authority, the US's Commodities Futures Trading Commission, the Federal Bureau of Investigation, the European Union's cartel busters and Switzerland's Financial Market Supervisory Authority (FINMA) for its part in an alleged criminal conspiracy to rig the $5.3 trillion-a-day foreign exchange market, which, incidentally, has grown by 60 per cent since 2007. Then, in October

2013, it emerged that Richard Usher, RBS's former chief dealer and EUR/USD spot trader who left for JPMorgan in 2010, had participated in electronic chat-room sessions with traders from some 15 other banks in a bid to manipulate the foreign exchange markets. The traders who took part were variously known as 'The Bandits' and 'The Cartel', according to the *Wall Street Journal*, which said the Edinburgh-based bank had handed records of the 'chats' to the FCA.[9] In November 2013, the global probe gathered momentum when the *Wall Street Journal* revealed that several big-hitting foreign exchange traders at global banks had been suspended from their duties. The *Journal* said they included Paul Nash and Julian Munson at RBS. Regulators suspect that RBS colluded with other global banks to jack up rates and rip off clients.[10] It may be that RBS is entirely innocent, but the impression is that the only way RBS and other banks could make decent profits in their markets business was by cheating.

Nevertheless, Hester continued to make it clear he strongly opposed any 'good bank'/'bad bank' split. He warned the chancellor that such a move would be destabilising for the bank, delay privatisation and cost the government some £10 billion. The fact that the profitability of RBS's markets division had collapsed by 66 per cent in the first quarter of 2013, when compared to the same quarter in 2012, undermined the claims of Hampton and Hester that the sunny uplands of reprivatisation were in sight and fuelled regulators' scepticism about their stewardship of the bank.

At the analysts' presentation on 3 May 2013, Van Saun described measures the bank was taking to try to boost its profitability but, to some analysts, they smacked of desperation. Van Saun seemed willing to cut to the bone in the pursuit of a few extra shekels – hardly a sustainable strategy, given it entailed the risk that customer service, staff morale and IT stability could deteriorate further. Considering Hester's consistent mantra was that he wished to put the customer 'front and centre' of what the bank was doing, Van Saun's cost-cutting zeal seemed strange, to say the least. Van Saun also talked of cutting the already paltry interest rates offered by RBS on deposit accounts.[11]

Manus Costello, an analyst at Autonomous Research, asked if the bank was still moving backwards and still had significant headwinds ahead of it, Hester didn't answer, instead waxing lyrical about reprivatisation as though it would be some sort of panacea for all RBS's ills: 'I think privatisation would be a symbol of recovery for the UK, just as nationalisation was a symbol of a crisis.'[12] Hester told analysts he saw nothing wrong with the government selling the first tranche of taxpayer-owned shares at a loss – that is for less than the average price per share paid by the taxpayer in 2008–09.

Both Hampton and Hester were positively gloating when, in October 2012, they revealed that RBS had exited the asset protection scheme – the giant government insurance scheme that saved it from collapse during the crisis. Tim Bush, head of governance and financial analysis at corporate governance watchdog Pensions and Investments Research Consultants (PIRC) said, 'My analysis was that RBS was aggressively puffing all the numbers in the hope of a quick and dirty sale. The numbers from the Prudential Regulation Authority and Osborne's Mansion House Speech bore that out.'[13]

As he plotted privatisation and presumably his own glorious escape Hester was exasperated by the constant buzz in political and business circles that RBS wasn't lending enough to small businesses. The bank's most prominent critics on this score were the UK Business Secretary Vince Cable, a former Shell executive whom Hester is said to have detested, and the fund manager and former Liberal Democrat Treasury spokesman Lord Oakeshott.

One of Hester's most outspoken and strange attempts to rebut their claims came in an interview in the *Sunday Times* published on 5 May 2013. In this, he claimed the bank had money 'coming out of our ears' – £20 billion ready and waiting to lend to small firms. He said it was only business's lack of confidence that was holding things back. Hester told the paper's deputy business editor Iain Dey, 'We're lending as much as we can. We are not constrained by either capital or funding. The only way I could see for us to lend more would be for someone to say we did not have to operate by any commercial standard – that we could undercut everyone because we did not have to make a profit.'[14]

The interview infuriated SMEs and entrepreneurs. In a tweet, Stuart Garner, chief executive of Derby-based Norton Motorcycles, said that Hester was 'taking the piss' and had the 'bare-faced front' to claim there was insufficient demand for credit.[15]

It was the beginning of the end for Hester. In May 2013, the UKFI chairman Robin Budenberg, a former UBS Warburg investment banker, having seemingly found a modicum of backbone, gave a presentation to the RBS board, in which he was scathing about RBS's investment bank and questioned its approach to capital deployment. The presentation fatally undermined Hester. Budenberg afterwards visited Hampton at his Bishopsgate office and the two men discussed whether it was appropriate for Hester to continue. Then, at the end of an RBS board meeting in the latter half of May 2013, Hampton told the bank's non-executive directors that he wanted a separate meeting with just non-executives present. So Hester and Bruce Van Saun, the only two executive directors on the board, left the room. Hampton then announced to the remaining nine directors – five men and four women – that he had been 'told to sack' Hester. The board asked who had requested the ousting and, once Hampton had told them, they immediately started discussing possible successors.

On Friday, 31 May 2013, according to *The Guardian*'s Jill Treanor, Hampton called a private meeting with George Osborne. The RBS chairman advised the chancellor that there was now no disagreement between the bank and the government – in other words, they both believed it was time for Hester to go. The following Wednesday, 5 June, Hampton headed to the Treasury on Horse Guards Road to confirm to Osborne, in person, that the RBS board had agreed to oust Hester.

The Bank of England's executive director for financial stability, Andy Haldane, was giving a presentation at the Festival of Economics in Trento, Italy that day. In it Haldane, a fierce critic of 'too big to fail' banks like Royal Bank of Scotland, was decrying their very existence. He had earlier pointed out how the Bank of England was astonished to discover the inadequacy of the IT and management information systems at banks like RBS and said he believed such inadequacies were the number one cause of their collapse during the crisis. Basically, Haldane believed it meant they were unable to tell their arse from their elbow. In his Trento presentation, Haldane said that banks like RBS had few, if any, discernible advantages. In fact, he said such banks had grown so large that they had become impossible to manage and impossible to regulate effectively. Not only are such banks inefficient, they are also dangerous, said Haldane. The central banker said none of the post-crisis bank reforms – including the Dodd–Frank Act, the Volcker Rule, the Vickers Ring-Fence and the Liikanen Separation – tackled the issue of 'too big to fail' banks. Far from fixing 'too big to fail', the problem had become aggravated, said Haldane.[16]

The board of RBS had been hoping to line up a successor before revealing that Hester was leaving the bank but this proved impossible. By Wednesday 12 June, Hampton felt ready to break the bad news to Hester. At 3 p.m., he called an impromptu 'virtual' board meeting. The non-executive members of the board, including remuneration committee chairperson, former Coca-Cola executive Penny Hughes, agreed that Hester should have a golden parachute of 'up to £5.8 million', made up of salary of £1.6 million from the date he was due to depart and up to £4.2 million in share awards. Hampton then let Hester know he was being fired, presenting it as a board decision and telling the portly horticulturalist in a one-to-one meeting it was a *fait accompli*. Hester was aggrieved and dismayed that he would not be able to see the bank through to privatisation. However, he made no attempt to fight back.

A press statement headlined 'Stephen Hester To Leave RBS' was issued at 5.10 p.m. on the Wednesday evening. This included quotes from both Hampton and Hester. Hester boasted of what he saw as his achievements at the bank while Philip Hampton said, 'On behalf of the Board I would like to thank Stephen for his leadership and dedication over the past five years. In the midst of a major crisis, he accepted the challenge of stabilising the bank, turning it around, and putting us in a position where we can begin to plan for returning the organisation to the private sector.'[17] Hampton also said, 'I think it is fair to say that it has been a particularly gruelling experience for Stephen.'[18] The bank's spin was that whoever led the reprivatisation of RBS was going to have to stay on for five years after the IPO but that there was no way that Hester, who had been CEO for nearly five years, was willing commit to staying on for that length of time. Financial journalists participating in a chaotic virtual press conference with Hampton and Hester wanted, above all else, to find out the true reasons for Hester's departure. And there were some fairly obvious giveaways, including that: (a) Hester was leaving before a successor was in place; (b) Hester said, 'It is the board's decision . . . I was prepared to carry on through privatisation . . . I'm co-operating amicably'; and (c) Hampton seemed uncomfortable when answering questions about the Treasury's role. All this led to them smelling a rat.

There was harrumphing in the wine bars and pubs of the Square Mile that night. Within an hour, the conventional wisdom was that

George Osborne, the chancellor, had knifed Hester in the back, a scenario that appalled many City workers. There was talk about how it would create a 'political risk discount', meaning RBS shares would be weighed down by fear of further political meddling. Brokers slapped sell signs on the shares with Nic Clarke at stock brokers Charles Stanley, saying Osborne's ousting of Hester 'smashes any lingering pretence that RBS is being run at an arms-length basis'.[19]

The shares were trading at 331p (34 per cent below the average price at which the government bought them) in the minutes prior to Hester's resignation. By Thursday morning they had collapsed by 9 per cent to 301p. At the time of writing, they had marginally recovered to 327p.

The former Conservative chancellor and member of the Parliamentary Commission on Banking Standards, Lord Lawson, welcomed the ousting of Hester. He said, 'First and foremost I think he was the wrong man for the job.'[20] And, perhaps hitting the nail on the head, one senior RBS insider said, 'The trouble for Stephen was that his strategy didn't work – and the buck stopped with him.'

McEwan's uncertain remedy

Chancellor George Osborne and Bank of England Governor Mervyn King spoke to 350 bow-tie-wearing bankers (and a few in evening gowns) on 19 June 2013, a week after Hester was dismissed. It was the annual Lord Mayor's Banquet in the Mansion House, a large neo-classical Georgian palace in the heart of the City of London. The tone could scarcely have been more different from that adopted by Gordon Brown when he genuflected before the City's finest six years earlier. Speaking in the Egyptian Hall, Osborne said that his main goal was to ensure that Britain's state-owned banks – RBS and Lloyds Banking Group – did whatever they could to support the UK economy. He also said, 'We want to get the best value for money for the taxpayer. And we want to do what we can to return them to private ownership.'[1] He then made several key points about RBS, none of which reflected particularly well on Hester:

- RBS was not 'healing' fast enough and was still weighed down by too many poor assets.
- Unlike Lloyds Banking Group, RBS was a long way from being ready to reprivatise – implying Hampton and Hester had been lying when claiming that RBS was ready to be reprivatised.[2]
- RBS would only be reprivatised 'when we feel the bank is fully able to support our economy and when we get good value for you, the taxpayer'.[3]
- Attempts to retain a global, full-service investment bank were unacceptable.
- RBS must sell Citizens as soon as possible.
- The government would consider a 'good bank'/'bad bank' split,

putting the toxic assets into a state-owned 'bad bank', something which Osborne said ought to have happened in October 2008, though he did not blame the previous government for not doing this.

As part of the final point, Osborne declared the Treasury would launch a review of whether a 'good bank'/'bad bank' split stacked up. Osborne added that the Treasury's review of the matter – on which investment bank Rothschild, fund management firm BlackRock and law firm Slaughter & May advised – would be completed by September. Wags, including the economist Ann Pettifor, joked that the result was a foregone conclusion – the Royal Bank of Scotland would not be broken up – and that the inquiry should be renamed the 'Rothschild BlackRock Stitch-Up'.[4]

The chancellor made no mention of the proposal from Justin Welby, the Archbishop of Canterbury, and a member of the Parliamentary Commission on Banking Standards, that RBS should be broken up into a number of regional banks which would be much more focused on the needs of their local economies, along the lines of Germany's *Sparkassen*. Welby's vision was that these baby Royal Banks could focus on funding local and regional businesses, of which they would have deep knowledge as a result of being entwined with their local communities. Mike Trippitt, an analyst with Numis Securities, described the 'good'/'bad' split as a 'very good idea, but four years too late' and argued it could delay the privatisation process.[5] On the day after the Mansion House event, the PRA identified RBS as the bank with the largest capital hole of any British bank, saying it needed to raise £13.6 billion. However, the bank pointed out that it had already put plans in place to raise £10 billion of this through disposals and some fancy financial footwork that entailed classifying future deferred tax as capital. The PRA also required RBS to make the biggest absolute adjustment of any British bank, increasing its risk-weighted assets by £56.3 billion which, some believe, suggested that Hampton and Hester had been trying to pull a fast one.

Shares in RBS plunged in the two days after Osborne's Mansion House speech – a drop of £4 billion in real money terms. The City detected a series of conflicting policies and U-turns from the Treasury and believed the chancellor was digging an ever deeper hole for himself via his belated openness towards the 'bad bank' idea.

Hester told shareholders he was willing to stay on until the end of the year or until a successor could be found but, given the poor state in which the bank remained, together with fears over endless government interference and uncertainty over its future status, strong candidates were not exactly pushing down the door in the hope of succeeding Hester. The most obvious internal candidate, RBS finance director Bruce Van Saun, ruled himself out. He wanted to return to his native US, where he was slated to take over as CEO of the soon-to-be-refloated Citizens Financial. That left Ross McEwan as the only credible internal candidate. The tall New Zealander had been RBS's head of UK retail banking since September 2012 and was previously head of retail banking at the Sydney-based Commonwealth Bank of Australia. Mark McCombe, a senior executive with the asset management firm BlackRock who had spent most of his career with HSBC in the Far East, was seen as a possible candidate but pulled out at the eleventh hour.

In the end, Hampton and the board plumped for McEwan. He was offered the job in late July and the appointment was announced on 2 August. When telling the 56-year-old Kiwi he'd got the job, Hampton said, 'I'm not too sure whether this should be congratulations or condolences'[6] and promised him that, at the very least, it would be an adventure. The next day's newspapers highlighted McEwan's credentials as a retail banker and the fact that he would not be accepting any bonuses in his first two years in the job. What many newspapers missed was that, over and above his £1-million annual salary, McEwan was getting a £350,000 cash contribution in lieu of pension and had also been awarded a £3.2 million golden hello on arriving from Australia the previous year. Nor was McEwan quite the dyed-in-the-wool retail banker some papers made him out to be. He had spent the bulk of his career in human resources, stockbroking and insurance and had worked in top management roles in retail banking for less than seven years.

The Royal Bank of Scotland board was confident that McEwan would be a 'safe pair of hands' who would have fewer unseemly bust-ups with the bank's majority shareholder, the UK government, or with regulators than his predecessor Stephen Hester had had. Under its revised 'significant influence functions' regime, the Prudential Regulation Authority had vetted McEwan for suitability and given him the all-clear. The fact that McEwan had twice failed his accountancy exams at New Zealand's Massey University didn't bother them (McEwan passed on the third attempt).

In his relatively short stint as RBS's head of retail, McEwan had kept a low profile. One of his few public outings came in March 2013 when he outlined plans for RBS's retail banking arm. In a presentation to analysts, McEwan admitted that, on arrival in the UK, he had been stunned by how far standards had slipped in British banking. He said, 'I've been quite surprised at how bad this industry is . . . I would even go [as far as] to say that there's not a good retail bank in the UK.' He vowed to ensure RBS would break the mould and become a really good bank again. He identified cost cutting and the simplification of procedures as the keys to driving change and boosting profits, but lacked any grand transforming vision for the bank. At another event a few weeks later, McEwan announced plans to axe 1,400 jobs in RBS's UK retail banking head office, with half of the cuts likely to be made in Edinburgh. That took redundancies at RBS since the bailout to more than 41,000 – almost the equivalent to the population of Kilmarnock. Then, at Hester's leaving dinner on 12 September, the outgoing CEO gave his successor the gift of a riding hat. He probably thought McEwan might need it to avoid a cracked skull in the event of the inevitable fall from grace – and Hester was also making a wry reference to the picture that he so abhorred of himself in full hunting regalia but which had been so loved by the *Daily Mail* and other tabloid newspapers.

On stepping up to chief executive on 1 October 2013, McEwan gave an impromptu address to about 300 staff in the bank's Bishopsgate office. He admitted to feeling a 'high level of trepidation, slight levels of fear, but absolute delight' on taking the controls. He concluded by saying that he wanted everyone at the bank to 'obsess all day, every day, about our customers'. However, in his first few months as chief executive, the sins of the past kept coming back to haunt the bank.

On 1 November, Osborne rather rudely gatecrashed McEwan's first results presentation as chief executive – and, mugs of tea in hand, the pair did a joint photocall at a branch of Swift Cycles, a bicycle shop in London's Spitalfields district. The aim was to convey the impression that the bank was still lending responsibly to successful, growing SMEs. The chancellor then proceeded to steal McEwan's thunder by announcing the results of the UK government's review of the 'good bank'/'bad bank' split. After four months of deliberation, he said the government had decided against a formal break-up. In a 153-page document, the Treasury said it preferred an internal restructuring. Government advisers Rothschild said a formal split would 'do more harm than good to RBS' as it would do nothing to improve its capital position, would be a distraction for management and would 'involve significant implementation challenge'.[7] The compromise solution agreed by Osborne and McEwan was for an internal 'bad bank' dubbed 'the RBS Capital Resolution Division' (RCD) which would ring-fence £38 billion of the bank's most hard-to-shift assets, with the goal of running off 70 per cent of these by 2015. RBS Capital Resolution would embrace £23.5 billion of dodgy assets from the bank's old non-core portfolio, £5.5 billion of troubled UK corporate loans, £4.1 billion of terrible Ulster Bank loans and a mixture of none-too-healthy assets from M&IB. McEwan said the aim was to free up capital so RBS could lend more to needy UK borrowers, accelerate its return to profitability, reduce 'tail' risk – the risk of negative events causing large losses – and give investors 'greater visibility'. He said RBS should be able to increase its core tier-1 capital ratio to 11 per cent by the end of 2015. He also argued that the creation of an internal bad bank would make it easier for the government to privatise its 81 per cent stake in the bank.

On 7 November 2013 Standard & Poor's said that the Treasury's decision to launch an internal 'bad bank' would undermine efforts to restore RBS to profitability – and downgraded RBS's long-term debt rating by one step to BBB+ from A–. S&P credit analyst Dhruv Roy said that lawsuits and enforcement proceedings relating to past misconduct would continue to weigh heavily over RBS's risk profile.[10] On 7 November, the bank reached a settlement in the first of many cases involving the sale of dodgy residential mortgage-backed securities (RMBSs) as the US housing market boomed between 2005 and 2007. The bank paid $153.7 million to the Securities and Exchange Commission (SEC), without admitting any wrongdoing, after selling $2.2 billion of defective RMBSs from April to May 2007. 'RBS cut corners and failed to complete adequate due diligence, with predictable results,' said George Canellos, director of the SEC's enforcement division. The SEC's lawsuit said that the credit division of RBS Greenwich Capital had wanted to undertake more due diligence but had been prevented from doing so by the lead banker in the deal, who wanted to press on. The Greenwich employee claimed that any further checks could 'blow up this trade'.[11] The SEC document also said RBS had 'engaged in transactions, practices or courses of business which would or did operate as a fraud and deceit upon the purchasers of [the] securities'.[12] The big question about no-fault regulatory settlements along these lines is whether they actually do anything to change bankers' behaviour. There is a growing view that most banks now treat them as a risk-taking motorist treats parking tickets – mildly inconvenient, but increasingly a cost of doing business. The cost of the fines is not borne by the executives responsible (who have anyway usually moved to other firms by the time the enforcement actions or litigation are completed) but by the bank's insurers and shareholders. As a result, they do not prompt soul-searching, behavioural change or stronger ethics.

In his first few months as chief executive, McEwan apprised investors of bad news to come, warning them the bank would almost certainly declare losses of some £8 billion for the full-year to 31 December 2013.

On 1 November he indicated that because it was setting up an internal 'bad bank' (RBS Capital Resolution) RBS would have to declare £4.5 billion in impairment losses during the fourth quarter of 2013. Then, in a surprise trading update on 27 January 2014, McEwan said the bank was taking a further £3.8 billion of provisions to pay for 'legacy' misconduct issues. The money would go towards compensating ripped-off customers, paying civil and criminal fines, and funding litigation.

So when Royal Bank of Scotland unveiled pre-tax losses of £8.24 billion on 27 February, investors were not surprised, even though the losses meant RBS had lost a cumulative £46 billion since being bailed out. In other words it had burned its way through the entire sum with which it was rescued by Gordon Brown. What unnerved investors more was the £2.3 billion of operating losses that the bank unveiled for 2013 – worse than the £1.7 billion that analysts had been expecting. More than anything else, this was what sent RBS's share price tumbling 9.3 per cent to 321 pence that morning.

In view of the massive losses, the bonuses the bank awarded seemed positively bizarre. Even though the losses the bank was declaring for 2013 were largely caused by reckless behaviour which was driven by, you guessed it, excessive bonuses; McEwan still saw fit to earmark £576 million for the payment of staff bonuses. The 56-year-old Kiwi insisted that RBS had no option, saying, 'A shrinking, but still important, part of our business operates in international markets, and our customers expect us to have the best people in the world supporting them in those markets.'

Many Britons found it incomprehensible. RBS seemed no less eager to reward people for failure than when it had given Fred Goodwin a £703,000 pension after he destroyed the bank. Unite national officer Rob MacGregor said, 'This is a state-sponsored grab by greedy senior bankers . . . In allowing this behaviour he [Chancellor George Osborne] is proving he has learnt nothing.'[13] Deputy Prime Minister Nick Clegg said RBS would have to show greater restraint. McEwan's mantra on results day was that RBS was determined to regain the trust of its customers and the public, but by doling out so much in bonuses to colleagues he was queering his own pitch. At least McEwan was candid about the bank's reputation, saying, 'We are the least trusted company in the least trusted sector of the economy. That must change.' He admitted the Tomlinson Report (not the actions it described) had been very damaging to the business, insisting it was being taken seriously. 'It has struck at the heart of our organisation,' he said, while continuing to deny all allegations of systematic fraud.[14] He also outlined various building blocks by which he felt RBS might transform itself from being a hated pariah to being a trusted and loved institution. These included:

- A renewed focus on the UK: McEwan said he would accelerate the retrenchment that started under Stephen Hester and focus on serving the needs of individuals and businesses in Britain.
- A simplified structure: he would crunch RBS's seven divisions into three: personal and commercial banking; commercial and private banking; and corporate and institutional banking.
- Simpler, more honest, products: McEwan said the bank would scrap 'teaser' rates; deals that penalise existing customers; and preferential online rates. He said it was 'abhorrent' that some rates and deals were not available to all customers.
- Business bankers back in the branches: RBS said it would reverse the decision, taken under Sir George Mathewson during Project Columbus, to remove business bankers from the branches, and speed up decision-making in this area.

- Slashing costs: McEwan said he was committed to cutting RBS's costs by £5.3 billion over the next four years but refused to confirm whether the media speculation was right and that this would mean 30,000 job losses.
- A reformed investment bank: McEwan said M&IB would cease proprietary trading, and refocus on serving the needs of UK and European businesses.

Among the challenges ahead, SVM Asset Management chief executive Colin McLean said, 'The biggest facing McEwan are getting a decent price for Citizens Financial Group, especially given it failed the Federal Reserve's "stress tests", and winding down the investment bank.'¹⁵

On results day, the Edinburgh-based insurance company Standard Life infuriated some Scottish nationalists by saying it had drawn up contingency plans to leave Scotland in the event of a 'yes' vote in the Scottish independence referendum, which was scheduled for 18 September 2014. Alliance Trust, a financial institution based in Dundee, also threatened to move parts of its operations south of Hadrian's Wall in the event of Scotland becoming independent. RBS was less explicit about how it might respond to such an eventuality. However, buried in the 'risk factors' section of its results announcement, the bank did quietly warn that Scottish independence 'would be likely to significantly impact the group's credit ratings and could also impact the fiscal, monetary, legal and regulatory landscape to which the group is subject'.

Many believed the bank would have no option other than to relocate its headquarters south of the border in the event of Scotland breaking away. The Scottish economy, with a GDP of £150 billion, would simply be too small to underwrite its total assets of £1.19 trillion. But McEwan preferred to keep schtum, saying the decision was one for the Scots.

In his address to investors and media in the incongruous setting of the Trampery – a fashionable 'shared workspace' for technology firms in east London, McEwan said: 'RBS lost its way before 2008 because it became detached from the customer-focused values that have to be at the heart of any bank. The bank, and of course the British taxpayer, paid a very heavy price for the self-serving decisions that were made at RBS . . . We cannot take trust for granted. We have to earn it by how we act and how we behave. Today won't be the end of bad headlines.

Past failures will continue to haunt us. But we can weather them . . .

'I also want to take this opportunity to be straight with the British people. We need to recognise that we are not yet a strong enough bank to privatise at a profit for the taxpayer in the immediate future. The journey to recovery and renewal is harder than was first anticipated back in 2008. There is no point avoiding this inconvenient truth . . .

'What I have learned [however] is that our customers and our staff have not given up on us. They know that everyone in the UK has a stake in RBS. They see often that we have good employees with good intentions. Our customers are often frustrated, but if we can get our house in order, they are eager for us to support them to meet their financial goals. They do want us to succeed. I really believe that. But they want us to do much better. I know we can.'[16]

McEwan's frankness and desire to introduce more honest pricing marked him out from his more disingenuous predecessors. However, it was undermined by his failure to address the bonus issue and worries about the viability of his plan.

A key problem he will face is that it is difficult to improve customer service at the same time as cutting costs. Mass redundancies would alienate the remaining staff, who would also have less time to complete each task, causing customer service to worsen. The only way in which McEwan can improve customer service while cutting costs is if the bank can develop state-of-the-art mobile apps and online transactional platforms, on a par with the sort of things already available from the likes of Amazon, Google and PayPal. That way McEwan might be able to secure the loyalty of sufficient numbers of younger consumers to take the sting out of branch closures and downsizing. The second challenge facing McEwan is financial. As the bank retreats to its native soil and becomes a mini-me to Lloyds Banking Group, a process that is likely to see the sale or closure of the Connecticut-based RBS Securities (formerly RBS Greenwich Capital) and the partial sale of Ulster Bank's Irish operations, RBS may struggle to generate sufficient revenues to cover its 'legacy' costs, which include the high cost of settling with customers whom it swindled or harmed, and the fallout from numerous ongoing regulatory and criminal probes.

A third challenge is avoiding a relapse. There is a danger that, under pressure to deliver McEwan's ambitious 15 per cent return on equity target, RBS's bankers will have no option other than to revert to the sort of behaviour – reckless lending, charging 'distressed' business borrowers extortionate fees, and mis-selling useless insurance products – that caused it to become such a hated institution in the first place. McEwan says he is determined to rebuild trust. But that will only be possible if the bank behaves in a trustworthy way right across its business.

The guilty men

Royal Bank of Scotland was not alone in being shabby, reckless, greedy, dysfunctional and corrupt during the build-up to the crisis. Nor was it alone in being like that in its aftermath. There were plenty of other banks around the world with these vices in spades. And many of them crashed and burned too. Others that failed and needed to be rescued include: Dexia and Fortis in Belgium; Allied Irish Banks, Anglo-Irish Bank and Bank of Ireland in Ireland; Kaupthing, Glitnir and Landsbanki in Iceland; HBOS and Northern Rock in the UK; and Bear Stearns, Citigroup, Lehman Brothers, Merrill Lynch, Wachovia and Washington Mutual in the USA. And many other banks only survived as a result of broader rescue programmes and money-printing by central banks. The Royal Bank, like these other banks, was very much a creature of its age. With growth its main focus, the board of directors and its management became wilfully blind to the riskiness of the assets they were buying. And the 'Greenspan doctrine' infected the thinking of financial regulators, auditors, credit-rating agencies, the Bank of England, governments and politicians. More than 200,000 people worked for the Royal Bank of Scotland at the time of its October 2008 collapse. But there was only one person in the driver's seat at the time of its collapse, and he had been in that position for the previous eight and a half years.

Fred Goodwin – RBS CEO 2000–08

Fred Goodwin had delusions of grandeur. He was determined to show the world that a plucky little bank from Scotland could play with the big guys. First, he wanted to take on England, then the USA and then the world. He wanted the fame and glory that would come from this, together with the money, power and lifestyle. He was self-confident, aggressive and contemptuous of anyone who questioned his vision but, with hindsight, he seems to have been a one-trick pony who became overly obsessed with the baubles of wealth. He believed that, after pulling off the £21-billion acquisition of NatWest, RBS had developed a secret formula for perpetual growth. The strategy was to make acquisitions without necessarily worrying too much about the price or how they would be paid for, since the assets could be sweated – which entailed sacking thousands of people and pressuring those who remained to sell more financial products – and it was assumed that the cumulative proceeds of the cost cuts and the revenue synergies would finance each deal. Goodwin pulled the trick off so often – he made 27 acquisitions as RBS chief executive – that he grew to believe he could keep on using it forever. His problem, however, was that he had no plan B for financing deals on the occasions when the cost cuts and revenue synergies failed to materialise – as happened with both Charter One and ABN AMRO. The assumptions were wrong and the model naive since it was dependent on the good ship RBS always having a fair economic wind to fill its sails.

In pursuit of his goal, Goodwin was prepared to take a lot of risks. One ex-executive director said that, given the speed with which RBS depleted deposits in the wake of the NatWest deal and became dependent on the wholesale funding market, it was almost certain to sink after it bought another large bank that was in a similar position. 'We were over-leveraged and we went for a crazy bank [ABN AMRO] and the economic climate changed. He was not rigged for bad weather. His mainsail was on full. Even a cheap merger can look bad if the economic conditions change. An expensive one can be disastrous.'

The City, having given Goodwin the thumbs-up during the battle for NatWest, almost fell in love with him because of the perceived skill and determination with which he crunched RBS and NatWest together. However, according to some former RBS executive directors the NatWest integration was massively over-hyped. The former chairman of Corporate Banking and Financial Markets Iain Robertson said, 'Lots about Fred's reputation was complete bloody nonsense. Fred was not that much better at cutting costs than many other people.'[1] However, the positive reception of the NatWest deal went to Goodwin's head.

As the storm gathered, a 'cult of Fred' inside RBS meant staff were unaware of how the bank was perceived and oblivious to the precariousness of its business model. Taken together with Goodwin's capricious and tyrannical management style, which discouraged dissent or challenge, this mass delusion played a big part in the bank's demise. For example, even after the bursting of the global credit bubble in July 2007, the bank's economists looked at the global economic outlook through rose-tinted spectacles, which in turn skewed the judgement of its top brass. On 6 June 2012, in his blog at www.evidencebasedhr.com, management expert Paul Kearns said, 'Fred Goodwin has undoubted talents but his management style is not one of them and it was the culture he created, above everything else, that ultimately condemned RBS to its inevitable fate.' And, in a separate interview, Kearns said, 'When the man at the top is a tyrant, the whole organisation becomes tyrannical. The only people who can survive in such a regime are other tyrants or people with absolutely no integrity, who will blow with the wind, and behave like the tyrant. In a terror regime the boss's motto is "either you agree with me or your career is dead in this organisation".'[2]

Goodwin's approach of verbally dismantling ('shredding') subordinates in front of their colleagues, his reluctance to heed advice and his lack of any internal confidants ensured he was increasingly out of touch and behaving like a medieval monarch, surrounded by cronies, courtiers and 'yes' men, without even a fool to remind him of his own human frailties. In an interview with *Institutional Investor Magazine*, published in August 2001, Goodwin said, 'It's hard for me to do my job if I don't have an understanding of how our business works.'[3] He was right. Yet, in allowing RBS's huge investment banking arm, which he has admitted he never fully understood, to balloon in size from 2003–04 onwards, he failed to abide by his own maxim. To imagine that he could play with the big boys of investment banking, such as Goldman Sachs, without really understanding what investment banking involved, was a dereliction of duty. So was allowing a bunch of traders at Greenwich Capital in Connecticut to abuse the enlarged NatWest/RBS balance without making sure he understood what they were doing or providing much oversight. So was the acceptance of a situation in which senior underlings like Leith Robertson were able to recklessly lend scores of billions of pounds into the private equity and commercial real estate sectors with insufficient supervision. Colin

McLean, chief executive of SVM Asset Management says, 'I think the biggest problem was that Fred didn't have enough banking experience to understand what's critical over a cycle for a banking model. He built an edifice that could fall over very easily.'[4]

One ex-executive director of RBS accuses Goodwin of squandering Mathewson's legacy. In a private document, he wrote:

- To the bank's cost, he did not understand corporate banking, corporate credit or the treasury function;
- He failed to build a credible management team, with many of Mathewson's praetorian guard heading quickly for the exit;
- He did not continue the investment in the bank's operating platform;
- The RBS culture was morphed from one of collegiate co-operation into a style characterised by fear and indecision.

Other errors that happened on Goodwin's watch included taking retail customers for granted, mis-selling products to UK and US retail and commercial customers and turning a blind eye to some of the shocking practices inside his bank (some of which involved multiple criminal acts). As hubris and vaingloriousness started to get the better of him, the bank became Goodwin's plaything. From 2005 onwards he was increasingly side-tracked by 'vanity' projects such as the Gogarburn headquarters and sponsorship of Formula One, which caused him to take his eye off the ball.

He appears to have abused the bank's resources to fund his own pampered lifestyle. He spent £18m on a corporate jet, £5.3 million on the conversion of a Grade A listed town house on St Andrew Square, £350 million on the campus-style headquarters at Gogarburn and $500 million on a US headquarters in Stamford, Connecticut with the world's second largest trading floor. Pantone 281-coloured Mercedes S600s with chauffeurs wearing peaked hats were on call 24/7 wherever he went. He indulged himself with a permanent suite in the Savoy hotel, complete with personal valet to look after his clothes. He recruited his boyhood heroes Sir Jackie Stewart and Jack Nicklaus as £3-million-a-year 'global ambassadors' for the bank, had fresh fruit flown daily from Paris and deluxe pies delivered on demand from his favourite pie-makers, Yorkes of Dundee. And then of course, during

2008, he had an extra-marital affair with a female colleague, reportedly a senior human resources professional at RBS Group who still cannot be named for legal reasons. Former colleagues and commentators suggest the alleged affair caused conflicts of interest. And, according to the *Sunday Times*, Goodwin failed to report it to either RBS's chairman or its board of directors, which was in breach of the bank's internal code of conduct.[5]

Even so, the FSA concluded that the picture was 'clearly more complex than the one-dimensional "dominant CEO" sometimes suggested in the media'. The regulator conceded that Goodwin could come across as 'somewhat cold, analytical and unsympathetic' but the report also says he could be courteous and professional and only infrequently intervened in board meetings.[6]

In an article published in online magazine *Slate* three months after Goodwin left the bank, the American journalist Daniel Gross asked, 'Who's the world's worst banker?' He chose Goodwin out of a long list because he had 'aced every requirement for a hubristic CEO' and 'designed a house that would teeter when the slightest ill wind began to blow'.[7] Gross gave six main reasons for choosing Goodwin:

- Carrying off mergers and acquisitions and calling them growth? Yes.
- Ill-advised, history-making, massive merger precisely at the top? Yep.
- Massive commitment of capital to investment banking, trading in funky securities, and poor credit controls? Yes, yes, and yes.
- Building an expensive, self-indulgent new headquarters building just in time for the collapse? Right-o.
- Telling shareholders you don't need more capital, and then raising it – and then having that capital lose value rapidly? Yep.
- And finally: dump problems on fellow citizens by messing things up so badly the bank has to be nationalised? Bingo.[8]

'The result? RBS's stock has lost 91 per cent of its value since March 2007 and retains value thanks only to massive government intervention. A job well-done, Sir Fred!'[9]

So what has Fred Goodwin been up to since the crisis he helped create? During 2010 he topped up his £342,500 annual pension with a £100,000-a year consultancy role at Edinburgh-based architects RMJM, majority-owned by his friend Sir Fraser Morrison. But the job was short-lived. Goodwin rubbed up his new colleagues the wrong way, and quit in January 2011 after his ruthless penny-pinching and abrasive management style precipitated a massed exodus from the troubled firm's Hong Kong office. Departing RMJM director David Pringle said Goodwin was 'deeply unpopular with most of the directors and staff that he came into contact with. A fantastic, lovely guy socially – but, in work mode, no empathy.'

In May 2011, it emerged that Goodwin had had an extra-marital affair with a still unnamed senior RBS colleague in his final years at the bank. The news, which prompted widespread speculation as to whether the liaison broke corporate governance guidelines or would have impaired his performance at the bank, surfaced in spite of a strict gagging order his lawyers managed to obtain from London's High Court. In court papers, the ousted RBS chief executive admitted that he concealed the relationship from bank colleagues for fear of their disapproval and that it might damage his career. He told the court he wanted to censor the media with a 'super injunction' because he suspected the news would have a 'serious negative impact' on his personal life.

He was right. When Joyce Goodwin learned of her husband's infidelity, she is said to have been so angry she ejected him from their recently-purchased family home in Edinburgh's leafy Colinton district. Goodwin returned to live in his former home in the Grange, which the family had fled after its windows were smashed in March 2009. In recent years, Goodwin has lived there pretty much as a recluse, occasionally surfacing for pheasant-shooting with a select group of trusted friends, including the double-glazing tycoon Gerard Eadie, the former chairman of stockbrokers Brewin Dolphin, Jamie Matheson, and former Merrill Lynch investment banker Matthew Greenburgh. He is also said to be a regular on the two championship golf courses at Archerfield, the Duke of Hamilton's former residence near Dirleton.

In January 2012, less than two months after the FSA published its report into RBS's failure, Sir Fred faced a further setback when he was formally stripped of his knighthood by the Queen on the recommendation of the Honours Forfeiture Committee. To an extent this was a diversionary tactic by the coalition government, aimed at taking the

sting out of public anger about the economic crisis the bank's collapse
had caused. Chancellor George Osborne justified the move by saying
RBS was emblematic of 'everything that went wrong in the British
economy over the last decade,' before adding, 'Fred Goodwin was in
charge, and I think it's appropriate that he loses his knighthood'. Only
a select band of despots, traitors, brigands and mountebanks – including Robert Mugabe, Nicolae Ceaucescu, Anthony Blunt and Lester
Piggott – have had knighthoods removed in the past.

Nicola Sturgeon, who became first minister of Scotland in November
2014, recently assured me that the Crown Office and Procurator Fiscal
Service continues to investigate alleged criminal wrongdoing by RBS
as part of the wide-ranging inquiry commenced in late 2011. In a letter
dated May 2015, Sturgeon said she agrees with the Crown Office that
'it is important that the fall of RBS is properly investigated to identify
any criminality there may be'. She added, 'The Crown Office and
Procurator Fiscal Service have advised that the inquiry is complex and
the volume of documentation that the investigators are considering is
huge. The inquiry is being conducted by the Serious and Organised
Crime Division of the Crown Office under the supervision of the Lord
Advocate [Frank Mulholland]. This involves police, prosecutors and
specialist forensic accountants. I am sure you appreciate that given the
task faced, the Lord Advocate anticipates the inquiry will take some
time to conclude. If criminality is uncovered, then the Lord Advocate
has indicated that criminal proceedings will be instructed.'

That sounds quite serious. However, by February 2015, Goodwin did
not see himself as being at risk of arrest. Indeed, he was welcomed back
into the heart of Edinburgh establishment. Early that month, he turned
up at the Oyster Club, an Edinburgh drinking society founded in the
1770s where he was a member, after an absence of about five years. The
first two people he met on crossing the threshold were two of Scotland's
most senior policemen. They greeted him like a long-lost friend.

Despite repeated requests, Goodwin has refused to be interviewed
for this book.

Tom McKillop – RBS chairman 2006–09

Senior executives at Royal Bank of Scotland were reassured by some
of the early noises made by Sir Tom McKillop, who was confirmed as

the bank's chairman in December 2005. McKillop, a Royal Bank of Scotland non-executive director from September 2005, took over the chairmanship from George Mathewson on 28 April 2006. When he arranged for one-to-one meetings with each of the divisional heads, they felt change was in the air. McKillop had such meetings with Johnny Cameron, Gordon Pell, Larry Fish, Cormac McCarthy and Annette Court, who joined Direct Line in 1994 and was chief executive of RBS's general insurance business from 2003 to 2006. At each session, the incoming chairman asked them if they had any concerns. Several told the Ayrshireman, then aged 63, that their overriding concern was Goodwin's management style. They told the chairman designate that Fred disliked bad news and could be a tyrant and a bully. One says, 'People were quite straight with McKillop about that.' At the time, McKillop told the directors, 'I have heard this from other people. I'll make sure that something gets done – it'll be dealt with.'

But to his eternal discredit McKillop didn't seem to do anything. Indeed, if anything, he seems to have been as much in denial about the problem as Mathewson was. One ex-executive director believes the former drugs company boss even egged Goodwin on, saying, 'Tom stood four-square alongside Fred and was a bully as well. He was pushing in the same direction as Fred.' History does not relate whether McKillop ever made any real effort to persuade Goodwin to change his ways. It's possible he was taken in by the smoke and mirrors surrounding Goodwin's achievements.

Insiders say that two months after becoming chairman McKillop was gung-ho about the bank's decision to push harder into investment banking – notably structured finance (CDOs, CLOs etc.), leveraged finance (funding private equity buyouts) and commercial real estate lending. He was also one of the most gung-ho about the acquisition of ABN AMRO in March 2007. Since these were the two decisions that arguably killed RBS, McKillop is clearly pretty culpable. He repeatedly said, 'The buck stops with me.' He later admitted that the ABN AMRO acquisition had been 'a bad mistake', adding that ABN AMRO was bought 'at the top of the market, so anything we paid was an error', confirming that ABN AMRO was, by February 2009, worth nothing.[10] As chairman he could have saved the bank. It is, therefore, surprising that McKillop's name is only mentioned twice in the FSA's report into the bank's failure.

During his time as chief executive of AstraZeneca, one of its drugs, the heartburn remedy Nexium, became a poster child of deceptive and unlawful marketing practices.[11] Also, the medical journal *The Lancet* accused AstraZeneca, under McKillop, of promoting one of its drugs using an 'unprincipled campaign' and urged McKillop to desist.[12] McKillop appears to have done little or nothing to stop deceptive and unethical sales and marketing practices at RBS – particularly for payment protection insurance and interest-rate swap agreements in the UK and for mortgage-backed securities in the US. The regulatory costs, litigation costs and damages arising from allowing such malpractice to persist at the bank will, in due course, run into scores of billions and could bankrupt the bank.

Another criticism of McKillop is that he could have restructured the board so that it was peopled with directors who were robust enough to challenge and stand up to Goodwin. He did manage to haul in three new non-executive directors with strong banking credentials in August 2008 – Arthur Ryan, Stephen Hester and John McFarlane. He also got rid of two directors who were tainted by the Charter One deal – Larry Fish and Bud Koch. Ultimately, however, McKillop's attempts to shape up governance at the bank fell far short of what was required.

McKillop could seem out of his depth in analyst presentations and is regarded as having glossed over some of the fundamentals as the bank sank further and further into the ordure over the course of 2007–08. One example was when he appeared to say that neither the FSA nor the Bank of England had any role in the Edinburgh-based bank's decision to proceed with a £12-billion capital-raising drive in April 2008. He sometimes came across as naive about the world of finance – for example, when speaking to the Treasury committee in February 2009, he revealed that he had had absolute faith in ratings from Standard & Poor's and Moody's saying, 'We never imagined the parts we were holding, a large part of it was AAA or super senior, we never imagined, as Fred said earlier, that could end up as 10 cents in the dollar.'[13]

In his favour, McKillop did offer one of the most grovelling apologies made by any banker or bank director in the wake of the crisis. Speaking at a shareholder meeting in the Assembly Hall of the Church of Scotland on Edinburgh's Mound on Thursday, 20 November 2008, he said, 'Both personally and in the office I hold, I am profoundly sorry about the position that we have reached. The buck stops with me as chairman and with the leadership of the group. Accountability has been allocated and fully accepted.'[14]

In reality, accountability has been neither allocated nor accepted. Like most of the bankers who led institutions to their doom, McKillop remains firmly in denial, blaming the global financial crisis on government and claiming that it was only with hindsight that the ABN AMRO deal looked ill-advised. There were plenty of commentators, including the *Daily Telegraph*'s Damian Reece, who publicly stated they thought it looked insane long before RBS signed along the dotted line.[15] McKillop also gave far too much credence to the advice of the bank's lawyers, Linklaters, on whether RBS could invoke the Material Adverse Change clause in order to scrap its offer for ABN in August to October 2007. If he had had more sense, the Ayrshireman would have ignored Linklaters' advice and pulled out anyway.

George Mathewson – RBS chairman 2000–06

As chief executive of Royal Bank of Scotland between 1992 and 2000, George Mathewson turned it around following the crisis of 1990–91 and pursued an innovative strategy that rebuilt the bank. He was very ambitious for RBS, seeing growing it both in the UK and internationally as the surest bulwark against its being taken over. He consistently ran the bank with an 'efficient' balance sheet – meaning within the parameters of the Basel Accord and using relatively low capital ratios and relatively high leverage to bolster returns – but he never took outrageous risks as chief executive. Indeed, in his period as chief executive, growth in earnings-per-share, profits and the share price were impressive and it was one of the UK's best performing banks during these years. Unfortunately, however, Mathewson also made three terrible errors. The first was to appoint Fred Goodwin as his successor. A simple phone call to Deloitte would have told him that Goodwin had misrepresented his role on the global liquidation of BCCI and a call to Clydesdale Bank would have told Mathewson that Goodwin was a poor manager who was despised by most of his staff. His second was to regard Tom McKillop as a suitable successor and to engineer the Ayrshireman's appointment.

Mathewson's third big mistake was that, on succeeding George

Younger as Royal Bank's chairman in April 2001, he erred towards being too hands-off. It was partly because he did not fancy having constant rows with Fred Goodwin. However, his detachment and lack of engagement with the bank intensified after Goodwin overpaid for Ohio-based Charter One in April 2004. Relations between Goodwin and Mathewson soured from this point onwards.

Mathewson acknowledges some mistakes that were made, including appointing Johnny Cameron to run Global Banking and Markets. Arguably, he also made some other unfortunate appointments, including several individuals who bank insiders claimed 'lacked any moral compass'. He blames other mistakes on 'pressure from the City' – that is institutional investors pressurising management to run the bank in a certain way so as to boost short-term shareholder returns. He says, 'After we had made RBS one of the most efficient banks in the UK, the City wanted to know what next? The pressure from the market was, if you don't find another way of increasing your return on capital, you will be taken over. So to some extent you get into this syndrome of take over or be taken over.'[16]

For Mathewson, the next pressure was to securitise the bank's loans – bundling them up into tradable bonds which could be sold to third-party investors, thereby removing them from the balance sheet. Mathewson said he and Iain Robertson would have preferred that the bank held leveraged loans until they matured, instead of securitising them. 'But Johnny Cameron was telling us we would not get such a good return on capital if we did that,' Mathewson said. 'Securitisation does have a place but, in my view, it also causes corruption. What does securitisation do? It takes the profits that you get from holding a loan over a period and pulls a big chunk of these profits into today's P&L, therefore contributing to bonuses. That gives flawed incentives for lending. Securitisation is a big problem and it lies behind a lot of the issues that have come up in recent years.'

So, to Mathewson's credit, he has thought through some of the flawed practices that fuelled the global financial crisis, but to his debit he did not do enough to control them. To vindicate himself fully, he needs to publicly acknowledge that he made errors of judgement in appointing Goodwin and McKillop.

Johnny Cameron – CEO/chairman RBS Global Banking and Markets 2000–08

Johnny Cameron had been a successful corporate banker at County NatWest, Dresdner Kleinwort Benson and Royal Bank of Scotland but he was out of his depth as the chief executive of a massive investment bank with operations in London, Connecticut, New York, Frankfurt, Madrid, Milan, Paris, Stockholm, Singapore, Japan, etc.

The urbane and affable Cameron says it was 'great fun' being a banker until the end of 2006. With economic conditions benign, regulators relaxed and liquidity plentiful, it was an unusually propitious environment to be building GBM.[17] He was a great salesman and motivator of people. Paradoxically, he was also, at the time, seen as a safe pair of hands. Writing after Cameron was elevated to the RBS main board in March 2006, Peter Thal Larsen, the *Financial Times*'s banking editor, said, '[S]hareholders have developed a growing regard for Mr Cameron, who has been able to avoid the mistakes previously made by British banks during their forays into investment banking.'[18] To his credit, Cameron did launch what he calls a 'drains-up' probe of the bank's mortgage-backed securities business, focused on RBS Greenwich Capital, in March 2007 and reined in the bank's use of conduits (off-balance sheet vehicles dependent on short-term funding). But where he fell down was his lack of in-depth knowledge of some areas of the markets business and in being too trusting of some of the individuals within it. One ex-Lazard investment banker said, 'If you're in investment banking but don't understand the mechanics of it, you're likely to come horribly unstuck. The traders will pretty much run rings around you, since you, as the manager, won't know what questions to ask. They will take bigger and bigger risks. In investment banking, everything is going round in circles. It's a game of musical chairs and the people who get left standing when the music stops are always the dim boys and, in this case, the dim boys were RBS. Yes, Cameron deserves a lot of blame because he exuded self-confidence, to the extent that many of the clearing bankers in the organisation probably thought he knew what he was doing.'

For at least ten months after the financial crisis intensified in July 2007, Cameron – like his boss Fred Goodwin – believed it would be a short-term phenomenon. In May 2008, he told a long-standing confidant over breakfast in London's Ritz hotel that he believed many of RBS's credit-market exposures could ultimately make huge profits for the bank. He believed they had been written down way below their true value and would ultimately come good.[19] It was a heroically sanguine mindset which ensured that insufficient steps were taken to prepare the bank for the coming storm. Cameron says his biggest regret is that when Fred Goodwin asked him to produce the numbers to justify the acquisition of ABN AMRO's investment banking arm he obliged him, rather than telling him the deal would be insane.[20]

Cameron was singled out for investigation by the Financial Services Authority in May 2009 and is the only RBS executive who has suffered any form of retribution from the regulator. In May 2010, the FSA reached a settlement with Cameron under which he agreed not to perform 'any significant influence function in relation to any regulated activity carried on by any authorised person, exempt person or exempt professional firm; or undertake any further full-time employment in the financial services industry.'[21] In exchange, the now disbanded regulator said it had not found any evidence of regulatory breach against Cameron and would not pursue any disciplinary action against him. As the American financial journalist Matt Levine said, '[Cameron], by reason of background and temperament, has been made to look like a bumbling moron who blew up his bank through incompetence, and has suffered the consequences of not being allowed near another bank.'[22] It is worth pointing out, however, that plenty of other people who worked for GBM are no less culpable than Cameron and many have also emerged from the wreckage of RBS as multi-millionaires. The people concerned include Brian Crowe, Leith Robertson, Euan Hamilton, Jay Levine, Ben Carpenter, John Walsh, Peter Nielsen, Symon Drake-Brockman and Vincent Dahinden. Despite their culpability for RBS's collapse, Robertson and Hamilton have not been prevented from establishing their own brand-new investment firm, Edinburgh-based Cramond Capital Partners.

Corporate governance/non-executive directors

The FSA report said it could find no procedural failure of governance at RBS board level during the review period but it did identify 'substantive failures of board effectiveness'.[23] It found evidence that the RBS board failed to challenge the management enough, failed to challenge the assumptions that underpinned its strategy, failed to appreciate the risks of proceeding with the ABN deal because they were obsessed by scale and failed to pay sufficient attention to banking fundamentals like capital, liquidity and asset quality.

Corporate governance expert Lucy Marcus says the size of the board, a lack of independence among its members, the board's failure to act in the interests of the business and its stakeholders and the board's over-dependence on carefully edited board papers were major contributors to the bank's near demise.[24]

The board's size definitely reduced its effectiveness. The FSA report said having a board of 18 members 'made it less manageable and more difficult for individual directors to contribute'.[25] Marcus says that having a board with more than nine members invariably means that a company ends up with a two-tier board, where some people are more committed or involved than others.

The RBS board was largely peopled by members of the establishment and suffered from 'group-think'. This was particularly evident during the ABN AMRO takeover battle, with the only real sceptics being Sir Steve Robson and Gordon Pell. As the FSA report makes clear, there was an absence of 'rigorous testing, questioning and challenge that would be expected in an effective board process dealing with such a large and strategic proposition' as the ABN takeover.[26] Most directors just took Fred's word for things and assumed that, because he had eked out more cost savings and revenue synergies than expected from NatWest and other takeovers, he would repeat the trick with ABN AMRO.

Board directors were hesitant about speaking their minds – an issue that could have been lessened if the board had had a wider range of people with a broader range of views. The FSA report also said the RBS board 'displayed inadequate sensitivity to the wholly exceptional and, compared with other companies, unique importance of customer and counterparty confidence in a bank and its chosen strategy'.[27] It was also 'much more focused on revenue and profit than on the size of the balance sheet'.[28]

Goodwin tended to package information and present things in ways that skewed and stifled board-level debate. For example, when seeking approval for the $10.5 billion Charter One deal in 2004, he presented this as a *fait accompli*. Marcus said that Part 2 of the FSA report, on management, governance and culture, 'is a reminder of what engaged, committed directors need to think about every time they read their board papers, walk into a board dinner, or attend a board meeting'.[29] It was, she said, an example of how not to do things. Writing in the newspaper he used to edit, former head of the CBI and former *Financial Times* editor Richard Lambert said, 'Since the underlying problem was about governance, it's vital that the broader lessons are learnt. These are that a forceful chief executive in a complex business and with the wrong incentives is unlikely to be constrained by an over-large board of directors drawn from the same establishment pool – and that the results can be calamitous.'[30]

However, some fund managers see the focus on corporate governance as a red herring. 'To expect the chairman or the non-executive directors to be able to change anything inside a bank is unrealistic,' said the head of financials at one of the UK's largest fund management firms. 'To be honest, they rarely have much of a clue about what's going on. All banks are led by the chief executive. Non-executives never have either the ammunition or the time to work out what's really going on inside a bank. As shareholders, we don't rely on them at all – we rely on the CEO plus other senior executives.'

Board and bank too Scottish

Samuel Johnson once said that 'patriotism is the last refuge of the scoundrel' but, at RBS, it was seen as a virtue. Having been the biggest fish in the small pond of the Scottish market, the bank became arrogant and disdainful of other banks once it embarked on its southward and international expansion, deluding itself into thinking it possessed a unique skill set that set it apart – and, in the minds of some of its top people, it was its Scottishness that set it apart. RBS also fell foul of 'small country syndrome'. In order to survive as an independent player, it felt that it had to expand into the English and overseas markets. It was driven to pursue a reckless growth strategy by its fierce rivalry with its cross-town neighbour, the Bank of Scotland.

Speaking ahead of the rights issue announcement in April 2008, Gordon Pell said, 'At that time [March 2000, when he joined RBS from NatWest], I was the only Englishman on the board of RBS, and I used to say quite openly that our attitude to diversity was that we didn't have a problem because we did occasionally recruit English people.'[31] And it is widely believed that the main reason that Sir Tom McKillop was appointed as the bank's chairman was that he was Scottish.

One former non-executive director at Royal Bank believes that having a preponderance of Scots on the board was an impediment to good corporate governance and a key reason for its failure. He said: 'It was dominated by Scots and there was almost a patriotic pride in the Royal Bank of Scotland. As far as I could make out, Scots, by and large, had seen their companies either collapse or be taken over by companies from outside Scotland. And here was a Scottish company that was doing the reverse – it was taking over English companies, American companies, Irish companies, Chinese companies, and it was being seen as successful. There was an element of national pride in all this, which you would never have had with an English company, and that coloured the view of most of the Scots on the board.

'Because there were so many Scots on the board and there was this element of national pride, I think it meant the Scottish directors were not disposed to challenge the management because they shared in this national pride. I think that got in the way of good governance. The board was too big and it was not diverse enough, and this Scottish thing went to the selection of senior executives. By and large, there was a preference for Scots and, if you talk to any headhunter that was working for the Royal Bank, they will tell you it was quite clear there was a genetic dimension. That restricted the skill set – there are not that many big international banks based in Scotland so, if you're looking for people with experience of running big international banks, it is not the best place to look.'

Gillian Tett also highlighted the bank's Scottishness in her testimony to the Scottish Parliament's banking inquiry. She said: 'Among the things that drove the Scottish banks to do what they did were – again – a sense of insecurity, a desire to catch up quickly and be big on the global stage, naivety, and the thrill of the glory of suddenly being Mr Big and of thinking that their balance sheets were going to be as big as the entire UK economy, when they were nobody a few years ago. That is a heady and toxic combination that is, as we now know, lethal. Scotland has some long-standing areas of strength; it can, for example, be very proud of its asset management business. However, that business was built not in three or four years but by a lot of hard graft over many years. If there is one big message to take from the crisis, it is that there are not many short cuts: that people should value and take pride in prudent, slow and steady building.'[32]

The majority of Scottish-based business and financial journalists who reported on RBS's rise and rise between 1999 and 2008 were, to an extent, complicit in the bank's collapse. As with some of the RBS non-executive directors and other Caledonian cheerleaders, their pride in this national champion to a large extent blinded them to its many flaws.

Risk management

As in other banks, risk management at RBS was a box-ticking exercise where independence of thought was discouraged. Most of the bank's risk managers and compliance officers were co-opted by so-called 'front-office' staff, including the bonus-crazed traders. Generally paid far less than front-office staff, risk managers had a much lower status inside the organisation, which contributed to their inability to success-fully challenge their fee-earning colleagues. Other problems were that Goodwin allowed the risk-management IT systems to atrophy to the extent that, as the bank expanded, it was increasingly oblivious to the risks it was taking. In an interview published in December 2012, John Hourican, former CEO of M&IB, said the back-office IT systems were so badly flawed that they 'helped bring down the bank', adding, 'It was like flying in the dark with no instruments.'[33] The use of models, such as 'Value at Risk' (discussed in Chapter 19), based on false assumptions, gave risk-taking traders and their managers a handy security blanket that dispelled anxiety. The FSA report into the bank's failure said there was too narrow a focus on VaR at the expense of examining risk in other ways.[34]

Speaking in November 2009, Hester said the failures in risk manage-ment were 'obvious to all'. He said, 'The failure of risk management was in macro risk management, as opposed to things that were hidden in drawers and not visible. That is not to say that things that are hidden in drawers and not visible should not be risk managed [but] it was not the detailed risks that made RBS and the banking system weak; it was the big, macro imbalances. In RBS's case, the weakness was in having a balance sheet that was too big, was vulnerable to funding and was not supported by adequate capital, and a management stretch that went alongside that.'[35]

The FSA report said that Global Banking and Markets was essentially flying blind because of a flawed approach to risk management, flawed reporting systems and flawed understanding of risk among its top executives. The report identified management information as being particularly deficient where CDOs were concerned. GBM also had some malleable prima donnas in senior risk roles. Gillian Tett said the silo-like structures within banks like RBS meant people always assumed that managing risk and being prudent was someone else's problem. She said, 'The banks that did better tended to have a much more collective attitude to and responsibility for risk.'[36]

The markets/institutional investors

The Bank of England executive director for financial stability, Andy Haldane, believes that the 'dictatorship of equity' – in which the ownership and control of banks are in the hands of a small and diminishing band of shareholders – played a key part in fomenting the crisis. Equity investors were constantly pressing the management of banks, including the Royal Bank of Scotland, to focus on growing short-term shareholder returns, both in terms of increased dividends and rising share prices, and to do so by running with 'efficient balance sheets'. That meant keeping capital reserves to the Basel-prescribed minimum and piling on leverage. Haldane added that shareholders' insistence that banks pursue increased return on equity as their core target contributed to bankers' recklessness. He said, 'RoE is not adjusted for risk but flattered by it' and this 'is fine for short-term investors' who benefit from a bumpy share price but means longer-term investors are on 'a road to nowhere ... What we have, then, is a set of mutually-reinforcing risk incentives. Investors shorten their horizons. They set RoE targets for management to boost their short-term stake. These targets in turn encourage short-term, risk-taking behaviour. That benefits the short-term investor at the expense of the long-term, generating incentives to shorten further horizons. And so the myopia loop continues.'[37]

Haldane said that, to boost equity returns, equity owners have a strong interest in increasing the volatility of the balance sheet. He believes that bank bosses and short-term investors at banks like RBS were effectively looting their institutions at the expense of longer-term investors.[38]

To break the myopia, or doom, loop, Haldane favours spreading governance and control right across banks' balance sheets – meaning depositors, bondholders and other creditors would have a greater say in the banks' strategic direction. He believes such a model would promote more responsible behaviour and curb the 'rent-seeking incentives' that predominate under the 'equity dictatorship' model.[39] Haldane concluded that it 'is the ultimate irony that an asset calling itself equity could have contributed to such inequity'.[40]

Haldane has separately blamed debt-holders in banks such as RBS, including the banks' depositors, for lending irresponsibly. They should have acted to restrain 'risk-hungry, excess-profit-seeking shareholders' by reining in the amount of credit they were providing and bumping up its cost at an earlier stage.[41] Haldane said, 'Debtors should act as a brake on risk-taking, but in practice they served as an accelerator.'[42]

Confident in the belief that the government would bail out any large British bank that got into difficulties, depositors and creditors came to believe their lending to such institutions was risk-free (which in turn persuaded them to lend at much lower rates of interest than if they had been exposed to true risk of default). As *The Economist* pointed out in a recent essay on financial crises, 'by loading risk onto the taxpayer, the evolution of finance had created a distorting subsidy at the heart of capitalism'.[43] Haldane has calculated this annual subsidy to be worth $350 billion (£230 billion) a year to British banks in 2007–11.[44]

Another problem is that most of the UK's investment management firms are not 'independent' but are tied to or else owned by investment banks or other financial institutions such as insurance firms. This creates conflicts of interest. For example, who is to know whether a fund manager pressurising a board of directors to embark on a takeover drive is not doing so in order that another part of their firm wins business and earns a fee?

Investors' constant refrain that Goodwin was a control freak, that they were not getting enough access to management and that RBS's levels of disclosure were poor, especially in the investment bank, was just carping from the sidelines. Investors were passive in communicating their dismay about the $10.5-billion Charter One acquisition in April 2004. The majority did so by dumping RBS's shares and walking away, though some investors put pressure on the RBS board and made their views plain via the Brunswick Report. But if they had genuine concerns about the bank and the way in which it was run, why did they endorse the takeover of ABN AMRO in August 2007, with 94.5 per cent of voting shareholders supporting the deal? There may be mitigating circumstances. It is possible Goodwin misrepresented the merits of the deal and, given that the RBS board unanimously supported the takeover plan, some shareholders feared that any failure to support it would prompt the entire board to resign, which would also be disastrous from a share-price perspective. This alone represented spectacular failure of the UK's supposedly superior 'comply or explain' corporate governance model.

Writing in *MoneyWeek*, the columnist Matthew Lynn said investors may have been 'frightened of offending such a major player in the markets'. He added, 'Whatever the explanation, they failed in their responsibilities to stand up to the management. Looking back, a significant vote against the deal – say 20 per cent – could well have derailed it. RBS might even have been saved.'[45]

Speaking in November 2009, City Minister Lord Myners said RBS was the 'worst-managed bank this country has ever seen' and that institutional investors were hugely to blame for its implosion. 'Where were the owners when these disastrous decisions were taken at RBS? They were egging the board on. The big question they need to answer is "What were you doing and what lessons have you learned?"'[46]

Regulators – the FSA, DNB and others

Like the institutional investors, the FSA was a watchdog that did not bark – or, if it did bark, it did so up the wrong tree. Its woefully inadequate pre-crisis approach to regulating banks was based on two false assumptions: that their boards of directors knew what they were doing and that they had integrity. The same was true of regulators elsewhere – De Nederlandsche Bank in particular should have been more alert to the state of ABN AMRO in the build-up to the crisis.

During RBS's supposedly successful years, the FSA was nonchalant about the quality of the bank's assets and didn't bat an eyelid as the bank became dangerously over-leveraged and geographically and organisationally stretched on the thinnest of capital layers. Nor did the regulator redeem itself in the final seven months before the bank failed. In ordering a rights issue on 9 April 2008 and failing to properly police the content of the prospectus document, the regulator failed again. It seems the regulator was not too worried if millions of investors got ripped off as long as the bank was saved.

The FSA chairman from 2003 to 2008, Sir Callum McCarthy, was the very model of a modern light-touch regulator, which made him the Blair government's favoured candidate for the job. The FSA has admitted that, right across the banking sector, supervision was under-resourced and that 'critically, the resources applied were far too low to adequately meet the challenges of supervising RBS'.[47] Only five FSA regulators were engaged in supervising the bank when it embarked on the world's biggest cross-border banking takeover in 2007. From 2003 onwards, the FSA was concerned about RBS's risk-management policies, its commercial property lending and Fred Goodwin's 'assertive and robust style'. However, the regulator did nothing to tackle any of these issues. It seems to have been scared of Fred, who repeatedly bullied it. Under McCarthy's chairmanship, the FSA was a largely toothless watchdog. The regulator would invariably back off at the first hint of menace from Fred – especially after Goodwin persuaded New Labour ministers to intervene on his behalf. Yet, if it suspected that something had gone seriously awry at RBS (as it had), it had the statutory powers under FSMA 2000 to obtain access and force change. Likewise the regulator's excuse that it was only supine because of political pressure to be 'light touch' and 'limited touch' is lame. The reason the regulator was given statutory independence was to ensure it would be impervious to political pressure.

The regulator should definitely have intervened to block the ABN AMRO takeover, and the reasons it has given for not doing so are specious. The Treasury committee said, 'The FSA's failure to assess the risks of the [ABN AMRO] deal represents a serious misjudgement on the part of the supervisory team and the senior management.'[48] The Treasury committee has recommended that the Prudential Regulation Authority and Financial Conduct Authority, the FSA's successor bodies, should completely overhaul the UK's approach to assessing and approving takeovers in the financial sector.

The 'revolving door' between regulators and regulated made proper regulation of the UK banking sector all but impossible. It meant the regulators shared the same world-view as the people they were supposed to be regulating. It also encouraged regulators to be unduly gentle with the banking sector. If an individual regulator were to embark on a crusade to root out corruption and take a few bankers' scalps for offences like false accounting or fraud, they would be seen as a boat rocker and they would be limiting their chances of getting a cushy job in the banking sector. The whole thing was almost absurdly cosy. FSA director James Crosby also served as CEO of HBOS until June 2006. A great many senior regulators came from an investment banking background – Sir Callum McCarthy was from Barclays Capital, Hector Sants from Credit Suisse and Lord Turner was ex-Merrill Lynch. Also, many senior regulators, including Hector Sants and Carol Sergeant, jumped ship to senior risk roles at banks when they left the regulator. Sants joined Barclays as head of conduct and government and regulatory affairs in January 2013 (but was forced to quit due to 'stress' ten months later), while Sergeant joined Lloyds TSB as chief risk director in February 2004. The FSA's managing director of supervision John Pain joined RBS, as head of conduct and regulatory affairs, in August 2013. There can of course be very good reasons for such moves but if a senior regulator's goal on leaving the regulator is a senior role at a bank, then it may be legitimate for the public to question how effectively they will perform their job.

Five years on from the crisis, I am afraid that in a great many cases the kneejerk response of senior regulators and the directors of British banks is still to sweep evidence of high-level financial wrongdoing, fraud and 'white-collar' crime under the rug. The long-standing leniency of regulators and prosecutorial authorities towards senior bankers, combined with the banks' ability effectively to sew up the legal profession with huge 'panels' of member law firms, arguably led many bankers to assume they were immune from prosecution and above the law.

In a speech to the Worshipful Company of Actuaries Robert Jenkins, a former member of the Bank of England's financial policy committee, said, '[The regulator] messed up in two ways: first it misjudged the breadth and depth of the risks that many banks were running. Second, it misjudged bankers' ability to judge and manage those risks. The latter is the more damning. How could we have been so dumb as to

believe that bankers were so smart? Both groups belong to the human
race and the human race is hubris-hungry and error-prone.'[49]

The way in which the FSA went about its investigation into the failure of RBS epitomised its flawed approach. The process started in May
2009 when the regulator launched a probe seemingly designed to 'nail'
Johnny Cameron. The FSA paid accountancy firm PwC £7.7 million
to sift through the evidence for signs of negligence or wrongdoing on
Cameron's part, as part of an examination of GBM's 'conduct, systems
and controls' and capital-raising exercises carried out by RBS in 2007
and 2008. Then, on 2 December 2010, the FSA admitted none of the
mud had stuck and effectively told the British public, 'There's nothing
to see here – move along. They may have been fools but they were not
knaves.' In a 298-word statement headlined 'FSA closes supervisory
investigation of RBS', the regulator said, 'The review confirmed that
RBS made a series of bad decisions in the years immediately before the
financial crisis, most significantly the acquisition of ABN AMRO and
the decision to aggressively expand its investment banking business.
However, the review concluded that these bad decisions were not the
result of a lack of integrity by any individual and we did not identify
any instances of fraud or dishonest activity by RBS senior individuals
or a failure of governance on the part of the Board. The issues we
investigated do not warrant us taking any enforcement action, either
against the firm or against individuals.'[50]

The statement was met with derision and disbelief. Goaded by
the Treasury committee chairman Andrew Tyrie and others, FSA
chairman Lord Turner eventually said the regulator would go back
to the drawing board and try to come up with something more credible. A year later the FSA produced a 450-page, 210,000-word report.
Published on 10 December 2011, this was not a total whitewash, but it
was certainly a 'greywash', to the extent that it skirted gingerly around
the defining issues. It seemed the regulator had started with two goals in
mind – to exonerate the RBS board and to exonerate itself – and had
marshalled its evidence accordingly. Under a 'Maxwell-isation' process,
lawyers for each of the former RBS directors and executives whom the
FSA interviewed were presented with draft copies of the report and
allowed to edit out critical references to themselves. So the references
to Goodwin having insufficient experience to run a major international
bank, which appeared in the draft report, were nowhere to be seen in

the final version. An FSA source said Goodwin and his lawyers Norton Rose were 'in and out of the FSA . . . fighting every word in the report. They have been crawling over every word.'[51]

Astonishingly, the FSA did not even bother to interview 7 of the 17 individuals who were on the Royal Bank of Scotland board at the time of its collapse – Larry Fish, Gordon Pell, Mark Fisher, Jim Currie, Charles 'Bud' Koch, Bill Friedrich and Janice Kong.[52] One former senior GBM executive says, 'The FSA report was a complete sham. No one from my level in the bank was even interviewed – it was just a minority of board-level and executive-level people. It's fairly obvious that nobody either in the government or the FSA wanted to uncover the truth.'

And, in compiling its report, the FSA sought to suppress evidence that went against its narrative flow. For example in November 2011, a few weeks before the report was published, two FSA enforcement officials called Victor Hong at 6 a.m. on Thanksgiving Day, a national holiday, in New York. A former head of price verification at RBS Greenwich Capital, Hong resigned on 8 November 2007 because he was unhappy with the heroically sanguine (some might say 'fraudulent') approach that the broker/dealer's management was taking to MBS and CDO valuations. According to sources close to Hong, the two officials sought to persuade Hong, firstly, to retract his 8 November 2007 resignation letter, in which he said, 'my expected oversight and sign-off responsibilities for monthly price verification would be intolerable, based upon persistent discrepancies between trader marks and analytical fair market values' and, secondly, to disavow the work he had done at RBS Greenwich Capital. They were apparently keen for Hong to approve a draft version of the FSA report that evidenced joint efforts by the FSA and RBS to convey the impression that neither Carol Mathis, chief financial officer of Greenwich Capital, nor the bank itself had any knowledge of the severe meltdown in the CDO market that kicked in in September 2007 and intensified in ensuing months. After Hong refused, one of the officials claimed it wasn't really that important anyway. A spokesman for the Financial Conduct Authority (which took over some of the functions of the FSA in April 2013), denied that the FSA enforcement officials had made the requests, claiming Hong was solely approached to see if he approved of what the report said about him as part of the 'Maxwell-isation' process.

In its published report, the FSA downplayed the significance of the Hong episode, arguing the FSA felt it inappropriate 'to take enforcement action in respect of the valuation of RBS's super-senior CDOs'. The FSA said this was because the debate about CDO pricing at RBS had taken place 'in the open' and that the alleged falsification of values 'did not in itself indicate an actionable failure of controls'.[53]

In the case of other banks, the falsification of CDO valuations was seen rather differently. Kareem Serageldin, former managing director of structured credit at Credit Suisse, was accused of falsifying the valuations of mortgage-backed securities, in order to hide losses and boost traders' bonuses during 2007. In April 2013, he was extradited from the UK to the US and pled guilty to conspiring to falsify books and records at a New York court. In November 2013, Serageldin was jailed for 30 months and told he would have to pay a $1-million forfeiture plus a substantial fine.[54] The *New York Times* reported:

> '[Serageldin] was in a place where there was a climate for him to do what he did,' the judge said. 'It was a small piece of an overall evil climate inside that bank and many other banks.'
>
> A spokesman for Credit Suisse disagreed with the judge's remarks, noting that when regulators decided not to charge the bank in connection with Mr. Serageldin's actions, they highlighted the isolated nature of the wrongdoing, the bank's immediate self-reporting to the government and the prompt correction of its results.[55]

RBS's chairman, Sir Philip Hampton, seems unsure about whether the directors who destroyed RBS deserved to be let off the hook. In a meeting with US Senators Richard Shelby and John Cornyn and Representatives Paul Kanjorski, Scott Garrett and Luis Gutierrez in September 2009, Hampton said the board's failure to question the ABN deal amounted to 'a failure of their fiduciary responsibilities'.[56]

Politicians – Bill Clinton, George Bush, Tony Blair and Gordon Brown

President Bill Clinton, who served two four-year terms in the White House from January 1993 to January 2001, was ostensibly a Democrat but he surrounded himself with free-market ideologues, some of whom had close links to Wall Street. They included former Goldman Sachs chairman Robert Rubin, who was Treasury Secretary from January 1995 until July 1999; Harvard economist Larry Summers, who was deputy Treasury Secretary under Rubin and served as Treasury Secretary from July 1999 until January 2001; and Alan Greenspan, a disciple of the libertarian Ayn Rand, who remained as chairman of the Federal Reserve from 1987 until 2006. Greenspan had a long-standing disdain for regulation and believed banks and financial firms should regulate themselves.

Errors made by the Clinton administration included the refusal to contemplate even modest regulation of the derivatives market (*see* Brooksley Born section in Chapter 7). Indeed, Clinton's administration went one further – it passed the Commodity Futures Modernization Act, which banned either the Securities and Exchange Commission or the Federal Reserve from regulating derivatives. This opened a Pandora's box of uncontrolled derivatives trading, distorted the global economy and financial markets and inflated the global credit bubble. Another error made on Clinton's watch was the partial repeal of the Glass–Steagall Act, which had prevented deposit-taking institutions from gambling depositors' cash in the global financial markets. The partial repeal of the 1933 Act – carried out by Clinton's administration to legalise *ex post facto* Citicorp's 1998 merger with Travelers, which gave birth to Citigroup – meant that banks became less stable, harder to manage and 'too big to fail'. The Clinton administration also pressurised lenders to make home ownership more affordable for lower-income groups and people with poor credit histories, by loosening underwriting requirements and introducing adjustable rate mortgages. This gave birth to the subprime fraud, which was the biggest single cause of the global financial crisis.

President George W. Bush threw fuel on the fire by turning a blind eye to the rampant mortgage fraud in the USA. In the US housing market between 2003 and 2007, the ability of borrowers to repay their mortgages became irrelevant – lenders were only concerned with whether they could shift the loans off their balance sheets via securitisations.

Margaret Thatcher's government freed up capital flows and the credit markets, creating an orgy of lending and the house-price bubble, which burst in 1989–90. Then, with the 'Big Bang' in October 1986, it introduced a more relaxed regulatory regime and smashed down the barriers that had separated retail banking from investment banking, making it possible for 'too big to fail' financial conglomerates to come into being. The governments of Tony Blair and Gordon Brown heightened the regulatory lassitude and embarked on an 11-year love affair with the banking sector. One reason Blair and Brown so adored the bankers was that, as they hawked consumer credit and business lending with huge success, the banks were making massive profits and so paying vast amounts of tax. In 2007 the banking sector paid £67.8 billion in tax – 13.9 per cent of the UK total that year.[57] Blair and Brown held up bankers like Goodwin as exemplars of all that was best about Britain, showered them with knighthoods and other honours and gave them a say in government policy. Invariably Brown and Balls sided with the bankers in their rare disputes with the FSA, insisting it must use as 'light a touch' as possible (*see* Chapter 18). Goodwin was like a prima donna in Westminster and expected the likes of Gordon Brown and Ed Balls to be at his beck and call.

The *Spectator* editor Fraser Nelson says, 'By working hand-in-glove with the financial sector, Labour ran a form of crony capitalism . . . Brown's government was so dazzled by the tax haul, so swept up in the party spirit, that it left the teenagers with the car keys and a case of tequila. The crash was inevitable.'[58] And this former closeness naturally meant Brown botched the bailouts, as he heavily relied on bankers to develop his rescue strategy and ended up sowing the seeds of the next crisis by being far too soft on his former friends.

The coalition government of Prime Minister David Cameron had no direct role in fomenting the banking crisis of 2008. The Tories' pre-election rhetoric included talk of jailing criminal bankers but Cameron has singularly failed to deliver where that is concerned. Cameron's government has instead launched two commissions into banking. Their proposals will do some good in terms of promoting better behaviour amongst bankers and making the sector safer. Cameron's government has faced constant accusations of meddling and irresolution where RBS is concerned. It is at risk of fuelling another credit bubble and house-price inflation with schemes like Funding for Lending and Help to Buy, the second of which provides first-time buyers with a state guarantee of up to 15 per cent of their mortgage. The overall problem is the seemingly simplistic relationship between banks and politicians has morphed into one in which the 'pinstripe Scargills' have been able to hold the government to ransom.

Central bankers – Alan Greenspan and Mervyn King

The Federal Reserve chairman Alan Greenspan responded to the dotcom crash and the terror attacks of 11 September 2001 by slashing US interest rates from 6.5 per cent to 1 per cent and holding it there. The so-called 'Greenspan Put' put a floor under the US housing market and restored confidence to the financial markets. But it also unleashed a tide of liquidity, a desperate hunt for yield by fixed-income managers and an inflationary spiral in housing.

Greenspan's libertarian beliefs infected political and regulatory thinking across the developed world. This was especially true of the UK where Chancellor Gordon Brown became an ardent disciple of the 'Greenspan doctrine'. It was Greenspan who ultimately gave the green light for the US bank consolidations of the late 1990s, which created a climate in which UK authorities didn't think twice about waving through RBS's acquisitions of NatWest and ABN AMRO. At the peak of his powers, Greenspan was considered to have quasi-divine abilities. His antics were rarely challenged by politicians, the media or the markets. One of Greenspan's most cherished beliefs was that derivatives were an appropriate vehicle for banks and investors to manage and unbundle their risk. Greenspan ignored multiple warnings that they were likely to become 'weapons of mass financial destruction'. In the run-up to the crisis, banks like RBS were using them to boost short-term profits and bankers' bonuses through speculation, obfuscation of the balance sheet, subversion of capital rules and gaming the system.

Mervyn King, governor of the Bank of England from 2003 to 2013, was another follower of the Greenspan doctrine. King was so obsessed with inflation that he turned a blind eye to asset price bubbles, including the UK's property bubble and the over-leveraged nature of many UK banks, which, under the tenets of the doctrine, could be expected to sort themselves out. As the crisis developed, King was in denial. At a press conference in August 2007, he repeated his belief that the trading of securitised credit had made British banks stronger. In answer to a question from the BBC *Newsnight* reporter Stephanie Flanders, King

said, 'Our banking system is much more resilient than in the past . . .
precisely because many of these risks are no longer on their balance
sheets . . . The growth of securitisation has reduced that fragility significantly . . . And I think it's quite difficult to imagine a major financial
crisis now.'[59] He was completely wrong of course. The crisis had started
the previous month.

In his *Today* programme lecture on 2 May 2012, King said, 'With
the benefit of hindsight, we should have shouted from the rooftops that
a system had been built in which banks were too important to fail,
that banks had grown too quickly and borrowed too much, and that
so-called "light-touch" regulation hadn't prevented any of this.'[60]

King's mantra, that there was nothing he or the Bank of England
could have done to steer Britain away from the rocks since banking
supervision had been removed from the Bank of England by Gordon
Brown in May 1997, is a cop-out. He could and should have done a
lot more, even if this only involved educating politicians, the Treasury
and the FSA of the dangers that were welling up in the system. King's
deputy governor for financial stability, Sir John Gieve, says that, after
ten years of unprecedented economic stability, there was little sign
of the impending blow-out or that the Bank of England had become
complacent. 'The big macro variables which we concentrated on,
particularly inflation, were not sending signals of danger, and the truth
is that we thought we had cracked it.'[61] Gieve, who became the fall guy
for the Bank of England's pre-crisis failures, admitted that, as the crisis
developed, the Bank completely underestimated the likely scale of the
crisis. He said 'We were expecting a shower, not a hurricane.'[62]

Gieve said King's entrenched views on 'moral hazard' made things
worse. He said King 'was very reluctant to provide support to the banking sector except on penal terms – and that goes back to Bagehot and
the role of the "lender of last resort", but also comes from the sense
that "these guys got themselves into trouble, they shouldn't be relying
on us, except on penal terms".'[63]

So despite King's insistence that there was nothing the Bank of
England could do to avert or quell the crisis, it could have done quite a
lot; here are just two items:

(1) it could have raised interest rates earlier to curb the UK's
     property bubble – which would also have had the advantage of

limiting the exposure of banks like RBS, Northern Rock and HBOS to collapsing property prices between 2007 and 2009;
(2) post-August 2007, the Bank of England could have come to the aid of flailing banks sooner by providing liquidity support at an earlier stage, along the lines of what both the Fed and the European Central Bank did, without necessarily insisting they could only borrow on penal terms.

Albert Edwards, global strategist at Société Générale, believes loose monetary policy was the primary cause of the great recession, not the over-exuberant actions of lenders and borrowers. 'Alan Greenspan's responsibility as chairman of the Fed requires little discussion in my view. My views on Mervyn King may be more controversial, but he has been in senior positions at the bank since 1991 as chief economist, then deputy governor, and governor since 2003. He has been at the helm and should, in my view, bear primary responsibility for the UK's economic collapse.'[64]

The hedge fund manager and *Planet Ponzi* author Mitch Feierstein summarises King's decade as governor by saying, 'The Bank was too slack during the long and indisciplined boom, under-prepared for the crash and playing catch-up thereafter. The legacy of Lord King's (and Gordon Brown's) career has been an economy still limping along far below peak output, with real wages caught in a vice. Few recent careers have more comprehensively failed.'[65] Feierstein says there is one redeeming feature of King's stewardship of the central bank – that he clung on to the principles of Walter Bagehot, to which Gieve referred. Feierstein said this was King's one 'shred of decency'.[66]

But King had his faith in Bagehot beaten out of him by Alistair Darling and was more pragmatic by March–April 2008. It seems Mark Carney, the former Goldman Sachs executive and former Bank of Canada governor who succeeded King on 1 July 2013, does not share King's old-fashioned beliefs. In a speech given four months after he became governor, he said the time for contrition was over and declared he was relaxed about the notion that UK banks should grow from their current size (total assets of four times the nation's GDP) to nine times the United Kingdom's GDP by 2050. Carney said, 'Some would react to this prospect with horror. They would prefer that the UK financial services industry be slimmed down, if not shut down. In the aftermath of the crisis, such sentiments have gone largely unchallenged. But, if organised properly, a vibrant financial sector brings substantial benefits.'[67] But if we were to allow our banks to balloon their balance sheets to the extent advocated by Carney they would become even more powerful and even more capable of subverting regulators and suborning politicians than was Fred Goodwin in his pomp.

Basel Committee on Banking Supervision

In the mid 1980s, the governments of the leading developed economies outsourced the setting of the most critical rules and regulations governing their banking sectors to an unaccountable private sector body – the Switzerland-based Basel Committee on Banking Supervision. The committee, largely made up of retired bankers and active central bankers, was expected to deliver a global 'capital adequacy framework' that would decree how much loss-absorbing capital banks must retain on their balance sheets – a critical measure for keeping the banks safe.

The Basel Committee's first accord, Basel I, came out in 1988 but the rot really set in with the second one, Basel II, which was developed in close partnership with the banking sector and was launched in June 2004. Basel II did even more to outsource regulation to the banks, giving them free rein to evaluate the riskiness of all the assets on their balance sheets. RBS saw this as a licence to game the system by, for example, using derivatives to 'reverse-engineer' assets so they could be made to seem less risky than they were. It was thanks to the Basel rules that Goodwin was able to balloon the RBS balance sheet with distinctly dodgy assets without the need to raise much additional capital. It enabled RBS to buy supposedly 'risk-free' assets like the super-senior tranches of CDOs and Greek government bonds without any commensurate need for additional capital. In its report into the failure of RBS, the FSA said that one of the flaws of Basel II was that it did not incorporate a leverage ratio as a backstop to risk-weighted asset measures, which meant that 'extremely high levels of leverage were compatible with the Basel II standards'.[68]

Don Cruickshank, the former regulator and author of the March 2000 'Review of Banking Services in the UK', believes that national governments, including that of the UK, made a catastrophic error of judgement in allowing bankers to write their own rules. 'We effectively let the banks decide what risk meant – and their balance sheets broadly doubled . . . in about six years.'[69]

Under Basel II, the holy grail for banks was to obtain Advanced Internal Ratings-Based (AIRB) status, which gave them *carte blanche* to calculate the risk weightings of the assets on their own balance sheets, without any regulatory oversight. On average, banks with AIRB status were able to reduce the amount of capital they needed by up to a third. Astonishingly, the FSA granted RBS temporary AIRB status in April 2008 before removing it again in August 2008. However, even the temporary AIRB status enabled RBS to run on an even thinner wafer of capital than it had beforehand. It is worth noting ABN AMRO, whose systems were as weak and whose credit issues were as severe as those of RBS, was unable to obtain AIRB status from the Dutch banking regulator De Nederlandsche Bank and withdrew its application in March 2008.

In 2012, Andrew Bailey, chief executive of the Prudential Regulatory Authority, conceded that banks 'should never have been allowed' to use their own models to determine capital requirements.[70]

Accounting Standards – International Accounting Standards Board (IASB)/the auditors

The Royal Bank of Scotland claimed that its vast £1.05-trillion loan book was in good health in its 2007 annual report. The bank said, 'Impairment losses in UK corporate bank fell 5 per cent, reflecting the strong quality of the portfolio.'[71] Overall provisions rose from £3.9 billion in 2006 to £6.4 billion in 2007. Total impairments rose from £6.4 billion to £11.4 billion (the increases were largely reflective of the absorption of the whole of ABN). We now know that the figures were false or misleading.

And the reason the figures did not reflect reality was not necessarily the result of calculated fraud but because of the bank's use of International Financial Reporting Standards (IFRS) to prepare its accounts. Under IFRS – which were adopted by all larger companies in the UK from January 2005 – a bank is not required to admit that loans are in trouble until they actually sour. Tim Bush, head of governance and financial analysis at corporate governance group PIRC, said that IFRS, as applied in the UK and Ireland, enabled banks to create phantom profits and phantom capital that 'misled creditors, misled shareholders, the Bank of England, FSA and others'.[72] Bush, a qualified accountant who was formerly a fund manager at Hermes, added that the use of IFRS had prompted the boards of banks to make illegal dividend payouts to shareholders while artificially inflating executive bonuses.

From about October 2006 onwards, traders and short-sellers suspected that RBS's supposedly 'clean' balance sheet was, in fact, riddled with toxic loans. We now know they were right. The bank ended up hiding an astonishing £32 billion of loan losses.

A Conservative MP, Steve Baker, introduced a Private Members' Bill in a bid to get accounting standards changed in May 2011.[73] He said, 'While complying with the rules, banks are producing accounts that grossly inflate their profits and capital in three ways. First, using IFRS mark-to-market and mark-to-model accounting, banks record unrealized gains in investments as profits. Second, IFRS prevents banks from making prudent provision for expected loan losses by allowing recognition only of incurred losses. Third, IFRS encourages banks not to deduct staff compensation from profits. Taken together, these flaws mean that banks' accounts under IFRS are at once rule-compliant and dangerously misleading.'[74] Instead of a licence to print money, IFRS had given banks an unprecedented opportunity to distort and magnify their financial strength.[75] A former executive with Lehman Brothers, Baker said that a bank's true solvency is not accounted for when it is audited under IFRS and the standards mean that banks that are loss-making and destroying capital look as though they are profitable and strong, which was exactly the situation with RBS during 2006 and 2007.

IFRS's biggest flaw is that it gives bank managements and their auditors too much latitude in the valuation of assets which, in the boom times, creates an illusion of capital strength and profitability and encourages managements to go out and take more risk by indulging in more and more poor-quality lending, which creates a Ponzi-like scenario in the frothiest market sectors. It also enabled bank managements to make ludicrously low provisions for bad debts. In an August 2010 letter to the Accounting Standards Board (ASB), Bush said that the adoption of IFRS had led directly to a 'regulatory fiasco' and the financial crisis, adding that the authorities' insistence on sticking with

IFRS, despite its well-documented flaws, continued to pose a severe risk to the financial system.[76]

Phil Hodkinson, who was finance director of HBOS from April 2005 until December 2007, struggled to understand IFRS's through-the-looking-glass approach to credit risk. In an email to the HBOS whistle-blower Paul Moore, in which he highlighted inconsistencies in how IFRS was applied in banking and insurance, he said:

> Banks weren't permitted to provide for future bad debts in their published accounts. They could only provide for loans that were delinquent today. Despite knowing that a percentage of today's customers would default at some time in the future, they could not put any money aside today in their accounts to provide for this.
>
> At the same time as companies and regulators (and tax authorities) wanted to move to one version of the truth (one set of accounts) from which to base their financial assessments, the IASB were, in my view, taking the published accounting basis (IFRS) in the direction of a more volatile, less intuitive version of the truth.[77]

A major related problem at RBS was that its auditors, Deloitte, are considered to have lacked professional scepticism for the duration of Goodwin's reign. For several years between 2000 and 2007 they were earning more in non-audit fees from RBS than they were in audit fees. Such disequilibrium can create a conflict of interest and undermine the independence of the audit – for example, it can make the auditor more willing to sign off on valuations for financial instruments which others might see as fanciful, along the lines of what happened with RBS's CDO and MBS valuations. The evidence suggests they had few qualms about going along with accounting which, although compliant with relevant standards, may have been deceptive. There was always a risk the firm would be inclined to side with management because Fred Goodwin was a former partner and regarded Deloitte's UK managing partner John Connolly as his mentor.

Conclusion

Fred Goodwin is deeply culpable for what happened to RBS, given that he was chief executive from 2000 to 2008. If he had run the bank differently, if he had been less blind to risk, if he hadn't pushed for rapid growth in leveraged finance, commercial property and structured finance at the worst point in the cycle and if he hadn't bought parts of ABN AMRO in order to assuage Santander chairman Emilio Botín and to avoid being sued by a bunch of hedge funds, Royal Bank might not have failed. If he hadn't crushed any internal dissent by being so vile to his colleagues, then sceptics would have been more willing to speak out at board and management meetings, questioning his strategy and reining him in.

Clearly though, there is a whole corporate governance superstructure in large companies whose role is meant to stop imperious chief executives from leading companies to their destruction. In the case of RBS, the superstructure was peopled by a chairman, non-executive directors, a chief financial officer, the group audit committee, a chief risk officer, risk managers, internal auditors, external auditors, institutional investors and credit rating agencies, as well as panoply of other extremely well-paid professional advisors, including actuaries, lawyers, investment bankers and consultants. However, where RBS was concerned, the preference of most of the people who fulfilled these roles was to go with the flow, suck up to Fred and flatter his ego in the hope of maximising their fees. None, with the possible exception of non-executive directors Sir Steve Robson, Gordon Pell and Peter Sutherland, seems to have challenged Goodwin over strategy. They were, to an extent, like the tailors (swindlers) in Hans Christian Andersen's 'The Emperor's New Clothes', persuading him he was elegantly clad. Among this bunch, blame must be widely shared, but Sir Tom McKillop, chairman from April 2006 until February 2009, is more blameworthy than most. As chairman, his job was meant to be to challenge the executive over strategy, not to be even more gung-ho than his chief executive. If there is to be one lesson from the RBS catastrophe from an internal company perspective, it is that Britain's much vaunted system of corporate governance is broken and is in need of an urgent overhaul.

However, the true villains of the piece are the politicians, central bankers, regulators and the Basel Committee on Banking Supervision. Despite his initial attempts to crack down on banker excess via the Cruickshank Report, Brown changed his tune towards banks and bankers in mid 2002. Seemingly pressurised by bankers, Tony Blair demanded that the already emasculated FSA give up any pretence of trying to regulate the banking sector. From that moment on, banks thought they could get away with virtually anything, whilst defying financial gravity and existing above the law. It meant morality and ethics were thrown out the window and we saw the mis-selling of rip-off products on an epic scale – including the scandals of payment protection insurance and interest-rate swap agreements sold to small and medium-sized enterprises. The Treasury, the FSA and the Bank of England all turned a deaf ear to the complaints from the banks' millions of 'victims' and paid scant heed to the overall balance-sheet strength – capital, liquidity and asset quality – of British banks. And, at various stages between 1988 and 2008, British politicians also outsourced critical aspects of banking regulation and supervision to the private sector body, the Basel Committee on Banking Supervision, which enabled the bankers to write their own rules. That, in itself, was an error easily as bad as any committed by Goodwin. So he is right. We can't just blame it all on him.

The government had an unprecedented opportunity to sort out RBS in the aftermath of its October 2008 collapse. It could have fully nationalised RBS and then split it into a 'good bank' and a 'bad bank', following the model adopted by the Swedish government for its bombed-out banking sector in 1992. That would have permitted a harsher treatment of certain categories of creditors and a much more profound restructuring than was possible under the Labour government's half-baked bailout. There should have been a more realistic approach to the marking-down of asset valuations, greater honesty and transparency in the way the bank was run and a less vindictive approach to smaller business customers whose businesses and lives the bank has destroyed.

RBS lost its moral compass under Fred Goodwin. It needed to find it again after the bailout, but under Hester it did not even look. In consequence, the bank continues to lose the confidence of customers and its own employees. After 25 years as a customer of the bank, I was delighted to move my accounts away in April 2013. And RBS continues to be seen as the most toxic bank brand on the British high street – with the possible exception of Barclays.

In failing to consider policies along these lines, the governments of both Gordon Brown and David Cameron have let the people of Britain down. The result has been that, at the time of writing, RBS is probably a worse bank than it was under Fred Goodwin, and it is certainly a much worse bank than it ever was under George Mathewson and Charles Winter.

At the time of writing, one resuscitation programme has, except in purely quantitative terms, largely failed. The approximately £100-billion unfunded liability the bank has for litigation and redress issues remains a massive albatross around its neck. These costs relate to five broad areas of alleged criminality and wrongdoing at RBS:

(1)   the mass 'mis-selling' of financial products to unsophisticated customers mainly in the US and UK;

(2)   the 'mis-selling' of mortgaged-backed securities to sophisticated investors in the US;

(3)   the alleged collusion with other global banks in the credit default swap market in the US and Europe;

(4)   the alleged rigging of key financial market benchmarks including Libor, ISDAfix and foreign exchange benchmark rates, which is already proven in the case of Libor and related interbank borrowing rates;

(5)   the alleged duping of investors ahead of a £12.3 billion rights issue in April 2008.

Even with its estimated £250-million-a-year legal budget and truculent approach to litigation, RBS will struggle to bat off these claims.[78]

The Royal Bank of Scotland is facing an uncertain future. If he genuinely believes in turning the place around rather than just extracting £3 million a year in pay and bonuses and spouting platitudes about being 'customer focused', McEwan is going to have to shape up his act. An ethical revolution is required. And that will be tough. At the very least, it will require the ousting of whole swathes of the bank's middle management. GRG needs to be shut down, with a new 'restructuring and recovery' division started from scratch. M&IB, if it survives at all, has to actually focus on serving the needs of large corporates – which is what Iain Robertson recommended it should do in his valedictory speech in March 2005. If the right moves are now made, RBS could become a great bank again. If they're not, I doubt it will even exist in ten years' time. Whatever happens, it now seems impossible that British taxpayers will ever see a return on their £45.5-billion investment in the bank.

Describing the Parliamentary Commission on Banking Standards report published on 19 June 2013, the *Financial Times*' chief economics commentator Martin Wolf said, 'One cannot read the commission's report without feeling real anger. The banking industry has taken the public for a ride. Despite substantial and welcome reforms, it still does so. The argument it makes is that it is too important to reform. In fact, it is too important not to be reformed.'[79]

Epilogue

Osborne's cunning plan

Ross McEwan has a mantra. Every time he gives an interview, or makes a presentation to analysts, the 58-year-old New Zealander says he wants to put customers first, and to treat them fairly. Otherwise, he says, RBS won't be able to get back on its feet or be successfully re-privatised. Speaking on the *Today* programme on 29 July 2015, McEwan said he wants RBS to return to being 'a sustainable bank that people in the UK will be proud of'. The front cover of the bank's most recent annual report and accounts is emblazoned with the words 'Earning our customers' trust', and contains about 150 mentions of the word 'trust' and 518 of the word 'customer' over the course of its 515 pages. Inside McEwan writes, 'We are determined to reach our aspiration of being number one for customer service, trust and advocacy.'[1]

These are admirable aims. And they're more likely to be realised under McEwan than they were under his predecessor, Stephen Hester, who, despite the odd platitude about customers, was more preoccupied with revving up RBS's investment bank. But there are some serious stumbling blocks ahead. One is what I'm going to call a 'Dr Jekyll and Mr Hyde approach': claims about being a customer-focused bank tend to lose credibility if the bank continues to treat customers unfortunate enough to be in the 'exit bank' with barely disguised contempt.

While customers of the 'go-forward bank' (the parts that RBS has decided to keep – predominantly its UK and Irish high street banking operations) are, supposedly at least, being showered with love and tenderness, those in the 'exit bank' (the parts that McEwan wants to shut or sell by 2017–19) are being brutalised as if by a cane-wielding maniac. And their complaints and cries of pain, lately amplified by the SME Alliance (a membership organisation founded in September 2014) risk drowning out any purrs of pleasure from 'go-forward' customers.

At the annual general meeting in Edinburgh on 23 June 2015, RBS's outgoing chairman, Sir Philip Hampton, was lambasted for well over an hour by customers, especially over allegations that the bank had set out to destroy viable and creditworthy business customers in order to seize their assets. Former Torex Retail chief executive Neil Mitchell said Hampton, who has since left to become chairman of drugs giant GlaxoSmithKline, was leaving a 'terrible legacy' at RBS. The former hotelier Nigel Henderson accused the bank of 'corruption' and said Hampton was 'wilfully blind'. Mitchell accused Hampton of burying his head in the sand. 'Global restructuring group has become a massive risk to this bank going forward,' said Mitchell. 'This is a real issue about culture. You didn't listen to me in 2010. In 2012 you pretended – you went through a sham of an investigation. The RBS business banking reputation has been trashed.'[2]

Hampton said two law firms had investigated GRG and refuted claims of 'systematic failings'. He did, however, express a willingness to meet aggrieved business customers 'if there is any fresh information'. McEwan did not comment on the allegations, preferring to tell shareholders about a two-way split at RBS. He said, 'Between now and 2019, the exit bank will occupy a diminishing amount of our time, allowing us to increasingly focus on becoming a substantially UK and Ireland focused retail and commercial bank with a core wholesale banking offer. At that point, we will be operating from a much lower risk profile, and be capable of delivering solid, sustainable returns.'[3]

To this end McEwan has in recent months stepped up the dismantling of RBS's once swaggering investment bank. The task includes reducing the unit's footprint in 54 countries in October 2007 to fewer than 13, and slashing investment banking assets from £147 billion in late 2013 to £30 billion in 2017. All that will remain will be a rump business in the UK and Western Europe. Already renamed 'corporate and institutional banking', this will be focused on RBS's 'traditional areas of strength' – debt financing, rates and currencies. What McEwan seems reluctant to acknowledge, however, is that the collateral damage from this headlong retreat could be immense. Any disposals he makes will almost certainly be sold at a loss. At least 14,000 of CIB's 18,000 employees will lose their jobs. Millions of customers will be left high and dry, their credit lines withdrawn or with their banking relationships sold, like so many sacks of boll-weevil-infested cotton, to mainly Asian banks. Speaking on results day on 26 February 2015, RBS finance director Ewen Stevenson said the cost – which includes generous redundancy cheques for sacked investment bankers and compensation for landlords whose leases are being torn up – will be '£2.5 billion to £3.5 billion'.[4]

A second problem facing McEwan as he focuses on his 'go-forward bank' is what he calls the 'noise' of misconduct-related explosions that keep ringing about his ears. Not only are these hurting the bank's bottom line, preventing the payment of dividends until 2017 at the earliest, they are also reputationally disastrous. In almost every jurisdiction of the world, the bank is being penalised for ripping off or otherwise harming its customers, and often in the not so distant past. The fact the regulatory settlements, which include deferred prosecution agreements, invariably let guilty bankers off the hook, while loading billions of dollars in fines onto shareholders – which at RBS means taxpayers – only adds to the sense of outrage.

Announcing half-year results on 30 July 2015, Hampton said the bank had been surprised by the relentless barrage of fines and demands for redress. 'These conduct and litigation costs have greatly exceeded the expectations of banks and their investors.' He added that it was hard to discern whether the level of fines and other penalties was going to rise or fall.[5] Analysts at Standard & Poor's believe massive conduct and litigation costs will be running sore for large banks such as RBS for the foreseeable future. McEwan agrees, telling *Sky News* on the same day, 'Will there ever be a time when we don't have any conduct or litigation [issues to resolve]? I don't think that will ever be the case.'[6]

One loud bang that will resonate across the UK and US before summer 2016 follows RBS's alleged mis-selling of £32 billion of residential mortgage-backed securities to the US mortgage finance firms Fannie May and Freddie Mac in the build-up to the crisis. For this, RBS faces a probable penalty of $13 billion (£8.5 billion) from the US regulator, the Federal Housing Finance Agency. If the estimate is accurate, this will be RBS's biggest fine yet – equivalent to the annual budget of the UK's Ministry of Justice.

The bank also faces other actions relating to alleged mortgage-backed securities mis-selling, including 25 lawsuits and criminal probes from the US Department of Justice and attorneys-general across the

United States. Many smelt blood after it lost an earlier case brought by the FHFA in May 2015. In that instance, the bank and its Japanese partner Nomura were ordered to pay $806 million after a judge ruled that the 'magnitude of [their] falsity, conservatively measured, is enormous'.[7]

Since the first edition of this book came out, US and UK regulators have slapped fines totalling $1.305 billion on RBS for forming a six-bank global cartel to rig the $5.3 trillion per day foreign-exchange market. In the process it was ripping off customers and counterparties, including multinational companies and investment funds. As part of a plea deal with the Department of Justice, RBS pled guilty in the Washington DC District Court to one count of forming an anti-competitive cartel between December 2007 and at least April 2010. RBS also entered into a 'cease and desist' order with the Federal Reserve in relation to the same crimes. RBS and co-conspirator banks face further severe penalties for forex rigging in other jurisdictions including Brazil[8] – where they are accused of manipulating the value of the country's currency, the real – and the European Union.[9] Not long after its chief executive Martin Wheatley was fired by UK chancellor George Osborne, the Financial Conduct Authority published a damning report, saying that, despite pledges made at the time of their 2012–13 Libor settlements, large banks had failed to tighten up their trading floor procedures, such that it was still possible for traders to fiddle around with benchmarks and indices. Simon Morris, regulatory partner at the law firm CMS, was stunned by the banks' seeming nonchalance. He said, 'This report is a clear wake-up call, and if things haven't speeded up by the autumn we can expect the next round of multimillion-pound fines to commence.'[10] RBS took a further £334 million provision for forex rigging in the first half of 2015.

A spate of civil litigation will follow the forex settlements, just as it followed the Libor settlements. Indeed some market participants are already suing the bank in the US, where RBS has failed to get their cases dismissed. Ed Coulson, a partner at law firm Hausfeld, said RBS's forex-rigging settlements with US and UK regulators have given rise to a 'treasure trove' of documentation, including incriminating instant messages and emails sent by members of the forex-rigging team who called themselves 'the Bandit's Club', giving pursuers' lawyers invaluable evidence with which to construct cases against banks. He added that RBS's guilty plea had 'bolstered the enthusiasm of claimants to bring these cases'.[11]

RBS thought that it had put a stake through the heart of its 'vampire unit' – the notorious global restructuring group which stands accused of deliberately destroying thousands of viable businesses in order to seize their assets – when it formally disbanded the group in August 2014. Many of the disputed assets wound up under the ownership of RBS's West Register property division, whose name the bank changed to SIG 1 Holdings Limited in November 2014. But it seems GRG and West Register could yet rise from the ashes to further damage RBS's reputation. The FCA has, for nearly two years, been investigating allegations swirling around them, but since the so-called section 166 probe was outsourced to Washington DC-based Promontory Financial Group and Paris-based accountancy firm Mazars in January 2014, nothing of any substance has been heard. The report is expected to be quite damning of the bank and to oblige it to compensate those who were affected. The estimated cost has been put at up to £5 billion.

RBS denies wrongdoing and hired the 'magic circle' law firm Clifford Chance to investigate the claims. On 17 April 2014, RBS published a report by the law firm which cleared the bank of systematic wrongdoing, but which did allude to certain questionable practices which it said it would eliminate. The bank says, 'Following the reckless lending leading up to the financial crisis, many of our customers and their businesses ended up in serious financial difficulty. GRG helped minimise losses where it could and successfully restructured a significant number of businesses it worked with, advancing over £100 million of new lending and safeguarding hundreds of thousands of jobs.' That, however, has done nothing to prevent a group of 371 firms from hiring Enyo Law and the QCs Lord Pannick and Andrew Hunter to sue the bank and four of its former executives – including Hampton and former GRG boss Derek Sach – for allegedly massacring their businesses. Problematically for the bank, leaked documents suggest that snuffing out certain types of business borrower in order to flatter the bank's capital strength became company policy from 2011 onwards. Writing in *The Times*, enterprise editor James Hurley revealed that GRG had put 800 of its staff through a bespoke 'capital tools' training programme during 2011, making it easier for them to identify companies whose extinguishments would flatter the bank's core tier one position. One

ex-GRG insider confirmed that, in cases where otherwise viable business customers were having a 'horrendous' impact on the bank's capital
position, the bank would 'manufacture' defaults, either by manipulating loan-to-value criteria or ratcheting up fees. The ex-insider said
GRG used a lot of 'smoke and mirrors' to keep customers in the dark.
He said, ' "You have to keep the plebs in their place" was the ethos.'[12]
Unnamed senior RBS insiders have said the GRG scandal has been
more damaging to the bank's reputation than either forex or Libor.[13]

Other scandals brewing for RBS include its alleged abuse and
mis-selling of the state-backed Enterprise Finance Guarantee (EFG),
which was introduced by Alastair Darling in January 2009 to bolster
lending to small firms that lacked security. Following a campaign led
by Welsh bricklayer Clive May, with the support of David Hanson MP
and Andy Keats of the Serious Banking Crimes Bureau, in January
2014 RBS issued a rare *mea culpa*, admitting it may have 'mis-sold'
many EFG loans. The bank undertook to trawl through its £940 million EFG portfolio for evidence of mis-selling. The police have also
been taking an interest.[14] Another developing scandal relates to RBS's
alleged mis-sale of 'inverse floater' lender option borrower option
(lobo) loans to dozens of UK local authorities, a debacle exposed by
Channel 4's *Despatches*.[15] The products, which contain hidden swaps,
are proving cripplingly expensive for many councils, necessitating
cuts to local services.

RBS's firesale of the bulk of its commercial property loan book in
Ireland has worked wonders for its capital position, but is coming back
to haunt it. The loans were sold to US 'vulture funds' run by the likes
of Cerberus Capital Management, Apollo Global Management and
Lone Star, which are generally considered to be less interested in customers' welfare than the banks' restructuring arms. Already Cerberus
has been forced to defend its treatment of borrowers, after it emerged
that it has become embroiled in a large number of lawsuits in both
Northern Ireland and the republic. RBS is essentially 'throwing its
customers to the wolves,' said Janine Alexander, a partner at law firm
Collyer Bristow.[16]

RBS may also have to spend hundreds of millions of pounds compensating people to whom it mis-sold packaged accounts. These bundle
current accounts with other financial products including breakdown,
mobile phone and travel insurance, and attract monthly fees of about

£25. The accounts became a money-spinner for the banks after they were precluded from selling further payment protection insurance, but may become 'the next PPI' (compensating customers who were 'mis-sold' PPI has already cost British banks at least £26 billion, of which RBS accounts for £3.8 billion).

On 8 June 2015, London's High Court opened a fresh can of worms for RBS when, as part of a £30 million lawsuit brought by the Manchester-based property company Property Alliance Group, the bank was ordered to hand over documents relating to its negotiations with the FSA ahead of its original February 2013 Libor settlement. This could prove damaging both for RBS and the regulator. The documents may reveal that, contrary to the FSA's findings, RBS did strive to rig sterling-based Libor. The FSA final notice says the bank only admitted to, and was only penalised for, rigging yen-based Libor and Swiss franc-based Libor – meaning the FSA, which morphed into the FCA in April 2013, had exonerated it of rigging the sterling equivalent.[17]

A court case over RBS's 'misleading' April 2008 rights issue is another massive bump in the road for the bank. The action has been brought by 35,000 investors – including the insurance and asset management firms Aviva, Legal & General, Scottish Widows, Standard Life, the pension fund Universities Superannuation Scheme and the sovereign wealth funds of Singapore and Kuwait. The investors, who are seeking up to £6 billion in damages, made a material breakthrough in March 2015 when the judge, Mr Justice Robert Hildyard, ordered the bank to hand over millions of private emails and other messages sent by senior executives at the time of the capital raising. These include messages sent and received by Fred Goodwin, Johnny Cameron, Guy Whittaker and Tom McKillop, who stand accused of seeking to pull the wool over investors' eyes. RBS and related parties have also been ordered to hand over correspondence between Goodwin and his favoured invest-ment bank adviser, Matthew Greenburgh of Merrill Lynch. These and other messages are expected to make uncomfortable reading for RBS and its legal advisers, Herbert Smith Freehills. One source close to the claimant group predicts they will 'shred' the bank's initial defence. 'RBS is now very much on the back foot. It seems that Goodwin and a tight-knit group of close colleagues were treating investors and their non-executive directors like idiots as they made their last throw of the dice.'

These are the sort of 'noises' with which McEwan and his team will struggle to suppress as they seek to shrink, simplify and reconstruct the bits of RBS they have decided to keep. Just occasionally, the 58-year-old McEwan seems willing to acknowledge the harm they are doing. In a phone-in with LBC's Nick Ferrari in March 2015, he admitted that 'bad behaviour is actually creating very bad lack of trust in this banking industry'.[18] Most of the time, however, McEwan and Stevenson, the only two executive directors the bank now has – both of whom are originally from New Zealand – seem to be in denial. Speaking to analysts on 26 February 2015, Stevenson said, 'We think we'll be through the litigation and conduct costs [some time in 2016].'[19] Sometimes McEwan seems to think the 'go-forward bank' can don a pair of mufflers and screen out the dreadful surround-sound cacophony that refuses to go away.

McEwan does, however, have a strong card up his sleeve. The largest brand in RBS's retail banking armoury, NatWest, remains relatively untainted by the crisis that's engulfing RBS. Indeed, a minority of British people don't even realise NatWest, acquired in March 2000, is part of RBS. The brand is becoming more dominant within the group, and will become more so once 308 Royal Bank of Scotland branches in England and Wales are rebranded as Williams & Glyn and once the RBS-branded investment bank is shrunk down to nothing. I suspect McEwan may be minded to take things further – for example, by rebranding the entire listed group under the English bank's name.

Despite continuing losses and the problems he euphemistically calls 'conduct and litigation', McEwan has in the past 18 months managed to bolster the bank's capital strength and make some tangible improvements to its UK retail bank. Through manoeuvres such as the sale of three-quarters of Rhode Island-based Citizens Financial Group and the offloading of unwanted overseas corporate loan-books, he has strengthened RBS's core tier one capital ratio from 10.9 per cent in December 2013 to 11.2 per cent in December 2014. He seems confident he can raise this to 13 per cent by the end of 2016.

Many commentators and investors believe that traditional, 'bricks and mortar' banks – hampered as they are by their employee-heavy organisational structures, inefficient processes and creaking Heath Robinson-esque information technology systems – have had their day. Their position at the top of finance's food chain will be usurped by so-called fin-tech players operating in areas like crowdfunding, cryptocurrencies, electronic transfers, mobile payments and peer-to-peer lending. Just as Uber is killing off taxi businesses, the fin-tech players will kill off mainstream banks – or so the theory goes.

When McEwan took over as chief executive, RBS was not well placed to meet this challenge. After a string of disastrous IT meltdowns which deprived customers of access to their cash and caused 600,000 payments to go 'missing', the bank's IT had become an industry joke. McEwan has responded by investing £1.75 billion on improving the resilience of RBS's core IT systems, as well as developing customer relationship management systems which will improve staff's understanding of individual customer's needs, for example by mapping all their interactions with the bank. RBS has traditionally exploited customers' apathy. For example, mortgage customers who neglected to renew their mortgage deals were automatically transferred into more expensive standard variable rate mortgages. RBS now uses data analytics to remind customers how much they could save by switching when they log into their digital banking and mobile app home pages.[20] Old timers worry about lost revenues, but advocates of greater transparency believe such developments will bring long-term rewards, partly through customers being more likely to trust RBS and to recommend it to their friends. As part of its bid to outpace rival banks where technology is concerned, RBS has entered into partnerships with scores of the world's leading fin-tech players in order to test out their gear, and has opened listening posts in California's Silicon Valley and Israel's Silicon Wadi.

Last year RBS made a big song and dance about the fact it had abolished 'teaser' rates on credit cards and savings accounts – practices McEwan deplores, seeing them as symptomatic of everything that's gone wrong with British banking. Television commercials that trumpeted the move bore the slogan 'Goodbye unfair banking; hello RBS', conveying the impression the bank was determined to be more honest with customers. John Hempton, co-founder and chief investment officer of Sydney-based fund management group Bronte Capital, which owns shares in RBS, is convinced McEwan is on the right track. 'I've watched Ross McEwan's career since 1998 and I've been impressed. He was flat-out-brilliant at customer service in his past roles.' Growing the bank's UK retail and commercial businesses, cutting costs without impairing customer service and sustaining or increasing its net interest margins (not always a particularly customer-friendly thing to do) are among the challenges. McEwan is convinced that savvy investors will 'see through the noise' and recognise that, with its rising operational profitability, the group's UK and Irish high street bank is 'a great business . . . a fantastic bank'.[21]

However, even in the sunnier uplands of retail banking, there are clouds. The darkest are the ones of the branch closure programme – a corollary of the tough-talking Kiwi's desire to cut RBS's costs by £5.3 billion by 2017. In order to minimise negative headlines, RBS is axing unwanted branches in batches of two or three. However there is a lot of anger about the programme, not least because the bank has reneged on its June 2010 commitment not to close branches where these are 'the last bank in town'. The introduction of additional mobile-banking vans and more cash machines, and the extension of a deal with Post Office counters, have done little to reduce the indignation that's being felt in affected communities. RBS had 2,400 UK branches following its NatWest takeover in March 2000. Goodwin avoided closing branches during his eight years at the helm, but the number of branches has fallen to 1,600 since he departed in 2008. If closures were to continue at their current rate fewer than 900 will remain by 2020 (bearing in mind that 314 'Project Rainbow' branches are to be transferred to a separately-owned Williams & Glyn by December 2016).

Speaking at the RBS annual shareholder event in June 2015, Fionn Travers-Smith, a campaigner with Move Your Money UK, told the RBS board that the closures are devastating local communities and asked for a moratorium. But Hampton, who was succeeded as chairman by the former FSA chairman Sir Howard Davies in September 2015, said closures had become a fact of life. Hampton said that when RBS made its 'last bank in town' pledge, the bank had underestimated the pace at which customers would switch to online and mobile banking, which he said had 'frankly surprised us'. Meanwhile fewer customers are visiting branches. Ex-insiders complain that the bank is deliberately 'massaging down' the number of people visiting its branches, for example by limiting counter staff in order to create longer queues at the same time as heavily promoting digital banking inside branches, with parallels to the way supermarket groups have pushed customers to use self-service tills by reducing the number of manned check-outs. That may be sour grapes. There is strong evidence that, particularly with regard to people in their forties and under, the use of mobile banking apps is sweeping all before it. In the UK banking market, mobile apps overtook online banking for the first time in March 2015, with 10.5 million mobile logins every day that month versus 9.6 million computer-based interactions, according to the British Bankers' Association.[22] Branch visits and call centre use are languishing in third and fourth places, with branch use down 10 per cent year-on-year.

Perhaps the biggest challenge for McEwan, though, is turning around the RBS's still rotten culture. In a conference call following the annual results in February 2015, he admitted that RBS was a 'bruising place to work'. As I said in Chapter 33 ('Hester's Ledger'), the internal culture, already poisonous under Goodwin, became more so under Hester. Insiders suggest McEwan is struggling to rectify this. The bank's apparent refusal to compensate customers such as Derek Carlyle, who spent seven years fighting its previous attempt to 'destroy' him and his family through the courts, even though he won a Supreme Court victory against the bank in 2015; its use of delaying tactics that include failing to divulge requested documents in order to stall and derail litigation in the hope of depleting claimants' legal budgets; its manipulation of the FCA's swaps 'redress' scheme to ensure the compensation it pays out to business customers it swindled through the 'mis-selling' of interest-rate swaps is minimised; the way atrocious standards of mortgage selling were allowed to persist in the UK retail bank until as recently as 2013, after McEwan took control; the attempts of former senior executives Derek Sach and Chris Sullivan to mislead the Treasury committee about the purpose of the global restructuring group; the bank's mendacious handling of the Highland Capital Management court case; its use of fake solicitors to terrify debtors into paying up; and the continued sense of entitlement of its remaining investment bankers and board directors – all these and more suggest something remains rotten in the state of RBS.

Speaking at his last AGM as chairman, Hampton admitted 'culture is a journey, not an end point. You don't change culture by flicking a switch.' At the same event, McEwan admitted, 'without the right culture and without the right leadership, we cannot, and will not, complete the journey'. In a June 2015 presentation to the St Paul's Institute, in a meeting held in the undercroft of Christopher Wren's imposing cathedral, RBS's George Graham admitted that improving RBS's culture was proving a thorny problem. Graham, a former editor of the *Financial Times*'s Lex column who joined RBS as deputy director of strategy in 2004 and became director of strategy in 2011, said that even though Goodwin's slogan, 'Make it happen', had been banished from the bank, the ethos lived on. He said, 'Shifting the culture of a bank doesn't lend itself well to 90-day plans and progress charts. Banks are trying, but it's not easy, and success is more likely to be visible by the absence of negatives than by any observable and tangible achievement of positives.'[23] He was no less gloomy about the future of the economics of banking, implying that without radical change and further savage cuts to RBS's bloated cost base, its survival looked uncertain, especially if UK interest rates were to remain low. The bank's cost-to-income ratio was 87 per cent in 2014, down from 95 per cent in 2013.

· Stockbrokers Jefferies, however, are impressed by McEwan's progress. In a May 2015 research note, they said that after a meeting with RBS management they were confident RBS would meet all its targets – including reducing its cost-to-income ratio to below 50 per cent and delivering operational efficiencies – arguing the bank would soon be in a position to start paying dividends again (although RBS must pay the government £1.5 billion to cancel the government's 'dividend access share' before this can happen). Jefferies hailed RBS's shares as a 'buy', believing they would rise to 510 pence.[24] David Madden, an analyst at IG, says McEwan is 'ramping up the rate of restructuring to try and whip the bank into shape as fast as he can'. He added, 'Even though it will be a number of years before the bank will return cash to shareholders, the firm is moving in the right direction.'[25] Others are less impressed. In the wake of the implementation of the European Union's Bank Recovery and Resolution Directive, which outlaws further state-funded bailouts of failing banks, credit rating agency Standard & Poor's downgraded RBS to BBB-, leaving the bank just one notch above 'junk'.

Against this backdrop, George Osborne is 'desperate' to sell the bank, through the agency of UK Financial Investments. Speaking at the Mansion House on 10 June 2015, the chancellor insisted that selling RBS was 'the right thing to do', adding that selling an initial few billion pounds' worth of shares at a loss (i.e. for less than the 502 pence-per-share that the Labour government paid for them in 2008–9) made sense, as enlarging the 'free float' should drive up the price and rehabilitate the bank. Emboldened by his party's recent general election victory Osborne claimed that any losses on the RBS stake would be overridden by profits from the sale of other bailed-out banks, including Lloyds, in which the government has already reduced its stake from 43 per cent at the time of the bailouts to 15 per cent in July 2015. 'Yes, we may get a lower price than Labour paid for it,' Osborne told a group of bow-tie wearing bankers, 'but the longer we wait, the higher the price the economy will pay.' At the time of writing, RBS's shares are worth 333.8 pence each, which means they have shed 33.5 per cent of their value, since Brown described the government's initial share purchase as a 'commercial investment' in October 2008 . If they were all to be sold at this price the UK government would lose £15.24 billion on its 'investment'. An initial sale to institutional investors didn't bode well. On 3 August 2015, UKFI sold a 5.4 per cent stake in RBS at 330 pence per share through a so-called 'accelerated bookbuild'. But the exercise left taxpayers short-changed. About 630 million shares for which taxpayers paid £3.2 billion seven years earlier were sold for just £2.1 billion, meaning the shortfall was £1.1 billion.

I asked some City friends whether Osborne is deranged in selling RBS at a loss, and whether he would have been better off waiting until the share price rises above 502 pence. They unanimously said that fund managers rarely consider the price at which shareholdings are bought, being more interested in what the price will do in the future. If investors believe a company's shares are about to crash – for example because its strategy is flawed, its sector has entered terminal decline (as Kodak's did at the dawn of digital photography), or because penalties for past wrongdoing could wipe it out – they prefer to dump the stock while it still has some value, rather than hold on until it has none. There will always be 'greater fools' in the market who are less alert to the risks or who are just more bullish about the firm's prospects. In view of RBS's multifarious problems, Osborne may be being quite canny in favouring a swift reprivatisation – even though most commentators believe it could take five to ten years before the government can sell all of its 79 per cent stake. Perhaps Osborne is the Lloyd Blankfein of politics, 'de-risking' the government's portfolio just as Blankfein 'de-risked' Goldman Sachs's by offloading subprime CDOs to the naive bankers of Dusseldorf in 2006 and 2007. However Osborne's haste to offload the government's RBS stake is more likely to be driven by political ambition: he wants to impress Conservative right-wingers, who will dictate who succeeds David Cameron as party leader, by privatising more state-owned assets than his heroine Margaret Thatcher.

John Hourican, who ran RBS's investment bank until he resigned over the Libor scandal in 2013, is disillusioned with what the government has done to RBS. He says the board under Hampton has been far too willing to acquiesce to the Treasury's flawed vision. Hourican said the RBS board has destroyed the entire £45.5 billion the taxpayer had put into the bank. 'There's no earnings power to generate a return. There's no capital going back to shareholders – it's just being used to shrink the bank. They have removed the investment capital.' He added that the government's strategy for banking is undermining Britain. 'We have given the keys of the global banking business to the American investment banks.'[26] And it's worth pointing out that none of the four investment banks that are handling the RBS re-privatisation is British. Three are American (Goldman Sachs, Citigroup and Morgan Stanley) while one is Swiss (UBS).

But while Hourican's views have some validity, they are essentially those of an old-school investment banker who is nonplussed that his alma mater is being retrenched out of existence, and who perhaps doesn't grasp that, in the world of investment banking, RBS was always going to be a second-rate player – and therefore at considerable risk of blowing itself up and breaking Britain's economy.

RBS ought to have been the catalyst for a radical rethink, both of banking and politics. But, as the reprivatisation gathers pace, we seem to have missed our chance. As Martin Wolf, the *FT*'s chief economics commentator, says, the political and financial elites' response to the crisis, especially since 2010, has been woeful and has stored up tremendous problems for the future. Writing in *The Shifts and the Shocks*, Wolf said, 'Ordinary taxpayers are being forced to suffer in order to save a banking system that has brought them only excess and ruin. This is intolerable: indeed, a form of debt-slavery. No industry should have the capacity to inflict economic costs that may even surpass those of a world war.'[27]

While banking's capacity to inflict such devastation has been marginally reduced since 2008, it is a long way from being exorcised.

Glossary

ABN AMRO – Algemene Bank Nederland Amsterdam Rotterdam
ABS – asset-backed security
ACT – advanced corporation tax
AIB – Allied Irish Banks
AIM – alternative investment market
AIRB – Advanced Internal Ratings-Based
ANZ – Australian and New Zealand Banking Group
APS – asset protection scheme
ASB – Accounting Standards Board
BBA – British Bankers' Association
BCCI – Bank of Credit and Commerce International
BIFU – Banking, Insurance and Finance Union
BIS – Bank for International Settlements
BoAML – Bank of America Merrill Lynch
BoS – Bank of Scotland
BoSI – Bank of Scotland (Ireland)
BPO – business process outsourcing
BCBS – Basel Committee on Banking Supervision
BTMU – Bank of Tokyo-Mitsubishi
BZW – Barclays de Zoete Wedd
C&G – Cheltenham and Gloucester Building Society
CBFM – Corporate Banking and Financial Markets
CCF – Credit Commercial de France
CDO – collateralised debt obligation
CDS – credit default swap
CFTC – Commodities Futures Trading Commission
CGNU – Commercial General Norwich Union

CIBD – Corporate and Institutional Banking Division
CLO – collateralised loan obligation
CMBS – commercial mortgage-backed security
CSCB – Committee of Scottish Clearing Bankers
CSFB – Credit Suisse First Boston
ECB – European Central Bank
EPS – earnings per share
ERM – Exchange Rate Mechanism
ESOP – employee share ownership plan
FCA – Financial Conduct Authority
FLS – Funding for Lending Scheme
FNBS – First National Building Society
FSA – Financial Services Authority
FSC – financial stability committee
FSMA – Financial Services and Markets Act 2000
GBM – Global Banking and Markets
GCS – group consolidation system
GEMC – group executive management committee
GRG – Global Restructuring Group
HBOS – Halifax Bank of Scotland
HCS – high-level consolidation system
HELOC – home equity line of credit
HMRC – Her Majesty's Revenue and Customs
HSBC – Hongkong and Shanghai Banking Corporation
IASB – International Accounting Standards Board
ICB – Independent Commission on Banking
ICFC – Industrial and Commercial Finance Corporation
IFA – independent financial advisor
IFRS – International Financial Reporting Standards
IFSC – International Financial Services Centre
IMD – International Institute for Management Development
IMF – International Monetary Fund
IMRO – Investment Management Regulatory Organisation
IPO – initial public offering
IRB – Internal Ratings Based
IRHP – interest rate hedging product
IRR – internal rate of return
IRSA – interest rate swap agreement

ISDA – International Swaps and Derivatives Association
J21 – Journey to One
JDS – Joint Disciplinary Scheme
KIO – Kuwait Investment Office
LEP – Leadership Excellence Profile
Libor – London Interbank Offered Rate
M&A – mergers and acquisitions
M&IB – markets and international banking
MAM – Mercury Asset Management
MBS – mortgage-backed security
NAB – National Australia Bank
NAPF – National Association of Pension Funds
PDFM – Phillips & Drew Fund Management
PEF – Performance Evaluation Framework
PEP – personal equity plan
PIRC – Pensions and Investments Research Consultants
PPI – payment protection insurance
PRA – Prudential Regulation Authority
PwC – PricewaterhouseCoopers
QE – quantitative easing
RBS – Royal Bank of Scotland
RCR – RBS Capital Resolution
RMBS – residential mortgage-backed security
RNS – Regulatory News Service
RoE – return on equity
ROSCO – Rolling Stock Operating Company
S&L – savings and loan (association)
S&P – Standard & Poor's
SAYE – save-as-you-earn
SBO – serviced by others
SCDI – Scottish Council for Development & Industry
SDA – Scottish Development Agency
SEC – Securities and Exchange Commission
SFA – Securities and Futures Authority
SFE – Scottish Financial Enterprise
SIB – Securities and Investment Board
SIV – structured investment vehicles
SLS – Specialised Lending Services

SLS – Special Liquidity Scheme
SME – small and medium-sized enterprises
TARP – Troubled Asset Relief Program
TCI – The Children's Investment Fund
TESSA – tax-exempt special savings account
TSB – Trustee Savings Bank
UBIL – Ulster Bank Ireland Limited
UBL – Ulster Bank Limited
UBS – Union Bank of Switzerland
UKFI – UK Financial Investments
UKLA – UK Listing Authority
VaR – Value at Risk

Endnotes

Website links are given for convenience of readers, who should be aware that they are owned and controlled by third parties. The publisher has no editorial control over these sites, and can accept no liability for their content.

INTRODUCTION

1   *Daily Mirror*, 4 November 2013, http://www.mirror.co.uk/money/city-news/royal- bank-scotlands-philip-hampton-2676822.
2   Stephen Hester, oral evidence given at Scottish Parliament, Economy, Energy and Tourism Committee, 'Official Report', 25 November 2009, http://www.scottish.parliament.uk/parliamentarybusiness/28862.aspx?r=343&mode=html.
3   Ha-Joon Chang, 'Economics is too important to leave to the experts', *The Guardian*, 30 April 2014 http://www.theguardian.com/commentisfree/2014/apr/30/economics- experts-economists.

CHAPTER 1

1   Adam Smith, *An Inquiry into the Nature and Causes of the Wealth of Nations*, 1776.
2   Ibid.
3   RBS Group, Minutes of Crisis Meeting of the Directors of the Royal Bank of Scotland, 1793, http://www.rbs.com/about/history-100/surviving-and-learning-from-times-of-turmoil/directors-crisis-meeting-minutes-1793.html.
4   Murray Rothbard, *The Mystery of Banking*, Richardson & Snyder, 1983.
5   Sydney G. Checkland, *Scottish Banking: A History, 1695–1973*, Collins, 1975.
6   Murray Rothbard, *The Mystery of Banking*.
7   'RBS History in 100 Objects', Royal Bank of Scotland website, http://www.rbs.com/about/history-100/doing-business-openly-and-fairly/royal-bank-rules-1819.html.
8   James Anderson, *The Story of the Commercial Bank of Scotland*, 1910.

9   Andrew Haldane, 'Control Rights (and Wrongs)', Wincott Annual Memorial Lecture, 24 October 2011, http://www.bankofengland.co.uk/publications/Documents/speeches/2011/speech525.pdf.
10 RBS Heritage Online, Alexander Kemp Wright, http://heritagearchives.rbs.com/wiki/Alexander_Kemp_Wright.
11 *The Glasgow Herald*, 4 June 1927, http://news.google.com/newspapers?nid=2507&dat=19270604&id=eP89AAAAIBAJ&sjid=dEkMAAAAIBAJ&pg=4503,5108462.
12 *The Scotsman*, 31 July 1981.
13 Ibid., 27 August 1981.
14 Ibid., 16 July 1981.
15 'Monopolies and Mergers Commission Report', 15 January 1982, http://webarchive.nationalarchives.gov.uk/+/http://www.competition-commission.org.uk/rep_pub/reports/1982/fulltext/150c12.pdf.
16 Ibid.
17 *The Glasgow Herald*, 16 January 1982.
18 David Boyle, *Broke: Who Killed the Middle Classes?*, Fourth Estate, 2013.
19 Peter Pugh, *Number One Charlotte Square*, privately published, 1987.
20 Ray Perman, *Hubris: How HBOS Wrecked the Best Bank in Britain*, Birlinn, 2012.

CHAPTER 2

1   *Business*, December 1987, p. 95.
2   Lord Younger obituary, *The Guardian*, 27 January 2003.
3   *The Glasgow Herald*, 3 March 1987, http://news.google.com/newspapers?nid=2507&dat=19870303&id=cS41AAAAIBAJ&sjid=_KULAAAAIBAJ&pg=2075,362770.
4   *The Glasgow Herald*, 19 March 1987, http://news.google.com/newspapers?id=eS41AAAAIBAJ&sjid=_KULAAAAIBAJ&pg=4450,4531346&dq=george-mathewson&hl=en.
5   Ibid.
6   *Business*, December 1987.
7   George Mathewson, speech at NCR's European Bankers Seminar in Cannes, 28 May 1992.
8   George Mathewson, speech to RBS executives, Esdaile training centre, 22 August 1990.
9   Nova Reda secret briefing document to RBS board, 21 November 1990.
10 George Mathewson, author interview.
11 George Mathewson, speech to branch banking managers' conference, 11–22 March 1991.
12 George Mathewson, author interview.

13 *Financial Times*, 29 April 2006, http://www.ft.com/cms/s/0/b6d5f46c-d71d-11da-b64c-0000779e2340.html.

14 David Torrance, *George Younger: A Life Well Lived*, Birlinn, 2008.

15 Building Societies Association http://www.bsa.org.uk/consumer/factsheets/100009.htm.

16 Anthony Sampson, *The Essential Anatomy of Britain: Democracy in Crisis*, Hodder & Stoughton, 1992.

CHAPTER 3

1 Richard Roberts, *The City: A Guide to London's Global Financial Centre*, Profile books, 2004.

2 Geoffrey Jones, *British Multinational Banking: 1830–1990*, The Clarendon Press, 1993.

3 *New York Times*, 22 July 1994, http://www.nytimes.com/1994/07/22/business/worldbusiness/22iht-ukbank.html.

4 Frank Kirwan, 'Strategy Review 1991', 26 June 1991.

5 George Mathewson, author interview.

6 David Lascelles, *Other People's Money: the Revolution in High Street Banking*, Institute of Financial Services, 2005.

7 Second RBS UK Commercial Banking Executive Conference, 5 December 1992.

8 *People Management*, 19 October 1995, http://www.caudatagroup.com/whitepapers/Re-engineerings_Missing_Ingredient.pdf.

9 George Mathewson, speech to NCR European Bankers' Seminar in Cannes, 28 May 1992.

10 Anonymous employee quoted in *Performance Management* and 'The New Workplace Tyranny Report', January 2013.

CHAPTER 4

1 Peter Wood interview, *Daily Telegraph*, 16 August 2003, http://www.telegraph.co.uk/finance/2860520/Business-profile-All-calmed-down-dear-but-just-as-direct-as-ever.html.

2 *The Independent*, 26 November 1993.

3 *Daily Telegraph*, 16 August 2003.

4 John Kay, *Foundations of Corporate Success*, Oxford University Press, 1993.

5 George Mathewson interviewed by Ian McConnell, 'Too bad I never got fired', *The Herald*, 29 April 2006, http://www.heraldscotland.com/sport/spl/aberdeen/too-bad-i-never-got-fired-sir-george-mathewson-the-man-least-likely-to-be-given-his-p45-tells-ian-mcconnell-a-spot-of-gardening-leave-would-however-not-have-gone-amiss-1.21869.

CHAPTER 5

1 'Royal Bank of Scotland Strategy Review', presented to the bank board, 26 June 1991.

2 *FX Week*, online financial magazine,12 July 1991.

3 *Financial Times*, 2 March 1992, http://data.synthesis.ie/site_media/trec/FT/FT921-5883.txt.

4 Alf Young, 'An offer that couldn't be refused', *The Glasgow Herald*, 13 January 1990, http://www.heraldscotland.com/sport/spl/aberdeen/an-offer-that-couldn-t-be-refused-1.595212.

5 Iain Robertson, author interview.

6 Ibid.

7 Ibid.

8 *Public Service Review*, 20 February 2001, http://www.publicservice.co.uk/article.asp?publication=PPP&id=94&content_name=Overview&article=2268.

9 *FX Week*, online financial magazine, 7 March 1994, http://www.fxweek.com/fx-week/news/1542889/royal-bank-plans-new-fx-hires-to-prepare-for-london-move.

10 Iain Robertson, author interview.

11 Richard Greensted (ed.), *Scrip Issue*, 24 March 1999, http://www.inservresource.com/website/archives/analysis%20archive.htm.

12 Iain Robertson, author interview.

13 Ibid.

14 'Royal Bank of Scotland Prospectus', 15 June 1994.

15 Iain Robertson, author interview.

CHAPTER 6

1 Frank Kirwan, author interview.

2 *The Hour*, Associated Press, 23 June 1993.

3 Simon Samuels, author interview.

4 George Mathewson, 'The Single European Market: European and non-European implications', speech, Money Europa Conference, Edinburgh, 1989.

5 Ibid.

6 *The Glasgow Herald*, 4 May 1989.

7 Frank Kirwan, author interview.

8 Simon Samuels, author interview.

CHAPTER 7

1 George Mathewson, presentation to RBS bank board, 26 June 1991.

2 Eric Baird, 'Adam Bank still paying for £21m flutter', *The Herald*, 19

December 1992, http://www.heraldscotland.com/sport/spl/aberdeen/ adam-bank-still-paying-for-21m-flutter-1.779898. Author's note: Sir Charles Fraser is my father.

3 Ibid.

4 'French rescuer hit by loss on Adam', *Financial Times*, 20 July 1993, http:// data.synthesis.ie/site_media/trec/FT/FT933-13294.txt.

5 'Adam gets new lease of life after RBS buy', *The Independent*, 20 July 1993, http://www.independent.co.uk/news/business/adam-gets-new-lease-of-life-after-rbs-buy-purchase-is-good-solution-after-last-years-crisis-1486041.html.

6 *The Scotsman*, 7 July 1998.

7 Iain Martin, *Making It Happen*, Simon & Schuster UK, 2013.

8 'Takeover battle that changed everything', *The Times*, 21 July 2003, http:// www.thetimes.co.uk/tto/business/columnists/article2623276.ece.

9 *The Scotsman*, 7 July 1998.

10 BBC News, 27 November 1998, http://news.bbc.co.uk/1/hi/business/ 223274.stm.

11 'The Andrew Davidson Interview: Martin Taylor', *Management Today*, 1 March 2002, http://www.managementtoday.co.uk/news/407684/ ANDREW-DAVIDSON-INTERVIEW-Martin-Taylor/?DCMP=ILC-SEARCH.

12 *Sunday Herald*, 25 April 1999, http://www.ianfraser.org/?p=7948.

13 Peter Burt, author interview.

14 George Mathewson, author interview.

15 Ibid.

16 Andrew Garfield, 'Ambition! The Scotsman Who's Banking on Buying Barclays', *The Independent*, 2 June 1999, http://www.independent.co.uk/ news/business/ambition-1097504.html.

17 Alf Young, 'Don't Sell Out Scotland PLC', *Sunday Herald*, 21 February 1999.

18 George Mathewson, speech to corporate and institutional bank dinner, Law Society, Chancery Lane, 16 June 1999.

19 Andrew Garfield, 'Ambition! The Scotsman Who's Banking on Buying Barclays'.

20 Jeffrey E. Garten, 'Too Big to Fail', op-ed in the *New York Times*, 1997, http://www.nytimes.com/1997/09/26/opinion/too-big-to-fail.html.

21 Ibid.

22 Ibid.

23 Brooksley Born, Chairperson Commodity Futures Trading Commission, testimony to the US House of Representatives Committee on Banking and Financial Services, concerning Long-Term Capital Management, 1 October 1998, http://www.cftc.gov/opa/speeches/opaborn-35.htm.

24   Simon Johnson and James Kwak, *13 Bankers: The Wall Street Takeover and the Next Meltdown*, Pantheon Books, 2010.

25   Gillian Tett, *Fool's Gold: How Unrestrained Greed Corrupted a Dream, Shattered Global Markets and Unleashed a Catastrophe*, Little, Brown, 2009.

26   Johnson and Kwak, *13 Bankers*.

CHAPTER 8

1   George Mathewson, author interview.

2   'RBS: Inside the Bank that Ran Out of Money', BBC One, October 2011, http://www.bbc.co.uk/programmes/601690y5.

3   'Perhaps coming out of Ferguslie Park was his undoing', *The Herald*, 2 February 2012, http://www.heraldscotland.com/news/home-news/perhaps-coming-out-of- ferguslie-park-was-his-undoing.16646739.

4   Peter Koenig, 'Is RBS's Fred the Shred too good to be true', *Sunday Times*, 2 November 2003, http://www.thesundaytimes.co.uk/sto/business/article42378.ece.

5   Ibid.

6   Alan Smart, 'Fred Goodwin was my chauffeur', Aye We Can blog, 27 February 2009, http://ayewecan.blogspot.co.uk/2009/02/sir-fred-goodwin-was-my-chaffeur.html.

7   Ben Borland, 'Fred's dream at uni was to be a pinball wizard . . .', *Scottish Daily Express*, 12 April 2009, http://www.express.co.uk/news/uk/94661/Fred-s-dream-at- uni-was-to-be-a-pinball-wizard.

8   Fred Goodwin interviewed by Ian Burrell, *Edinburgh Evening News*, July 1998.

9   Australian Broadcasting Corporation, 4 September 2001.

10   'Goodwin for Clydesdale', *The Herald*, 3 March 1995, http://www.herald-scotland.com/sport/spl/aberdeen/goodwin-for-clydesdale-1.691836.

11   Fred Goodwin interviewed by Amanda Hall, *Sunday Telegraph*, December 1999.

12   Alf Young, author interview.

13   Iain Martin, *Making It Happen*.

14   Ibid.

15   George Mathewson, speech to branch banking managers' conference, 11–22 March 1991.

16   George Mathewson, author interview.

CHAPTER 9

1   'Securities and Futures Authority Final Notice', 18 May 2000, http://www.fsa.gov.uk/pubs/additional/545.pdf.

2   'Who pushed NatWest?', *Euromoney*, 1 November 1999, http://www.euromoney.com/Article/1005082/BackIssue/50093/Who-pushed-NatWest.html.

3   Peter Burt, author interview.

4   'The Bidding for NatWest', *The Economist*, 30 September 1999, http://
    www.economist.com/node/244328.

5   'Cheque mate?', *Sunday Times*, 26 September 1999.

6   George Mathewson, author interview.

7   Ian Fraser, 'Banking on a future', *Sunday Herald*, 3 October 1999, http://
    www.ianfraser.org/banking-on-a-future.

8   'Rowland's riposte', 'Lex' column, *Financial Times*, 28 October 1999.

9   John White, Oral History, Computerworld Honors Program, International
    Archives, transcript of a Video History Interview with John White, Head of
    Manufacturing, RBS Americas, Recipient of the 2008 EMC Information
    Leadership Award, 1 April 2008.

10 George Mathewson, author interview.

11 'Revealed: RBS's secret plan for NatWest takeover', *Daily Express*, 14
    November 1999.

12 Diana Younger, author interview.

13 Ian Fraser, 'Royal Bank to pounce on NatWest', *Sunday Herald*, 28 November
    1999, http://www.ianfraser.org/royal-bank-to-pounce-on-natwest.

14 'NatWest rejects Royal Bank bid', BBC News, 28 November 1999, http://
    news.bbc.co.uk/1/hi/business/540532.stm.

15 Ian McConnell, 'Burt gives Royal a mugging', *The Herald*, 1 December 1999,
    http://www.heraldscotland.com/sport/spl/aberdeen/burt-gives-royal-a-
    mugging-1.259642.

16 *Sunday Herald*, 11 May 2003, http://www.ianfraser.org/410.

17 Andrew Ross Sorkin, 'Market Place; The Bank of Scotland raises ante
    in hostile bid for NatWest', *New York Times*, 9 December 1999, http://
    www.nytimes.com/1999/12/09/business/markets-market-place-bank-
    scotland-raises-ante-hostile-bid-for-natwest.html.

18 HSBC NatWest research note, 1 December 1999.

19 'Royal to renew efforts in battle for NatWest', *Sunday Herald*, 5 December 1999.

20 NatWest press release.

21 'Queen's bank manager puts his head above the parapet', *Daily Mail*, 23
    December 2001.

22 George Mathewson, author interview.

23 Simon Samuels, author interview.

24 Iain Robertson, author interview.

25 Simon Samuels, Nick Lord and Stuart Young, 'NatWest – The End
    Game', Citigroup, Salomon Smith Barney, 1 February 2000.

26 Michael Lever, David Raye and Jonathan Pierce, 'Reject both bids – too
    much risk, too little reward', HSBC company report – NatWest Group, 3
    February 2000.

27 Ian Fraser and Kenny Kemp, 'The Giant Killer', *Sunday Herald*, 13 February 2000.

28 George Mathewson, author interview.

29 Ian Fraser and Kenny Kemp, 'The Giant Killer'.

30 Jim Mahar and Kristina Polson, 'The Battle for NatWest', St Bonaventure University, 2003.

CHAPTER 10

1 Peter Smith, 'The fall of NatWest – an insider's account', *Supply Management*, 2 November 2000, http://www.supplymanagement.com/analysis/features/2000/the-fall-of- natwest-an-insiders-account.

2 Ibid.

3 Fred Goodwin, presentation to analysts and investors hosted by Merrill Lynch, New York, 2 November 2005.

4 'RBS press release Re: Directorate', 17 March 2000, http://www.investors.rbs.com/news-item?item=7700876424847.

5 'NatWest press release Changes to the board of directors', 6 March 2000, http://www.investegate.co.uk/article.aspx?id=200003061502297507G.

6 'RBS Annual Report and Accounts 2000'. The 2000 figures are for the 15 months ended 31 December 2000, owing to a change of year end. Four RBS executive directors – Mathewson, Goodwin, McLuskie and Robertson – received controversial 'special bonuses' following the successful completion of the NatWest acquisition.

7 Alf Young, author interview, 23 October, 2012.

8 'Delivering on our promises', RBS investor presentation, 19 April 2000, http://www.investors.rbs.com/download/corporate_actions/acquisition/0_30_day-Slides.pdf.

9 RBS press release, 2000.

10 Frances Coppola, author interview.

11 Matthew Norman, 'Chef in the City', *Daily Telegraph*, 31 July 2002, http://www.telegraph.co.uk/foodanddrink/4815091/Chef-in-the-city.html.

12 Gordon Pell, author interview.

13 Ibid.

14 Ibid.

15 *Daily Telegraph*, 2 August 2000, http://www.telegraph.co.uk/finance/4460697/Kirsty-takes-the-high-road-as-Sally-comes-marching-home.html.

16 Iain Robertson, author interview.

17 Ibid.

18 Ibid.

19 Ibid.

20 John White, Oral History, Computerworld Honors Program, International Archives, transcript of a Video History Interview with John White, Head of Manufacturing, RBS Americas, Recipient of the 2008 EMC Information Leadership Award, 1 April 2008.

21 'Why Fred is getting credit', *Scotland on Sunday*, 6 August 2000, http://www.scotsman.com/business/banking/why-fred-is-getting-credit-1-1285545.

22 Ibid.

23 *The Scotsman*, March 2000.

24 'RBS rewards staff for NatWest "delivery"', *Daily Telegraph*, 28 February 2003.

25 'Questor' column, *Daily Telegraph*, 8 August 2002, http://www.telegraph.co.uk/finance/markets/questor/2770171/The-Questor-Column.html.

26 Frances Coppola, author interview.

27 Ibid.

28 Ibid.

CHAPTER 11

1 AFX, 'RBoS delights mrkt with strong FY results; shares show sharp gains', 1 March 2001, http://www.iii.co.uk/investment/detail/?display=news&code=cotn:RBS.L&action=article&articleid=3131842.

2 'Imprudent capitalist who risked and lost the respect of his friend Gordon Brown', *The Guardian*, 21 January 2009, http://www.guardian.co.uk/business/2009/jan/21/sir-fred-goodwin-gordon-brown.

3 Simon Targett, 'Funds furious over RBS bonuses', *Financial Times*, 27 March 2001.

4 Patience Wheatcroft, 'The Human Factor', *Management Today*, 1 May 2001, http://www.managementtoday.co.uk/news/408120/HUMAN-FACTOR-Fred-Goodwins-pounds-814000-bonus-smacked-ofthe-insensitivity-made-banks-unpopular-high-streetand-high-places/?DCMP=ILC-SEARCH.

5 Mary Mackenzie's obituary, *The Herald*, 9 November 2012, http://www.heraldscotland.com/comment/obituaries/mary-mackenzie.19350890.

6 George Mathewson, David Torrance interview, 2007.

7 'The Roles of the Chairman, Chief Executive and Senior Independent Director under the Combined Code', ICSA Guidance Note 041001, September 2004.

8 'RBS, Inside the Bank That Ran Out of Money', BBC Scotland, October 2011, http://www.bbc.co.uk/programmes/b01690y5.

9 George Mathewson, author interview.

10 Ibid.

11 Stewart Hamilton, author interview.

12 Ibid.

13 Grant Ringshaw, 'The Bionic Bank', *Daily Telegraph*, 22 February 2004, http://www.telegraph.co.uk/finance/2877749/The-bionic-bank.html.

14 Robert Winnett and Tracy Corrigan, 'RBS was 'disaster waiting to happen', *Daily Telegraph*, 21 March 2009, http://www.telegraph.co.uk/finance/recession/5025315/RBS-was-disaster-waiting-to-happen.html.

15 Tim Sharp, 'RBS admits retail arm was a cash cow to fund acquisitions', *The Herald*, 13 November 2010, http://www.heraldscotland.com/business/corporate-sme/rbs-admits-retail-arm-was-a-cash-cow-to-fund-acquisitions-1.1068037.

16 Anthony Bianco and Heather Timmons, 'Crisis at Citi', *BusinessWeek* magazine, 8 September 2002, http://www.businessweek.com/stories/2002-09-08/crisis-at-citi.

17 'Dixon Motors falls to RBS', *Daily Telegraph*, 23 April 2002, http://www.telegraph.co.uk/finance/2760655/Dixon-Motors-falls-to-RBS.html.

18 *Automotive Management*, 28 September 2005, http://www.am-online.com/news/2005/ 9/28/mystery-surrounds-dixon-s-exit/9978.

19 *Daily Mirror*, 4 November 2013, http://www.mirror.co.uk/money/city-news/royal-bank-scotlands-philip-hampton-2676822.

20 Andrew G. Haldane, executive director for financial stability, Bank of England, 'Control rights (and wrongs)', speech given at Wincott Annual Memorial Lecture, 24 October 2011, http://www.bankofengland.co.uk/publications/Documents/speeches/2011/speech525.pdf.

21 Anat Admati and Martin Hellwig, *The Bankers' New Clothes: What's Wrong With Banking and What to Do About It*, Princeton University Press, 2013.

22 Nick Cohen, *You Can't Read this Book: Censorship in an Age of Freedom*, Fourth Estate, 2012.

23 Peter Koenig, 'Special report: Is RBS's Fred the Shred too good to be true?', *Sunday Times*, 2003, http://www.thesundaytimes.co.uk/sto/business/article42378.ece.

CHAPTER 12

1 'Social Banking', a seminar held by the Smith Institute in 11 Downing Street on 20 October 1999, http://www.smith-institute.org.uk/file/SocialBanking.pdf.

2 'PwC Hour Glass', January 2008, http://www.evidencebasedhr.com/wp-content/uploads/2011/12/RBS-Neil-Roden-PwC-Hourglass9-Feb2008.pdf.

3 Jack Welch, *Jack: What I've Learned Leading A Great Company and Great People*, Headline, 2002.

4 Ibid.

5 W. E. Deming, quoted in Kenneth Hopper and William Hopper, *The Puritan Gift*, I. B. Tauris, 2009.

6 Professor Phil Taylor, 'Performance Management and the New Workplace Tyranny', a report for the STUC, January 2013.

7 Rob MacGregor, author interview.

8 Gerry Duffy, 'Eye spy Scotland's biggest fraudster', *The Sun*, 16 October 2009, http://www.thesun.co.uk/sol/homepage/news/scottishnews/2686873/Eye-spy-Scotlands-biggest-fraudster-Donald-MacKenzie.html.

9 'FSA in pledge to crack down on misselling by bank salesforces', *Money Marketing*, 4 December 2003, http://www.moneymarketing.co.uk/news/

fsa-in-pledge-to-crack-down-on-misselling-by-bank-salesforces/54309. article.

10   Richard Dyson, '£40m kickback', *Mail on Sunday*, 25 January 2004, http://www.thisismoney.co.uk/money/mortgageshome/article-1515987/16340m-kickback.htm.

11   Parliamentary Commission on Banking Standards, 13 November 2012, http://www.publications.parliament.uk/pa/jt201213/jtselect/jtpcbs/c710-i/c71001.htm.

12   Ibid.

13   *The Guardian*, 26 May 2011, http://www.theguardian.com/business/2011/may/26/jayne-anne-gadhia-virgin-money-interview.

14   Professor Phil Taylor, 'Performance Management and the New Workplace Tyranny', January 2013.

15   Brian Pitman, 'Evidence to the Future of Banking Commission', June 2010, http://www.which.co.uk/documents/pdf/future-of-banking-commission-report-276591.pdf.

16   Ron Kerr and Sarah Robinson, 'From Symbolic Violence to Economic Violence: The Globalizing of the Scottish Banking Elite', *Journal of Organization Studies*, January 2012, http://oss.sagepub.com/content/33/2/247.

17   Tom Peters and Robert Waterman, *In Search of Excellence*, Harper & Row, 1982.

Chapter 13

1   Michael Lafferty, author interview.

2   Giles Barrie, author interview.

3   Iain Robertson, author interview.

4   Ian Fraser, 'RBS faces a hit on profits', *Sunday Herald*, 24 November 2004.

5   Teresa Hunter, 'Small Change' column, *Sunday Herald*, 18 May 2003.

6   Iain Martin, *Making It Happen*.

7   *Sunday Times*, 9 January 2005, http://www.thesundaytimes.co.uk/sto/business/article98046.ece.

8   Ibid.

Chapter 14

1   RTÉ News, December 1999, http://www.youtube.com/watch?v=nqu3TkuhhVg.

2   Ibid.

3   Mike Soden, interviewed by journalist Jamie Mann, who helped with the research for this chapter.

4   RBS Heritage, http://heritagearchives.rbs.com/companies/list/ulster-bank-ltd.html.

5   'NatWest Group annual report and accounts year to 31 December 1999', http://www.rbs.co.uk/Group_Information/Investor_Relations/Financial_Results/1999/natwest1999.pdf.

6   John Meagher, 'Moving house ... stone by stone', *Irish Independent*, 6 March 1999, http://www.independent.ie/national-news/moving-house-stone-by-stone-415158.html.

7   Kyran Fitzgerald, 'McCarthy takes a gamble on redemption', *Irish Examiner*, 26 May 2012.

8   Ciaran Hancock, 'Focus: Banking on Braveheart', *Sunday Times Ireland*, 12 October 2003, http://www.thesundaytimes.co.uk/sto/business/article246481.ece.

9   Simon Carswell, interviewed by Jamie Mann.

10 Johnny Ronan, interviewed by Jamie Mann.

11 Ibid.

12 Ita Gibney, 'Getting the story right', *Finance Magazine*, March 2004, http://www.finance-magazine.com/display_article.php?i=4434&pi=180.

13 Ciaran Hancock, *Sunday Times Ireland*.

14 RTÉ News, *Prime Time* debate (part one), 16 October 2003, http://youtu.be/cxtkjZFfuZI.

15 Simon Carswell column, *Irish Times*, 18 July 2012, http://www.irishtimes.com/newspaper/finance/2012/0718/1224320306803.html.

16 IMDb, http://www.imdb.com/character/ch0009155/quotes.

17 'Irish government accuses First Active of "reckless' advertising"', *Mortgage Introducer*, July 2005, http://www.mortgageintroducer.com/mortgages/11199/135/News_in_depth/Irish_government_accuses_First_Active_of_'reckless'_advertising.htm.

18 RTÉ Television, *Freefall*, 7 and 14 September 2010, http://www.rte.ie/tv/programmes/freefall.html.

19 Ibid.

20 'The global housing boom: in come the waves', *The Economist*, 16 June 2006, http://www.economist.com/node/4079027.

21 'Davy Research Note', 29 March 2006, http://www.davy.ie/other/email/econcr20060329.pdf.

22 'Drivers of Growth', RBS Investor Day, 2006 Divisional Conference, http://www.investors.rbs.com/download/transcript/2006PrimaryInvestorDayTranscript.pdf.

23 Simon Carswell, interviewed by Jamie Mann.

24 Anne Harris, 'Gayle-force wedding shows A-listers how to do it with style', *Sunday Independent*, 18 July 2004, http://www.independent.ie/lifestyle/independent-woman/celebrity-news-gossip/gayleforce-wedding-shows-alisters-how-to-do-it-with-style-482264.html.

25 *Sunday Tribune*, 25 October 2009.
26 John Walsh, 'Ulster Bank asked to finance Dunne deal', *Irish Examiner*, 8 December 2012, http://www.irishexaminer.com/archives/2012/1208/business/ulster-bank-asked-to-finance-dunne--deal-216379.html.
27 *Sunday Tribune*, 25 October 2009.
28 George Garvey, 'Developer wanted to bring "Knightsbridge" to D4', *Irish Independent*, 10 March 2012, http://www.independent.ie/national-news/developer-wanted-to-bring-knightsbridge-to-d4-3045909.html.
29 Ibid.
30 Kaupthing board papers, via WikiLeaks, http://wlstorage.net/file/kaupthing-bank-before-crash-2008.pdf.
31 Matt Cooper, *How Ireland Really Went Bust*, Penguin Ireland, 2012.
32 'The Failure of The Royal Bank of Scotland', FSA board report, 10 December 2011.
33 'Ulster Bank takes more space at George's Quay', Irish Property Unit Trust, 28 February 2007, http://www.iput.ie/news/article/news-news-article-ulster-bank-takes- more-space-at-georges-quay/#.UPF4aG93arg.
34 ' "Big four" banks called to account', *Portadown Times*, 15 May 2007, http://www.portadowntimes.co.uk/news/local/big_four_banks_called_to_account_1_1645598.

CHAPTER 15

1 Richard C. Morais, 'Businessman of the Year: Brisk and brusque', *Forbes*, 6 January 2003, http://www.forbes.com/global/2003/0106/034_print.html.
2 Richard C. Morais, author interview.
3 Rob MacGregor, author interview.
4 Ibid.
5 'The Prince's Trust Annual Review 2008–09'.
6 HRH The Prince of Wales, speech at The Prince's Trust Celebrate Success Awards, The Barbican, London, 15 March 2007, https://www.princeofwales.gov.uk/media/speeches/speech-hrh-the-prince-of-wales-the-prince%E2%80%99s-trust-celebrate-success-awards-the.
7 Howard Williamson, 'When Fred Goodwin Steered Clear of Risk', Children & Young People Now, 17 March 2009, http://www.cypnow.co.uk/cyp/opinion/1038903/when-fred-goodwin-steered-risk.
8 'UK honours awarded to RBS's Goodwin, Vodafone's Horne-Smith', Bloomberg, 11 June 2004, http://www.bloomberg.com/apps/news?pid=newsarchive&sid=aFSUY9anOmmo.
9 Brian Reade, 'Fred Goodwin scandal shows Labour's cred has been torn to shreds', *Daily Mirror*, 22 January 2009, http://www.mirror.co.uk/news/uk-news/fred-goodwin-scandal-shows-labours-372402.

CHAPTER 16

1   Alan Taylor, 'The damnation of Fred Goodwin', *Sunday Herald*, 5 February 2012, http://www.heraldscotland.com/news/home-news/the-damnation-of-fred- goodwin.16662411.

2   Iain Martin, *Making it Happen*.

3   Decline of West Where Mathewson Rues What RBS Wrought', Bloomberg, 19 June 2009, http://www.bloomberg.com/apps/news?pid=newsarchive&sid=anU5X5BaNe4M.

4   'Edinburgh golfers sink bank's course bid at the first hole', *The Scotsman*, 21 February 2003, http://www.scotsman.com/news/edinburgh-golfers-sink-bank-s-course-bid-at-the-first-hole-1-870495.

5   'Sir Fred's crowning glory', *The Scotsman*, 9 January 2005.

6   Jane Simpson, 'The Bankers' Draft; RBS Staff Are Ordered out to Meet the Queen', *Mail on Sunday*, 18 September 2005.

7   'New RBS headquarters', Scottish Government news release, 14 September 2005, http://www.scotland.gov.uk/News/Releases/2005/09/14110145.

8   Opening of a new headquarters, Royal Bank of Scotland, 14 September 2005, http://www.royal.gov.uk/LatestNewsandDiary/Speechesandarticles/2005/TheQueenopensanewbankcomplexinEdinburgh.aspx.

9   Jane Simpson, 'The Bankers' Draft; RBS Staff Are Ordered out to Meet the Queen', *Mail on Sunday*.

10 'Laughing all the way to the bank: three Royal Bank of Scotland personnel tell how they are finding life inside the firm's £350-million state-of-the-art headquarters', *Sunday Mail*, 30 October 2005, http://www.thefreelibrary.com/Laughing+ all+the+way+to+the+bank%3B+Three+Royal+Bank +of+Scotland. . .-a0138102542.

11 Simon Hattenstone, 'Sir Fred just say sorry', *The Guardian*, 24 January 2009, http://www.guardian.co.uk/business/2009/jan/24/fred-goodwin-rbs/print.

12 'Furniture makers built to last', *Financial Times*, 7 October 2009, http://www.ft.com/cms/s/0/23881884-b2d9-11de-b7d2-00144feab49a.html.

13 Eric Gershon, 'RBS Building Headquarters in Stamford, Conn.', *Hartford Courant*, 29 April 2008, http://www.securityinfowatch.com/news/10545618/royal-bank-of-scotland-building-headquarters-in-stamford-conn.

14 'FLIGHT TEST: Dassault Falcon 900EX – Easy does it', *Flight International*, 18 November 2003, http://www.flightglobal.com/news/articles/flight-test-dassault- falcon-900ex-easy-does-it-173964.

15 Edward Simpkins, 'Revealed: Royal Bank's secret jet', *Sunday Telegraph*, 4 April 2004, http://www.telegraph.co.uk/finance/2882151/Revealed-Royal-Banks-secret-jet.html.

16 Robert Peston, 'Three in a featherbed romp for RBS, WPP and Courts',

Sunday Telegraph, 4 April 2004, http://www.telegraph.co.uk/finance/comment/2882145/City-comment.html.

17 Edward Simpkins, 'Revealed'.

18 Gary O'Shea, 'Welcome to Fred's Pleasure Dome', *The Sun*, 23 March 2009, http://www.thesun.co.uk/sol/homepage/news/scottishnews/2334777/RBS-boss-Sir-Fred-Goodwin-alleged-to-have-spent-millions-creating-a-palace.html.

19 Mark Gallagher, 'F1investor – The crash F1 cannot avoid', Pitpass.com, 14 October 2008, http://www.pitpass.com/fes_php/pitpass_print_article.php?fes_art_id=36277.

20 Kevin Garside, 'Williams land £36m deal', *Daily Telegraph*, 7 January 2005, http://www.telegraph.co.uk/sport/columnists/kevingarside/2353382/Williams-land-36m-deal.html.

21 Maurice Chittenden and Jon Ungoed-Thomas ' "Reckless" RBS blew £200m on top sports stars under Sir Fred Goodwin.'

22 Iain Martin, *Making It Happen*.

23 Mike Lawrence, 'Sold to the Highest Bidder', Pitpass.com, 26 October 2008, http://www.pitpass.com/fes_php/pitpass_print_article.php?fes_art_id=36400.

24 PJR Executive Coaching website, http://www.pjrcoaching.co.uk/index.html.

CHAPTER 17

1 Tom McKillop, author interview (from November 2004).

2 George Mathewson, author interview.

3 Jason Nissé, 'A Parochial Power Play, Starring a Scot on the Rocks', *The Independent on Sunday*, 31 July 2005, http://www.highbeam.com/doc/1P2-1947330.html.

4 Tom Stevenson, 'Business Comment', *Daily Telegraph*, 22 December 2005, http://www.telegraph.co.uk/finance/comment/2928858/Business-comment.html.

CHAPTER 18

1 Victor Keegan, 'Economics Notebook, Raising the risk stakes', *The Guardian*, 28 October 1998, http://www.guardian.co.uk/Columnists/Column/0,,325036,00.html.

2 Alan Greenspan, *The Age of Turbulence: Adventures in a New World*, Allen Lane, 2007.

3 Chris Skinner, 'How the City developed, Part 14', *The Finanser*, 23 December 2011, http://thefinanser.co.uk/fsclub/2011/12/how-the-city-developed-part-fourteen-crisis.html.

4 Lord Jenkin, House of Lords debate on the FSMA 2000, 16 March 2000, http:// hansard.millbanksystems.com/lords/2000/mar/16/financial-services-and-markets-bill.

5 Arup Daripa, Sandeep Kapur and Stephen Wright, 'Labour's Record on Financial Regulation', Working Paper, Department of Economics, Birkbeck, University of London, 26 September 2012, http://www.ems.bbk.ac.uk/faculty/wright/pdf/oxrep.

6 City Editor's Comment, 'What Equitable Life shows on power of regulation', *Daily Telegraph*, 20 December 2000, http://www.telegraph.co.uk/finance/personalfinance/comment/4475894/What-Equitable-Life-shows-on-power-of-regulation.html.

7 *Financial Services and Markets Act 2000*, http://www.lme.com/~/media/Files/Corporate%20Structure/FSMA%202000.pdf.

8 Rowan Bosworth-Davies, 'Regulation by prosecution', part 3 of a submission to the Parliamentary Commission on Banking Standards, 27 March 2013, http://rowans-blog.blogspot.co.uk/2013/03/why-british-banking-industry-has-become_27.html.

9 Jeremy Warner, 'A sensible solution to the Eddie George problem', *The Independent*, 13 September 1997, http://www.independent.co.uk/news/business/a-sensible-solution-to-the-eddie-george-problem-1238918.html.

10 Clive Briault, 'The Rationale for a Single National Financial Services Regulator', FSA Occasional Paper, May 1999, http://www.fsa.gov.uk/pubs/occpapers/op02.pdf.

11 Gordon Brown writing in *The Times*, quoted in 'Ministers warned over spending plans', BBC News, UK Politics, 8 March 2002.

12 John Wilson (ed.), 'Social Banking', a seminar held at 11 Downing Street, London, 20 October 1999, published by The Smith Institute. Speakers included Patricia Hewitt, Ed Mayo and Fred Goodwin. http://www.smith-institute.org.uk/file/SocialBanking.pdf.

13 FSA Press Release, 'Coutts fined £8.75 million for anti-money laundering control failings', 26 March 2012, http://www.fsa.gov.uk/library/communication/pr/2012/032.shtml.

14 Don Cruickshank, 'Review of Banking Services in the UK', 20 March 2000, http://webarchive.nationalarchives.gov.uk/+/http://www.hm-treasury.gov.uk/fin_bank_reviewfinal.htm.

15 Ibid.

16 Ibid.

17 Julia Kollewe, 'Ex-Treasury chief Robson accused of "suppressing" Cruickshank', *The Independent*, 23 February 2005, http://www.independent.co.uk/news/business/news/extreasury-chief-robson-accused-of-suppressing-cruickshank-6151954.html.

18   Andy McSmith, 'Brown attacks "greedy" big four banks', *Daily Telegraph*, 15 March 2002, http://www.telegraph.co.uk/news/uknews/1387786/Brown-attacks-greedy-big-four-banks.html.

19   Gordon Pell, author interview. These remarks were said off the record but, in this one instance, I felt obliged to breach journalistic etiquette.

20   Robin Fellgett, financial sector director, HM Treasury, council minutes, CFSI, November 2002, http://www.csfi.org.uk/Advisory%20Council%20Minutes%20Nov%2002%20.pdf.

21   Nick Kochan, author interview.

22   Tony Blair, 'Risk and the State', speech at The Institute for Public Policy Research, 26 May 2005, http://www.number10.gov.uk/Page7562.

23   Callum McCarthy, FSA chairman, letter to Tony Blair, 31 May 2005. McCarthy's remarks about the FSA only deploying six staff to regulate HSBC are ironic given that the rather more vigilant US authorities later fined the bank $1.9 billion for laundering money for drug lords, terrorists, criminal gangs and rogue states, http://www.fsa.gov.uk/pubs/foi/foi_0256.pdf.

24   James Moore, 'FSA bows to criticism and promises reform', *Daily Telegraph*, 20 July 2005, http://www.telegraph.co.uk/finance/markets/2919272/FSA-bows-to-criticism- and-promises-reform.html.

25   Nils Pratley, 'The City is in denial as oligarchs from Wild East shred its reputation', *The Guardian*, 26 April 2013, http://www.guardian.co.uk/business/nils-pratley-on-finance/2013/apr/26/city-denial-oligarchs-wild-east-reputation.

26   Philip Augar, *Chasing Alpha: How Reckless Growth and Unchecked Ambition Ruined the City's Golden Decade*, Bodley Head, 2009.

27   Tyler Durden, 'Why the UK Trail of the MF Global Collapse May Have "Apocalyptic" Consequences for the Eurozone, Canadian Banks, Jefferies and Everyone Else', *Zero Hedge*, 12 August 2011, http://www.zerohedge.com/news/why-uk-trail-mf-global-collapse-may-have-apocalyptic-consequences-eurozone-canadian-banks-jeffe.

28   FSA whistle-blower's letter to Vince Cable MP, forwarded to FSA chairman Lord Turner on 15 April 2009, http://www.ianfraser.org/wp-content/uploads/2010/12/VC.pdf.

29   Charles Lavery, *Daily Record*, 2 December 2000.

30   Hector Sants, speech to AIFA conference, 21 November 2007.

31   Gordon Brown, *Beyond the Crash: Overcoming the First Crisis of Globalisation*, Simon & Schuster 2010. (In this book, Brown wrote, 'People will rightly ask why we did not know earlier of the fundamental weakness of Royal Bank of Scotland. The simple answer is: we were misled. The story on paper was of the world's most successful growing bank: making huge

profits paying high dividends, able to acquire new assets, one of the first into China, and on its way to become the world's biggest bank.' But surely it was his duty, as prime minister, to ensure that the UK regulatory apparatus was capable of recognising that RBS's 'success' was largely mythical?)

32 Ed Balls, Economic Secretary to the Treasury, speech to the British Bankers Association, 11 October 2006, http://webarchive.nationalarchives. gov.uk/+/http:/www.hm-treasury.gov.uk/newsroom_and_speeches/ speeches/econsecspeeches/speech_est_111006.cfm.

33 Ed Balls, evidence to the House of Lords Select Committee on regulators, 22 May 2007, http://www.publications.parliament.uk/pa/ld200607/ ldselect/ldrgltrs/189/ 7052202.htm.

34 Ibid.

35 Daniel Johnson, dialogue with Andrew Rawnsley and Nick Cohen, 'Is the party really over for Labour?', *Standpoint Magazine*, April 2010, http:// standpointmag.co.uk/node/2824/full.

36 Andrew Rawnsley, *The End of the Party: the Rise and Fall of New Labour*, Viking, 2010.

37 Mervyn King, Oral Evidence Taken before the Treasury Committee on 28 June 2011, http://www.publications.parliament.uk/pa/cm201012/ cmselect/cmtreasy/874/ 110628.htm.

38 'The failure of the Royal Bank of Scotland', FSA board report, 12 December 2011.

39 Sir Steve Robson speaking to Andrew Rawnsley and quoted in 'Is the party really over for Labour?', *Standpoint Magazine*, April 2012, http:// standpointmag.co.uk/node/2824/full. Lord Turnbull was giving verbal testimony to the Treasury Select Committee on 28 October 2010.

40 Andrew Rawnsley, *The End of The Party*.

41 Sir Nicholas Macpherson, Oral Evidence Taken Before the Committee of Public Accounts on 17 September 2012, http://www.publications.parliament.uk/pa/cm201213/cmselect/cmpubacc/552/120917.htm.

CHAPTER 19

1 Andrew G. Haldane, Capital Discipline, remarks based on a speech given at the American Economic Association, Denver, 9 January 2011, http:// www.bankofengland.co.uk/publications/Documents/speeches/2011/ speech484.pdf.

2 Ibid.

3 'Getting Basel Right', *The Economist*, 21 February 2002, http://www. economist.com/node/998606.

4 The trading book is where a bank holds instruments that it intends to buy

and sell for a profit; the banking book is where it holds more traditional 'hold-to-maturity' loans.

5   'The Jorion–Taleb debate', *Derivatives Strategy*, April 1997, http://www.derivativesstrategy.com/magazine/archive/1997/0497fea2.asp.

6   Jon Danielsson, Paul Embrechts, Charles Goodhart, Con Keating, Felix Muennich, Olivier Renault and Hyun Song Shin, 'An Academic Response to Basel II', Financial Markets Group, special paper 130, London School of Economics, 2001, ftp://ftp.math.ethz.ch/users/embrecht/Basel2.pdf.

7   Yves Smith, *ECONned: How Unenlightened Self-Interest Undermined Democracy and Corrupted Capitalism*, Palgrave Macmillan, 2010.

8   Yalman Onaran, 'Basel becomes Babel as conflicting rules undermine safety', *Bloomberg News*, January 2013, http://www.bloomberg.com/news/2013-01-03/basel-becomes-babel-as-conflicting-rules-undermine-safety.html.

9   Reserve Bank of New Zealand, 'Your bank's disclosure statement: what's in it for you?', http://www.rbnz.govt.nz/nzbanks/3359149.html.

10 Jon Danielsson et al., 'An Academic Response to Basel II', ibid.

11 George Mathewson, speech to the European Banking Federation in Brussels,11 March 2003.

12 Ibid.

13 Ibid.

14 Avinash Persaud, quoted by Duncan Wood in 'Basel II: The Backlash', *Risk Magazine*, 1 January 2008, http://www.risk.net/risk-magazine/feature/1510752/basel-ii-backlash.

15 Andy Haldane, 'Capital Discipline', remarks based on a speech given at the American Economic Association, Denver, 9 January 2011, http://www.bankofengland.co.uk/publications/Documents/speeches/2011/speech484.pdf.

16 Don Cruickshank, author interview.

CHAPTER 20

1   Shanny Basar, 'RBS offers second largest bookbuild', *Financial News*, 15 October 2001, http://www.efinancialnews.com/story/2001-10-15/rbs-offers-second-largest-bookbuild.

2   Peter Panepento, 'New Bank in Town Forces Change', *Erie Times-News*, 25 November 2001.

3   Joseph DiStefano, 'Citizens CEO: City back from the brink', *Philadelphia Inquirer*, 8 May 2005, http://articles.philly.com/2005-05-08/business/25441506_1_lawrence-k-fish-royal-bank-greater-philadelphia-chamber.

4   'Annual Report 2005', Citizens Financial Report, http://www.citizens-bank.com/au/CitizensAnnualReport05.pdf.

5 'Fred Goodwin', *Bloomberg BusinessWeek Magazine*, 6 June 2004, http://
   www.businessweek.com/stories/2004-06-06/fred-goodwin.

6 Ian Rowley, 'Banking on US acquisitions', *CFO Europe*, 1 February 2003,
   http://www.cfo.com/printable/article.cfm/3008062.

7 John Engen, 'Hitting for the Cycle', *American Banker*, 1 August 2003, http://
   www.americanbanker.com/magazine/113_8/-203069-1.html.

8 'RBS to buy Commonwealth', *Daily Telegraph*, 1 October 2002, http://
   www.telegraph.co.uk/finance/2828828/RBS-to-buy-Commonwealth.
   html.

9 John Engen, 'Hitting for the Cycle'.

10 Caroline Merrell, 'Record-breaking RBS plays down move on US', *The
   Times*, 20 February 2004, http://www.thetimes.co.uk/tto/business/indus-
   tries/banking/article2153451.ece.

11 'Out Of The S&L Ashes', *BusinessWeek* magazine, 23 March 1997, http://
   www.businessweek.com/stories/1997-03-23/out-of-the-s-and-l-ashes.

12 Rob Wherry, 'The Forbes Platinum List: The Best Big Companies
   "Banking on profits"', *Forbes*, 1 June 2003, http://www.forbes.com/
   free_forbes/2003/0106/113.html.

13 Katherine Griffiths, 'RBS takeover to net US directors $1bn', *The
   Independent*, 7 May 2004, http://www.independent.co.uk/news/business/
   news/rbs-takeover-to-net-us-directors-1bn-6170344.html.

14 Steven Syre, 'The next Larry Fish?', *The Boston Globe*, 8 December 2005,
   http://www.boston.com/business/articles/2005/12/08/the_next_larry_fish.

15 George Mathewson, author interview.

16 Simon Samuels, author interview.

CHAPTER 21

1 Colin McLean, author interview.

2 Julia Kollewe, 'RBS feels lure of China but rules out Standard Chartered
   bid', *The Independent*, 21 April 2005, http://www.independent.co.uk/news/
   business/news/rbs-feels-lure-of-china-but-rules-out-standard-chartered-
   bid-6147806.html.

3 This is based on interviews with RBS directors and executives who were
   present.

4 Kelly Jenkins, 'Exclusive: Disgraced ex-RBS boss Fred Goodwin wrecks
   £195k sports car', *Daily Mirror*, 15 March 2009, http://www.mirror.co.uk/
   news/uk-news/exclusive-disgraced-ex-rbs-boss-fred-382616.

5 Harry Wilson, Philip Aldrick and Kamal Ahmed, 'Royal Bank of Scotland
   investigation: the full story of how the "world's biggest bank" went bust',
   The Telegraph, 5 March 2011, http://www.telegraph.co.uk/finance/
   newsbysector/banksandfinance/8363417/Royal-Bank-of-Scotland-

investigation-the-full-story-of-how-the-worlds-biggest-bank-went-bust.
html.

6 RBS interim results, transcript of analysts' presentations, 4 August 2005, http://www.investors.rbs.com/download/transcript/Interim-Aug05-Transcript.pdf.

7 Cathy Chan, 'Goldman hired for Bank of China's IPO', Bloomberg, 26 August 2005, http://www.bloomberg.com/apps/news?pid=newsarchive &sid=aCQkBeNOi1og&refer=us.

8 Mark Kleinman, 'Eastern promise: Scots take the Silk Road', *Sunday Telegraph*, 10 December 2006, http://www.telegraph.co.uk/finance/migrationtemp/2952136/Eastern-Promise-Scots-take-the-Silk-Road. html.

9 Aude Lagorce, 'RBS buys a stake in Bank of China', *MarketWatch*, 18 August 2005, http://articles.marketwatch.com/2005-08-18/news/30750855_1_china-construction-bank-guangdong-development-bank-royal-bank.

10 'RBS announces formation of strategic partnership with Bank of China', RBS press release, 18 August 2005.

11 Mark Kleinman, 'RBS aims to trouser China's nouveaux', *Sunday Telegraph*, 12 November 2006, http://www.telegraph.co.uk/finance/2950557/RBS-aims-to-trouser-Chinas- nouveaux.html.

12 Fred Goodwin, presentation to analysts and investors hosted by Merrill Lynch, New York, 2 November 2005.

13 Ibid.

14 Guest List for the Dinner in Honour of Prince Charles and Camilla, Duchess of Cornwall, published 2 November 2005, as provided by the White House, http://www.nytimes.com/2005/11/02/politics/03royals-list.html.

15 Associated Press, 2 November 2005, http://usatoday30.usatoday.com/news/washington/2005-11-02-camillacharles_x.htm.

16 Geraldine Lambe, 'Why RBS needs spin', *The Banker*, 7 November 2005, http://www.thebanker.com/World/Western-Europe/UK/Why-RBS-needs-spin.

17 Jason Nissé, 'RBS directors fear early exit by Sir Fred', *The Independent on Sunday*, 20 November 2005, http://www.independent.co.uk/news/business/news/rbs-directors-fear-early-exit-by-sir-fred-516014.html.

18 Chris Hughes, 'How Goodwin can close his personal discount at Royal Bank', *BreakingViews*, 20 November 2005, http://www.telegraph.co.uk/finance/2926397/Breaking-views-How-Goodwin-can-close-his-personal-discount-at-Royal-Bank.html.

19 'Lowering the Bar', *The Economist*, 18 May 2006, http://www.economist.com/node/ 6950339.

20   Harry Wilson et al., 'Royal Bank of Scotland investigation: the full story of how the "world's biggest bank" went bust'.

CHAPTER 22

1   Barry L Ritholtz, 'A Memo Found in the Street', *Barron's*, 29 September 2008, http://online.barrons.com/article/SB122246742997580395.html.

2   Gillian Tett, *Fool's Gold: How Unrestrained Greed Corrupted a Dream, Shattered Global Markets and Unleashed a Catastrophe*, Little, Brown, 2009.

3   Glen Newey, 'Who Rates the Rating Agencies?', *London Review of Books*, 12 November 2013, http://www.lrb.co.uk/blog/2013/11/12/glen-newey/who-rates-the-ratings-agencies/#sthash.Uhi9i9eE.dpuf.

4   Nicholas Dunbar, *The Devil's Derivatives*, Harvard Business Review Press, 2011.

5   Vivek Ahuja, 'RBS sets up new structured credit products group', *Financial News*, 10 July 2002, http://www.highbeam.com/doc/1G1-92618052.html.

6   A 'Gaussian copula' model was developed by Chinese-born actuary David Li in 2000. This was adopted across the global banking sector in the early 2000s as it enabled them to downplay the price linkages ('correlations') between bundled fixed-income securities.

7   Ron den Braber, 'Credit Tranche and Nth To Default: Model Assumptions Gaussian Copula Model', RBS Financial Markets, 3 September 2002.

8   Ron den Braber, author interview.

9   Ibid.

10   Ibid.

11   Ibid.

12   Iain Robertson, author interview.

13   International Directory of Company Histories, Vol. 2, St. James Press, 1990, via website Funding Universe, http://www.fundinguniverse.com/company-histories/long-term-credit-bank-of-japan-ltd-history.

14   Gillian Tett, oral evidence given at Scottish Parliament, Economy, Energy and Tourism Committee, 'Official Report', 25 November 2009, http://www.scottish.parliament.uk/parliamentarybusiness/28862.aspx?r=343&mode=html.

15   Michael Lewis, http://truthaboutwallstreet.ca/michael-lewis.php.

16   *Sunday Times*, 27 November 2005.

17   Daniel Gross, author interview.

18   Sophie Roell, 'Niche Bond Firm Greenwich Capital Has a Mutually Beneficial Relationship with Parent Bank Royal Bank of Scotland', *The Banker*, 1 October 2005.

19   Ibid.

20 Ibid.

21 Gillian Tett, *Fool's Gold*.

22 Federal Housing Finance Agency lawsuit against RBS Group PLC and numerous RBS subsidiaries, September 2011.

23 Johnny Cameron, transcript of RBS CBFM analysts' conference, 3 October 2005.

24 'RBS hires Merrill top gun', *Institutional Investor*, 12 February 2004, http://www.institutionalinvestor.com/Article/1031448/RBS-Hires-Merrill-Top-Gun.html.

25 *Mail on Sunday*, 17 February 2013, http://www.thisismoney.co.uk/money/news/article-2279661/Tax-dodge-crusader-act-film-scheme-Sir-Alex-Ferguson-used.html.

26 Warren Buffett, letter to Berkshire Hathaway Inc. shareholders, published with the '2002 Berkshire Hathaway Inc. Annual Report', 4 March 2003, http://www.berkshirehathaway.com/letters/2002pdf.pdf.

27 Ibid.

28 Ibid.

29 Ibid.

30 BIS, '73rd Annual Report', June 2003, http://www.bis.org/publ/arpdf/ar2003e.htm.

31 BIS, 'The role of ratings in structured finance: issues and implications', January 2005, http://www.bis.org/publ/cgfs23.pdf.

32 Raghuram G. Rajan, 'Has financial development made the world riskier?', 2005, http://www.nber.org/papers/w11728.pdf?new_window=1.

33 Patrick Hosking, 'The Business: Patrick Hosking warns the house bubble will burst', *New Statesman*, 26 April 2004, http://www.newstatesman.com/node/147799.

34 Iain Martin, *Making It Happen*.

35 Nouriel Roubini, '"The Biggest Slump in US Housing in the Last 40 Years" . . . or 53 Years?', *Economonitor*, 23 August 2006 http://www.economonitor.com/nouriel/2006/08/23/the-biggest-slump-in-us-housing-in-the-last-40-yearsor-53-years.

36 Shawn Tully, 'Jamie Dimon's Swat Team', *Fortune Magazine*, 2 September 2008, http://money.cnn.com/2008/08/29/news/companies/tully_dimon.fortune.

37 Fred Goodwin, 'Risk Return and Growth – Getting the Balance Right', presentation at Merrill Lynch Banking Conference, 6 October 2006, http://www.investors.rbs.com/download/transcript/MLConference-transcript.pdf.

38 Bloomberg, 8 February 2007, http://www.bloomberg.com/apps/news?pid=newsarchive&sid=aPB3Ict11jwc.

39 'The Failure of the Royal Bank of Scotland', FSA board report, 12 December 2011, http://www.fsa.gov.uk/pubs/other/rbs.pdf.
40 Ibid.

CHAPTER 23

1 Christian Sylt, 'RBS "careless" with $2.7bn loan to Formula One', *The Independent*, 29 November 2013, http://www.independent.co.uk/news/business/news/rbs-careless-with-27bn-loan-to-formula-one-8974034.html.
2 YouTube video of PEX 2006 conference, 14 November 2006, http://www.youtube.com/watch?v=b3W47b39hy0.
3 *Financial Times*, 22 May 2007, http://www.ft.com/cms/s/0/8d7aaf52-0801-11dc-9541-000b5df10621.html.

CHAPTER 24

1 Jeroen Smit, *The Perfect Prey*, Quercus, 2010.
2 Dominic Elliott, 'Orcel takes on emerging markets', *Financial News*, 10 May 2010, http://www.efinancialnews.com/story/2010-05-10/orcel-takes-on-emerging-markets.
3 Jonathan Kandell, 'Super Santander', *Institutional Investor*, 11 November 2008, http://www.institutionalinvestor.com/Popups/PrintArticle.aspx?ArticleID=2043952.
4 Iain Dey, 'Hedge fund investing is child's play', *Sunday Telegraph*, 6 January 2008, http://www.telegraph.co.uk/finance/newsbysector/banksandfinance/2782131/Hedge-fund-investing-is-childs-play.html.
5 Louise Armitstead, 'Activist investors flex their biceps', *Sunday Times*, 17 June 2007, http://www.thesundaytimes.co.uk/sto/business/article66497.ece.
6 James Mackintosh, 'Tiger cub makes Toscafund roar', *Financial Times*, 23 March 2007, http://www.ft.com/cms/s/0/d90b2828-d8e2-11db-a759-000b5df10621.html.
7 Werner Seifert and Hans-Joachim Voth, *Invasion of the Locusts: intrigues, power struggles, market manipulation*, published in German by Econ, 2006.
8 Letter to ABN AMRO's Arthur Martinez and Rijkman Groenink from The Children's Investment Fund, 20 February 2007, http://online.wsj.com/public/resources/documents/tciletter-0918.pdf.
9 'Wens splitsing ABN Amro brug te ver', *NRC Handelsblad*, 24 February 2007, http://www.nu.nl/economie/987760/wens-splitsing-abn-amro-brug-te-ver.html.
10 'Dutch disease', *The Economist*, 1 March 2007, http://www.economist.com/node/ 8782343.

11 'McCreevy was irresponsible, says Dutch banker', *Irish Independent*, 5 February 2010, http://www.independent.ie/business/world/mccreevy-was-irresponsible-says-dutch-banker-26629436.html.

12 'RBS: Inside the Bank that Ran Out of Money', BBC One, October 2011, http://www.bbc.co.uk/programmes/b01690y5.

13 Patrick Hosking, 'Goodwin exits "sin-bin" as RBS pays big dividend', *Sunday Times*, 2 March 2007, http://www.thetimes.co.uk/tto/business/industries/banking/article2154066.ece.

14 'RBS annual results 2006', transcript of analysts' conference, 1 March 2007, http://www.investors.rbs.com/download/transcript/2006ResultsAnalystsConferenceTranscript.pdf.

15 Grant Ringshaw, 'Barclays in £80bn offer to ABN AMRO', *Sunday Times*, 18 March 2007, http://www.thesundaytimes.co.uk/sto/business/article61579.ece.

16 Ibid.

17 Steve Slater, 'ABN, Barclays in exclusive merger talks', Reuters, 19 March 2007, http://uk.reuters.com/article/2007/03/19/uk-abnamro-barclays-takeover- idUKL1829161620070319.

18 Jeroen Smit, *The Perfect Prey*.

19 Rijkman Groenink, author interview.

20 The Barclays deal nearly didn't happen. When its CEO John Varley was told that LaSalle was being sold without his knowledge, he was furious since it formed part of the Barclays–ABN merger agreement. One retired bank chairman said, 'Rijkman double-crossed Barclays. John was disgusted and nearly pulled out that day.'

21 'Media Briefing Transcript', Fortis, Royal Bank of Scotland, Santander, 25 April 2007, http://www.rbspresentations.co.uk/Group_Information/Investor_Relations/Analyst_Conferences/25apr2007/files/Media_Briefing_-_Fortis,_RBS,_Santander_25_April_2007.pdf.

22 Ibid.

23 Ibid.

24 Grant Ringshaw, 'Battle of the banks'.

25 'The failure of Royal Bank of Scotland', FSA board report, December 2011.

26 Jeroen Smit, *The Perfect Prey*.

27 Gordon Pell, verbal testimony to the House of Commons Scottish Affairs Committee (Banking in Scotland), 19 March 2009, http://www.publications.parliament.uk/pa/cm200910/cmselect/cmscotaf/70/9031903.htm.

28 'The failure of Royal Bank of Scotland', FSA board report, December 2011.

29 Ibid.

30   Simon Goodley, 'Business Diary', *Daily Telegraph*, 26 May 2007, http://
     www.williamsf1.com/news/view/45http://www.telegraph.co.uk/
     finance/comment/citydiary/2809511/Business-diary-Was-Stalin-a-
     Rothschild.html.

31   'RBS consortium offer for ABN AMRO', transcript of analyst question
     and answer session, 29 May 2007, http://www.investors.rbs.com/ir/rbs/
     jsp/sec_filings_item.jsp?source=1587&ipage=4965865.

32   Ibid.

33   Ibid.

34   Ibid.

35   'Braveheart Two', *The Economist*, 31 May 2007, http://www.economist.
     com/node/9262505.

36   Alex Salmond, letter to Sir Fred Goodwin, May 2007, http://www.scot-
     land.gov.uk/Resource/Doc/919/0103329.pdf.

CHAPTER 25

1   'Goodwin's bid spurns investors as Royal Bank trails U.K. rivals', quoted
     by Bloomberg, July 2007, http://www.bloomberg.com/apps/news?pid=n
     ewsarchive&sid=aKjFdUOOVAH0&refer=news.

2   Matt Taibbi, 'Bank of America: Too Crooked to fail', *Rolling Stone*, 14 March
     2012, http://www.rollingstone.com/politics/news/bank-of-america-too-
     crooked-to-fail-20120314.

3   Jeroen Smit, *The Perfect Prey*.

4   Iain Robertson, author interview.

5   Steve Slater, 'Barclays lift ABN offer with China, Singapore help',
     Reuters, 23 July 2007, http://www.reuters.com/article/2007/07/23/
     us-abn-takeover-idUSWLB918320070723.

6   Damian Reece, 'RBS and Barclays should be getting the jitters', *Daily
     Telegraph*, 28 July 2007, http://www.telegraph.co.uk/finance/comment/
     2813039/RBS-and-Barclays-should-both-be-getting-the-jitters.html.

7   Damian Reece, 'McKillop may be apologetic over RBS woes, but he
     remains in denial', *Daily Telegraph*, 20 November 2008, http://www.
     telegraph.co.uk/finance/comment/damianreece/3492281/McKillop-
     may-be-apologetic-over-RBS-woes-but-he-remains-in-denial.html.

8   Roger Hunt with Kenny Kemp, *Be Silent or Be Killed: The True Story of a
     Scottish Banker Under Siege in Mumbai's 9/11*, Corskie, 2010.

9   'One "Quant" Sees Shakeout for the Ages – "10,000 years"',
     Wall Street Journal, 13 August 2007, http://online.wsj.com/article/
     SB118679281379194803.html.

10   Emma Davis, 'Fortis Wins Shareholder Backing For ABN Takeover',
     Reuters, 6 August 2007.

11   Fair Pensions, written evidence to the Parliamentary Commission on
     Banking Standards, September 2012.

12 Steve Slater, 'RBS investors back ABN deal', Reuters, 10 August 2007, http://www.reuters.com/article/2007/08/10/us-abn-takeover-rbs-vote-idUSL1076842520070810.
13 Colin McLean, author interview.
14 Ibid.
15 Patrick Hosking, 'Cash vs connections', The Times, 14 August 2007, http://www.thetimes.co.uk/tto/business/columnists/article2617543.ece.
16 Jeroen Smit, The Perfect Prey.
17 Peter de Vink, author interview.
18 Jeremy Warner's Outlook: 'Stock market correction heads for crash', The Independent, 17 August 2007, http://www.independent.co.uk/news/business/comment/jeremy-warners-outlook-stock-market-correction-heads-for-crash-461943.html.
19 Rijkman Groenink, author interview.
20 Ibid.
21 Iain Martin, Making It Happen.
22 Ariane van Caloen, 'Chapitre 1 – La revanche ratée de Votron', La Libre Belgique, 22 November 2008, http://www.lalibre.be/actu/belgique/article/461895.
23 Harry Wilson et al., 'Royal Bank of Scotland investigation: the full story of how the "world's biggest bank" went bust'.
24 Grant Ringshaw, 'Barclays falls to earth', Sunday Times, 2 September 2007, http://www.thesundaytimes.co.uk/sto/business/article70720.ece.
25 Iain Martin, Making It Happen.
26 Monza, Mediastorehouse.com, http://www.mediastorehouse.com/low.php?xp= gm&xg=34285.
27 Andrew Foxwell, 'RBS defiant as shareholders' revolt grows', Mail on Sunday, 9 September 2007, http://www.thisismoney.co.uk/money/markets/article-1613816/RBS-defiant-as-shareholders-revolt-grows.html.
28 Bank of England Governor Mervyn King interviewed by Robert Peston, File on 4, BBC Radio 4, 6 November 2007, http://www.guardian.co.uk/business/2007/nov/06/21.
29 'ABN AMRO outlook for FY2007', Press Release, 17 September 2007, http://www.sec.gov/Archives/edgar/data/1038727/000095010307002282/dp06922_425.htm.
30 Sir Fred Goodwin, Oral Evidence to the House of Commons Treasury Committee, 10 February 2009, http://www.publications.parliament.uk/pa/cm200809/cmselect/cmtreasy/uc144_vii/uc14402.htm.
31 Ibid.
32 'The failure of Royal Bank of Scotland', FSA board report.
33 Lina Saigol, 'The Real Deal: The sobering message of RBS's sky-high ABN bid', FT Alphaville, 1 October 2007, http://ftalphaville.ft.com/blog/2007/10/01/7720/the-real-deal-the-sobering-message-of-rbss-sky-high-abn-bid.
34 Peter Thal Larsen, 'Sir Fred's heady firsts', Financial Times, 4 October 2007, http://www.ft.com/cms/s/0/79037fd2-72ae-11dc-b7ff-0000779fd2ac.html.

35 Jon Menon and Ben Livesey, 'Royal Bank Pays "Big Price", Takes Control at ABN', Bloomberg, 8 October 2007, http://www.bloomberg.com/apps/news?pid= 20601087&sid=afWu1.qzHTX0&refer=home.

36 Peter Thal Larsen, 'Victory formally declared in ABN tussle', *Financial Times*, 9 October 2007, http://www.ft.com/cms/s/0/b014e75c-75da-11dc-b7cb-0000779fd2ac.html.

37 Magnus Linklater, 'Ah, a bit of rapacious capitalism. How we've missed it', *The Times*, 20 October 2007, http://www.thetimes.co.uk/tto/opinion/columnists/magnuslinklater/article2043772.ece.

38 Melanie Reid, 'Is this man the world's greatest banker?', *The Times*, 11 October 2007, http://www.thetimes.co.uk/tto/business/industries/banking/article2155528.ece.

39 'Consortium banks' offer for ABN AMRO unconditional', press conference, 10 October 2007, http://www.sec.gov/Archives/edgar/data/1038727/000119312507216954/d425. htm.

40 Ibid.

41 Peter de Vink, author interview.

42 Ibid.

43 'Scots on the rocks', *The Economist*, 25 February 2010, http://www.economist.com/node/15579813.

44 Rijkman Groenink, author interview.

45 Sir Fred Goodwin, Oral Evidence to the House of Commons Treasury Committee, ibid.

46 George Mathewson, author interview.

CHAPTER 26

1 Colin McLean, author interview.

2 Simon Clark, 'Goodwin's $140 Billion Binge May Doom RBS to Nationalization', *Bloomberg News*, 24 November 2008, http://www.bloomberg.com/apps/news?pid=newsarchive&sid=a_6BKzvwAYCY.

3 John Hourican, author interview.

4 Ibid.

5 David Rothnie, 'RBS speeds ABN AMRO integration', *Financial News*, 15 October 2007, http://www.efinancialnews.com/story/2007-10-15/rbs-speeds-abn-amro-integration.

6 Ibid.

7 Peter Thal Larsen, 'Goodwin's undoing', *Financial Times*, 24 February 2009, http://www.ft.com/cms/s/0/dbcc20aa-02a0-11de-b58b-000077b07658.html.

8 Neil Hume and John O'Doherty, 'RBS stakebuilding talk helps Footsie take a positive turn', *Financial Times*, 14 November 2007, http://www.ft.com/cms/s/0/4cd03aec-9255-11dc-8981-0000779fd2ac.html.

9 RBS chairman puts half a million into the bank', *Sunday Times*, 11 November 2007, http://www.thesundaytimes.co.uk/sto/business/money/investments/article75097.ece.

10 Peter Thal Larsen, 'Aiming to repeat NatWest purchase trick', *Financial*

Times, 17 October 2007, http://www.ft.com/cms/s/0/56d837a6-7c16-11dc-be7e-0000779fd2ac.html.

11 'The failure of Royal Bank of Scotland', FSA board report.

12 Ibid.

13 Harry Wilson et al., 'Royal Bank of Scotland investigation: the full story of how the "world's biggest bank" went bust'.

14 Ibid.

15 Kilian Wawoe, author interview.

16 RBS, transcript of analyst conference, 6 December 2007, http://www.investors.rbs.com/download/transcript/RBS_1H08_Analysts_Presentation_Transcript.pdf.

17 Fons Trompenaars, author interview.

18 David Rothnie and Harry Wilson, 'Shake-up starts at new-look RBS', *Financial News*, 3 March 2008, http://www.efinancialnews.com/story/2008-03-03/shake-up-starts- at-new-look-rbs-1.

CHAPTER 27

1 'Sir Fred Goodwin's fortunes have seen him fall from hero to zero in 11 years', *The Daily Telegraph*, 21 March 2009, http://www.telegraph.co.uk/finance/recession/5025423/Timeline-Sir-Fred-Goodwin.html.

2 SEC, 7 November 2013, http://www.sec.gov/litigation/complaints/2013/comp-pr2013-239.pdf.

3 'Is Merrill the tip of the iceberg? If so who is the Titanic?', *The Economist*, 28 October 2007, http://www.economist.com/node/10048962.

4 On 7 July 2007, Charles 'Chuck' Prince was quoted in *Financial Times* as saying, 'As long as the music is playing, you've got to get up and dance. We're still dancing.' This was in response to a question about whether the bank would continue to pour money into private equity and leveraged buyouts.

5 James J Cramer, 'Street Justice', *New York Magazine*, 12 November 2007, http://nymag.com/news/businessfinance/bottomline/40639.

6 Christopher T. Mahoney, 'What caused the crash? An autopsy', Project Syndicate, 20 May 2013, http://www.project-syndicate.org/blog/what-caused-the-crash--an-autopsy-by-christopher-t--mahoney#GtK8bE3jE3lCSWXW.99.

7 Michael Lewis, *The Big Short: Inside the Doomsday Machine*, Allen Lane, 2010.

8 Victor Hong's LinkedIn entry, http://www.linkedin.com/pub/victor-hong/10/b79/a03.

9 As a PwC partner, Carol Mathis led the Greenwich Capital audit until March 2000. She then joined Greenwich as chief financial officer in December 2000 – giving rise to a possible conflict of interest.

10 Victor Hong's LinkedIn entry.

11 Consolidated Complaint, In Re: RBS Group PLC Securities Litigation, United States District Court, Southern District of New York, 15 July 2009.

12 Ibid.

13 Chris Flanagan, 'JPMorgan, Global ABS/CDO', *Weekly Market Update*, 2 November 2007.

14 Paul Murphy, 'Beware the "uber leveraged" trio – Barclays, RBS and Deutsche', *FT* Alphaville, 7 November 2007, http://ftalphaville.ft.com/2007/11/07/8705/beware-the-%E2%80%9Cuber-leveraged%E2%80%9D-trio-%E2%80%94-barclays-rbs-and-deutsche.

15 John Glover, 'Banks face $100bn of writedowns on Level 3 rule', *Bloomberg News*, 7 November 2007.

16 Consolidated Complaint, In Re: RBS Group PLC Securities Litigation, United States District Court, Southern District of New York, 15 July 2009.

17 Sanford Bernstein Research Note, 'RBS: Highly Positive Trading Update Confirms Our Expectations. Reiterate Outperform £6.75 PT' 6 December 2007.

18 Royal Bank of Scotland: details of Asset Protection Scheme and launch of the Asset Protection Agency, HM Treasury, http://www.hm-treasury.gov.uk/d/rbs_aps_apa.pdf.

19 Fred Goodwin, oral evidence, Treasury Select Committee, 10 February 2009.

20 Iain Martin, *Making It Happen*.

21 Helen Thomas, 'Sighs all round as RBS takes £1.5bn write-downs', *FT* Alphaville, 6 December 2007, http://ftalphaville.ft.com/blog/2007/12/06/9430/sighs-all-round-as-rbs-details-%C2%A315bn-write-down.

22 Colin McLean, author interview.

23 Ibid.

24 Andrew McLaughlin, RBS communications director, email statement, 20 February 2013.

25 Alastair Darling, *Back from the Brink: 1,000 Days at Number 11*, Atlantic Books, 2011, edited extract via *The Guardian*, 11 September 2011, http://www.guardian.co.uk/politics/2011/sep/11/alistair-darling-start-worrying.

26 Walter Bagehot, *Lombard Street: A Description of the Money Market*, 1873.

27 Alistair Darling, *Back from the Brink*.

28 Sir Tom McKillop, oral evidence, Treasury Select Committee, 10 February 2009.

29 Steve Slater, 'RBS profits up despite write-downs', Reuters, 28 February 2008, http://uk.reuters.com/article/2008/02/28/uk-rbs-idUKL2890137 20080228.

30 RBS, transcript of analysts' conference, February 2008.

31 Ibid.

32 Brian O'Connor, 'RBS rolls with the punches', *Daily Mail*, 29 February 2008, http://www.thisismoney.co.uk/money/markets/article-1621145/City-Focus-RBS-rolls-with-the-punches.html.

33 RBS, transcript of analysts' conference, February 2008.

34 Ibid.

35 'The Failure of Royal Bank of Scotland', FSA Board Report, http://
www.fsa.gov.uk/pubs/other/rbs.pdf.

36 'Bearing All', *The Economist*, 5 March 2009, http://www.economist.com/
node/13226308.

37 'European Banks', 'Lex' column, *Financial Times*, 18 March 2008, http://
www.ft.com/intl/cms/s/0/8c29bd5af48c-11dc-aaad-0000779fd2ac.html.

38 Johnny Cameron, speaking at Sheffield University SPERI seminar, 'The
Banking Crisis and the Future of Banking', 15 October 2013, http://
youtu.be/ribZd8Wb6Vc.

39 Nicholas Dunbar, 'The FSA, RBS and the "Pack of Lies" ', 23 December 2011,
http://www.nickdunbar.net/article/the-fsa-rbs-and-the-pack-of-lies/

40 Helen Power, 'Investors torn about fate of Royal Bank of Scotland's Fred
the Shred', *Sunday Telegraph*, 20 April 2008, http://www.telegraph.co.uk/
finance/newsbysector/banksandfinance/2788558/Investors-torn-about-
fate-of-Royal-Bank-of-Scotlands-Fred-the-Shred.html.

41 Sarah John, Matt Roberts and Olaf Weeken, Bank of England's
Sterling Markets Division, 'The Bank of England's Special Liquidity
Scheme', March 2012, http://www.bankofengland.co.uk/publications/
Documents/quarterlybulletin/qb120105.pdf.

42 Alistair Darling, *Back from the Brink: 1,000 Days at Number 11*, Atlantic Books,
2011.

43 RBS, transcript of analysts' conference (with US analysts), 22 April 2008,
http://www.investors.rbs.com/download/transcript/2pm_US_Call_
Transcript_FINAL.pdf.

44 Katherine Griffiths and Philip Aldrick, 'Shareholders tell Royal Bank
of Scotland to solve "Scottish question" ', *Daily Telegraph*, 24 April
2008, http://www.telegraph.co.uk/finance/newsbysector/banksand
finance/2788837/Shareholders-tell-Royal-Bank-of-Scotland-to-solve-
Scottish-question.html.

45 RBS, transcript of analysts' conference (with US analysts).

46 Ibid.

47 Nicholas Dunbar, *The Devil's Derivatives*, Harvard Business Review Press,
2011.

48 RBS, transcript of analysts' conference (with US analysts).

49 Ibid.

50 Ibid.

51 Reuters, 23 April 2008, http://www.reuters.com/article/2008/04/23/
rbs-idUSL2373614720080423.

52 Patrick Hosking, 'Royal Bank of Scotland announces Britain's biggest

rights issue', *The Times*, 23 April 2008, http://www.thetimes.co.uk/tto/business/industries/banking/article2156980.ece.

53 'RBS chiefs face flak from shareholders at Edinburgh AGM', *The Herald*, 23 April 2007, http://www.heraldscotland.com/rbs-chiefs-face-flak-from-shareholders-at- edinburgh-agm-1.879146.

54 Ibid.

55 Peter Taylor, 'Former RBS chief backs Sir Fred Goodwin', *Daily Telegraph*, 24 April 2007, http://www.telegraph.co.uk/finance/newsbysector/banksandfinance/2788871/Former-RBS-chief-backs-Sir-Fred-Goodwin.html.

56 Ian Fraser, 'The bankers' new clothes', *Sunday Herald*, 27 April 2008, http://www.ianfraser.org/the-bankers-new-clothes.

57 Colin Barr, 'RBS chief gets off Scot-free', *Fortune*, 22 April 2008, http://money.cnn.com/2008/04/22/news/newsmakers/rbs.goodwin.fortune/index.htm.

58 US District Court, District of Connecticut, Federal Housing Finance Agency vs. Royal Bank of Scotland Court, including RBS Greenwich Capital, 7 September 2011, http://www.fhfa.gov/webfiles/22598/fhfa%20v%20royal%20bank%20of%20scotland.pdf.

59 Clark McGinn, *Out of Pocket: How Collective Amnesia Lost the World Its Wealth, Again*, Luath Press, 2010.

CHAPTER 28

1 Terry Murden, 'Chastened Goodwin faces his biggest building task', *Scotland on Sunday*, 26 April 2008, http://www.scotsman.com/business/terry-murden-chastened-goodwin-faces-his-biggest-building-task-1-1432485.

2 'RBS rights issue prospectus', the Royal Bank of Scotland Group plc, Proposed 11 for 18 Rights Issue of 6,123,010,462 New Shares at 200 pence per share, 30 April 2008, http://www.investors.rbs.com/download/corporate_actions/rights_issue/ProspectusFINAL.pdf.

3 Speaking to the Treasury Select Committee on 30 January 2012, FSA chief executive Hector Sants referred to a meeting he had with Goodwin on 9 April 2008, saying, 'I specifically required [Fred Goodwin] to have a rights issue, which certainly, as far as I could judge from that meeting, he was not intending to do when he came into the meeting with me. I asked him to raise as much capital as he possibly could.' http://www.publications.parliament.uk/pa/cm201012/cmselect/cmtreasy/uc1780-ii/uc178001.htm.

4 ICG is a bank-specific minimum capital requirement, laid down by the FSA.

5 Gordon Brown, *Beyond the Crash: Overcoming the First Crisis of Globalisation*.

6   'Share Register Analysis', RBS Group PLC, 4 June 2007 to 1 September 2008.

7   Martin Delgado, 'Fury as bailed-out RBS plans to blow £300,000 on lavish Wimbledon bash for top executives', *Daily Mail*, 2 June 2009, http://www.dailymail.co.uk/news/article-1194449/RBS-bailed-20bn-taxpayers-money--goes-blows-300-000-tennis-freebies.html.

8   Louise Armitstead and Mark Kleinman, 'Sir Philip Hampton approached by investors to take helm at RBS', *Sunday Telegraph*, 15 June 2008, http://www.telegraph.co.uk/finance/newsbysector/banksandfinance/2791666/Sir-Philip-Hampton-approached-by-investors-to-take-helm-at-RBS.html.

9   Felix Salmon, 'The defenestration of Bill Winters', Reuters, 7 October 2009, http://blogs.reuters.com/felix-salmon/2009/10/07/the-defenestration-of-bill-winters.

10 Harry Wilson, et al., 'Royal Bank of Scotland investigation: the full story of how the "world's biggest bank" went bust'.

11 Iain Martin, *Making It Happen*.

12 Steve Slater, 'RBS confident on insurance sale', Reuters, 11 June 2008, http://uk.reuters.com/article/2008/06/11/uk-rbs-trading-idUKWLA466620080611.

13 Ambrose Evans-Pritchard, 'RBS issues global stock and credit crash alert', *Daily Telegraph*, 18 June 2008, http://www.telegraph.co.uk/finance/newsbysector/banksandfinance/2791861/RBS-issues-global-stock-and-credit-crash-alert.html.

14 Tim Sharp, 'Royal Bank shares rise as £691m deficit not as dire as predicted', *The Herald*, 9 August 2008, http://www.heraldscotland.com/royal-bank-shares-rise-as-pound-691m-deficit-not-as-dire-as-predicted-1.886711.

15 RBS, 2008 Interim Results Proceedings at an Analysts Presentation, 8 August 2008, http://www.investors.rbs.com/download/transcript/RBS_1H08_Analysts_Presentation_Transcript.pdf.

16 Ibid.

17 Ibid.

18. Ibid.

19 Ibid.

20 As reported by Anthony Reuben, 'What is it like to lose millions of pounds?', 8 August 2008, http://news.bbc.co.uk/1/hi/business/7550130.stm.

21 'Brown aims to get housing market moving again', Reuters, 30 April 2008, http://uk.reuters.com/article/2008/04/30/uk-britain-brown-idUKLAC00282120080430.

22 Alistair Darling, *Back from the Brink*.

23 Jill Treanor, 'Sir Victor Blank: The City grandee who could soon be heading a bank of Britain', *The Guardian*, 26 September 2008, http://www.theguardian.com/business/2008/sep/26/lloydstsbgroup.hbosbusiness.

24 Chris Blackhurst, 'The revenge of the nerds', *Evening Standard*, 18 September 2008, http://www.standard.co.uk/news/the-revenge-of-the-nerds-6850307.html.

25 Harry Wilson, et al., 'Royal Bank of Scotland investigation: the full story of how the "world's biggest bank" went bust'.

26 Decca Aitkenhead, 'Storm Warning', *The Guardian*, 29 August 2009, http://www.guardian.co.uk/politics/2008/aug/30/alistairdarling.economy.

27 Damian McBride, *Power Trip: A Decade of Policy, Plots and Spin*, as serialised in the *Mail on Sunday*, 23 September 2013, http://www.dailymail.co.uk/news/article-2429682/Useless-Darling-just-Damian-McBride-reveals-poor-Alistair-played-martyr-amid-2008-economic-crisis.html#ixzz2fl3jKKd3.

28 Alistair Darling, *Back from the Brink.*

29 Rachel Johnson, 'Life gets tough-ish in Notting Hell', *Sunday Times*, 21 September 2008, http://www.thesundaytimes.co.uk/sto/style/fashion/trends/article237359.ece.

30 Edward Harrison, 'Lehman fallout: HBOS and RBS are getting slaughtered', *Credit Writedowns*, 15 September 2008, http://www.creditwritedowns.com/2008/09/lehman-fallout-hbos-and-rbs-are-getting.html.

31 Harry Wilson et al., 'Royal Bank of Scotland investigation: the full story of how the "world's biggest bank" went bust'.

32 'ABN Amro Staff Told to Prepare for "The Visit"', *Here Is the City*, 22 September 2008, http://hereisthecity.com/2008/09/20/abn_amro_staff_told_to_prepare.

33 Alistair Darling, *Back from the Brink*.

34 'The Failure of the Royal Bank of Scotland', FSA Board Report.

35 Shane Ross, *The Bankers: How the Banks Brought Ireland to Its Knees*, Penguin, 2010.

CHAPTER 29

1 James Quinn, 'Gordon Brown meets Wall Street financiers', *Daily Telegraph*, 25 September 2008, http://www.telegraph.co.uk/finance/financialcrisis/3081161/Gordon-Brown-meets-Wall-Street-financiers.html.

2 George Parker, 'His finest moment', *Financial Times*, 13 October 2009, http://www.ft.com/cms/s/0/9d296c26-b859-11de-8ca9-00144feab49a.html.

3 Gordon Brown, *Beyond the Crash*.

4   WikiLeaks, US Embassy Cable, 17 March 2008: Subject: Banking Crisis Now One of Solvency Not Liquidity Says Bank of England Governor http:// www.guardian.co.uk/world/us-embassy-cables-documents/146196.

5   Ian Fraser, 'RBS will get "billions" in US bailout of economy', *Sunday Herald*, 28 September 2008, http://www.heraldscotland.com/ rbs-will-get-billions-in-us-bail-out- of-economy-1.826927.

6   Senior Labour ministers, author interviews.

7   Alastair Darling, *Back from the Brink: 1,000 Days at Number 11*, Atlantic Books, 2011, edited extract via *The Guardian*, 11 September 2011, http://www. guardian.co.uk/politics/2011/sep/11/alistair-darling-start-worrying.

8   Lord Myners attended ahead of the formal announcement of his appointment as City minister on 3 October.

9   Sir John Gieve, speaking at Sheffield University SPERI seminar, 'The Banking Crisis and the Future of Banking', 15 October 2013, http:// youtu.be/ribZd8Wb6Vc.

10 Alistair Darling, *Back from the Brink*.

11 Scottish Parliament Economy, Energy and Tourism Committee, 25 November 2009, Financial Services Inquiry http://archive.scottish.parliament.uk/s3/committees/eet/or-09/ee09-3102.htm.

12 Johnny Cameron, speaking at Sheffield University SPERI seminar, 'The Banking Crisis and the Future of Banking', 15 October 2013, http:// youtu.be/ribZd8Wb6Vc.

13 George Parker and Peter Thal Larsen, 'Calm gives way to storm over bailout', *Financial Times*, 8 October 2008, http://www.ft.com/cms/ s/0/45d9dc5a-94a9-11dd-953e-000077b07658.html.

14 'Banks ask Chancellor for Capital', Peston's Picks, 7 October 2008, http://www.bbc.co.uk/blogs/thereporters/robertpeston/2008/10/ banks_ask_chancellor_for_capit.html.

15 Fred Goodwin, presentation to Merrill Lynch banking conference, 7 October 2008, http://www.investors.rbs.com/download/slides/ ML100708.pdf.

16 Iain Dey, 'How the government bailout saved our banks', *Sunday Times*, 3 October 2009, http://www.thesundaytimes.co.uk/sto/business/article186710.ece.

17 Alistair Darling, *Back from the Brink*.

18 Philip Aldrick, 'Royal Bank of Scotland: why is one of Britain's biggest banks trading like a penny stock?', *Daily Telegraph*, 7 October 2009, http:// www.telegraph.co.uk/finance/newsbysector/banksandfinance/3151276/ Royal-Bank-of-Scotland-Why-one-of-Britains-biggest-banks-is-trading-like-a-penny-stock.html.

19 Alistair Darling, *Back from the Brink*.

20   'The Failure of the Royal Bank of Scotland', FSA Board Report.

21   Alistair Darling, *Back from the Brink.*

22   Simon Watkins, 'Alistair Darling Interview: Britain was two hours away from total social collapse – Former Chancellor on the crisis that erupted five years ago this week', *Mail on Sunday*, 7 September 2013, http://www.thisismoney.co.uk/money/news/article-2415003/ALISTAIR-DARLING-INTERVIEW-Britain-hours-away-total-social-collapse--Former-Chancellor-crisis-erupted-FIVE-years-ago-week.html.

23   Alistair Darling, *Back from the Brink.*

24   Harry Wilson et al., 'Royal Bank of Scotland investigation: the full story of how the "world's biggest bank" went bust'.

25   Press Association, 7 October 2008, http://www.independent.co.uk/news/uk/politics/brown-pledges-to-maintain-financial-stability-953966.html.

26   Landon Thomas Jr, 'Their shares hurting, UK banks are pressing the Exchequer', *New York Times*, 7 October 2008, http://www.nytimes.com/2008/10/07/business/worldbusiness/07iht-pound.4.16758212.html?_r=0.

27   Iain Dey and Dominic Rushe, 'Five days that shook the world', *Sunday Times*, 12 October 2008, http://www.thesundaytimes.co.uk/sto/business/article241532.ece.

28   'The Love of Money', Part 3, BBC, October 2009, http://youtu.be/-0UhmUI-WbQ.

29   'Leading Questions', Lord Myners interviewed inside the Treasury by Robert Peston, BBC, 1 August 2009.

30   Patrick Wintour, Jill Treanor and David Teather, 'How an era in banking was brought to an end – over a curry', *The Guardian*, 9 October 2008, http://www.guardian.co.uk/politics/2008/oct/09/economy.alistairdarling1.

31   Alistair Darling, *Back from the Brink.*

32   Damian McBride, ' "I'll put troops on the streets": Gordon Brown's spin doctor reveals just how close to anarchy Britain came when the banks crashed', *Daily Mail*, 21 September 2013, http://www.dailymail.co.uk/news/article-2427617/Gordon-Brown-considered-putting-troops-streets-banks-crashed-reveals-Damian-McBride.html.

33   Alistair Darling, *Back from the Brink.*

34   Andrew Rawnsley, *The End of the Party.*

35   George Osborne, 'The job needs doing – but this bail-out is no triumph', *London Evening Standard*, 12 October 2008, http://www.standard.co.uk/news/the-job-needs-doing--but-this-bailout-is-no-triumph-6923097.html.

36   'Britain's bail-out', *Financial Times*, 9 October 2008.

37   George Parker, 'His finest moment', *Financial Times*, 14 October 2008, http://www.ft.com/cms/s/0/9d296c26-b859-11de-8ca9-00144feab49a.html.

38   Andrew Rawnsley, *The End of the Party*.

39   Fred Goodwin, oral evidence given to the Treasury Select Committee, 10 February 2009.

40   Nick Goodway, 'Pressure on RBS to ditch Goodwin and McKillop', *Daily Mail*, 8 October 2008 http://www.thisismoney.co.uk/money/markets/ article-1643638/Pressure-on-RBS-to-ditch-Goodwin-and-McKillop.html.

41   Alan Cochrane, 'Is Alex Salmond's "Arc of Prosperity" done for?', *Daily Telegraph* (Scottish edition), 9 October 2008, http://www.telegraph.co.uk/ comment/columnists/alancochrane/3562699/Is-Alex-Salmonds-Arc-of-Prosperity-done-for.html.

42   Lord Myners, author interview.

43   Ibid.

44   Ibid.

45   Alistair Darling, *Back from the Brink*.

46   Lord Myners, author interview.

47   Colin McLean, author interview.

48   Response from Sir Tom McKillop to the Treasury committee, 31 March 2009, http://image.guardian.co.uk/sys-files/Business/pdf/2009/03/31/ mckillop_to_mcfall.pdf.

49   George Parker, 'Faces of the Crisis: John Kingman', *Financial Times*, 2 January 2009, http://www.ft.com/cms/s/0/8215a934-d8e1-11dd-ab5f-000077b07658.html# axzz2b5rLjmjP.

50   Harry Wilson, Philip Aldrick and Kamal Ahmed, 'RBS investigation: Chapter 4: the bail-out', *Daily Telegraph*, 11 December 2011, http://www. telegraph.co.uk/finance/newsbysector/banksandfinance/8947559/RBS-investigation-Chapter-4-the-bail-out.html.

51   Alistair Darling, *Back from the Brink*.

52   RBS chairman's committee minutes of conference call, 13 October 2008, http://www.publications.parliament.uk/pa/cm200809/cmselect/ cmtreasy/144/144iii21.htm.

53   'Bank chiefs quit after rescue bid', BBC News, 13 October 2008, http:// news.bbc.co.uk/1/hi/scotland/7666647.stm.

54   Paul Krugman, 'Gordon does good', *New York Times*, 12 October 2008, http://www.nytimes.com/2008/10/13/opinion/13krugman.html?_r=0.

55   Simon Clark, 'U.K. Banks Should Shut Tax Haven Units, Cable Says', Bloomberg, 14 October 2008, http://www.bloomberg.com/apps/news?p id=newsarchive&sid=a_0KFH3SRWhY&refer=uk.

56   Felicity Lawrence and David Leigh, 'RBS avoided £500m of tax in global deals', *Guardian*, 13 March 2009, http://www.theguardian.com/ business/2009/mar/13/rbs-tax-avoidance.

CHAPTER 30

1   Alistair Darling, *Back from the Brink.*

2   Philip Aldrick, 'Ding Ding, End of Round Two of the Banking Bailout', *Daily Telegraph*, 8 November 2008, http://www.telegraph.co.uk/finance/newsbysector/banksandfinance/6521119/Ding-ding-end-of-round-two-of-the-banking-bail-out.html.

3   Andrew Sparrow, 'Gordon Brown and Alistair Darling press conference – live', *The Guardian*, 19 January 2009, http://www.guardian.co.uk/politics/blog/2009/jan/19/gordonbrown-alistairdarling.

4   Andrew Rawnsley, *The End of the Party.*

5   Alistair Darling, *Back from the Brink.*

6   Stuart MacDonald, 'Ian Hamilton sues RBS over shares', *Sunday Times*, 18 February 2009, http://www.thesundaytimes.co.uk/sto/news/uk_news/article143998.ece.

7   Gillian Bowditch, 'Ian Hamilton – our last defender', *Sunday Times*, 22 February 2009, Sundaytimes.co.uk/sto/news/uk_news/article151816.ece.

8   Ambrose Evans-Pritchard, 'Let banking fail', says Nobel economist Joseph Stiglitz, *Daily Telegraph*, 2 February 2009.

9   Peter Thal Larsen, 'RBS chairman leaves early', *Financial Times*, 4 February 2009, http://www.ft.com/cms/s/0/d08b734e-f25b-11dd-9678-0000779fd2ac.html.

10   'RBS directorate change', RBS press release, 6 February 2009, http://www.bloomberg.com/apps/news?pid=newsarchive&sid=agYaQBjXv.zk.

11   Andrew Rawnsley, *The End of the Party.*

12   Fred Goodwin, oral evidence to the House of Commons Treasury committee, 10 February 2009, http://www.publications.parliament.uk/pa/cm200809/cmselect/cmtreasy/144/09021014.htm.

13   Robert McDowell, 'Banking on Economics', 11 February 2009, http://bankingeconomics.blogspot.co.uk/2009/02/treasury-select-committee-hbos-and-rbs.html.

14   Stephen Hester, oral evidence to the House of Commons Treasury committee, 10 February 2009, http://www.publications.parliament.uk/pa/cm200809/cmselect/cmtreasy/144/09021014.htm.

15   Simon Hattenstone, 'Sir Fred just say sorry', *The Guardian*, 24 January 2009, http://www.guardian.co.uk/business/2009/jan/24/fred-goodwin-rbs/print.

16   BBC, 25 February 2009, http://www.bbc.co.uk/blogs/thereporters/robertpeston/2009/02/fred_goodwin_to_receive_650000.html.

17   Andrew Rawnsley, *The End of the Party.*

18   'Group claims responsibility for attack on Fred Goodwin's home', Scotsman.com, 25 March 2009, http://www.scotsman.com/news/

group-claims-responsibility-for-attack-on-fred-goodwin-s-home-1-468354.

19 'David Starkey: This Much I Know', *The Observer*, 29 March 2009, http://www.guardian.co.uk/lifeandstyle/2009/mar/29/david-starkey-historian.

20 'G20 protests: Rioters loot RBS after clashes in the City', *Daily Telegraph*, 1 April 2009, http://www.telegraph.co.uk/finance/g20-summit/5089240/G20-protests-Rioters-loot-RBS-office-after-clashes-in-City.html.

21 RBS Press Release, 18 June 2009, http://www.investors.rbs.com/newsitem?item= 169296873400365.

CHAPTER 31

1 Arthur Martin, 'Inside RBS chief's very own Versailles', *Mail Online*, 1 May 2012, http://www.dailymail.co.uk/news/article-2137090/Inside-RBS-chiefs-Versailles-Hester-opens-gardens-public-bailed-bank.html.

2 Douglas Fraser, 'RBS "not a toxic brand", says boss', BBC News, 25 August 2009, http://news.bbc.co.uk/1/hi/business/8218043.stm.

3 RBS 2008 Annual Review, 9 March 2009, http://files.shareholder.com/downloads/RBS/826828100x0x278478/df821101-a4f3-459b-80a8-a45141002a84/RBS_Annual_Review_2008_09_03_09.pdf.

4 Alexander Smith, 'Hester must ditch RBS investment bank', Reuters, 26 February 2009, http://uk.reuters.com/article/2009/02/26/us-column-rbs-idUKTRE51P3GR 20090226.

5 Liam Vaughan and Howard Mustoe, 'RBS Bankers Preparing for Nuclear Winter as Hester Undoes Goodwin Empire', *Bloomberg News*, 10 January 2012, http://www.bloomberg.com/news/2012-01-10/rbs-faces-nuclear-winter-as-ceo-hester-dismantles-goodwin-s-bank.html.

6 Ian Fraser, 'O'Neil appointment confirms UKFI's warped priorities', 19 July 2010, http://www.ianfraser.org/oneil-appointment-confirms-ukfis-warped-priorities/.

7 Lord Myners, author interview.

8 'Willem Buiter's Maverecon', 26 February 2009, http://blogs.ft.com/maverecon/2009/02/a-tax-payer-rip-off-of-surprising-boldness/#axzz2qkaRhzFe.

9 Huw Jones, 'RBS fined for reporting flaws worsened by ABN Amro deal', Reuters, 24 July 2013, http://uk.reuters.com/article/2013/07/24/uk-britain-rbs-fine- idUKBRE96N0BS20130724.

10 James Titcomb, 'Ex RBS worker "infiltrated bank" after posing as bond salesman', *Daily Telegraph*, 5 August 2013, http://www.telegraph.co.uk/finance/newsbysector/banksandfinance/10222666/Ex-RBS-worker-infiltrated-bank-after-posing-as-bond-salesman.html.

11 John Hourican, speech to ABN AMRO investment bankers Gustav Mahlerlaan, Amsterdam early March 2009.

12   Neelie Kroes, European Competition Commissioner, speech to the British Bankers Association international conference, 30 June 2009, http://europa.eu/rapid/press-release_SPEECH-09-324_en.htm?locale=en.

13   'State aid: Commission approves impaired asset relief measure and restructuring plan of Royal Bank of Scotland', EC press release, 14 December 2009, http://europa.eu/rapid/press-release_IP-09-1915_en.htm.

14   Vince Cable, *Hansard*, Commons Debates, 9 November 2009: Column 724, http://www.publications.parliament.uk/pa/cm200809/cmhansrd/cm091103/debtext/91103-0005.htm.

15   Michael Meacher/Alistair Darling, *Hansard*, Commons Debates, 3 November 2009: Column 729, http://www.publications.parliament.uk/pa/cm200809/cmhansrd/cm091103/debtext/91103-0006.htm.

CHAPTER 32

1   This may sound far-fetched but the Labour government does seem to have been wrong-footed by the intervention of EU Competition Commissioner Neelie Kroes in June 2009, and her plans for RBS certainly undermined what the government had had in mind for the bank.

2   'Eurozone Crisis: In-Country Bank Analysis', *Navigant*, July 2012, http://www.navigant.com/~/media/WWW/Site/Insights/Financial%20Services/EurozoneCrisis_BankAnalysis_07_12_FS_UK.ashx.

3   Patrick Hosking and Roland Watson, 'RBS record £4bn loss as Greek gamble backfires', *The Times*, 23 February 2012, http://www.thetimes.co.uk/tto/business/industries/banking/article3329146.ece.

4   Bess Levin, 'Layoffs watch '11', *Dealbreaker*, 7 November 2011, http://dealbreaker.com/2011/11/layoffs-watch-11-rbs-3.

5   Stephen Hester, 'Annual Review & Summary Financial Statement 2011', RBS Group, 23 February 2012, http://www.investors.rbs.com/download/pdf/video_interview/stephen_hester.pdf.

6   Van Saun interviewed by Gavin Hinks, *Finance Director*, 22 February 2012, http://www.financialdirector.co.uk/financial-director/interview/2154190/fd-interview-bruce-van-saun.

7   George Osborne, *Hansard*, Commons Debates, 19 December 2011: Column 1072, http://www.publications.parliament.uk/pa/cm201011/cmhansrd/cm111219/debtext/111219-0001.htm#1112195000653.

8   Bess Levin, 'Layoffs watch '11', *Dealbreaker*, 7 November 2011, http://dealbreaker.com/2011/11/layoffs-watch-11-rbs-3.

9   Harry Wilson, 'Civil war breaks out at Royal Bank of Scotland', *Daily Telegraph*, 19 February 2012, http://www.telegraph.co.uk/finance/newsbysector/banksandfinance/9090330/Civil-war-breaks-out-at-Royal-Bank-of-Scotland.html.

10   Phillipa Leighton-Jones and Vivek Ahuja, 'RBS: "We're a Global Flow Powerhouse"', Moneybeat, *Wall Street Journal*, 13 June 2013, http://blogs. wsj.com/moneybeat/ 2013/06/13/rbs-were-a-global-flow-powerhouse.

11   Ibid.

12   Keith Mullin, 'Stephen Hester, have I got a job for you!', *International Financing Review*, 14 June 2013, http://www.ifrasia.com/stephen-hester-have-i-got-a-job-for-you/21091396.article.

13   Jessica Hodgson, 'RBS Sets Radical Cutback of Investment Bank, Layoffs', *Wall Street Journal*, Dow Jones Newswires, January 2012, http:// online.wsj.com/article/BT-CO-20120112-703653.html.

14   Matthew Oakeshott, 'The Treasury needs a new team to stop the slide back into recession', *The Guardian*, 26 July 2012, http://www.guardian. co.uk/commentisfree/2012/jul/26/treasury-new-team-slide-recession.

15   Jill Treanor, 'Royal Bank of Scotland future divides coalition', *The Guardian*, 2 August 2012, http://www.guardian.co.uk/business/2012/ aug/02/royal-bank-of-scotland- future-divides-coalition.

16   David Enrich and Jean Eaglesham, 'Clubby London Trading Scene Fostered Libor Rate-Fixing Scandal', *Wall Street Journal*, 2 May 2013, http://online.wsj.com/article/SB10001424127887323296504578396670651342096.html.

17   FSA Final Notice, The Royal Bank of Scotland plc, 36 St Andrew Square, Edinburgh, EH2 2YB, FSA Ref. No: 121882, 6 February 2013.

18   'RBS Securities Japan Limited Agrees to Plead Guilty in Connection with Long-Running Manipulation of Libor Benchmark Interest Rates', Department of Justice Press Release, 6 February 2013, http://www.justice. gov/opa/pr/2013/February/13-crm-161.html.

19   CFTC, Press Release, 6 February 2013, http://www.cftc.gov/PressRoom/ PressReleases/pr6510-13.

20   CFTC, Order Instituting Proceedings against RBS, 6 February 2013, http://www.cftc.gov/ucm/groups/public/@lrenforcementactions/docu-ments/legalpleading/enfrbsorder020613.pdf.

21   FSA, Final Notice To: The Royal Bank Of Scotland PLC of: 36 St. Andrew Square, Edinburgh, EH2 2YB, FSA Ref. No: 121882, 6 February 2013, http://www.fsa.gov.uk/static/pubs/final/rbs.pdf.

22   Ian Fraser, 'Stephen Hester: the great escape artist', *Sunday Herald*, February 2013, http://www.ianfraser.org/the-great-escape-artist/.

23   John McDonnell, *Hansard*, Commons Debates, 6 February 2013: Column 316, http://www.publications.parliament.uk/pa/cm201213/cmhansrd/ cm130206/debtext/130206-0002.htm.

24   Stephen Hester interviewed by Krishnan Guru-Murthy, Channel 4 News, 6 February 2013, http://youtu.be/ighdbxkxan4.

25 Sir Philip Hampton, Oral Evidence Taken before the Parliamentary Commission on Banking Standards.

26 'RBS boss admits banks became "detached from society"', BBC News, 3 August 2012, http://www.bbc.co.uk/news/business-19107542.

27 Harry Wilson, 'EU fines Royal Bank of Scotland £324m over Libor rigging', http://www.telegraph.co.uk/finance/libor-scandal/10493940/EU-fines-Royal-Bank-of-Scotland-324m-over-Libor-rigging.html.

28 Sandy Chen, quoted by Alistair Osborne, 'Banks face crippling Libor litigation costs', *Daily Telegraph*, 28 June 2012, http://www.telegraph.co.uk/finance/newsbysector/banksandfinance/9363260/Banks-face-crippling-Libor-litigation-costs.html.

29 Lisa Abramowicz, 'RBS US Credit Sales Head Britton Departs as Debt Unit Shrinks', *Bloomberg*, 30 July 2013, http://www.bloomberg.com/news/2013-07-30/rbs-u-s-credit-sales-head-britton-departs-as-debt-unit-shrinks.html.

30 'Heads Roll as banks react to PPIP probe', Asset-Backed Alert 11 April 2014.

31 Iain Dey, 'Ejected', *Sunday Times*, 16 June 2013, http://www.thesunday-times.co.uk/sto/business/Companies/article1274249.ece.

CHAPTER 33

1 Faisal Islam, 'Should RBS be able to use losses to not pay tax?', Channel4News, 20 June 2013, http://blogs.channel4.com/faisal-islam-on-economics/should-rbs-be-able- to-use-losses-to-not-pay-tax/18282.

2 Edward Robinson, 'RBS on Brink of Profit Seen by Van Saun as King Urges a Breakup', *Bloomberg Markets Magazine*, 4 April 2013, http://www.bloomberg.com/news/2013-04-03/rbs-on-brink-of-profit-seen-by-van-saun-as-king-urges-a-breakup.html.

3 Stephen Hester interviewed on *The Andrew Marr Show*, BBC One, 26 February 2012, http://news.bbc.co.uk/1/hi/programmes/andrew_marr_show/9699854.stm.

4 Patrick Jenkins, 'RBS nears end of non-core rundown', *Financial Times*, 2 January 2013, http://www.ft.com/cms/s/0/35137d56-4a15-11e2-a7b1-00144feab49a.html#axzz2YZGyUndo.

5 Edward Robinson, 'RBS on Brink of Profit Seen by Van Saun as King Urges a Breakup'.

6 Howard Mustoe, 'RBS May Consider US Citizens Unit Sale on U.K.-First Strategy', *BusinessWeek* magazine, 20 December 2011, http://www.businessweek.com/news/2011-12-20/rbs-may-consider-u-s-citizens-unit-sale-on-u-k-first-strategy.html.

7 James Quinn, 'RBS hopes dashed by one phone call', *Daily Telegraph*,

13 October 2012, http://www.telegraph.co.uk/finance/newsbysector/banksandfinance/9606927/RBS-hopes-dashed-by-one-phone-call.html.

8 James Quinn, 'RBS to create new challenger bank under revived "Williams & Glyn's" brand', *Daily Telegraph*, 27 September 2013, http://www.telegraph.co.uk/finance/newsbysector/banksandfinance/10322675/RBS-to-create-new-challenger-bank-under-revived-Williams-and-Glyns-brand.html

9 Edward Robinson, 'RBS on Brink of Profit Seen by Van Saun as King Urges a Breakup'.

10 Patrick Wintour and Jill Treanor, 'RBS bonuses to reach £775m despite Treasury tough talk', *The Guardian*, 18 February 2009, http://www.guardian.co.uk/business/2009/feb/18/rbs-bonuses.

11 Ambereen Choudhury and Andrew MacAskill, 'RBS Says "Restrictive" Bonuses May Prompt Staff Exits', *Bloomberg News*, 2 December 2009, http://www.bloomberg.com/apps/news?pid=newsarchive&sid=aSaDT TfsRwCg.

12 Jill Treanor, 'RBS's top nine executives handed £28m in shares', *The Guardian*, 8 March 2011, http://www.theguardian.com/business/2011/mar/08/rbs-executives- handed-28m-shares-disgrace.

13 Robert Peston, 'RBS's Hampton: "Journeymen" bankers are paid too much', Peston's Picks, BBC News, 17 January 2011, http://www.bbc.co.uk/blogs/thereporters/robertpeston/2011/01/rbss_hampton_journeymen_banker.html.

14 Michael Seamark and Nick McDermott, 'The £8m mansion RBS chief Stephen Hester gave to his ex-wife . . . while he rents £4m apartment', *Daily Mail*, 28 January 2012, http://www.dailymail.co.uk/news/article-2092914/Stephen-Hester-The-8m-home-RBS-chief-gave-ex-wife-She-keeps-mansion--Hester-rents-4m-apartment.html.

15 Peter Oborne, 'Stephen Hester and Chris Huhne are symbols of a country in moral freefall', *Daily Telegraph*, 25 January 2012, http://blogs.telegraph.co.uk/news/peteroborne/100132665/hester-and-huhne-are-symbols-of-a-country-in-moral-freefall.

16 'RBS boss Hester rejects £1m bonus', BBC News, 30 January 2012, http://www.bbc.co.uk/news/uk-16783571.

17 Stephen Hester, Oral Evidence Taken before the Parliamentary Commission on Banking Standards, 11 February 2013, http://www.publications.parliament.uk/pa/jt201213/jtselect/jtpcbs/c606-xxxvi/c606xxxvi.pdf.

18 Sir David Walker, Treasury Select Committee, 22 May 2012, http://www.publications.parliament.uk/pa/cm201213/cmselect/cmtreasy/uc72i/uc72i.htm.

19 Harry Wilson, 'FSA informed of interest rate swap mis-selling scandal over a year ago', *Daily Telegraph*, 8 April 2012, http://www.telegraph.co.uk/finance/newsbysector/banksandfinance/9193091/FSA-informed-of-interest-rate-swap-mis-selling-scandal-over-a-year-ago.html.

20 Sky News, 8 July 2012, http://news.sky.com/story/957537/miliband-wants-banking-revolution.

21 Lawrence Tomlinson, 'Banks' Lending Practices: Treatment of Businesses in Distress', redacted report available at http://www.tomlinsonreport.com/docs/tomlinsonReport.pdf.

22 Lawrence Tomlinson in response to a question from Mark Garnier MP, verbal testimony to Treasury Select Committee, 29 January 2009.

23 Lawrence Tomlinson, 'Banks' Lending Practices: Treatment of Businesses in Distress'.

24 Lawrence Tomlinson, verbal testimony to Treasury Select Committee, 29 January 2014.

25 Lawrence Tomlinson, 'Banks' Lending Practices: Treatment of Businesses in Distress'.

26 Greg Harkin, 'Ulster Bank forced firms to default, then took their assets: claim', *Sunday Independent*, 1 December 2013, http://www.independent.ie/business/irish/ulster-bank-forced-firms-to-default-then-took-their-assets-claim-29798794.html.

27 Siobhan Kennedy, 'Whistleblower: how RBS "deliberately destroyed" firms', Channel 4 News, 11 Feb 2014.

28 Lawrence Tomlinson, 'Banks' Lending Practices: Treatment of Businesses in Distress'.

29 James Moore, 'RBS used vampire practices to strangle viable companies, MPs told', *The Independent*, 29 January 2014, http://www.independent.co.uk/news/business/news/rbs-used-vampire-practices-to-strangle-viable-companies-mps-told-9094631.html.

30 Ian Fraser, 'Bank Robbery?', *Sunday Herald*, 1 December 2013, http://www.ianfraser.org/bank-robbery.

31 Dominic Kennedy, 'Cashing in on property crash', *The Times*, 30 September 2012, http://www.thetimes.co.uk/tto/business/industries/banking/article3554103.ece.

32 Heidi Blake and Jonathan Calvert, 'RBS kills off good firms for profit', *Sunday Times*, 24 November 2013, http://www.thesundaytimes.co.uk/sto/news/uk_news/National/article1344412.ece.

33 Jill Treanor, 'New RBS chief Ross McEwan denies "systematic" profiteering', *The Guardian*, 27 November 2013, http://www.theguardian.com/business/2013/nov/27/rbs-chief-mcewan-denies-profiteering.

34 Philip Stafford, 'RBS faces possible criminal probe', *Financial Times*, 27

November 2013, http://www.ft.com/cms/s/0/ea9d30c0-537b-11e3-9250-00144feabdco.html.

35 Empty Wheel, 'Lanny Breuer deputizes banks rather than prosecuting them', 1 January 2013, http://www.emptywheel.net/tag/promontory-financial-group.

36 Lawrence Tomlinson, verbal testimony to Treasury Select Committee, 29 January 2014.

37 Ian Fraser, 'Corruption allegations, major fraud inquiries, links to pornographic magazine . . . and a luxury yacht. Welcome to the world of banking in 2012', *Sunday Herald*, 22 July 2012, http://www.ianfraser.org/?p=7711.

38 ' "Vampire" Bank Practices Outlined', *Evening Standard*, 29 January 2014, http://www.standard.co.uk/panewsfeeds/vampire-bank-practices-outlined-9094092.html.

39 Jim Hood, *Hansard*, Commons Debates, 10 March 2010: Column 96WH, http://www.publications.parliament.uk/pa/cm200910/cmhansrd/cm100310/halltext/100310h0004.htm.

40 Simon Bain, 'Landmark RBS court case result overturned', *The Herald*, 16 September 2013 http://www.heraldscotland.com/business/company-news/landmark-rbs-court- case-result-overturned.22170807.

41 Simon Bain, 'RBS face £4m bill after seven-year pursuit of bankrupt developer fails', *Herald*, 12 March 2015 http://www.heraldscotland.com/business/13205356.RBS_face_4m_bill_after_seven_year_pursuit_of_bankrupt_developer_fails.

42 Doug Morrison, 'Uncharted territory', *Property Week*, 8 October 2010, http://www.propertyweek.com/uncharted-territory/5007029.article.

43 Neil Mitchell, author interview.

44 Ibid.

45 Ibid.

46 Ibid.

47 Ibid.

48 Ibid.

49 This is one of many hundreds of emails the author has received from business people who claim that RBS and its Global Restructuring Group have deliberately destroyed their businesses and taken away their livelihoods. The sender preferred to remain anonymous for fear of further persecution. The email has been edited for clarity and brevity.

50 Clifford Chance LLP: Independent Review of the Central Allegation Made by Dr Lawrence Tomlinson in Banks' Lending Practices: Treatment of Businesses in Distress, 17 April 2014 http://www.rbs.com/news/2014/04/clifford-chance-report-into-allegations-of-systematic-fraud.html.

51 Ian Fraser, 'RBS accused of diversion over malpractice report', *Sunday Herald*, 20 April 2014 http://www.heraldscotland.com/business/company-news/rbs-accused-of- diversion-over-malpractice-report.24001423.

52 In the Court of Appeal (Civil Division), on appeal from the Queen's Bench Division, The Royal Bank of Scotland PLC v. Highland Capital Management and others, before Lord Justice Maurice Kay, Lord Justice Toulson and Lord Justice Aikens, 11 April 2013, http://www.cyklaw.com/assets/1861001.pdf.

53 LexLaw Solicitors and Advocates, 'RBS v Highland Financial Partners: Culture of denial at RBS?', 14 April 2013, http://lexlaw.co.uk/solicitors-london/rbs-v-highland-financial-partners-culture-of-denial-at-rbs.

54 'RBS said to settle Highland suits over $100m CDO losses', *Bloomberg News*, 17 September 2013.

55 James Quinn, 'Stephen Hester: Banking culture change "will take a generation"', *Daily Telegraph*, 29 September 2012, http://www.telegraph.co.uk/finance/newsbysector/banksandfinance/9576646/Stephen-Hester-Banking-culture-change-will-take-a-generation.html.

56 John Nolan, author interview.

57 Rob MacGregor, Banking in Scotland – Scottish Affairs Committee, 2 December 2009, Q572, http://www.publications.parliament.uk/pa/cm200910/cmselect/cmscotaf/70/9120204.htm.

58 Rob MacGregor, author interview.

CHAPTER 34

1 'Changing Banking for Good', Report of the Parliamentary Commission on Banking Standards, House of Commons, House of Lords, 19 June 2013, http://www.parliament.uk/documents/banking-commission/Banking-final-report-vol-ii.pdf.

2 Iain Dey, 'Ejected', *Sunday Times*.

3 Andy Haldane, Bank of England, speech at the Festival of Economics, Trento, Italy, 31 May 2013, http://2013.festivaleconomia.eu/programma/conferenza/-/asset_publisher/6ffIhSNOsu9P/document/id/165653?redirect=http%3A%2F%2F2013.festivaleconomia.eu%2Fen%2Fprogramma%2Fconferenza.

4 Sir Mervyn King, Oral Evidence to the Parliamentary Commission on Banking Standards, 6 March 2013, http://www.publications.parliament.uk/pa/jt201213/jtselect/jtpcbs/c606-xl/c60601.htm.

5 Ibid.

6 George Osborne, Oral Evidence to the Parliamentary Commission on Banking Standards, 25 February 2013, http://www.publications.parliament.uk/pa/jt201213/jtselect/jtpcbs/c606-xl/c60601.htm.

7 Iain Dey, 'Ejected', *Sunday Times*.

8 Alex Brummer, 'A poisonous relationship between a top banker and a determined Chancellor ended with a blow from the political knife', *Daily Mail*, 14 June 2013, http://www.dailymail.co.uk/debate/columnists/article-2341368/A-poisonous-relationship-banker-determined-Chancellor-ended-blow-political-knife.html.

9 David Enrich, Jenny Strasburg and Katie Martin, 'Richard Usher Allegedly Took Part in "Bandits Club" Chat Sessions', *Wall Street Journal*, 14 October 2013, http://on.wsj.com/17pVVGz.

10 David Enrich and Katie Martin, 'Currency probe widens as major banks suspend traders', *Wall Street Journal*, 1 November 2013, *http://on.wsj.com/1aIOOAE*.

11 Bruce Van Saun, Royal Bank of Scotland finance director, 'RBS Q1 interim management statement'.

12 Stephen Hester.

13 Tim Bush, author interview.

14 Iain Dey, 'Hester: no takers for £20bn RBS wants to lend', *Sunday Times*, 5 May 2013, http://www.thesundaytimes.co.uk/sto/business/Finance/article1255004.ece.

15 Tweet from Stuart Norton, @norton_ceo, 5.30pm on 7 May 2013, https://twitter.com/norton_ceo/status/331808227979325440.

16 Marshall Auerback, 'Andy Haldane: The Counter-Reformation in Banking Has Just Begun', Institute for New Economic Thinking, *The Institute Blog*, 31 May 2013, http:// ineteconomics.org/blog/inet/andy-haldane-counter-reformation-banking-has-just-begun.

17 'Stephen Hester to leave RBS', RBS press release, 12 June 2013, http://www.investors.rbs.com/news-item?item=1526744909611008.

18 'RBS's Stephen Hester quits with £5.6m golden parachute', *The Herald*, 12 June 2013, http://www.heraldscotland.com/news/home-news/rbss-stephen-hester-is-stepping- down.1371053976.

19 Nic Clarke, banking analyst at Charles Stanley, 'Research Note on Royal Bank of Scotland', 13 June 2013.

20 Jennifer Thompson and George Parker, 'George Osborne "clear" on vision for RBS', *Financial Times*, 13 June 2013, http://www.ft.com/cms/s/0/ea8bf5fc-d442-11e2-8639-00144feab7de.html.

CHAPTER 35

1 'Speech by Chancellor of the Exchequer, RT Hon George Osborne MP, Mansion House 2013', 19 June 2013, https://www.gov.uk/government/speeches/speech-by-chancellor-of-the-exchequer-rt-hon-george-osborne-mp-mansion-house-2013.

2 In numerous articles and radio broadcasts from September 2012 to June

2013, including in the *Sunday Herald*, the *Yorkshire Post*, LBC 93.7 and BBC Radio 4's *Today* programme, I said that Hampton and Hester were wrong to suggest that the bank was ready to be reprivatised.

3   'Speech by Chancellor of the Exchequer, RT Hon George Osborne MP, Mansion House 2013'.

4   Ann Pettifor, 'Just Money', on Twitter, https://twitter.com/AnnPettifor/status/ 376348644498096132.

5   James Salmon, 'RBS chaos: Politicians and City clash over giant bank's future as speculation continues', *This Is Money*, 13 June 2013, http://www.thisismoney.co.uk/money/markets/article-2341286/CITY-FOCUS-Its-chaos-politicians-City-clash-RBS-future-speculation-continues.html.

6   Ross McEwan, speech to RBS staff in 250 Bishopsgate, 1 October 2013, http://www.ibtimes.co.uk/articles/510543/20131001/ross-mcewan-new-rbs-ceo-stephen-hester.htm#.UkrHv4iTx1k.twitter.

7   'RBS and the case for a bad bank: The Government's Review', 1 November 2013, https://www.gov.uk/government/uploads/system/uploads/attachment_data/file/254540/PU1581_RBS_bad_bank_Govt_review.pdf.

8   'A message from our chief executive', RBS News Headlines, 1 November 2013, http://www.rbs.com/news/2013/11/letter-from-our-chief-executive.html.

9   RBS Independent Lending Review, 1 November 2013, http://www.independentlendingreview.co.uk/RBSILRSummary_and_Recommendations.pdf.

10   'Royal Bank of Scotland credit ratings downgraded by S&P', BBC News Scotland, 7 November 2013 http://www.bbc.co.uk/news/uk-scotland-scotland-business-24856832.

11   SEC vs RBS Securities, 7 November 2013, http://www.sec.gov/litigation/complaints/2013/comp-pr2013-239.pdf.

12   Ibid.

13   Press release: 'RBS in state sponsored land grab', Unite The Union 27 February 2014 http://www.unitetheunion.org/news/rbs-in-state-sponsored-grab/.

14   Ross McEwan, Q&A, media conference in the Trampery, 27 February 2014.

15   Colin McLean, author interview.

16   Ross McEwan, speech in the Trampery, 27 February 2014 http://www.bbc.co.uk/news/business-your-money-26365616.

CHAPTER 36

1   Iain Robertson, author interview.

2   Paul Kearns, author interview.

3 Jane Adams, 'The Unconventional Mr. Goodwin', *Institutional Investor Magazine*, 1 August 2001 http://www.institutionalinvestor.com/Article/1027830/The-unconventional-Mr-Goodwin.html.

4 Colin McLean, author interview.

5 Iain Dey, 'RBS directors were kept in dark over Goodwin's alleged affair', *Sunday Times*, 22 May 2011, http://www.thesundaytimes.co.uk/sto/business/Finance/article631743.ece.

6 'The failure of the Royal Bank of Scotland: Financial Services Authority Board Report', Part 2, Management, governance and culture, paragraph 610, December 2011, http://www.fsa.gov.uk/static/pubs/other/rbs.pdf.

7 Daniel Gross, 'Who's the World's Worst Banker?', *Slate*, 1 December 2008, http://www.slate.com/articles/business/moneybox/2008/12/whos_the_worlds_worst_banker.html.

8 Ibid.

9 Ibid.

10 Tom McKillop, Commons Select Committee, Treasury, Banking Crisis, Examination of Witnesses, Q1666, 10 February 2009, http://www.publications.parliament.uk/pa/cm200809/cmselect/cmtreasy/144/09021003.htm.

11 Thomas Ginsberg, 'Aggressive stance AstraZeneca's passionate CEO, Sir Tom McKillop, is too busy fighting the dragons of the drug industry to retire just yet', *Philadelphia Inquirer*, 24 April 2005, http://articles.philly.com/2005-04-24/business/25425965_1_crestor-astrazeneca-plc-exanta.

12 'The statin wars: why AstraZeneca must retreat', *The Lancet*, 25 October 2003, http://www.thelancet.com/journals/lancet/article/PIIS0140-6736(03)14669-7/fulltext?_eventId=login. Tom McKillop quoted in 'AstraZeneca defends its new bestseller', BBC News, 24 October 2004, http://news.bbc.co.uk/1/hi/business/3210409.stm.

13 Tom McKillop, Commons Select Committee, Treasury, Banking Crisis, Examination of Witnesses, Q949, 10 February, http://www.publications.parliament.uk/pa/cm200809/cmselect/cmtreasy/uc144_vii/uc14402.htm.

14 Katherine Griffiths, 'RBS apologises for near collapse', *Daily Telegraph*, 20 November 2008, http://www.telegraph.co.uk/finance/newsbysector/banksandfinance/3491617/RBS-apologises-for-near-collapse.html.

15 Damian Reece, 'McKillop may be apologetic for RBS's woes but he remains in denial', *Daily Telegraph*, 20 November 2008, http://www.telegraph.co.uk/finance/comment/damianreece/3492281/McKillop-may-be-apologetic-over-RBS-woes-but-he-remains-in-denial.html.

16 George Mathewson, author interview.

17 Johnny Cameron, speaking at Sheffield University SPERI seminar, 'The Banking Crisis and the Future of Banking', 15 October 2013, http://youtu.be/ribZd8Wb6Vc.

18 Peter Thal Larsen, 'Rising star could have further to go', *Financial Times*, 1 March 2006, http://www.ft.com/cms/s/0/f74ac48e-a8c7-11da-aeeb-0000779e2340.html.

19 Iain Dey and Kate Walsh, 'How Fred shredded RBS', *Sunday Times*, 8 February 2009 http://www.thesundaytimes.co.uk/sto/business/article148906.ece.

20 Iain Martin, *Making It Happen*.

21 'The failure of the Royal Bank of Scotland: Financial Services Authority Board Report', Executive summary, paragraph 44, December 2011, http://www.fsa.gov.uk/static/pubs/other/rbs.pdf.

22 Matt Levine, 'Jon Corzine Must Be Pretty Happy To Hear About This Jonny Cameron Character', *Dealbreaker*, 12 December 2011 http://dealbreaker.com/2011/12/jon-corzine-must-be-pretty-happy-to-hear-about-this-jonny-cameron-character.

23 'The failure of the Royal Bank of Scotland: Financial Services Authority Board Report', Part 2, Management, governance and culture, paragraph 591.

24 Lucy P. Marcus, 'RBS's board lessons', Reuters, 19 December 2011, http://blogs.reuters.com/lucy-marcus/2011/12/19/rbss-board-lessons/.

25 'The failure of the Royal Bank of Scotland: Financial Services Authority Board Report', Part 2, Management, governance and culture, paragraph 593, ibid.

26 Ibid., paragraph 599.

27 Ibid.

28 Ibid., Paragraph 606.

29 Lucy P. Marcus, 'RBS's board lessons'.

30 Richard Lambert, 'Unchecked excess: The lessons of RBS failure', *Financial Times*, 12 December 2011, http://www.ft.com/cms/s/0/c91ca412-24b6-11e1-ac4b-00144feabdc0.html#axzz2MUkBzkw4.

31 Gordon Pell, Stonewall Workplace Conference, Queen Elizabeth II Conference Centre, 16 April 2008, http://www.stonewallcymru.org.uk/other/startdownload.asp?openType=forced&documentID=1344.

32 Gillian Tett, oral evidence to the Scottish Parliament Economy, Energy and Tourism Committee, 'Official Report', 25 November 2009, http://archive.scottish.parliament.uk/s3/committees/eet/or-09/ee09-3102.htm.

33 Gareth Gore, 'The fall and (partial) rise of RBS', *International Financing Review*, December 2012, http://www.ifre.com/the-fall-and-(partial)-rise-of-rbs/21052458.article.

34 'The failure of the Royal Bank of Scotland: Financial Services Authority Board Report', Part 2, Factors contributing to RBS's failure, paragraph 67.

35 Stephen Hester, oral evidence, given to the House of Commons Treasury Committee, Banking Crisis – Banks, 11 February 2009, http://www.publications.parliament.uk/pa/cm200809/cmselect/cmtreasy/uc144_viii/uc14402.htm.

36 Gillian Tett, oral evidence to the Scottish Parliament Economy, Energy and Tourism Committee, 'Official Report', ibid.

37 Andrew G Haldane, executive director for financial stability, Bank of England, 'Control rights (and wrongs)', speech given at Wincott Annual Memorial Lecture, Westminster, London, 24 October 2011, http://www.bankofengland.co.uk/publications/Documents/speeches/2011/speech525.pdf.

38 Ibid.

39 Ibid.

40 Ibid.

41 Andy Haldane, 'The Doom Loop: equity and the banking system', London Review of Books, 23 February 2012, http://www.lrb.co.uk/v34/n04/andrew-haldane/the-doom-loop.

42 Ibid.

43 The slumps that shaped modern finance, The Economist, 12 April 2014 http://www.economist.com//news/essays/21600451-finance-not-merely-prone-crises-it-shaped-them-five-historical-crises-show-how-aspects-today-s-fina?fsrc=scn/tw/te/bl/ed/slumpsthatshaped.

44 Andrew Haldane, 'Control Rights (and Wrongs)', Wincott Annual Memorial Lecture, 24 October 2011, http://www.bankofengland.co.uk/publications/Documents/speeches/2011/speech525.pdf.

45 Matthew Lynn, 'Forget Fred Goodwin – the worst RBS offenders got away scot-free', MoneyWeek, 20 December 2011, http://www.moneyweek.com/news-and-charts/economics/uk/sir-fred-goodwin-social-pariah-offenders-scot-free-from-rbs-56818.

46 David Teather, 'Myners tells investors to rein in banks', The Guardian, 3 November 2009, http://www.guardian.co.uk/business/2009/nov/03/myners-lloyds-rbs-banking- bailouts.

47 'The failure of the Royal Bank of Scotland: Financial Services Authority Board Report', Part 2, Supervisory approach, priorities and resources, paragraph 743.

48 'The FSA's report into the failure of RBS', House of Commons Treasury Committee, 16 October 2012, http://www.publications.parliament.uk/pa/cm201213/cmselect/cmtreasy/640/640.pdf.

49 Robert Jenkins, Member of the Bank of England's Financial Policy

Committee, speech given at the Worshipful Company of Actuaries, Haberdashers' Hall, 10 July 2012, http://www.bankofengland.co.uk/publications/Documents/speeches/2012/speech593.pdf.

50 FSA, 2 December 2010, http://www.fsa.gov.uk/pages/Library/Communication/Statements/2010/investigation_rbs.shtml.

51 Becky Barrow and Rob Davies, 'Fred the Shred "tries to dilute RBS report": Banker's lawyers challenge criticism of his role', *Daily Mail*, 7 December 2011, http://www.dailymail.co.uk/news/article-2070900/Sir-Fred-Goodwin-tries-dilute-RBS-report-Bankers-lawyers-challenge-criticism-role.html.

52 Jill Treanor, 'FSA failed to interview key RBS board members for controversial report', *The Guardian*, 23 February 2012, http://www.theguardian.com/business/2012/feb/23/fsa-failed-interview-rbs-board-report?CMP=twt_fd.

53 'The failure of the Royal Bank of Scotland: Financial Services Authority Board Report', Part 3, Global Banking and Markets, paragraph 181, ibid.

54 Rachel Abrams and Peter Lattman, 'Ex-Credit Suisse Executive Sentenced in Mortgage Bond Case', Dealbook, *New York Times*, 22 November 2013, http://dealbook.nytimes.com/2013/11/22/ex-credit-suisse-executive-sentenced-in-mortgage-case.

55 Ibid.

56 US Embassy Cable, leaked by Bradley Manning to WikiLeaks, 11 September 2009, http://www.theguardian.com/world/us-embassy-cables-documents/224740.

57 Total tax contribution of UK financial services, PwC report for the City of London, December 2008.

58 Fraser Nelson, 'Don't blame the HBOS bankers, blame the politicians who cosied up to them', *Daily Telegraph*, 5 April 2013, http://www.telegraph.co.uk/finance/newsbysector/epic/hbos/9971610/Dont-blame-the-HBOS-bankers-blame-the-politicians-who-cosied-up-to-them.html. (Note that, in my view, there are some errors in Nelson's piece but the passage quoted is reflective of New Labour's behaviour.)

59 Bank of England, transcript of Inflation Report Press Conference, 8 August 2007, http://www.bankofengland.co.uk/publications/Documents/inflationreport/conf080807.pdf.

60 'Sir Mervyn King rejects criticism for crisis', BBC News, Business, 3 May 2012, http://www.bbc.co.uk/news/business-17929120.

61 Sir John Gieve speaking at Sheffield University SPERI seminar, 'The Banking Crisis and the Future of Banking', 15 October 2013, http://youtu.be/ribZd8Wb6Vc.

62 Ibid.

63 Ibid.

64 Albert Edwards, 'Time to strip Sir Alan Greenspan and Sir Mervyn King of their knighthoods', *Deflation*, 9 February 2012, http://www.deflation.com/time-to-strip-sir-alan-greenspan-and-sir-mervyn-king-of-their-knighthoods-too/.

65 Mitch Feierstein: 'We put out one fire but now Mark Carney wants to start another', *The Independent*, 30 October 2013 http://www.independent.co.uk/news/business/comment/mitch-feierstein-we-put-out-one-fire-but-now-mark-carney-wants-to-start-another-8911902.html.

66 Ibid.

67 Mark Carney, speech at 125th anniversary of *Financial Times*, 24 October 2013, http://www.bankofengland.co.uk/publications/Documents/speeches/2013/speech690.pdf.

68 'The failure of the Royal Bank of Scotland: Financial Services Authority Board Report', Part 2, Appendices.

69 Sir Donald Cruickshank, Oral Evidence Taken Before The Parliamentary Commission On Banking Standards, 24 October 2012, http://www.publications.parliament.uk/pa/jt201213/jtselect/jtpcbs/c606-iv/c60601.htm.

70 Brooke Masters, 'UK bank supervisors tighten their grip', *Financial Times*, 21 October 2012, http://www.ft.com/cms/s/0/1b95422a-1b5c-11e2-90cb-00144feabdco.html.

71 RBS Annual Report and Accounts, 2007, http://www.investors.rbs.com/download/report/RBS_GRA_2007_21_4_08.pdf.

72 Tim Bush, author interview.

73 Financial Services (Regulation of Derivatives) Bill, 2010–11, http://services.parliament.uk/bills/2010-11/financialservicesregulationofderivatives.html.

74 Steve Baker, press release to announce Private Members' Bill, 15 May 2011, http://www.cobdenpartners.co.uk/pdf/FinRegDerivs-PR.pdf.

75 Ibid.

76 Tim Bush, letter to the Accounting Standards Board, assessing the impact of the Accounting Standards Board ('ASB') proposals for the future of UK and Irish financial reporting, 19 August 2010, http://www.taxresearch.org.uk/Documents/ASBUKIrishFinalResponse.pdf.

77 Email from Phil Hodkinson to Paul Moore dated 3 March 2011.

78 For a more detailed round-up of Royal Bank of Scotland's unexploded time bombs, see my '£1trn timebombs RBS must defuse', *Sunday Herald*, 3 November 2013, http://www.heraldscotland.com/business/company-news/1trn-timebombs-rbs- mustdefuse.22584590.

79 Martin Wolf, 'Reform of British banking needs to go further', *Financial Times*, 20 June 2013, http://www.ft.com/cms/s/0/28d640fc-d8d4-11e2-84fa-00144feab7de.html.

EPILOGUE

1   RBS Annual Report and Accounts 2014 http://www.investors.rbs. com/~/media/Files/R/RBS-IR/2014-reports/annual-report-2014.pdf.

2   STV News, 'Outgoing RBS chairman lambasted by shareholders at final AGM', 23 June 2015 http://news.stv.tv/scotland/1323491-rbs-chairman-sir-philip-hampton-lambasted-by-shareholders-at-final-agm.

3   Ross McEwan, speech to RBS annual general meeting, 23 June 2015 http://www.rbs.com/news/2015/june/rbs-2015-agm.html.

4   Transcript of RBS annual results 2014 analysts' conference, 26 February 2015 http://www.investors.rbs.com/~/media/Files/R/RBS-IR/results-center/management-presentation-transcript-270215.pdf.

5   Jill Treanor, 'RBS expects further fines with no let-up from regulators', *The Guardian*, 29 July 2015 http://gu.com/p/4b54q/stw.

6   Sky News, 'Ross McEwan says bank may never see end of misconduct costs', 29 July 2015 http://news.sky.com/video/1527705/rbs-boss-fears-misconduct-treadmill.

7   United States District Court, Southern District of New York, Federal Housing Finance Agency v Nomura, Opinion & Order, 11 May 2015 http://1.usa.gov/1cqlRuS.

8   Ministério da Justiça, Conselho Administrativo de Defesa Econômica, CADE, Notice, 1 July 2015 http://bit.ly/seibrazil.

9   Transcript of RBS first quarter results analysts' conference, 30 April 2015 http://www.investors.rbs.com/~/media/Files/R/RBS-IR/download/transcript/q1-2015-results-analyst-call-transcript.pdf.

10 Caroline Binham, 'Banks still failing to manage benchmark risks, warns UK watchdog', *Financial Times*, 29 July 2015 http://on.ft.com/1I2VJBq.

11 Martin Arnold and Lindsay Fortado, 'Banks in forex probe braced for legal barrage', May 2015 http://on.ft.com/1KIFdJ4.

12 James Hurley, 'In my worst nightmares I never thought the bank would do this to me', *The Times*, 5 May 2015 http://thetim.es/1IdKdWo.

13 Matt Suffham, 'Exclusive – RBS hires advisers to look at treatment of small businesses', Reuters, 22 July 2015 http://reut.rs/1SQVHzD.

14 James Hurley, 'We mis-sold taxpayer-backed loans to small businesses, confesses RBS', *The Times*, 15 January 2015 http://thetim.es/1Goblre.

15 Channel 4 Press Release, 'How Councils Blow your Millions: Channel 4 Despatches', 6 July 2015 http://www.channel4.com/info/press/news/how-councils-blow-your-millions-channel-4-despatches.

16 Ian Fraser, 'The dog that eats up debt', *Sunday Herald*, 21 December 2014 http://www.ianfraser.org/?p=10969.

17 Lindsay Fortado, 'RBS order to hand over FCA Libor documents in £30m lawsuit', *Financial Times*, 8 June 2015 http://www.ft.com/

cms/s/0/7f71330a-0dec-11e5-9a65-00144feabdco.html.

18   RBS press release: CEO Ross McEwan takes calls live on LBC, 13 March 2015 http://www.rbs.com/news/2015/march/ceo-ross-mcewan-takes-calls-live-on-lbc.html.

19   Transcript of RBS annual results 2014 analysts' conference, 26 February 2015 http://www.investors.rbs.com/~/media/Files/R/RBS-IR/results-center/management-presentation-transcript-270215.pdf.

20   Bill Goodwin, 'RBS goes back to the 1970s with big data', *Computer Weekly*, 17 June 2015 http://bit.ly/1eHPrwy.

21   BBC News, 'RBS £153m first half loss after litigation costs', 29 July 2015 http://www.bbc.co.uk/news/business-33714228.

22   Tim Wallace, 'Rise of the machines: Bank customers shun staff for mobile phones', *Daily Telegraph*, 26 July 2015 http://www.telegraph.co.uk/finance/newsbysector/banksandfinance/11766002/Rise-of-the-machines-bank-customers-shun-staff-for-mobile-phones.html.

23   George Graham, RBS's head of strategic insight, speaking at St Paul's Institute's Unfinished Business: Reform and Innovation in Finance event; St Faith's Chapel, Crypt of St Paul's Cathedral; 10 June 2015 https://youtu.be/SC8PsLDD_OE.

24   'RBS is more than a restructuring story, says Jefferies', Sharecast , 29 May 2015 http://www.sharecast.com/news/rbs-to-deliver-on-overhual-says-jefferies/22854510.html.

25   David Madden, 'Fed's enthusiasm fades', FX Street, 29 July 2015 http://www.fxstreet.com/analysis/market-insight/2015/07/30.

26   Nick Kochan, 'We have given the keys of the global banking business to the Americans', *Daily Telegraph*, 2 August 2015 http://www.telegraph.co.uk/finance/newsbysector/banksandfinance/11778378/We-have-given-the-keys-of-the-global-banking-business-to-the-Americans-says-John-Hourican.html.

27   Martin Wolf, *The Shifts and the Shocks: What We've Learned – and Have Still To Learn – from the Financial Crisis*, Allen Lane, 2014.

Bibliography

Admati, Anat and Hellwig, Martin, *The Bankers' New Clothes: What's Wrong With Banking and What to Do About It*, Princeton University Press, 2013.

Augar, Philip, *Chasing Alpha: How Reckless Growth and Unchecked Ambition Ruined the City's Golden Decade*, The Bodley Head, 2009.

Augar, Philip, *Reckless: The Rise and Fall of the City, 1997–2008*, Vintage Books, 2010.

Bermingham, David, *A Price to Pay: The Inside Story of the NatWest Three*, Gibson Square Books Ltd, 2012.

Bower, Tom, *Gordon Brown: Prime Minister*, Harper Perennial, revised and updated edition, 2007.

Boyle, David, *Broke: Who Killed the Middle Classes?*, Fourth Estate, 2013.

Brown, Gordon, *Beyond The Crash: Overcoming the First Crisis of Globalisation*, Simon & Schuster Ltd, 2010.

Cameron, Alan, *Bank of Scotland 1695–1995: A Very Singular Institution*, Mainstream Publishing, 1995.

Carswell, Simon, *Anglo Republic: Inside the Bank that Broke Ireland*, Penguin, 2012.

Chancellor, Edward, *Devil Take the Hindmost: A History of Financial Speculation*, Plume Books, 2000.

Coggan, Philip, *The Money Machine: How the City Works*, Penguin Books, 6th edition, 2009.

Cohan, William D., *Money and Power: How Goldman Sachs Came to Rule the World*, Penguin Books, 2011.

Cohen, Nick, *You Can't Read This Book: Censorship in an Age of Freedom*, Fourth Estate, 2012.

Cooper, Matt, *How Ireland Really Went Bust*, Penguin Ireland, 2012.

Darling, Alistair, *Back from the Brink: 1,000 Days at Number 11*, Atlantic Books, 2011.

Dunbar, Nicholas, *The Devil's Derivatives: The Untold Story of the Slick Traders and Hapless Regulators Who Almost Blew Up Wall Street . . . And Are Ready to do it Again*, Harvard Business Review Press, 2011.

Elliott, Larry and Atkinson, Dan, *Going South: Why Britain Will Have a Third World Economy by 2014*, Palgrave Macmillan, 2012.

Financial Crisis Inquiry Commission, *The Financial Crisis Inquiry Report: Final Report of the National Commission on the Causes of the Financial and Economic Crisis in the United States*, Public Affairs, January 2011.

Financial Services Authority, *The Failure of the Royal Bank of Scotland: Financial Services Authority Board Report*, December 2011.

Greenspan, Alan, *The Age of Turbulence: Adventures in a New World*, Allen Lane, 2007.

Harvie, Christopher, *Broonland: The Last Days of Gordon Brown*, Verso, 2010.

Heffernan, Margaret, *Wilful Blindness: Why We Ignore the Obvious at Our Peril*, Simon & Schuster, 2011.

Hunt, Roger, and Kemp, Kenny, *Be Silent or Be Killed: The True Story of a Scottish Banker Under Siege in Mumbai's 9/11*, Corskie, 2010.

Johnson, Simon and Kwak, James, *13 Bankers: The Wall Street Takeover and the Next Financial Meltdown*, Pantheon Books, 2010.

Kerr, Andrew William, *History of Banking in Scotland*, David Bryce & Son, 1884.

Kynaston, David, *The City of London, Volume IV: A Club No More 1945–2000*, Chatto & Windus, 2001.

Lascelles, David, *Other People's Money: The Revolution in High Street Banking*, Institute of Financial Services, School of Finance, 2005.

Lewis, Michael, *Liar's Poker: Two Cities, True Greed*, Hodder & Stoughton, 1989.

Lewis, Michael, *The Big Short: Inside the Doomsday Machine*, Allen Lane, 2010.

McGinn, Clark, *Out of Pocket: How Collective Amnesia Lost the World Its Wealth, Again*, Luath Press, 2010.

Martin, Iain, *Making It Happen: Fred Goodwin, RBS and the Men Who Blew Up the British Economy*, Simon & Schuster, 2013.

Munro, Neil, *The History of the Royal Bank of Scotland, 1727–1927*, [1928], reprinted by The Grimsay Press, 2011.

Nevin, Michael, *The Golden Guinea – The International Financial Crisis: 2007–2014: Causes, Consequences and Cures*, Southdown Books, 2012.

O'Toole, Fintan, *Ship of Fools: How Stupidity and Corruption Sank the Celtic Tiger*, Faber & Faber, 2009.

Perman, Ray, *Hubris: How HBOS Wrecked the Best Bank in Britain*, Birlinn, 2012.

Peston, Robert and Knight, Laurence, *How Do We Fix This Mess?: The Economic Price of Having It All and the Route to Lasting Prosperity*, Hodder & Stoughton, 2012.

Rawnsley, Andrew, *The End of the Party: The Rise and Fall of New Labour*, Penguin Books, 2010.

Ross, Shane, *The Bankers: How the Banks Brought Ireland to Its Knees*, Penguin, 2011.

Roubini, Nouriel and Mihm Stephen, *Crisis Economics: A Crash Course in the Future of Finance*, Penguin Books, 2010.

Sampson, Anthony, *The Money Lenders: Bankers and a World in Turmoil*, Viking Press, 1982.

Sampson, Anthony, *The Essential Anatomy of Britain: Democracy in Crisis*, Hodder & Stoughton, 1992.

Shaxson, Nicholas, *Treasure Islands: Tax Havens and the Men Who Stole the World*, Vintage Books, 2011.

Simms, Andrew and Boyle, David, *Eminent Corporations: The Rise and Fall of the Great British Corporation*, Constable, 2010.

Smit, Jeroen, *The Perfect Prey: The Fall of ABN AMRO, or What Went Wrong in the Banking Industry*, Quercus, 2009.

Smith, Yves, *ECONned: How Unenlightened Self-interest Damaged Democracy and Corrupted Capitalism*, Palgrave Macmillan, 2010.

Sorkin, Andrew Ross, *Too Big To Fail: Inside the Battle to Save Wall Street*, Viking Penguin, 2009.

Stewart, Jackie, *Winning Is Not Enough: The Autobiography*, Headline, 2007.

Stiglitz, Joseph E., *Globalisation and its Discontents*, Allen Lane, 2002.

Stiglitz, Joseph E., *The Roaring Nineties: Seeds of Destruction*, Allen Lane, 2003.

Tett, Gillian, *Saving the Sun: Shinsei and the Battle for Japan's Future*, Random House, 2004.

Tett, Gillian, *Fool's Gold: How Unrestrained Greed Corrupted a Dream, Shattered Global Markets, and Unleashed a Catastrophe*, Abacus, 2010.

Torrance, David, *George Younger: A Life Well Lived*, Birlinn, 2008.

Index